# Selected Readings in Human Factors

*Edited by*
Michael Venturino

Human Factors Society

Copyright © 1990 by The Human Factors Society, Inc.

Individual readers of this book and nonprofit libraries acting for them are freely permitted to make fair use of the material in it, such as to copy an article for use in teaching or research. Permission is granted to quote excerpts from articles in scientific works with the customary acknowledgment of the source, including the author's name and the book's title. Permission to reproduce any article or a substantial portion (more than 500 words) thereof, or any figure or table, must come from the first-named author of the article and from the Managing Editor of the Society. Republication or systematic or multiple reproduction of any material in this book is permitted only under license from The Human Factors Society, Inc. Address inquiries and notices to the Managing Editor, The Human Factors Society, P.O. Box 1369, Santa Monica, CA 90406, U.S.A.

The opinions and judgments expressed here are those of the authors and are not necessarily those of the editor; neither are they to be construed as representing the official policy of The Human Factors Society, Inc.

In the case of authors who are employees of the United States government, its contractors, or grantees, The Human Factors Society, Inc., recognizes the right of the U.S. government to retain a nonexclusive, royalty-free license to use the author's copyrighted article for U.S. government purposes.

Additional copies of this book may be obtained from The Human Factors Society, Inc., P.O. Box 1369, Santa Monica, CA 90406 U.S.A.; (213) 394-1811, 394-9793, fax (213) 394-2410.

**Reprint Acknowledgments**

The Society is grateful to the following publishers and authors for permission to reprint their works in this book:

Chapter 1, from R. J. Corsini, ed., *Encyclopedia of Psychology*, vol. 1. Copyright 1984 by John Wiley & Sons, Inc. Reprinted by permission of John Wiley & Sons, Inc.

Chapter 3, reprinted by permission of the publisher from W. B. Rouse and K. R. Boff, eds., *System Design: Behavioral Perspectives on Designers, Tools, and Organizations*. Copyright 1987 by Elsevier Science Publishing Co., Inc.

Chapter 5, from the *Journal of Applied Psychology*, vol. 47, 1963. Copyright 1963 by the American Psychological Association. Reprinted by permission.

Chapter 6, copyright 1983, IEEE. Reprinted, with permission, from *IEEE Transactions on Systems, Man and Cybernetics*, SMC-13, pp. 257-266, 1983.

Chapter 7, from the *Psychological Review*, vol. 88, 1981. Copyright 1981 by the American Psychological Association. Reprinted by permission.

Chapter 14, from the *Journal of Experimental Psychology*, vol. 67, 1964. Copyright 1964 by the American Psychological Association. Reprinted by permission.

Chapter 17, from P. A. Hancock and N. Meshkati, eds., *Human Mental Workload*. Copyright 1988 by Elsevier Science Publishers B.V. and reprinted by permission.

Chapter 20, from R. Glaser, ed., *Training Research and Education*, 1965. Copyright by R. Glaser and reprinted by permission.

Chapter 23, from *Ergonomics*, vol. 21, 1978. Copyright 1978 by Taylor & Francis Ltd and reprinted by permission.

Chapter 24, from *Communications of the ACM*, vol. 26, 1983. Copyright 1983 by the Association for Computing Machinery and reprinted by permission.

The Society also thanks the following authors of articles that appeared in past issues of *Human Factors*: Alphonse Chapanis (Chap. 2), Harold P. Van Cott (Chap. 4), Nehemiah Jordan (Chap. 5), Richard E. Christ (Chap. 8), Stanley N. Roscoe (Chap. 9), Stephen R. Ellis (Chap. 10), Ralph E. Geiselman (Chap. 11), Carol A. Simpson (Chap. 12), William B. Knowles (Chap. 15), Douwe B. Yntema (Chap. 16), Barry H. Kantowitz (Chap. 18), Christopher D. Wickens (Chap. 19), Walter Schneider (Chap. 21), Dennis C. Wightman (Chap. 22), and Thomas S. Tullis (Chap. 25).

# Contents

*Preface* .................................................................. vii

**Part I: Prologue** ......................................................... 1
1. Engineering Psychology ................................................. 3
   *H. McIlvaine Parsons*
2. Some Generalizations about Generalization ............................ 11
   *Alphonse Chapanis*
3. An Experimental View of the Design Process .......................... 27
   *Joseph M. Ballay*

**Part II: Human-Machine Systems** ......................................... 45
4. From Control Systems to Knowledge Systems ........................... 47
   *Harold P. Van Cott*
5. Allocation of Functions between Man and Machines in Automated Systems .......... 55
   *Nehemiah Jordan*
6. Skills, Rules, and Knowledge: Signals, Signs, and Symbols,
   and Other Distinctions in Human Performance Models .................. 61
   *Jens Rasmussen*
7. Categorization of Action Slips ....................................... 71
   *Donald A. Norman*

**Part III: Information Representation and Displays** ...................... 87
8. Review and Analysis of Color Coding Research for Visual Displays .... 89
   *Richard E. Christ*
9. Airborne Displays for Flight and Navigation ......................... 119
   *Stanley N. Roscoe*
10. Perspective Traffic Display Format and Airline Pilot Traffic Avoidance .............. 131
    *Stephen R. Ellis, Michael W. McGreevy, and Robert J. Hitchcock*
11. Perceptual Discriminability as a Basis for Selecting Graphic Symbols ............... 143
    *Ralph E. Geiselman, Betty M. Landee, and Francois G. Christen*
12. System Design for Speech Recognition and Generation ............... 153
    *Carol A. Simpson, Michael E. McCauley, Ellen F. Roland, John C. Ruth,
    and Beverly H. Williges*

**Part IV: Stimulus-Response Compatibility and Motor Control** ............. 181
13. S-R Compatibility: Spatial Characteristics of Stimulus and Response Codes .......... 183
    *Paul M. Fitts and Charles M. Seeger*
14. Information Capacity of Discrete Motor Responses .................. 195
    *Paul M. Fitts and J. R. Peterson*

**Part V: Time-Sharing and Mental Workload** .............................. 205
15. Operator Loading Tasks ............................................ 207
    *William B. Knowles*
16. Keeping Track of Several Things at Once ........................... 215
    *Douwe B. Yntema*
17. Properties of Workload Assessment Techniques ...................... 227
    *F. Thomas Eggemeier*
18. On Scaling Performance Operating Characteristics: Caveat Emptor ... 249
    *Barry H. Kantowitz and Marysue Weldon*
19. POCs and Performance Decrements: A Reply to Kantowitz and Weldon .............. 267
    *Christopher D. Wickens and Yei-Yu Yeh*

**Part VI: Skill Acquisition and Skilled Performance** ...............................**273**
20. Factors in Complex Skill Training ............................................275
    *Paul M. Fitts*
21. Training High-Performance Skills: Fallacies and Guidelines ......................297
    *Walter Schneider*
22. Part-Task Training for Tracking and Manual Control ...........................313
    *Dennis C. Wightman and Gavan Lintern*

**Part VII: Human-Computer Interaction** ........................................**331**
23. Evaluation of Mouse, Rate-Controlled Isometric Joystick,
    Step Keys, and Text Keys for Text Selection on a CRT .........................333
    *Stuart K. Card, William K. English, and Betty J. Burr*
24. The Evaluation of Text Editors: Methodology and Empirical Results ................347
    *Teresa L. Roberts and Thomas P. Moran*
25. The Formatting of Alphanumeric Displays: A Review and Analysis .................371
    *Thomas S. Tullis*

*Suggested Reading* ...........................................................397

*Index* ......................................................................401

# Preface

The impetus for publishing this book was quite simple: it has been almost 20 years since the appearance of a book of readings in human factors. In the last two decades the technological capabilities, systems, and types of problems encountered in the field of human factors have changed considerably. Advances in technology, in part made possible by the proliferation of computers and computer technology, have permeated all walks of life and have significantly enhanced the potential of systems, machines, and organizations. Through all this technology-driven change, the human element has been a common denominator.

The basic capabilities and limitations of the human as a processor of information and solver of problems have not changed over the years; however, modern, complex systems are demanding more sophisticated skills from an operator. The human factors practitioner's ongoing challenge has been to make complex systems simple to monitor and operate in all types of environments. In essence, the goal in making systems "friendlier" is to create an interface that not only employs but also takes advantage of the human's natural and intuitive abilities. Easier said than done.

Technology-driven changes and people's attempts to cope with them effectively have been reflected in the human factors literature. The pinnacles and pitfalls characteristic of scientific inquiry have formed an important data base for researchers and practitioners alike. Over the years a number of important articles have appeared, and with time they have increased in stature. Some areas of investigation have matured, and researchers in those areas have produced a stable, empirically derived knowledge base. Other areas have emerged from developing technology. In addition, stimulating controversies have arisen within the field.

This book of readings constitutes a survey of six traditional subdisciplines in human factors: human-machine systems, information display, stimulus-response compatibility, mental workload, training, and human-computer interaction. It is a compilation of articles that are informative and representative of work in specific areas. The choice of these traditional subdisciplines was deliberate and represents an attempt to, first, consolidate important contributions in established topic areas and, second, provide students and professionals an overview of established areas of study within the human factors discipline. Although a number of emerging areas in human factors currently are gaining popularity (e.g., artificial intelligence, telepresence and telerobotics, forensics), to some extent these areas are still maturing and therefore were not included in this collection. Space limitations prevented the inclusion of articles from other topic areas, such as anthropometry, environmental design, and organizational design and management. A brief introduction precedes each section and provides the context for the selections. Each selection is in turn introduced and contributions to the field noted.

It is doubtful that consensus can ever be reached in selecting articles and chapters for a book such as this. Some selections are obvious choices because of their seminal contribution or classic status; others might seem to have been chosen arbitrarily. Despite the possible lack of consensus, I believe this collection is representative of many important areas in human factors. Overall a broad range of topics are covered, and readings concerned with method, empirical review, and theory are included. This breadth is achieved, however, at the expense of depth in any single area. Such a trade-off is unfortunate but inevitable. The readings are highly selective, and most are drawn from the applications literature. With a few exceptions, the readings do not stray too far into the theoretical literature on which many human factors principles are based; nonetheless, they provide worthwhile examples of the application of such principles.

The articles and chapters included here meet at least one of the following criteria: (a) frequently cited benchmark papers that stimulated research in a particular area; (b) articles representative of a large number of papers, which adequately characterize research in an area; (c) critical reviews of research in a particular area; and (d) in a few limited cases, representative research in an area of emerging technology or capability. All journal articles and book chapters are reproduced in their entirety.

This book is aimed at students, but it should be useful for practitioners as well. A significant reason for compiling this material is to provide a high-quality and convenient supplement to a human factors textbook. Reducing the time students spend searching through library stacks is a worthwhile endeavor, freeing valuable time for learning.

*Selected Readings in Human Factors* reflects the intellectual insight, hard work, and devoted interest of a group of individuals. I would like to acknowledge their significant contributions and express heartfelt appreciation. First, sincere thanks go to Arthur D. (Dan) Fisk, who as past HFS Managing Editor championed the idea of a book of readings to the Society's Executive Council. His support was substantial and his tenacity and patience in the initial stages admirable. Diane L. Damos picked up the challenge when she succeeded Dan as Managing Editor, carrying the project through its final stages (and accompanying difficult decisions) to completion. Her insight and perseverance are appreciated.

A number of individuals helped to generate selections within the various topic areas, providing the backbone for the book. Phillip L. Ackerman, Ray E. Eberts, John M. Flach, and Paul Green deserve accolades and considerable credit for their suggestions. After initial selection and organization of articles were completed, the overall structure and content were subjected to the scrutiny of a handful of senior members of the Human Factors Society. Their comments and suggestions helped to polish and refine the book. The authors of often-used human factors textbooks—including Jack A. Adams, Barry L. Kantowitz, and Mark S. Sanders—made helpful comments and suggestions.

Among those who provided insight on the appropriateness of the selections were F. Thomas Eggemeier, Richard J. Hornick, Richard J. Jagacinski, Dieter W. Jahns, and David Meister. Thanks many times over to Lois Smith, Marian G. Knowles, and Lynn Strother at the Human Factors Society's Central Office; their diligence and behind-the-scenes work on the details of management and publication allowed the project to run smoothly during all stages. Most important, I gratefully acknowledge the authors of the selections included here. Theirs is the real work in this book of readings. I am thankful to Charles Bates, Jr., who fosters a stimulating and rewarding research environment. Finally, I would like to thank John W. Senders, who stimulated my interest in human factors and lured me into this exciting discipline.

# Part I
# PROLOGUE

Human factors is a multidisciplinary endeavor dedicated to designing objects and environments for safer, more effective, and more efficient use by humans. As such it is a fascinating field that brings together elements of psychology, engineering, computer science, anthropometry, and systems design. What are the backgrounds of people employed in this field? Where do they work, and what kind of work do they do? Where do they publish, and where do they get their information? The three selections included in Part I describe the people in human factors and their activities, discuss important issues in the empirical activities of human factors engineers, and characterize the design process.

The first selection, by H. McIlvaine Parsons (Chapter 1), presents a sketch of human factors engineering beginning with a historical overview. Although some elements of human factors—such as time and motion studies—existed in the late nineteenth and early twentieth centuries, Parsons notes that the development and maturity of human factors as we know it today were accelerated by requirements to solve the training and equipment design problems that arose in the 1940s during World War II. These problems resulted from psychomotor and information-processing overloads imposed by operating complex machines and systems in stressful environments. Parsons provides examples of major organizations that employ engineering psychologists, the professional societies in which they hold membership, and the publications that are used in the dissemination of their empirical work. He also gives examples of the techniques of investigation typical in human engineering, as well as the independent and dependent variables used in these studies. Parsons concludes by noting the growing importance of the human factors discipline in our technologically oriented society.

Most principles of behavior used in human factors engineering are empirically derived and based on the scientific method of inquiry. One of the most important aspects of scientific investigation is the extent to which the results of controlled studies may be generalized beyond the parameters and samples used in the studies. *Generalizability* is the conceptual mechanism by which results obtained under a given set of specified conditions would be obtained under similar but slightly different conditions. It is an extrapolation factor that forms a foundation of related facts permitting the systematic and logical advance of scientific knowledge.

The selection by Alphonse Chapanis (Chapter 2) is an insightful discussion of the generalizability of human factors investigations. Chapanis asks sobering questions about the concept of generalizability, gives empirical evidence for generalization drawn from behavioral science, and discusses several fallacies about generalization. He reviews factors that limit generalizability and provides suggestions for designing studies with generalizability of results in mind. Despite the many questions that surround this issue, Chapanis concludes that human factors research has produced general guidelines and recommendations that are of use to designers. He also notes that such guidelines and recommendations will never supersede the designer's need for detailed, system-specific knowledge. Consequently, it is important for human factors researchers to determine the limits of generalizability of their empirical work.

The focus of many human factors researchers and practitioners is on design. Yet adequate knowledge of the design process is often lacking. For example, it is important to know the stages involved in the creative design process, the kinds of information that are useful in each stage, and the demands the design process imposes on the designer's cognitive and information-processing system. The selection by Joseph M. Ballay (Chapter 3) is an empirically based illustration of the factors involved in the design process, from concept to product. The information in this article provides insight into the activities, needs, and requirements involved in the design/problem-solving process.

According to Ballay, design is portrayed first as a poorly defined construction task, which leads to variability in the creative process, which in turn depends on the degree to which the final product is specified. Design is also viewed as a visual task that may involve any number of representations, including mock-ups and models, orthographic and perspective drawings, and procedural representations. Third, design may be viewed from the perspective of human information processes, including the translating and integrating of both the designer's ideas and information provided by design aids, such as computers, CAD images, and drawings. Also discussed are factors involved in sketching preliminary ideas and representations and the management of the large amounts of information needed to create and implement a design. Although the creative process investigated by Ballay differs from that involved in complex system design, it should nonetheless be informative and provide some insight for human factors researchers and practitioners.

# Engineering Psychology

**H. M. PARSONS**

Though perhaps several thousand psychologists in the United States and as many elsewhere call their subdiscipline "engineering psychology," the term is both unclear and somewhat of a misnomer, persisting through tradition and organizational inertia; Division 21 of the American Psychological Association until 1983 was "The Society of Engineering Psychologists," and its hybrid composition long frustrated efforts to adopt a more suitable name. The field might better be named "psychology for modern technology." It is that branch of psychology that examines human behavior as it relates to the equipment, computer software, environments, and human-machine systems that characterize modern technology. Primarily, it has asked: what are the capabilities and limitations of human performance in using technology and its products? How should people and machines be shaped to fit each other? Here "machines" must be interpreted to include the creations not only of engineers but also of computer programmers and analysts, architects, training developers, and planners.

Clearly, engineering psychologists often find themselves closely associated with these other disciplines, as well as with physical anthropology and physiology. The title of this article reflects an initial and continuing association with engineering, the principal source of technology, and the subdiscipline's vocabulary has drawn on engineering for such terms as input, output, coding, feedback, and information channel. Within psychology, engineering psychologists border not only on experimental psychology, in which most early engineering psychologists were trained, but also on organizational and industrial, personnel, and operant subdisciplines. But they are distinguished by their emphasis on the physical features of technology as the sources of inputs to human behavior and the recipients of outputs. Because technology so greatly influences modern life, engineering psychology would seem to have considerable significance. Its growth is tied to that of the multidisciplinary field of human factors (overseas, ergonomics). Many, if not most, American engineering psychologists identify themselves also as human factors scientists, and some who engage in applications as human factors engineers.

## HISTORY

Conventionally, the origin of engineering psychology is placed in World War II, with its major technological innovations in weaponry, aircraft, submarines, and radar. The demands these imposed on psychomotor skills and information processing seemed at times to exceed human capabilities. As a result, lives might be lost and worse, the battle. Things had to work right the first time; traditional trial-and-error development was not enough. With such a driving influence, military organizations began to foster engineering psychology to find out what operators of such new equipment could actually accomplish with it—where they might succeed and where fail. Problems lay not only in the designs of displays and controls but in the workloads operators confronted and the environments in which they functioned. Tasks had to be accomplished within certain time limits and as free of error as possible. Past laboratory studies of psychophysics and psychomotor activity did not disclose enough about what people can and cannot do; investiga-

From R. J. Corsini (Ed.), *Encyclopedia of Psychology*. Copyright 1984 by John Wiley & Sons, Inc.

tions had to be directed toward special, more complex sensing, processing, and control activation, involving particular inputs from equipment to operators and their outputs to manage it. Because some of the new technological marvels had to be operated in high-altitude and undersea environments hostile to human beings, it became necessary to find out how their performance was affected by increased or reduced atmospheric pressures, increased or reduced accelerations, noise, heat and cold, and vibration. The biological impacts of these conditions were studied by medical investigators and psychophysiologists such as Ross A. McFarland, who was also a distinguished engineering psychologist.

With the advent of space missions, such inquiry became even more urgent. Equipment had to be designed (with engineering psychologists' support) to allow for human inadequacies, then tested (again with such support) to see whether it did the job. Combinations of humans and machines—especially air defense centers, shipboard combat information centers, and ballistic missile complexes—were called "human-machine systems." Engineering psychologists helped engineers design and test these systems—a far cry from the "knobs and dials" focus with which engineering psychology started. Later such involvement in system design extended to other human-machine complexes, such as air-traffic control centers and power plants; the driving force behind the development was again life and death—as well as financial loss.

Military support continued for engineering psychology in a number of ways after World War II. For example, the Office of Naval Research funded a substantial research program led by Alphonse Chapanis at Johns Hopkins University, also an early one at New York University and later ones at many other universities and locations. The Army established a Human Engineering Laboratory that employed many engineering psychologists. The Air Force's Aerospace Medical Research Laboratory conducted extensive research itself and supported it elsewhere. When the Air Force began to require its contractors to conform to new requirements for human factors engineering in system and equipment design, contractors formed human factors groups in their engineering departments that included engineering psychologists. The first was at Hughes Aircraft under the aegis of Alexander Williams; other major aerospace concerns followed: Lockheed, Douglas, McDonnell (becoming McDonnell Douglas), Boeing, and Honeywell. The Navy and Army established similar requirements, which became consolidated in Department of Defense regulations and standards.

Given such employment opportunities, experimental psychologists moved into engineering psychology, and graduate courses were established. Some engineering psychologists worked in laboratory research, some in development or applications, some in both. Military aircraft absorbed most of the effort, though engineering psychologists worked on almost all new equipment and systems. When the National Aeronautics and Space Administration was established, it also supported research and development by engineering psychologists. A large number of consulting companies were formed, funded largely by Department of Defense or NASA contracts. Although a National Academy of Sciences report urged more support for engineering psychology, it received very little assistance from the National Science Foundation, perhaps because its orientation seemed too applied.

Engineering psychology had actually begun before World War II—on a very small scale—with the printed word. Though printing as a technological development had been with us for a long time, experimental psychology had not. Early in the twentieth century a few psychologists sought to apply the experimental method to printing to make print easier to use—that is, read—in work described by D. G. Paterson and M. A. Tinker in *How to make type readable*, and by M. A. Tinker in *Legibility of print*. Some research on legibility and readability continued over the years, involving not only books and media but also highway signs, instruction manuals, license plates, and cathode ray tubes. More recently engineering psychologists have investigated comprehension of printed commands, data, error messages, and the like in interactive computer systems. Since a purchaser might prefer the interactive system that was more comprehensible, financial motivation invigorated this field of research and application.

Although military work has been given the credit for the growth of engineering psychology since World War II, some commercial support also developed early, first at the Bell Telephone Laboratories, then at International Business Machines and other large corporations. In subsequent years nonmilitary research, development, and applications increased, as evidenced in the number and size of in-house human factors groups as well as human factors consulting organizations, though often it was difficult to sort out what proportions could be claimed by engineering psychology. Product effectiveness for the user resulting from engineering psychology has seldom been an outstanding advertising feature in the competition for sales, though it might become so if prospective purchasers were more aware of it. However, product hazard has indeed become a "driver," and engineering psychologists have been testifying more and more as expert witnesses in product liability litigation.

Product effectiveness is not the concern of engineering psychologists alone. Engineers can design automobiles to brake better or accelerate faster without their help. However, the threat to life and limb in motorcars fostered some engineering psychology as early as 1928, as reported by A. R. Lauer in *The psychology of driving: Factors of traffic enforcement*, and as subsequently recorded by Theodore Forbes in *Human factors in highway traffic safety research*. Thanks in part to Ralph Nader, the Federal government eventually established the National Highway Traffic Safety Administration, which along with the Federal Highway Administration employs a number of engineering psychologists, as do the major automobile manufacturers—General Motors, Ford, and Chrysler. The Federal Aviation Administration has also made use of engineering psychology. Stanley Roscoe's *Aviation psychology* described a substantial body of technology-oriented research in commercial aviation. The National Institute of Occupational Safety and Health and the Bureau of Mines have also turned to engineering psychology for help in reducing occupational accidents and loss of life, limb, or money. But engineering psychology has rarely penetrated the factory. The work-related design of industrial machinery was preempted early by industrial engineers, while industrial psychologists concerned themselves with organizational and personnel problems. Eventually, however, engineering psychologists began to investigate robotics as a significant form of automation still requiring human involvement. They also studied quality control, since human error is a major target of engineering psychology—and an important factor in productivity.

For more complete accounts of engineering psychology's history, the reader can consult chapters on engineering psychology in the *Annual Review of Psychology* (1958, 1960, 1963, 1966, 1971, 1976) and articles or chapters by Paul Fitts (1951, 1963), Franklin Taylor (1957, 1963), Walter Grether (1968), and Julien Christensen (1971).

## FOCAL POINTS IN REAL-WORLD APPLICATIONS

Outside academia, engineering psychology has concentrated on some particular aspects of human performance as dependent variables, and on various categories of equipment, environments, and systems as independent variables affecting these. Its work has been applied to diverse human-machine aggregates. The dependent variables have largely though not exclusively consisted of the time needed and accuracy attained in a particular performance, components of human information processing, decision making, monitoring and vigilance, inspection and signal detection, accidents, auditory communication, psychomotor skills and skill acquisition, continuous manual control (tracking), reading, stress and fatigue, and various kinds of workload capacity. Categories of independent variables include systems, automation, tasks, controls and control devices, displays (including print), equipment and tool design, workload (mental and physical), work-rest cycles, procedures, maintenance activities, information feedback, training techniques, training devices, and ambient conditions (illumination, glare, noise, temperature, vibration, acceleration, and atmospheric pressure).

Among the human-machine aggregates have been aircraft (military and commercial), submarines, spacecraft, radar, sonar, undersea habitats, air traffic control, highway transportation, automobiles, urban transportation, postal operations, residential environments, offices, telephonic and radio communications, nuclear power plants, mining, interactive computers, missile systems, command and control systems, health care delivery, and law enforcement.

## UNIVERSITIES

Despite overlaps, engineering psychology has had a somewhat different role within American university psychology departments than elsewhere. For one thing, engineering psychologists in universities teach graduate students (who subsequently receive essential on-the-job training in industry or government, if they enter these to make a living). A number of American universities have graduate curricula and give graduate degrees in engineering psychology, and some (for example, the Air Force Academy) teaches it to undergraduates. However, the number has been shrinking for several reasons: (1) graduate work in human factors, including much of engineering psychology, has been shifting to engineering departments, notably industrial engineering; (2) employer needs have emphasized training in cross-disciplinary applications rather than in experimental research, though quite a few employers still regard the latter as an important qualification; (3) Psychology departments dominated by experimental psychologists tend to derogate engineering psychologists on the grounds that their research is too mundane—that is, insufficiently theoretical (though at the same time, ironically, experimental psychologists have been exploring potentials in applied research so their students can obtain employment after graduation).

Most university research in engineering psychology tries to be "basic"—that is, abstract or highly generalizable—although some is applied: applicable to the processes and products of modern technology. Strong views have been expressed on behalf of each emphasis. A major research interest is human information processing, which largely originated in engineering psychology in the United States and Great Britain and in technological problems. But human information processing has become a major focus also of experimental psychology, which takes it as a virtual synonym for cognition. Where, then, is the dividing line in research between engineering and experimental psychology?

In human information processing, "information" seems to be a newer term for stimuli—inputs into an individual's sensory apparatus; processing involves what might earlier have been subsumed under perception, attention, memory, and choice or discrimination. Reaction time is a favorite dependent variable. A number of examples illustrate the difference between applied (engineering) and basic (experimental) research. Applied research showed that if an actual switch, knob, or stick on a console were moved to the right, the indicator or signal it controlled should appear or be moved to the right—not to the left—so as to reduce errors and reaction times. Further research with synthetic stimulus and response arrays of pushbuttons and lamps in a variety of spatial arrangements further demonstrated "stimulus-response compatibility." Conducted in a laboratory, this early research was published in an "experimental," not an "applied," journal (but probably would not have been later). More recently, research under the joint label of human information processing and experimental psychology has sought to identify some theoretical stage of in-the-head processing to explain S-R compatibility.

In another illustration, a British investigator studied air traffic controllers receiving coinciding messages from pilots over the same loudspeaker. Success in getting clearer messages with a loudspeaker for each sound source led to research in processing stimuli close to each other or coinciding in time, and to models or theories of human "channel" capacity and "filtering." The visual and auditory stimuli were simpler and thus more abstract: they were no longer pilots' messages. Together with its modeling and theorizing, this research has come to be viewed by some as "experimental" rather than "engineering."

In still another example, engineering psychologists have employed extraneous secondary tasks to increase the workload faced, for instance, by a pilot operating a cockpit simulator; the purpose can be to determine maximum capacity on the primary task, when any reserve capacity is exhausted. Such time sharing has been investigated in experimental psychology laboratories to find out how different kinds of nonpilot primary and secondary tasks interact, and to construct theoretical models of information-processing capacities.

Whatever it is called, such basic research in academia may be able to guide engineering psychologists facing practical problems, such as helping an engineer design a complex display panel in a nuclear power plant, so an operator will not be overloaded with information and can filter out data of less importance. But such translations may not be easy, if the information (the stimuli) is very different in the laboratory from that in the power plant. On the other hand, if the translation is too easy, the laboratory research risks being called "engineering" rather than "experimental," and the investigator receives less credit as a scientist from departmental colleagues. Similar dilemmas have marked interfaces between other basic and applied sciences.

Theorizing, to which many experimental psychologists appear partial, comes more easily when variables seem unrelated to some technological problem. Thus color discrimination in coding for a display belongs to engineering psychology, but experimental psychology examines its theoretical basis. Coding means some way of representing the external world. Such representation in a machine, for operator processing, has been a major interest in engineering psychology; information is "coded." When the machine is a computer, most of such coding is alphanumeric (including language). With an increasing focus on computers, engineering psychology has been investigating language as an information-processing medium—but so has experimental psychology, or at least it has been investigating information processing with language as the medium. Thus the difference between them has become blurred; inputs as well as outputs are much alike in each, in contrast to the marked differences when engineering psychology was oriented more toward psychomotor skills.

## TECHNIQUES

Experimentation has been the primary investigative technique of both university and nonuniversity engineering psychology—one reason why academic training in experimental psychology has been useful. Experiments are conducted in laboratories, in field settings, and in mixes of the two. Some experiments outside academia are oriented toward general problems but most have some particular goal, such as to evaluate how well an operator performs with some specific equipment, or to compare alternative displays or machines when operated by humans. The dependent variables are not necessarily the same in these two kinds of particular experiments. In the former, the time an individual takes or the errors the individual makes in reacting to a component can (but may not) be isolated, so only human performance is being measured—although, as an early engineering psychologist, Franklin Taylor, pointed out, it is often difficult to exclude that of the machine component entirely. In the latter kind of experiments—the comparison of alternative devices—the investigator measures the joint output of the device and the operator. It has been questioned whether the study of such combinations constitutes "psychology." One reason justifying a psychologist's participation is the relative unfamiliarity of most engineers with experimental design, especially with respect to human variables.

When combinations of human operators and machines become large and complex, experiments evaluating them have been called "human-machine system experiments," and the investigators, "system psychologists." Such experiments are similarly large and complex, and experimental subjects function as teams or crews. Investigators have made comparisons between two designs for an operations center; have assessed system capabilities, as for example how many aircraft an air control center can bring into an airport in an hour; and have diagnosed problems, such as which system components or subsystems (including operators) should be held responsible for some particular level of system performance. In addition to design factors, such system experiments have investigated procedures, skill levels, and training methods. Generally they simulate parts of the system or its environment. Though such research rarely gets reported in journals, more than 200 experiments in approximately 50 programs between 1950 and 1970 were described by H. McIlvaine Parsons in *Man-machine system experiments;* the most cited investigator was H. Wallace Sinaiko.

Most nonacademic experimentation in engineering psychology takes place, however, on components within a system—on display design, maintenance procedure, skill requirement, or training device. Here, too, simulation is one of the principal tools, often created for the study. It consists, for example, of a mockup or of signals seen on a cathode ray tube. Some experimentation is exploration, for discovery; some is verification, for certainty. Experimental designs have been developed to combine these stages by putting all seemingly important independent variables into an experiment at the start, screening them by means of fractional factorials with only two states per variable, then sequentially refining the design with fewer variables and more replication. "Response surface methodology" adapted by Charles W. Simon has exemplified such approaches, as has central composite design described by Robert C. Williges (1981).

Engineering psychology employs additional ways to gather data such as observations of real-world operations, examination of archival sources, and systematic querying of operators and maintainers to obtain their self-reports. Such self-report data from interviews or questionnaires are particularly useful in providing insights into problems that can then be studied more objectively; for example, an operator is asked to recall "critical incidents" resulting from a design flaw, a faulty procedure, or inadequate training. Operators are not too reliable in reporting their own levels of performance or the relative advantages of two different equipments; however, if they have been trained to become experts and are furnished well-tested rating scales, their self-report data may be better than no data at all.

A number of analytic techniques are used by engineering psychologists. Foremost is task description and analysis. This technique sets forth in detail what a person does step by step in operating or maintaining some equipment, relating each action to some input (e.g., from a display), to some control device, perhaps to some choice or decision, and to any feedback. In a sense, such analysis constitutes a verbal simulation of performance. When added to such a description, the time taken for each action, the probability of error, and the skill level needed furnish a substantial basis for equipment design, procedure development and documentation, skill requirements, and the development of training methods and equipment. However, it is often difficult to provide reliable time and error data before equipment is built, since there has been no comprehensive task taxonomy or accompanying data base. A related technique is computer modeling of human and machine performance. Data similar to those for task analysis are programmed into a computer, which can then be used to vary nontask factors such as workload, design changes, or procedural differences, to determine how these alter the time and accuracy of a task. The computer model's findings are reliable, however, only to the extent that the inputs it gets are reliable.

On the basis of their data gathering, experimentation, and analysis, engineering psychologists produce reports, briefings, and face-to-face consultation with system developers, design engineers, and others. Reports contain generalizable knowledge or specific findings. They may be transformed into presentations at professional gatherings or journal articles, or may remain reports with little circulation, possibly for proprietary or security reasons. Briefings and consultation are more effective methods of getting recommendations adopted, but are evanescent. As a result, much of what engineering psychologists accomplish in the actual design of some equipment or system remains unknown to other psychologists and to the public. (In that sense they resemble clinical psychologists in private practice.) Further, their contribution may not be apparent within a team effort. It is difficult to determine from the published work what engineering psychology has actually done to shape technology.

## ORGANIZATIONS AND PUBLICATIONS

Engineering psychologists make up a division of the American Psychological Association and participate in that association's annual meetings. Without a technical journal of their own, they generally publish in *Human Factors,* the journal of the Human Factors Society, to which many or most belong, or in *Ergonomics,* the journal of the Ergonomics Society (in England) and the International Ergonomics Association. The APA division of Applied Experimental and Engineering Psychology is an amalgam of varied professionals, some from universities, some from government, some from industry; some concentrate on research, some on development or applications; some identify more as experimental psychologists, some as human factors engineers. One of its members, Conrad Kraft, was the first recipient of the American Psychological Association's annual Distinguished Scientific Award for Applications of Psychology. Alphonse Chapanis and Edwin A. Fleishman were later winners of the award.

Outside the United States, engineering psychology occupies a strong position in the Soviet Union, where it is a well-supported field of psychology with considerably more public recognition than in the United States. At least one of its leading investigators and teachers, Boris Lomov, is also prominent in the U.S.S.R. Academy of Science. (Two American psychologists who worked in engineering psychology have belonged to the National Academy of Sciences, though their work in engineering psychology was apparently not the primary basis for such recognition.) Great Britain and various continental nations have produced distinguished engineering psychologists as well, such as D. E. Broadbent and Frederic Bartlett.

## PROSPECTS

As long as technology continues to evolve and produce new processes in which humans participate or new products they use, there will be a continuing need for engineering psychology, or at least for psychologists concerned with the interactions between technology and people. The term "engineering psychology," however, may not survive, nor the separate identity of such psychologists in universities. For those elsewhere, their continuity and growth will depend on various factors: involvement in new technological innovations such as robotics, interactive computers, and office automation; extending their interests beyond skilled performance; and the driving factors (such as life and death and financial gain or loss) that make their contributions to a technological world seem important to those who create it. (In the absence of such factors, for example, work in environmental design as a facet of engineering psychology has languished for lack of funding, despite much intellectual interest.)

The outstanding development in technology is automation—in the factory and office as well as in various products. Of increasing uncertainty is the extent to which something can or should be automated—an industrial process, paperwork, transportation, teaching, a toothbrush, or the game of chess. To proponents of artificial intelligence there appear to be no limits technically—at least, in the future. Presently, human beings remain in the act. But what should their roles be? What will they continue to do that intelligent machines cannot? Engineering psychologists can help resolve that issue, by continuing to reveal human capabilities and limitations (especially cognitive) in technology-related performance, at the same time examining with some skepticism what intelligent machines can and cannot do. Adopting J. C. R. Licklider's notion of "man-machine symbiosis," engineering psychology can investigate how humans and machines can best work together to cope with the complexity and variety that characterize our world, which neither humans nor machines can comprehend alone.

But engineering psychology is also challenged to broaden its perspective. There is more to the impact of technology on human behavior than skilled performance. How people feel, why they act as they do, their relationships with others—these emotional, motivational, and social variables are also influenced by technology, and in turn influence the shape it takes. Because these considerations demand systematic inquiry into the physical world of technology, virtually all psychologists have left them unattended, or attended only superficially. Engineering psychology—or psychology for modern technology—seems the logical candidate to fill this void. Indeed, one of its pioneers, Paul Fitts, once said it should encompass stressors, motivation, and social consequences. In this way it can orient technology to human advantage.

## FURTHER REFERENCES

Christensen, J. M. The emerging role of engineering psychology. In W. C. Howell & I. L. Goldstein (Eds.), *Engineering psychology. Current perspectives in research.* New York: Appleton-Century-Crofts, 1971.

De Greene, K. B. *Systems psychology.* New York: McGraw-Hill, 1970.

Fitts, P. M. Engineering psychology. In S. Koch (Ed.), *Psychology: A study of a science,* Vol. 5: *The process areas, the person, and some applied fields: Their place in psychology and in science.* New York: McGraw-Hill, 1963.

Fitts, P. M. Engineering psychology and equipment design. In S. S. Stevens (Ed.), *Handbook of experimental psychology.* New York: Wiley, 1951.

Forbes, T. W. (Ed.). *Human factors in highway traffic safety research.* New York: Wiley/Interscience, 1972.

Grether, W. F. Engineering psychology in the United States. *American Psychologist,* 1968, *23,* 743-751.

Howell, W. C., & Goldstein, I. L. (Eds.). *Engineering psychology: Current perspectives in research.* New York: Appleton-Century-Crofts, 1971.

Kantowitz, B. H. Interfacing human information processing and engineering psychology. In W. C. Howell and E. A. Fleishman (Eds.), *Human performance and productivity: Information processing and decision making,* Vol. 2. Hillsdale, N.J.: Erlbaum, 1982.

Lauer, A. R. *The psychology of driving. Factors of traffic enforcement.* Springfield, Ill.: Thomas, 1960.

Parsons, H. M. *Man-machine system experiments.* Baltimore, Md.: Johns Hopkins Press, 1972.

Parsons, H. M. Psychology for engineering and technology. In P. J. Woods (Ed.), *Career opportunities for psychologists. Expanding and emerging areas.* Washington, D.C.: American Psychological Association, 1976.

Paterson, D. G., & Tinker, M. A. *How to make type readable.* New York: Harpers, 1940.

Roscoe, S. N. *Aviation psychology.* Ames, Iowa: Iowa State University Press, 1980.

Taylor, F. V. Human engineering and psychology. In S. Koch (Ed.), *Psychology: A study of a science,* Vol. 5: *The process areas, the person, and some applied fields: Their place in psychology and in science.* New York: McGraw-Hill, 1963.

Taylor, F. V. Psychology and the design of machines. *American Psychologist,* 1957, *12,* 249-258.

Tinker, M. A. *Legibility of print.* Ames, Iowa: Iowa State University Press, 1963.

Williges, R. C. Development and use of research methodologies for complex system/simulation experimentation. In M. J. Moraal & K. F. Kraiss (Eds.), *Manned system design.* New York: Plenum, 1981.

*Since the original publication of the foregoing article, several outstanding works have appeared in the field. Some of them are listed below.* — Ed., 6/90

Adams, J. A. (1989). *Human factors engineering.* New York: Macmillan.

Kantowitz, B. H., and Sorkin, R. D. (1983). *Human factors: Understanding people-system relationships.* New York: Wiley.

Klemmer, E. T. (Ed.). (1989). *Ergonomics: Harness the power of human factors in your business.* Norwood, NJ: Ablex.

Parsons, H. M. (1988). Psychology and modern technology. In P. J. Woods (Ed.), *Is psychology for them? A guide to undergraduate advising* (pp. 140-144). Washington, DC: American Psychological Association.

Sanders, M. S., and McCormick, E. J. (1987). *Human factors in engineering and design* (6th ed.). New York: McGraw-Hill.

Wickens, C. D. (1984). *Engineering psychology and human performance.* Columbus, OH: Merrill.

# 2

# Some Generalizations about Generalization

ALPHONSE CHAPANIS,[1] *Alphonse Chapanis, Ph.D., P.A., Baltimore, Maryland*

*Three fallacies about generalization are that so-called basic research is more generalizable than applied research, that general findings are immediately useful for design purposes, and that the use of taxonomies increases the generalizability of human factors studies. Some factors that limit generalizability are the use of unrepresentative subjects, insufficient training subjects receive before measurements are begun, inadequate sampling of tasks and situations, inappropriate selection of dependent variables, long-term changes in the world of work, and artifacts attributable to the measurement process itself. In designing a study to predict behavior in a specific application, the guiding principle is similarity. The study should be as similar as possible to the real situation. Two principles should be followed to design studies whose findings can be extrapolated to a wide range of situations: (1) design heterogeneity into the studies and (2) replicate earlier studies with variations in subjects, variables, or procedures.*

## INTRODUCTION

That "there has been little or no advancement in human factors or ergonomics in . . . the last 25 years" is the thesis of Smith's recent (1987) harsh evaluation and challenge to the human factors profession. The main reason there has been no progress in the accumulation of general knowledge in human factors, he goes on to argue, is that practically all the studies conducted in our field have been to solve specific design problems and have been conducted in such a way that they lack generalizability.

What is this thing called generalizability, and why is it so important? We say that a finding has generality, or that it can be generalized, if the finding holds in situations other than the one in which it was observed. By definition, then, generalizing always means extrapolating to conditions not identical to those at the time original observations were made—to other groups of people, to other variations of independent or dependent variables, to modifications of variables that were originally held constant, or to other environments.

The belief that findings can be generalized is widely accepted. It lies at the heart of all science and governs the way we live. Generality is important for the scientist because if all findings from empirical studies held only under the exact conditions in which they were obtained, science would be in deep trouble. Moreover, all of us—scientists and nonscientists alike—constantly generalize from observations we make about events in the world around us in order to have a basis for coping with the behavior of persons we have not yet met and situations we have not yet encountered.

Despite the importance of generality for all of us, few researchers consider it in their

[1] Requests for reprints should be sent to Alphonse Chapanis, Suite 210, Ruxton Towers, 8415 Bellona Lane, Baltimore, MD 21204.

work. Indeed, it is difficult to find the topic even mentioned in textbooks of statistics or methodology. Perhaps the reason for this neglect is that we cannot bring ourselves to face reality—the reality that there may be no logical basis for generalizing or extrapolating from particular observations. Although he did not use the exact words I have used, this is clearly what the philosopher David Hume meant when in 1739 he wrote in *A Treatise on Human Nature*:

> Our foregoing method of reasoning will easily convince us, that there can be no *demonstrative* arguments to prove, *that those instances of which we have no experience resemble those of which we have had experience.* (Lindsay, 1911, p. 91; italics in original)

And in another place:

> It is impossible for us to satisfy ourselves by our reason, why we should extend that experience beyond those particular instances which have fallen under our observation. We suppose, but are never able to prove, that there must be a resemblance betwixt those objects, of which we have had experience, and those which lie beyond the reach of our discovery. (p. 94)

This dismaying point of view has been echoed more recently by experts such as Fromkin and Streufert (1976):

> Although it is important to determine if a relationship is relevant outside the confines of a particular laboratory experiment, generalizations are never logically justified and, to further complicate the issue, there are no objective criteria which yield unequivocal answers to the question of generality. (p. 431)

Are Hume and his more modern proponents correct? Can we never generalize? The idea seems to run counter to what we all believe and the way we behave. Isn't it possible to design studies in such a way that at least some generalization can be justified? This article is the result of my attempts to come to grips with questions like these. Although I believe my ideas apply to all studies in the behavioral sciences, my primary focus is on those in the area of human factors. Because human factors methods include a variety of investigative techniques such as critical incident studies, activity analyses, and task analyses (see, for example, Meister, 1985), I have not confined my thinking to controlled experimentation but, rather, have considered the total range of empirical studies in which the human factors specialist might engage.

## SOME COMMON FALLACIES ABOUT GENERALIZATION

I begin with what I think are three common fallacies about generalization as it relates to empirical studies.

### On the Generality of Basic versus Applied Research

Although I view basic and applied research as two ends of a continuum, people often talk about them as though they are discrete categories. A common misconception that I want to put to rest immediately is epitomized in this quotation from Anastasi: "A closely related difference [between basic and applied research] pertains to the specificity or generality of the results. The findings of basic research can usually be generalized more widely than those of applied research" (1979, p. 9). Simon is another writer who clearly agrees with Anastasi as regards generality and specificity: " 'Basic' indicates the degree to which results can be applied to many situations. 'Applied' indicates the degree to which there are situations within the boundaries of the experiment that match some current problem" (1987, p. 2).

In my view basic research is neither more nor less generalizable than applied research. Although no single description applies to all basic research, many, perhaps most such studies have several of the following characteristics:

> Subjects are solicited, or conscripted, from some conveniently accessible population. They are brought into a laboratory and are confronted

with an experimental setup—a particular piece or arrangement of apparatus. The apparatus may be something that has been used before and so, in the interests of economy, is made to serve again, or it may be an apparatus fashioned according to the experimenter's predilections. Carefully controlled stimuli with defined characteristics are presented to the subject. Often the stimuli are things a subject may never or rarely experience in a lifetime, such as spectrally pure lights, pure tones, nonsense syllables, or nonsense forms. From a large number of possible dependent variables the experimenter selects one or a few that, in his or her opinion, are most likely to yield meaningful results. The subject is instructed about what is to be done, is given a few trials to become familiar with the apparatus and procedures, is tested for perhaps an hour or so, and is then dismissed.

I maintain that nothing in that catalogue of conditions should give an experimenter any confidence that the findings will generalize to conditions other than those that held at the time the study was done. Indeed, the findings from basic studies done this way are sometimes less generalizable than the findings of applied studies in which subjects, variables, and other conditions are allowed to vary widely. One of the principal advantages of controlled experimentation is that it allows the experimenter to find *statistically* significant results more easily. But that, in itself, has nothing to do with the generalizability of the findings.

In short, the basic versus applied issue adds nothing to our search for generalizability.

*A General Finding Is Not Necessarily Useful*

The second fallacy is especially relevant to applied research. Under the general heading of threats to external validity, Cook and Campbell write that "tests of the extent to which one can generalize across various kinds of persons, settings, and times are, in essence, tests of statistical interactions" (1979, p. 73). To take an example, if an experimenter finds a relationship between $X$ and $Y$, and if the relationship does not interact with a third variable $Z$, then the investigator may generalize across levels of $Z$. Although that knowledge may be sufficient for basic research, it is not good enough for applied work. Let me explain.

Figure 1 shows a relationship between the logarithm of the smallest visible target ($Y$) and the logarithm of the least visible contrast of the target ($X$). Because the *shape* of this function is essentially the same for a wide range of luminance levels $Z$—that is, there is no interaction between $Y$ and $Z$—we can generalize and say that the function in Figure 1 holds across levels of luminance. Knowing that, however, is not sufficient for applied work. Design engineers are not interested in generalities—they want definite answers and precise numbers. As it relates to this example, a design engineer might want to know exactly what level of background luminance and what contrast should he or she design for in order that a target of size $X$ will be visible. As Figure 2 shows, the curves for different luminance levels are essentially parallel, showing no interaction, but the precise levels of $Y$ are just as dependent on luminance level as they are on contrast.

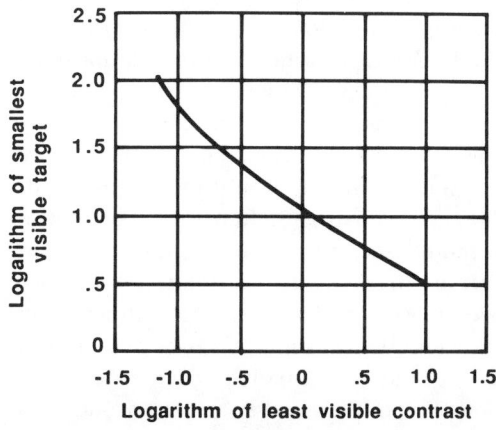

Figure 1. *The smallest visible target as a function of the contrast between the objects and their backgrounds. Background luminance was $10^{-3}$ footlamberts. Data of Blackwell from Chapanis, Garner, and Morgan, 1949.*

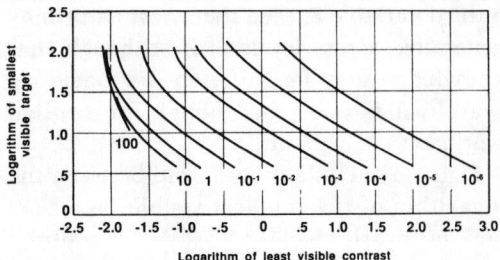

Figure 2. *The smallest visible target as a function of the background luminance (in footlamberts) and the contrast between the objects and their backgrounds. Data of Blackwell from Chapanis, Garner, and Morgan, 1949.*

So far my example involves only two variables. To complicate things even further, most applied work requires that we take into account a very large number of interacting variables. Our design engineer might, for example, tell us that the target will be green, visible for only a fraction of a second, and have to be detected in peripheral vision by overworked 40-year-old traffic controllers who may have been on the job for eight hours.

As I see it, the basic problem is not that, as Smith asserts, we have no general design guidelines in particular areas. Psychology in general—and human factors in particular—has hundreds of general laws, relationships, and guidelines. That is not the stumbling block for design. Where we stumble is in our ability to provide design engineers with precise numerical data to put into their specifications. Those specifications are almost without exception for machines or systems that are in some respects different from their predecessors and that are sometimes genuinely unique. They may never have been built before and may involve specific combinations of conditions never before encountered. A great deal of human factors research has to be specific because we are asked to provide definite answers and numbers for specific designs. Typical design guidelines, even when derived from generalizable findings, are useful only in telling us what variables we should consider when we do our specific studies. Although they have not yet been integrated into the general methodological literature, screening designs devised by Simon (1973, 1977) appear to provide an efficient way of coping with the multiplicity of factors encountered in practical research.

*A Rose Is Not a Rose Is Not a Rose*

The third and perhaps most important fallacy is that taxonomies—at least those that are currently available—will solve our problems of generalizability. I agree that it is useful to classify things into common categories, but all things bearing the same label are not necessarily equivalent. We all have an unfortunate tendency to overgeneralize about names and labels, but not all studies about fatigue, for example, investigate the same phenomenon simply because their titles contain the word *fatigue*. The same could be said about studies that profess to study decision making, feedback, psychomotor performance, stress, usability, workload, or any other of a large number of topics. These words—fatigue, decision making, and so on—are, in Aronson and Carlsmith's terms (1968), *conceptual variables*. Conceptual variables cannot be studied directly. They have to be defined operationally, and operational definitions of the same conceptual variable may vary greatly. Although investigators seldom state operational definitions explicitly, they can be inferred from the kinds of measurements that are made and the purposes for which the investigator says they were made.

Differences among diverse operational definitions are illustrated in a study by Wierwille, Rahimi, and Casali (1985), who investigated 16 assessment techniques all of which purportedly were measures of mental workload. The techniques ranged from physiological measures (heart rate and eyeblinks) to performance measures (tapping regularity and time estimation) and subjective estimates (rating scales). When the measures were validated in a simulated flight task, only one measure was able to distinguish reliably between high, medium, and low workloads. Six other measures were able to distinguish between two of the three workload conditions, and the remaining nine were not able to differentiate between any of the workloads.

Operational definitions that measure different things even when they presumably define the same conceptual variable may sometimes thwart our attempts to generalize when it seems intuitively obvious that we should be able to do so. For instance, Koelega and Brinkman (1986) reported recently on their attempts to find consistency among the findings of studies on the effects of noise on vigilance. To help achieve consistency they confined their survey to studies of vigilance that had similar task demands. Their efforts ended in failure. Part of the reason for the conflicting results, they state, is that various studies do not define and measure *noise* in the same way. Not only do noises vary in both intensity and frequency composition, but they may be continuous and meaningless, continuous and meaningful, continuous and variable, attractive or unattractive, real "live" sounds, intermittent bursts of white noise with random or fixed components, and so on. Their observations about the conceptual variable *noise* apply also to *vigilance*. Their survey led them to conclude the following:

> Only when very specific noise parameters and very specific task variables are investigated might a coherent body of results eventually emerge; but the very nature of this specificity means that attempts to generalize to other noise and vigilance situations would not make sense. (p. 478)

The lesson to be learned from this and similar studies is that we should be careful in generalizing about conceptual variables. Although it is tempting to assume that studies identified with a common key word all refer to the same phenomenon, in reality there may be little or no commonality among them. Taxonomies will have to become much more detailed and specific than they are at present if they are to help us cope with this reality.

## SOME EMPIRICAL EVIDENCE FOR GENERALIZATION

I turn now from the negative to the positive—to some empirical evidence to support our intuitive notion that under certain conditions we *can* generalize. The evidence all comes from psychological studies of learning.

### Generalization in Learning— Respondent Conditioning

Consider the following kind of experiment: An animal is harnessed in an apparatus with one paw resting on an electrode. If a tone, say, of 1000 Hz is sounded, the animal will probably merely prick up its ears. This tone is the stimulus to be conditioned, or, more briefly, the conditioned stimulus. If a shock—the unconditioned stimulus—is delivered to the animal's paw through the electrode, the animal will reflexly lift its paw— an unconditioned response. Now if the tone and shock are delivered simultaneously a sufficient number of times, the tone itself will eventually cause the animal to lift its paw reflexly. The animal, which previously had been neutral toward the tone, has been conditioned to produce automatic paw lifting upon hearing it.

Once a conditioned response has been established, tests show that the response generalizes—that is, it will be elicited by stimuli similar to the original conditioned one. So, for example, a tone of 1250 Hz, and perhaps even tones of 1500 or 2000 Hz, will elicit reflex paw withdrawal. The more nearly the test tone resemble the original one, the more likely it is that it will evoke the conditioned response. It is as though the biological system were defining a range of stimuli that it will consider equivalent.

*Generalization in Learning— Behavior Modification*

Behavior modification, the more applied derivative of operant conditioning, is essentially a procedure for changing behavior so that individuals will function more effectively in society (Martin and Pear, 1978). Examples are reducing tantrums in children, decreasing drug use, increasing verbal behavior, and increasing socially acceptable behavior such as thanking others who have helped or stopping at stop signs and traffic lights when driving. In general, the procedure uses positive reinforcement to reward desired behavior and the absence of reinforcement or punishment to eliminate or extinguish undesirable behavior.

Generalization is essential for behavior modification to be effective because without it, learning would be of limited value. What the behavior modifier hopes is that the behavior learned in training situations will hold up or transfer to new stimuli, other behaviors, new settings, and people other than those involved in training. As Gambrill (1977) points out, however, "one cannot simply count on generalization effects" (p. 273). Although the literature contains numerous examples of successful generalizations, one can also find many studies in which the expected generalization did not occur (see, for example, Foxx, McMorrow, and Mennemeier, 1984; Haring, 1985; Kogel, Glahn, and Nieminen, 1978; Odom, Hoyson, Jamieson, and Strain, 1985; Parsonson and Baer, 1978; Sprague and Horner, 1984). As in the case of respondent conditioning, the key appears to be similarity. "Conditions provided in the training situation should match those in the natural environment as closely as possible" (Gambrill, 1977, p. 272), and "The first effort of the behavior modifier attempting to program generalization should be to make the final stages of the training situation similar to the test situation (natural environment) in as many ways as possible" (Martin and Pear, 1978, p. 164).

*Generalization in Learning—Transfer of Training*

Even better evidence comes from studies of the transfer of training, a phenomenon somewhat similar to the generalization that occurs in conditioning or behavior modification but much more relevant to human factors. Once a skill—for example, riding a bicycle, operating a computer, or driving an automobile—is learned, that learning will generalize, or transfer, to situations similar but not identical to the one in which the original learning occurred. For example, it may take days for a novice to learn how to drive a specific automobile, but having mastered that skill, he or she can learn in a matter of minutes to drive almost any other automobile. As in the case of conditioning, transfer of training is more complete the greater the similarity between the original learning situation and the one to which learning transfers. Having learned to drive an automobile with automatic drive, it is easy to transfer to any other vehicle with automatic drive but more difficult to transfer to a vehicle that has a manual shift.

Training on actual systems to be operated is not essential for this kind of transfer, or generalization, to occur. In human factors many operators learn skills on a simulator— for example, a simulator of an aircraft cockpit or a simulator of the control room of a nuclear power plant. The skills they learn on the simulator then make it possible for them to learn more quickly how to operate a real aircraft or nuclear power plant. As is the case with behavior modification, not all training simulators result in positive transfer of training to real tasks. Some training simulators may actually produce *negative* transfer—that is, make it more difficult to learn the real task than would have been the case if the learner had had no experience with the simulator. Once again the key word is "similarity": more effective transfer occurs the more closely the simulator matches the real operating system—a condition usually referred to as *fidelity of simulation*.

### Extension of the Foregoing to Scientific Generalization

To use somewhat different words, studies of conditioning, behavior modification, and transfer of training tell us that people will react or perform in essentially the same way for a range of similar conditions. Now a human factors study is basically a simulation in which certain kinds of behavior are observed. It follows, then, that the closer the research situation matches some real one, the more justified we are in generalizing from the empirical findings to what would happen in a real environment. Even though we cannot measure precisely the fidelity of simulations, or the similarity between two situations, we have here some empirical support for generalization.

### Generalization through Replication

In the foregoing arguments I have made some generalizations—about conditioning, behavior modification, and transfer of training. By what kind of logic am I justified in making those generalizations?

We can generalize about conditioning because literally thousands of studies on this phenomenon have been done around the world in hundreds of laboratories. Moreover, these studies have been done with animals ranging from earthworms to human beings.

They have been done with hundreds of different stimuli, and those stimuli have been conditioned to a multiplicity of responses. In other words, our rationale for generalizing about conditioning is that conditioning experiments have been replicated with a wide variety of subjects, procedures, environmental surroundings, stimuli, and responses, and all those replications have yielded similar findings.

Much the same holds for behavior modification and transfer of training. Transfer of training studies have been done with all kinds of subjects, with tasks ranging from the simple to the complex and from the trivial to the highly significant, and with different investigators using a variety of procedures.

*A human factors example.* Smith's skepticism notwithstanding, I would assert that we have generalizations of this kind in human factors—findings that we can generalize because they have been observed in a variety of different situations.

One of my favorite examples comes from a critical incident study reported by Fitts and Jones some 40 years ago (and reprinted in the open literature in 1961) on errors made by Air Force pilots in operating aircraft controls. Their main finding was that the errors could be grouped into six major categories as follows:

- Operating the wrong control
- Failing to adjust a control properly
- Forgetting to operate a control
- Moving a control in the reverse direction
- Inadvertently activating a control
- Inability to reach a control when needed

Although this study was done on Air Force pilots 40 years ago, the findings are as valid today as they were then. They are valid because we find exactly the same kinds of control errors being made in the operation of washing machines, power lawnmowers, automobiles, nuclear power plants, modern airplanes, and hundreds of other machines and systems. In short, the Fitts and Jones findings have generality in part because similar findings have been observed formally and informally in a wide range of settings and with a large number of machines and systems.

## SOME FACTORS THAT LIMIT GENERALIZABILITY

What are some factors that restrict our ability to generalize? Recognizing them explicitly should make it easier for us to guard against them when we design our studies.

### Internal versus External Validity

Campbell and Stanley (1963) and Cook and Campbell (1979) make a useful distinction between what they call *internal* and *external validity* and list *threats* to each of these. *Internal validity* means, in essence, that the findings of a particular study follow logically and unequivocally from the way the study was designed and conducted. A study is internally valid if there are no contaminating factors (for example, confounding of variables) that vitiate the conclusion(s) of that study. *External validity* refers to the generalizability of the findings of an internally valid study to other situations.

Internal validity is, of course, a prerequisite to generalizability. One cannot generalize a finding if that finding is not supported by the data. In what follows I shall assume that studies were done properly, that safeguards against internal invalidity were observed, and that conclusions follow logically from the data. My concern is with threats to external validity—factors that restrict or limit our ability to generalize from the findings of an internally valid study. In their enumeration of these threats to external validity, Campbell, Cook, and Stanley were generally concerned with one or another form of formal experimentation. My concern here is with the broader range of human factors methods.

### Unrepresentative Subjects

Using unrepresentative subjects, the most obvious threat to external validity, is the one most often mentioned (sometimes the only one mentioned) in textbooks on methodology. It is so well known that it merits no elaboration beyond repeating the generally accepted rule that subjects should be representative of the persons to whom one wants to generalize.

### Inadequate Training

A seldom recognized threat to external validity is the inadequate preparation and training that subjects receive before measurements begin. To develop proficiency in many skills requires months and sometimes years. The classic study of telegraphy done by Bryan and Harter nearly a century ago (1897, 1899) is perhaps the first to provide quantitative evidence on this point. More recent data on other kinds of skills are summarized in the textbook by the Eastman Kodak Company (Ergonomics Group, 1986, pp. 262–265).

Even more important than the time required to acquire proficiency is the change in the nature of skills as training progresses. The Bryan and Harter study found that the nature of telegraphic skill changed as learning progressed. That finding has been substantiated by several studies (see Fleishman and Quaintance, 1984, pp. 336–340) showing that the combinations of abilities contributing to the performance of tasks early in training are different from those later in training.

Our skills in driving an automobile, flying an airplane, operating a computer, controlling air traffic, typing, navigating a ship, and many other kinds of tasks improve and change over long periods of time (Schneider, 1985). Yet most research studies in human factors give subjects no more than a few minutes to familiarize themselves with the task before measurements are begun. This may be one of the major sources of external invalidity in human factors studies.

*Inadequate Sampling of Situations*

Another subtle threat to external validity arises from inadequate sampling of the variations in real-life work that occur at different times. For example, activities of office workers may be quite different when payrolls have to be prepared than they are at any other times. Driving on interstate highways in the mid-West is not the same as driving in mid-Manhattan. Sales activities vary depending on the day of the week, the month, and the season. Navigating a large tanker through a narrow channel at night during a rainstorm is quite different from navigating the same ship in the open ocean on a calm sunlit day. Function analyses, action-information analyses, task analyses, activity analyses, workload analyses, and even controlled experiments involving these and many other kinds of tasks may give distorted and invalid results if variations in tasks that may occur at different times are not adequately sampled.

*Improper Choice of Dependent Variables*

Another threat to external validity that is seldom discussed has to do with the choice of dependent variables. All too often dependent variables are picked because they are easy to measure, because instruments or devices for measuring them are readily available, because the investigator or other people have used them, or simply because they are most likely to yield statistically significant results. As I pointed out in an article I wrote some years ago (Chapanis, 1971), in human factors work the researcher should always be asking himself or herself, "Of all the dependent variables I could pick for my study, which one(s) will have the greatest amount of transfer to the design or evaluation of a machine or system?"

To illustrate what I meant, I compared a "baker's dozen" of systems criteria—that is, criteria that are important to the designer or engineer—with an equal number of criteria typically used in research (Table 1). The list of research criteria in this table is, to be sure, a highly abbreviated one. Nonetheless, these are criteria that one can find used over and over again in human factors studies.

The two columns in this table indicate that there seems to be little correspondence between them. It is difficult to see what some of the research criteria in the left-hand column have to do with any of the systems criteria in the right-hand column. Moreover, a number of systems criteria do not seem to be measured by any of the research criteria. This, I believe, is one major reason that it is often difficult to generalize from research studies

TABLE 1

Some Common Dependent Measures (or Criteria) Used in Ergonomic and Human Factors Research (Left Column) and Some General Systems Criteria (Right Column)

| Research Criteria | Systems Criteria |
| --- | --- |
| Accuracy (or, conversely, errors) | Anticipated life of the system |
| Cardiovascular responses | Appearance |
| Critical flicker fusion | Comfort |
| EEG | Convenience |
| Energy expenditure | Ease of operation or use |
| Muscle tension | Familiarity |
| Psychophysical thresholds | Initial cost |
| Ratings (e.g., of annoyance, comfort, etc.) | Maintainability (e.g., mean time to repair) |
| Reaction time | Manpower requirements |
| Respiratory responses | Operating cost |
| Spare mental capacity | Reliability (e.g., mean time to failure) |
| Speed | Safety |
| Trials to learn | Training requirements |

From Chapanis (1971)

to applications—the dependent variables studied have little or nothing to do with the criteria that are important in the design world.

*Long-Term Changes*

Still another source of external invalidity is likely to become even more important as our profession matures and acquires some history. It is that long-term changes in the world of work may invalidate studies done even a few years ago. Driving an automobile, flying an aircraft, doing secretarial work, checking out groceries in a supermarket—all these and many more activities are different today from the way they were as recently as ten years ago. Changes in technology and in our environment are responsible for many of these changes. But we must not overlook equally important changes in our population. We are becoming an aged population, and a greater proportion of women are entering the labor force. Both of these changes have consequences for the design of work and leisure activities. Much more subtle are changes in the skills available in our population (see, for example, National Commission on Excellence in Education, 1983). At the very time when the demand for highly skilled workers is increasing, there is evidence that the intellectual skills of our population are decreasing.

Because of these important but gradual changes, the results of activity analyses, function analyses, action-information requirements analyses, task analyses, time-line analyses, fault-tree analyses, failure modes and effects analyses, workload analyses, and even controlled experiments done today may not be valid 10 or 20 years from now.

*Measurement Artifacts*

Finally, the research process itself may be the source of several kinds of invalidity (Webb, Campbell, Schwartz, and Sechrest, 1966), and the classic Hawthorne studies (Roethlisberger and Dickson, 1939) are a dramatic example. An example from my own experience comes immediately to mind. A number of years ago we studied the activities of workers in large law offices in Baltimore and Washington using, among other techniques, activity analyses. By subtle means we were able to compare certain activities of workers who did not know they were being observed with those of workers who knew they were being observed. It should come as no surprise that workers behaved differently when they knew they were being studied than when they did not.

Other sources of invalidity may come from subtle interactions between the experimenter and subjects and the intrusiveness of measurement devices on the behavior and performance of subjects. These and related sources of invalidity are very difficult to guard against, particularly in the human factors domain, where so much of our work involves simulations of complex equipment and systems and such elaborate tests that it is almost impossible to disguise them. Nevertheless it is important to be aware of these problems and to use, whenever possible, unobtrusive kinds of research and measuring devices.

## DESIGNING STUDIES FOR GENERALITY

In human factors work we use the word *generalization* to refer to two somewhat different situations. In the first, we want to generalize or extrapolate from a particular study to some specific application. We want to design a study to predict how nuclear power plant operators will respond to a computerized display in an emergency, or we want to predict how well drivers will be able to drive with a novel type of steering mechanism.

The second way we use the word *generalization* is when we want to design a study whose findings will apply to or be valid over a wide range of situations. Such generalizations are contained in the hundreds of guidelines and recommendations one can find in the human factors literature, of which the following two are examples:

> When comparing alternative designs from the human engineering point of view, the simplest design will be one that is easiest to operate and maintain because it will require less crew training, less crew workload, and will have the least potential for human error. (NASA, 1987, p. 2.0-1)
>
> Simple tasks can be performed effectively at much higher levels of fatigue than more complex tasks. Thus, in designing the daily schedules, it would be beneficial to place the complex tasks during periods of least fatigue. (p. 4.0-18)

Different rules apply to the design of studies that are to be generalized in these two ways.

*Extrapolating to a Specific Design Application*

In designing studies that are to be used to predict behavior in a specific situation, the guiding principle can be summed up in one word: *similarity*. The study should be as similar as possible to the real situation. This means that subjects, apparatus, tasks, dependent variables, and the test environment should simulate or match those of the application as closely as possible.

*What feature of the data do you want to generalize?* A complexity in extrapolating from research studies to applications is that different applications may require different kinds of data. Most researchers in the behavioral sciences are interested only in averages and the differences among those averages. That is also true of human factors studies in which the designer, engineer, or human factors professional is interested only in a simple comparison between two or more alternatives. For example, which of warning devices A, B, or C is likely to alert an overloaded operator most quickly, or which of four brake pedals will result in the fastest braking reaction time? For applications of this kind, the primary purpose of the study is to discover whether there are significant differences among average measures of performance. These are then used as the basis for a prediction about what will happen in the application environment.

Often, however, design engineers are faced with trade-offs, and the resolution of some trade-offs requires slightly different kinds of data. In evaluating two complex training simulators, for example, one of them, A, may cost more, be more complex to operate, require more personnel to operate, or be more complex to maintain than B. In such a case, the engineer may still decide to go with simulator A if the human factors professional can demonstrate that A compensates for its disadvantages by doing a much better job of training. Applications of this kind require not only that there be a difference between means but that the difference be greater than some specific amount. Although this is only an extension of the simpler case discussed earlier, it does require a somewhat different statistical analysis.

Other trade-off studies, particularly those that may be subjected to a sensitivity analysis, require data showing how human performance varies for incremental changes in design. For example, how much is human performance degraded for each degree change in temperature, for each change in oxygen concentration, or for each extra hour of work? To obtain data of this kind, an adequate number of tests must be made over a wide range of conditions so that regression lines or equations may be computed.

A third kind of application is the most difficult for which to get data. We accept as a general human factors guideline that in many cases we should design not for the average person but, rather, for the middle 90%, the top 95%, or the bottom 95% of people depending on the application. As an example, we might want to know exactly how to design the displays, instructions, and sequence of operations for an automated banking terminal so that at least 95% of typical users will be able to complete a transaction successfully on their first exposure to the machine. Designing studies to get answers to questions of this kind requires careful attention to the selection of subject-users and the number of them that will be used in the study.

*A final word on similarity.* It's easy enough to say that research studies should simulate closely the situations to which they are to be extrapolated, but the rule is difficult to apply because we have no way of measuring similarity or of knowing how similar is similar enough. Although attempts have been made to formulate general laws relating generalization to dimensions of psychological similarity (see, for example, Shepard, 1987), they are still much too theoretical and apply to too restricted situations to be of use to the human factors practitioner. Under the circumstances, we have to fall back on the experience, sophistication, and good judgment of the investigator. Familiarity with the literature and experience with what works and what does not work are invaluable aids to the investigator in deciding how similar is similar enough.

## Studies Supporting Broad Generalizations

There are two ways one can go about doing studies that will extrapolate to a wide range of situations. The first is by deliberately building heterogeneity into studies, a tactic recommended by Brunswik (1956) over 30 years ago; the second is by replication.

*Designing heterogeneity into studies.* To design heterogeneity into studies, the subjects, apparatus, tasks, response measures (dependent variables), and environmental conditions should be as heterogeneous as is feasible. This notion is so contrary to what we have generally been taught in courses on experimental design that I think it is worth clarifying with some examples.

I refer first to a study by Lutz and Chapanis (1955), not because I think it is the best exemplar of the point I want to make but, rather, because I am familiar with the unwritten reasoning that led us to do what we did. Our study was done for the telephone company at a time when push-button telephone sets had not yet been designed for public use. Our purpose was to try to find out what a push-button telephone set should look like—in particular, where numbers and letters should be located on a keyset. Given that the keyset would be used by the general population, we deliberately selected subjects broadly, or, to use Cook and Campbell's terminology (1979, p. 75), we deliberately sampled for heterogeneity. We used equal numbers of men and women, selected subjects from three age groups, and used equal numbers of subjects who claimed to be either naive or sophisticated with regard to their experience with keysets.

Similar reasoning applied to the keysets. The configuration of the keyset had not yet been decided upon, so we deliberately chose six different possible configurations.

One of the principal findings of our study was that the most commonly selected pattern of assigning numbers or letters was from left to right and then from top to bottom. Our findings had considerable generalizability because of the following:

- We found no significant differences between the choices of (a) men and women, (b) naive and experienced subjects, and (c) persons in the different age groups.
- The same assignment rule held for both numerals and letters.
- The same finding held for all configurations of the keyset.

That is much greater generalizability than would have come from a study that had used a more homogeneous group of subjects, had used only one task, and had tested only one keyset.

The second study I shall cite was done by Ledgard, Singer, and Whiteside (1981), who worked with a commercially available computer program, Control Data Corporation's NOS Version I Text Editor. Briefly, they modified the program by replacing the original notational commands with more English-like words. They then tested the two editors with three groups of subjects: inexperienced users (persons who claimed having fewer than 10 hours of computer experience), familiar users (persons with between 11 and 100 hours of computer experience), and experienced users (persons who claimed over 100 hours of terminal use).

Figure 3 shows one part of their findings. Although the percentage of the task completed is clearly related to prior computer experience, the more important finding was that performance on the English editor was better for all three groups of subjects. Ledgard et al. (1981) also used four dependent measures: percentage of the task completed, percentage of erroneous commands used, editing efficiency (the average number of commands needed to make a single editing change), and subjective preferences. All four measures were consistent in showing that the experimental editor was superior to the original one. From the standpoint of this article, however, the point I want to make is that the findings of this study are more generalizable because of the heterogeneity of the subjects and dependent measures used.

In the critical incident study by Fitts and Jones to which I have already referred, their findings have generality in part because of the heterogeneity of the aircraft from which data were collected. Although this point is not made explicitly by the authors, data were collected from pilots of single-engine and multiengine aircraft, pursuit aircraft and bombers, cargo aircraft, and combat vehicles. Another factor contributing to greater generality was the heterogeneity of the situations from which data were collected: training flights, cross-country flights, and combat missions.

I could list further examples, but I think these are sufficient to substantiate my point: Generality is enhanced when the same findings can be demonstrated to appear with heterogeneous subjects, tasks, and ecological conditions. To search for that kind of generality, one must deliberately build heterogeneity into one's studies.

*A word of caution.* At this point a word of caution is in order. When I say that one should deliberately introduce heterogeneity into one's studies, I don't mean that all controls and order should be thrown to the winds. There are ways of introducing heterogeneity into human factors studies that do not compromise their validity. To elaborate on this point would mean discussing technical matters of methodology that would take us beyond the scope of this article. Suffice to say that the studies by Lutz and Chapanis and by Ledgard et al. are two examples of how heterogeneity can validly be built into a research study.

*Achieving generalizability through replica-*

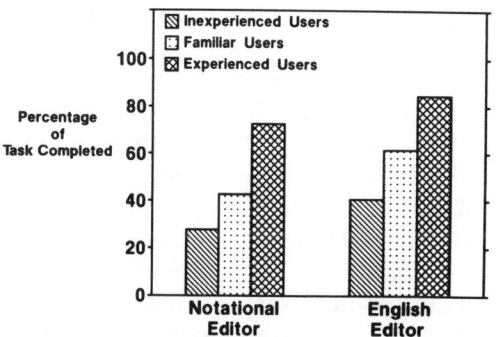

Figure 3. *Percentage of editing tasks completed by three groups of subjects using either the original (notational) editor or an experimental, more English-like editor. Data from Ledgard, Singer, and Whiteside, 1981.*

*tion.* The second way of achieving generalizability is, unfortunately, used all too seldom. It is simply to replicate, to repeat, studies that have already been done. Ideally, a replication should match some original study with a minor change in conditions, with the addition of a new variable, or with the deletion of a variable originally used. However, we should not overlook the value of repeating studies exactly, or as exactly as possible. In a strict sense, it is impossible to duplicate research exactly. If for no other reason, the repeated study will have been done at some later time, with a different investigator, with different subjects, and with at least subtle differences in the environment or context of the study. If the replicated study yields the same findings as the original one, this means that the findings are robust enough to appear in two different time periods, with two different investigators, with a different group of subjects, and under somewhat different environmental conditions. Knowing that adds a small but important increment to our confidence about the generalizability of the original findings.

There is antipathy in the scientific community about repeating studies, and journal editors are reluctant to publish such studies. I hope that these attitudes will change and that we shall begin to see at least short notes stating that some original study was repeated and that the findings were or were not confirmed. If we are indeed seriously committed to increasing the store of true generalizations in our profession, we should encourage our students to replicate studies already done and should do so ourselves without feeling that we are wasting our time.

*But what if the same findings don't appear?* What I have just said may sound as though I think studies will always yield the same results when one builds heterogeneity into them, or when one replicates them. That's not true, of course. In fact, it's more the exception than the rule. Different groups of subjects often do respond differently, different tasks usually produce different kinds of behavior, and variations in the environment often cause people to perform differently. But that's no reason for abandoning heterogeneity as an approach and going back to single-variable, tightly controlled kinds of studies. And, if anything, it's all the more reason for replicating. Knowing that one can't generalize some findings across subjects, tasks, or environments is itself a generalization that is worth having.

## CONCLUSION

So what do we conclude? Is the human factors literature too full of specific applied studies and too deficient in studies that can be generalized? Having thought about this business of generalization and having clarified in my own mind what it means and how to get it, I think that considering the youthfulness of our profession and the complexity of the problems we deal with, our discipline is in good shape. We have many general guidelines and recommendations, but these will never be enough. One reason for our existence is that we supply design engineers not only with general statements but with definite numbers and specifications that they can design to. Because the devices and systems that engineers design are almost invariably novel in some respect and are used in novel circumstances, general guidelines and recommendations will never be enough. We shall always have to have specific studies to obtain the exact answers and precise values that engineers need for particular applications. In the final analysis, however, every study, whether basic or applied, can be generalized to some extent. The real challenge for investigators is to find out how much and to what other situations any particular study can be generalized.

# REFERENCES

Anastasi, A. (1979). *Fields of applied psychology* (2nd ed.). New York: McGraw-Hill.

Aronson, E., and Carlsmith, J. M. (1968). Experimentation in social psychology. In G. Lindzey and E. Aronson (Eds.), *The handbook of social psychology. Vol. 2: Research methods* (2nd ed., pp. 1–79). Reading, MA: Addison-Wesley.

Brunswik, E. (1956). *Systematic and representative design of psychological experiments.* Berkeley: University of California Press.

Bryan, W. L., and Harter, N. (1897). Studies in the physiology and psychology of the telegraphic language. *Psychological Review, 4,* 27—53.

Bryan, W. L., and Harter, N. (1899). Studies on the telegraphic language: The acquisition of a hierarchy of habits. *Psychological Review, 6,* 345–375.

Campbell, D. T., and Stanley, J. C. (1963). *Experimental and quasi-experimental designs for research.* Chicago: Rand McNally.

Chapanis, A. (1967). The relevance of laboratory studies to practical situations. *Ergonomics, 10,* 557–577.

Chapanis, A. (1971). The search for relevance in applied research. In W. T. Singleton, J. G. Fox, and D. Whitfield (Eds.), *Measurement of man at work* (pp. 1–14). London: Taylor and Francis.

Chapanis, A., Garner, W. R., and Morgan, C. T. (1949). *Applied experimental psychology: Human factors in engineering design.* New York: Wiley.

Cook, T. D., and Campbell, D. T. (1979). *Quasi-experimentation: Design and analysis issues for field settings.* Chicago: Rand McNally.

Ergonomics Group, Health and Environment Laboratories, Eastman Kodak Company. (1986). *Ergonomic design for people at work* (Vol. 2). New York: Van Nostrand Reinhold.

Fitts, P. M., and Jones, R. E. (1961). Analysis of factors contributing to 460 "pilot-error" experiences in operating aircraft controls. In H. W. Sinaiko (Ed.), *Selected papers on human factors in the design and use of control systems* (pp. 332–358). New York: Dover.

Fleishman, E. A., and Quaintance, M. K. (1984). *Taxonomies of human performance.* New York: Academic Press.

Foxx, R. M., McMorrow, M. J., and Mennemeier, M. (1984). Teaching social/vocational skills to retarded adults with a modified table game: An analysis of generalization. *Journal of Applied Behavior Analysis, 17,* 343–352.

Fromkin, H. L., and Streufert, S. (1976). Laboratory experimentation. In M. D. Dunnette (Ed.), *Handbook of industrial and organizational psychology* (pp. 415–465). Chicago: Rand McNally.

Gambrill, E. D. (1977). *Behavior modification: Handbook of assessment, intervention and analysis.* San Francisco: Jossey-Bass.

Haring, T. G. (1985). Teaching between-class generalization of toy play behavior to handicapped children. *Journal of Applied Behavior Analysis, 18,* 127–139.

Koelega, H. S., and Brinkman, J-A. (1986). Noise and vigilance: An evaluation review. *Human Factors, 28,* 465–481.

Kogel, R. L., Glahn, T. J., and Nieminen, G. S. (1978). Generalization of parent-training results. *Journal of Applied Behavior Analysis, 11,* 95–109.

Ledgard, H., Singer, A., and Whiteside, J. (1981). *Directions in human factors for interactive systems.* New York: Springer-Verlag.

Lindsay, A. D. (Ed.). (1911). *A treatise on human nature by David Hume* (Vol. 1). London: J. M. Dent.

Lutz, M. C., and Chapanis, A. (1955). Expected locations of digits and letters on ten-button keysets. *Journal of Applied Psychology, 39,* 314–317.

Martin, G., and Pear, J. (1978). *Behavior modification: What it is and how to do it.* Englewood Cliffs, NJ: Prentice-Hall.

Meister, D. (1985). *Behavioral analysis and measurement methods.* New York: Wiley.

National Aeronautics and Space Administration. (1987). *Man-system integration standards,* Vol. 1, (NASA-STD 3000). Washington, DC: Author.

National Commission on Excellence in Education. (1983). *A nation at risk: The imperative for educational reform.* Washington, DC: U.S. Department of Education.

Odom, S. L., Hoyson, M., Jamieson, B., and Strain, P. S. (1985). Increasing handicapped preschoolers' peer social interactions: Cross-setting and component analysis. *Journal of Applied Behavior Analysis, 18,* 3–16.

Parsonson, G. S., and Baer, D. M. (1978). Training generalized improvisation of tools by preschool children. *Journal of Applied Behavior Analysis, 11,* 363–380.

Roethlisberger, F. J., and Dickson, W. J. (1939). *Management and the worker.* Cambridge, MA: Harvard University Press.

Schneider, W. (1985). Training high-performance skills: Fallacies and guidelines. *Human Factors, 27,* 285–300.

Shepard, R. N. (1987). Toward a universal law of generalization for psychological science. *Science, 237,* 1317–1323.

Simon, C. W. (1973). *Economical multifactor designs for human factors engineering experiments* (Tech. Report P73-326A). Culver City, CA: Hughes Aircraft Company.

Simon, C. W. (1977). *Design, analysis and interpretation of screening designs for human factors engineering experiments* (Tech. Report CWS-03-77). Westlake Village, CA: Canyon Research Group.

Simon, C. W. (1987). Will egg-sucking ever become a science? *Human Factors Society Bulletin, 30*(6), 1–4.

Smith, L. L. (1987). Whyfore human factors? *Human Factors Society Bulletin, 30*(2), 6–7.

Sprague, J. R., and Horner, R. H. (1984). The effects of single instance, multiple instance and general class training on generalized vending machine use by moderately and severely handicapped students. *Journal of Applied Behavior Analysis, 17,* 273–278.

Webb, E. J., Campbell, D. T., Schwartz, R. D., and Sechrest, L. (1966). *Unobtrusive measures: Nonreactive research in the social sciences.* Chicago: Rand McNally.

Wierwille, W. W., Rahimi, M., and Casali, J. G. (1985). Evaluation of 16 measures of mental workload using a simulated flight task emphasizing mediational activity. *Human Factors, 27,* 489–502.

# 3

## AN EXPERIMENTAL VIEW OF THE DESIGN PROCESS

Joseph M. Ballay

Center for Art & Technology
Carnegie-Mellon University
Pittsburgh, Pennsylvania

## ABSTRACT

Patterns of design problem solving are revealed by experiments with designers using traditional methods and computer-aided systems to solve a typical industrial design problem. Comparing a model of the design process with the products of designers' problem solving suggests that the early stages of the process are particularly important to the production of successful designs. The early stages of the design process are defined from three viewpoints—as an ill-defined construction task, as a visual task, and as a series of information transactions. These viewpoints provide a context for considering several patterns: patterns of planning, routine processes, information management, and the use of visual representations. In particular, the process of sketching visual representations is examined as it fits within the larger context of design problem solving.

## I. INTRODUCTION

In this paper, I intend to convey some insights about the design process that I and my colleagues gained during a recent research project. We were trying to understand how the design process, particularly the design of mass-produced, durable products, was affected by the use of CAD systems. Our aim was, and still is, to improve the usability of computer systems in designing, especially during the most creative phases of the process. As a part of the research project, we defined a design scenario. This design scenario is typical of industrial design tasks and is portable, which allowed us to observe designers working on it in a traditional design environment as well as on a CAD system.

The scenario required designers to design *Easybanker*, a hypothetical but plausible product which allows the payment of credit card bills from home through the telephone system to the bank. It was imagined to be about the size of a typical telephone modem and included a card reader, a keypad, an LCD display, and a miniaturized voice recognition cell. In addition to the product concept, the designers were given a package of information including functional requirements for *Easybanker*, specifications on alternative components, component costs, and production constraints.

The design sessions were videotaped and observed. The designers were asked to verbalize their actions as they went along. Significant events were then organized into a protocol of each designer's session.

The insights reported here are based on the observation of approximately fifty designers, design students, engineers, and draftsmen. Of these, eighteen were the subjects of detailed protocol analysis, and one subject was studied in-depth for approximately twenty hours of design activity.

## II. MODELING THE DESIGN PROCESS

For the purpose of organizing our observations, we agreed on a tentative model of the design process. It was based on existing literature (Jones, 1970) about the design process and on a preliminary analysis of the design process as we observed it. The model had five subtask segments which were assumed to run more or less sequentially:

1. *Criteria Formulation* - collecting and analyzing information to establish design criteria.
2. *Space Organization* - volumetric decisions concerning fit, function, ergonomics, and aesthetics.
3. *Details and Structure* - engineering refinement of previously defined concepts.
4. *Appearance Decisions* - decisions that merge concepts with aesthetic criteria.
5. *Release Package* - producing and assembling final documents for release.

In comparison to this model, the design process which was actually observed turned out to be mostly sequential, with some parts of the segments running in parallel and with only a little backtracking. In order to evaluate the designs produced by this process, we established five categories of product

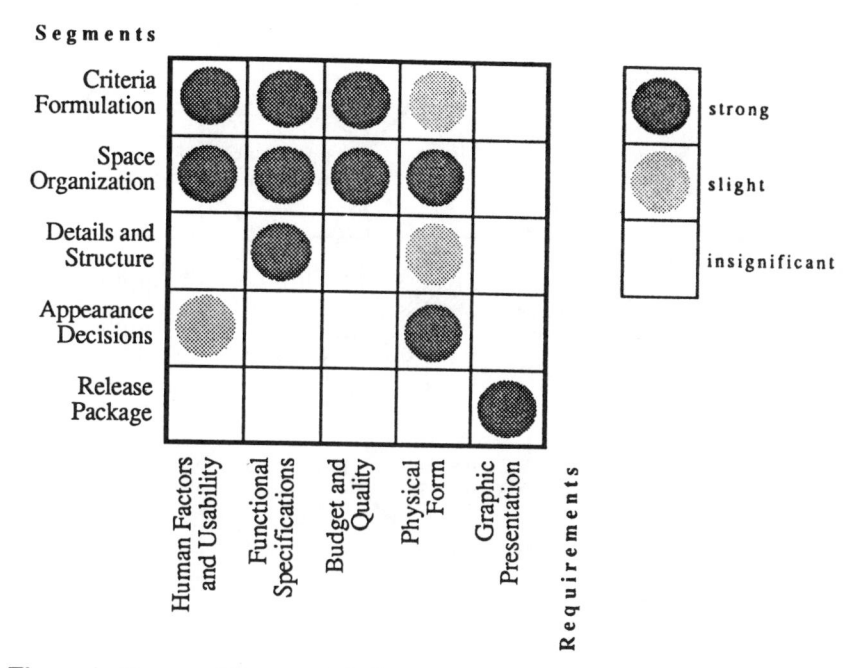

**Figure 1.** Degree of Segment's Influence on Meeting Product Requirements.

requirements. The designers were told that their designs would have to respond to these requirements, but no priority or weighting was given. These categories were the following:

o  *Human Factors and Usability* - meeting the needs of the user.
o  *Functional Specifications* - meeting the engineering requirements for production and functional performance.
o  *Budget and Quality* - achieving an appropriate balance of cost/performance in the use of alternative components.
o  *Physical Form* - assuring size, shape, and appearance are appropriate to the environment in which it will be used.
o  *Graphic Presentation* - assuring the release package is appropriate to professional standards.

One analysis of the observed design process involved comparing the five segments of the sequential model against the five categories of product requirements in a simple interaction matrix (see Figure 1). Each cell of the matrix represented the degree (strong, slight, or insignificant) to which design decisions made during that segment influenced the eventual success in meeting that product requirement. In other words, when in the design process were the significant decisions made which influenced the eventual success of the design?

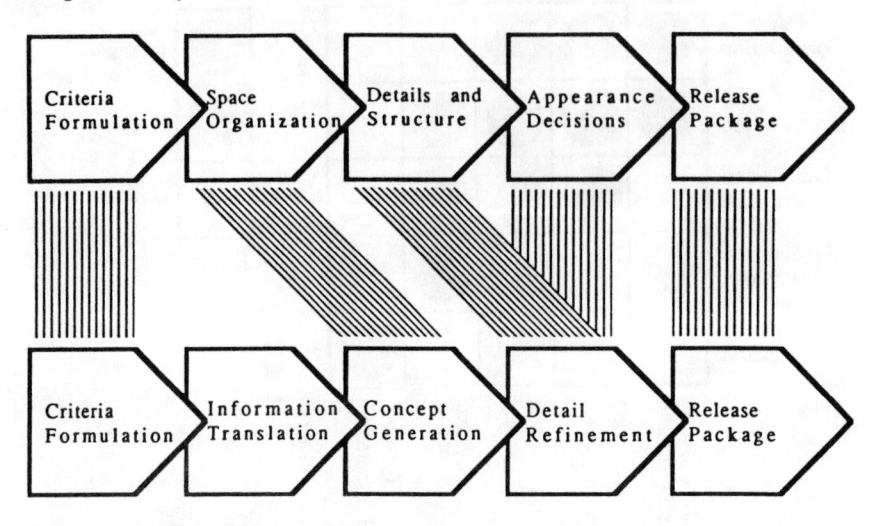

Original Sequential Model

Criteria Formulation → Space Organization → Details and Structure → Appearance Decisions → Release Package

Criteria Formulation → Information Translation → Concept Generation → Detail Refinement → Release Package

Revised Sequential Model

**Figure 2.** Revised Sequential Model.

The cells of the matrix were assigned degrees of significance based on reviews of the session protocols. It was immediately clear that the early segments were the most significant. Decisions made during the Criteria Formulation and Space Organization segments, in particular, were of prime significance in influencing the design with respect to the Human Factors and Usability, Functional Specifications, and Budget and Quality requirements. The Physical Form requirement was influenced throughout the design process, and the Graphic Presentation requirement was influenced only at the end.

This exercise confirmed our beliefs that the early stages of the design process deserved the most detailed study if we were to affect the ability of designers to design better products on computer systems.

As observational data accumulated, it became clear that our sequential model would have to be revised (see Figure 2). The Details and Structure segment and the Appearance Decisions segment ran so consistently in parallel that they were combined into a single segment named Detail Refinement. Space Organization was renamed Concept Generation to more accurately reflect the scope of activities which occurred during that segment. Most importantly, it became clear that the model needed a new segment named Information Translation. It reflects the designer's significant subproblem of translating the information he receives, such as written briefs, drawings, and specifications, into a format or mode that is useful in the problem solving process. For example, several designers in the traditional environment converted alternative components—part of the information package—into crude models made of plastic foam, paper, or foamboard. Designers in the CAD environment would convert these drawings into CAD drawing files.

This new Information Translation segment and the recognized importance of the early segments of the design process set the priorities for our research, which I will try to reflect in the rest of this paper. I will focus on the patterns we observed designers using to manipulate and use information during the early parts of the design process.

## III. THREE VIEWS OF THE DESIGN PROCESS

At various times during the analysis of the protocols, we found it enlightening to think about the early phases of the design process from different points of view. Three of the most useful viewpoints are described briefly below. The first derives from the literature on the psychology of problem solving. The second responds directly to the tangible output we observed from the design process. The third is a more abstract view derived from an information processing model of human cognition.

### A. Design as an Ill-defined Construction Task

If we examine design from the viewpoint of the individual designer as a problem solver, we find that two aspects of design tasks have an important impact on the way design problems are solved: design tasks are *construction tasks*, and design tasks are *ill-defined*.

By a construction task we mean a task which has as its main goal the creation, by cumulative action, of a persisting external product—a product which must satisfy a demanding set of criteria before the task is said to have been successfully completed. Industrial design is an example of a construction task because its main goal is the production of an external representation of the solution which must satisfy criteria of utility, clarity, aesthetics, etc. Other examples of construction tasks are computer programming, sculpting, carpentry, and assembling a HEATHKIT amplifier.

Construction tasks vary widely in the demands they place on the problem solver for decisions about the product form. Tasks such as routine carpentry and HEATHKIT amplifier assembly place minimal demands on the problem solver for decisions about the nature of the end result. In contrast, tasks such as sculpting and computer programming impose major demands on the problem solver to contribute to the shaping of the final product. Tasks such as these two are described (Reitman, 1965) as ill-defined because they do not provide the problem solver with sufficient information to specify the final product. Problem solvers must, therefore, provide information through their own decisions which further specify the task and define the form of the final product. There are a number of consequences which follow if a task is an ill-defined construction task:

- The partially completed product becomes part of the task environment. That is, what has been constructed up to now influences the subsequent course of problem solution and the shape of the final product. In design, the designer's current sketches are used as a source of ideas and inferences which shape later design decisions.
- Because the partially completed product is continually changing, the task environment is continually changing. These changes in environment stimulate new ideas and inferences. As a result, invention (finding a new way) is stimulated continuously throughout the course of the solution, right up to the moment when the final drawing is completed.
- Because construction tasks produce a final product which must satisfy external criteria, such tasks necessarily involve a commitment of resources. The more expensive the commitment of resources in producing the final product, the more desirable it will be to plan. All construction tasks benefit from planning because all involve commitment of expensive resources.

## B. Design as a Visual Task

As we have seen, design resembles other ill-defined construction tasks. However, there are also some important ways in which design differs from the others. Perhaps the most important difference has to do with the "visual" nature of design. If a designer has several ideas in mind, he typically cannot evaluate the relationship among them until they are made visible. A drawn external representation is a very important aid to the designer in making spatial inferences. Experienced design teachers find that students who claim to have designed wonderful things "in their heads" usually discover disastrous flaws in their designs when they try to put them on paper.

Furthermore, experienced designers mix drawing with other types of external representations. The designer in our in-depth study made use of seven distinct types of representation in the course of designing the *Easybanker*. Each of these appears to serve unique functions in aiding the design process:

- *Procedural Representations* - encoded action scenarios. A designer engages in a brief play. For example, he uses a procedural representation to describe how the user will operate the *Easybanker*.
- *Solid Models* - three-dimensional materials. They help a designer perceive volumetric relations, to orient volumes in space, and to facilitate the arrangement of volumes with respect to one another in space.
- *Matrices* - two-dimensional (usually) grids of information. A designer constructs a matrix to help him to choose which of the alternative parts he wants to work with. The rows of the matrix represent part types

(keyboards, displays, etc.) and the columns represent alternative models of each type. Information concerning each model is contained in the cells. Thus, keyboard number 1 costs $1.20 and is "big," while keyboard number 2 costs $1.10 and clicks when the keys are pressed.

o *Orthographic Projections* - views perpendicular to the principal Cartesian planes. Many orthographic views were produced, including one with a Polaroid camera. The photograph provided a crude plan view of an arrangement of the solid models. It was used as a record of the locations of the parts with respect to each other.

o *Notations* - words, numbers, letters, and related symbols. The notations may vary in length from a single character to a few lines. Usually, they were no longer than a few words.

o *Perspective Drawings* - graphic conventions which imply a "spatial" view of objects. Many perspective views were produced. The perspective sketches served to record the designer's decisions about the orientation of the parts and about the appearance of the envelope that contained them.

o *Dimensions* - representation which combines symbolic and graphic components. In this representation, meaning is conveyed by both the symbolic and the graphic components. If a designer changes either the numbers or the positions of the arrows, the meaning of the representation changes.

It is evident from the session protocols that a designer uses the various representations episodically, tending to do all the work he can in one representational mode at a time. When that work is done, he switches to another representational mode to do the next block of work. Figure 3 shows some of these episodes graphically.

## C. Design as a Series of Information Transactions

At the procedural level, the design process can be explained by the cyclical model shown in Figure 4. The model is based on principles of human cognition (Newell & Simon, 1972) and is useful in describing where information comes from and goes to at any stage of the design process. It accounts for the information held in the designer's head and the information held in the external environment, or held in a computer in the case of an automated design system. Most importantly, the model puts representations in a position of central importance as the medium of exchange between the designer and the computer.

We have observed that designers do not know many details about what they are going to sketch until part of the sketch is made; "knowing" is in the observing of the external sketch. According to the information transaction model, a designer begins sketching (enters the transaction) with only partial information, retrieved from his own memory, about the sketch that will be

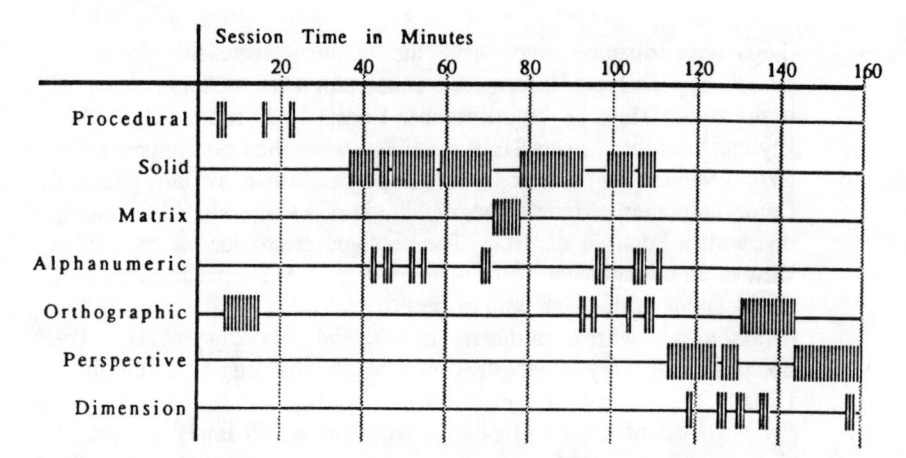

**Figure 3.** Alternation of Representational Modes. The seven modes of representation were used by a designer during an experimental session that lasted about 160 minutes. The horizontal bands of marks indicate where each model was actively used, with each mark indicating about two minutes of activity. The episodic use of representations can be seen in the clustering of activity in each of the modes. In particular, note the long episodes of solid modeling early in the session and the alternation between orthographic and perspective toward the end of the session. Aside from some time in the first 30 minutes of the session, when the subject was studying the information package, there was nearly continuous activity in one or more modes.

produced. Additional information is retrieved from the task environment, including computers in the environment. A record of the information processes is encoded in a representation, which then becomes a part of the designer's memory and of the task environment. The representations are external and can take a variety of modes, as described above.

If one imagines putting these information transactions end to end, the external artifacts of the design process would appear as a chain of representations, the majority of which are sketches. The large number of sketches produced in the protocols indicates the importance of sketching to the creative design process.

## IV. PATTERNS IN DESIGN PROBLEM SOLVING

By using any of our views of the design process, patterns of design problem solving behavior began to emerge. I believe these patterns represent the most interesting and useful insights we gained from this research. We observed idiosyncratic variations in the overall design process depending on the experiences and preferences of the individual designers. Regardless of how the

Experimental View of the Design Process 35

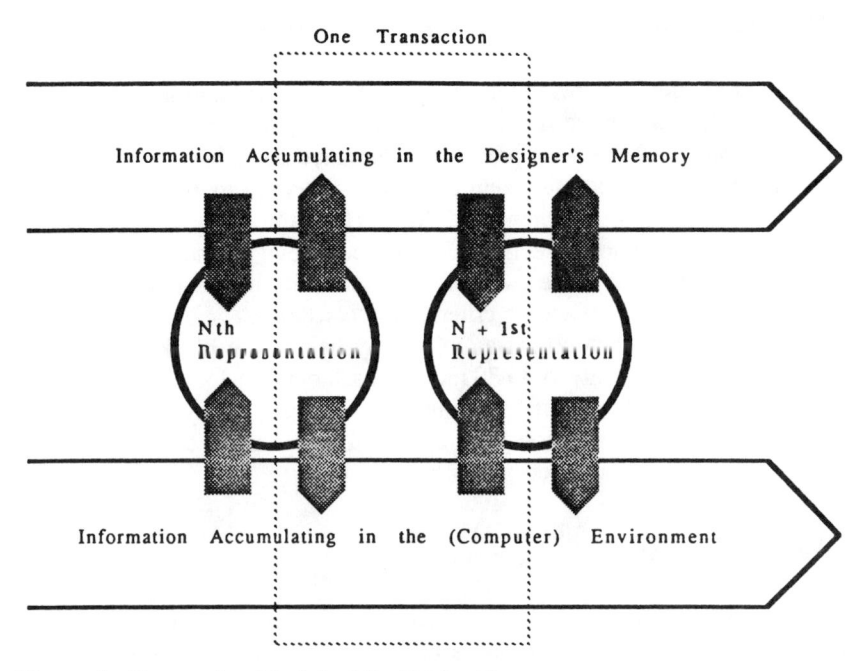

**Figure 4.** Transaction Model of the Design Process.

process varied in its organization between these basic patterns, there was consistency within the patterns. Figure 5 graphically describes the patterns of three kinds of activity in the overall design process—*Planning, Routine Primary Processes,* and *Workplace Management.*

**Figure 5.** Overall Design Activity Patterns. These three kinds of design activity constituted the process of a designer during a 160-minute experimental session. The horizontal bands of marks indicate the duration of each activity, with each mark indicating about two minutes of activity. Routines involve the use of well-rehearsed professional skills toward an interim goal. Note how bursts of planning (setting new interim goals) separate the routines. The management activities focus on organizing the designer's work environment to facilitate the routine activities.

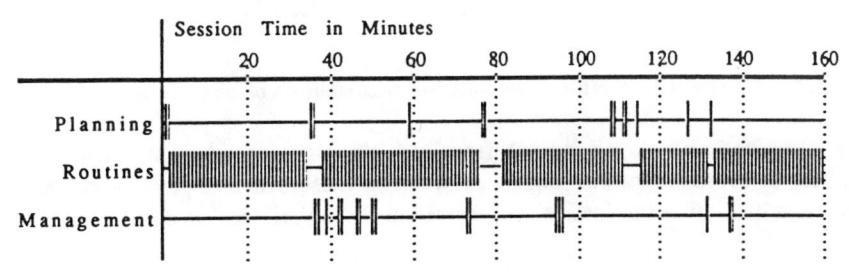

## A. Pattern: Alternating Planning and Routine Primary Processes

As shown in Figure 5, the overall design process is divided into large blocks of primary processes which are similar to the process segments of our initial model (e.g., understanding the criteria, producing alternative component arrangements, etc.). These primary processes seem to be well-rehearsed routines. While the routine processes may be interrupted for such purposes as evaluating and editing, these interruptions are germane to the ongoing process. Periods of planning occur between these routines. They are an intense combination of reviewing alternatives, reviewing criteria and constraints, and making major decisions regarding which processes to employ next. The blocks of primary processes are long, typically 20 to 30 minutes each out of a 160-minute session. The planning periods are short, less than a minute each. They represent only about 2% of the total session, but appear to be crucial to the effective management of the primary process blocks.

## B. Pattern: Workplace Management

This is the organization and reorganization of the immediate environment in which the designer works. It includes preparation and maintenance of tools; selection of materials; and arrangement of notes, drawings, or other information for comparison and easy reference. While some workplace management is distributed throughout the design process, there are periods of concentrated management following a period of planning. In these, the designer reorganizes in order to carry out the plans he has just made. He responds to the anticipated needs of the next primary process. These periods of concentrated management can exceed 10% of the session when many changes in the design process are called for.

The designer needs to consider a large amount of information in order to create a good design. However, this requirement also means that the designer needs some techniques for organizing or managing this information in his workplace. These techniques help to make the design process more efficient by minimizing the amount of time spent on retrieving, searching, and sorting information. Additionally, these techniques can also minimize errors such as losing or regenerating information. These techniques are discussed in more detail in section D.

## C. Pattern: Selective Refinement and the Dimensions of Sketching

We examined the sketch output from our design scenario along with the videotaped protocols of the sequences in which these sketches were produced. As a result of this examination, we identified three variables or dimensions of sketching which help describe the process by which information is put into sketches. This process is more structured than the traditional view of sketching (i.e., merely fast, inaccurate drawing) and has been given the name "selective refinement."

Most sketches do not start "from scratch." In keeping with the information transaction model, they build on information that is extracted from previous representations. In paper-based systems, it is common to use tracing paper to extract information in an obvious external way. We also have evidence that a transaction happens at the cognitive level, too. In one protocol segment, a subject sketched four different component arrangements without involving any tracing. The first sketch took 13 minutes, the others about 5 minutes each. Clearly some information, probably in the form of partial solutions, was being extracted from the first arrangement and being used in the succeeding arrangements. We call this a decision about inclusion.

Inclusion, coherence, and precision are the three dimensions that describe the ways in which sketches can differ from "finished work."

o *Inclusion* - the amount of information about a form that is represented in a sketch. It can be thought of as the level of detail or as the "grain size" of the information in the sketch.
o *Coherence* - the degree to which different pieces of information agree with or support another. It reflects whether the partial solutions to subproblems have been reconciled to one another.
o *Precision* - the dimensional refinement with which an intended configuration is represented. This is the most commonly understood of the dimensions.

While planning, a designer makes several choices. He chooses a mode of representation and levels of precision, inclusion, and coherence. The choices are made, based on training and experience, to be appropriate to the state of the problem as the designer understands it at that time. The choice of a representation mode is obviously an important decision. Perspectives show information that numerical dimensions do not and vice versa. That is why a completed page of sketches is often a combination of modes. The decisions about inclusion, coherence, and precision are involved in the design process in other ways which will be discussed. The important point is that for experienced designers, these variables are under the designer's control. The looseness of a sketch is a conscious choice, not simply the result of being sloppy or in a hurry. Sketching is not so much the precursor of a drawing as it is the record of a thought. It is a way of controlling the information in the early representations of a design solution. The process can be applied to a wide range of representational modes including sketch perspectives, sketch cross sections, and sketch diagrams.

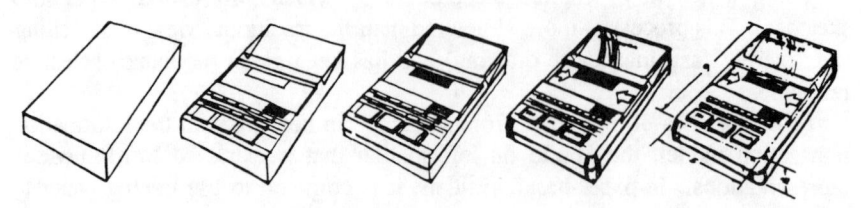

**Figure 6.** Sequence of Designer's Sketches.

*1. Inclusion Pattern*

Through inclusion, a sketch can accumulate information as it is worked on. Interestingly, the information in a sketch seems to get added in a consistent sequence that is partly idiosyncratic (the result of a designer's training and experience) and partly a response to the demands of the particular design problem. This implies that computer-supported design might include a personalized expert system that responds by adjusting to specific problem types or to specific users. One designer added information in the following sequence in every orthographic and perspective sketch he produced (see Figure 6):

1. Proportion of envelope (the product housing).
2. Component locations.
3. Mechanical and aesthetic refinements.
4. Material and surface attributes (surface reaction to light).
5. Notations and dimensions.

*2. Coherence Pattern*

A complete page of sketches often includes several views of an object. Coherence requires that these be in agreement with one another. We have some interesting protocol evidence of a subject dealing with the coherence of a sketch. In reconciling between the orthographic and perspective views, two patterns were observed.

First, as shown in Figure 7, while the subject alternated between orthographic and perspective views, the amount of time spent on each view decreased in a very regular sequence. Less time was spent with each alternation, starting with 15 or 20 minutes on each view and decreasing to a minute or less per view. The typical number of alternation cycles was three or four.

Second, the piece of information, such as a shadow or a detail line, that was the last to be included in one view was consistently first to be included in the next view. For example, while the designer worked on the perspective sketch, the last detail he added was a representation of light reflection to indicate that the digital readout was covered by a transparent window. The first detail he

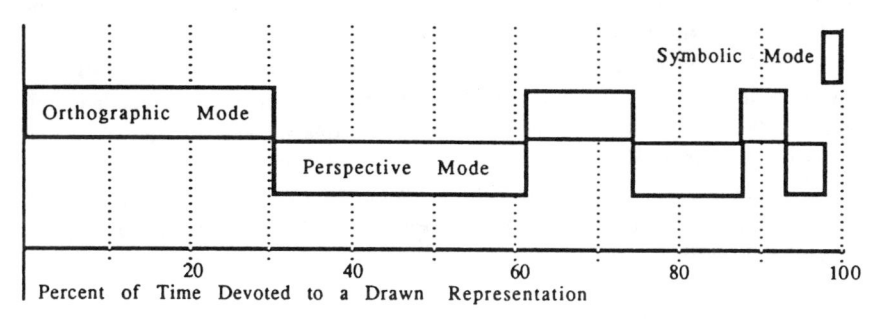

```
                                                          Symbolic  Mode  ┌┐
      ┌──────────────────────┐                       ┌────────┐   ┌─┐
      │ Orthographic  Mode   │                       │        │   │ │
      └──────────────────────┘     ┌─────────────┐   └─┐    ┌─┘   └─┘
                                   │ Perspective Mode│   │    │
                                   └─────────────────┘   └────┘
            20          40          60          80          100
      Percent of Time Devoted to a Drawn Representation
```

**Figure 7.** Pattern of Alternating Views.

added upon returning to the orthographic sketches was the same representation of light reflection.

The information processing model of human problem solving indicates a very limited capacity to carry complex information in short-term memory. These patterns of alternation and information carry-over seem to be an effective way of minimizing the amount of information that has to be dealt with at one time. The subject stays in one view and switches from one subproblem to the next until the current view is insufficient for solving the next subproblem, or he stays with one subproblem (representing the window, in the example above) and shifts to another view.

*3. Precision Pattern*

Choosing a level of precision is clearly related to decisions about economy and available time; a rough sketch is not simply the effect of sloppiness. If that were the case, we could expect a randomness to the precision of line making within a sketch or between sketches. We have made comparative measurements of line precision and the results do not support the sloppiness hypothesis. Rather, the overall precision of an entire sketch changes systematically from low to high as the design process moves toward completion.

Imprecision seems to have a value of its own. In ill-defined construction tasks, we should expect that invention (the substitution or addition of new ideas) will go on throughout the design process. By implication, there is the prediction that we should see final solutions being postponed as long as possible. Both patterns show up in the protocols. Low precision can be seen as evidence of the tendency to postpone final solutions, thus contributing to invention throughout the design process. At any stage of the design process, a designer is more willing to abandon the ideas represented in economical, low precision sketches than those that represent a large commitment of time, thought, or money.

Also, sketches that are low in inclusion, coherence, or precision can provide a dissonant visual field which encourages and sometimes demands invention for the solution of subproblems that were ignored at the beginning of the sketch.

The dissonances that occur may be partly intentional and partly the result of errors in information carried over between views. However these mutations occur, the designer periodically checks for agreement between views and discovers the dissonances. They tend to be located in areas of a sketch which have not been thoroughly solved; thus, the dissonance can be interpreted as representing a range of possible solutions which will require further refinement or the invoking of additional constraints. Alternatively, the dissonance can be interpreted as a spatial paradox or geometric impossibility which will require some invention for its resolution.

### D. Pattern: Information Management

A noticeable feature of the design process is the large amount of external information the designer uses in reaching a final solution. In the first 160 minutes of our in-depth study, the designer used a nine-page text, drawings of ten components, foamboard models of seven components, cost analyses of four partial solutions, photographs of four partial solutions, rough perspective drawings of three partial solutions, and partially rendered perspective drawings of three partial solutions.

The large amount of information present in a design task poses the problem of how best to retrieve and store it. We have identified four techniques by which designers manage information: *Partitioning, Grouping, Labeling,* and *Combining.*

#### 1. Partitioning Pattern

The designer maintains three distinct areas for storing information which are ordered by the accessibility of the information contained in them. The most accessible area is the designer's desktop, and this contains the information and representations currently being worked on. The next most accessible area is the wall area around the desk on which the designer pins various drawings of partial solutions. The third is out-of-the-way storage. In it the designer has access to an enormous amount of information that is not kept on the desktop or on the walls; e.g., drawings from previous design projects, tables of standards, etc. This type of information differs from the other two because it is not all contained in any single area. Furthermore, this information is not as accessible as that contained in either of the other areas because most of it is not immediately visible.

The desktop contains most of the information the designer uses for decision-making at any one time. Information needed for making a decision, but not present on the desktop, is typically brought here. For example, the designer would occasionally take a drawing from the wall and trace some aspect of it. Information on the walls is generally used for reference. For example, the designer would take a measurement from a drawing pinned to the wall and use it to confirm some dimension of a drawing on the desktop.

Partitioning is useful as an information management technique because locating information in separate areas reduces the workload of retrieving information from any single area. Furthermore, the ordering of the areas by their accessibility ensures that there will be minimal interference between the information contained in the different areas.

*2. Grouping Pattern*

The two characteristics of this technique are that sets of information are grouped together, and the groups are defined by virtue of having different locations. This technique is similar to partitioning, except that the groups are only temporarily assigned to locations. In contrast, the areas used in partitioning are unchanged throughout the design process.

Probably the simplest and most common example of grouping was the designer's tendency to create triads of drawings on a single sheet of paper: a plan view, a side view, and a perspective view. In this way, the designer groups several sets of information (the different views) at a single location (the sheet of paper). Another example occurred at the beginning of the second session when the designer placed all photographs, models, and rough sketches from the first session into separate groups around his desktop while he was reacquainting himself with the design problem.

*3. Labeling Pattern*

This is simply the act of giving an identifying label or name to a partial solution. The label identifies an object or a collection of objects as being part of a labeled solution. The designer maintained labels for each of four partial solutions he generated. These labels were transferred as each new representation of a partial solution was generated, for example, from photograph to rough perspective to rendered perspective.

During one session, the designer made an error that illustrates the importance of maintaining a labeling scheme. He began to remake, unintentionally, a perspective drawing that he had already completed. Indeed, he used the original perspective to help format the new one on the page. When the designer was asked which partial solution he was working on, he first compared the labels of the new and old perspectives and wondered if he had mislabeled one of them. However, after he had compared the drawings themselves he realized his mistake. This example suggests that the labels provide the designer with a quick method of distinguishing different solutions instead of comparing details in the drawings, which is a relatively slow process.

*4. Combining Pattern*

In this type of activity, the designer appends information to a representation which did not include that information. For example, the designer always wrote the price of a component onto its foamboard model. Thus, the cost information, something that is not inherently represented in a foamboard model, was appended to the representations of the components. In other instances of combining, the designer wrote the cost of each component in a configuration of models and glued it to the photograph of that configuration. Later, he annotated the rough perspective sketches with approximate dimensions.

Combining information on the various representations appears to free the designer from unnecessary searching. The designer added information which was not inherent in the representation but was useful for making decisions which involved considering information from different representations. One implication of this technique is that the designer already has a good idea of what information will be useful in making decisions.

## V. CONCLUSION

### A. Observations

1. In sketching, designers are engaging in a set of intentional acts. They make an economic choice about what kind of representation and what level of inclusion, coherence, and precision is most appropriate to explore the problem at hand.
2. The designers perform complex information processing by extracting information out of their own experience and out of previous sketches, adding information and reconciling information conflicts in their sketches.
3. Through *ex*clusion, *in*coherence, and *im*precision, the designers provide their sketches with enough ambiguity so they can take advantage of inventive opportunities right up to the end of the design process.
4. It seems clear that the more kinds of representation a designer can use, the better able he is to work through complex problems. Systems which force a designer to make an early decision about the inclusion, coherence, or precision of information will be counterproductive. They will tend to close down a designer's inventiveness too early in the design process.
5. It is important to recognize how the role and function of the computer changes as the design process progresses. At the beginning, it is a tool for individual problem solving, and sketchy representations are appropriate. Toward the end, it becomes a tool for group management or communication, and complete representations are required. I have been focusing on the earliest phases of the process. For this role, we have identified several qualities that a computer-aided design system should have:

- Users should feel like they are working on the representation, not on the computer.
- In graphics applications, the primary information is the image itself; image manipulation must be direct and intuitive.
- Solid models assist cognitive aspects of spatial problem solving; computer-aided design systems need a surrogate for solid models.
- A model's system of spatial reference should be natural to the task; coordinates are appropriate for specifications but not for ideation.

## B. Proposed Studies

There are many areas of incomplete knowledge about the design process. We have proposed three kinds of experiments which we believe would help to bring the requirements for computer-aided design systems into focus:

o   *Composition/Decomposition Experiment* - explores the processes by which simple spatial objects are composed or assembled into more complex objects. It also explores the related process of decomposing or analyzing a complex object into simpler parts.

o   *Orthographic/Perspective Experiment* - focuses on two conventional systems for representing spatial objects on a simple two-dimensional plane. It is known that experts alternate between these systems when solving problems, but it is not clear how the conventions affect problem solving.

o   *Default Representations Experiment* - is a survey of the actual representational parameters used by architects, engineers, and designers in the process of sketching to solve spatial problems. Experts have many available options for such parameters as viewing angle, eye height, hidden lines, and line weights, but in the early stages of the design process, they frequently resort to a small set of default representations.

## ACKNOWLEDGMENTS

The research referred to in this paper was supported by contracts with the Kingston, NY, Laboratory of the IBM Corporation. I am grateful for their support. This research required the talents of my colleagues in several departments at Carnegie-Mellon. Thanks are due in particular to Karen Graham of the Department of Design and to John R. Hayes and David Fallside of the Department of Psychology.

## REFERENCES

Jones, J.C. (1970). *Design methods*. London: John Wiley & Sons.
Newell, A., & Simon, H.A. (1972). *Human problem solving*. Englewood Cliffs, NJ: Prentice-Hall.
Reitman, W.R., (1965). *Cognition and thought*. New York: Wiley.

# Part II
# HUMAN-MACHINE SYSTEMS

The human as an element or component in a system has tremendous capability. The machine also has tremendous capability as a system element. Unfortunately, their combined potential is not usually realized because of the limitations of the human-machine interface. The heart and soul of most systems operations is that interface, but designing it to be efficient and functionally effective has been problematic. A number of factors are important in designing any system, training to use that system, and operating it under all conditions. The four selections in Part II address issues in system design and operation, including allocation of function, mental models of system functioning, and human error.

What kind of relationship do humans have with the machines they build? It should not be surprising that the very tools, machines, and systems humans build have a substantial influence on human thought and behavior. The selection by Harold P. Van Cott (Chapter 4) makes this point in an eloquent fashion. He traces how the evolution of the human activities of controlling, knowing, and understanding has paralleled—and may have been shaped by—the development of tools and machines that humans constructed. For example, the invention of mechanical linkages was a visible and tangible manifestation of the concept of cause-and-effect relationships and became a useful analog for describing and explaining events and phenomena in the environment. The relationship between human thought and technology is apparently a very intimate one. Van Cott leaves us with the thought-provoking notion—and challenge to human factors—that our use of intelligent environments today may shape how we view ourselves and our world tomorrow.

In all complex systems the human and machine elements must work together to achieve satisfactory performance levels. During the design process, determination of which tasks are performed by the human and which by the machine is known as *allocation of function*. Over the years it has proved to be a problematic aspect of system design. The basis for allocation-of-function decisions has typically been a comparison of human and machine capabilities. In other words, what can the human do best and what can the machine do best?

In Chapter 5, Nehemiah Jordan suggests that using such a comparative basis in allocating functions between human and machine is misdirected. He suggests an approach based on *complementarity* rather than *comparability*. His point is that the conceptual basis for allocation-of-function decisions should be how humans and machines can complement or augment each other, not whether one is superior in performing a given function. Thinking of humans and machines as working together is an appropriate orientation toward system design. Although it is certainly necessary to have a basis for comparison, an approach adopting a philosophy of complementarity in allocation of function may be a more effective one that, in turn, may lead to a superior system interface design.

The types of tasks people perform in operating machines and systems vary widely, as do the types of skills and abilities they bring to the human-machine interface. The quest for a suitable, robust taxonomy of human performance in systems is a noble one—it is the basis for describing how a human operator performs tasks in a variety of systems and situations. The selection by Jens Rasmussen (Chapter 6) presents an insightful and potent method of classifying human behavior and representing the thought-action relationship.

Rasmussen describes three levels of behavior: skill-based, rule-based, and knowledge-based. Skill-based behavior is the relatively autonomous execution of well-learned perceptual-motor sequences. Rule-based behavior involves procedural subroutines stored in memory; this knowledge is based on previous experience. Knowledge-based behavior is goal oriented and is derived from functional reasoning using a mental representation of the system or environment. Rasmussen's behavioral categories are based on the way humans represent "constraints in the behavior of a deterministic environment or system." Rasmussen characterizes human thought and action and describes the type of environmental information that is salient for that class of behavior. He points out that the relevance of a type of environmental information to a particular class of behavior is determined by the context in which it is perceived rather than by the specific form in which it is displayed.

Because of its characterization of the human-environment relationship, the concepts espoused by Rasmussen should be considered as interface design essentials. This paper has been influential in stimulating conceptualization of mental models of the human-machine interface.

Everyone makes mistakes, but not everyone knows how informative mistakes and errors can be. For this reason one of the important aspects of human-system behavior is error—specifically human error. Unfortunately, human error is notoriously difficult to predict and incorporate into system design. In Chapter 7, Donald A. Norman presents a categorization of one type of human error: an action slip. Simply put, an action slip is the unintentional performance of some behavior or action. Norman categorizes a large number of slips and forms the basis of a theoretical model of action. He identifies three major sources of action slips: errors in formation of intention, faulty activation of knowledge structures, and faulty triggering of active knowledge structures. According to Norman, the analysis of patterns of slips and their underlying causes allows insight into how an intention is represented in the cognitive system and how that intention activates a number of potential action sequences. Knowing how intent is represented, and understanding the basis on which intent activates a particular action sequence, is an essential step in understanding the nature of human error. Comprehending human error is a vital part of designing an appropriate human-machine interface. This is especially important as we move into intelligent environments, where future systems will infer human intent.

# 4

# From Control Systems to Knowledge Systems

HAROLD P. VAN COTT,[1] *Essex Corporation, Alexandria, Virginia.*

*Historically, the human species has been dependent upon technology for survival. This dependency placed people in a control loop from which they learned that mechanical cause-and-effect models were useful as explanatory mechanisms. These models were selectively reinforced to the exclusion of other forms of explanation. As the human's role shifts from that of a controller to a supervisor, new forms of rationality are reinforced. This process is being facilitated by new information technologies that demassify images and allow the individual to construct a highly personal understanding of human beings and nature.*

## INTRODUCTION

Most engineering psychologists are not inclined to be philosophical. We may occasionally turn to musings when things go wrong in the laboratory or the field or when we finally run out of things to do. But, by and large, we prefer to stick to the practical and serious business of persons and machines and leave philosophizing to others. Division presidents, in particular, are expected to be serious. And serious means reporting research rather than wool gathering. Today, however, I have decided to gather wool about a topic that has long been of interest to me, namely, human knowledge and understanding, and how people acquire them.

Engineering psychology is rooted in technology. Without technology there would be no engineering psychology, and all of us here today would be off at some other convention. Historically, our discipline has centered upon the interaction of technology with human performance. By performance, we have usually meant the overt behavior or response that a person makes when using some system, machine, or device. We have called this human activity *control*, and much of our endeavor has centered on methods for measuring, modeling and optimizing the human's behavior as a controller. We have paid scant attention to how technology affects human thought.

This paper examines the human activities of controlling, knowing, and understanding as stages in human evolution. It considers these activities in relation to technology and shows how they have been shaped by it. It illustrates how the technology of the past has produced certain forms of thought and how the technology of the future is likely to change thought. Finally, it discusses what all of this may mean for future generations of engineering and applied experimental psychologists.

## HUMAN SURVIVAL DEPENDS ON TECHNOLOGY

History can be told in terms of the history of the technologies that people have devised

[1] This paper is based on the Presidential Address given to the Division of Applied Experimental and Engineering Psychologists, American Psychological Association, Anaheim, California, August 28, 1983. Requests for reprints should be sent to Harold P. Van Cott, Essex Corporation, 333 N. Fairfax Street, Alexandria, VA 22314.

to ensure their survival and of the skills, rules, and knowledge that have been instrumental to the use of that technology.

The first human beings had no technological aids to survival. Most of their waking time and energy was devoted to surviving in a hostile environment. They had nothing with which to protect themselves but the raw materials about them. But they must have been able to observe, remember, and reason. Out of the cause-and-effect lessons of a harsh daily life, they learned the basic skills of survival. These simple skills were transmitted by imitation from person to person and from generation to generation. Human behavior during this most primitive period is most appropriately characterized as coping rather than control. Coping not only must have occupied many of the waking hours of early humans, it must also have fueled their thinking and their fears.

In time, the discovery that some materials worked better than others improved the chances of survival. A sharp rock was found to cut better than a round one. A pointed stick pierced leather more easily than a dull one. These muscle-powered artifacts made the human a manual controller. The axe, spear, and drill are examples of simple manual control systems. Later, devices that replaced or augmented muscle-power with an external power source, such as the bow, extended the human-tool control system. At about this time it can be said that human survival had become completely dependent upon technology. The human had become part of a manual control loop whose efficiency determined whether or not that person perished or lived. And efficiency depended not only on the devices and tools used for survival, but also on the skills learned and refined by its users.

As time passed, some quirk in genetic structure gave humans a larger and more efficiently organized cerebrum. This made possible the development of speech. Speech gave everything a name and permitted the world of natural objects and events to be differentiated from human-made objects and events. It allowed one person to designate to another the different tools used for hunting, fishing, and other survival strategies. Speech was found to be a better way than imitation to transmit the performance skills necessary to make effective use of technology. In time, these skills became codified into rules that increased the efficiency of tool use and further improved the chances of human survival.

Tribes with gifted tool designers and skilled users fared better than those without them. This meant that the more inventive clans with more advanced technology—especially those that inhabited mild climates—survived better than the less creative tribes in harsher environments. A culture competent at survival was able to spend less time in practicing survival skills and more time in other endeavors, such as the pursuit of knowledge for its own sake. The Egyptians were an example of a civilization in a benign climate and with an advanced technology that could devote time to philosophy, religion, literature, art, and music. The Eskimo and the Laplander could not. Thus under certain conditions, technology and climate allowed human thought to explore a new dimension—the understanding of humans and their universe. These explorations, however, were limited in scope and restricted to a few privileged individuals.

As technology became more elaborate, it created the need for measurement methods and concepts. Construction and trade required standard units of length, volume, and weight. For example, the cubit (the measurement from the elbow to the tip of the middle finger) came into general use throughout Egypt in the tenth century B.C. Larger units of linear measure were required to survey the land along the Nile after the annual flood waters receded. As the art of measurement became more sophisticated, the concrete rules of arithmetic and geometry developed for building, surveying, and trade became abstract. Once abstract, they could be applied to other measurement problems such as astronomy and weapons design. For example, the effective use of a Roman crossbow depended upon a knowledge of the concepts of distance, mass, and angle. Thus the concrete rules for using technology when augmented by knowledge became generalizable. The rules themselves were not generalizable, but the knowledge was. This generalized knowledge formed the basis for the development of scientific theories.

## TECHNOLOGY SHAPES HUMAN THOUGHT

For most of human history, the rate of technological advance has been slow. Survival technology and skills changed little for thousands of years. However, in the 15th century, an intellectual renaissance took place that surpassed that of the Egyptians, Greeks, and Romans and rivaled the development of human speech as a step in human evolution. In quick succession a number of inventions left an indelible stamp on human thought that persists to this day. The mechanical clock and printing press are outstanding examples. The clock introduced the concept of precise time—time in hours and minutes, not in sunrises, sunsets, and seasons. Human life became organized about clock time. The concept of time has driven us ever since, appearing to move us inexorably from the past into the future. The printing press extended human memory and linearized human thought. Other inventions altered the human's role as a controller. The fly-ball governor of 1780 regulated engine speed so that people no longer had to perform that function on a continuous basis. Other inventions followed. One of the most significant was the Jacquard loom, which used a punched template to control textile design. Inventions such as these introduced the concept of a programmable machine capable of carrying out human plans and intentions.

Each of these technological inventions contained an assembly or linkage of interacting mechanical parts. The form of a linkage was a physical expression of a set of cause-and-effect relationships. Being visible, a machine produced, in the minds of those familiar with its structure and function, a mental model, image, or analog of the cause-and-effect process embodied in the machine. These models became useful for describing and explaining other phenomena and events. It is said that the mechanical clock led to the formulation of the theory of planetary movements. Mechanical analogs were easy to grasp, and quickly became assimilated as popularly held explanatory concepts. They provided models that could be used to explain the complex questions of nature and life that could not be readily understood as a result of direct observation. Machines had now taken on a theoretical significance. In time it was believed that the working of the mind itself would be explained by mechanical forces. Was it not Descartes who said that the soul was influenced by pressure upon the pineal gland?

Each new generation of technology was the genesis of a new, expanded, and more complete view of the world that had not existed before. Although technology had great explanatory power, it also constrained human thought and understanding. Physical and mechanical models discouraged other modes of explanation; they displaced magic and reshaped philosophy and theology.

How are we to account for the fact that machines have had such a profound effect on human thought? I believe the answer may be found in the simple principles of operant conditioning. In operant conditioning, consequences, in the form of reinforcements or rewards, occur as a result of human performance. Any stimulus in the environment that is present when an operant response is reinforced acquires control. Stimuli that occur frequently, and that do not change, acquire greater control than other less constant stimuli. Now it happens that all of the stimuli in the environment (human-made tools, implements, devices, and systems) represent the least variable set of stimuli. Other stimuli change in one or more dimensions almost continually. The amount of entropy in a machine is far less than in nature.

Technological devices reward their users by providing reinforcement that satisfies a need. Each device and gadget we use is analogous to a Skinner box. From the earliest age, we learn that sucking a bottle will bring milk; flipping a switch, light; turning a faucet, water; tuning a radio, music; and tuning a TV, images. The reinforcement function fulfilled by a given technology also extends to the skills, rules, and knowledge required to use it. Just as the responses associated with the operation of a device are reinforced, so too are the skills, rules, and knowledge that must accompany these responses. In this way, mental models derived from the use and understanding of technology are constantly rewarded and strengthened. They imprint on us a way of viewing the world. This perhaps has always been so.

When technology was primarily mechanical, mechanical models were used as explanatory concepts. As electricity came into use, current flow, resistance, and switching became useful explanatory concepts. With the introduction of the computer, the concepts of information storage, search, and retrieval have been added.

## ANALOGS AS EXPLANATIONS

We need only consider our own discipline of psychology to discover that the origins of many of our theories and models come from physics and engineering. Descartes explained the reflexes of humans in terms of the functioning of a mechanical statue that moved as water was forced through pipes in its limbs. The Gestalt theory of perception was borrowed from electrical field theory. In engineering we have likened the human to an amplifier. Our account of human information processing comes from communication theory. We have used computer storage as an analog to describe human memory. Our physics and engineering envy has dominated our science so thoroughly that, until recently, we have refused to admit cognition as a legitimate object of study because we could find no physical analog to account for it. Penis envy never captured our attention as much as our envy of physics. The history of our profession is the history of the development of physical models of human behavior and of human thought.

Figure 1 summarizes the major points I have made so far. It shows that for much of human history we were manual controllers who used simple tools and implements for survival. During this period the intellectual content of the human species was derived from the rudimentary skills learned in the use of simple devices. With the development of speech, skills were codified into rules for the design, manufacture, and use of technology. As more complex technologies were devised, survival rules were generalized into knowledge that formed the basis for scientific theory. Scientific theory, in turn, became the creed and dogma of popular belief. Each new invention was accompanied by a parallel genesis in the structure of human thought: from simple to more complex skills, from simple to more complex rules, and from simple to more complex knowledge.

Looking to the future—and barring genocide or some natural cataclysm—human beings will continue to use technology to

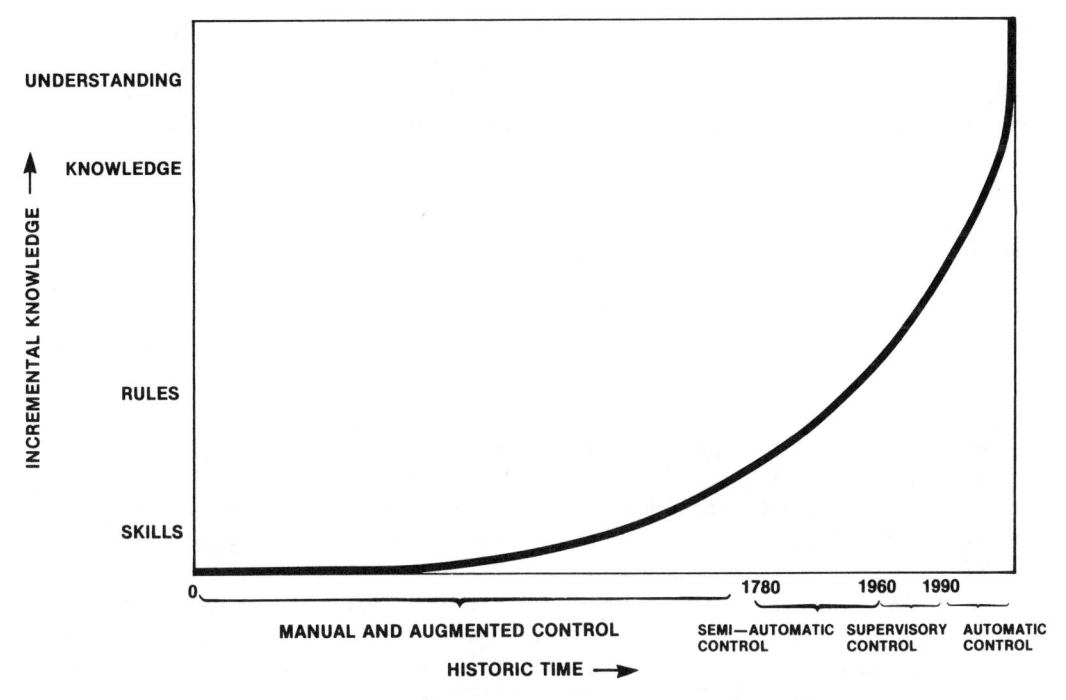

Figure 1. *Knowledge as it relates to technology.*

transform more and more of the resources of nature into human-made resources. And a time will come (it is already beginning to unfold before us) when people will be able to blueprint a world controlled largely by automation. In this new world of the future, the office and factory, the home and the hospital, the store and transportation, will be automatic. Robots will perform the control functions once performed by people. The human race will have become the instrument of its own evolution. This freedom from the necessity for humans to be in direct control of the machines necessary for their survival will create an opportunity for large numbers of individuals to experience the greatest adventure in human history—understanding. It will be an intellectual adventure, not a physical one. It will be an adventure in which new forms of information technology will become a vital force in human evolution that will cause a major restructuring of human life and thought.

## THE INFORMATION BOMB

In the recent book, *The Third Wave*, Toffler (1980) said: "An information bomb is exploding in our midst, showering us with a shrapnel of images and drastically changing the way each of us perceives and acts. . . . In shifting from a technosphere to an infosphere we are transforming our own psyches."

Before the advent of mass media, children grew up in a slowly changing community and built up a model of reality out of images received from a limited number of sources. The teacher, the minister, and particularly the family, interpreted life and imparted the skills, rules, and knowledge of a simple world and its simple technology. Knowledge came largely from the speech and images learned from first-hand experience with other individuals and with artifacts. There was no radio and no television to provide different images and models of the world. Images were narrow in range, and the knowledge conveyed by them was limited.

Later (and in parallel with the growth of industrialization), books, newspapers, magazines, radio, and television multiplied the number of channels of information from which an individual formed models of reality. Information, like products, was mass produced. Certain images were so widely distributed and fixed into so many people's memories that they were transformed into icons. The images of the Hindenberg in flames, of Hitler and Stalin, of Roosevelt, and of the weapons of World War II dominated my youth. They recurred again and again in the newsreels; in *Life, Look,* and *Time.* Scientific knowledge was also mass-produced and digested. It appeared in *Reader's Digest* and *Scientific American.* Conventional wisdom held that most nearly all phenomena could be understood and explained by physical models and a science based on these models.

In the past decade, the number of information channels and the number of images available to us has continued to multiply. These new images reach us at a faster rate than ever before. They are temporary images. Polaroid snapshots, Xerox copies, paperback books, and disposable graphics appear and disappear. More ideas, beliefs, and explanations flood into consciousness, are developed, and then vanish. The mass-produced images of what we took to be reality and the explanations of reality have begun to crumble and fade. A subtle but startling change has begun to occur. The once powerful, monolithic mass media are being "demassified." Information is becoming more personalized. Cable television and video and audio cassettes provide us with a greater individual choice of images, models, analogs, and knowledge. Communication satellites shrink and warp the dimensions of time and space that once were measured in clock time and travel distance. We need not visit a place to know it. Video games teach children how to use television sets and computers in an interactive manner. We are becoming a generation of message senders as well as message receivers. We are learning to manipulate and control information rather than being controlled by it. We are learning to use information as humans once used technology as a means for acquiring understanding as well as a means for survival.

## THE DEMASSIFICATION OF INFORMATION

The most significant of all of these changes in information technology is the personal computer. It allows me not only to selectively retrieve images, but also to create images of my own design. My visual frame of reference is no longer restricted to an 8-1/2 × 11 page; it has become a video window past which I can move, manipulate, create and examine graphics, diagrams, spread-sheets, and text. Instead of passively adopting a mental model of reality produced for me by others, I can invent and reinvent one of my own design.

This demassification of information will lead to greater individuality. It will explain why opinions on everything from science to religion will become less uniform. Consensus will shatter. And all of this will have a far-reaching effect on the way we think. Taken together, these changes in information technology will revolutionize our view of the world and our ability to sense and understand it.

As we become more familiar with the intelligent environment provided by the computer and computer networks, and learn to converse with them as we now do with people, we will use computers with the ease and naturalness with which we now drive a car or ride a bicycle. And they will help us to understand ourselves and the world in a way that has never before been possible. Computers can be expected to alter our view of causality, to heighten our awareness of the interrelatedness of things, and to permit us to synthesize meaningful wholes out of the disconnected sense data that surround us.

For the past 200 years, the study of nature at all levels has relied upon physical reductionism as a major explanatory concept. This approach has attempted to comprehend phenomena at one level in terms of concepts at a lower and presumably more fundamental level. It has been widely held that human thought and behavior can be explained by the activity of the nervous system. The nervous system was believed to be reducible to processes in the cell; the cell to be explained in terms of chemical processes; and chemical processes, in terms of atomic physics. Finally, atomic physics has been believed to be explainable by means of quantum mechanics. Each of these levels of explanation is physical. They are derived from a paradigm of nature and are causally driven, at least in part, by our heritage of mechanical analogs. Recently, however, an unusual thing has begun to happen. Many physicists now say that quantum mechanics cannot be understood without introducing cognition as a component of the system. Physicists in increasing numbers claim that until we understand cognition and intelligence we will never understand the human or the universe.

I do not wish to suggest by what I have said that physical science and physical models are invalid. Rather, I propose that there may be alternative models that are not only less constraining but also are as rational as the mechanical models of physical science. I believe that we may be able to devise these alternative models by our interactions with the intelligent environment created by networks of computers and information media. These networks will be able to tap nearly any data set of our choosing or devising. These data sets will not be limited to numerical and scientific data, but will include and integrate other representations of reality in the form of images, poetry, literature, history, and philosophy.

## IMPLICATIONS FOR ENGINEERING PSYCHOLOGY

Throughout most of its brief history, engineering psychology has been concerned with the human as a component of closed-loop control systems. We have used engineering and physical models and concepts to account for human performance. It was not considered necessary to explore the cognitive process of the human controller. This approach was fitting and proper because it was responsive to the technology of the time and to the human's role in relation to it.

More recently, with the development of process control systems, engineering psychology has become concerned with the human as a supervisor and monitor of a process. This new technology has required us to develop concepts and models that express the cognitive content of these new process control tasks. We have had to become concerned with the operator's mental model or map of a system and its states. This approach has been fitting and proper because it is responsive to the human's role in relation to process control technology.

Even more recently, as computers and information systems have become almost a direct extension of the human brain, engineering psychologists have shifted attention from the human as a controller of technology to the role of the computer as an aid to human planning and decision making. Our concern is not with how humans can support a system, but how systems can be used to support humans.

The day is at hand when engineering psychologists will direct much of their attention to the problem of coupling machine intelligence with human intelligence. Their focus will be on educational systems and on knowledge systems. Their goal will be to promote human understanding. The object of their study will be what J. C. R. Licklider once called the "symbiosis of man and machine." The variables of interest will be the variables associated with the structure of the universe in relation to the structure of human cognition.

We can now only dimly perceive the types of questions that the applied study of human knowing and understanding will raise. Few of the methods available to us now appear to be suitable for answering these questions. For example, we now have a reasonably good method for the analysis of physical tasks; however, we do not have a method for the description or analysis of cognitive tasks. We must devise one.

In the future the engineering psychologist will need to understand how people aggregate the bits and pieces of images and data from different data sources into larger concepts. We will need to develop a method for evaluating and validating the data from information networks because the data in these networks will always be secondhand or surrogate data. And we will need to study the larger questions of the differences among information, knowledge, and understanding. These are but a few of the issues engineering psychology will face as it approaches its new frontier.

## CONCLUSION

Throughout history human rationality has taken different forms. I have tried to show how one form of rationality has been derived from our relationship to technology and technological systems. This form of rationality has permitted us to survive, but it has constrained our ability to fully understand. I believe that future generations of engineering psychologists will help to develop the new systems that will permit humans to better understand themselves and their relationship to the world about them in a way that has never before been possible.

Alfred Lord Tennyson said:

> *Our little systems have their day;*
> *They have their day and cease to be,*
> *They are but broken lights of Thee;*
> *And Thou, O Lord, are more than they.*
>
> *Let knowledge grow from more to more;*
> *But more of reverence in us dwell;*
> *That mind and soul, according well,*
> *May make one music as before.*

## REFERENCE

Toffler, A. *The third wave.* New York: Morrow, 1980.

# ALLOCATION OF FUNCTIONS BETWEEN MAN AND MACHINES IN AUTOMATED SYSTEMS

## NEHEMIAH JORDAN, RAND *Corporation*

With the growing complexity of the man-machine systems the problem of allocation becomes more critical. Little progress has been made towards its solution since the publication of Fitts' article in 1951 which has dominated thinking in this area. Fitts recommended that man be compared to machines and be chosen for those functions which he does better than machines and vice versa. To do so is wrong; when we can compare a man to a machine, we find that we can also build a machine for the function involved. Hence the lack of progress. Men and machines are complementary, rather than comparable. Once the problem is so reformulated, new ways of thinking which appear to be promising open up.

In a document entitled *Factors Affecting Degree of Automation in Test and Checkout Equipment* which, among other things, reviews the problems of allocation of functions, Swain and Wohl (1961) assert:

A rather stark conclusion emerges: *There is no adequate systematic methodology in existence for allocating functions* (in this case, test and checkout functions) *between man and machine.* This lack, in fact, is probably the central problem in human factors engineering today.... It is interesting to note that ten years of research and applications experience have failed to bring us closer to our goal than did the landmark article by Fitts in 1951 (p. 9).

These two competent and experienced observers summarize 10 years of hard and intensive labor as having basically failed. This is a serious problem. Why this failure?

We can attempt to seek a possible answer to the question by seeking a similar case in other fields of scientific endeavor and seeing what can be learned from it. And another case is easy to find; it is in fact a classical case. In their book, *The Evolution of Physics*, Einstein and Infeld (1942) spend some time discussing the problems which beset prerelativity physics in which they focus upon the concept of "ether."

They point out that ether played a central role in physical thinking for over a century after having first been introduced as a necessary medium for propagating electromagnetic waves. But during all this time all attempts to build and expand upon this concept led to difficulties and contradictions. A century of research on ether turned out to be sterile in that no significant advance was made during that time. They conclude: "After such bad experiences, this is the moment to forget ether completely and try never to mention its name" (p. 184). And they do not mention the concept anymore in the book. The facts underlying the concept were not rejected, however, and it was by focusing upon the *facts* while rejecting the *concept* that Einstein could solve the problems which bedeviled the physics of his day.

The lesson to be learned from this momentous episode is that when a scientific discipline finds itself in a dead end, despite hard and diligent work, the dead end should probably not be attributed to a lack of knowledge of facts, but to the use of faulty concepts which do not enable the discipline to order the facts properly.

From *Journal of Applied Psychology*, 47(3), June 1963. Copyright 1963 by the American Psychological Association.

The failure of human factors engineering to advance in the area of allocation of functions seems to be such a situation. Hence, in order to find an answer to the question, "Why this failure?", it may be fruitful to examine the conceptual underpinnings of our contemporary attempts at allocating functions between men and machines. And this brings us back to the landmark article by Fitts (1951) mentioned earlier.

This article gave rise to what is now informally called the "Fitts list." This is a two-column list, one column headed by the word "man" and the other, by the word "machine." It *compares* the functions for which man is superior to machines to the functions for which the machine is superior to man. Theoretically, this leads to an elegant solution to the allocation of functions. Given a complex man-machine system, identify the functions of the system and then, based on such a list which was expected to be refined with time and experience, choose machines for the functions they are best suited for and men for the functions they are best suited for. This is a clean engineering approach and it is not surprising that great hopes were placed upon it, in *1951*. The only gimmick is that it did not and does not work.

The facts to be found in all the existing versions of the Fitts list are all correct, just as the facts underlying the concept of ether were all correct. Hence the inutility of these lists must be attributed to what we are told to do with these facts, to the instruction to compare man to the machine and choose the one who fits a function best. I question the *comparability* of men and machines. If men and machines are not comparable, then it is not surprising that we get nowhere when we try to compare them. Just as the concept of ether led to inutility, perhaps the concept of man-machine comparability does the same. Let us explore somewhat the background to the concept *comparability*.

The literature on the place of a man in man-machine systems converges to two posthumous articles by K. J. W. Craik (1947a, 1947b). These articles are recognized by almost all as being the basis upon which much that followed is built. Craik argues that in order to best be able to plan, design, and operate a complex system man functions and machine functions should be described in the same concepts, and, by the very nature of the case, these concepts have to be engineering terms. In other words, Craik recommends that we describe human functions in mathematical terms *comparable* to the terms used in describing mechanical functions.

In fairness to Craik's memory it must be stressed that these two papers published after his death were notes for a discussion and probably not meant for publication. Hence he should not be blamed for failing to recognize the simple fact that anytime we can reduce a human function to a mathematical formula we can generally build a machine that can do it more efficiently than a man. In other words, to the extent that man becomes comparable to a machine we do not really need him any more since he can be replaced by a machine. This necessary consequence was actually reached but not recognized in a later paper, also a fundamental and significant paper in the human factors engineering literature. Birmingham and Taylor (1954) in their paper, "A Design Philosophy for Man-Machine Control Systems," write: "speaking mathematically, he (man) is best when doing least" (p. 1752). The conclusion is inescapable—design the man out of the system. If he does best when he does least, the least he can do is zero. But then the conclusion is also ridiculous. Birmingham and Taylor found themselves in the same paradoxical situation in which Hume found himself some 200 years earlier when his logic showed him that he could not know anything while at the same time he knew he knew a lot.

This contradiction, so concisely formulated by Birmingham and Taylor yet not recognized by them or, it seems, by their readers, should have served as a warning that something was wrong with the conceptualization underlying the thinking in this area. But it did not.

Now we can see why the Fitts lists have been impotent. To the extent that we compare, numerically, human functions to machine functions we must reach the conclusion that wherever possible the machine should do the job. This may help to explain a curious aspect in designers' behavior which has annoyed some:

an annoyance expressed trenchantly by a human factors engineer over a glass of beer thusly: "Those designers, they act as if they get a brownie point every time they eliminate a man."

Let us return to the Fitts lists. They vary all over the place in length and in detail. But if we try to abstract the underlying commonalities in all of them we find that they really make one point and only one point. Men are flexible but cannot be depended upon to perform in a consistent manner whereas machines can be depended upon to perform consistently but they have no flexibility whatsoever. This can be summarized simply and seemingly tritely by saying that men are good at doing that which machines are not good at doing and machines are good at doing that which men are not good at doing. Men and machines are not comparable, they are *complementary*. Gentlemen, I suggest that complementarity is probably the correct concept to use in discussing the allocation of tasks to men and to machines. Rather than compare men and machines as to which is better for getting a task done let us think about how we complement men by machines and vice versa to get a task done.

As soon as we start to think this way we find that we have to start thinking differently. The term "allocation of tasks to men and machine" becomes meaningless. Rather we are forced to think about a task that can be done by men *and* machines. The concept "task" ceases to be the smallest unit of analysis for designing man-machine systems though still remaining the basic unit in terms of which the analysis makes sense. The task now consists of actions, or better still activities, which have to be shared by men and machines. There is nothing strange about this. In industrial chemistry the molecule is the fundamental unit for many purposes and it does not disturb anybody that some of these molecules consist of hundreds, if not thousands, of atoms. The analysis of man-machine systems should therefore consist of specifications of tasks and activities necessary to accomplish the tasks. Man and machine should complement each other in getting these activities done in order to accomplish the task.

It is possible that with a shift to emphasizing man-machine comparability new formats for system analysis and design will have to be developed, and these formats may pose a problem. I am convinced, however, that as soon as we begin thinking in proper units this problem will be solved with relative ease. Regardless whether this is so, one can now already specify several general principles that may serve as basic guidelines for complementing men and machines.

Machines serve man in two ways: as tools and as production machines. A tool extends man's ability, both sensory and motor; production machines replace man in doing a job. The principle underlying the complementarity of tools is as follows: man functions best under conditions of optimum difficulty. If the job is too easy he gets bored, if it is too hard he gets fatigued. While it is generally silly to use machines to make a job more difficult, although this may be exactly what is called for in some control situations, tools have, since their inception as eoliths, served to make a difficult job easier and an impossible job possible. Hence tools should be used to bring the perceptual and motor requirements of a task to the optimum levels for human performance. We have had a lot of experience with tools and they present few, if any, problems.

The problem is more complex with machines that do a job in place of man. Here we can return with benefit to the commonalities underlying the Fitts list. To the extent that the task environment is predictable and a priori controllable, and to the extent that activities necessary for the task are iterative and demand consistent performance, a production machine is preferable to man. To the extent, however, that the environment is not predictable, or if predictable not controllable a priori, then man, aided by the proper tools, is required. It is in coping with contingencies that man is irreplaceable by machines. This is the essential meaning of human flexibility.

Production machines pose a problem rarely posed by tools since they replace man in doing a job. They are not perfect and tend to break down. When they break down they do not do the job. One must always then take into account the criticality of the job for the system. If the job is critical, the system should be so designed that man can serve as a manual backup to the machine. Although he will then not do it as well as the machine, he still can do it well enough to pass muster. This is another aspect of human flexibility—the ability for graceful degradation. Machines can either do the job as specified or they botch up; man degrades gracefully. This is another example of complementarity.

Planning for feasible manual backup is a difficult job in the contemporary complex systems that we are constructing. It has generally been neglected. In most simple systems explicit planning is not necessary since man's flexibility is generally adequate enough to improvise when the relatively simple machines break down. But this changes with growing system complexity.

It is here that "automation" should be mentioned. Some of you may have been bothered by the fact that automation is in the title of this paper but has, as yet, still to be introduced. The reason is rather simple. Although automation represents a significant technological breakthrough which has generated many specific problems, the allocation of tasks to men and machines being one of them, conceptually, an automated machine is just another machine, albeit radically different in its efficiency and performance characteristics. The problems that were generally latent or not too critical in the older, simpler man-machine systems became both manifest and critical, however, with its introduction. One of the most critical areas is manual backup.

We customarily design automated systems by allocating those functions which were either difficult or too expensive to mechanize to man and the rest to machines. As many articles in the literature indicate, we have looked upon man as a *link* in the system and have consequently given him only the information and means to do the job assigned to him as a link. When the system breaks down a man in a link position is as helpless as any other machine component in the system. We have tended to design out his ability to take over as a manual backup to the system. At the same time the jobs performed by the machine have become more and more important and the necessity for a manual backup consequently greater. How to design a complex automated system to facilitate its being backed up manually is a neglected area. One thing seems certain. It will most probably call for "degradation" in design, that is, systematically introducing features which would not have been necessary were no manual backup needed. This is an important area for future human factors engineering research.

Another area of complementarity which is gaining in significance as the systems are getting more and more complex is that of responsibility. Assuming we lick the problems of reliability we can depend upon the machines to do those activities assigned to them consistently well, but we never can assign them any responsibility for getting the task done; responsibility can be assigned to men only. For every task, or for every activity entailed by the task, there must be a man who has assigned responsibility to see that the job be done as efficiently as warranted. This necessitates two things: the specification of clear-cut responsibilities for *every* man in the system and supplying the men with means which will enable them to exercise control over those system tasks and activities for which they are responsible. You may think that this is obvious—yes it is. But it is surprising how rare, and then how ineffective, our planning and design in this area are. Experience to date with automated systems shows that the responsibilities of the individuals involved are generally nebulous so that when something unexpected occurs people often do not know who is to do what. Even to the extent that these responsibilities are clarified with time and experience, the system hardware often makes it difficult for men to assume these responsibilities, the means for man to exercise control over the areas of his responsibility being inadequate or lacking.

The complementarity of men and machines is probably much more profound and subtle than these aspects which I have just highlighted. Many other aspects will undoubtedly be identified, elaborated, and ordered to the extent that we start thinking about how one complements the other. In other words, to the extent that we start *humanizing* human factors engineering. It is not surprising that the 10 years of lack of progress pointed to by Swain and Wohl (1961) were accompanied by the conceptual definition of treating man as a machine component. Man is not a machine, at least not a machine like the machines men make. And this brings me to the last point I would like to make in this paper.

When we plan to use a machine we always take the physical environment of the machine into account; that is, its power supply, its maintenance requirements, the physical setting in which it has to operate, etc. We have also taken the physical environment of man into account, to a greater or lesser extent; that is, illumination and ventilation of the working area, noise level, physical difficulties, hours of labor, coffee breaks, etc. But a fundamental difference between men and machines is that men also have a psychological environment for which an adequate physical environment is a necessary condition but is ultimately secondary in importance. This is the truth embedded in the adage: Man does not live by bread alone. The psychological environment is subsumed under one word: motivation. The problems of human motivation are at present eschewed by human factors engineering.

You can lead a horse to water but cannot make him drink. In this respect a man is very similar to a horse. Unless the human operator is motivated he will not function as a complement to machines, and the motivation to function as a complement must be embedded *within the task itself*. Unless a task represents a challenge to the human operator he will *not* use his flexibility or his judgment, he will *not* learn nor will he assume responsibility, nor will he serve efficiently as a manual backup. By designing man-machine systems for man to do *least* we also eliminate all challenge from the job. We must clarify to ourselves what it is that makes a job a challenge to man and build in those challenges in every task, activity, and responsibility which we assign to the human operator. Otherwise man will not complement the machines but will begin to function like a machine.

And here too men differ significantly from machines. When a man is forced to function like a machine he realizes that he is being used inefficiently and he experiences it as being used stupidly. Men cannot tolerate such stupidity. Overtly or covertly men resist and rebel against it. Nothing could be more inefficient and self-defeating in the long run than the construction of man-machine systems which cause the human components in the system to rebel against the system.

Herein lies the main future challenge to human factors engineering.

## REFERENCES

Birmingham, H. P., & Taylor, F. V. A design philosophy for man-machine control systems. *Proc. IRE, N.Y.*, 1954, 42, 1748-1758.

Craik, K. J. W. Theory of the human operator in control systems: I. The operator as an engineering system. *Brit. J. Psychol.*, 1947, 38, 56-61. (a)

Craik, K. J. W. Theory of the human operator in control systems: II. Man as an element in a control system. *Brit. J. Psychol.*, 1947, 38, 142-148. (b)

Einstein, A., & Infeld, L. *The evolution of physics*. New York: Simon & Schuster, 1942.

Fitts, P. M. (Ed.), *Human engineering for an effective air navigation and traffic control system*. Washington, D. C.: National Research Council, 1951.

Swain, A. D., & Wohl, J. G. *Factors affecting degree of automation in test and checkout equipment*. Stamford, Conn.: Dunlap & Associates, 1961.

(Received July 15, 1962)

# Skills, Rules, and Knowledge; Signals, Signs, and Symbols, and Other Distinctions in Human Performance Models

JENS RASMUSSEN, SENIOR MEMBER, IEEE

*Abstract*—The introduction of information technology based on digital computers for the design of man–machine interface systems has led to a requirement for consistent models of human performance in routine task environments and during unfamiliar task conditions. A discussion is presented of the requirement for different types of models for representing performance at the skill-, rule-, and knowledge-based levels, together with a review of the different ways in which information is perceived at these different levels in terms of signals, signs, and symbols. Particular attention is paid to the different possible ways of representing system properties which underlie knowledge-based performance and which can be characterized at several levels of abstraction—from the representation of physical form, through functional representation, to representation in terms of intention or purpose. Furthermore, the role of qualitative and quantitative models in the design and evaluation of interface systems is mentioned, and the need to consider such distinctions carefully is discussed.

## INTRODUCTION

MANY technical systems in modern times are highly automated and do not rely on human intervention in the control of normally planned functions. Yet their existence depends on extensive support from a human staff to maintain the necessary conditions for satisfactory operation and to cope with all the badly structured and probably unforeseen states of affairs in the system. Due to the high risk involved in the potential for accidents in large centralized production units, concern with being able to predict human performance during complex rare events has increased. We therefore need systematic descriptions of human performance in total, from the observation of information to the physical actions on the process plant, and the descriptions should cover a wide range of work situations from daily routine to stressed encounters with accidental events.

We need tools for reliable prediction of human performance and of the various error modes for this purpose. A long tradition exists within vehicle control to use quantitative models for systems design and performance analysis, such as the models based on optimal control theory. During recent years, attempts have been made to extend these models to higher level human decisionmaking to conform with the increasing levels of automation in aviation, and to transfer such models for process control applications. Whether or not this approach is fruitful depends on the nature of the human task. The optimal control part of the model may not be needed if the manual acts are no longer an integral part of the control task but merely a general interface manipulation skill. In that case, independent development of a decision model may lead to a more direct approach. What we need is not a global quantitative model of human performance but a set of models which is reliable for defined categories of work conditions together with a qualitative framework describing and defining their coverage and relationships. In some areas, particularly in reliability engineering, several premature attempts have been made to quantify human performance due to the pressing need for prediction. This tendency to rush to measurement and quantification is, however, not only a modern trait of engineers. Indeed, the stranger in Plato's *Statesman* remarked:

> There are many accomplished men, Socrates, who say, believing themselves to speak wisely, that the art of measurement is universal, and has to do with all things.... But these persons, because they are not accustomed to distinguish classes according to real forms, jumble together two widely different things, relating to one another, and to a standard, under the idea that they are the same, and also fall into the converse error of dividing other things not according to their real parts.

The aim of the present paper is to discuss some basic distinctions which are useful in defining the categories of human performance for which separate development of models is feasible. In this effort we have to consider that humans are not simply deterministic input–output devices but goal-oriented creatures who actively select their goals and seek the relevant information. The behavior of humans is teleological by nature. In their classical paper Rosenbluth and Wiener [1] define teleological behavior as behavior which is modified *during its course* by signals from the goal. This restrictive definition seems, however, to be due to an inadequate distinction between two concepts: *causes* of physical events and *reasons* for physical functions, a distinction which has been discussed in detail by Polanyi [2]. Teleological behavior is not necessarily dependent on feedback during its course but on the experience from previous attempts, i.e., the reason for choosing the particular approach. *Reasons* act as the classical "final causes" and can control functions of behavior systems by selection,

Manuscript received April 1, 1982; revised December 10, 1982.
The author is with the Risø National Laboratory, DK 4000 Roskilde, Denmark.

From *IEEE Transactions on Systems, Man and Cybernetics*, SMC-13. Copyright 1983 by IEEE.

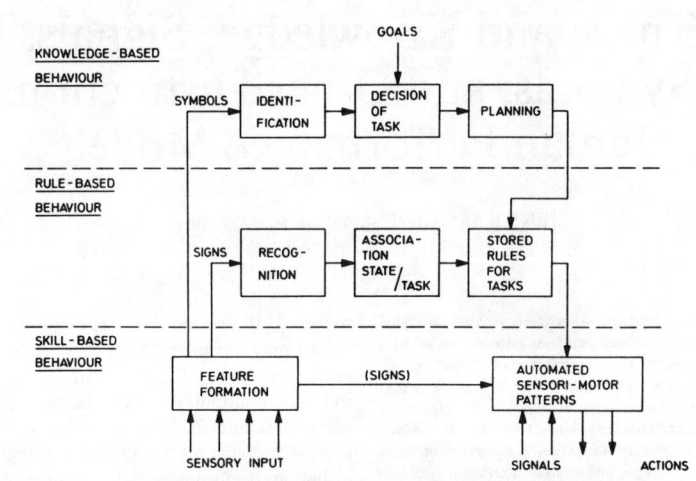

Fig. 1. Simplified illustration of three levels of performance of skilled human operators. Note that levels are not alternatives but interact in a way only rudimentarily represented in diagram.

be it natural selection in biological evolution or through human design choices for man-made systems. *Causes*, on the other hand, control functions through the physical structure of the system. Since all technical systems are designed for very definite reasons, it follows directly that teleological explanations—in the classical sense—of the functions of man-made systems derived from their ultimate purpose are as important as causal explanations based on engineering analysis. The same is the case for explanations of purposive human behavior.

Actually, even human position and movement in the physical environment are only occasionally directly controlled during the course of action by simple feedback. It may be the case in unfamiliar situations calling for accurate and slow time–space coordination, but in more complex rapid sequences, the sensory equipment is too slow for direct feedback correction, and adaptation is based on means for selection and regeneration of successful patterns of behavior for use in subsequent situations, i.e., on an internal dynamic world model.

At a higher level of conscious planning, most human activity depends upon a rather complex sequence of activities, and feedback correction during the course of behavior from mismatch between goal and final outcome will therefore be too inefficient, since in many cases it would lead to a strategy of blind search. Human activity in a familiar environment will not be goal-controlled; rather, it will be oriented towards the goal and controlled by a set of rules which has proven successful previously. In unfamiliar situations when proven rules are not available, behavior may be goal-controlled in the sense that different attempts are made to reach the goal, and a successful sequence is then selected. Typically, however, the attempts to reach the goal are not performed in reality, but internally as a problem-solving exercise, i.e., the successful sequence is selected from experiments with an internal representation or model of the properties and behavior of the environment. The efficiency of humans in coping with complexity is largely due to the availability of a large repertoire of different mental representations of the environment from which rules to control behavior can be generated *ad hoc*. An analysis of the form of these mental models is important to the study of human interaction with complex man-made systems.

Basically, meaningful interaction with an environment depends upon the existence of a set of invariate constraints in the relationships among events in the environment and between human actions and their effects. The implications of the foregoing discussion is that purposive human behavior must be based on an internal representation of these constraints. The constraints can be defined and represented in various different ways which in turn can serve to characterize the different categories of human behavior.

## SKILLS, RULES, AND KNOWLEDGE

When we distinguish categories of human behavior according to basically different ways of representing the constraints in the behavior of a deterministic environment or system, three typical levels of performance emerge: skill-, rule-, and knowledge-based performance. These levels and a simplified illustration of their interrelation are shown in Fig. 1.

The *skill-based behavior* represents sensory–motor performance during acts or activities which, following a statement of an intention, take place without conscious control as smooth, automated, and highly integrated patterns of behavior. Only occasionally is performance based on simple feedback control, where motor output is a response to the observation of an error signal representing the difference between the actual state and the intended state in a time–space environment, and where the control signal is derived at a specific point in time. Typical examples are experimental tracking tasks. In real life this mode is used rarely and only for slow, very accurate movements such as assembly tasks or drawing. In most skilled sensory–motor tasks, the body acts as a multivariable continuous control system synchronizing movements with the behavior of the environment. Performance is based on feedforward control and depends upon a very flexible and efficient dynamic internal world model. Feedforward control is necessary to explain rapid coordinated movements, for instance, in handwriting, sports, etc. The role of feedforward control for industrial control tasks has been demonstrated experimentally by Crossman and Cooke [3]. Pew [4] found a shift from error correction mode to pattern generation mode between 0.5 and 1 Hz in sinus tracking.

The control of voluntary movements is even more complex. Since the success of rapid movements is independent of the initial positions of limbs, and since the topology of movements can be transferred to other metric proportions and limbs, the function must depend on schemata for generating complex movements with reference to a dynamic internal map of the environment. Sensory input is probably not used to control movements directly but to update and align this internal map (see Bernstein [5] and the excellent review by Pew [4]). The case in point is that the behavioral complexes necessary to perform an intention to "pick up a glass" or "place finger on nose" [6] are integrated wholes which cannot be decomposed into separate elements (without changing the level of description to neurophysiology). From this discussion the constraints in the behavior of the environment at the skill level appear to be represented only by prototypical temporal–spatial patterns.

Characteristically, skilled performance rolls along without conscious attention or control. The total performance is smooth and integrated, and sense input is not selected or observed: the senses are only directed towards the aspects of the environment needed subconsciously to update and orient the internal map. The man looks rather than sees.

In some cases, performance is one continuous integrated dynamic whole, such as bicycle riding or musical performance. In these cases the higher level control may take the form of conscious intentions to "modulate" the skill in general terms, such as "Be careful now, the road is slippery," or "Watch out, now comes a difficult passage." In other cases, performance is a sequence of rather isolated skilled routines which are sequences of a conscious "executive program." In general, human activities can be considered as a sequence of such skilled acts or activities composed for the actual occasion. The flexibility of skilled performance is due to the ability to compose, from a large repertoire of automated subroutines, the sets suited for specific purposes.

At the next level of *rule-based behavior*, the composition of such a sequence of subroutines in a familiar work situation is typically controlled by a *stored rule* or procedure which may have been derived empirically during previous occasions, communicated from other persons' know-how as instruction or a cookbook recipe, or it may be prepared on occasion by conscious problem solving and planning. The point here is that performance is goal-oriented but structured by "feedforward control" through a stored rule. Very often, the goal is not even explicitly formulated but is found implicitly in the situation releasing the stored rules. The control is teleological in the sense that the rule or control is selected from previous successful experiences. The control evolves by "survival of the fittest" rule. In effect, the rule will reflect the functional properties which constrain the behavior of the environment, but usually in properties found empirically in the past. Furthermore, in actual life, the goal will only be reached after a long sequence of acts, and direct feedback correction considering the goal may not be possible. Feedback correction during performance will require functional understanding and analysis of the current response of the environment, which may be considered an independent concurrent activity at the next higher level (knowledge-based).

The boundary between skill-based and rule-based performance is not quite distinct, and much depends on the level of training and on the attention of the person. In general, the skill-based performance rolls along without the person's conscious attention, and he will be unable to describe how he controls and on what information he bases the performance. The higher level rule-based coordination is generally based on explicit know-how, and the rules used can be reported by the person.

During unfamiliar situations, faced with an environment for which no know-how or rules for control are available from previous encounters, the control of performance must move to a higher conceptual level, in which performance is goal-controlled and *knowledge-based*. In this situation, the goal is explicitly formulated, based on an analysis of the environment and the overall aims of the person. Then a useful plan is developed—by selection—such that different plans are considered, and their effect tested against the goal, physically by trial and error, or conceptually by means of understanding the functional properties of the environment and prediction of the effects of the plan considered. At this level of functional reasoning, the internal structure of the system is explicitly represented by a "mental model" which may take several different forms. We will return to this point in discussion of reasons and causes later.

Similar distinctions between different categories of human behavior have been proposed elsewhere. Fitts [7] distinguishes between three phases of learning a skill: the early or cognitive phase, the intermediate or associative phase, and the final or autonomous phase. If we consider that in real life a person will have a varying degree of training when performing his task depending on variations and disturbances, the correspondence with the three levels in the present context is clear.

Whitehead [8, pp. 92–98], discussing symbolism, operates with three categories of human performance: instinctive action, reflex action, and symbolically conditioned action, which are also related to the present discussion:

> Pure instinct is the most primitive response which is yielded by organisms to the stimulus of their environment....
> Reflex action is a relapse towards a more complex type of

instinct on the part of an organism which enjoys, or has enjoyed, symbolically conditioned action.... Reflex action arises when, by the operation of symbolism, the organism has acquired the habit of action in response to immediate sense-perception, and has discarded the symbolic enhancement of causal efficacy.... [In symbolic conditioned action] the causal efficacy is thereby perceived as analyzed into components with the locations in space primarily belonging to the sense-perceptions.... Finally mankind also uses a more artificial symbolism, obtained chiefly by concentrating on a certain selection of sense-perceptions, such as words for example. In this case there is a chain of derivations of symbol from symbol whereby finally the local relations between the final symbol and the ultimate meaning are entirely lost. Thus these derivative symbols, obtained as they were by arbitrary association, are really the result of reflex action suppressing the intermediate portions of the chain.

Whitehead's discussion of symbols and derived symbols, the meaning of which is lost, leads to the distinction between signals, signs, and symbols.

## SIGNALS / SIGNS / SYMBOLS

One aspect of the categorization of human performance in skill/rule/knowledge-based behavior is the role of the information observed from the environment, which is basically different in the different categories. The fact that information or indications from the environment can be perceived in basically different ways by a human observer is no new discovery, but curiously enough it has so far not been considered explicitly by man–machine interface designers. This is the case even though major problems during unfamiliar situations may be caused by the fact that the same indication may be perceived in various different roles and that it is a well-known psychological phenomenon that shift between different modes of perception is difficult.

At the *skill-based* level the perceptual motor system acts as a multivariable continuous control system synchronizing the physical activity such as navigating the body through the environment and manipulating external objects in a time–space domain. For this control the sensed information is perceived as time–space *signals*, continuous quantitative indicators of the time–space behavior of the environment. These signals have no "meaning" or significance except as direct physical time–space data. The performance at the skill-based level may be released or guided by value features attached by prior experience to certain patterns in the information not taking part in the time–space control but acting as cues or *signs* activating the organism.

At the *rule-based* level, the information is typically perceived as *signs*. The information perceived is defined as a sign when it serves to activate or modify predetermined actions or manipulations. Signs refer to situations or proper behavior by convention or prior experience; they do not refer to concepts or represent functional properties of the environment. Signs are generally labeled by names which may refer to states or situations in the environment or to a person's goals and tasks. Signs can only be used to select or modify the rules controlling the sequencing of skilled subroutines; they cannot be used for functional reasoning, to generate new rules, or to predict the response of an environment to unfamiliar disturbances.

To be useful for causal functional reasoning in predicting or explaining unfamiliar behavior of the environment, information must be perceived as *symbols*. While signs refer to percepts and rules for action, symbols refer to concepts tied to functional properties and can be used for reasoning and computation by means of a suitable representation of such properties. Signs have external reference to states of and actions upon the environment, but symbols are defined by and refer to the internal conceptual representation which is the basis for reasoning and planning. Cassirer notes [9]:

> Symbols—in the proper sense of the term—cannot be reduced to mere signs. Signs and symbols belong to two different universes of discourse: a sign is part of the physical world of being, a symbol is part of the human world of meaning.

The difference between signs and symbols, and the difficulty in the shift from rule-based reliance on signs to knowledge-based use of symbols, is clearly illustrated in the testimony of the Three Mile Island operators to the Congress [10, p. 138].

> Mr. Frederick: "Let me make a statement about the indications. All you can say about them is that they are designed to provide indications for whatever anticipated casualties you might have. If you go out of the bounds of an anticipated casualty, if you go beyond what the designers think might happen, then the indications are insufficient and they may lead you to make wrong inferences. In other words, what you are seeing on the gage, like what I saw on the high pressurizer level, I thought it was due to excess inventory. In other words, I was interpreting the gage based on the emergency procedure, where the emergency procedure is based on the design casualties. So the indications then are based upon my interpretation. Hardly any of the measurements that we have are direct indications of what is going on in the system. They are all implied measurements."

If to this is added the difficulty in abandoning a search for a rule which is not there, the point becomes clear [10, p. 139].

> Mr. Faust: "What maybe you should try to understand here is that we are trying to gain the proper procedure to go at it. We were into possibilities of several procedures, not just one, to cover what was happening. It has not been written, in fact. So we were still trying to determine which procedure to go by."

The distinction between the perception of information as signals/signs/symbols is generally not dependent on the form in which the information is presented but rather on the context in which it is perceived, i.e., upon the intentions and expectations of the perceiver. Whorf expresses

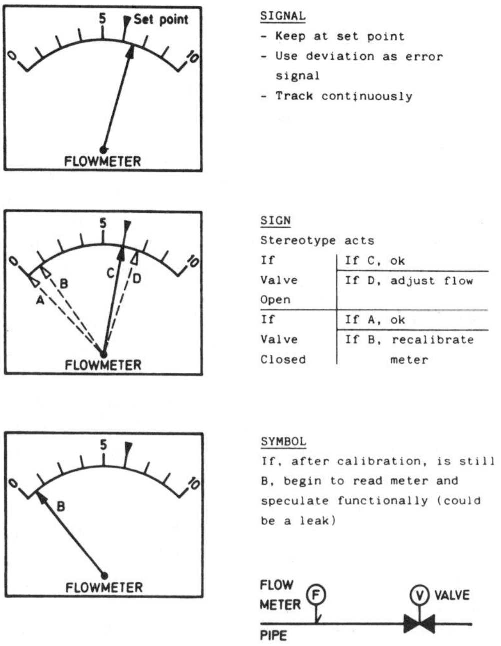

Fig. 2. Same physical indication on control panel can serve to communicate to operator in form of signal, sign, and symbol.

this well-known fact in the following way [11]:

> The categories and types that we isolate from the world of phenomena we do not find because they stare every observer in the face; on the contrary, the world is presented to us in a kaleidoscopic flux of impressions which has to be organized by our minds....

Fig. 2 illustrates how the same instrument can serve to transmit all three kinds of message.

The discussion of the different perception of information is a classical topic within biology and philosophy, and similar distinctions have been drawn. Dewey and Bentley [12] apply the same definition for sign and symbol as discussed but use the term signal in a different way which is more related to its use in classical discussions of reflexive behavior such as that of Pavlov's dogs. They

> have employed the word "sign" to name this technically characteristic 'indirectness' as it is found across the entire behavioural field... Within the range of sign, the word "signal" was chosen to name the underlying sensory-perceptive level; the word "designation" for the next higher evolutionary level—namely, that of linguistic sign operation; and the word "symboling" for a still higher range in the evolutionary sense....

In the present man–machine context, it seems to be important to keep the role of information as time–space signals, which are processed directly in a dynamic control of the motor performance, separate from the role as signs which serve to modify actions at a higher level.

The distinction between signs and symbols is also treated by von Foerster [13]. However, he focuses upon the difference between humans and animals.

> Communication among social insects is carried out through unalterable signs which are linked to the genetic make-up of the species... To communicate acquired knowledge by passing through generations, it must be communicated in symbols and not signs. This separates man from beasts.

This may be the case sometimes, but operating from signs may also be the normal way to be efficient for humans.

To sum up, the three levels of behavior in the present context are characterized by different uses of the information available, and the distinction is very clear from an information processing point of view.

*Signals* are sensory data representing time–space variables from a dynamical spatial configuration in the environment, and they can be processed by the organism as continuous variables.

*Signs* indicate a state in the environment with reference to certain conventions for acts. Signs are related to certain features in the environment and the connected conditions for action. Signs cannot be processed directly, they serve to activate stored patterns of behavior.

*Symbols* represent other information, variables, relations, and properties and can be formally processed. Symbols are abstract constructs related to and defined by a formal structure of relations and processes—which by conventions can be related to features of the external world.

## Reasons / Causes

As previously mentioned, in the knowledge-based domain the functional or causal properties of the environment can be represented in different ways. Several problems meet the human data processor at this level in the interaction with a complex physical environment. Only a few elements of a problem can be within the span of attention simultaneously. This means that the complex net of causal relations of an environment must be treated in a chain of mental operations, often leading to effects like the law of least resistance and the point of no return. That is, strategies which depend on sequences of simple operations are intuitively preferred, and little tendency will exist to pause in a line of reasoning to backtrack and develop alternative or parallel paths [14].

An effective way to counteract limitations of attention seems to be to modify the basis of mental data processing —the mental model of the causal structure—to fit it to the specific task in a way which optimizes the transfer of previous results and minimizes the need for new information. The efficiency of human cognitive processes seems to depend upon an extensive use of model transformations together with a simultaneous updating of the mental models in all categories with new input information, an updating which may be performed below the level of conscious attention and control.

From the analysis of verbal protocols, it appears that several strategies for model transformation are generally

## LEVELS OF ABSTRACTION

**FUNCTIONAL PURPOSE**
Production flow models, system objectives

**ABSTRACT FUNCTION**
Causal structure, mass, energy & information flow topology, etc.

**GENERALISED FUNCTIONS**
"Standard" functions & processes, control loops, heat transfer, etc.

**PHYSICAL FUNCTIONS**
Electrical, mechanical, chemical processes of components and equipment

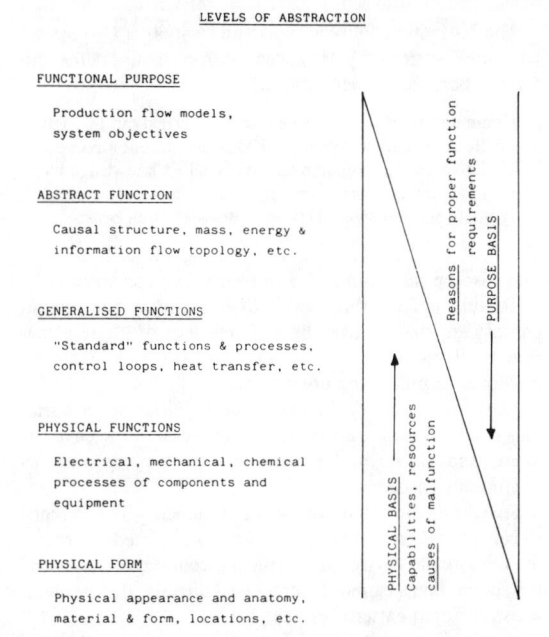

**PHYSICAL FORM**
Physical appearance and anatomy, material & form, locations, etc.

PHYSICAL BASIS — Capabilities, resources, causes of malfunction
PURPOSE BASIS — Reasons for proper function requirements

Fig. 3. Properties of system will be used in operators' decisionmaking in terms of concepts at several levels of abstraction; frequently even during single decision sequence.

used to facilitate mental data processing, such as the following.

- *Aggregation*: Elements of a representation are aggregated into larger units, chunks, within the same model category as familiarity with the context increases.
- *Abstraction*: The representation of the properties of a system or an environment is transferred to a model category at a higher level of abstraction.
- *Analogies and Use of Ready-Made Solutions*: The representation is transferred to a category of model for which a solution is already known or rules are available to generate the solution.

In the *abstraction hierarchy*, which has been identified from analysis of verbal protocols from computer maintenance and process plant control, the system's functional properties are represented by concepts which belong to several levels of abstraction (see Fig. 3). The lowest level of abstraction represents only the system's physical form, its material configuration. The next higher level represents the physical processes or functions of the various components and systems in a language related to their specific electrical, chemical, or mechanical properties. Above this, the functional properties are represented in more general concepts without reference to the physical process or equipment by which the functions are implemented, and so forth.

At the lower levels, elements in the description match the component configuration of the physical implementation. When moving from one level of abstraction to the next higher level, the change in system properties represented is *not* merely removal of details of information on the physical or material properties. More fundamentally, information is added on higher level principles governing the cofunction of the various elements at the lower level. In man-made systems, these higher level principles are naturally derived from the purpose of the system, i.e., from the *reasons* for the configurations at the level considered. Change of level of abstraction involves a shift in concepts and structure for representation as well as a change in the information suitable to characterize the state of the function or operation at the various levels of abstraction. Thus an observer will ask different questions regarding the state of the environment depending on the nature of the currently active internal representation.

In other words, models at low levels of abstraction are related to a specific physical world which can serve several purposes. Models at higher levels of abstraction are closely related to a specific purpose which can be met by several physical arrangements. Therefore, shifts in the level of abstraction can be used to change the direction of paths which are suitable for transfer of knowledge from previous cases and problems. At the two extreme levels of models, the directions of the paths available for transfer are in a way orthogonal, since transfer at one level follows physical, material properties, while at the other it follows purpose.

Important human functions in man–machine systems are related to correction of the effects of errors and faults. Events can only be defined as errors or faults with reference to intended state, normal function, or other variants of system purpose or functional meaning. The functional models at the different levels of abstraction play different roles in coping with error struck systems. *Causes of improper functions* depend upon changes in the physical or material world. Thus they are explained "bottom-up" in the levels of abstraction, whereas *reasons for proper function* are derived "top-down" from the functional purpose (see Fig. 3). The clear difference between the propagation of causes of faults and reasons for function in the hierarchy has been discussed in detail by Polanyi [2]. This role of the abstraction hierarchy can be seen clearly in verbal protocols recorded during diagnostic search in information processing systems. The diagnostician will frequently be forced to consider the functions of the system at several levels. He will typically have to identify information flow paths and proper functional states by arguing top-down from the level of symbolic information, while he will utilize bottom-up considerations to analyze and explain the actual functional state from physical causes.

Another human task for which the use of representations at several levels of abstraction is of obvious value is the *design of technical systems*. Basically, system design is a process of iteration between considerations at the various levels rather than an orderly transformation from a description of purpose to a description in terms of physical form. A many-to-many mapping exists between the two levels; a purpose can be served by many physical configurations, and a physical system can serve many purposes or have a variety of effects. The use of different categories of representation in a design strategy has been explicitly discussed by Alexander [15, p. 89, 90]:

> Every form can be described in two ways: from the point of view of what it is, and from the point of view of what it does. What it is, is sometimes called the formal description. What it does, when put in contact with other things, is sometimes called the functional description.... The solution of a design problem is really only another effort to find a unified description. The search for realization through constructive diagrams is an effort to understand the required form so fully that there is no longer a rift between its functional specification and the shape it takes.

If we accept the complex of strata between physical form and functional meaning of technical systems, an "invention" is related to a jump of insight which happens when one mental structure upward from physical form and another downward from functional meaning, which have previously been totally unconnected, suddenly merge to "a unified description."

Each level of abstraction or category of representation depends upon a special set of concepts and relationships. Shifting the level of modeling can be very effective in a problem situation since data processing at another level can be more convenient, the process rules can be simpler or better known, or results can be available from previous cases. A special instance of this strategy is the solution of a problem by simple analogy which depends upon the condition that different physical systems have the same description at higher levels of abstraction.

In some cases, efficient strategies can be found where symbols are transferred to another level of abstraction and reinterpreted. A simple example will be the subconscious manipulation of symbols which are reinterpreted as artificial objects, e.g., Smith's [16] solution of scheduling problems by manipulation of rectangles; or the reinterpretation of numbers in terms of actions for calculations by means of an abacus. This recursive use of the categories of functional models adds another dimension to the variety of tricks to cope with complexity. The most general is, of course, the use of natural language which can be used to make statements about models and operations at all levels of abstraction. However, this generality is frequently offset by the difficulty of keeping track of the context, i.e., the category of model behind the symbols.

Another consideration should be added to this discussion. Frequently, other persons will be part of the environment with which a particular person interacts and for which he has to use mental models in order to cope with unfamiliar situations. As for technical systems, various levels of abstraction can be used to model human functional properties, and an analogy of the levels discussed in Fig. 3 is drawn for "models of man" in Fig. 4. All the levels are used in various professional contexts, but what is of particular interest here is that, in ordinary working life, human interaction is based on a top-down prediction drawn from perceptions of other persons' intentions, motives, and on common sense representations of human capabilities,

FUNCTIONAL PURPOSE

Value structures,
myths, religions,
intentions

ABSTRACT FUNCTION

Information processing

GENERALISED FUNCTIONS

Psychological mechanisms
cognitive, affective

PHYSICAL FUNCTIONS

Physiological functions

PHYSICAL FORM

Anatomical structure
"sculptures"

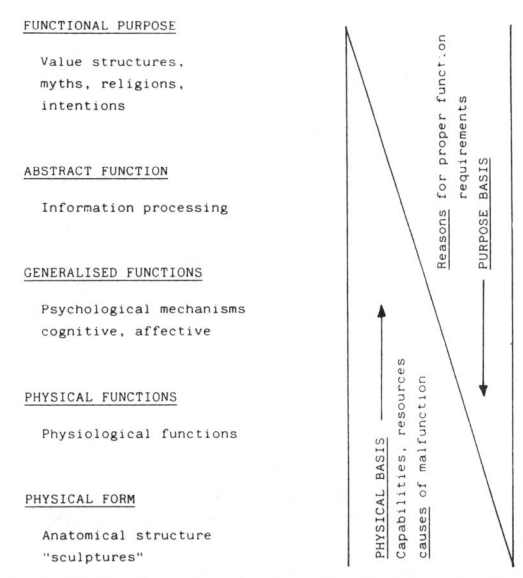

Fig. 4. Models of man also exist at several levels of abstraction. Note that interaction with work environment will require consideration of all levels from physical injuries at bottom to perception of goals and policies at top.

together with knowledge of accepted practice. Causal bottom-up arguments play literally no role, and the most important information to use for planning human interactions for unfamiliar occasions is therefore knowledge of the value structures and myths of the work environment. The obvious reason for this is the complexity and flexibility of the human organism. However, it should be emphasized that due to the growing complexity of information and control systems, the role of such intentional models [17] is rapidly increasing, and for interaction with such technical systems as well.

## QUALITATIVE VERSUS QUANTITATIVE MODELS OF HUMAN PERFORMANCE

A discussion of models of human behavior raises immediately the distinction between qualitative and quantitative models. Frequently, qualitative models are considered to be merely premature descriptive models which, after further work, will develop into or be replaced by proper quantitative models. However, this is not necessarily the case. The two kinds of models have in several respects different and equally important roles for analysis and prediction of performance. This difference in significance is related to the distinction between categories of behavior and the members of such categories, i.e., the specific behavior in particular situations. Bateson [18, p. 46] discusses this distinction in detail with reference to Whitehead and Russells' logical types:

> ... there is a deep gulf between statements about an identified individual and statements about a class. Such statements are of *different logical types*, and prediction from one to the other is always unsure.

The fact that "the generic we can know, but the specific eludes us" [18, p. 45] has different implications depending upon the purpose of the modeling effort. For systems design, qualitative models will serve important purposes if they are able to predict the category of behavior which will be activated by different possible interface configurations and display formats. The model will then support the choice of an interface design which will activate a category of behavior having limiting properties compatible with the functions allocated the human operator. In a way, research on human performance in order to support system design should not focus on modeling actual performance in existing environments but on *possible* performance in optimal future systems, as has been discussed by Sloman [19] in a philosophical context. Qualitative models identifying categories of behavior and the limiting properties of the related human resources will serve designers a long way in the design of systems which allow humans to optimize their behavior within a proper category [20]. Compare this with Norman's arguments [21] for the importance of considering the proper mental image for design of "friendly" systems and the need for a profession he calls "cognitive engineering." The distinctions between models of categories and of particulars have different implications depending also on the cognitive level of behavior considered. At the skill-based level we are considering highly trained people, similar to experimental psychologists' "well trained subjects" who have adapted to the particular environment. In this domain, models of optimal human performance are mainly models of the behavior of the *environment*, as seen through the man. Therefore, generic quantitative models of human performance in well structured tasks can be—and have been—developed at this level of performance. At the level of knowledge-based behavior, we are dealing with individual reactions to unfamiliar situations, and models will be more a question of qualitative matching of categories of system requirements with human resources. For unfamiliar tasks, these resources depend on a specific person's subjective preferences, experience, and state of training. In this context, training means supplying people with a proper repertoire of possible behaviors for unexpected situations, and qualitative models matching categories will be highly effective. Until recently, the training of industrial operators has not been based on models of human performance compatible with those used for systems design. However, the explicit use of qualitative models for matching categories of system requirements and human resources for planning of training programs by Rouse and his coworkers [22] has turned out successfully and proves the value of qualitative models.

To be useful, qualitative as well as quantitative models must reflect the structure underlying the mental processes, i.e., the internal or mental *models*; the kind of *data* dealt with by the processes; and the *rules* or *strategies* used to control the processes. In addition, the models must reflect the limits of human capabilities so that human "errors" are also modeled properly.

This question of also modeling errors properly leads directly to the issue of analog parallel processing models versus the sequential digital models of human information processes of the artificial intelligence (AI) community. Can holistic human perception, for instance, be properly modeled by the sequential "production rule" systems? In the present context of models for system design and evaluation, the fundamental question appears to be not whether a model is implemented for experimental evaluation by means of one or another physical information processing system but whether or not a theoretical framework exists formulated independently of the tools for experimental implementation. This framework must have a one-to-one correspondence to human psychological mechanisms, their processing limitations, and error characteristics. If such a separation between model and implementation were maintained, many of the arguments between psychologists and AI researchers [23] could be circumvented. An implication of this point is that computer programs based, for instance, on the production systems of Newell and Simon [24] cannot in general be accepted as theories unless they adequately represent limiting properties and error characteristics of the human processes. Proper representation of the failure properties of human information processes will be difficult, for instance, if holistic perception is modeled by sequential scene analysis. Therefore, proper evaluation of a model requires analysis of instances when the model breaks down rather than a search for correspondence with human performance in successful instances. This is the essence of Simon's statement [25]:

> A thinking human being is an adaptive system;... To the extent he is effectively adaptive, his behaviour will reflect characteristics largely of the outer environment... and will reveal only a few limiting properties of his inner environment....

Successful performance does not validate a model, only tests of its limits and error properties can do this.

## Conclusion: Implications for Design

In our work, concern is with the timely development of models of human performance which can be useful for the design and evaluation of new interface systems. For this purpose, we do not need a single integrated quantitative model of human performance but rather an overall qualitative model which allows us to match categories of performance to types of situations. In addition, we need a number of more detailed and preferably quantitative models which represent selected human functions and limiting properties within the categories. The role of the qualitative model will generally be to guide overall design of the structure of the system including, for example, a set of display formats, while selective, quantitative models can be used to optimize the detailed designs.

In many cases, the use of quantitative models for optimizing a design can be replaced by experimental evaluation. Unfortunately, however, it is the categories of performance for which experimental evaluation is most feasible—i.e., skill- and rule-based performances—which are also most readily modeled quantitatively. A major difficulty is the modeling of the knowledge-based control of performance during unfamiliar situations as well as the interaction among the different levels of performance depending upon the state of training. In particular, experimentally as well as analytically, studying the interference from overlearned routines during situations calling for knowledge-based responses is very difficult. Several problem areas for research can be identified for which we find it important to separate the categories of performance while keeping in mind the distinctions discussed previously. The first problem we meet in design of interface systems based on modern information technology is the tradition from the one-sensor–one-indicator technology that the operator task is expressed in terms of actions on the system, the state of which the operator is supposed to "figure out for himself" from readings of a number of physical variables and his training in system fundamentals. However, if computer technology is to be used to optimize man–machine communication, information presentation must be structured according to the nature of the control tasks the operator is supposed to perform. To do this properly, it is necessary to design the hierarchy of functions called for in the control of complex systems as one consistent whole —regardless of whether the individual functions are automated or allocated to operators. In a supervisory control task, the operator will have to face tasks at several levels in the hierarchy of control functions; i.e., the concepts used in a proper description of the various tasks will vary in the level of abstraction between physical implementation and overall system purpose, as discussed in relation to causes and reasons [26], [27]. In order to plan the formats of data presentation and the integration of measured data needed to derive the related variables, a *formalized description of the categories of control tasks* at the various levels of abstraction is necessary. An attempt to develop such a description is given by Lind [28].

A further requisite to structuring the man–computer interaction will be a description of these various categories of control tasks in information processing terms, together with a description of the strategies the operator is supposed to use; i.e., the *control task must be described in terms referring to human mental functions* rather than system requirements. This is particularly important, since several strategies which have very different requirements for human information processing capacity and data formats may be used for a specific external control task. As an example, consider the identification of the actual state of the system to be controlled: should identification be based on recognition of a specific symptom, on a decision table look-up, or on genuine diagnosis based on functional reasoning? However, as stated earlier, to match the interface to human capabilities in a specific task, we do not need a model of the detailed data process which will be performed but rather of the characteristics of different possible categories of performance in terms of the strategy and the related representation of system structure and state variables, together with requirements for processing capacity. In addition, information on the subjective human preferences or performance criteria which will control the selection of strategy in a given environment is necessary for design.

This situation leads to the need for human *performance analyses in real-life situations* to identify mental strategies and subjective performance criteria. From the analysis of task performance by observation, interviews, verbal protocols, error reports, etc., leading to descriptions of actual performance in a number of situations, generalization across instances can lead to descriptions of prototypical performance [29] from which a repertoire of formal strategies can be identified and described with reference to the distinctions described in the present paper. For instance, see [30] for a discussion of diagnostic strategies.

*Evaluation of a specific interface design* will require different types of experiments for which the distinctions discussed in the present paper have proved useful in our research [31]. For *evaluation of the system design concepts*, experiments involving the total set of display formats to be used in a work scenario are necessary to validate the design; i.e., to see whether the data presentations in actual work situations activate the strategies on which the display formats are based. In most cases, this validation is more readily based on a qualitative evaluation of the match between the predicted strategy and the strategy that was actually used than upon a quantitative performance measure. An effective tool in the qualitative evaluation is analysis of verbal reports and interviews. Although it may be doubtful whether verbal reports reveal mental data processes, they can be very valuable in identifying categories of performance by means of the distinction discussed previously on the basis of the concepts used to name tasks, models, and variables for the different categories of behavior.

Other kinds of experiments are required to *verify the internal consistency* in models. For this purpose, computer simulations related, for instance, to optimal control models or production rules for intelligent artifacts can be used. In addition, selective laboratory experiments with human subjects using quantitative performance measurements can be useful. See, for instance, the diagnostic experiments of Rouse and his coworkers [32]. Such experiments may also be used to optimize the ergonomic design of a display or set of displays for a specific selected task. However, even when quantitative performance measures are used, verbal statements are valuable in verifying that the performance trials analyzed in an experiment belong to the same category.

A general conclusion from our research has been that, in order to switch from the traditional one-sensor–one-indication technology to effective use of modern information technology for interface design, we have to consider in an integrated way human performance which is normally studied by separate paradigms. In addition, it is evident that we, like Eddington's ichthyologist [33], will be able to obtain some of the results needed more readily by conceptual analysis before experiments than by data analysis afterwards.

## References

[1] A. Rosenbluth, N. Wiener, and J. Bigelow, "Behaviour, purpose and teleology," *Phil. Sci.*, vol. 10, pp. 18–24, 1943.
[2] M. Polanyi, *Personal Knowledge*. London: Routledge & Kegan Paul, 1958.
[3] E. R. F. W. Crossman and J. E. Cooke, "Manual control of slow-response systems," presented at the Int. Cong. Human Factors in Electronics, Long Beach, CA, 1962. Also in E. Edwards and F. Lees, *The Human Operator in Process Control*. London: Taylor & Francis, 1974.
[4] R. W. Pew, "Human perceptual-motor performance," in *Human Information Processing: Tutorials in Performance and Cognition*, B. H. Kantowitz, Ed. New York: Erlbaum, 1974.
[5] N. Bernstein, *The Coordination and Regulation of Movement*. New York: Pergamon, 1967.
[6] J. C. Eccles, *The Understanding of the Brain*. New York: McGraw-Hill, 1972.
[7] P. M. Fitts and M. I. Posner, *Human Performance*. Brooks/Cole, 1962.
[8] A. N. Whitehead, *Symbolism, Its Meaning and Effect*. New York: Macmillan, 1927.
[9] E. Cassirer, *Essay on Man*. New Haven, CT: Yale Univ. Press, 1944.
[10] Oversight Hearings, "Accident at the Three Mile Island nuclear power plant," U.S. Gov. Printing Office, Washington, DC, 1979.
[11] B. Whorf, "Science and linguistics," *Technol. Rev.*, vol. XLII, 1940. Also in *Language, Thought and Reality. Selected Writings of Whorf*, J. B. Carroll, Ed. Cambridge, MA: MIT Press, 1956.
[12] A. F. Bentley, "Kennetic inquiry," *Sci.*, vol. 112, pp. 775–783, 1950.
[13] H. von Foerster, "From stimulus to symbol: The ecology of biological computation," in *Sign, Image and Symbol*, G. Kepes, Ed. London: Studio Vista, 1966.
[14] J. Rasmussen and A. Jensen, "Mental procedures in real life tasks: A case study of electronic trouble shooting," *Ergonomics*, vol. 17, pp. 293–307, 1974.
[15] C. Alexander, *Notes on the Synthesis of Form*. Cambridge, MA: Harvard Univ. Press, 1964.
[16] H. T. Smith, "Perceptual organization and the design of the man-computer interface in process control," in *Monitoring Behaviour and Supervisory Control*, Sheridan and Johannsen, Eds. New York: Plenum, 1976.
[17] D. C. Dennett, "Intentional systems," *J. Phil.*, vol. LXVIII, Feb. 25, 1971.
[18] G. Bateson, *Mind and Nature*. New York: Elsevier-Dutton, 1979.
[19] A. Sloman, *The Computer Revolution in Philosophy: Philosophy, Science, and Models of Mind*. Sussex, England: Harwester, 1978.
[20] J. Rasmussen and M. Lind, "Coping with complexity," presented at European Ann. Conf. Human Decision and Manual Control, Delft, 1981, Risø-M-2293.
[21] D. A. Norman, "Steps toward a cognitive engineering: Systems images, system friendliness, mental models," presented at the Symp. Models of Human Performance, ONR Contractor's Meeting, La Jolla, CA, June 19, 1981.
[22] W. B. Rouse, "Panel on human performance theories and models," presented at the IEEE Standards Workshop on Human Factors in Nuclear Safety, Proceedings to be published. 1982.
[23] H. L. Dreyfus, *What Computers Can't Do*. New York: Harper and Row, 1972.
[24] A. Newell and H. A. Simon, *Human Problem Solving*. Englewood Cliffs, NJ: Prentice-Hall, 1972.
[25] H. A. Simon, *The Sciences of the Artificial*. Cambridge, MA: MIT Press, 1969.
[26] L. P. Goodstein and J. Rasmussen, "Man/machine system design criteria in computerized control rooms," abbreviated version in *Proc. ASSOPO 80—an IFIP/IFAC Symp.*, Trondheim, Norway, June 16–18, 1980.
[27] L. P. Goodstein, "Computer-based operating aids," presented at Design 82, Birmingham, UK, Sept. 22–23, 1982.
[28] M. Lind, "Generic control tasks in process plant operation," to be published, 1982.
[29] E. Hollnagel, O. M. Pedersen, and J. Rasmussen, "Notes on human performance analysis," Risø-M-2285, 1981.
[30] J. Rasmussen, "Models of mental strategies in process plant diagnosis," in *Human Detection and Diagnosis of System Failures*, J. Rasmussen and W. B. Rouse, Eds. New York: Plenum, 1981.
[31] E. Hollnagel, "The methodology of man–machine systems: problems of verification and validation," Risø-M-2313, 1981.
[32] W. B. Rouse, "Experimental studies and mathematical models of human problem solving performance in fault diagnosis tasks," in *Human Detection and Diagnosis of System Failures*, J. Rasmussen and W. B. Rouse, Eds. New York: Plenum, 1981.
[33] A. Eddington, *The Philosophy of Physical Science*. New York: Cambridge Univ. Press, 1939 (also Ann Arbor, MI: Univ. of Michigan Press, 1958).

# Categorization of Action Slips

## Donald A. Norman
University of California, San Diego (La Jolla)

A slip is the error that occurs when a person does an action that is not intended. In this article I examine several collections of slips, primarily of actions, with the aim of devising a theoretical explication. A theory of action is outlined in which an action sequence is represented by a parent schema and numerous child schemas, in which several action schemas can be active at any one time, and in which each schema has a set of triggering conditions and an activation value. The path from intention to action consists of the activation of the parent schema that corresponds to the intention, the activation of child schemas for the component parts of the action sequence, and then the appropriate triggering of schemas when the conditions match those required for their operations. This action system allows slips to be organized into three major categories and a number of subcategories. The three major categories of slips are: (a) errors in the formation of the intention (which includes the subcategories of mode and description errors); (b) faulty activation of schemas (which includes the subcategories of capture errors, data-driven and associative activations, loss of intention, and misordering of action components); and (c) faulty triggering (which includes the subcategories of spoonerisms, blends, intrusions of thoughts, and premature triggering).

A slip is a form of human error defined to be the performance of an action that was not what was intended. Slips can often be interpreted. They often appear to result from conflict among several possible actions or thoughts, from intermixing the components of a single action sequence, or from selection of an appropriate act but in some inappropriate way. From an analysis of slips of action it is possible to construct the outlines of a theory of action that suggests how an intention is represented and acted upon.

One of the first large collections of verbal slips was put together by Meringer (1908; Meringer & Mayer, 1895/1978). The best early theoretical account was provided by Freud (1901/1966), who made use of Meringer's collection. Freud's analyses made important contributions to our understanding of the mind. Freud's contribution can be reinterpreted in modern terminology by separating the two different aspects of cognitive machinery that he made use of: processing

---

Partial support for this research was provided by Office of Naval Research (ONR) Contract N00014-79-C-0323 and by the Defense Applied Research Agency, monitored by ONR under Contract N00014-79-C-0515. Support was also provided by Grant MH-15828 from the National Institutes of Mental Health to the Center for Human Information Processing.

I am grateful for the help of the LNR research group, both in building up the collection of slips and in providing useful comments upon the analysis of the examples. In particular, Jonathan Grudin was an avid collector and analyzer of slips. His help is much appreciated. I appreciate the comments and help of various readers, especially Peter Lindsay, J.L. McClelland, and George Mandler. Bernard Baars, Elliot Saltzman, and Dedre Gentner provided useful comments. I gratefully acknowledge Marigold Linton's living room floor.

Requests for reprints should be sent to Donald A. Norman, Center for Human Information Processing, University of California, San Diego, La Jolla, California 92093.

From *Psychological Review*, 88. Copyright 1964 by the American Psychological Association.

and knowledge. Freud believed that slips resulted from competition among underlying mechanisms, often working in parallel with one another and almost always beneath the consciousness of the owner. The resulting notions were of mental operations controlled by a quasi-hierarchical control structure, with parallel activation of thoughts and memories and with conscious access to only a limited amount of this activity. The ideas are sophisticated even for today's theorists, who only recently have introduced the differences between conscious and subconscious processing into their models of cognitive functioning and who are just beginning to develop notions of independently operating computational units. Freud also was concerned with the particular knowledge contents of the memories and beliefs of his patients, but these analyses are not required for the understanding of the mechanisms that underlie slips.

Slips are indeed compelling sources of data. To Freud, the interpretations of some were clear, "for the meaning in them is unmistakable, even to the dullest intelligence, and strong enough to impress even the most critical judgment" (Freud, 1924, p. 59). It is indeed true that slips appear manageable and that they cry out for interpretation. The examination of any large collection of slips reveals that they can be categorized and that they fall into patterns. (See, for example, the collection and categories of verbal slips in Fromkin, 1973, Appendix.) However, the meaning in them is not at all clear; their categorization and interpretation are theory dependent, yet contemporary theories of cognitive behavior are not really up to the task. Several workers have tried to categorize human error in terms of behavioristic criteria (errors of commission, of ommission, of substitution). These classifications do not aid in understanding the underlying mechanisms. Moreover, they quickly become large and unwieldy. A complete error theory seems likely to require autonomous, subconscious processing, with intentions, past habits, thoughts, and memories all playing some role in corrupting the intended behavior.

Consider the following slip. I was leading a conference discussion for a group of papers on the topic of "Representation of Knowledge." In my coverage of one of the speakers' presentation, I said, "This tells us nothing of the reputation [pause] *representation* of the information." A clinical (Freudian) interpretation is easy to perform; the slip revealed my underlying concern about the reputation of the speaker. But note that the slip itself did not occur at a random time: The hidden intent apparently was able to select just the right opportunity to reveal itself, a situation where the syntactical and phonological components would match properly. The words *reputation* and *representation* share a common ending and a common beginning and are the same part of speech. The erroneous sentence is just as grammatical and meaningful as the intended sentence. What mechanisms can account for these aspects of slips? These different aspects of a slip point out an important point: Most slips have multiple causes. Many sources of information are likely to be interacting to give rise to any particular action. When the act is an error, it is apt to be the result of numerous underlying forces, so that the resulting slip is multiply determined and consistent with a number of constraints and explanations.

Analyses of verbal slips indicate that the pronunciation of words is not a unitary concept associated with the words. Otherwise, once having started a word, we would go all the way through with it. But people say such things as *canpakes* for *pancakes* and *relevation* for *revelation*; or they interchange sounds among several words, as in *the sweeter hitch* instead of *the heater switch*. One form of error is a blend: when a person is undecided about two words, out comes a mixture, as in *momentaneous* for the mix of *momentary* and *instantaneous* (all these examples come from Fromkin, 1973, Appendix). There appear to be notions of individual parts of an action or of an utterance, perhaps differentially activated, waiting to be picked up and executed. As with the slip of *reputation* for *representation*, slips probably have several contributing causes, with the actual word selection being influenced by a combination of syntactical considerations, meaning, and phonological selection from the set of possible words, as well as by activation of underlying motives and plans.

Verbal slips have been widely studied (see the collections of articles in Fromkin, 1973, 1980). In the present article I concentrate on slips of actions rather than of words. These have not been so thoroughly studied as verbal ones, but they have been noted. One form of action slip is the performance of a well-formed habit in inappropriate circumstances, as in the report by William James (1890) that

very absent-minded persons in going to their bedroom to dress for dinner have been known to take off one garment after another and finally to get into bed, merely because that was the habitual issue of the first few movements when performed at a later hour. (p. 115)

Other action slips result when a thought that was not intended to be voiced or performed gets done anyway. Sometimes the complementary slip occurs. Having thought about the need to do some action or to say some utterance, the person does not do it but believes that it has been done (or, at least, later remembers it to have been done). In one case, thoughts cause actions, in the other, thoughts replace actions.

One interesting aspect of slips is people's ability (or inability) to detect them. Many slips are caught at the time they are made. Sometimes they are caught just prior to their occurrence, but with insufficient time to prevent the act, or at least the initial stages of the act. For a slip to be started, yet caught, means that there must exist some monitoring mechanism of behavior—a mechanism that is separate from that responsible for the selection and execution of the act.

## Outline of an Activation–Trigger–Schema System

The proposed model, an activation–trigger–schema system (ATS), assumes that action sequences are controlled by sensorimotor knowledge structures: *schemas*. A schema is an organized memory unit, much along the lines proposed for perception and memory (Norman & Bobrow, 1976; Rumelhart & Ortony, 1977). The extension of these ideas to include motor actions seems natural, both from the demands of the situation and from historical precedent (Head originally introduced the term *schema* specifically for motor action—see Bartlett, 1932; also see Schmidt, 1975, 1976). The operation of the model is based on activation and selection of schemas and uses a triggering mechanism that requires that appropriate conditions be satisfied for the operation of a schema. This model of schema activation is consistent with the literature on memory and models of schemalike computational mechanisms, as well as with the literature on the heterarchical nature of the motor control system (Szentagothai & Arbib, 1975).

The ATS model is novel only in its combination of previously stated ideas; all the components of the model have been stated elsewhere, although not in this combination and not for this purpose. Thus, the notion of schemas is well established in the study of perception and memory and somewhat so in the study of motor skills. The notion of activation values among schemas has been discussed for the related concepts of semantic networks by Collins and Loftus (1975) and for memory knowledge structures by Anderson (1976). The importance of trigger conditions is widely recognized in the literature on computational systems, the development most pertinent to this model being the production system (Newell, 1973; Waterman & Hayes-Roth, 1978). The formulation used here was partially developed by Rosenbloom (Note 1) and has been elaborated by Norman and Shallice (Note 2). The ATS framework is being explored for perceptual processing (McClelland & Rumelhart, Note 3; Rumelhart & McClelland, Note 4) and for the control of motor sequences in typing (Rumelhart & Norman, Note 5).

The novelty of the current model lies in several of its aspects: first, the combination of schemas, activation values, and triggering conditions; second, the application of motor action sequences; third, the role of intention; fourth, the consideration of the operation of cognitive systems when several different action sequences are operative simultaneously; and fifth, the specific application of this framework to the classification of slips. In order to analyze most slips, the model need only be specified in its general principles of operation. More detailed specification is, of course, required for the understanding of any specific action sequence, but at the moment there are not sufficient data to justify more details. Fortunately, a general analysis suffices for the analysis of most slips.

*Intention, Parent and Child Schemas*

For the current analysis, details of the structure of schemas are not necessary. It suffices to view a schema as an organized body of knowledge, including procedural knowledge that can direct the flow of control of motor activity. Each schema is assumed to cover only a limited range of knowledge or actions. As a result, any given action sequence must be specified by a rather large ensemble of schemas, organized in a heterarchical control structure. One schema may need to invoke other schemas, passing to them particular values that the variables of the schemas must assume for the particular actions to be performed. Information passes both down from the higher-order schemas to the lower ones and also back up from lower-order schemas to higher ones.

For now, what is important is that a given action sequence has a number of different schemas that control the various aspects of the action. The highest-level schema is called the *parent* schema, with the subschemas that are initiated by the parent schema for the control of component parts of the action sequence being called *child* schemas. Each child schema may act as a parent schema to further child schemas. The concept of intention is equated with the initial, highest-level parent schema.

A major assumption of the ATS theory for slips is that skilled actions—actions whose components are themselves all highly skilled—need only be specified at the highest levels of their memory representations. Once the highest-level schema is activated, the lower-level parent components of that action sequence complete the action, to a large extent autonomously, without further need for intervention except at critical choice points. (This argument is developed in more detail by Norman & Shallice, Note 2.)

A major justification for the use of activation values comes from consideration of the forms of interactions that are required of schemas in such domains as perception and action. In these domains, activation values offer a mechanism for considerable interaction among schemas, allowing a schema to constrain and support any others that share common data bases or require similar resources. These issues are addressed in the papers by McClelland and Rumelhart (Note 3), Rumelhart and McClelland (Note 4), and Rumelhart and Norman (Note 5).

Note that numerous schemas will be activated at any given time. This implication results from two factors. First, any given action sequence is usually quite complex, involving a large number of component schemas. Second, because many (most) action sequences may require considerable time to be completed (consider the act of eating dinner or of walking to a restaurant), multiple intentions and schemas are usually active at any one time. The determination of the appropriate triggering conditions for a given schema then becomes a critical factor in the correct performance of an act. Activation values do not provide a sufficient mechanism for determining the appropriate temporal ordering of sequences. The model provides each schema with a set of specific conditions that are required for it to be triggered. An activated schema can be triggered by current processing activity whenever the situation matches its conditions sufficiently well. Exact match is not required—otherwise it would not be possible to account for many of the observed slips—but we assume there is a trade-off between level of activation and the goodness-of-match to the trigger conditions. The mechanism that is being considered here is that of "descriptions" (Norman & Bobrow, 1979). There are a number of different possible theoretical specifications of schemas, but for current purposes it is only important that there is selectivity of activation and triggering.

Consider an example. When I drive home from the University, the intention to go home activates a host of relevant child schemas. These schemas then get triggered at appropriate times by satisfaction of their conditions by previous actions, by the environment, or by perceptions. I need not consider the details: I intend only that I should drive home. I can now do other tasks such as talk to a passenger, listen to the radio, and think about things other than the driving. The normal schemas required for avoiding obstacles, maintaining speed, braking properly, and following the correct route all have been activated and all trigger themselves when appropriate conditions arise. Conscious attention to the task can vary, with the task itself demanding attention at critical action points. Suppose, however, that I wish to drive to the fish store, not to my home. Because the fish store route is almost identical to the route required to go home, it is specified as a deviation from the better-learned, more frequently used home route schema. For this purpose I must set up a new schema, one that is to be triggered at a critical location along the usual path. If the relevant schema for the deviation is not in a sufficiently active state at the critical time for its triggering, it is apt to be missed, and as a result, the more common home route followed: I find myself home, fishless.

What I have given is a preliminary, high-level statement of a theory of act selection. Although the details are not presented, the specification is sufficient for current purposes. The essential assumptions are that any given action sequence is controlled by an ensemble of child schemas, that at any one time numerous schemas for a number of different sequences may be active. Schemas only invoke actions when they have been triggered, and this requires satisfaction of trigger conditions plus a sufficiently high level of activation.

Application of the Theory of Action to the Interpretation of Slips

In this article, I concentrate on action errors. Verbal errors are analyzed when they exhibit semantic properties or some interaction with planning or motor operations.[1] In addition, I use the examples of motor slips from the work of Reason (1975, 1976, 1977, 1979). Some examples come from the book by Hurst (1976) and from official government accident reports. I have also used the collection of pilot errors by Fitts and Jones (1961a, 1961b), although a number of these errors are not relevant to the analyses that I am performing. In total, I have examined roughly 1,000 incidents, 200 of which were from my own collection.

The theory of action permits numerous opportunities for slips. There can be error in the selection of the intention or errors in the specification of the components. Even if the appropriate schemas are all activated, there can be errors of performance when schemas are triggered out of order or when a relevant schema is missed. There can also be errors resulting from the intrusion of unwanted activities from thoughts, from the occurrence of some event in the world that triggers an unintended response, or from a well-learned, familiar habit's taking control of action.

The basic classification of slips has three major headings, each corresponding to a different aspect of act formation or performance, and each contributing a source of error. These three major sources of action slips are (a) the formation of the intention, (b) activation, and (c) triggering. The complete classification is given in Table 1.

*Slips During the Formation of an Intention*

The formation of an intention is the result of many considerations, including the overall goals of the person, decision analyses, problem solving activities, situational analyses, and so on. Any or all of these can be faulty, but most are not within the focus of this article. Here I start with intentions as given and therefore ignore errors that result from the decision-making or problem-solving aspect of intention formation. However, there are still two classes of intentional problems that do lead to relevant action slips: errors in classifying the situation and errors that result from ambiguous or incompletely specified intentions.

---

[1] I only analyzed slips that had been recorded immediately after the incident by either the perpetrator or an observer. I attempted to get as complete a record as possible, including what the person had been thinking and how the slip was discovered. Some of the other sources of slips were not collected in this way (e.g., those of Fitts & Jones). For the purposes of mapping slips to the theory, a precise determination of the occurrence is required.

Table 1
*A Classification of Slips Based on Their Presumed Sources*

Slips that result from errors in the formation of the intention
    Errors that are not classified as slips: errors in the determination of goals, in decision making and problem solving, and other related aspects of the determination of an intention
    Mode errors: erroneous classification of the situation
    Description errors: ambiguous or incomplete specification of the intention
Slips that result from faulty activation of schemas
    Unintentional activation: when schemas not part of a current action sequence become activated for extraneous reasons, then become triggered and lead to slips
        Capture errors: when a sequence being performed is similar to another more frequent or better learned sequence, the latter may capture control
        Data-driven activation: external events cause activation of schemas
        Associative activation: currently active schemas activate others with which they are associated
    Loss of activation: when schemas that have been activated lose activation, thereby losing effectiveness to control behavior
        Forgetting an intention (but continuing with the action sequence)
        Misordering the components of an action sequence
        Skipping steps in an action sequence
        Repeating steps in an action sequence
Slips that result from faulty triggering of active schemas
    False triggering: a properly activated schema is triggered at an inappropriate time
        Spoonerisms: reversal of event components
        Blends: combinations of components from two competing schemas
        Thoughts leading to actions: triggering of schemas meant only to be thought, not to govern action
        Premature triggering
    Failure to trigger: when an active schema never gets invoked because
        The action was preempted by competing schemas
        There was insufficient activation, either as a result of forgetting or because the initial level was too low
        There was a failure of the trigger condition to match, either because the triggering conditions were badly specified or the match between occurring conditions and the required conditions was never sufficiently close

## *Mode Errors: Erroneous Classification of the Situation*

When a situation is falsely classified, then the resulting action may be one that was intended and appropriate for the analysis of the situation but inappropriate for the actual situation. There are a number of possible reasons for the misclassification, but the one of most theoretical interest for the purpose of this paper is a *mode error*.

The name results from experience with computerized text editors that have explicit modes for entering text (text mode) and for giving commands (command mode). Failure to identify which mode the system is in leads to (frequent) errors of attempting to insert new text while the system is in command mode or to specify commands while it is in text mode. These errors can have serious effects: In one experimental text editor, attempting to insert the word *edit* into a manuscript while the system is actually in command mode leads to destroying the entire manuscript and then destroying the ability to invoke the normal "undoing" of such widespread damage. Similarly, many devices have visual displays or buttons whose meaning depends on the mode the system is in (e.g., aircraft automatic pilots, digital wristwatches). Failure to identify the mode correctly leads to erroneous interpretation of the display or erroneous action. In all these cases, the intentions, the act specification, and the carrying out of the acts are done properly; the fault lies in specification of the situation.

The most numerous examples of mode errors in my collection come from the use of computers. There are numerous instances of people typing the "end-of-text" symbol required by the text editor to signify the completion of the text when they were actually using other systems that did not require the symbol or attempting to delete a file by using the editor command that deletes a line of text.

In other situations, one person reported attempting to move the carriage on his typewriter by hand while using a typewriter that did not have a movable carriage. Reason (1979) tells of a person who reported: "I sat down to do some work and before starting to write I put my hand up to my face to take my glasses off, but my fingers snapped together rather abruptly because I hadn't been wearing them in the first place." Reason also tells of a person who reported: "My office phone rang. I picked up the receiver and bellowed 'Come in' at it." From my collection there is the person who had been dictating for an hour with a hand-held microphone. He left the room to ask a question, then returned to complete the dictation. He picked up the telephone handset instead of the microphone.

As is usual, these errors most likely have several causes. But they share the characteristic that an action entirely appropriate for a situation is being performed, except that this is not the current situation. Errors of partial specification (description errors) seem also to be involved in the last two examples. The episodes of the bellowed "Come in" and the removal of the nonexistent eyeglasses could also be caused by capture errors.

*Description Errors: Insufficient Specificity*

Some slips of selection occur either when all the relevant information needed to form the appropriate intention is not available or when an appropriate intention has been formulated, but the description of the desired act is insufficient. This latter situation gives rise to what has earlier been called an incomplete description (Norman & Bobrow, 1979), leading to ambiguity in the selection of information from memory. These ambiguities can lead to such performance slips as the replacing of the lid to the sugar container on the coffee cup (they are similarly shaped containers) or throwing a soiled shirt into the toilet rather than the laundry basket (again, they are similarly shaped containers: the laundry basket was in a different room from the toilet). Verbal slips frequently involve the substitution of one word of a related semantic field, such as *door* for *window* or *trampoline* for *hammock*. Table 2 presents some of the motor and verbal errors of specification in my collection.

It is obvious that a number of the slips in Table 2 have alternative categorizations. Saying "You need a pencil to turn that slot" instead of "You need a coin . . ." could result from several causes. The resulting behavior, however, is a substitution of one word for another.

The ATS framework provides the mechanisms that allow these classes of errors to occur. However, the theory does not address the issue of why the particular word *pencil* might have been substituted for *coin*. Here, it is quite possible that further knowledge of situational factors, or knowledge of the thoughts active at the time, or a clinical analysis of the person would demonstrate the existence of contributing factors that, working through the mechanisms of the ATS formalism, gave rise to this particular slip at this particular time. Unfortunately, in most of the situations analyzed here, there is insufficient information to determine these other factors.

*Slips That Result From Faulty Activation of Schemas*

The activation of a schema can be faulty in one of two ways: A schema may be unintentionally activated, thereby causing an action to intrude where it is not expected; or a schema may lose its activation before its appropriate time to control behavior has occurred, thereby leading to omission of its components of the action sequence.

*Unintentional Activation*

Unintended activation of a schema can occur for several reasons, including the reasons discussed in the section on errors in the formation of the intention. More interesting, however, are errors that result from capture, by data-driven activations or by associations.

Table 2
*Slips of Selection: Description Errors or Errors in Specificity of Description*

| Situation and intention | Action (or speech) |
|---|---|
| Eating bread. A's piece on plate, B's piece on counter (several feet apart). B intends to eat B's piece. | B picks up A's bread, bites into it, says "Oh my goodness, I'm eating yours." |
| Put toothbrush away in glass on counter. | Put toothbrush in hairbrush location: in cabinet, under counter, on opposite side. |
| Put lid on sugar bowl. | Put lid on coffee cup (same size opening). |
| Toss soiled T-shirt into laundry basket. | Toss shirt into toilet (different room than laundry basket). |
| Glass and coffee cup side by side (both empty). Intend to pour orange juice into glass. | Pour orange juice into cup. Notice only when later attempting to pour coffee into cup. |
| Intend to take rice from storage jar and measure in measuring cup. | Pour cooking oil into measuring cup: (both oil and rice kept in glass containers on counter top). |
| Turn on automobile engine. Intend to shift into gear. | Put on lights. (It was daytime.) |
| Intend to step on motorcycle brake (by depressing pedal with right foot). | Push gearshift lever (left foot). |
| Type a tab (large bar at top of keyboard). | Type space (large bar at bottom of keyboard). |
| Stop car. Intend to unbuckle seatbelt. | Stop car. Unbuckle watchband. |
| Push button to turn off exposure meter of camera. | Push shutter button (take picture). |
| Intend to say, "You need a coin to turn that slot." | "You need a pencil to turn that slot." |
| Intend to say, "The only language they had in common was Russian." | "The only language they had in common was English." (Observation recorded in Moscow.) |
| Intend to say, "I am a sheep in wolf's clothing." | "I am a sheep in lamb's clothing." (Said correctly 40 minutes previously.) |
| Intend to say, "Speech is very much overspecified." | "Speech is very much oversimplified." |
| Intend to say, "New flight started to Amsterdam." | "New flight started to Chicago." |

*Capture slips.* A capture error occurs when a familiar habit substitutes itself for the intended action sequence. The basic notion is simple: Pass too near a well-formed habit and it will capture your behavior. This set of errors can be described by concepts from the traditional psychological literature on learning—strong habits are easily provoked. The traditional mechanism is stimulus generalization. In current terms, if the habit is strong enough, even partial matches from the situation are apt to activate the relevant parent schema, and once activated, it can get triggered.

A capture error is a form of error of activation, closely related to errors caused by thoughts or by external activation. Still capture errors have a certain flavor about them that set them off. Reason (1979) described them in this way:

Like the Siren's call, some motor programs possess the power to lure us into unwitting action, particularly when the central processor is occupied with some parallel mental activity. This power to divert action from some intention seems to be derived in part from how often and how recently the motor program is activated. The more frequently (and recently) a particular sequence of movements is set in train and achieves its desired outcome, the more likely it is to occur uninvited as a "slip of action."

The classic example of a capture error has already been mentioned: the example from James of the person who went to his room to change for dinner and found himself in bed. Here are two more examples, one from my collection and one from Reason's:

I was using a copying machine, and I was counting the pages. I found myself counting "1, 2, 3, 4, 5, 6, 7, 8, 9, 10, Jack, Queen, King." (I have been playing cards recently.)

I meant to get my car out, but as I passed through the back porch on my way to the garage I stopped to put on my Wellington boots and gardening jacket as if to work in the garden. (Reason, 1979).

*External activation (data driven).* In the class of slips called "data driven," the intrusions result from the analysis of external events: The environment forces an intrusion. This class is similar to the other forms of activation error, with the distinguishing feature being that there is some obvious environmental cause for the act. The most prominent example is the Stroop phenomenon, a classic demonstration experiment in psychology in which the names of colors (e.g., *blue*) are printed in colors that differ from the name (so that the word *blue* might be printed with red ink). The task is to look at the word as rapidly as possible and say aloud the name of the ink color in which it is printed. There is extreme difficulty caused by the intrusion of the printed names. Here are some other examples of data-driven slips:

I had just given away my last cigarette. A smoker never lives with the knowledge that he does not have cigarettes available. At that time I did not have enough change to buy a pack from the vending machine. I went to my friend's room in the dormitories and got the exact amount needed to buy a pack of cigarettes. I went directly to the vending machines, put my money in and pressed the selection button. The pack was not delivered but the machine did not return my money. So I went to the laboratory to borrow some more money and headed back to the vending machines. I intended to try a different selection button, hoping the machine would work this time.

When I got to the vending machines, I put twenty cents in the *coffee machine*, when I realized that I was there to buy cigarettes, not coffee. Since the money was not recoverable, I got the coffee even if I did not really want it.

I then went back to the laboratory, got some more change, and headed back again to the vending machines, this time successfully. (The story has been shortened from the original.)

B was assigning a visitor a room to use. Standing in front of the room, at the telephone in an outside alcove, B decided to call the department secretary to tell her the room number. Instead of her telephone number, B dialed the room number. (B knew the phone number well; for the past four years it was his phone number when B served as department chair.)

*Associative activation.* This class differs from capture activations in that there need not be any formal similarity between the action sequences involved, but simply a strong association between them. Thus, the intention activates a relevant set of schemas that, by association to other schemas in memory, cause those others to become activated. This is the mechanism of "being reminded of." However, once the reminded-of schemas are activated, it may be they that control the resulting actions rather than the intended schemas.

Errors of associative activation seem to occur most frequently in speech. One example occurred during discussion of the difficulty of viewing the stars from the La Jolla/Del Mar area (because the nights are often foggy or cloudy): "You want to see stars? Go to Lick Observatory (Pause) Why did I say that? I was thinking Palomar. I was even visualizing Palomar." (The speaker had lived for several years at Stanford, where the Lick Observatory is located, hence the strong association of "Lick" to the concept of "observatory.")

Similar examples are easy to find, such as the following conversation: "She stopped off in Cambridge, England. She used to live in Cambridge, Boston. Cambridge, umm, Massachusetts." Or the comment by a person while driving along the street of a town looking for a place to eat, as the car passed El Nopalito (a Mexican restaurant): "They have Chinee—Japa—Mexican food to go."

## Loss of Activation

When the appropriate schemas for an action schema are activated, some may lose activation as a result of the normal decay and interference properties of primary memory. The result shows up in several different ways, depending upon the exact schema that was lost and when in the temporal events of the action the schema was lost.

One result can be that of losing the desired intention but allowing the behavioral repertoire to continue to its next logical junction. This led one of my informants to stand staring into the refrigerator wondering why he was there. Here is another, more complete example:

I have to go to the bedroom before I start working (writing) in the dining room. I start going there and realize as I am walking that I have no idea why I go there. Knowing myself, I keep going, hoping that something in the bedroom would remind me.... I get there but still cannot recall what I wanted... so I go back to the dining room. There I realize that my glasses are dirty. With great relief I go back to the bedroom, get my handkerchief, and wipe my glasses clean.

Sometimes the components of an action

are misordered. Thus, a student reported the following incident:

> I was at the end of a salad bar line, sprinkling raisins on my heaping salad, and reached into my left pocket to get a five-dollar bill. The raisins knocked a couple of croutons from the salad to the tray. I reached and picked them up, intending to pop them into my mouth. My hands came up with their respective loads simultaneously, and I rested the hand with the croutons on the tray and put the bill in my mouth, actually tasting it before I stopped myself.

Verbal misordering of components can follow similar patterns as in this report:

> Once while jogging with a colleague early in the morning, I reported my academic history as "I got my degree at Harvard and was a post-doc and faculty member at Penn." (Exactly the reverse of the facts.)

Another class of errors is to leave out a step in a sequence, such as to forget to put the water in the coffee maker. Studies of aircraft accidents (Fitts & Jones, 1961a, 1961b) reveal that skipped steps are a frequent cause of accidents.

Yet another obvious class of error would be the repetition of a step in a sequence or the restarting of a sequence at some earlier stage. I have observed people (and myself) engaging the starter of an automobile after the engine had already been started. (This could, of course, also be classified as a mode error.) No incidents of this sort are in my collection, but Reason (1979) does provide a number of examples:

> I started to pour a second kettle of boiling water into a teapot full of freshly made tea. I had no recollection of having just made it.

> As I was leaving the bathroom this morning, it suddenly struck me that I couldn't remember whether or not I had shaved. I had to feel my chin to establish that I had.

> I put a cigarette into my mouth, got my matches out, then instead of lighting the cigarette I took another one out of the packet.

## Slips That Result From Faulty Triggering

A schema may be properly selected and activated but lead to a slip because it is triggered improperly, either at the wrong time or not at all. The most famous examples of inappropriate triggering that lead to reversals of event components are Spoonerisms, in which components of words are interchanged, as in Spooner's example of "You have tasted the whole worm" instead of the intended "You have wasted the whole term."[2]

One form of error is to blend the components of actions. Presumably, these errors occur when two or more active schemas are triggered simultaneously, sometimes resulting in the merging of two schemas that are appropriate for the situation, sometimes merging a relevant schema with one that is not relevant (or, under the clinical interpretation, not desired). Blends sometimes result when a person is unsure which of two actions to perform: The result is a mixture of both, as when indecision between the choice of the words *close* and *shut* yields the response *clut*. Merges tend to involve activation and anticipation components, such as in the saying of "financed by the Rockebrothers, uh, the Rockefeller Brothers Foundation", or mixtures of related names, as when a speaker commented on "some interesting studies by Lynn Shepard." (The speaker did not notice the slip; Lynn Cooper has worked with Roger Shepard and has published numerous joint articles with him.)

A large class of errors occurs from false triggering of acts among the things currently active in mind. Thus, one can have an anticipation error such as "She presented these to American subjects and she presented these to Chinese—um, Japanese. I'll get to Chinese in a minute." Or, "Suppose you put a string around a ten-foot earth," where the intent was to say "ten-foot ball," but the speaker was simultaneously planning ahead how to talk about the problem of putting a string around the earth.

With a computer system, many errors come from doing the desired result rather than the action that leads to the result. Thus, because typing the "break" key terminates the program and leads to the appearance of the symbol % on the screen, several students have reported typing the % directly rather than the break key. (The % sign is never

---

[2] There is reasonable evidence that Spooner's reversals were often deliberate, carefully planned and thought out. Thus, this example stretches credulity. Nonetheless, the basic phenomenon is real and numerous examples are well documented (see Fromkin, 1973, 1980). For example, one of my colleagues said "Ruman and Normalhart" instead of "Norman and Rumelhart."

used as a command in this particular computer.) Additional examples of anticipation errors are the following:

I was typing a note to some students, stating when I could meet with them. I was mentally reviewing my day as I typed. I had a lunch appointment at 12:00 p.m., so I decided I could meet with them at 2:00 p.m. I typed "can we eat." I then realized the error and changed the "eat" to "meet."

One day as I was running on my morning trek, I saw a woman ahead. I was counting steps, but as I neared the woman I decided to say "Good morning." When I got to the woman, she smiled and said "Good morning," and I responded "Thirty-three."

A related class of errors comes from confusing thoughts with deeds. This is a lack of action rather than an intruded action, but the cause is related: An activation in primary memory was misused, in this case to substitute for the act.

I think of asking A to make more coffee and later complain of the lack. My thought, it turns out, was never voiced.

I make an error typing a line on the computer, think of typing the special character that deletes the line (@), and then continue typing, only to find that the computer responds with an error message. The @ sign was only thought, not actually typed.

Slips that result from failure to perform some action are more difficult to detect than errors that result from a falsely executed action. Indeed, if both the action components and the intention are forgotten, there is little to signal the error to either the person or an onlooker. Slips resulting from failure to do something are common in experience, however, such as forgetting to mail a letter or to stop at the bank on the way to work. Some of these cases are covered in the section on lack of activation.

## The Detection of Slips

### The Need for Feedback Mechanisms in Cognitive Behavior

Many slips are detected by the perpetrator, often as the act is being initiated and before any real headway has been made for the discrepant behavior. Sometimes slips go undetected for relatively long periods, and sometimes they are never detected. I presume that some slips are caught so early in their cycle that they are unseen by the observer and are perhaps even unconscious in the producer.

In order for discrepant behavior to be detected, two things are necessary: a feedback mechanism with some monitoring function that compares what is expected with what has occurred; a discrepancy between expectations and occurrences. The task is nontrivial, for the specification of the intention is at a considerably different level than are the mechanics of the act.

The existence of feedback mechanisms seems a logical necessity in the control of human behavior (or almost any complex behavior, animal or machine). In cognitive psychology, feedback mechanisms have played almost no role, probably because the emphasis has been on the reception of information rather than the performance of acts (but see Miller, Galanter, & Pribram, 1960). Those areas of psychology that study output—manual control, human factors, and motor skills—do worry about feedback, but there has been little interaction with cognitive psychology.

### Some Examples of Error Monitoring

Many, but not all, of the errors in my collection of slips were caught by the perpetrator. (Unfortunately, in most collections of slips, this information is not recorded. Even in my own collection, this information is not always available.) Slips are caught at various levels of action, from the start of the activity to after considerable delay. Table 3 presents examples of the catching (or failing to catch) of slips at different points in the act. Note that many of these slips are caught only with the active cooperation of the observer or the listener. And sometimes even the cooperative effort fails. With motor slips, at times the slip is discovered only because the incorrect action leads to a situation that reveals itself later. Thus, one subject reported pouring orange juice into the coffee mug, drinking the juice, and noticing the problem only when desiring to pour a cup of coffee; the remnants of the juice attracted her attention.

Note the critical point of the feedback analysis: For a slip to be detected, the monitoring mechanism must be made aware of the discrepancy between intention and act.

Table 3
*Examples of Detecting Slips at Various Stages in the Action*

Caught in the act
"I caught myself as I was about to pour the tea into the opened can of tomatoes that was just next to (left of ) the teacup." (The can was empty.)

Caught just after the act
"One of the problems with the TV guide—*the TV guide*—the restaurant guide."
"Financed by the Rockebrothers, uh, the Rockefeller Brothers Foundation."

Multiple corrections
"This is paid for by NSF, I mean CHIP, I mean Sloan."
"I think it's time he cleaned up his office, too. Umm, desk; umm, room."
"They have Chinee—Japa—Mexican food to go."

Not caught (by the perpetrator)
A: We're not very good at badminton anymore.
B: What?
A: Badminton.
B: Badminton?
A: Oh, I did say badminton, didn't I. Table tennis.
B: Where did that come from?
A: I was thinking about planning the yard, and thinking of putting in a badminton court.

"I told the water skiing story in which the skier is almost hit by another boat. I said, '. . . almost hit by another car.' A listener interrupted to point out the error. I was skeptical, but another listener confirmed the error."

Caught after a very long delay
A noticed that B was using his special (and expensive) scissors with serrated blades to cut some loose threads from clothes. (Both A and B had agreed that the scissors were reserved for trimming hair.)
A: Hey—No! That's a hair comb.
B: Oh—sorry.
The normal activities then continued. There was no further conversation. B went and got another pair of scissors. About a minute or two after the conversation:
A: I meant that was a hair *scissors*, only to be used to cut hair.
B: I knew what you meant. I did have the vague feeling that something was wrong, but I wasn't sure what. Now I realize that you called the scissors a comb. I understood you though.

---

But if the monitoring function only has access to the act specification, it can only say how well the act is performed, not if it is the correct one. The following example demonstrates a form of error that was not detected by the speaker:

A was driving a van and noticed that the rearview mirror on the passenger side was not adjusted properly. A meant to say to the passenger on the right, "Please adjust the mirror," but instead said, "Please adjust the window." The passenger, B, was confused and asked, "What should I do? What do you want?" A repeated the request: "Adjust the window for me." The situation continued through several frustrating cycles of conversation and attempts by the passenger to understand just what adjustment should be made to the window. The error correction mechanism adopted by the driver was to repeat the erroneous sentence more and more loudly.

The apparent difficulty here is that the feedback monitoring was at the wrong level to detect the failure in the word selection. Instead, it attempted to correct failure in word enunciation. Suppose that A's intention had been imprecisely specified as "Adjust that (ill-specified) object on the right side of the van," and suppose that this intention had spawned a set of schemas and action units that eventually chose "window" as the name of an object on the right side of the vehicle. This would lead to a failure to detect the error, for whatever mechanism monitors the speaking of the word would be checking to see that the erroneous word, *window*, was pronounced properly. (The error itself is possibly also a form of data-driven slip, for the window was in the visual path to the mirror, and the sight might have helped select the incorrect word. Whatever the cause, the point is that the error was made at a level undetectable by the monitoring function.)

## Levels of Feedback Systems

In the terms used in this article, the basic control sequence is from intention to triggering to action. Note that the only way that an error can be detected is for it to occur within the action triggering mechanism or in the actual mechanics of performing the response. If the intention is incorrectly specified, the error cannot be noted—not by this system, anyway. There is much too large a difference in the level of specification of the intention and the actual acts that get done: The comparison mechanisms would have to be horrendously complex. Suppose a person is carrying out the intention to drive home. One of the actions performed along the way is to move the right hand down while simultaneously moving the left hand up. (The driver is rotating the steering wheel of the automobile in order to turn the car to the right.) Is this an appropriate set of actions for the intention? The difficulty is that the intention is specified at a very high level of abstractness ("drive home"), whereas the act is specified either in terms of muscle signals or limb movements. To compare intentions and actions, the two must be at the same level of specification.

Consider the problem of language behavior. The intention is specified at some abstract, "idea" level, but the output of the motor control system is the production of sound waves. To match how well the sound conveys the idea requires the monitoring function to go through the whole process of speech understanding, first to identify the words that have been spoken, then to determine if the interpretation of those words matches the intention.

The solution to this difficulty is for the action system to have many feedback comparison processes, each monitoring different levels of the operation of the system. In speech, at some low level, feedback processes probably monitor how well sound frequencies and intensities match the intended voice pitch and loudness. Other systems probably monitor rhythm and stress, intonation and pronunciation. A different system must compare the intended word selection with that actually being uttered (or triggered for utterance), and another system monitors the meaning and affect. Different levels of feedback are required for different purposes.

With motor actions, similar division among levels is required. Each level of specification of the intention must be decomposed into more basic levels in order for an action to take place, each new decomposition more finely dividing the actions required and more precisely specifying what must be done. And each new level of specification is, in turn, decomposed into its basic components, until some primitive level of act specification is reached. Feedback and monitoring is required at each level.

## Comments on Naturalistic Errors

The collection and analysis of naturally occurring errors forces us to consider behavior that is not constrained by the limitations and artificiality of the experimental laboratory. By examining errors, we are forced to demonstrate that our theoretical ideas can have some relevance to real behavior. There are situations that are simply too complex to be reproduced in the laboratory; for example, naturalistic observations are the only way to obtain data of people under extreme stress (in some cases, while they face severe injury or death during an emergency situation).

But naturalistic observations have disadvantages. It is difficult—sometimes impossible—to record exactly what went on. Observers are not always around, and even when they are, they are not always ready to make the detailed observations that would be required. Records from memory (and even from direct perception) are notoriously unreliable.

One common question about these errors concerns their frequency of occurrence, both with respect to each other (relative frequency) and in absolute terms (absolute frequency). Naturalistic observations cannot be used to determine these numbers. I have not provided percentages for my observations, because I believe that the numbers would be misleading. Observers are selective in what they record. It is sometimes difficult to determine what should count as an error. The records are incomplete, for the goal was to collect a general sampling of all forms of errors, and exhaustive recording was not used. If the goal is to determine relative frequency, then only a complete record will do. Accurate sampling and statistics probably require video recording of large segments of behavior and then careful perusal of the tapes in order to transcribe in detail the situations identified as errors (see Deese, 1978). Mackay (1973, 1980) has argued that naturalistic data can be used to give reasonable statistical estimates when "a strong case can be made that the missing data are random or unselected with regard to what you're analyzing" (Mackay, Note 6).

To validate what has been theoretically postulated as the cause of errors, laboratory tests are useful. It should be possible to cause many of the errors in the classification scheme to occur within the experimental laboratory. Errors of activation and of capture seem especially likely to be reproducible. MacKay, Baars, and Motley have been quite successful in generating verbal errors in laboratory situations (Baars 1980; Baars & MacKay, 1978; Baars & Motley, 1976; Baars, Motley, & MacKay, 1975; MacKay, 1973; MacKay & Soderberg, 1971; Motley & Baars, 1976). I believe their techniques and others can be adapted to the study of motor behavior.

## Summary

In this article I have attempted to draw from a reasonably large collection of slips sufficient components and constraints for a theory of action. I propose that a system of activated schemas with a triggering mechanism for determining appropriate time for activation provides a satisfactory framework for the categorization and analysis of slips. To perform a well-learned action sequence, only the highest-level parent schema must be specified: This corresponds to the intention. This schema will, in turn, activate whatever child schemas are required to guide the various components of the action sequence. Each activated component is a sensorimotor schema, with conditions that specify when it is to be triggered into action. Were this all there were to the theory, the only errors that could occur would be errors of ordering in which a relevant component missed its triggering situation, or an erroneous one was mistriggered when the existing situation provided a sufficient match for its trigger conditions.

However, the theory allows for multiple sources of activations, for example from the external world (data-driven activation), from internal processing (thoughts, associations, prior or future action components), or by capture by well-learned familiar habits. The likelihood that a given schema will be triggered is a joint function of its level of activation and of the match between the goodness with which the current conditions match the triggering conditions. This trade-off provides an obvious place to develop experimental tests of the theory. Slips occur for only three reasons: the formation of the intention is in error; there is faulty activation of schemas; there is a failure in satisfying the conditions for triggering.

Feedback plays an essential role in complex behavior. With slips, it is of interest to discover under what conditions a slip can be discovered and when it cannot. The monitoring of actions is a basic component of a feedback control system, but the monitoring function requires that the comparison of intention and action be done at the same level of specification. Because complex acts have many differing levels of specification, each with its own relevant schemas and operations, the monitoring function must also be performed at many different levels. The performance of an action, from initial conceptualization through realization, is then the process of decomposing the original intention into a sequence of physically performable acts, with multiple levels of feedback analysis accompanying the acts.

## Reference Notes

1. Rosenbloom, P. *The XAPS reference manual.* (Experimental Activation Production System). University of California, San Diego, July 17, 1979.
2. Norman, D. A., & Shallice, T. *Attention to action: Willed and automatic control of behavior.* Unpublished manuscript, 1980.
3. McClelland, J. L., & Rumelhart, D. E. *An interactive activation model of the effect of context in perception. Part 1* (CHIP Technical Report). Center

for Human Information Processing, University of California, San Diego (La Jolla), 1980.
4. Rumelhart, D. E., & McClelland, J. L. *An interactive activation model on the effect of context on perception, Part 2* (CHIP Technical Report). Center for Human Information Processing, University of California, San Diego (La Jolla), 1980.
5. Rumelhart, D. E., & Norman, D. A. *Simulating a skilled typist: A study of skilled cognitive-motor performance.* Manuscript in preparation, 1980.
6. MacKay, D. Personal communication, 1978.

## References

Anderson, J. R. *Language, memory and thought.* Hillsdale, N.J.: Erlbaum, 1976.
Baars, B. J. On eliciting predictable speech errors in the laboratory: Methods and results. In V. Fromkin (Ed.), *Errors of linguistic performance: Slips of the tongue, ear, pen, and hands.* New York: Academic Press, 1980.
Baars, B. J., & MacKay, D. G. Experimentally eliciting phonetic and sentential speech errors: Methods, implications and work in progress. *Language in society: Experimental linguistics*, 1978, *7*, 105–109.
Baars, B. J., & Motley, M. T. Spoonerisms as sequencer conflicts: Evidence from artificially elicited errors. *American Journal of Psychology*, 1976, *89*, 467–484.
Baars, B. J., Motley, M. T., & MacKay, D. G. Output editing for lexical status in artificially induced slips of the tongue. *Journal of Verbal Learning and Verbal Behavior*, 1975, *14*, 382–391.
Bartlett, F. C. *Remembering.* Cambridge, England: Cambridge University Press, 1932.
Collins, A. M., & Loftus, E. F. A spreading activation theory of semantic processing. *Psychological Review*, 1975, *82*, 407–428.
Deese, J. Thought into speech. *American Scientist*, 1978, *66*, 314–321.
Fitts, P. M., & Jones, R. E. Analysis of factors contributing to 460 "pilot-error" experiences in operating aircraft controls. In W. H. Sinaiko (Ed.), *Selected papers on human factors in the design and use of control systems.* New York: Dover, 1961. (a)
Fitts, P. M., & Jones, R. E. Psychological aspects of instrument display: 1. Analysis of 270 "pilot-error" experiences in reading and interpreting aircraft instruments. In W. H. Sinaiko (Ed.), *Selected papers on human factors in the design and use of control systems.* New York: Dover, 1961. (b)
Freud, S. *A general introduction to psychoanalysis.* (J. Riviere, trans.). London: Allen & Unwin, 1924.
Freud, S. *Psychopathology of everyday life.* J. Strachey (Ed. and trans.). London: Ernest Benn, 1966. (Originally published, 1901.)
Fromkin, V. (Ed.). *Speech errors as linguistic evidence.* The Hague: Mouton, 1973.
Fromkin, V. (Ed.). *Errors of linguistic performance: Slips of the tongue, ear, pen, and hands.* New York: Academic Press, 1980.
Hurst, R. (Ed.). *Pilot error: A professional study of contributory factors.* London: Butler & Tanner, 1976.
James, W. *The principles of psychology.* New York: Holt, 1890.
MacKay, D. G. Spoonerisms: The structure of errors in the serial order of speech. In V. Fromkin (Ed.), *Speech errors as linguistic evidence.* The Hague: Mouton, 1973.
MacKay, D. G. Speech errors: Retrospect and prospect. In V. Fromkin (Ed.), *Errors of linguistic performance: Slips of the tongue, ear, pen, and hands.* New York: Academic Press, 1980.
MacKay, D. G., & Soderberg, G. A. Homologous intrusions: An analogue of linguistic slips. *Perceptual and Motor Skills*, 1971, *32*, 645–646.
Meringer, R. *Aus dem Leben der Sprache.* Berlin: B. Behr, 1908.
Meringer, R., & Mayer, C. *Versprechen und Verlesen: Eine psychologisch-linguistische Studie.* Amsterdam: John Benjamins, 1978. (Originally published, 1895.)
Miller, G. A., Galanter, E., & Pribram, K. H. *Plans and the structure of behavior.* New York: Holt, Rinehart & Winston, 1960.
Motley, M. T., & Baars, B. J. Semantic bias effects on the outcome of verbal slips. *Cognition*, 1976, *4*, 177–187.
Newell, A. Production systems: Models of control structures. In W. C. Chase (Ed.), *Visual information processing.* New York: Academic Press, 1973.
Norman, D. A., & Bobrow, D. G. On the role of active memory structures in perception and cognition. In C. F. Cofer (Ed.), *The structure of human memory.* San Francisco: Freeman, 1976.
Norman, D. A., & Bobrow, D. G. Descriptions: An intermediate stage in memory retrieval. *Cognitive Psychology*, 1979, *11*, 107–123.
Reason, J. T. How did I come to do that? *New Behaviour*, April 24, 1975.
Reason, J. T. Absent minds. *New Society*, November 4, 1976.
Reason, J. T. Skill and error in everyday life. In M. Howe (Ed.), *Adult learning.* London: Wiley, 1977.
Reason, J. T. Actions not as planned. In G. Underwood & R. Stevens (Eds.), *Aspects of consciousness.* London: Academic Press, 1979.
Rumelhart, D. E., & Ortony, A. The representation of knowledge in memory. In R. C. Anderson, R. J. Spiro, & W. E. Montague (Eds.), *Schooling and the acquisition of knowledge.* Hillsdale, N.J.: Erlbaum, 1977.
Schmidt, R. A. A schema theory of discrete motor skill learning. *Psychological Review*, 1975, *4*, 229–261.
Schmidt, R. A. The schema as a solution to some persistent problems in motor learning theory. In G. E. Stelmach (Ed.), *Motor control: Issues and trends.* New York: Academic Press, 1976.
Szentagothai, J., & Arbib, M. A. *Conceptual models of neural organization.* Cambridge, Mass.: MIT Press, 1975.
Waterman, D. A., & Hayes-Roth, F. (Eds.). *Pattern directed inference systems.* New York: Academic Press, 1978.

Received May 20, 1980 ■

# Part III
# INFORMATION REPRESENTATION AND DISPLAYS

Perhaps one of the most challenging tasks in human factors engineering is designing a display interface that allows effective and efficient communication of information from one entity (e.g., the environment or a system) to another (e.g., the human). A number of reasons underlie the difficulty of this challenge, including the diversity of types of information to be represented, the large range of environmental conditions in which the information is displayed, the tremendous variety of people who use the information, the diversity of the information requirements for different kinds of tasks, and the constraints that technology places on display design. However, because of increasing capabilities, display technology is no longer a limiting factor in formatting and portraying information. It is up to human factors engineers to use this emerging display flexibility to achieve an effective and efficient coupling between the information requirements and the formatting or display of that information. The selections in Part III attempt to cover the more salient types of information representation; they include visual coding of discrete information, visual representation of spatial information, the development and selection of symbology, and speech displays and voice-interactive systems.

One of the more effective ways of highlighting information in visual displays is through the use of color. Color is unquestionably a salient stimulus for our visual system, but under what conditions is its use in displays helpful, and when is its use detrimental or confusing? The selection by Richard E. Christ (Chapter 8) contains a critical review of the use of color in visual displays. The paper deals with the effects of color coding on the accuracy and reaction time of visual search through display elements. A number of factors are considered, including the effectiveness of color code as the primary stimulus attribute, color as one of a number of relevant stimulus attributes, and color as a redundant code. In general color is an effective code, but its effectiveness depends on other factors, such as the number of colors in a code, the presence of other codes (brightness, shape, size, alphanumerics), and display density. Christ also discusses a number of design guidelines based on information distilled from his review. Once again we find that the answer to a design question is that it depends on a number of factors. Christ does an admirable job of distilling the details of "it depends."

Representation of the dynamic environment and portrayal of information elements essential for display-control relationships has always been a challenge. Chapters 9 and 10 deal with the representation and formatting of visual information for flight displays. The flight environment typifies environments in which it is necessary to portray large amounts of information for highly complex tasks and sequences of tasks. Some types of information are discrete in nature; others are from the continuous time-space domain. The issue treated in the next two selections is how best to put these very different types of information into visual displays.

Stanley N. Roscoe's selection (Chapter 9) discusses the tasks and information requirements for the flight environment. Many varied tasks are required of pilots and other flight deck personnel, and there are substantial demands to integrate information that may be coded and displayed in different modalities and in different locations in the cockpit. The overall amount of information needed to perform these tasks is significant. Roscoe maintains that there is room for improvement in grouping and coding displayed information for the flight environment based on the fact that flight tasks are by nature integrated. Roscoe presents the case that information from different sources required to perform an integrated flight task should be presented in a common frame of reference or coordinate system. As suggestions for accomplishing this he presents and discusses a number of display principles that deal with spatial analogue information, movement compatibility, and scale factors, among others.

How does the way information is formatted affect the way one plans and executes action sequences? Stephen R. Ellis, Michael W. McGreevy, and Robert J. Hitchcock address this question in Chapter 10. Their article complements aspects of the Roscoe study by investigating the visual portrayal of spatial dimensions. Ellis et al. present empirical work comparing representations of three-dimensional space in perspective and plan-view formats of a cockpit display of air traffic. The perspective display represents an attempt to more closely mimic spatial relationships in the world and more closely match the pilot's mental model of the flight environment. This display type is a good example of two of Roscoe's display principles: the principle of *pictorial realism* and the principle of *display integration*. Of significant interest here is the display-control relationship, the manner in which display formats affect control options. Ellis and his colleagues found that the perspective display, which presents altitude information in a relatively natural manner, elicited more vertical maneuver responses from pilots than did the plan-view display. In essence, providing information about the vertical dimension in a natural way afforded greater use of that dimension in pilots' maneuvering. Findings such as this enable information representations in complex systems to be made more usable and to facilitate the design of more effective information displays. This knowledge also provides a basis for conceptualizing the human-machine interface and for making important display design decisions, especially as display technology allows a more accurate imitation of the physical aspects of the environment.

A common manner of representing discrete information is through the use of symbols. A symbol is an abstract representation of an object or concept based on some established relationship or association. How to select among candidate symbols for use in a symbol set is addressed by Ralph E. Geiselman, Betty M. Landee, and Francois G. Christen (Chapter 11). The authors maintain that two factors must be considered for any symbol to represent a concept: meaningfulness and discriminability from other symbol characters. The proposed method of selecting candidate symbols is based on discriminability between features of the candidate symbol and those already existing in the symbol set. In selecting among candidate symbols, the entire symbol domain for that specific application must be considered. The authors derive a discriminability index formula for evaluating new candidate symbols and present empirical results that support the predictability of the index.

The results of the empirical validation showed that the similarity of figural details and configural attributes (e.g., shape) of symbols was an important basis for discrimination but that configural attributes were a more salient basis for discrimination. The authors note that other factors, such as meaningful association, are important in choosing symbols, and these must also be considered when selecting among candidate symbols. Nonetheless, perceptual attributes are an important factor in the design of symbol sets.

Another way of putting information into the human system is through the auditory sense modality, often via auditory displays. The types of auditory displays are numerous, ranging from warning tones, beeps, and buzzers to synthesized speech displays. Chapter 12 contains a discussion of issues in speech technology, a relatively recent addition to the human-machine interface provided by technological advances. In today's systems, speech displays are becoming increasingly common and inherently more valuable because of the extended display capability they bring to the human-system interface.

Carol A. Simpson, Michael E. McCauley, Ellen F. Roland, John C. Ruth, and Beverly H. Williges present a thorough review of speech technology that is organized around when, how, and where automated speech technology should be used as a display interface (Chapter 12). Both sides of the display interface are discussed: speech recognition systems as a form of user control or information input, and speech generation systems as a form of information display. Simpson et al. review terminology commonly used in speech recognition and speech generation systems, present information for identifying applications of speech recognition and voice display, discuss factors relevant for selecting tasks amenable to speech recognition and selecting functions for speech display, and discuss factors that may affect the selection of speech recognition and speech generation characteristics. Finally, they identify task design and interface dialogue design as important factors in integrating speech technology into a system. The importance of properly designed auditory/speech aspects of the human-machine interface cannot be stressed enough. The day is near when we will be talking to our cars or central control systems in the home—and they will talk back to us!

# Review and Analysis of Color Coding Research for Visual Displays

RICHARD E. CHRIST, *Department of Psychology, New Mexico State University, Las Cruces, New Mexico*

*The experimental literature on the effects of color on visual search and identification performance was reviewed. Forty-two studies published between 1952 and 1973 were located that gave results which could be used to determine the effectiveness of color codes relative to various types of achromatic codes. Quantitative analyses of these results indicated that color may be a very effective performance factor under some conditions, but that it can be detrimental under others. Tentative conclusions about the nature of these conditions were derived from the results. A guide for design decisions and an indication of knowledge gaps are also provided.*

## INTRODUCTION

This paper reports an analysis of the experimental literature on the effects of color on visual search and identification performance. The goal was that of evaluating the basis of possible design recommendations for or against the use of color in aircraft displays. More specifically, the aim of the study was concerned with the issue of whether or not color, relative to achromatic target features, can be expected to affect search and identification performance and, if so, in what manner and to what degree. The study was not concerned with related questions such as that of specifying optimal colors for targets and backgrounds to maximize the correct location and identification of colored targets. The secondary aim of the study was to identify the gaps in knowledge and to recommend a research program aimed at closing those gaps.

## PROCEDURE

A literature search was conducted of studies published since 1950 which reported accuracy of identification or search time as dependent measures and color as an independent variable. The literature search utilized the Defense Documentation Center bibliographic services and the *Psychological Abstracts*. Potentially useful papers were obtained (when possible) and read to determine their appropriateness. The relevant references cited in these papers were also located and reviewed. In addition, communications were established with personnel at Wright-Patterson Air Force Base, Griffiss Air Development Center, Army Behavioral Science Research Laboratory, Federal Aviation Commission, and various industrial research groups. These efforts yielded a total of 42 studies.

Acceptance of a paper as relevant was based on the following criteria:

(1) The dependent measure was percent correct, information transmitted, or time to locate targets.
(2) Data relevant to a comparison between chromatic and achromatic attributes (*e.g.*, size, shape, *etc.*) were provided.
(3) The tasks required information extraction from symbolic or pictorial displays rather than from direct real-world viewing.

(4) The observers were young, normal adults.
(5) The procedures and general experimental design were acceptable.

Articles which did not meet the criteria, but which did pertain to the use of color in visual displays are listed in the annotated bibliography for possible future use (see Appendix A).

One problem which became apparent during the search for relevant literature needs special mention. In spite of ample evidence that target factors such as size, energy, and spectral purity interact with target background features to affect the appearance of colors, many, if not most, of the studies did not control these factors nor have they provided information from which it could be determined that color (*i.e.*, hue) as such was really the variable being investigated when what was called "color" was varied. Hence, it was assumed that when color was introduced and varied in a given experiment, differential hues were primarily responsible for the discriminability of targets from the background and from each other. The contribution to discrimination provided by factors such as differential brightness and saturation were assumed to be minor unless these latter factors were specifically introduced as independent variables.

*Data Handling*

As in previous investigations by Teichner (1974) and Teichner and Krebs (1972, 1974), an iterative process was employed. Absolute values of the dependent variable as a function of one or more major independent variables were plotted across studies. However, probably due to the wide variation in the methods used and amount of practice permitted, plots of accuracy and of search time as dependent measures were grossly inconsistent at comparable values of the independent variables. For example, in the search literature, at least three methods are employed to determine search time. In some studies the subject must merely say "stop" upon location of the target; in others, the subject must identify some distinguishing feature of the located target; and, in still others, the subject must touch a pointer to the location of the target. These experimental differences necessarily produce different search times. Consequently, and since the primary goal was to compare the relative effectiveness of color and other target attributes, the time and accuracy measures were used to calculate relative scores. Specifically, the difference between performance with color in the display and with no color in the display was divided by the results obtained with no color in the display, *i.e.*,

% Difference Score =

$$\frac{\text{Color} - \text{Achromatic}}{\text{Achromatic}} \times 100. \qquad (1)$$

These calculations were always made within a given experiment while holding other task parameters constant. Positive scores indicated an advantage for color, negative scores a disadvantage for color, both relative to a particular achromatic target attribute (*e.g.*, size).

The results are presented separately for identification and search performance. Within each type of performance measures, a distinction was made between the use of color as a nonredundant target attribute and the use of color as a redundant target attribute. Target attributes were considered to be nonredundant if the targets could be identified (or located) only in terms of their color or, for example, only in terms of their shape. Target attributes were considered to be redundant if the targets could be identified (or located) either in terms of their color or their shape; that is, the color and shape of the target were perfectly correlated.

## RESULTS FOR ACCURACY OF IDENTIFICATION

*Nonredundant Colors Relative to Nonredundant Achromatic Codes*

There are two ways to use color and achromatic attributes as nonredundant or independent features of a target. In the first case, the targets may be unidimensional. That is, targets differ from each other in terms of only one stimulus dimension; all other attributes of the targets are held constant. For example, targets may differ from each other only in terms of their colors; the shape, size, brightness, and all other possible target features are held constant. Or, targets may differ from each other only in terms of their unique shapes (*e.g.*, alphanumeric symbols) with all other possible stimulus attributes held constant.

A second way to use color and other stimulus attributes as nonredundant features of a target is to identify one attribute as the critical target feature and allow one or more other target attributes to vary at random. For example, if targets are defined as objects which differ in color, targets in the display may be a small, red square in one instance and a large, blue circle in another, but in either case, the targets are correctly identified as red and blue, respectively. In this example, targets vary independently in size, color, and shape but only color is relevant for target identification. Using this same example, the targets could be defined as objects which differ in shape and therefore the correct identification responses would be square and circle, respectively. It is important to emphasize that *nonredundant* multidimensional attributes of a target must vary independently of each other. Knowing one attribute of a target (*e.g.*, its shape) provides no information as to its other attributes (*e.g.*, its size or color).

This distinction between the unidimensional and multidimensional use of color and achromatic attributes as nonredundant features of a target allowed for three different types of comparisons: (1) accuracy in identifying target colors relative to other target attributes, each used in comparable unidimensional displays; (2) accuracy in identifying different target attributes in the same multidimensional display; and (3) accuracy in identifying a nonredundant target attribute in a multidimensional display relative to the same target attribute in a unidimensional display. The results for each of these comparisons will be reported separately.

*Between unidimensional displays.* Ten studies reported data for the accuracy of identifying colors and for the accuracy of identifying various achromatic stimulus attributes, each in unidimensional displays. These studies represent a wide range of experimental tasks and dependent measures. Three studies reported only information transmitted in an absolute identification task (Anderson and Fitts, 1958; Egeth and Pachella, 1969; Garner and Creelman, 1964); four reported only the percent correct in an identification task (Allport, 1971; Alluisi and Muller, 1958; Mackworth, 1963a; 1963b); one reported the number of trials on which a counting error occurred (Smith and Thomas, 1964); and one reported the percent correct in what was clearly a short-term running memory task (Kanarick and Petersen, 1971).

The results of the primary analysis of these studies are presented in Figure 1, which shows the effectiveness of color relative to each of the achromatic features indicated on the abscissa. The relative effectiveness of color was calculated using Equation 1. The data points with a slash through them represent the derived scores based on information transmission measures; the others are based upon percent correct data.

It can be seen from this figure that, in general, color is superior to size, brightness, and

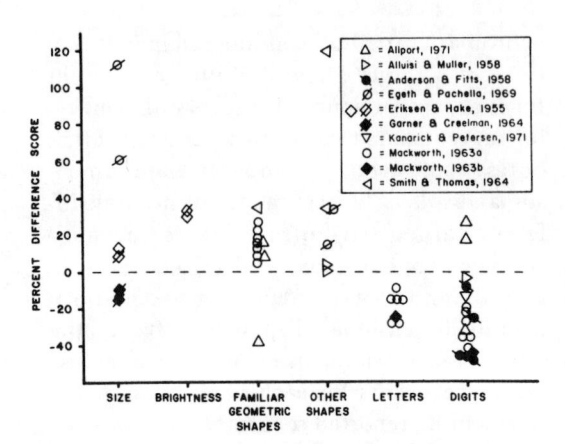

Figure 1. *The accuracy of identifying colors in unidimensional displays relative to the achromatic codes indicated on the abscissa.*

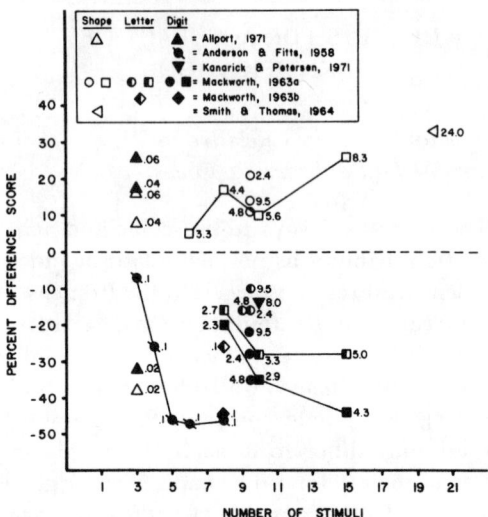

Figure 2. *The accuracy of identifying colors in unidimensional displays, relative to familiar shapes, letters, and digits, as a function of the number of stimuli displayed and exposure time.*

shape as unidimensional target features, but inferior to alphanumeric symbols. The relative scores shown in Figure 1 probably depend upon the particular experimental values selected for color and for the other variables. On the other hand, a wide variety of colors and a large number of different values for each comparison attribute are represented in these data. Given these considerations, the consistency of results is relatively high.

The data shown in Figure 1 based on familiar geometric shapes, letters, and digits were further analyzed in terms of the number of different stimuli in the display (density) and the exposure time of the display. The results of this analysis are shown in Figure 2. As in Figure 1, the ordinate of this figure shows the relative advantage of color determined from Equation 1; the abscissa shows the number of stimuli in the display. The achromatic attributes and exposure times are shown as parameters. The lines shown in this figure connect data points from single experiments which varied stimulus density. Note that in the Mackworth (1963a) experiment where density was varied, density and exposure time are confounded. Comparisons across different experiments also generally confounded exposure time and the number of stimuli to be identified.

Figure 2 shows that, except for one deviant point, identification accuracy in unidimensional color displays was superior, relative to identification accuracy in unidimensional shape displays. Furthermore, the relative superiority of color over shape appeared to generally increase with increased numbers of stimuli to be identified and with increased exposure time. This latter trend was true for the Allport (1971) data but was only partially true in the Mackworth (1963a) experiments. The increasing superiority of color relative to shape as a function of density can be seen in one of the Mackworth (1963a) experiments (shown by the line connecting those data points) and also across all four experiments which permitted this comparison.

Figure 2 also shows that, except for two deviant points, identification accuracy in unidimensional color displays was inferior, relative to identification accuracy in displays varying only in digits or letters. This figure also shows that the inferiority of identifying colors relative to identifying alphanumeric symbols increased as the number of stimuli to be identified increased. This is shown by the lines connecting data points from the Anderson and Fitts (1958) study and from the Mackworth (1963a) experiment which varied density. There is also a suggestion that the inferiority of color identification relative to alphanumeric symbol identification increased as exposure time decreased. This general trend may be seen both within and across experiments at any given level of density. Given the overall confounding of exposure time and the number of stimuli to be identified, the more conservative conclusion that should be drawn from the data shown in Figure 2 is that the effectiveness of identifying colors relative to shape, letters, and digits varied with task difficulty.

Two additional studies were found which used color and achromatic stimulus attributes, each within a unidimensional display, to encode various types of target categories, *e.g.*, types of radar sites or types of industrial plants (Christner and Ray, 1961; Hitt, 1961). Subjects in both experiments were given a series of questions designed to sample several subtasks such as identifying ("What type of aircraft is in cell 4-C?") and counting ("How many aluminum plants are in the display?"). In each case, the subject's ability to discriminate among the various values within each dimension was at least a major part of the total task requirements, as was his ability to remember the associations between target attributes and code categories. The stimulus exposure times in both of these studies were determined by how long the subject took to respond. Probably as a result of this extended exposure time, errors of identification or counting were negligible and presumably did not vary over the different target attributes used. The experiments did not report any error data.

*Within uncorrelated multidimensional displays.* Eight studies reported the accuracy of identifying colors and uncorrelated achromatic attributes within the same multidimensional display. A good example of this type of experiment is the Allport (1971) study in which subjects were shown displays which varied in two dimensions. In one of his conditions, outline shapes were each drawn with one of three randomly selected colors. The subject's task was to identify both the shape and the color of the shape. For our purposes, this type of study used a display which will be described as a nonredundant multidimensional display where all the variable dimensions are relevant. If, in the Allport study, subjects had been asked to identify only the shapes and to ignore the colors, or vice versa, the stimulus display would have been called a nonredundant multidimensional display with one irrelevant dimension. With this latter type of display, different dimensions may be relevant on different presentations of the same display.

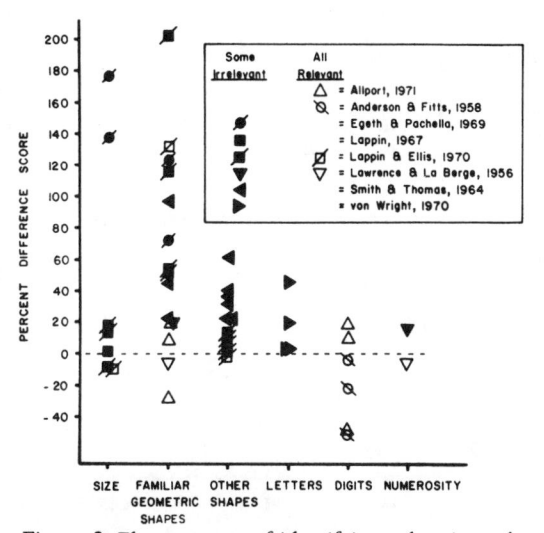

Figure 3. *The accuracy of identifying colors in multidimensional displays, relative to the achromatic codes indicated on the abscissa, when only some and when all the target attributes were to be identified.*

The analysis of the data from these studies, presented in Figure 3, shows the effectiveness of identifying colors relative to each of the achromatic features indicated on the abscissa, as derived from Equation 1. In this case, the comparisons were all made within the same multidimensional display. Figure 3 also shows the breakdown of studies by dependent measure (data points with a slash are based on information transmission scores; the rest on percent correct) and whether the attributes were all relevant or if some of the attributes were to be ignored. The results shown in Figure 3 are generally consistent with those shown in Figure 1 for shape and size attributes. That is, comparisons between unidimensional displays and within uncorrelated multidimensional displays both show colors to be more accurately identified than sizes and shapes. The results for alphanumeric symbols were less consistent. Hence, while color was clearly inferior to letters and digits when compared across unidimensional displays, the color-alphanumeric comparison within uncorrelated multidimensional displays was equivocal.

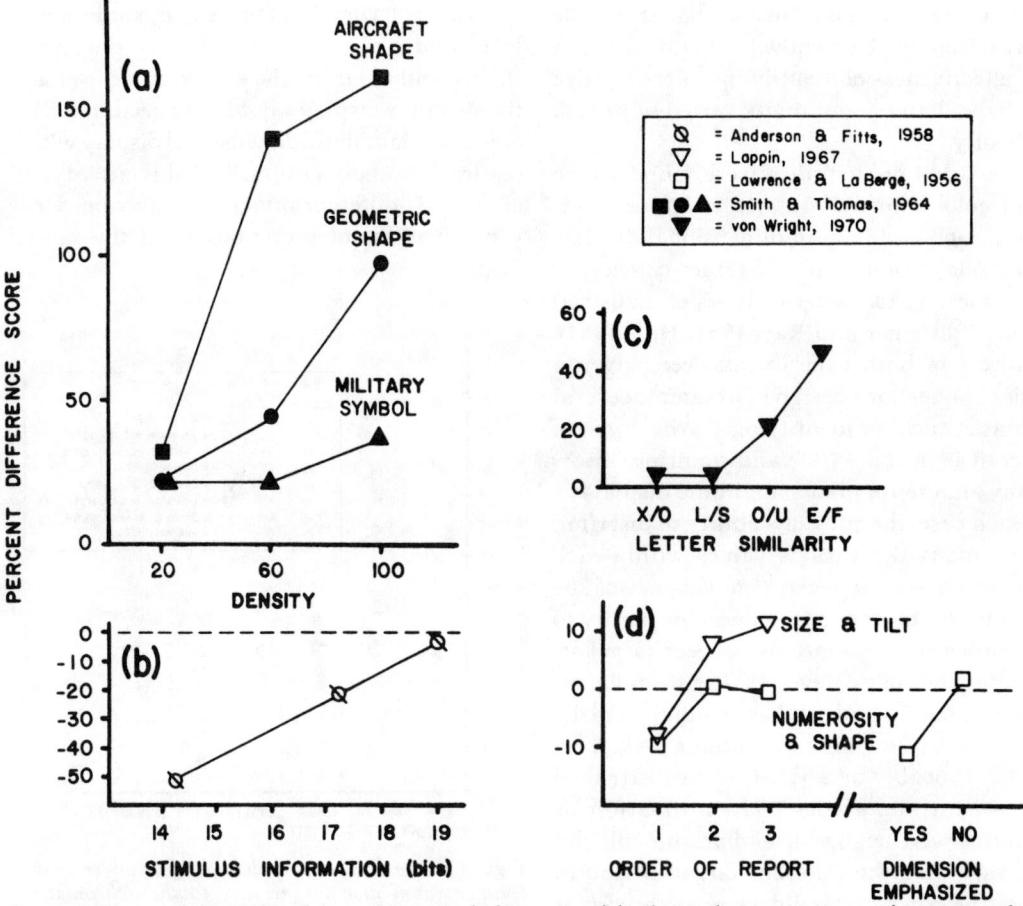

Figure 4. *The accuracy of identifying colors in multidimensional displays, relative to various achromatic codes, as a function of task difficulty.*

Figure 4 shows the effects of task difficulty on the relative effect of colors, as derived from five different experiments. Figure 4a shows the effectiveness of color in a counting task relative to three kinds of shape codes. In this study (Smith and Thomas, 1964), five levels of one of the three kinds of shapes were shown in five independently selected colors. Subjects were asked to count the number of times a specific color or a specific shape appeared in the display. Previous work had shown that the relative similarities of the five shapes within each shape dimension were greater for aircraft shapes than for geometric shapes and were greater for geometric shapes than for military symbols. Thus, the task of identifying and counting a particular shape would be more difficult for geometric shapes than for military symbols and most difficult for aircraft shapes. It is also reasonable to assume that the task was increasingly difficult as the total number of colors and shapes (density) increased in the display. Using either definition of task difficulty, the data presented in Figure 4a show that the identification of colors is increasingly superior relative to shapes as task difficulty increases.

Figure 4b shows the effectiveness of identifying colors relative to digits as the amount of information in the stimulus increases. In this study (Anderson and Fitts, 1958), subjects were shown three randomly selected digits, each presented on an independently sampled color background. The subject's task was to identify each color-digit pair. Each digit was selected from a population of nine possible digits. The colors were selected from a population of three, six, or nine possible colors. As the number of possible colors increased, the total information in the display increased from 14.25 bits to 19.02 bits. While the colors were always identified less accurately than the digits, this inferiority decreased as stimulus information increased.

Figure 4c shows the analysis of an experiment by von Wright (1970). In this study, subjects were shown a 4 × 4 matrix in which each cell was one of two colors and contained one of two letters. The subject's task was to name either the color or the letter in each cell. The relative similarity of the two letters within each pair was varied; the letter pairs were, in increasing order of similarity, X and O, L and S, O and U, and E and F. Figure 4c shows that the identification accuracy of colors was always superior relative to letters and that it became increasingly superior as the difficulty of identifying letters increased.

Figure 4d summarizes the analysis of parts of two experiments (Lappin, 1967; Lawrence and LaBerge, 1956) which varied the order of report of color relative to other attributes in the display and which varied which of three attributes were emphasized when all three were to be identified. In the latter case, the emphasized dimension was almost always reported first. Figure 4d shows the effectiveness of color identification relative to different achromatic attributes as the order of reporting (or the emphasis on) color was varied. It can be seen that color became increasingly more effective as recall was delayed or as importance was de-emphasized.

Given the widely differing procedures employed in the studies shown in Figure 4, it seems clear that the identification of colors became increasingly superior (or less inferior) to achromatic target features as the difficulty of identifying achromatic targets increased (Figure 4a and 4c). This is reasonable since in those comparisons the same colors were used as the difficulty of discriminating among achromatic targets was increased. What is less clear (cf., Figure 4b and 4d) is why the effectiveness of color relative to digit and shape attributes should increase as the number of colors, and the delay in reporting colors, was increased. However, the identification of colors may be superior to other attributes in a nonredundant multidimensional display because identification of the achromatic attributes is reduced and not necessarily because color identification improves in any absolute sense.

*Between unidimensional and multidimensional displays.* One problem inherent in comparing the effect of color and achromatic attributes within uncorrelated multidimensional displays is that the relative measure employed in this report does not indicate the possible effects on one attribute due to the addition of other uncorrelated attributes. Two interrelated questions need to be answered: (1) Does the addition of color to an achromatic display affect the accuracy of identifying the achromatic attribute?; and (2) Does the addition of an achromatic feature to a color display affect the accuracy of identifying colors? In either case, performance data on the accuracy of identifying the attribute in question are needed for both unidimensional and multidimensional displays. For (1), the appropriate derived score is the difference in the accuracy of identifying the achromatic attribute between multidimensional and unidimensional displays relative to the unidimensional display, *i.e.*,

$$\% \text{ Difference Score} = \frac{(\text{Color} + \text{Achromatic}) - \text{Achromatic}}{\text{Achromatic}} \times 100; \quad (2)$$

and for (2), the difference in accuracy of identifying color between multidimensional and unidimensional displays relative to the unidimensional display, *i.e.*,

$$\% \text{ Difference Score} = \frac{(\text{Color} + \text{Achromatic}) - \text{Color}}{\text{Color}} \times 100. \quad (3)$$

Only five studies were found which would permit both derived scores to be determined (Allport, 1971; Anderson and Fitts, 1958; Egeth and Pachella, 1969; Mackworth, 1963b; Smith and Thomas, 1964). One additional study (Morgan and Alluisi, 1967), where colors were added as an irrelevant attribute in a size judgment task, permitted only the score from Equation 2 to be derived. The results of these analyses are shown in Figure 5.

Figure 5a presents the effects of color on the accuracy of identifying an achromatic target attribute in a multidimensional display relative to the accuracy of identifying this achromatic attribute in a comparable unidimensional display, calculated by Equation 2. The four achromatic attributes used in this comparison are indicated on the abscissa of Figure 5a. It may be seen that, in general, color in a multidimensional display interfered with the correct identification of achromatic attributes in that display. This seems to be true whether the color was relevant (*e.g.*, Anderson and Fitts, 1958) or irrelevant (*e.g.*, Morgan and Alluisi, 1967) and, based upon these same two studies, the interference increased as the number of different colors increased. Hence, the three data points shown from the Anderson and Fitts study differ according to how many colors were possible in the multidimensional display.

As the number of possible colors increased from three to nine, the interference they had upon digit identification increased relative to a unidimensional digit display. The three vertical clusters of four points shown from the Morgan and Alluisi study represent, from left to right in Figure 5a, 2, 4, and 8 irrelevant colors. The four points within each cluster represent, from top to bottom in Figure 5a, increasing similarity of target sizes. This study showed that, as the number of irrelevant colors increased, size identification accuracy decreased relative to a unidimensional display of different target sizes. This was especially true when the discriminability between target sizes was reduced. The data from the other three experiments, which are shown in Figure 5a, are less clear about the effects of the

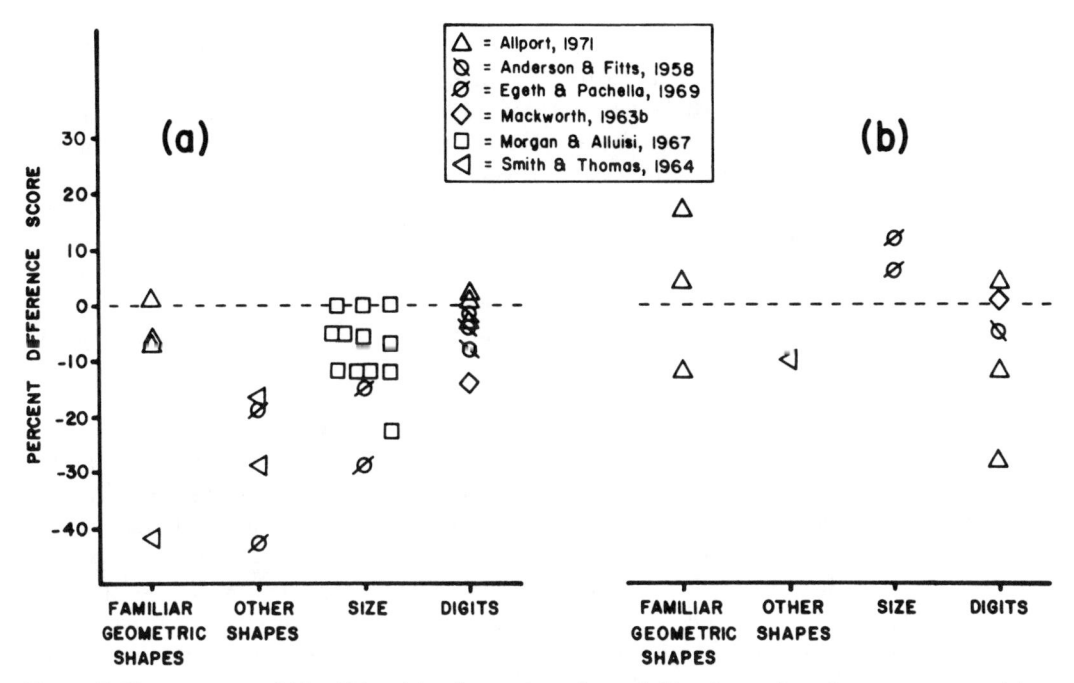

Figure 5. *The accuracy of identifying (a) achromatic codes and (b) colors, when they were presented in a multidimensional display relative to when they were presented in a unidimensional display.*

number of colors or about the effects of achromatic target discriminability.

The effect of achromatic attributes on the accuracy of identifying colors in a multidimensional display relative to the accuracy of identifying color in a unidimensional color display is shown in Figure 5b. The relative scores in this figure were calculated by Equation 3; the achromatic attributes investigated are shown on the abscissa. Figure 5b shows that the effects of an achromatic attribute on the accuracy of identifying colors in a nonredundant multidimensional display are equivocal; some studies suggest that the addition of achromatic attributes increases the accuracy of identifying colors, while others suggest a decrease.

Before presenting the results obtained when color is used as a redundant target attribute in identification tasks, six other studies using color as a nonredundant variable need to be discussed. None of these experiments could be analyzed or interpreted in the manner used for the other nonredundant color studies.

Five studies reported the use of color and other achromatic stimulus attributes as criteria for target selection. In all five studies the subject was presented with an array of alphanumeric symbols and was required to identify only a part of the total array. The task usually involved three distinct stages: (1) the presentation of a cue (most frequently a high- or low-pitched tone) which indicated which of two categories of stimuli were to be reported, or, additionally, the presentation of a third cue (a medium-pitched tone) to indicate that all the items in the display were to be reported; (2) the use of a stimulus criterion variable to select those items specified by the cueing stimulus, *e.g.*, red or black, letter or digit, top row or bottom row; (3) the identification (recall) of the selected alphanumeric symbols.

Three studies used the procedure defined above (Dick, 1969; 1970; von Wright, 1970), one replaced the tones with verbal instructions (Brown, 1960), and one equated the cueing stimulus and the selection criterion, putting them in the stimulus array as a single red, inverted, or fragmented letter (Snyder, 1972).

The four studies which used position (top or bottom row) as a stimulus selection criterion found that color was inferior to position. These same four studies found different results concerning the efficiency of color relative to target class (letter or digit). Brown (1960) and Dick (1969; 1970) found color to be inferior to class as a selection criterion; von Wright (1970) found the opposite result. The apparent discrepancy may be due to three factors. One is related to the way the data were reported: Brown used and reported data only from the partial report condition; Dick, in both of his studies, reported only the average accuracy pooled over partial and whole report conditions; and, von Wright reported the data from the whole and partial report conditions separately. We were able to convert von Wright's data to make them compatible with the data of Brown and of Dick, but not both in any one transformation. The second factor, which may account for the different results, relates to when the cue was given concerning which stimulus selection criterion to employ. Brown gave his subjects this information either 2 sec before or simultaneous with the stimulus exposure. Dick systematically varied the time between stimulus offset and cue onset over a range extending from 850 msec before stimulus offset to 850 msec after stimulus offset. Von Wright always presented his tone cue 5 msec after stimulus offset. The third possibly very relevant distinction between these studies is that all subjects in the studies by Dick used the same multidimensional displays, so that the relative effectiveness of color as a selector is based upon comparisons within multidimensional displays. The subjects in the Brown and von Wright studies viewed different displays depending upon whether color, position, or class was the selection criterion. Hence, in these latter two studies the relative effectiveness of color was based upon comparisons between multidimensional displays.

Figure 6 shows the results of one analysis of these four studies. This figure shows the effectiveness of color as a selection criterion relative to class and location criteria as a function of stimulus offset-cue onset differences. The relative effectiveness of color as a stimulus selection criterion was calculated using Equation 1. It may be seen in Figure 6 that color was always less effective as a stimulus selection criterion relative to position and that, except for the moment of stimulus exposure, color was also less effective than alphanumeric class. At stimulus onset or 5 msec after stimulus offset, color was superior as a stimulus selection criterion relative to class.

Von Wright also employed a number of

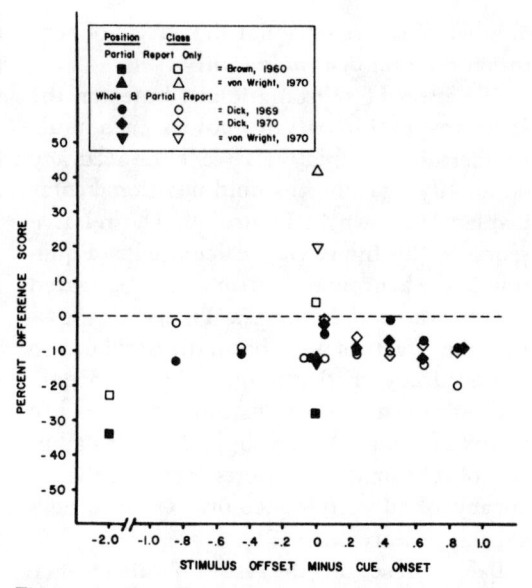

Figure 6. *The effectiveness of color as a selection (partial-report) criterion, relative to position and alphanumeric class, as a function of stimulus offset minus cue onset differences.*

other achromatic attributes as stimulus selection criteria. He found that, in general, location, color, brightness, and size were all effective as selection criteria and that orientation or tilt of the items, class (letters and digits), phonetic attribute (vowel and consonant), and normal and mirrored images were ineffective as selection criterion. The relative scores, derived using Equation 1, showed that color was superior as a stimulus selection criterion relative to all these attributes except location (location, −12; size and brightness, +11; orientation, +24; class, phoneme, and mirrored attributes, +19). Von Wright did report that two of his subjects were able to use class and one other subject was able to use a phoneme attribute as effective selection criterion. Those subjects had considerably more practice with the experimental task than did the other subjects. When the selection criterion was given in the visual display rather than in an auditory cue (Snyder, 1972), color was superior to inversion (+19) and to fragmentation (+30).

A related issue, that of using color as an aid in organizing stimulus input, was examined by Kanarick and Petersen (1971) in a short-term running memory study. They required subjects to monitor a row of 10 channels of information. The 10 inputs were all digits, all colors, or five digits followed in the row by five colors. They found no difference between the all digit and all color conditions but a pronounced advantage in using two different types of information. The analysis shows a 31% savings for color and digit combined relative to either attribute alone.

*Color as a Redundant Attribute*

If multidimensional targets can be identified accurately on the basis of any of several different attributes, those attributes are said to be redundant. Redundancy in this case simply means that more information is provided by the target than is minimally necessary for it to be identified. For example, targets may differ from each other in terms of both their shape and their color, *e.g.*, red squares, blue circles, or green triangles. If these target attributes are completely redundant, squares are always red, and red objects are always squares. The same reasoning may be applied to the examples of blue circles and green triangles. If these targets were the only ones used in a display, subjects could attend only to their shapes or only to their colors and still be able to identify the targets correctly.

Another case of redundancy is called partial (as opposed to complete) redundancy. In this form of redundancy, targets may differ from each other both in their shapes and colors, but with only one attribute unique to the target. That is, targets may be defined as squares, circles, triangles, and diamonds, and blue may be associated with only squares and circles, while green is associated with only triangles and diamonds. In this case, color is partially redundant with shape since knowing the color of the target partially reduces target uncertainty but is not sufficient for actual identification.

Only three studies were located which reported using colors completely correlated with relatively simple and well-controlled achromatic attributes. Eriksen and Hake (1955) used 17 levels of brightness, 20 hues, and 20 target sizes in three unidimensional displays and all possible completely redundant two- and three-way multidimensional combinations. Garner and Creelman (1964) used 20 hues and 20 sizes both singly and in redundant combinations. Kanarick and Petersen (1971) combined six colors in a completely redundant fashion with six digits.

In addition to these, five additional studies were located which reported accuracy of target identification from colored and achromatic displays of the same stimulus materials. Wong and Yacoumelos (1973) had their subjects identify various features shown on a map. Markoff (1972) used static ground-level photographs of one of three alternate targets (soldier, tank, and truck) embedded in a wooded scene. Jeffrey and Beck (1972) used prearranged targets in static aerial photographs. Kraft and Anderson (1973) used dynamic aerial motion picture film in either a stereoscopic or a nonstereoscopic display. Fowler and Jones (1972) used television displays of a three-dimensional ground terrain to simulate a real-time airborne sensor display. In all of these studies, subjects were prebriefed as to the types of targets they were to detect and identify. The subjects in the Fowler and Jones (1972) and the Jeffrey and Beck (1972) studies were experienced pilots and experienced photointerpreters, respectively. In all cases it was assumed that the subjects knew the color of the designated targets even though it may not have been specified during prebriefing. Thus, color was at least a partially redundant dimension in these latter five studies.

Figure 7 shows the results of an analysis of all eight studies. This figure shows the relative change in performance produced by adding a redundant dimension to the target attributes indicated on the abscissa. The formula used to calculate relative change was:

$$\% \text{ Difference Score} = \frac{\left[\begin{array}{c}\text{With redundant attribute}-\\ \text{Without redundant attribute}\end{array}\right]}{\text{Without redundant attribute}} \times 100. \quad (4)$$

On the left of this figure are the data from Eriksen and Hake (1955), Garner and Creelman (1964), and Kanarick and Petersen (1971). It can be seen that the addition of a completely redundant color to size, brightness, and already redundant combinations of size and brightness facilitated absolute identification performance. For purposes of comparison, the effect of adding a redundant brightness to size and the effect of adding a redundant size to brightness are also shown. It can be seen that either of these latter redundant combinations also produced increases in identification accuracy relative to size alone or brightness alone but not as much as did redundant color.

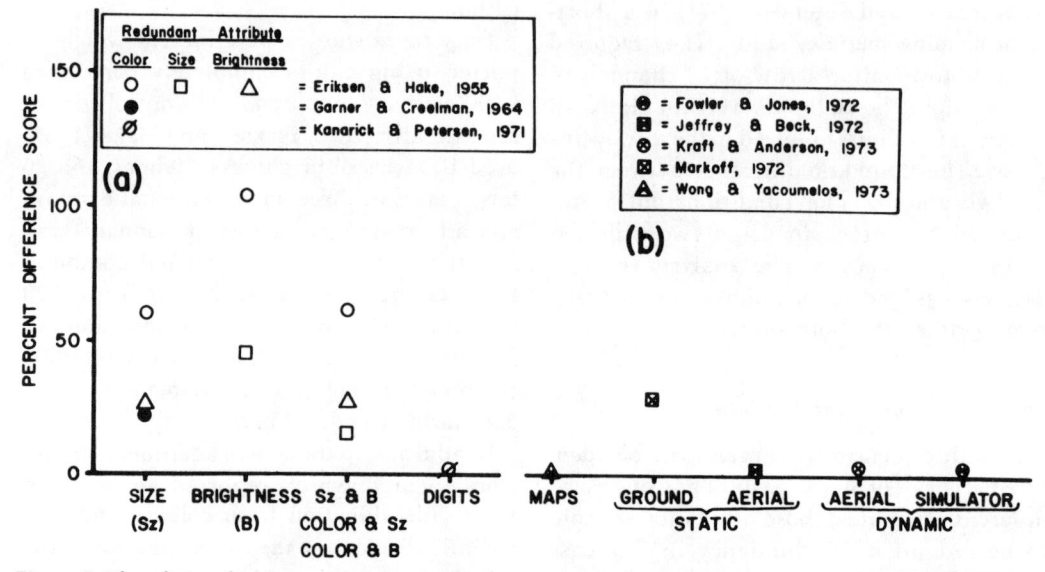

Figure 7. *The relative change in accuracy of identification produced by adding (a) a redundant attribute to the target codes indicated on the abscissa and (b) "natural" color representation to achromatic maps and pictures.*

Also shown for the purpose of comparison are the effects of adding a redundant size to an already redundant combination of color and brightness and the effects of adding a redundant brightness to an already redundant combination of color and size. Again, identification accuracy was improved, but not as much as when redundant color is added to size-brightness combinations. The addition of redundant color to digits had only a very small positive effect over digits alone in the running memory study of Kanarick and Petersen (1971).

Figure 7b compares colored displays with achromatic displays of maps, static ground and aerial photographs, and dynamic aerial photographs and simulated sensor displays. Only Markoff's (1972) static ground photographs suggested an advantage in using color. The other four studies found essentially no effect. It may be significant that the mean accuracy of identifying targets in the Markoff study was based upon four separate levels of display resolution. Hence, on the average, the displays used in the Markoff study were spatially degraded relative to those used in the other four studies.

## RESULTS FOR SEARCH TIME

This section is concerned with the effects of color in search tasks. The dependent measure is the time required to find predesignated targets. Since superior performance is indicated by smaller numerical values, the appropriate form of Equation 1 is:

$$\% \text{ Difference Score} = \frac{\text{Achromatic} - \text{Color}}{\text{Achromatic}} \times 100. \quad (5)$$

*Nonredundant Colors Relative to Nonredundant Achromatic Codes*

Only four studies were found in which subjects had to search for a specified color or for a specified achromatic stimulus attribute in nonredundant displays. Eriksen (1952) used four unidimensional displays, each varying in only color, brightness, shape, or familiar geometric form. Color and a number of different achromatic variables were used as unidimensional codes by Hitt (1961) in a matrix display and by Christner and Ray (1961) in a map-type display. Both of these studies required the subjects to locate or count designated code items. In either case, the data they reported were the number of responses their subjects were able to make to a series of five questions divided by the time it took to make these responses. Although this rate measure is not really equivalent to search time, it does depend on it. It was used, therefore, to calculate the effectiveness of colors in their studies. Smith and Thomas (1964) used both multidimensional displays, with nonredundant combinations of colors and shapes, and unidimensional displays each varying in only shape or color. The subject's task was to count the frequency of occurrence of a specified value of a given attribute. This study was the only source of data for the multidimensional display comparison and for the multidimensional-unidimensional displays comparison.

Figure 8a shows the difference scores based on each of the achromatic attributes indicated on the abscissa. It may be seen that the time needed to locate or count colors in the unidimensional displays was short compared to the time needed to locate or count achromatic attributes. The least advantage of color suggested may be relative to alphanumeric symbols. The advantage of color over shape appears to be even greater when the comparisons are made within multidimensional displays (Figure 8b). Finally, as shown in Figure 8c, the effect of colors in a multidimensional display was to decrease counting speed for shapes compared to shapes in a unidimensional display. On the other hand, it would

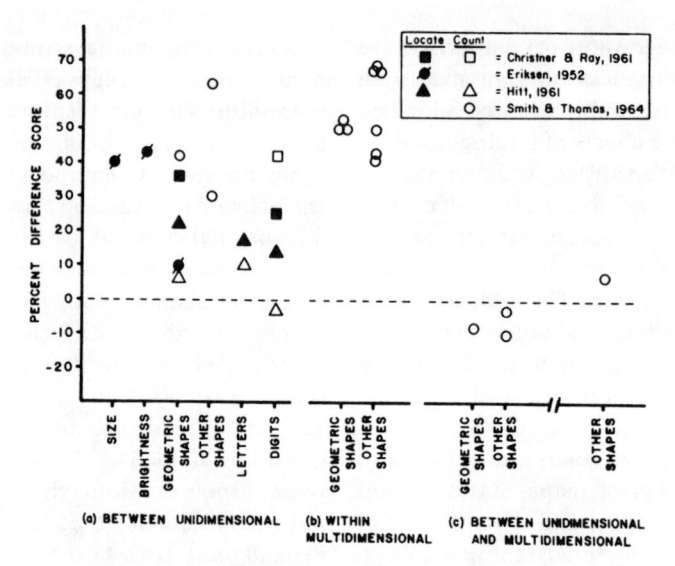

Figure 8. *The time required to locate colored targets relative to the achromatic target codes indicated on the abscissa in (a) unidimensional and (b) multidimensional displays. (c) The time required to locate achromatic targets and colored targets in multidimensional displays relative to unidimensional displays.*

appear that the effect of shapes in a multidimensional display was to increase counting performance for colors relative to colors in a unidimensional display. These latter two types of comparisons are based on relative scores derived from reversing the terms in the numerators of Equations 2 and 3, respectively.

Two additional studies which used color and achromatic stimulus features as nonredundant target variables must be handled separately since they both involved comparisons between nonredundant multidimensional displays. Lehtiö (1970) used displays consisting of digits (0-9) which could vary in size (large and small) and in color (red and blue). In one part of his study a target was defined as the only small digit, the only red digit, or the only digit "3" in displays which varied randomly in each of the other two nontarget dimensions. The data showed that considerably less time was required to locate the only red digit relative to the only small digit or the only digit "3". The percent difference scores, determined using Formula 5, showed a 70% gain with red relative to small, and an 81% gain using red relative to the digit "3".

In another part of the Lehtiö study, the target was defined multidimensionally as the single occurrence of a small, red, digit "3"; nontargets were other combinations of values from each of the three stimulus dimensions. In six different experimental conditions, the proportion of nontargets which were red, small, or "3" was either 0.20 or 0.80. This frequency manipulation occurred for only one stimulus dimension in each condition; the other two dimensions were divided equally between the target and the nontarget values. Since there was no appropriate achromatic control condition, a percent difference score could not be computed. However, the effect of frequency manipulation was much larger when the relative proportion of the different colors was varied than when the relative proportions of different sizes or of different digits were varied. An increase in the proportion of nontargets with the target's color led to larger increases in search time than did increases in the proportion of nontargets which were small or the digit "3".

Newman and Davis (1962) used 36 stimuli in six differently encoded displays: (1) 36 different abstract shapes; (2) 18 shapes in each of two colors; (3) 18 shapes in each of two levels of brightness; (4) 18 shapes each flashing at two different rates; (5) 12 shapes in each of three colors; and (6) 12 shapes each flashing at three different rates. Comparisons of the latter five two-dimensional conditions with the shapes-only condition showed that the two that utilized color as an encoding variable were most superior. The percent different score for each of the two-dimensional display conditions relative to the unidimensional shape condition was as follows: +43 for three colors, +35 for two colors, +20 for two brightnesses, +10 for two flash rates, and −2 for three flash rates. Comparisons between the color encoded two-dimensional displays and each of the other three achromatically encoded two-dimensional displays showed that two colors were superior, relative to two brightnesses (+17) and to two flash rates (+28); and that three colors were superior, relative to three flash rates (+44).

*Color as a Redundant Attribute*

Fifteen studies were found that used color as a redundant variable in a search task. Six studies used color as a completely redundant variable; three studies compared color and achromatic representations of the same stimulus materials; and six employed color as a partially redundant variable.

The left-hand side of Figure 9 presents the difference scores from the studies using completely redundant color coding. The remainder of the figure provides the data from the three studies which compared chromatic with achromatic representations of the same stimuli. This figure shows the relative change

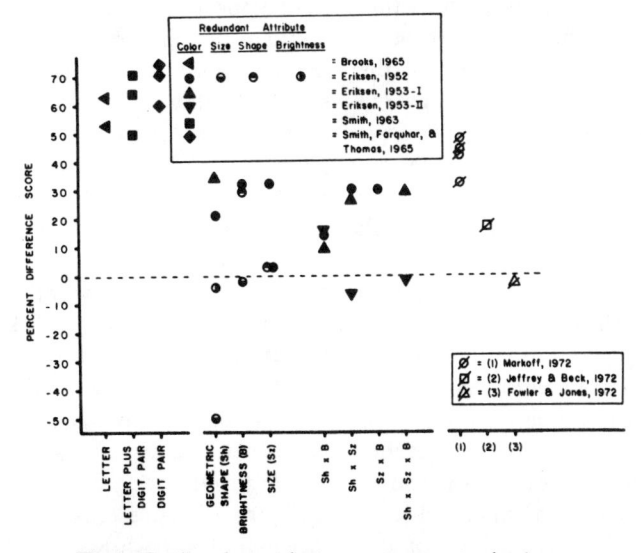

Figure 9. *The relative change in time required to locate targets produced by adding a redundant attribute to the target codes indicated on the abscissa.*

in search time produced by adding a redundant attribute to the targets indicated on the abscissa. The formula used to calculate these relative scores was obtained by reversing the terms in the numerator of Equation 4.

The extreme left-hand side of the figure shows that the addition of redundant color has a large positive effect on the time needed to locate and count alphanumeric targets. The data from Smith (1963) and Smith, et al. (1955) showed an increasing advantage for redundant color as stimulus density increased. The two data points from Brooks' (1965) study represent the effects of using only one color which was correlated with the target letter, and the effects of using a different color correlated with each letter in the display. As the number of colors increased, there was a slight decrease in the benefit derived from redundant color.

The data representing the addition of redundant colors to shape, size, and brightness, shown in the center of Figure 9, are from two studies by Eriksen (1952; 1953). Two points should be made concerning those studies. First, comparing the data from Eriksen's 1952 and 1953-I experiments, it may be seen that redundant color had a similar pattern of effects when no particular dimension of the multidimensional target was emphasized (1952) and when the shape dimension of the target was emphasized (1953-I). The second point to be made concerns the data shown from Eriksen's 1953-II experiment. Although the same displays were used in this experiment as in the others, in this one the targets were defined only as circles, even though the circles were always correlated with a unique color and with other achromatic features.

The effect of adding redundant colors to the display, but not informing the subjects of this redundancy, was different from that found in the other two experiments in which subjects were informed. Specifically, for two of the three conditions shown in Figure 9, the effect of adding redundant color to the display but not informing the subjects of the redundancy was to decrease performance relative to when the colors were not added. For the purpose of comparison, the effects of adding a redundant achromatic attribute to the achromatic targets indicated on the abscissa are also shown for the Eriksen (1952) data. It can be seen that these redundant achromatic attributes generally added very little or even decreased search performance when they were added to other achromatic target dimensions. The one exception was adding redundant shape to brightness. In this case, the relative improvement in search performance was comparable to that found for adding redundant color to brightness.

Relative scores, calculated as above and based on data from the three studies identified on the extreme right-hand side of Figure 9, suggest that color photographs (Jeffrey and Beck, 1972; Markoff, 1972) were superior to black-and-white photographs in search tasks. The four data points from Markoff represent four levels of display resolution. As spatial resolution decreased, the advantages of redundant color increased. Fowler and Jones (1972) found no advantage (in fact, a slight disadvantage) for color in a simulated, forward-looking sensor display.

Only three of the studies using color as a partially redundant variable included a monochromatic or achromatic control condition. Hence, only these three studies permitted calculation of a difference score. In two of these studies (Green and Anderson, 1956; Smith, 1962), the subject's knowledge of the target color was varied. When subjects did not know the target color, color was irrelevant even though it was partially redundant with the target. The target in all three studies was a two-digit number.

Figure 10 represents one way to view the three studies. It shows the effect of partially redundant color coding relative to a monochromatic control as a function of the number of different colors, the total number of stimuli in the display (density), and the subject's knowledge of the target color. It is apparent that when the subject knew the target color, his performance was better in a multicolored display than in a monochromatic display. It also appears that when a subject knew the target color, the advantages of partially redundant color coding increased as the number of different colors in the display increased and as the overall display density increased.

Figure 10 also suggests that adding partially redundant colors to the displays without giving the subjects knowledge of the color of the target produced a decrement in performance relative to the monochromatic display condition. There is also some suggestion that this detrimental effect of irrelevant color increased as the number of different colors employed increased and as the overall display density increased.

An important consideration in the use of color as a partially redundant coding variable is the number of nontargets which have the same color as the target. More specifically, the issue is concerned with how relevant the color of the target is. As the number of nontargets which have the same color as the target increases, the usefulness of color as a critical target feature decreases. Figure 11 shows the effect of known and unknown partially redundant target colors relative to a monochromatic control as a function of the proportion of elements in the display which have the target color. The data show a definite trend for a decreasing advantage of color coding as the proportion of nontargets which have the same color as the target increase. The advantage becomes a disadvantage when the proportion exceeds about 0.70. Partially redundant colors are almost always detrimental to subjects who are not aware of the target color. Difference scores from Shontz, Trumm, and Williams (1971) are shown at the left side of Figure 11. These investigators used maps with 196 different identifiable points. The proportion of nontargets having the same color as the target in these displays ranged from 0.015 to 0.200. These data also suggest a trend of decreasing effectiveness of partially redundant color rela-

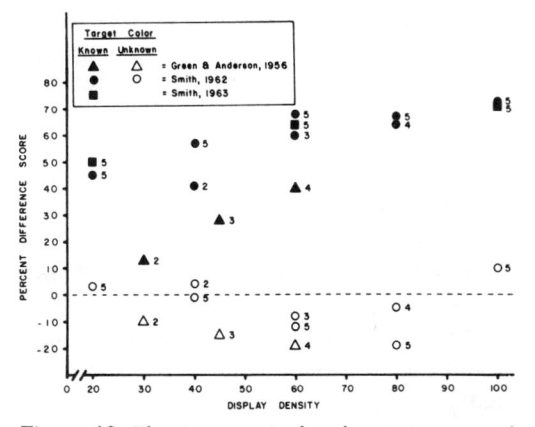

Figure 10. *The time required to locate targets with partially redundant color codes, relative to monochromatic displays, as a function of the display density, the number of different colors used in the displays (shown as a parameter), and the subject's awareness of the target color.*

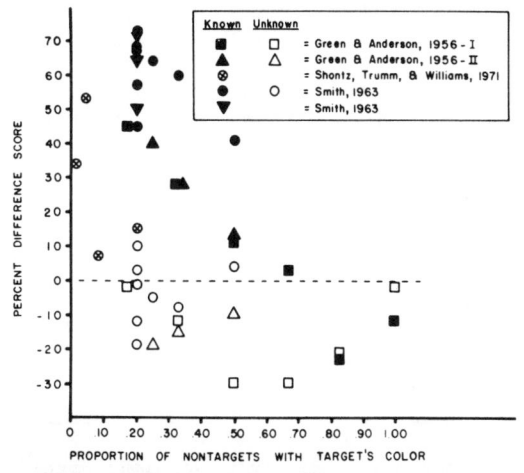

Figure 11. *The time required to locate targets with partially redundant color codes, relative to monochromatic displays, as a function of the proportion of nontargets having the target color. The parameter indicates whether or not the subject was aware of the target color.*

tive to monochrome as the proportion increases.

The remaining two studies which employed a partially redundant color code (Williams, 1966; Williams and Wallen, 1965) did not use a monochromatic or an achromatic control. Instead, their subjects always viewed a display containing 100 two-digit numbers each surrounded by one of the nonredundant combinations of five colors, five shapes, and five sizes. Subjects were always told the unique target number but were or were not informed of the color, shape, and size features of the target.

Figure 12 shows the data from these two studies along with those of Green and Anderson (1956) and Smith (1962). In this figure, the relative score represents the effects of knowing the target color relative to not knowing the target color. The values are plotted as a function of the proportion of the nontargets which have the target color in the total display. As may be seen, knowledge of the target color is advantageous when the proportion was low. However, as the proportion of colors identical to the target color increases, knowledge of the target color becomes less and less useful and eventually becomes a disadvantage as the display approaches a monochromatic display.

## RESULTS FOR THE SUBJECTIVE ADVANTAGES OF COLOR

Five of the studies reviewed included the results of subjective preference ratings and questionnaire responses. Schutz (1961) and Christner and Ray (1961) had subjects rank order or rate their preference for stimulus codes. Both of these studies reported that the subjects preferred color codes relative to achromatic codes.

Munns (1968, p. 1221) concluded his article by saying, "... the use of color made S's task somewhat easier but did not increase S's effectiveness. S's report feeling more secure with the color coding."

Jeffrey and Beck (1972) and Chase (1970) both used intensive questionnaire and interview techniques to obtain subjective evaluations of the effectiveness of color. It may be significant that both of these studies used experienced personnel as subjects: Jeffrey and Beck had experienced photointerpreters compare chromatic and achromatic aerial photographs; Chase had experienced pilots compare chromatic and achromatic visual simulations of a landing approach. In both studies, subjects emphasized the increased naturalness of the color displays and their belief that color improved their ability to detect details. Color did not actually improve detection or identification in the Jeffrey and Beck study. Perhaps most challenging was the general subjective report that color in displays is less monotonous and that it produces less eye strain and fatigue.

## DISCUSSION

The most clear-cut finding is that if the color of a target is unique for that target, and if that

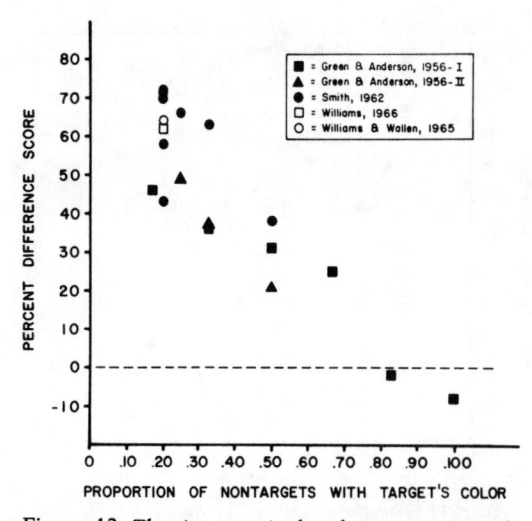

Figure 12. *The time required to locate targets with partially redundant color codes when subjects are aware of the target color, relative to when they were not aware, as a function of the proportion of nontargets having the target color.*

color is known in advance, color aids both identification and searching. The gain over black-and-white or monochrome may be as large as 200%. If this were the only conclusion, the investigation would have demonstrated what to many people is obvious. However, the conclusion does not hold for all display conditions to the same degree, and it must be considered in light of what appear to be still other effects of the use of color.

More specifically, if the subject's task is to identify some feature of a target, colors can be identified more accurately than sizes, brightnesses, familiar geometric shapes, and other shape or form parameters, but colors are identified with less accuracy than alphanumeric symbols. This is generally true, both when comparisons are made between unidimensional displays and within multidimensional displays, although the differences tend to be larger within multidimensional displays. There is also a tendency for the relative superiority (or inferiority) of color to increase as the density of targets in the display increases. Compared to the use of achromatic coding dimensions, the gain in accuracy with the use of colors can be at least 176% better than size, 32% better than brightness, and 202% better than shape. Conversely, the loss in accuracy using colors relative to alphanumeric symbols can be at least 48%.

The most parsimonious explanation for these results may be that the accuracy of identifying attributes of visual targets is directly related to the subject's prior experience in responding to values within these dimensions. It is reasonable to assume that most subjects will have had extensive practice identifying alphanumeric symbols, somewhat less practice in identifying colors, and relatively little practice identifying many of the achromatic target features employed in the experiments reported.

A problem with the use of colors may occur when they are used in a multidimensional display. Specifically, when colors are added to an achromatic display, the subject's accuracy in identifying achromatic target features decreases relative to when the display elements are monochromatic or achromatic. The loss in accuracy for identifying achromatic attributes of the target when colors are varied can be at least 29% for size, 43% for shapes, and 14% for alphanumeric symbols. This interfering effect of color can occur whether the color is relevant, *i.e.*, part of the target code, or irrelevant.

Very few studies are available concerning the use of color as a redundant variable in identification tasks. One study found that a redundant color could increase identification accuracy of simple targets. Compared to the absence of redundant color the gain using redundant color was 60% for size, 104% for brightness, and 61% for size and brightness combinations. The only other study which found an effect for redundant color was the study by Markoff (1972) who compared recognition performance for targets in an open field using color and black-and-white photographs. That study was also unique in that the spatial resolution of the display was degraded. Markoff found a 29% advantage for recognition using the color photographs relative to the black-and-white photographs.

The same relative advantages and disadvantages apply to the use of color when the subject's task is to locate or count some feature of targets in a search display. Specifically, subjects required less time to locate or count colors in a search display relative to every achromatic condition used in the experiments reviewed for this report (including alphanumeric symbols). Compared to the use of achromatic codes, search time with the use of colors can be at least 40% less than size, 43% less than brightness, 63% less than shape, and 43% less than alphanumeric symbols. On the other hand, irrelevant colors in a display interfere with the subject's ability to locate achromatic target features relative to a monochromatic display.only one study was available for this comparison. It found that search time for shapes can increase 10% when irrelevant colors were added to the display.

Redundant colors can decrease search time in symbolic displays if the subject knows the color of the targets. This advantage of redundant colors increases as the density of symbols in the display increases and as the number of nontarget colors increases. Specifically, compared to the absence of redundant color, search time decreases with color as a redundant variable up to at least 32% for size and brightness, 34% for shape, and 74% for alphanumeric symbols. Given that subjects know the color of the target, the gain using color exists whether color is completely redundant or partially redundant.

Using color in a pictorial display to provide a "natural" representation of the real world has also been shown to decrease search time. Compared to black-and-white photographs, color photographs reduce search time by as much as 32% when the display is in focus and by as much as 48% when the display is presented with degraded spatial resolution. With aerial photographs, the relative advantage of color can be as much as 18%, but one study showed a relative disadvantage (−3%) for color television displays relative to black-and-white.

In partially redundant color-coded displays, the gain in search performance derived from knowing the color of the target decreases as the proportion of nontargets which have the same color as the target increases. When the proportion of nontargets with the target's color exceeds about 0.70, knowing the color of the target can be a disadvantage; *i.e.*, an increased search time relative to a monochromatic display. The increase can be as much as 23%.

When partially redundant color is added to a search display and the subject does not know the color of the target, search performance is generally degraded. Search time under these conditions can increase at least 23% relative to a monochromatic display and at least 72% relative to when the subject knows the color of the target. However, not knowing the color of the target may be an advantage when the proportion of nontargets with the same color as the target is quite high. This is not likely to occur until the proportion of irrelevant target colors exceeds 0.80. Beyond that, not knowing the target's color still results in a loss, relative to a monochromatic display, but not as great a loss as when the target color is known.

In addition to those effects of color already noted, which can be accepted with some degree of confidence, two other more tentative conclusions concerned with memory factors are available:

(1) Subjects can use the color of elements in a briefly exposed display as a partial report criterion better than any other information about the elements, except position, if this information is provided at the moment of stimulus onset or up to 5 msec after stimulus offset. However, if the cue for which elements of the display are to be identified occurs either before or after this brief time interval, color is a poorer partial report criterion than either position or alphanumeric class; and

(2) The memory of target color deteriorates less during a retention interval than does the memory of target size, orientation, or shape. Hence, when subjects must identify and remember several independent features of a briefly exposed target, the accuracy of delayed reports of colors is only slightly reduced over the immediate reports. By comparison, the accuracy of shape and size reports is more affected if the report is delayed.

## A GUIDE FOR DESIGN DECISIONS

The data in Table 1 show the maximum and the minimum gain (or loss) that has been reported with the use of colors as target codes relative to the indicated achromatic coding dimensions. Minimum and maximum gain (or loss) are expressed in terms of the percent change relative to the achromatic codes shown in the first column. Positive scores indicate a gain, negative scores a loss with the use of color. These data are given separately for target identification tasks and for search tasks. Within each task, the data are further divided into five major categories based upon the use of color and upon the type of comparison used to derive the data:

(1) The use of color as a nonredundant code; comparisons are made between unidimensional displays.

(2) The use of color as a nonredundant code; comparisons are made within multidimensional displays.

(3) The effects of nonredundant colors on the accuracy of identifying achromatic features of targets within multidimensional displays; comparisons are made between multidimensional displays and unidimensional displays.

(4) The use of color as a completely redundant coding variable; comparisons are made between displays with completely redundant colors and achromatic displays.

(5) The use of color as a partially redundant coding variable; comparisons are made between displays with partially redundant colors and monochromatic or achromatic displays. Studies using "natural" color representation in pictorial displays are included in this category.

For each range of effects listed in Table 1, the total number of comparisons *(n)* available in the literature is indicated. It should be noted that some of these data are based only on one or two comparative data points.

The values given in Table 1 should be used only as a starting point by any designer considering the use of color in displays. The figures given in this report should be consulted for additional information. Studies cited in this report, as well as others which are listed in Appendix A, should also be reviewed for more detailed descriptions of the specific types of targets used as well as other methodological details.

Several overriding considerations should be mentioned. It is quite possible that the larger gain scores are based upon comparisons in which the colors are more discriminable than the achromatic codes. Likewise, the achromatic codes could be more discriminable than the comparative color codes when the larger losses are recorded. Relatively few studies have been conducted to scale discriminability of target elements within a given dimension. Even fewer studies have been done scaling differences between stimulus dimensions. Furthermore, target background and luminance and the ambient lighting conditions may have been such that either the color or the achromatic coding variable was given an advantage. The point is that the values given in the table merely represent the range of results reported in the literature.

It is not always possible to determine whether hue is really the variable being introduced when what was called "color" was varied. Such factors as the saturation and brightness of the target were not as carefully controlled as would be desirable.

The data in the table are, for the most part, derived from subjects having minimal practice in the experimental task. There is substantial evidence that practice with a perceptual task increases overall performance; this is true for both identification and search tasks. As a result, if subjects are given extensive practice in identifying or locating colors, the maximum gain scores shown in the table would probably be exceeded. Likewise, if subjects are given extensive practice identifying and locating values within any of the achromatic codes, the minimum scores shown in the table would be too high.

TABLE 1

Range of Percent Difference Scores for the Use of Color

|  | Identification Task |  |  | Search Task |  |  |
|---|---|---|---|---|---|---|
|  | Minimum | Maximum | n | Minimum | Maximum | n |
| *Unidimensional* | | | | | | |
| Brightness | + 29 | + 32 | 2 | +43 | +43 | 1 |
| Size | − 6 | +111 | 6 | +40 | +40 | 1 |
| Geometric Shape | − 38 | + 33 | 11 | + 6 | +42 | 5 |
| Other Shapes | 0 | +118 | 6 | +30 | +63 | 2 |
| Letters | − 29 | − 15 | 6 | +10 | + 7 | 2 |
| Digits | − 48 | + 26 | 17 | − 3 | +42 | 4 |
| *Multidimensional* | | | | | | |
| Size | − 10 | +176 | 7 | | | 0 |
| Geometric Shape | − 28 | +202 | 15 | +50 | +53 | 3 |
| Other Shapes | − 2 | + 62 | 12 | +41 | +69 | 6 |
| Letters | + 4 | + 46 | 4 | | | 0 |
| Digits | − 51 | + 19 | 6 | | | 0 |
| *Interference* | | | | | | |
| Size | − 29 | 0 | 14 | | | 0 |
| Geometric Shape | − 42 | + 1 | 4 | − 8 | − 8 | 1 |
| Other Shapes | − 43 | − 17 | 4 | −10 | − 3 | 2 |
| Digits | − 14 | + 2 | 7 | | | 0 |
| *Complete Redundancy* | | | | | | |
| Size | + 22 | + 60 | 3 | +32 | +32 | 1 |
| Brightness | +104 | +104 | 1 | +32 | +32 | 1 |
| Geometric Shape | | | 0 | +21 | +32 | 2 |
| Letters | | | 0 | +53 | +63 | 2 |
| Digits | + 2 | + 2 | 1 | +60 | +74 | 3 |
| *Partial Redundancy* | | | | | | |
| Digits | | | 0 | −23 | +73 | 20 |
| Maps | + 1 | + 1 | 1 | | | 0 |
| Static-Ground Photo | + 29 | + 29 | 1 | +32 | +47 | 1 |
| Static-Aerial Photo | + 2 | + 2 | 1 | +17 | +17 | 1 |
| Dynamic-Aerial Film | + 3 | + 3 | 1 | | | 0 |
| Dynamic-Aerial TV | + 3 | + 3 | 1 | − 3 | − 3 | 1 |

## KNOWLEDGE GAPS

The secondary aim of this study was to identify gaps in knowledge which prevent a reasonable evaluation of the utility of color in aircraft displays. The data presented in this report point to many general and absolute gaps in knowledge. There simply are *no* data available for making some color code-achromatic code comparisons. Furthermore, even when several comparative values are available in the literature, they have often been obtained under relatively restricted conditions. Thus, there is a general need for more parametric research designed to provide data that would allow a broader and a more representative comparison between color codes and various achromatic codes.

In addition to these literal gaps in knowledge, this report makes it possible to identify several more specific knowledge gaps:

(1) The bulk of the data available from the experimental literature is derived from subjects with minimal experience. This fact may severely restrict the conclusions and recommendations that are based on these data.

(2) Without exception, the data available for this report were obtained under conditions where the subjects could devote their full attention to a single experimental task. If display design guides are to be developed which

can maximize the use of inflight aircraft displays, for example, there is a need to examine the relative effectiveness of different display codes when different displays and tasks compete for the operator's attention.

(3) There is some suggestion that display density and the exposure time of the display interact in their joint effects on identification accuracy. While this would be an important consideration for display design, the data that are available generally confound these two variables.

(4) The data from just two experiments strongly suggest that memory for colors deteriorates less during a retention interval than does memory for various shape attributes. These effects have strong implications for how information can best be extracted from multidimensional displays.

(5) The data from several studies have implications for the use of color to enable subjects to select part of a briefly exposed display for identification. These data suggest that subjects can use information about relevant color to select material from immediate memory storage better than they can use any other stimulus selection criteria except position. The issue of when the subject can most effectively use a selection criterion based on color and the range of possible application of this partial report technique has not been fully explored.

(6) At several points in this report the data suggested that colors interfere with the accuracy of identifying and the speed of locating achromatic target attributes. This finding for the use of color could severely limit its use in situations where color is not the only target feature of concern or where color might be irrelevant. Practically no data are available which indicate why color interferes with the accuracy of identifying or the speed of locating achromatic targets. Egeth and Pachella (1969) suggest three possible reasons: (1) color interferes with the discriminability of other target dimensions, (2) color distracts the observer so that he does not attend to other target dimensions, and (3) color-naming responses are more highly practiced than are the naming responses for other target dimensions, so that the effect could be a result of response competition. Each of these hypotheses has strong implications for the use of color and, more particularly, for the question of how to reduce the interference effects which apparently accompany its use.

(7) The data from identification studies which used color as a redundant target dimension, particularly those which used "natural" representations of color, have not generally found a great advantage for color displays relative to black-and-white displays. These results lead to several questions. First, is the redundant color an integral part of the target? Garner (1972) has suggested that, for redundant dimensions to aid identification, there must be integrality of all target dimensions. Secondly, will practice with a redundant color help it gain integrality with other target features? Finally, is color redundancy more likely to be useful if other features of the target are degraded?

## APPENDIX A
## BIBLIOGRAPHY OF LITERATURE PERTAINING TO THE USE OF COLORS IN DISPLAYS

This bibliography is an annotated list, identified only by author and date of publication, of those studies which did not meet the criteria for inclusion in the literature analysis, but which did pertain to the use of color in visual displays. The studies are annotated in terms of factors which affect the use of color and in terms of purposes for which color might be used. In addition, where possible, a statement is provided which summarizes the major findings for each category of studies. The bibliography is considered inclusive at least between 1952—1973 for interests of the present study, *i.e.*, search and identification performance. Some studies reflecting other kinds of performance or color sensitivity are presented to provide a starting point for those intererested in other related topics. A complete reference for all the annotated studies is included in the list of references.

## General Reviews

The following papers review display problems in general and the use of color codes in particular.

Crumley, Divany, Gates, Hostetter, and Hurst, 1961
Fletcher and Siegel, 1968 (particularly Chapter 5)
Graham, 1965 (particularly Chapters 12–16)
Jones, 1962
Meister and Sullivan, 1969
Payne, 1964
White, Dainoff, and Reynolds, 1972 (Section 1)

## Variables Affecting Detection and Recognition of Colors

*Limited stimulus energy.* The detection and recognition of target colors are limited, both in foveal and peripheral viewing conditions, when the targets are small in area, low in intensity, and brief in exposure time.

Conners, 1968, 1969, 1970
Kaiser, 1968
Siegel, 1968
Siegel and Siegel, 1971
Weitzman and Kinney, 1967, 1969

*Location of target in visual field.* The detection and recognition of different colors vary as a function of their location in the visual field.

Dudek and Colton, 1970
Middleton and Wyszecki, 1961
von Fieandt and Harlahti, 1970
Wissman, 1965

*Eye movements.* Color recognition is poor, at best, during voluntary saccades relative to conditions of steady fixation.

Lederberg, 1970

*Ambient illumination.* The illumination provided by an external source or by the display lights may differentially affect dark adaptation (detection thresholds) and visual acuity (discrimination performance).

Barnes, 1970
Bauer, 1968
Cavonius and Hilz, 1970
Dudek and Colton, 1970
Jainski, 1971 (relevant to glare sources)
Reynolds, 1971
Smith and Goddard, 1967 (includes an extensive review of the literature)
von Fieandt and Harlahti, 1970
Walraven and Leebeek, 1960

*Target background.* The hue, saturation, and brightness of the target and the background interact in affecting the perception of the target.

Barnes, 1970
Bishop and Crook, 1961
Graham, 1965 (Chapter 16)
Reynolds, White, and Hilgendorf, 1972
Tinker and Paterson, 1931
White, Dainoff, and Reynolds, 1972

*Color vision deficiencies.* Color vision deficiencies of observers produce performance decrements and limit the colors which can be recognized.

Chen, 1971
Feallock, Southard, Kobayashi, and Howell, 1966
Hidalgo, 1969
Hurvich, 1973
Paulson, 1973
Sloan and Habel, 1955
Wallace, Hextor, and Hecht, 1943

Walraven and Leebeek, 1960

*Other factors affecting color perception: Visual masking.*
Bevan, Jonides, and Collyer, 1970
Teft, 1969

*Other factors affecting color perception: Luminance flicker.*
Crook, Bishop, Feehrer, and Wade, 1960
Hidalgo, 1969

*Other factors affecting color perception: Figural aftereffects.*
Crawford and Kingaman, 1966

*Other factors affecting color perception: Auditory noise.*
Chason and Berry, 1971

*Other factors affecting color perception: Target overlap.*
Newman and Davis, 1962
Rizy, 1967
Smith, 1963b
Snadowsky, Rizy, and Elias, 1966

## Influence of Color Contrast on Visual Acuity

Color contrast may enhance the spatial resolution of targets but there remains some controversy as to how good color contrast is in this regard relative to brightness contrast.

Cavonius, 1965 (also Cavonius and Schumacher, 1966)
Chen, 1971
Crook, Hanson, Shor, and Winterberg, 1959
Eastman Kodak Co., 1944
Guth and Eastman, 1970
Hilz and Cavonius, 1970a, 1970b
McLean, 1965

## Absolute Identification of Colors

The following studies were concerned with specifying the maximum number of colors which can be identified and specifying which colors are best under different conditions of the target and the background hue, saturation, and brightness. The studies are divided into those concerned with luminous targets and those concerned with surface colors. The latter are further grouped according to whether they use the Munsell or the Federal color specifications.

*Luminous sources of colored light.*
Bishop and Crook, 1961
Chapanis and Halsey, 1956
Das, 1966
Halsey, 1959a, 1959b
Halsey and Chapanis, 1951, 1954
Indow and Stevens, 1966
Kintz, Parker, and Boynton, 1969

*Munsell color specification.*
Chapanis, 1965
Chapanis and Overbey, 1971
Conover, 1959
Conover and Kraft, 1958
Hanes and Rhoades, 1959
White, Dainoff, and Reynolds, 1972

*Federal color specification.*
Feallock, Southard, Kobayashi, and Howell, 1966
Horowitz and Fromer, 1959

## Memory for Target Colors

The retention of target colors may be superior, relative to other achromatic target features depending upon when and how the color of the target is specified.

Alden, Wedell, and Kanarick, 1971
Brown, 1960
Clark, 1969
Crannell, 1964
Dick, 1969, 1970
Heider, 1972
Herring and Bryden, 1970
Kanarick and Petersen, 1971
Lappin, 1967
Lawrence and LaBerge, 1956
Rabbitt, 1962
Tate and Springer, 1971
von Wright, 1968a, 1968b, 1970

*Reaction Time to Color Targets*

The following studies were usually designed to investigate theoretical concepts for information processing rather than to investigate reaction time to color targets, *per se*. They are listed here due to their implications for the use of color in displays.

Bernstein and Segal, 1968
Berry, 1967
Downing and Gossman, 1970
Ellis and Chase, 1971
Finn and Lit, 1971
LaBerge, 1971
Lit, Young, and Shaffer, 1971
Stone, 1969, 1971
Stone and Peeke, 1971
Warm, Loeb, and Alluisi, 1967

*Some Miscellaneous Studies Using Color Targets*

*Visibility of color underwater.*
Behan, Behan, and Wendhausen, 1972
Kinney, Luria, and Weitzman, 1967, 1968
*Detection of markers and warning signals.*
Hilgendorf, 1969, 1970, 1971
Judd, 1973
Kurke, 1956
Lamar, 1956
Lavender and Ekstrom, 1968
MacNeill, 1965
Papaloïzos, 1961
Reynolds, White, and Hilgendorf, 1972
*Color in maps.*
Christner and Ray, 1961
Shontz, Trumm, and Williams, 1971
Wong and Yacoumelos, 1973
*Aerial reconnaissance: Photography.*
Anson, 1966, 1967, 1970
Jeffrey and Beck, 1972
Kraft and Anderson, 1973
*Aerial reconnaissance: Television.*
Fowler and Jones, 1972
*Camouflage.*
Fletcher and Siegel, 1968
Gee and Humphreys, 1965
Siegel and Fletcher, 1969
*Filing tasks.*
Konz and Koe, 1969
Long, Lebo, and Ogden, 1969
*Task organization.*
Krulee, Gapp, Landi, and Manelski, 1964

Poock, 1969
Promisel, 1961
Puig and Zenhausern, 1967
*Display attraction.*
Cohen and Nelson, 1966
Crannell, 1964
Dooley and Harkins, 1970
Richards and Macklin, 1971
*Observer preference and evaluation.*
Chase, 1970
Christner and Ray, 1961
Jeffrey and Beck, 1972
Munns, 1968
Shutz, 1961

## ACKNOWLEDGMENTS

This project was performed for the Joint Army Navy Aircraft Instrumentation Research (JANAIR) program and was sponsored by the Office of Naval Research, Contract N00014-70-A-0147-003. I wish to express my appreciation to Commander John E. Hammack, contract monitor, for his encouragement and understanding of the problems associated with this kind of research. I am especially grateful to Warren H. Teichner, the principal investigator, for his many helpful suggestions and comments. I am grateful as well to Diane H. Harmon who directed the literature research and kept track of the papers upon which this research is based, and to Nancy E. Hutchcroft who prepared the figures used in the paper.

## REFERENCES

Alden, D. G., Wedell, J. R., and Kanarick, A. F. Redundant stimulus coding and keeping-track performance. *Psychonomic Science*, 1971, *22*, 201-202.

Allport, D. A. Parallel encoding within and between elementary stimulus dimensions. *Perception & Psychophysics*, 1971, *10*, 104-108.

Alluisi, E. A. and Muller, P. F., Jr. Verbal and motor responses to seven symbolic visual codes: A study in S-R compatibility. *Journal of Experimental Psychology*, 1958, *55*, 247-254.

Anderson, N. S. and Fitts, P. M. Amount of information gained during brief exposures of numerals and colors. *Journal of Experimental Psychology*, 1958, *56*, 352-369.

Anson, A. Color photo comparison. *Photogrammetric Engineering*, 1966, *32*, 286-297.

Anson, A. The stereoscopic effect of color. *Photogrammetric Engineering*, 1967, *33*, 371-376.

Anson, A. Color aerial photos in the reconnaissance of soils and rocks. *Photogrammetric Engineering*, 1970, *36*, 343-354.

Barnes, J. A. The effect of cockpit lighting systems on multicolored displays. Human Engineering Labs, Aberdeen Proving Ground, Technical Memorandum 30-70, December, 1970.

Bauer, R. W. Night flight vision: II. Psychophysical comparisons of three colors of cockpit lighting. Human Engineering Labs, Aberdeen Proving Ground, Technical Memorandum 13-68, October, 1968.

Behan, F. L., Behan, R. A., and Wendhausen, H. W. Color perception underwater. *Human Factors*, 1972, *14*, 41-44.

Bernstein, I. H. and Segal, E. M. Set and temporal integration, *Perception & Psychophysics*, 1968, *4*, 233-236.

Berry, C. Timing of cognitive responses in naming task. *Nature*, 1967, *215*, 1203-1204.

Bevan, W., Jonides, J., and Collyer, S. C. Chromatic relationships in metacontrast suppression. *Psychonomic Science*, 1970, *19*, 367-368.

Bishop, H. P. Separation thresholds for colored bars with and without luminance contrast. *Psychonomic Science*, 1966, *4*, 223-224.

Bishop, H. P. and Crook, M. N. Absolute identification of color for targets presented against white and colored backgrounds. Wright Air Development Division, Technical Report 60-611, March, 1961.

Brooks, R. Search time and color coding. *Psychonomic Science*, 1965, *2*, 281-282.

Brown, J. Evidence for a selective process during perception of tachistoscopically presented stimuli. *Journal of Experimental Psychology*, 1960, *59*, 176-181.

Cavonius, C. R. Human visual acuity measured with colored stimuli. Human Sciences Research, Inc., McLean, Virginia, Research Report 65/8-CR, September, 1965.

Cavonius, C. R. and Hilz, R. Visual performance after preadaptation to colored lights. *Journal of Experimental Psychology*, 1970, *83*, 359-365.

Cavonius, C. R. and Schumacher, A. W. Human visual acuity measured with colored test objects. *Science*, 1966, *152*, 1276-1277.

Chapanis, A. Color names for color space. *American Scientist*, 1965, *53*, 327-346.

Chapanis, A. and Halsey, R. M. Absolute judgments of spectrum colors. *Journal of Psychology*, 1956, *42*, 99-103.

Chapanis, A. and Overbey, C. M. Absolute judgment of colors using natural color names. *Perception and Psychophysics*, 1971, *9*, 356-360.

Chase, W. D. Evaluation of several TV display system configurations for visual simulation of the landing approach. *IEEE Transactions on Man-Machine Systems*, 1970, *MMS-11*, 140-149.

Chason, L. R. and Berry, G. A. Effect of white noise on color vision. Proceedings, 79th Annual Convention of the American Psychological Association, 1971, 585-586.

Chen, Y. W. Visual discrimination of color normals and color deficients. *AV Communication Review*, 1971, *19*, 417-431.

Christner, C. A. and Ray, H. W. An evaluation of the effect of selected combinations of target and background coding on map-reading performance: Exp. V. *Human Factors*, 1961, *3*, 131-146.

Clark, S. E. Retrieval of color information from preperceptual memory. *Journal of Experimental Psychology*, 1969, *82*, 263-266.

Cohen, D. B. and Nelson, W. H. Effect of differently colored incidental stimuli on cued discriminations. *Perceptual and Motor Skills*, 1966, *22*, 143-146.

Conners, M. M. Luminance requirements for hue perception in small targets. *Journal of the Optical Society of America*, 1968, *58*, 258-263.

Conners, M. M. Luminance requirements for hue identification in small targets. *Journal of the Optical Society of America*, 1969, *59*, 91.

Conners, M. M. Luminance requirements for hue perception and identification for a range of exposure durations. *Journal of the Optical Society of America*, 1970, *60*, 958.

Conover, D. W. The amount of information in the absolute judgment of Munsell hues. WADC TN-58-262, Wright Air Development Center, WPAFB, Ohio, 1959.

Conover, D. W. and Kraft, J. The use of color in coding displays. WADC TR-55-471, Wright Air Development Center, WPAFB, Ohio, 1958.

Crannell, C. W. Code learning and color. *Journal of Psychology*, 1964, *58*, 295-299.

Crawford, F. T. and Klingaman, R. L. Figural aftereffects as a function of hue. *Journal of Experimental Psychology*, 1966, *72*, 916-918.

Crook, M. N. and Bishop, H. P. The discriminability of simulated achromatic radar scope targets. Institute for Applied Experimental Psychology, Tufts University, June, 1957.

Crook, M. N., Bishop, H. P., Feehrer, C. E., and Wade, E. A. Luminance reintensification at frequencies from 40 to 300 cycles per second as a factor in the reading of simulated visual displays. Institute for Psychological Research, Tufts University, Final Report, October, 1960.

Crook, M. N., Hanson, J. A., Shor, R. E., and Winterberg, R. P. The discrimination of simulated colored radar scope targets. Institute for Applied Experimental Psychology, Tufts University, November, 1959.

Crumley, L., Divany, R., Gates, S., Hostetter, R., and Hurst, P. Display problems in aerospace surveillance systems. Part I. A survey of display hardware and analysis of relevant psychological variables. HRB-Singer, Inc. 256-R-2, Part I., June, 1961.

Das, S. R. Recognition of signal colors by a different set of color names. *Journal of the Optical Society of America*, 1966, *56*, 789-794.

Dick, A. O. Relations between the sensory register and short-term storage in tachistoscopic recognition. *Journal of Experimental Psychology*, 1969, *82*, 279-284.

Dick, A. O. Visual processing and the use of redundant information in tachistoscopic recognition. *Canadian Journal of Psychology*, 1970, *24*, 133-141.

Dooley, R. P. and Harkins, L. E. Functional and attention-getting effects of color on graphic communications. *Perceptual and Motor Skills*, 1970, *31*, 851-854.

Downing, B. D. and Gossman, J. R. Parallel processing of multidimensional stimuli. *Perception & Psychophysics*, 1970, *8*, 57-60.

Dudek, R. A. and Colton, G. M. Effects of lighting and background with common signal lights on human peripheral color vision. *Human Factors*, 1970, *12*, 401-407.

Eastman Kodak Company. Influence of color contrast on visual acuity. Report, NDRC contract number OEmsr-1070, 1944.

Egeth, H. and Pachella, R. Multidimensional stimulus identification. *Perception & Psychophysics*, 1969, *5*, 341-346.

Ellis, S. H. and Chase, W. G. Parallel processing in item recognition. *Perception & Psychophysics*, 1971, *10*, 379-384.

Eriksen, C. W. Location of objects in a visual display as a function of the number of dimensions on which the objects differ. *Journal of Experimental Psychology*, 1952, *44*, 56-60.

Eriksen, C. W. Object location in a complex perceptual field. *Journal of Experimental Psychology*, 1953, *45*, 126-132.

Eriksen, C. W. and Hake, H. W. Multidimensional stimulus differences and accuracy of discrimination. *Journal of Experimental Psychology*, 1955, *50*, 153-160.

Feallock, J. B., Southard, J. F., Kobayashi, M., and Howell, W. C. Absolute judgment of colors in the Federal Standards System. *Journal of Applied Psychology*, 1966, *50*, 266-272.

Finn, J. P. and Lit, A. Effect of photometrically matched wavelength on simple reaction time at scotopic and photopic levels of illumination. Proceedings, 79th Annual Convention of the American Psychological Association, 1971, 5-6.

Fletcher, D. E. and Siegel, A. I. Literature survey-visual data relevant to aircraft camouflage. Applied Psychological Services, Wayne, Pennsylvania, Report Number NADC-AC-6806, March, 1968.

Fowler, F. D. and Jones, D. B. Target acquisition studies: (2) Target acquisition performance–color vs. monochrome TV displays. Martin Marietta Corp., OR 11,768, January, 1972.

Garner, W. R. Information integration and form of encoding. In A. W. Milton and E. Martin (Ed.) *Coding processes in human memory*. New York: John Wiley, 1972.

Garner, W. R. and Creelman, C. D. Effect of redundancy and duration on absolute judgments of visual stimuli. *Journal of Experimental Psychology*, 1964, 67, 168-172.

Gee, D. L. and Humphreys, A. H. User review of camouflage for the individual combat solider in the field. U.S. Army Engineer Research and Development Labs., Fort Belvoir, Virginia, Report 1834, October, 1965.

Graham, C. H. (Ed.) *Vision and visual perception*. New York: John Wiley, 1965.

Grant, D. A. and Curran, J. F. Relative difficulty of number, form and color concepts of a Weigl-type problem using unsystematic number cards. *Journal of Experimental Psychology*, 1952, 43, 408-413.

Green, B. F. and Anderson, L. K. Color coding in a visual search task. *Journal of Experimental Psychology*, 1956, 51, 19-24.

Guth, S. K. and Eastman, A. A. Chromatic contrast. *American Journal of Optometry and Archives of American Academy of Optometry*, 1970, 47, 526-534.

Halsey, R. M. Identification of signal lights: I. Blue, green, white, and purple. *Journal of the Optical Society of America*, 1959, 49, 45-55. (a)

Halsey, R. M. Identification of signal lights: II. Elimination of the purple category. *Journal of the Optical Society of America*, 1959, 49, 167-169. (b)

Halsey, R. M. and Chapanis, A. On the number of absolutely identifiable spectral hues. *Journal of the Optical Society of America*, 1951, 41, 1057-1058.

Halsey, R. M. and Chapanis, A. Chromaticity-confusion contours in a complex viewing situation. *Journal of the Optical Society of America*, 1954, 44, 442-454.

Hanes, R. M. and Rhoades, M. V. Color identification as a function of extended practice. *Journal of the Optical Society of America*, 1959, 49, 1060-1064.

Heider, E. R. Universals in color naming and memory. *Journal of Experimental Psychology*, 1972, 93, 10-20.

Herring, B. S. and Bryden, M. P. Memory colour effects as a function of viewing time. *Canadian Journal of Psychology*, 1970, 24, 127-131.

Hidalgo, Z. D. Effects of intermittent stimulation on hue and saturation discrimination of color defectives and normals. *American Journal of Optometry and Archives of American Academy of Optometry*, 1969, 46, 929-938.

Hilgendorf, R. L. Optimal colors for markers and signals. Survival and Flight Equipment (SAFE) Association. Proceedings of the Seventh National Flight Safety, Survival and Personal Equipment Symposium, October, 1969, 121-131.

Hilgendorf, R. L. An optimal hierarchy of colors for markers and signals. Survival and Flight Equipment (SAFE) Association. Eighth Annual Symposium Proceedings, September, 1970, 143-155.

Hilgendorf, R. L. Colors for markers and signals: Inflight validation. Survival and Flight Equipment (SAFE) Association, Ninth Annual Symposium Proceedings, September, 1971, 123-127.

Hilz, R. and Cavonius, C. R. Sehschärfe bei Farbunterschieden ohne Helligkeitsunterschiede. *Vision Research*, 1970, 10, 1393-1398. (a)

Hilz, R. and Cavonius, C. R. Wavelength discrimination measured with square-wave gratings. *Journal of the Optical Society of America*, 1970, 60, 273-277. (b)

Hitt, W. D. An evaluation of five different abstract coding methods. Exp. IV. *Human Factors*, 1961, 3, 120-130.

Hodge, M. H. Influence of irrelevant information upon complex visual discrimination. *Journal of Experimental Psychology*, 1959, 57, 1-5.

Horowitz, M. W. and Fromer, R. A set of discriminable surface colors and symbols for coding in animated training panels. U.S. Naval Training Device Center, Technical Report NAVTRADEVCEN 20-0S-52, May, 1959.

Hurvich, L. M. Color vision deficiencies. In Committee on Vision, Division of Behavioral Sciences, National Research Council, *Color vision*, National Academy of Sciences, 1973, 1-33.

Indow, T. and Stevens, S. S. Scaling of saturation and hue. *Perception & Psychophysics*, 1966, 1, 253-271.

Jainski, P. The effect of dazzle on electronic display visibility in modern high-performance aircraft cockpits: A summary. German Federal Ministry of Defence, Research project T II 3, (No. T-808-I-203). Royal Aircraft Establishment Library Translation 1545, March, 1971.

Jeffrey, T. E. and Beck, F. J. Intelligence information from total optical color imagery. U.S. Army Behavior and Systems Research Laboratory, Research Memorandum 72-4, November, 1972.

Jones, M. R. Color coding. *Human Factors*, 1962, 4, 355-365.

Judd, D. B. Color in visual signaling. In Committee on Vision, Division of Behavioral Sciences, National Research Council, *Color vision*, National Academy of Sciences, 1973, 65-82.

Kaiser, P. K. Color names of very small fields varying in duration and luminance. *Journal of the Optical Society of America*, 1968, 58, 849-852.

Kanarick, A. F. and Petersen, R. C. Redundant color coding and keeping-track performance. *Human Factors*, 1971, 13, 183-188.

Kinney, J. A. S., Luria, S. M., and Weitzman, D. O. Visibility of colors underwater. *Journal of the Optical Society of America*, 1967, 57, 802-809.

Kinney, J. A. S., Luria, S. M., and Weitzman, D. O. The underwater visibility of colors with artificial illumination. Naval Submarine Medical Center, Research Report No. 551, October, 1968.

Kintz, R. T., Parker, J. A., and Boynton, R. M. Information transmission in spectral color naming. *Perception & Psychophysics*, 1969, 5, 241-245.

Konz, S. A. and Koe, B. A. The effect of color coding on performance of an alphabetic filing task. *Human Factors*, 1969, 11, 207-212.

Kraft, C. L. and Anderson, C. D. Prediction of target acquisition performance of aerial observers and photointerpreters with and without stereoscopic aids. Aerospace Medical Research Lab, Wright-Patterson AFB, Ohio, 1973, in prep.

Kraft, C. L., Booth, J. M., and Boucek, G. P., Jr. Achromatic and chromatic stereoscopic performance. Paper presented at the Color Symposium for Commission 1, 12th Congress of the International Society for Photogrammetry, Ottawa, Canada, July, 1972.

Krulee, G. K., Gapp, A., Landi, D. M., and Manelski, D. M. Organizing factors and immediate memory span. *Perceptual and Motor Skills*, 1964, *18*, 533-548.

Kurke, M. I. Evaluation of a display incorporating quantitative and check-reading characteristics. *Journal of Applied Psychology*, 1956, *40*, 233-236.

LaBerge, D. On the processing of simple visual and auditory stimuli at distinct levels. *Perception & Psychophysics*, 1971, *9*, 331-334.

Lamar, E. S. Vision in air sea rescue search. Center for Naval Analysis Operations Evaluation Group, Study 250, February, 1946.

Lappin, J. S. Attention in the identification of stimuli in complex visual displays. *Journal of Experimental Psychology*, 1957, *75*, 321-328.

Lappin, J. S. and Ellis, S. H. The span of apprehension: Form identification as a function of amount of information displayed. *Perception & Psychophysics*, 1970, *7*, 65-72.

Lavender, H. J., Jr. and Ekstrom, R. M. A red-green paradox? *Human Factors*, 1968, *10*, 63-66.

Lawrence, D. H. and LaBerge, D. L. Relationship between recognition accuracy and order of reporting stimulus dimensions. *Journal of Experimental Psychology*, 1956, *51*, 12-18.

Lederberg, V. Color recognition during voluntary saccades. *Journal of the Optical Society of America*, 1970, *60*, 835-841.

Lehtiö, P. K. The organization of component decisions in visual search. *Acta Psychologica*, 1970, *33*, 93-105.

Lit, A., Young, R. H., and Shaffer, M. Simple time reaction as a function of luminance for various wave lengths. *Perception & Psychophysics*, 1971, *10*, 397-399.

Long, T. R., Lebo, D., and Ogden, D. A simplified method for increasing mailsorting efficiency. *Journal of Applied Psychology*, 1969, *53*, 510-512.

Mackworth, J. F. The relation between the visual image and post-perceptual immediate memory. *Journal of Verbal Learning and Verbal Behavior*, 1963, *2*, 75-85. (a)

Mackworth, J. F. The duration of the visual image. *Canadian Journal of Psychology*, 1963, *17*, 62-81. (b)

MacNeill, R. F. Color and legibility: Caution and warning data-plates. Human Engineering Labs, Aberdeen Proving Ground, Maryland, Technical Note 3-65, November, 1965.

Markoff, J. I. Target recognition performance with chromatic and achromatic displays. Honeywell, Inc. SRM-148, January, 1971.

McLean, M. V. Brightness contrast, color contrast and legibility. *Human Factors*, 1965, *7*, 521-526.

Meister, D. and Sullivan, D. J. Guide to human engineering design for visual displays. Bunker-Ramo Corporation, August, 1969.

Middleton, W. E. K. and Wyszecki, G. W. Visual thresholds in the retinal periphery for red, green and white signal lights. *Journal of the Optical Society of America*, 1961, *51*, 54-56.

Morgan, B. B., Jr. and Alluisi, E. A. Effects of discriminability and irrelevant information on absolute judgment. *Perception & Psychophysics*, 1967, *2*, 54-58.

Munns, M. Some effects of display symbol variation upon operator performance in aircraft interception. *Perceptual and Motor Skills*, 1968, *26*, 1215-1221.

Newman, K. M. and Davis, A. R. Nonredundant color, brightness, and flashing rate encoding of geometric symbols on a visual display. *Journal of Engineering Psychology*, 1962, *1*, 47-67.

Papaloïzos, A. Some characteristics of instrument measuring dials. *Ergonomics*, 1961, *4*, 169-182.

Paulson, H. M. Comparison of color vision tests used by the armed forces. In Committee on Vision, Division of Behavioral Sciences, National Research Council, *Color vision*, National Academy of Sciences, 1973, 34-64.

Payne, M. C., Jr. Color as an independent variable in perceptual research. *Psychological Bulletin*, 1964, *61*, 199-208.

Poock, G. K. Color coding effects in compatible and noncompatible display-control arrangements. *Journal of Applied Psychology*, 1969, *53*, 301-303.

Promisel, D. M. Visual target location as a function of number and kind of competing signals. *Journal of Applied Psychology*, 1961, *45*, 420-427.

Puig, J. and Zenhausern, R. Visual perception in the determination of spacecraft attitude. *Psychonomic Science*, 1967, *8*, 397-398.

Rabbitt, P. M. Short-term retention of more than one aspect of a series of stimuli. *Nature*, 1962, *195*, 102-103.

Reynolds, H. N. The visual effects of exposure to electroluminescent instrument lighting. *Human Factors*, 1971, *13*, 29-40.

Reynolds, R. E., White, R. M., Jr., and Hilgendorf, R. L. Detection and recognition of colored signal lights. *Human Factors*, 1972, *14*, 227-236.

Richards, O. W. and Macklin, P. Colored overhead transparencies: Contrast gain or seeing loss? *AV Communication Review*, 1971, *19*, 423-432.

Rizy, E. F. Dichroic filter specification for color additive displays: II. Further exploration of tolerance areas and the influence of other design variables. Rome Air Development Center, Technical Report No. RADC-TR-67-513, September, 1967.

Schutz, H. G. An evaluation of methods for presentation of graphic multiple trends. Exp. III. *Human Factors*, 1961, *3*, 108-119.

Shontz, W. D., Trumm, G. A., and Williams, L. G. Color coding for information location. *Human Factors*, 1971, *13*, 237-246.

Siegel, A. and Fletcher, D. E. Guide to aircraft in-flight camouflage. Applied Psychological Services, Inc., Wayne, Pennsylvania, Report No. NADC-AC-6904, March, 1969.

Siegel, M. H. The influence of exposure time on color discrimination. *Psychonomic Science*, 1968, *12*, 227-228.

Siegel, M. H. and Siegel, A. B. Color name as a function of surround luminance and stimulus duration. *Perception & Psychophysics*, 1971, *9*, 140-144.

Sloan, L. L. and Habel, A. Recognition of red and green point sources by color-deficient observers. *Journal of the Optical Society of America*, 1955, *45*, 599-601.

Smith, H. A. and Goddard, C. Effects of cockpit lighting color on dark adaptation. Bunker-Ramo Corp. Technical Report AFFDL-TR-67-56, May, 1967.

Smith, S. L. Color coding and visual search. *Journal of Experimental Psychology*, 1962, *64*, 434-440.

Smith, S. L. Color coding and visual separability in information displays. *Journal of Applied Psychology*, 1963, *47*, 358-364. (a)

Smith, S. L. Legibility of overprinted symbols in multicolored displays. *Journal of Engineering Psychology*, 1963, *2*, 82-96. (b)

Smith, S. L., Farquhar, B. B., and Thomas, D. W. Color coding in formatted displays. *Journal of Applied Psychology*, 1965, *49*, 393-398.

Smith, S. L. and Thomas, D. W. Color versus shape coding in information displays. *Journal of Applied Psychology*, 1964, *48*, 137-146.

Snadowsky, A. M., Rizy, E. F., and Elias, M. F. Symbol identification as a function of misregistration in color additive displays. *Perceptual and Motor Skills*, 1966, *22*, 951-960.

Snyder, C. R. R. Selection, inspection, and naming in visual search. *Journal of Experimental Psychology*, 1972, *92*, 428-431.

Stone, G. C. Response latencies in matching and oddity performance: Effects of format, stimulus, and demand variables. *Perceptual and Motor Skills*, 1969, *29*, 219-232.

Stone, G. C. Response latencies in visual search involving redundant or irrelevant information. *Perception & Psychophysics*, 1971, *9*, 9-14.

Stone, G. C. and Peeke, S. Stimulus characteristics, output requirements, and latencies of response to visual stimuli. Proceedings, 79th Annual Convention of the American Psychological Association, 1971, 3-4.

Tate, J. D. and Springer, R. M. Effects of memory time on successive judgments. *Psychological Bulletin*, 1971, *76*, 394-408.

Teft, L. W. The effects of stimulus hue on backward masking under conditions of monoptic and dichoptic stimulus presentation. *Psychonomic Science*, 1969, *16*, 287-288.

Teichner, W. H. The detection of a simple visual signal as a function of time of watch. *Human Factors*, 1974, *16*, 339-353.

Teichner, W. H. and Krebs, M. J. Laws of simple visual reaction time. *Psychological Review*, 1972, *79*, 344-358.

Teichner, W. H. and Krebs, M. J. Laws of visual choice reaction time. *Psychological Review*, 1974, *81*, 75-98.

Tinker, M. A. and Paterson, D. G. Variations in color of print and background. *Journal of Applied Psychology*, 1931, *15*, 471-479.

von Fieandt, K. and Harlahti, J. New studies on perimetric thresholds of pigment colours. *Annales Academiae Scientiarum Fennicae*, 1970, B-167, 1 (Helsinki).

von Wright, J. M. Selection in visual immediate memory. *Quarterly Journal of Experimental Psychology*, 1968, *20*, 62-68. (a)

von Wright, J. M. Selection in visual immediate memory, II. *Reports from the Institute of Psychology, University of Turku* (Finland), No. 31, 1968. (b)

von Wright, J. M. On selection in visual immediate memory. *Acta Psychologica*, 1970, *33*, 280-292.

Wallace, S. R., Hextor, P. L., and Hecht, S. Color vision and its relation to the detection of camouflage. Psychological Section, Office of the Surgeon Hqs., Army Air Forces Training Command. Research Bulletin Hq. 43-6, Oct., 1943.

Walraven, P. L. and Leebeek, H. L. Recognition of color code by normal and color defectives at several illumination levels. An evaluation study of the N.R.R. plates. *American Journal of Optometry*, 1960, *37*, 82-92.

Warm, J. S., Loeb, M., and Alluisi, E. A. Effects of color, relative position, and the onset or offset of signals in a watchkeeping task. *Psychonomic Science*, 1967, *9*, 95-96.

Weissman, S. Effects of luminance on the perception of red and green at various retinal positions. *Journal of the Optical Society of America*, 1965, *55*, 884-887.

Weitzman, D. O. and Kinney, J. A. S. Appearance of color for small, brief, spectral stimuli in the central fovea. *Journal of the Optical Society of America*, 1967, *57*, 665-670.

Weitzman, D. O. and Kinney, J. A. S. Effect of stimulus size, duration, and retinal location upon the appearance of color. *Journal of the Optical Society of America*, 1969, *59*, 640.

White, R. M., Jr., Dainoff, M. J., and Reynolds, R. E. Factors affecting the detection and recognition of colored targets. Aerospace Medical Research Lab. Technical Report, 72-38, May, 1972.

Williams, L. G. The effect of target specification on objects fixated during visual search. *Perception & Psychophysics*, 1966, *1*, 315-318.

Williams, L. G. Studies of extrafoveal discrimination and detection. In Committee on Vision, Division of Behavioral Sciences, National Research Council, *Visual search*, Symposium at spring meeting, 1970. National Academy of Sciences, 1973.

Williams, L. G. and Wallen, D. J. Generalizing from the corneal reflection technique: A methodological study. *Perceptual and Motor Skills*, 1965, *21*, 807-810.

Wong, K. W. and Yacoumelos, N. G. Identification of cartographic symbols from TV displays. *Human Factors*, 1973, *15*, 21-31.

# Airborne Displays for Flight and Navigation

STANLEY N. ROSCOE, *Display Systems Department, Hughes Aircraft Company, Culver City, California*

*This paper deals with certain types of airborne displays, specifically, those used in navigating and flying aircraft. Consideration is given to the nature of the crew's flight task, to certain principles of flight display, and to some of the experimental evidence bearing on principles of display.*

## FOREWORD

Commercial aviation is on the threshold of Category II instrument flight and is working concurrently toward the longer-range goal of all-weather Category III flight capability. Category II certification will allow an aircraft to land when the visual ceiling is as low as 100 feet and the runway visual range (RVR) is as little as 1200 feet. For Category III the corresponding values become zero-zero. While Category II will be an impressive achievement, the final step to Category III is indeed a big one. To achieve Category III means that a flight crew can complete all phases of a flight from takeoff to landing without ever seeing the outside world from the cockpit. Thus Category III requires a complete instrument flight capability. The demands of this ultimate step warrant a reevaluation of traditional approaches to cockpit instrumentation and of the basic pilot techniques used in aircraft navigation and control.

## THE NATURE OF THE FLIGHT TASK

The flight task is inherently a goal-directed activity (Williams, 1947). Every flight has a start and an end, and in order to complete the flight successfully, sub-goals must be set up and met for all phases of flight from takeoff to landing. Thus it is necessary to equip the aircraft with onboard data management and display systems that will allow the crew (1) to set up these sub-goals of flight, or "indices of desired performance," and (2) to control the aircraft in such a manner that these sub-goals are all met with precision and safety.

Throughout the flight, sub-goals must be set up for (1) the altitude to fly, (2) the direction to fly, (3) the time or distance to fly, and (4) the mechanical operation of the aircraft including all its sub-systems.

In order to set up these sub-goals the crew must take into account the physical facts of the flight. These include the performance characteristics of the aircraft itself, the presence and flight paths of other aircraft in the traffic flow to the extent required to avoid collision, the weather, the terrain over which the flight is being made, any characteristics of the crew and the passengers that might impose constraints upon the flight, and finally the body of rules that governs flight in the National Airspace System.

Thus from a knowledge of the goal of the flight and the physical facts involved, the crew must set up and achieve the various sub-goals leading to a successful flight. It is the express function of onboard data management and display systems to facilitate this process.

If the systems employed in the aircraft are to perform this function most effectively, they must provide the crew with the proper information, logically grouped for ease of interpretation, and

effectively coded to allow positive and precise control of the aircraft. Through analysis and experimentation it is possible to establish:
(1) the information requirements,
(2) logical rules for grouping related information into integrated displays, and
(3) principles for encoding information for ease of interpretation and control.

Since the information required for the navigation and control of aircraft is reasonably well established, the most profitable areas for potential improvement in aircraft instrumentation are first, in the grouping of information into integrated displays and, second, in the modes of presentation of the displayed information.

In order to develop an analytical rationale for the grouping and coding of displayed information, it is helpful to consider the nature of the crew's task in navigating and controlling an aircraft (Carel, 1965). The aircrew's overall task consists largely of the iterative asking and answering of four basic questions:
(1) What should be my route to my destination, and where am I with respect to my desired route and destination?
(2) What should be my velocity vector, and what is it now?
(3) What should be my attitude, thrust, and configuration, and what are they now?
(4) What should I do with the controls to correct discrepancies that may exist in items 1, 2, and 3?

These questions constitute categories of information, ranging from the most general to the most specific, and for each of these categories there is a desirable state of affairs at any particular moment; that is, sub-goals must be set up and achieved for each of these categories.

The categories of information, however, are not independent but are inherently related since the only way the crew can affect any of the sub-goals of flight is by manipulating the controls. Doing so directly causes changes in the attitude, thrust, and external configuration of the aircraft, which in turn indirectly affects its velocity vector, and this in turn indirectly affects its position in space and/or time. Thus the sub-goals of flight are in fact related in a hierarchical fashion in the order stated, and the crew's overall job is therefore comprised of a hierarchical series of tasks in which they are required to realize a goal at one level of the hierarchy by programming a set of sub-goals for the task at the next subordinate level in the hierarchy. Ultimately this all boils down to the manipulation of controls.

Figure 1 is a diagram illustrating this concept and is intended to show that the crew's tasks are interrelated in a hierarchical fashion and that the higher order loops impose forcing functions on subordinate loops. Each of these loops can be considered as a closed loop system, but it is a mistake to consider only the closed loop aspect of each loop taken separately. The consequence is that we have in current aircraft flight-director-type tracking displays that deal with loop 4, attitude displays that deal with loop 3, navigation displays that deal with loop 2, and maps that are used in dealing with loop 1. The fact that the information required in adjacent loops is related is seldom taken into account in display design, and

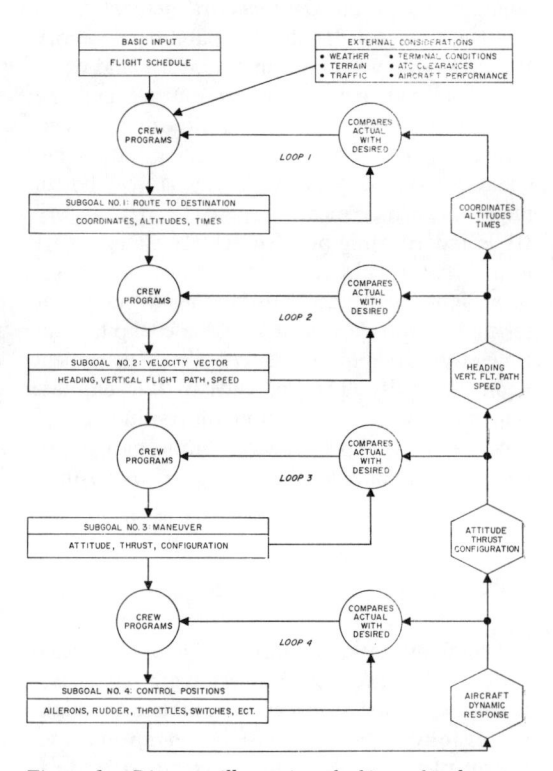

*Figure 1. Diagram illustrating the hierarchical nature of the flight task.*

the way the subordinate variables affect the attainment of the next superior set of goals is not often displayed.

The concept of the hierarchical nature of the aircrew's tasks provides the rationale for the logical grouping of information into a relatively small number of integrated displays. The basic notion is that hierarchically related information should be presented in a common frame of reference or coordinate system. The first problem is to decide how far to carry this integration process. Analysis and experience suggest that at least two views of the flight domain should be presented, a horizontal or downward-looking view used for navigation and a vertical or forward-looking view used for flight control. Furthermore, it is evident that certain categories of information, such as altitude and speed, for various reasons cannot readily be incorporated into either view and therefore require separate displays.

Finally, since visual displays convey information largely by the movement of their indices, it is necessary to decide upon a consistent and natural set of movement relationships. This is a central problem in the design of visual displays. Fortunately there is some experimental evidence providing an empirical basis for deciding upon appropriate movement relationships.

## PRINCIPLES OF DISPLAY

Let us consider some principles or rules that bear upon the design of flight and navigation display systems. First I will state the principles, then discuss them one at a time, giving experimental evidence supporting the validity of the principles.

### The Principle of Display Integration

The first principle has already been introduced in the preceding discussion, but just what we mean when we say that a display is integrated requires further amplification. Simply combining a large number of information items into a single display unit does not necessarily result in an integrated display. The basic notion of display integration requires that related information is presented in a common reference system which allows the relationships among the items to be perceived directly.

Perhaps the clearest example of display integration and its benefits can be provided by a brief consideration of map-type navigation displays. These relatively new devices have been in military service since 1959, are being incorporated into most military aircraft currently under development, and appear certain to be adopted by the airlines in the near future. A photograph of a typical map-type navigation display is shown in Figure 2.

Basically, map-type horizontal situation displays present the position and heading of the aircraft relative to a map of the area. Information required to provide this presentation has traditionally been shown on the following separate cockpit indicators:

(1) a magnetic compass or directional gyro showing aircraft heading,
(2) a manually settable course selector dial, establishing a desired radial flight path to or from a VORTAC or TACAN radio facility,
(3) a course deviation indicator showing the direction and relative magnitude of the deviation of the aircraft's position from the selected radial,
(4) a TO/FROM indication showing whether the aircraft's present position is along the inbound or outbound leg of the selected radial course, and
(5) a DME counter showing the slant range of the aircraft to or from the radio facility.

By observing and integrating these various indications and continually referring to hand-held charts, it is possible for a pilot to determine his approximate position relative to a VORTAC or TACAN station, and by flying the proper series of headings, he can cause the aircraft to make good a flight path to or from a radio facility along a desired radial.

With a map-type navigation display, the various quantities and discrete indications just listed are combined into a single, integrated presentation showing graphically the horizontal flight situation represented by the numerous separate indications with all of the relationships among the indications being immediately apparent. No transformations are required by the pilot to interpret the display's indications.

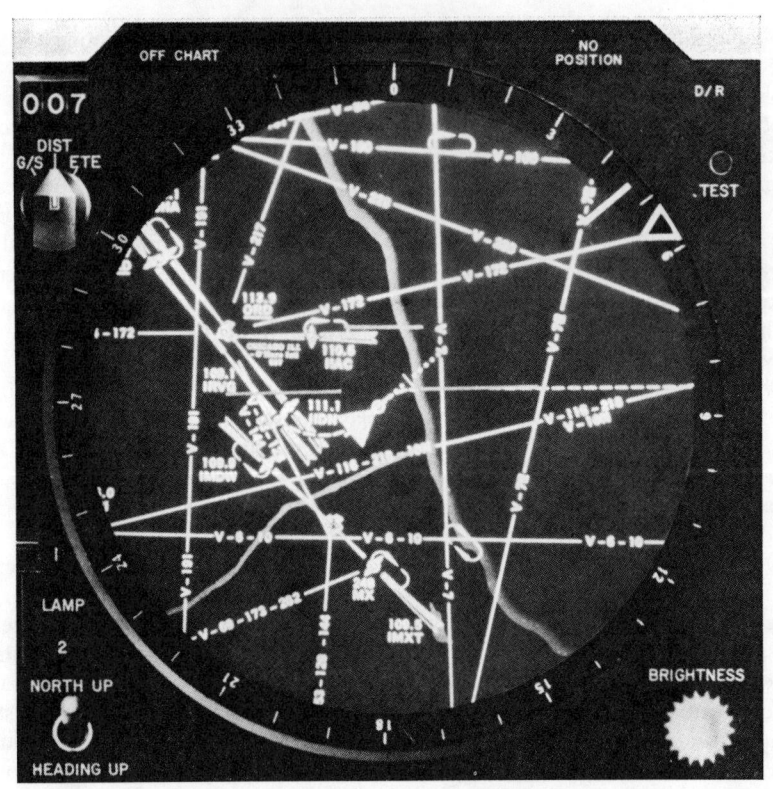

*Figure 2. A typical map-type navigation display.*

The differences in a pilot's ability to control the flight path of the aircraft using the two types of presentations are truly dramatic as indicated by the actual flight path recordings shown in Figure 3. These recordings show the best and worst flight paths flown by several instrument-rated pilots on four terminal area navigation problems using the two types of display presentations (Roscoe, *et al*, 1950). Included in the recordings for the conventional separated indicators are several completely incorrect problem solutions. There were no such cases with the map-type display. It is safe to say that no pilot has ever become lost or failed to solve a terminal area navigation problem while using a map-type navigation display that was working properly.

As an important fringe benefit, the pilots controlled their airspeed, altitude, and attitude significantly better when using the map display than when using the separated indicators. This was true despite the fact that the map display showed none of these items. Presumably the pilots could devote more attention to the control of the aircraft because, with the map display, less attention was required by their basic navigation task.

As stated previously, map displays offer perhaps the best example of the benefits of display integration, but there are many other notable examples. Equally dramatic results can be achieved through the proper integration of related information in vertical situation displays and even altimetry displays.

*The Principle of Pictorial Realism*

Not all of the benefits of map displays and vertical situation displays can be attributed to the fact that they are integrated. It is also true that they lend themselves to the application of pictorial realism because they are basically analog as

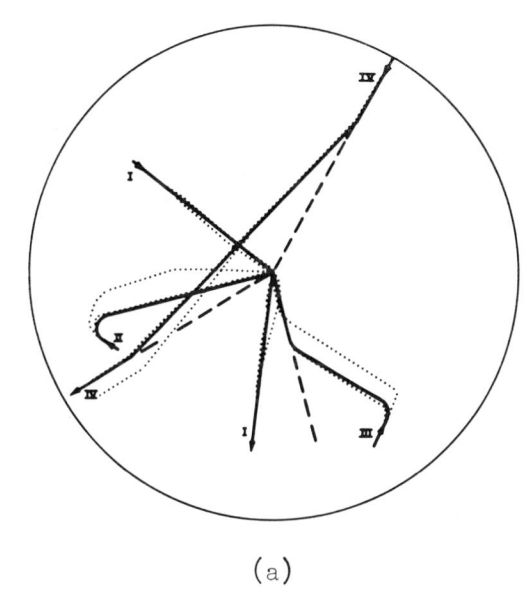

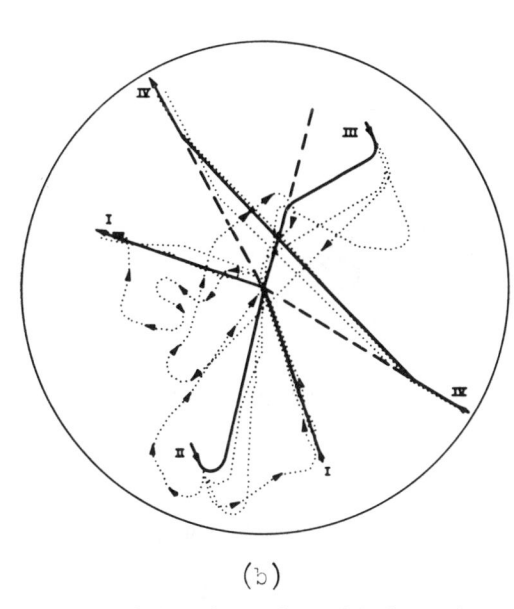

*Figure 3. Flight path recordings of the best and worst solutions to four terminal area navigation problems flown by instrument pilots using a map-type pictorial navigation display (a) and using conventional separated symbolic flight displays (b).*

opposed to digital presentations. Their information content is encoded graphically so that the symbols presented can be readily identified with what they represent. It is extremely difficult if not impossible to achieve a similar effect with displays that are basically digital such as counter readouts or moving tapes read against a fixed lubber line index.

An altimetry experiment bears directly on this subject (Simon and Roscoe, 1956). In that experiment, subjects were tested on their ability to solve altitude control decision problems using the various displays shown in Figure 4. The displays used were selected to sample three design variables:

(a) Vertical linear scales versus circular scales,
(b) Integrated presentations versus separated presentations of related parameters, and
(c) Spatial analog versus decimal counter presentations.

Time and error performance scores for the four displays are shown in Figures 5 and 6, respectively. In addition to demonstrating once again the superiority of integrated over separated displays, these results show that undistorted spatial analogs having a high degree of pictorial realism—as represented by the vertical linear scale—are superior to distorted spatial analogs—as represented by the circular scale display. It should be noted that the scale of the circular display was the same length and had the same symbols and markings as the vertical scale display. It was as if the linear vertical scale had been wrapped around to form a circle, thereby creating a distorted as opposed to an undistorted spatial analog. It should also be noted that the pictorially realistic spatial analog display of altitude, in which *up* means *up* and *down* means *down* in terms of the aircraft's position and motion in space, was vastly superior to the digital presentation of related values.

*The Principle of the Moving Part*

There is an impressive body of experimental and operational evidence that the part of the display that represents the aircraft should move against a fixed scale or coordinate system rather than having the scale move against a fixed index representing the aircraft. Despite this seemingly overwhelming evidence, the question of what should move on a display is by far the most controversial subject in display design. The issue

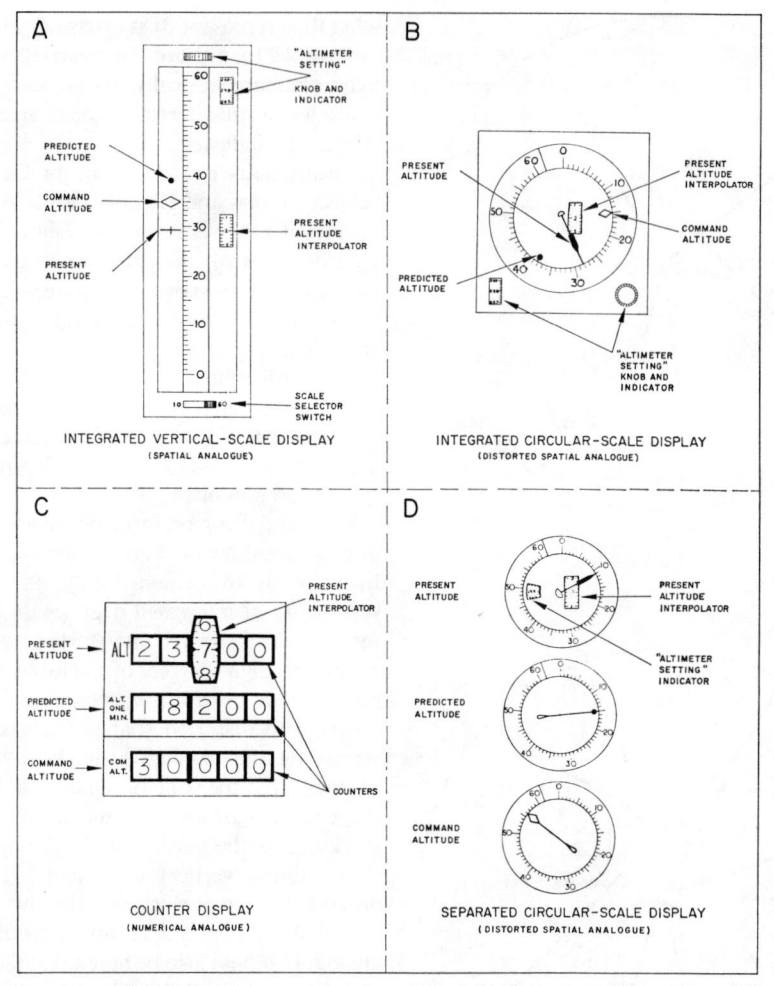

*Figure 4. Four methods of displaying present altitude, predicted altitude in one minute, and command altitude.*

manifests itself in many separate issues. Here are some of them:

(1) Heading—should the compass rose rotate against a fixed lubber line so that heading can always be read at the top of the display, or should a pointer rotate relative to a fixed compass rose so that display movement is clockwise when the aircraft is turning to the right and vice versa?

(2) Altitude—should altitude be represented by one or more pointers moving against a fixed altitude scale or should a moving scale be read against a fixed lubber line index?

(3) Attitude—should the horizon bar move against a fixed aircraft symbol or should the aircraft symbol move against a fixed outside world?

These issues are not simple despite the fact that the bulk of the experimental evidence favors having the aircraft symbol move. The simple explanation of why the aircraft symbol should move is that when a pilot moves a control he "naturally" expects the display indication result-

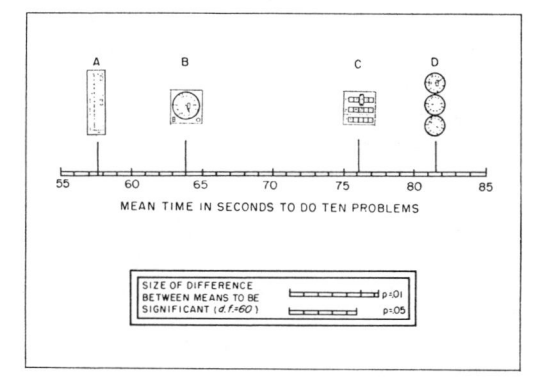

*Figure 5. Time-score performance for all pilots combined in altimetry display comparison.*

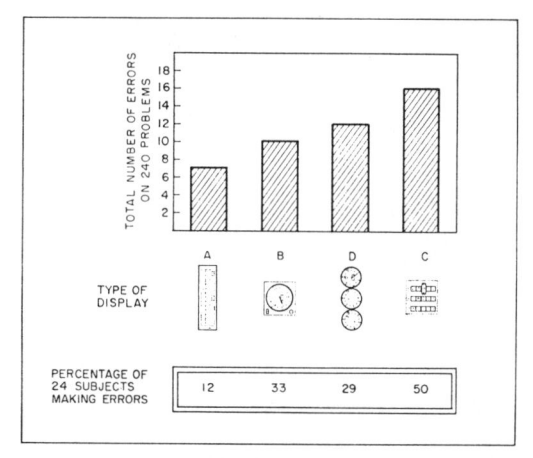

*Figure 6. Number of errors and percentage of subjects making errors on four altimetry displays.*

ing from that control movement to move in the same direction so that up means up, down means down, right means right or clockwise, left means left or counterclockwise, forward means faster, backward means slower, etc. Even more basically, one might say that when a pilot moves a control, he knows he is controlling his aircraft, not the outside world relative to his aircraft, and therefore he expects his aircraft symbols to move. Unfortunately the issue is not that simple.

Before attempting to analyze the problem further, let us consider some of the relevant operational and experimental evidence. During and shortly after the end of World War II a great deal of scientific attention was directed to the question of optimum movement relationships for flight displays.

By studying the patterns of eye movements and fixations of pilots flying ILS approaches, it was discovered that the pilots spent most of their time looking at three instruments: the attitude indicator, the heading indicator, and the cross-pointer indicator (Fitts, Jones, and Milton, 1949). Very little time was spent on the airspeed indicator, the vertical speed indicator, and the altimeter, even though these instruments also provided critical information. It was then noted that the first three displays were ones in which the scales, or the parts of the display representing the outside world, moved.

On the displays in the latter group, pointers moved against fixed scales so that unique positions on the displays had unique meaning. For example, if one were to remove the scale from the airspeed indicator, an experienced pilot would still be able to use it in making an approach to a landing because he would know where the needle was supposed to be when the aircraft was at its proper approach speed. The same thing is true of the vertical speed indicator and to some extent of the altimeter, both of which had pointers that moved against fixed scales. Of course if one were to remove the scale from a moving-scale instrument it would convey no information whatever.

This led to the intensive investigation of the effects of dial design variables upon the speed and accuracy of quantitative instrument reading (Christensen, 1955). Special attention was given to the comparison of moving-pointer versus moving-scale displays. Test conditions were arranged to be as much as possible like those encountered in flight. First, subjects knew what display would be presented (in contrast to a number of previous experiments in which this had not been the case). Second, subjects knew the approximate position on the display at which the reading would occur. This was realistic because in flight the pilot knows what the display read the last time he looked at it.

Under these conditions, at all exposure times, reading was more accurate with displays that had their scales fixed so that a given place on the display represented a given value. One could get a good deal of approximate information from looking at such displays even if they had no scale markings. This is particularly important in rapid check reading. With moving-scale displays, even check reading requires careful attention to the numbers on the scales.

Of all the display movement issues, the one that has received the most thorough researching is the comparison between "inside-out" and "outside-in" attitude displays. Conventional gyro horizon attitude indicators are "inside-out." Aircraft attitude is indicated by the position and movement of a small "artifical horizon" bar read against a fixed aircraft symbol. The presentation represents the geometric relationships one would see if he viewed the outside world through a small, circular port hole at the front of the aircraft. Thus, when the aircraft rolls to the right, the artificial horizon rotates to the left, or counter-clockwise, and vice versa. Its position maintains congruence with the real horizon.

Many experiments have compared this type of "inside-out" presentation with the opposite type, or "outside-in," presentation in which a miniature aircraft symbol moves against a fixed horizon line representing the outside world. The presentation is analogous to the geometric relationships one would see if he viewed the aircraft from behind and observed its movements against a fixed earth and sky. Thus, when the pilot rolls his aircraft to the right, or clockwise, he observes his miniature moving aircraft symbol rotate in the same direction. Figure 7 presents a simple schematic representation of the two types of displays, in each case showing the aircraft in a climbing turn to the right. One can think of an inside-out display as a "worm's eye view" and an outside-in display as a "bird's eye view."

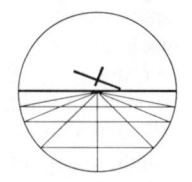

*Figure 7. Schematic representation of an inside-out moving-horizon attitude display and an outside-in moving-airplane attitude display.*

Results of both simulator and flight experiments generally favor the outside-in moving-airplane presentation over the conventional moving-horizon presentation by a very great margin. In one simulator experiment the conventional inside-out display with an aircraft-stabilized steering error dot was compared with an experimental outside-in display with a space-stabilized error dot (Bauerschmidt and Roscoe, 1960). Diagrams of the two displays are shown in Figure 8. The pilot's task was to fly a radar-directed air-to-air attack in a simulated high-performance interceptor aircraft. The steering error dot continuously indicated the computed instantaneous angle-to-turn-through to get onto and maintain a typical lead-collision co-altitude attack geometry.

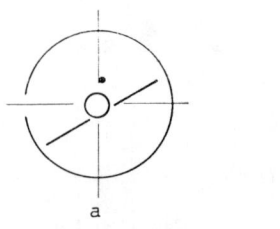

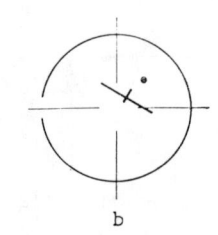

*Figure 8. Experimental display: a. moving-horizon display with aircraft-stabilized error dot, b. pursuit-type moving-airplane display.*

The results of this comparison are shown in Figure 9. The curves show the average azimuth steering errors at the instant of firing made by independent groups of seven pilots each, with each pilot flying a series of 30 trials using the display to which he was assigned.

On the average, azimuth steering errors at firing were approximately one-fifth as large with the experimental moving-airplane display as they were with the conventional moving-horizon display; elevation steering errors showed similar differences. A secondary finding was that pilots made approximately 18 times as many control reversals with the conventional display as they did with the experimental display. This was true despite the fact that all of the pilots' previous flight experience had been with the conventional moving-horizon type of presentation.

Results such as these have frequently been discounted because they were obtained in a fixed-base (i.e., non-moving) simulator rather than in a real aircraft. However, not all of the evidence in favor of moving-airplane attitude displays comes from simulator experiments. Flight experiments

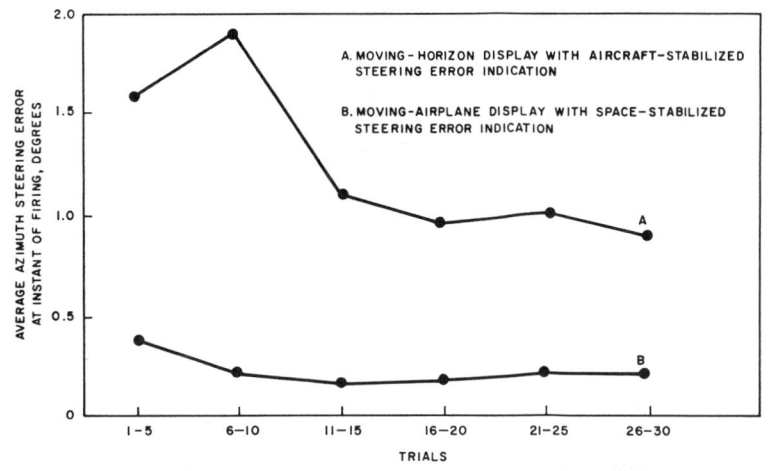

*Figure 9. Comparison of moving-horizon and moving-airplane displays: Average azimuth steering errors at the instant of firing on simulated radar-directed air-to-air attacks in interceptor aircraft.*

performed at the University of Illinois, at Hughes Aircraft Company, and at the Miramar Naval Air Station have all shown that pilots can rapidly make the transition to the moving-airplane display and that non-pilots can use it immediately, which is not the case with the conventional artificial horizon. Operational airline experience with a moving-airplane-type attitude display supports these findings.

*The Principle of Pursuit Tracking*

In many aircraft steering displays, the pilot's task is to track and null a computed steering error indication, typically showing the azimuth and elevation angles-to-turn-through to get onto and maintain a desired flight path. Such a task is required in both air-to-air and air-to-surface weapon delivery, in flying ILS landing approaches, and in numerous similar maneuvers. In some cases displays, rather than showing angles-to-turn-through, present highly quickened error indications which are more nearly proportional to the required control movements that will cause the aircraft to make good the desired flight path.

In almost all such cases, the displayed indications tell the pilot nothing about what his aircraft is doing or what his target is doing but merely the differences between the two, in other words, the errors that must be nulled in order to make good the desired flight path. Such displays typically present their error indications by means of a single moving element, for example, a steering error dot, or by means of a pair of cross-pointer indices showing the horizontal and vertical components of the steering error. Displays of this type are known as compensatory tracking displays, and the task of using such displays is known as compensatory tracking.

There is considerable experimental evidence indicating that tracking performance is significantly improved when such displays are modified so that the index of desired performance, or target, and the index of actual performance, your own aircraft, both move independently against a common coordinate system. Such displays are known as pursuit, as opposed to compensatory, displays because the pilot's task is to cause his own aircraft symbol to pursue the independently moving target symbol. Thus he has uncontaminated, independent indications of both the actual performance of his own aircraft and that of the target.

A direct comparison of pilot performance with pursuit and compensatory displays was made in a simulated air-to-air attack steering simulation study (Bauerschmidt and Roscoe, 1960). Diagrams of the two displays are shown in Figure 10.

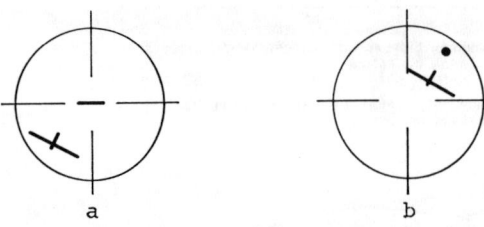

*Figure 10. Experimental display: a. Compensatory-type moving-airplane displays, b. Pursuit-type moving airplane display*

In the compensatory display, a command to fly up and to the right was indicated by the displacement of the aircraft symbol downward and to the left by amounts proportional to the angles-to-turn-through. The symbol was rotated clockwise or counterclockwise to indicate the aircraft's bank angle. Pitch angle was not shown. The pilot's task was to compensate for the indicated steering errors by flying the aircraft symbol always to the center of the display.

In the pursuit display there were two independently moving symbols, a steering error dot representing the target and an aircraft symbol showing the attitude of the pilot's own aircraft. The aircraft was rotated and displaced laterally to indicate bank angle and was displaced vertically to indicate pitch. The error dot was displaced laterally to indicate horizontal angle-to-turn-through and was displaced vertically by an amount proportional to the vertical angle-to-turn-through plus the pitch angle of the aircraft. Thus the pilot's task was to fly the aircraft symbol to the moving error dot wherever the dot might be. When the two symbols were coincident, the pilot was making good his desired flight path, even though the two symbols might not be in the center of the display.

The results of the experimental comparison of the two displays are shown in Figure 11. The curves show the average azimuth steering errors at the instant of firing made by independent groups of seven pilots each, with each pilot flying a series of 30 trials using the display to which he was assigned.

Performance was excellent with both displays, but there was still approximately a two-to-one difference favoring the pursuit display over the compensatory display, and elevation steering performance also showed a similar difference.

*The Principle of Frequency Separation*

In the preceding discussions it has been shown that pilot performance is facilitated by displays in which the symbol representing the pilot's own aircraft moves against a fixed reference system representing one or more dimensions of the outside world. It has also been shown that pilot performance is further improved when the index of desired performance, such as a target symbol or other command indication, moves independently against the same external reference system.

The reasons for these findings seem to be intimately involved with the dynamics of the display and most specifically with the high frequency components of the display's indications. In other

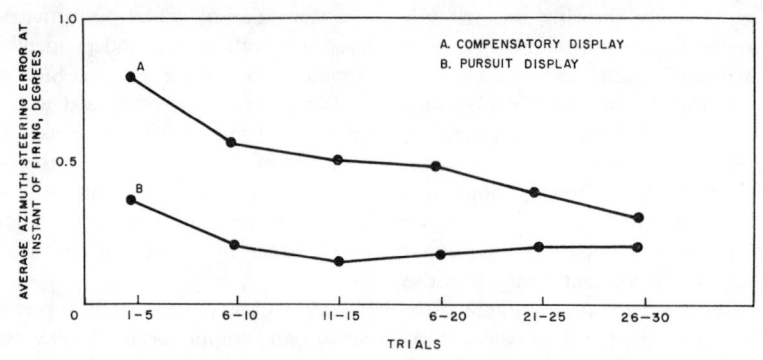

*Figure 11. Comparison of pursuit and compensatory displays: Average azimuth steering errors at the instant of firing on simulated radar-directed attacks in interceptor aircraft.*

words, it appears that the critical consideration is that the elements of a display that respond immediately to the pilot's control inputs move in the expected direction. It appears that the direction of movement of the more slowly responding display indications is far less critical.

This observation leads to the notion of the frequency separation principle of display which has been put forth by various people but never explicitly tested in any formal experimental program. The best known example of the frequency separation principle is the so-called "kinalog" display system proposed by Lawrence Fogel (1959).

Fogel demonstrated an attitude-director display system in which the initial response of the attitude presentation followed the principle of the moving part. For example, if the pilot moved his stick to the right to initiate a right turn, the aircraft symbol initially rotated clockwise. As the aircraft established its right turn, the horizon line on the display and the aircraft symbol both gradually rotated counterclockwise so that in a steady-state turn the aircraft's bank angle was indicated by a tilted horizon line. Upon rolling out of the turn, once again the first indication of the display was the counterclockwise rotation of the aircraft symbol followed more slowly by the clockwise rotation of the horizon line and aircraft symbol back to level.

While this display system was never tested experimentally, the simple laboratory demonstration of its operation was extremely easy to interpret and showed enough promise to warrant further investigation.

If it turns out that the frequency separation principle is valid and that it is only important for the initial indication of a display to follow the outside-in principle of the moving part, then a number of possibilities for ingenious display designs present themselves. Referring back to the diagram presented in Figure 1 showing the hierarchical nature of the pilot's flight task, one might postulate that only those display indications used for loop 4 and possibly loop 3 control need to be presented outside-in while those used for loop 2 and loop 1 functions can be presented inside-out. Thus bank angle and/or turn rate might be presented by a moving-airplane symbol while heading might be presented by a moving compass rose. Certainly such possibilities warrant experimental investigation.

*The Principle of Optimum Scaling*

Whether a display presentation is outside-in or inside-out, or a frequency-separated combination of the two, it is important that spatial displays present as much of the total situation as is consistent with scale-factor requirements. This appears to be important because of the goal-directed nature of flying. It helps to see where you are going on a display—not just a small region about where you are, but all the places you might go. This enables the pilot to predict in advance the outcome of any course of action he might select, and this is important because the selection of the proper course of action is just as critical as his execution of that course of action.

The selection of optimum scale factor, which in combination with display size determines the "field of view," presents a delicate set of trade-offs in display design. Proper choice of scale factor is important, not only because of the desire to present the greatest possible field of view, but also because, for any given display size, control performance deteriorates as scale factor changes in either direction from some optimum value. In general, as you increase scale factor, precision of control improves up to some point at which the system becomes unstable, and the pilot's task blows up on him. As scale factor is reduced, precision deteriorates, but stability of control improves.

The increase in control precision that comes with increasing scale factor is achieved only at the price of increased pilot attention and effort. To fly a high gain display precisely, the pilot must work hard at his control task, and consequently he has less attention left over to time-share on other tasks. In servo theory terms, he will have to increase his gain to keep it properly matched with the gain of the display. As display gain is reduced, the converse is true: the pilot can reduce his gain, and less attention will be required to maintain stable control. He will have more attention left over for other tasks.

Thus it is important to determine just what degree of precision is necessary for any phase of a flight mission, that is, what limits of control error are permissible. The pilot should not be asked to control the aircraft more accurately than is necessary. If the accomplishment of a mission means not running into another airplane that has been assigned a slightly different altitude, then the pilot must control his own altitude only precisely enough not to run into the other airplane. However, for years altitude has been presented on a scale that can be read to the nearest 20 feet or less, even though we cannot begin to measure altitude that accurately. Consequently, we have an instrument that is unnecessarily sensitive and difficult to control and actually misleading in its pretended accuracy. So, while the usual reason for reducing scale factor is to present a greater range of values, it appears that there is some advantage in reducing scale factor to improve stability of control and reduce work load, as long as the scale factor is sufficient to allow the required precision of control.

No general rules can be given concerning optimum scale factors. For each particular application, the optimum scale factor must be determined empirically by experimentation, and the required precision of control must be determined independently.

## CONCLUSION

The design of flight and navigation displays is far from an exact science, despite the fact that a respectable amount of experimental research has been done in the field. The display principles discussed represent some of the generalizations that can be drawn from that experimental research. While they do not represent a complete formula for display design, there is little doubt that pilot performance in the navigation and control of aircraft would be vastly improved if cockpit displays were designed in accordance with these principles.

## REFERENCES

Bauerschmidt, D. K. and Roscoe, S. N. A comparative evaluation of a pursuit moving-airplane steering display. *IRE Trans. Human Factors in Electronics*, 1960, **HFE-1**(2), 62–66.

Carel, W. L. Pictorial displays for flight. Culver City, Calif.: Hughes Aircraft Company TR 2732.01/40, December 1965.

Christensen, J. M. The importance of certain dial design variables in quantitative instrument reading. USAF: WADC TR 55-376, October 1955.

Fitts, P. M., Jones, R. E. and Milton, J. L. Eye fixations of aircraft pilots: 2. Frequency, duration, and sequence of fixations when flying the USAF instrument low approach system (ILAS). USAF: AMC TR 5839, October 1949.

Fogel, L. J. A new concept: The Kinalog Display System. *Human Factors*, 1959, **1** (2), 30–37.

Roscoe, S. N., Smith, J. F., Johnson, B. E., Dittman, P. E. and Williams, A.C. Comparative evaluation of pictorial and symbolic VOR navigation displays in the 1-CA-1 link trainer. Washington, D. C.: CAA Division of Research Report No. 91, July 1950.

Simon, C. W. and Roscoe, S. N. Altimetry studies: II. A comparison of integrated versus separated, linear versus circular, and spatial versus numerical displays. Culver City, Calif.: Hughes Aircraft Company Technical Memorandum 435, May 1956.

William, A. C., Jr. Preliminary analysis of information required by pilots for instrument flight. USN: ONR, Special Devices Center Report 70-16-1, April 1947.

# 10

# Perspective Traffic Display Format and Airline Pilot Traffic Avoidance

STEPHEN R. ELLIS,[1] and MICHAEL W. McGREEVY, *NASA–Ames Research Center, Moffett Field, California and the School of Optometry, University of California, Berkeley, and* ROBERT J. HITCHCOCK, *Department of Cybernetics, San Jose State University, San Jose, California*

*Part-task experiments have examined perspective projections of cockpit displays of traffic information as a means of presenting aircraft separation information to airline pilots. Ten airline pilots served as subjects in an experiment comparing the perspective projection with plan-view projections of the same air traffic situations. The pilots' task was to monitor the traffic display in order to decide if an avoidance maneuver was needed. Pilots took more time to select avoidance maneuvers with a conventional plan-view display than with an experimental perspective display. In contrast to previous results, if the pilots selected a maneuver with the perspective display, they were more likely to choose one with a vertical component. Tabulation of the outcomes of their initial avoidance decisions with both perspective and plan-view displays showed that they were more likely to achieve required separation with maneuvers chosen with the aid of perspective displays.*

## INTRODUCTION

The search for a natural display format for a cockpit display of traffic information is as old as the concept itself. The idea for a cockpit traffic display probably originated at the RCA Princeton Electronics Laboratory in 1941, but it was not implemented until after World War II (Herbst, Wolff, Ewing, and Jones, 1946). The basic RCA proposal was to transmit a televised image of the air traffic controller's radar display to a receiver in the cockpit. Terrain and navigation information was provided by optical overlays on both the controller's display and the pilot's video display. Limitations in the existing technology, however, restricted the flexibility with which the display could be formatted. The map format, for example, was north-up rather than heading-up, and thus would have presented a disorienting display when the aircraft was heading south (Baty, Wempe, and Huff, 1974; Ellis, Kim, Tyler, McGreevy, and Stark, 1985; Wickens, 1984).

During the intervening years, various investigators have examined possible cockpit traffic displays for use by the airlines for traffic separation and as a collision-avoidance aid (Boeing Commercial Airplane Company, 1977; Verstynen, 1980). Display formats have generally adhered to the plan-

[1] Requests for reprints should be sent to Stephen R. Ellis, MS 239-3, NASA–Ames Research Center, Moffett Field, CA 94035.

view format originally used for the RCA project, though most now use either heading or track-up formats with a north-up option.

More recently, studies of cockpit traffic displays conducted at the Ames Research Center have focused on the display *format* as opposed to other considerations such as system integration questions and operational procedures. These studies have examined the effect of display background, display update rate (Palmer and Ellis, 1983; Palmer, Jago, Baty, and O'Connor, 1980), and aircraft symbology (Hart and Loomis, 1980) on pilots' estimates of spatial separation and on their patterns of avoidance maneuvers (Ellis and Palmer, 1981; Smith, Ellis, and Lee, 1984).

All of these previous studies concerned with traffic display format have been conducted with plan-view type displays. In such displays, the vertical separation is represented by text displays of aircraft altitude attached to the aircraft symbol. This kind of displayed text is called a *data tag*. An alternative mode of indicating relative altitude is to change the shape of the aircraft symbols. This technique is called *shape encoding*. An example of shape encoding is the use of a full hexagonal symbol to represent an aircraft at the pilot's own altitude. An upper half of the hexagon would then be used to represent aircraft above the pilot's altitude, and the lower half would represent aircraft below the pilot's altitude.

Since none of these previous formats had provided a convenient representation of the vertical dimension of separation, we developed a more natural way of presenting combined horizontal and vertical traffic separation to airline pilots. We selected a perspective format because its dimensionality matches the three-dimensional characteristics of traffic separation. We hoped that this perspective format would match pilots' visualizations of their situations in three-dimensional space, and that the format would be a significant improvement over previous uses of perspective projections to show aircraft separation (e.g., Bird, 1975). We believed that the more natural characteristics of a perspective display, compared with plan-view, would assist in the detection and resolution of traffic conflicts.

The development of this format was also experimentally useful because it allowed investigation of previously observed biases in pilots' maneuver patterns. Earlier investigations in part-mission (Palmer, 1983) and part-task simulation (Smith et al., 1984) had shown, for example, that when pilots were given sufficient time (at least 60 s) they preferred to use horizontal maneuvers to avoid intruding aircraft.

In general, the justifications given for the horizontal maneuvers were procedural. The pilots often based their selection on the extra freedom the usual FAA rules give them for horizontal as compared with vertical maneuvers. For example, justifications for the turns were often "to keep the other aircraft in sight" or "to avoid leaving the assigned altitude." The turns frequently were toward the intruding traffic.

This turning-towards bias, however, is not always observed. It has been found, for example, to be modulated by other aspects of the encounter, especially the heading difference between the aircraft involved (Smith, et al., 1984). Thus, we suspected that the preference for horizontal avoidance maneuvers might not be due to the procedural justification given and also could be modified by the characteristics of the display and the encounter.

Specifically, we thought that the preference for horizontal maneuvers was not based merely on the procedural factors cited by the pilots, but might actually arise from their own difficulties in using the supplementary text written on the plan-view displays—the data tags—to visualize three-dimensional separation. Accordingly, the following experiment was conducted, in which pilots viewed identical sets of traffic encounters presenting identical separation information. The information was presented on either a plan-view or a perspective display. If the display format were influencing the pattern of pilot avoidance maneuvers, pilots using the perspective display should have selected more maneuvers with vertical components.

Analysis of the factors influencing a pilot's decision to initiate an avoidance maneuver while monitoring traffic on a cockpit traffic display is particularly important since these displays may by installed along with automatic collision-avoidance systems. The designers of such systems will need to be familiar with the avoidance decision logic that airline pilots have developed from years of flight experience. Clearly, potential inconsistencies, both in the pilots' collision-avoidance logic, and in the logic of automatic systems, must be identified and resolved. The following experiment extends previous investigations into the kind of initial-maneuver techniques and biases airline pilots may bring to the interpretation of cockpit traffic displays (Palmer et al., 1980; Smith et al., 1984).

## METHODS

*Subjects*

Ten current or recently retired airline pilots served as subjects in this experiment.

*The Perspective Display*

The perspective display presented a view of the airspace surrounding the pilot's ownship through a "synthetic camera" that was positioned above and behind it, viewing it slightly from one side. The vertical scale was expanded by a factor of five, in a manner corresponding to usual practice in the construction of three-dimensional topographical maps (Jenks and Brown, 1966). The use of a perspective projection to present the traffic situation entailed a choice of many specific parameters of the projection; for example, the effective focal length of the synthetic lens and consequent field of view, the position and direction of the viewing vector, and the amount of expansion of the vertical scale. Since we could find little theoretical or practical guidance for making these choices, we based them primarily on structured interviews with five pilots before the experiment began. During these interviews, the pilots commented on the appearance of the display when a great variety of different projections were used. This interaction with the pilots was made possible by providing an interactive design tool that quickly generated pictures with various perspective parameters for perusal and permutation. The specific projection we chose was nevertheless somewhat ad hoc; the choice of a display remains an area for considerable future investigation.

The projection we ultimately used was a correct-perspective view from an eyepoint 30 km behind ownship, looking down on ownship from an elevation angle of 30 deg with a 50-deg field-of-view angle, and rotated 8 deg so that ownship could be viewed a bit on its right side. The viewing vector was oriented directly toward ownship. Because we were dealing with a synthetic camera, we were able to select the sizes of the aircraft independently of the position of the eyepoint. The size of ownship was constant at 8.0 mm across on the display and was chosen so that it would be clearly visible. The display was 127 mm square. The sizes of all other aircraft were than rescaled relative to ownship according to their perspective projection. It is important to note that the rescaling of all aircraft with respect to ownship and the differential scaling of the vertical axis resulted in an actual projection significantly different from a strictly "correct" projection with the

PLAN-VIEW DISPLAY       PERSPECTIVE DISPLAY

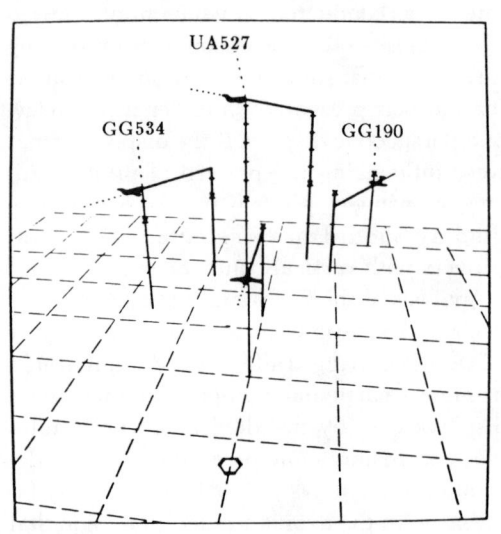

Figure 1. *Comparison of a plan-view (left) and a perspective traffic display (right) for an identical traffic situation.*

perspective parameters we used. All displays were viewed about 60 cm from the display surface under photopic conditions. Display line luminances were about 30 cd/m².

Aircraft on the display were represented by schematic airplane-like symbols and were positioned so that their correct current location was under the nose of the symbol. Ownship was always presented so that it was in the center of the display. Each aircraft was presented with a 60-s ground-referenced predictor and trailed 10 dots separated by 4-s periods, representing previous positions. Horizontal separation and aspect were unambiguously presented by placing reference lines from the present and future positions of all aircraft onto a grid ruled with 3-nautical-mile intervals that were shown 5000 feet below ownship. The grid appeared to move under ownship in proportion to its ground speed and was aligned so that its centerline always corresponded to ownship's instantaneous ground track. Thus, the grid could serve as a moving two-dimensional frame of reference for judging present and future horizontal separation.

Vertical separation was presented by calculating a level plane at ownship's altitude passing through all of the reference lines. The intersection of this plane with each reference line was shown by small $x$'s drawn on the reference lines. The intervals between the $x$'s and all present or future positions of aircraft were divided into 1000-foot intervals by tick marks.

An important aspect of all of the symbology selected for use with the perspective display was that it presented "ownship-relative" information. For example, the 1000-foot altitude tick marks indicate relative vertical separation, and the alignment of the grid to ownship's ground track provides a relative horizontal-separation metric. In this way, the display presents what Falzon (1982) calls the "variables" of an encounter as opposed to "properties," which are the specific characteristics of the aircraft involved such as speed, heading, and absolute altitude.

## Plan-View Control Display

A plan-view format with ground-referenced, one-minute predictors and 40 seconds of history similar to that on the perspective display served as a control (see left side of Figure 1). The data tags on this display showed speed (knots) and altitude (hundreds of feet) on the middle line, and vertical rate information (hundreds of feet per minute) on the bottom line. Upward- and downward-pointing arrows indicated climb and descent, respectively. Dashed lines three nautical miles on each side of ownship's ground track and route lines provided a sense of motion over terrain. Thus, this display presented separation information similar to that presented on the perspective display and served as a control for testing the hypothesis regarding horizontal-maneuver bias.

## Experimental Design

Display type was crossed with subjects in a repeated-measures design with counterbalanced order of presentation and independent groups analysis to control for asymmetric transfer. The encounters used on all displays were designed so that in each situation there were two aircraft displayed with ownship: an intruder, 90 s from time of minimum separation, and a pseudo-intruder, 110 s from minimum separation. The trajectory of the pseudo-intruder was selected so that it never produced a spacing violation with ownship.

The traffic environment was that of a terminal control area (TCA) under true instrument meteorological conditions. All aircraft were medium commercial transports and were to be considered under air traffic control. No other aircraft were equipped with cockpit traffic displays. Ownship was in straight-and-level flight in conformance with its current clearance to maintain 10 000 feet and 240 knots if no spacing violation occurred for the duration of the scenario, which lasted 90 s at most.

## Encounter Geometry

The intruder's trajectories were selected to randomly provide 108 geometrically different encounters with a variety of horizontal and vertical speeds, horizontal and vertical miss distances, and heading differences. This was done by systematically varying the intruder's heading difference with ownship (0, ±30, ±60, ±90, ±120, ±150 deg) and randomly pairing these heading differences with horizontal miss distances (±0.5, ±1.5, ±4.0 nautical miles), vertical miss distances (±300, ±750, ±1500 feet), and intruder vertical speeds (0, ±2000 feet/min) in a repeated-measures design in which heading difference was crossed with display type. The algebraic sign of the other variables was ignored. This variation served to provide the 108 different traffic scenarios to be presented to each subject. Thus, any systematic selection of maneuvering would be collected from a wide variety of potential traffic encounters. This wide variety points to an advantage of using a part-task technique, since neither full-mission nor part-mission experiments are capable of allowing exploration of such a wide experimental space.

## Subject's Task

The pilot's task was to monitor the developing conflict situation as if he were flying in ownship, and to recommend an avoidance maneuver. Maneuvers were to be selected if the pilot determined that an intruding aircraft would pose a spacing violation by coming within 3 nautical miles horizontally and 1000 feet vertically. If the pilot foresaw a violation, he was then to select an avoidance maneuver (climb, descent, turn, or combined maneuver) by moving the stick of the simulator in the direction he would use if actually flying an aircraft. He also could signal with a stick-mounted button when he had seen enough of the developing conflict to determine that no avoidance maneuver would be necessary. Either of these decisions would terminate the encounter scenario. The pilot's decision time was measured from the beginning of the encounter, when the traffic display first appeared on the CRT screen, to the time when he either selected a maneuver or decided he no longer needed to monitor the traffic display because the danger of a conflict had passed. The times and types of maneuvers selected were automatically recorded by the simulation computer.

Immediately after making an avoidance decision, the pilot answered several questions on a questionnaire concerning the specific characteristics of the avoidance maneuver he had selected. He indicated the desired bank angle, the desired degree of angular course deviation, the desired rate of climb or descent, and the desired amount of change in altitude. The pilots took from one to two minutes, immediately after termination of the encounter, to complete the questionnaire. This information allowed the experimenters to simulate the maneuver on a data analysis computer to determine some of the consequences had the pilot been allowed to execute the maneuver he selected.

Significantly, the pilot was never allowed to see the consequences of his selected avoidance decision. This condition, which was successfully used for a similar purpose in a previous experiment (Smith et al., 1984), was specifically intended to reduce the effects of practice and training on the results. The experiment was thus intended to take an inventory of pilots' maneuver predispositions based on their extensive flying experience.

To prevent this inventory from being corrupted by the experience of the experiment itself, we carefully avoided training the pilots either explicitly or implicitly in specific avoidance procedures or in the consequences of their own decisions. No pilot, however, was allowed to participate in the experiment until he had demonstrated complete understanding of the symbology used on the display and successful operation of the simulator controls. This understanding was provided by approximately one hour of briefing and practice before the beginning of any particular experimental run.

*Experimental Environment*

The experiment was conducted in two sessions separated by about one week. Each session, including initial instructions, lasted between four and five hours. All sessions were conducted in the NASA–Ames Multicab room, which allowed the subjects to sit in simple aircraft simulators and monitor the displays on an Evans and Sutherland PS II calligraphic display positioned on the control panel. This test facility is described in detail elsewhere (Hart, 1982). It provided a fairly realistic cockpit environment in which the pilots could monitor the developing traffic conflicts. All of the usual flight controls are present: stick, rudder, and pedals. No external visual scene could be provided. The cabs were partially closed to isolate the pilot and increase the realism of the simulation. The pilots were kept in audio contact with the experimenter by an intercom link.

Each subject received written instruction booklets that described the purpose and assumptions of the experiment and the operation of the simulator cockpits. The pilots were told to adopt one of the roles of the "pilot not flying," whose usual duties include a radio watch to keep track of potential traffic conflict. The cockpit traffic display provided the source of this information instead of the usual aircraft radio communications. The subjects were told to assume that the traffic display presented true conditions unaffected by weather, tracker lags, or radar noise, and that wind was negligible.

## RESULTS

The statistical tests on the results reported in this section have been checked to eliminate the possibility of asymmetric transfer (Poulton, 1974) by using a repeated-measures analysis with 10 subjects and then confirming any significant effect with an independent-groups analysis with 5 subjects per group.

The pilots' mean decision time either to initiate a maneuver or to decide that no maneuver would be necessary was 38 s for the plan-view display and 35 s for the perspective display. This difference was not statistically significant, $F(1,9) = 0.447, p > 0.05; F(1,8) = 0.555, p > 0.05$. However, an analysis of variance conducted on the data showed a highly significant interaction between type of display and heading difference, $F(5,45) = 3.51, p < 0.01; F(5,40) = 5.71, p < 0.001$, which on inspection showed that for all but head-on traffic, the pilots' decision time with the perspective display was from 3 to 6 s faster than with the plan-view display (see Figure 2). For head-on traffic, the reverse was true, and the perspective display actually took about 5 s longer to interpret. This undoubtedly resulted from that fact that an intruder's symbology was practically impossible to interpret when it flew along the axis of the viewing vector, as was the case for head-on traffic. Under these conditions, the reference lines from both present and future positions were practically superimposed, and it was hard to tell if the intruder was coming or going. Thus, it is reasonable to conclude that, for the task used in this experiment, the perspective display provided a time advantage for the conditions in which its symbology could be seen.

The pilots selected avoidance maneuvers somewhat more frequently when using the plan-view displays than when using the perspective display. The mean number of maneuvers with plan-view was 59.3, versus 49.6 for the perspective display. This difference is, however, not statistically significant, $t(9) = 1.40, p > 0.05; t(8) = 0.07, p > 0.05$.

However, a breakdown of the types of maneuvers chosen shows a striking difference in the maneuver patterns for the two displays.

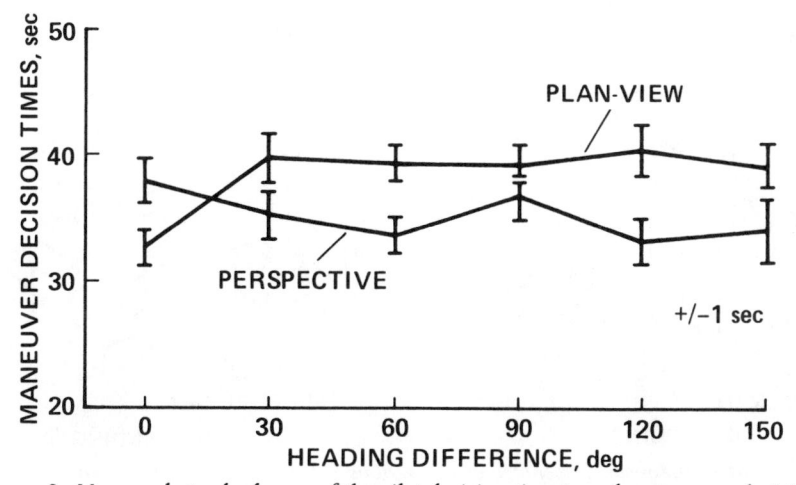

Figure 2. Mean and standard error of the pilot decision time to make maneuver decisions.

The left part of Figure 3 shows the maneuver pattern for the plan-view display. This pattern replicates an earlier finding from both part-mission and part-task experiments. These results showed that when intruding aircraft are seen at least 60 s before minimum separation, horizontal maneuvers seem to be preferred (Palmer, 1983; Smith et al., 1984). The right part of Figure 3 clearly shows a shift to more maneuvers with vertical components when pilots used the perspective display.

This tendency may be analyzed subject by subject by calculating the ratio of each pilot's maneuvers with vertical components to those without vertical components. Though correlated with a percentage, this score is superior for statistical analysis because it is not constrained to a fixed range of 0 to 100. Tabulation of this score for each pilot separately showed that all pilots had a greater preference for vertical maneuvers with the perspective display (sign test, $p < 0.002$). The mean of the vertical maneuver score for the plan-view display was 0.77 and the mean for the perspective display was 2.33. This difference can be analyzed by a $t$ test for repeated measures and double-checked by an independent groups $t$ test. Both confirm the relatively increased number of vertical maneuvers with the perspective display that is clear from Figure 3, $t(9) = 4.30, p < 0.002; t(8) = 2.62, p < 0.03$.

We have assessed some aspects of the quality of the initial maneuvers that the pilots selected with both types of display, such as the frequency of the pilots' failure to maneuver when necessary for safe spacing. This analysis of the patterns of the pilots' avoidance maneuvers was accomplished by tabulating each extrapolated encounter outcome into one of six possibilities. For each encounter, a pilot decided whether or not a maneuver would be required to avoid a separation violation. A decision to make no maneuver was "correct" if, in fact, no separation violation would have occurred. If, however, a no-maneuver decision resulted in a separation violation, this decision was "incorrect." A decision to make a maneuver was termed necessary if the planned separation for an encounter resulted in a separation violation.

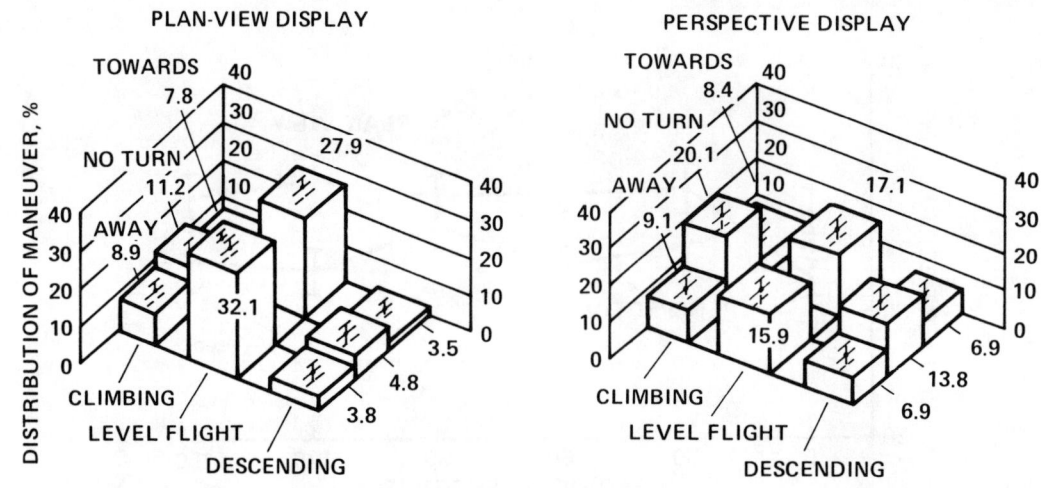

Figure 3. *Histograms of the mean percentage of the various categories ($\pm 1$ SE) of avoidance maneuvers broken down by display type.*

Furthermore, a necessary maneuver was "successful" if it would have avoided the violation, or "unsuccessful" if it would not. On the other hand, a decision to maneuver was termed unnecessary if no separation violation would have occurred. Such an unnecessary maneuver was a "blunder" if it would have created a separation violation. An unnecessary maneuver that would not create a separation violation was categorized as a "wasted" maneuver.

Frequency counts of each possible outcome were analyzed for each pilot and each display. All categories except incorrect show an overall advantage for the perspective display. Two categories show statistically significant differences insensitive to the statistical method of repeated-measures analysis: unsuccessful, $t(9) = 5.71$, $p < 0.001$; sign test $p < 0.002$; and blunder, $t(9) = 3.464$, $p < 0.0085$; sign test $p < 0.04$. The smaller number of unsuccessful maneuvers with the perspective display remained statistically significant when checked with the more conservative independent groups $t$ test, $t(8) = 3.58$, $p < 0.01$.

## DISCUSSION

### Patterns of Maneuver Selection

The difference in maneuver patterns shown in Figure 2 clearly demonstrates that pilots' avoidance maneuvers in the vertical dimension are strongly affected by the manner in which vertical separation is presented. The more natural presentation of vertical separation on the perspective display approximately doubled the number of maneuvers in the vertical dimension. Thus, the pilots' previous explanations that their preference for horizontal maneuvers was due to procedural reasons must be seen as rationalizations (Dreyfus and Dreyfus, 1986). The same pilots, when provided a second chance to interpret a given encounter (and unaware of the repetition because of the large number of different encounters and the intervening time between test sessions), chose more vertical maneuvers when using a perspective display.

The presence or absence of a vertical component in a pilot's initial avoidance maneuver is practically important because the planned implementation by the FAA of the Traffic-Alert and Collision Avoidance System (TCAS) will initially only command vertical maneuvers. Such maneuvers would be in conflict with pilots' overall biases if traffic information were presented on a plan-view format with sufficient preview time for pilots to consider a horizontal maneuver. Significantly, the pilots' preference for horizontal maneuvers is reduced if they are allowed to monitor a developing conflict for 60 s or less (Palmer, 1983). The horizontal bias almost disappears if a preview of only 40 or 25 s is allowed (E. A. Palmer, personal communication, October 9, 1986). This dependence on preview time probably reflects the fact that vertical maneuvers, particularly descents, are quicker than turns. Thus, when the time for maneuvering is short, vertical maneuvers are preferred.

Accordingly, plan-view cockpit traffic displays in collision-avoidance systems that command only vertical avoidance maneuvers should display traffic only long enough so that the pilot does not begin to consider a horizontal maneuver. Some current designs for traffic-avoidance systems that also display aircraft position conform to this recommendation. In these designs, conflicting traffic is displayed only if it is less than 40 s to a point of minimum separation (Radio Technical Commission for Aeronautics, 1983).

Use of a perspective display format for a cockpit traffic display would relax the restriction on preview time, since with such

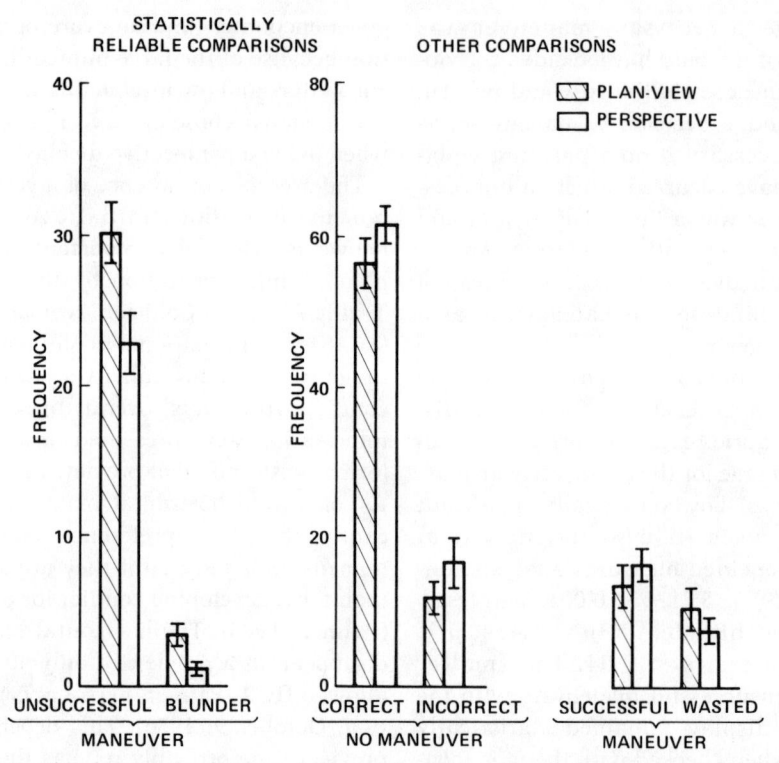

Figure 4. *Barplot showing the means and the standard errors for the frequency of possible outcomes.*

displays pilots would be less inclined to make purely horizontal maneuvers. However, because a constraint on preview time also has the advantage of reducing the amount of traffic shown on the display, the selection of a display format should not be based solely on its probable effect on pilot maneuver biases.

*Timing of Maneuver Selection*

The absolute response times used by the pilots to evaluate whether avoidance maneuvers would be required are undoubtedly closely related to the specific task and instructions. The approximate 10% time reduction for interpretation of the perspective display, however, probably does reflect a *relative* difference and shows that decision time can be reduced by avoiding the use of data tags that must be read to find vertical separation. The requirement that the pilot read four sets of numbers associated with each vehicle in the plan-view display—as opposed to only the aircraft identification tag on the corresponding aircraft symbol on the perspective display—probably accounts for the difference in decision times.

The particular problem of superimposition of the display symbology seen with the perspective format for head-on traffic is analogous to the problem of superimposition of data tags on the plan-view display. Since the plan-view display had the advantage of an automatic algorithm that prevented superimposition of the data tags, a similar system for adjusting the eyepoint to provide a less frontal view of head-on traffic might have helped the perspective display and further reduced pilot decision time while using it. Clearly, any implementation of a perspective display will require a solution to the problem of superimposed symbology. As an alternative to automatic decluttering, pilots might be given some control over the position of the eyepoint.

Elaborate quantitative evaluation of the quality of the pilots' avoidance maneuvers while using each display is beyond the scope of this experiment. This is primarily because the experiment was designed as a way to inventory pilots' initiation of traffic avoidance, not to assess the proficiency with which they could carry out such a maneuver. The latter analysis would require substantial training (to asymptotic behavior) in order to provide a realistic and useful comparison of display formats. The reported relative differences are worth noting, however, because they suggest that use of the perspective display resulted in improved avoidance maneuvering with fewer blunders and fewer unsuccessful attempts to achieve a specified separation. Furthermore, the relative decision times and maneuver patterns reported above are significant in themselves because they reflect the biases and opinions with which pilots would greet the introduction of a cockpit traffic display into the cockpit. In the cases of our subjects, these opinions are based on thousands of hours, in some cases more than 10 000 hours, of airline experience and thus reflect the kind of ingrained opinion and perception that might appear in time of stress.

In summary, the results of the current experiment point toward the usefulness of investigating more natural display formats for the integrated presentation of three-dimensional separation information. The improvements in decision time and avoidance performance that can be attributed to the perspective format in this experiment are probably not the maximum achievable, since the format itself was not systematically optimized for the pilot's use. Our research on the influence of the parameters of a projection on picture perception will provide a basis for further improvements in parameter selection (McGreevy and Ellis, 1986; McGreevy, Ratzlaff, and Ellis, 1985). These improvements could also be integrated into intelligent perspective display systems that automatically configure themselves to provide their users with the most interpretable perspective projection possible.

## ACKNOWLEDGMENTS

A preliminary version of this report were presented at the May 1984 AGARD Conference on Human Factors Considerations in High Performance Aircraft. The research reported here was partially supported by NASA Cooperative Agreement NCC-2-86 to L. Stark at the University of California, Berkeley.

## REFERENCES

Baty, D. L., Wempe, T. E., and Huff, E. M. (1974). A study of aircraft map display location and orientation. *IEEE Transactions on Systems, Man and Cybernetics, SMC-4,* 560-568.

Bird, J. M. (1975). *On the display of three dimensional air traffic control situations. Applied psychology* (Note A.P. 47). Birmingham, England: University of Aston.

Boeing Commercial Airplane Company. (1977). *Cockpit displayed traffic information study* (Report No. D6-42968). Seattle, WA: Author.

Dreyfus, H. L., and Dreyfus, S. (1986). *Mind over machine.* New York: Free Press.

Ellis, S. R., and Palmer, E. A. (1981). *Threat perception while viewing single intruder encounters on a cockpit display of traffic information* (NASA TM 81341). Moffett Field, CA: NASA–Ames Research Center.

Ellis, S. R., Kim, W. S., Tyler, M., McGreevy, M. W., and Stark, L. (1985). Visual enhancements for perspective displays: Perspective parameters. In *Proceedings of the 1985 International Conference on Systems, Man and Cybernetics* (pp. 815-818). New York: IEEE.

Falzon, P. (1982). Display structures: Compatibility with the operator's mental representations and reasoning processes. In *Proceedings of the 2nd European Annual Conference on Human Decision Making and Manual Control* (pp. 297-305). Wachtberg-Werthoven, West Germany: Forschungsinstitut für Anthropotechnik.

Hart, S. G. (1982). Effect of VFR aircraft approach traffic with and without cockpit display of traffic information. In *Proceedings of the 18th Conference on Manual Control* (AFWAL-TR-3021; pp. 522-544). Wright-Patterson AFB, OH: Air Force Flight Dynamics Laboratory.

Hart, S. G., and Loomis, L. L. (1980). Evaluation of the potential format and content of a cockpit display of traffic information. *Human Factors, 22*, 591-604.

Herbst, P. J., Wolff, D. E., Ewing, D., and Jones, L. R. (1946). The TELERAN proposal. *Electronics, 19*, 125-127.

Jenks, G. F., and Brown, D. A. (1966). Three dimensional map construction. *Science, 154*, 837-846.

McGreevy, M. W., and Ellis, S. R. (1986). The effects of perspective geometry on judged direction in spatial information instruments. *Human Factors, 28*, 421-438.

McGreevy, M. W., Ratzlaff, C., and Ellis, S. R. (1985). Virtual space and two-dimensional effects in perspective displays. In *Proceedings of the 21st Annual Conference on Manual Control.* (NASA CP 2428; pp. 29.1-29.14). Moffett Field, CA: NASA–Ames Research Center.

Palmer, E. A. (1983). Conflict resolution maneuvers during near miss encounters with cockpit traffic displays. In *Proceedings of the Human Factors Society 27th Annual Meeting* (pp. 757-761). Santa Monica, CA: Human Factors Society.

Palmer, E. A., and Ellis, S. R. (1983). Potential interactions of collision avoidance advisories and cockpit displays of traffic information. In *Proceedings of the Society of Automotive Engineers* (Paper 831544; pp. 433-443). Warrendale, PA: Society of Automative Engineers.

Palmer, E. A., Jago, S. J., Baty, D. L., and O'Conner, S. L. (1980). Perception of horizontal aircraft separation on a cockpit display of traffic information. *Human Factors, 22*, 605-620.

Poulton, E. C. (1974). *Tracking skill and manual control.* New York: Academic Press.

Radio Technical Commission for Aeronautics. (1983). *Minimum operation performance standards for the traffic-alert and collision avoidance system (TCAS) (airborne equipment)* (RTCA/DO-185, prepared by committee SC-147). Washington, DC: Author.

Smith, J. D., Ellis, S. R., and Lee, E. (1984). Perceived threat and avoidance maneuvers in response to cockpit traffic displays. *Human Factors, 26*, 33-48.

Verstynen, H. A. (1980). *Potential roles for the cockpit traffic display in the evolving ATC system* (Report No. SAE-800736). Warrendale, PA: Society of Automotive Engineers.

Wickens, C. D. (1984). *Engineering psychology and human performance.* Columbus, OH: Charles Merrill.

# 11

# Perceptual Discriminability as a Basis for Selecting Graphic Symbols

RALPH E. GEISELMAN, *University of California, Los Angeles*, BETTY M. LANDEE,[1] *and* FRANCOIS G. CHRISTEN, *Perceptronics, Inc., Woodland Hills, California*

*The purpose of this research was to develop a performance-based criterion for selecting among alternative symbols to be used in graphic displays. The specific criterion developed was an index of perceptual discriminability. Through regression analyses of an intersymbol similarity-rating matrix, it was concluded that symbols are judged more or less similar on the basis of the number of shared versus unique configural attributes (an X, a triangle, etc.), as opposed to primitive attributes (number of lines, arcs, etc.). An easy-to-use discriminability-index formula was derived from the regression analysis involving the configural attributes, and this formula was used to predict the results of an experiment involving a search for specific symbols embedded in an array. Indices obtained from a formula such as the one developed here could be used as part of the basis for choosing among alternative candidate symbols for inclusion in an existing symbol domain.*

## INTRODUCTION

A major goal of this research was to develop a human-factors-based criterion for selecting among candidate symbols for inclusion in an existing graphic-display symbology data base, the U.S. Army's conventional symbol set, FM 21-30 (U.S. Army, 1970). Symbolic displays are evolving independently, on a system-by-system basis, with few standards to follow. Consequently, there is little agreement as to how a given concept is to be portrayed. Guidance is needed both in future symbology development and for standardization of existing symbol sets. In choosing a candidate symbol to represent a particular concept, at least two factors must be considered: (1) the meaningfulness of the symbol, that is, how well the symbol portrays its referent; and (2) the discriminability of the symbol, as reflected in the speed and accuracy of detecting and/or identifying the form in the context of the existing symbol domain. Symbol meaning was not studied in this research. Although symbol discrimination is not the only task that is a component of the more complex tasks involved in graphic-display usage, logically it is a precursor to several other behavioral-task primitives such as search, comparison, and multiple-symbol pattern recognition. Symbol discrimination should therefore be given primary emphasis in a research effort, as suggested by Williams and Teichner (1979).

Selecting one candidate symbol over another cannot be carried out optimally without taking into account the symbol domain in which the candidate symbol is to be used (Easterby, 1970). Identifying the symbol attributes that are most influential in affecting intersymbol discriminability seems basic to any effort to resolve symbol conflicts (Attneave and Arnoult, 1966). We propose that consideration be given to an existing symbol

[1] Requests for reprints should be sent to Betty M. Landee, Perceptronics, Inc., 6271 Variel Ave., Woodland Hills, CA 91367.

domain in assessing the potential discriminability of new candidate symbols, and that the standards for accomplishing this can be determined empirically using the methodology outlined below.

## EXPERIMENT 1

The methodology used here is based on two assumptions: (1) the more similar to existing symbols a new symbol is perceived to be, the less discriminable the new symbol will be, and (2) knowing the attributes by which people judge the similarity of existing symbols will allow designers to generate new symbols using other attributes or characteristics, resulting in highly discriminable symbols. Thus, the approach was to assess the perceived similarity among a sample of symbols, to determine which symbol attributes lead to the perceived similarity, and to construct and validate a formula for quantifying a symbol's perceived discriminability. The approach was implemented using the following five-step procedure.

First, the Army's standard symbology, FM 21-30, was defined as the symbol domain. A representative sample of 20 symbols was selected from this domain for use in Experiment 1. (The precise method of selection is outlined in the Materials section that follows.) Second, each symbol in the symbol set was defined in terms of primitive symbol attributes, such as number of lines, arcs, 90-deg angles, etc., and also in terms of such configural symbol properties as an X or an oval.

The third step was to determine which symbol attributes predict the intersymbol perceived similarity. This was accomplished with a stepwise multiple regression procedure, in which the similarity ratings constituted the variable to be predicted, and the symbol descriptors constituted the predictors. This procedure was carried out separately for the primitive attributes and the configural attributes to determine which type of attributes can be used to predict the greater amount of variance in the intersymbol similarity ratings. The fourth step was to develop an equation that would enable a symbol designer to estimate the discriminability of any given candidate symbol to be included into the symbol domain. The fifth and final step was to validate the derived discriminability-index formula. This was done in Experiment 2.

### Method

*Subjects.* The subjects were 24 undergraduate volunteers from the introductory psychology course at the University of California at Los Angeles. The subjects participated in groups with two to six members.

*Materials.* Twenty symbols from the conventional Army symbology (FM 21-30) were selected for use in this investigation. It was decided that symbol elements external to the basic symbol shape would not be considered in this study since to do so would require an unmanageable number of sample symbols. The symbols were chosen from three military categories (combat, combat support, and combat service support), and an effort was made to include a wide variety of symbol characteristics. The 20 symbols used here are presented in Figure 1.

The symbols shown in Figure 1 could all be described in terms of nine primitive symbol attributes. One of these pertained to the external symbol shape, namely the number of lines in the perimeter (circle = 1, triangle = 3, etc.). The internal portion of the symbol could be described in terms of the following eight attributes: (1) number of straight lines, (2) number of arcs, (3) number of completed circles, (4) number of 90-deg angles, (5) number of non–90-deg angles, (6) number of quasi angles (such as a straight line meeting an arc), (7) number of blackened-in elements (e.g., a solid bar), and (8) number of alphanumeric characters. Most of these symbol

SYMBOL DOMAIN

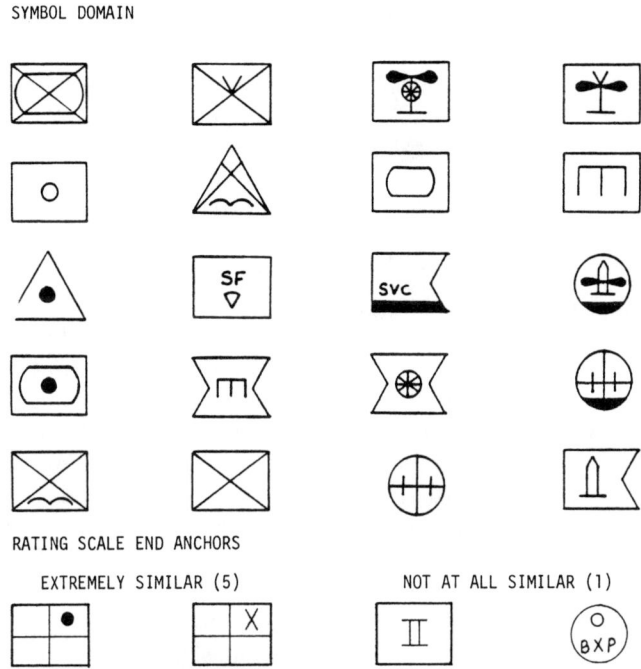

Figure 1. *Twenty symbols from the conventional Army symbology (FM 21-30) used in Experiment 1.*

attributes either have been shown to affect symbol perceptibility in controlled experiments, or could be predicted theoretically from Gestalt principles. Thus, this set of attributes has some degree of psychological validity. A second set of symbol attributes was constructed based upon configural properties of the symbols, and this set is presented in Figure 2. This set is different from the one described above in that attention is given to how the primitive symbol attributes tend to combine to form more complex configurations. Two judges independently decomposed the 20 symbols into the set of configural attributes. They were in perfect agreement. These judges were undergraduate research assistants at UCLA who knew nothing about the current research and who had not seen any of the symbols previously.

*Procedure.* Each participant was given a booklet containing instructions for the similarity-judgment task and 190 pages of symbol pairs representing all pairwise comparisons among the 20 symbols studied. The subject's task for each pair of symbols was to rate the similarity of the pair on a scale of one to five: (1) not at all similar, (2) slightly similar, (3) moderately similar, (4) very similar, and (5) extremely similar. Pairs of symbols representing end anchors for this scale were provided, and these pairs are included in Figure 1. The order in which the pairs appeared was randomized across subjects. The average time taken to complete the task was 35 min.

*Results and Discussion*

The intersymbol similarity ratings were predicted from a comparison of the primitive symbol attributes among symbols in the first analysis, and from a comparison of configural

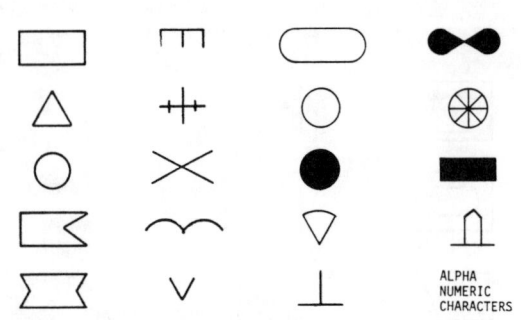

Figure 2. *Configural symbol attributes of the symbols shown in Figure 1.*

symbol attributes among symbols in the second analysis. Each analysis was carried out to determine how well each type of attribute set accounts for the similarity ratings (the percentage of variance accounted for), and to derive a discriminability-index formula. The subjects showed considerable agreement on the 190 intersymbol similarity ratings, with only 8% of the variation among the ratings being attributable to the interaction between subjects and symbols.

*Primitive symbol attributes.* One hypothesis as to how two symbols appear to be similar to an observer is that similarity on primitive symbol attributes combines to produce an overall sensation of "sameness." That is, to the extent that one symbol has the same number of straight lines, arcs, etc., as another symbol, the two symbols will be seen as more similar. This hypothesis is non-Gestalt in the sense that is does not explore the various ways in which the primitive parts could be combined to form the different symbols; however the simplicity of this hypothesis lends itself to a straightforward evaluation.

For this analysis, the log mean similarity rating for each of the 190 pairwise comparisons of the 20 symbols was used as the criterion in a stepwise multiple regression procedure. The log transformation was applied to this variable because its distribution was skewed and leptokurtic. The nine predictors of the similarity ratings were absolute difference scores obtained by subtracting the two vectors of nine values in the primitive symbol attribute set for each pair of symbols. Thus, the rationale was that any two symbols given a high average similarity rating would have similar values on the attributes in the attribute set (i.e., small absolute difference scores).

The results of the stepwise multiple regression procedure showed that the similarity ratings could be partially accounted for from absolute difference scores on a combination of four symbol attributes. These four attributes, in the order of their entry into the multiple regression equation, are (1) number of lines in the external symbol shape, (2) number of straight lines in the internal symbol shape, (3) number of alphanumeric elements, and (4) number of arcs. No other attribute difference scores, when added to the equation, significantly increased the percentage of variance accounted for ($p < 0.05$) in the similarity ratings. Although the predictive power of the above four variables was significant, $F(4,185) = 14.55, p < 0.001$, the difference scores on these attributes accounted for only 25% of the variance.

*Configural symbol attributes.* A second hypothesis as to how two symbols appear to be similar to an observer is that similar configural symbol elements, such as those shown in Figure 2, combine to produce an overall sensation of "sameness." This hypothesis differs from the one discussed above in that higher-order symbol attributes are the focus of analysis. It is, of course, the aim of this analysis to account for a greater percentage of the variance in the similarity ratings than was possible with the primitive elements.

For this analysis, the log mean similarity rating for each of the 190 pairwise comparisons of the 20 symbols was again used as the criterion in a stepwise multiple regression procedure. This time, 20 predictors of the similarity ratings were obtained by subtracting the two vectors of 20 values in the configural symbol attribute set for each pair of symbols. The aim of this analysis was to account for a greater percentage of the variance in the similarity ratings than was possible with primitive elements. The results showed that 12 of the predictors were significant independent sources of information about the similarity ratings (as determined by tests of significance for increases in $R^2, p < 0.05$). The rectangular external symbol shape accounted for 14% of the variance, while 11 other configural properties accounted for an additional 5% each, on average. Thus, 67% of the variance in the similarity ratings could be accounted for in all on the basis of the configural properties. This represents a marked advance over the variance accounted for when primitive symbol elements were considered (25%).

Since 12 configural attributes out of 20 were found to be important, and 11 of these 12 each accounted for nearly an equal amount of variance, it seemed appropriate to summarize these results into a form that would perhaps be more manageable. One potential methodology in this regard has been offered by Tversky (1977). This method suggests that the perceived similarity of two forms is a function of the number of elements that they have in common, and also the number of elements that are held uniquely by only one of the forms. Thus, an attempt was made to predict the similarity ratings in the present experiment from both (1) the number of configural attributes held in common by two symbols, and (2) the number of configural attributes held uniquely by only one symbol in the pair.

The results of this regression analysis showed that 65% of the variance could be explained simply on the basis of the number of configural attributes that two symbols held in common. An additional 5% of the variance could be explained through consideration of the number of unique configural attributes in a symbol pair. Thus, the 12 predictors from the configural attribute set can be summarized in the form of two predictors: number of configural attributes held in common and number of unique configural attributes.

From this result, a discriminability-index ($D$) formula for evaluating a new candidate symbol $c$ with $n$ configural attributes is as follows ($i$ refers to the $i$th configural attribute of the candidate symbol). This procedure is analogous to comparing the candidate symbol to each of the 20 symbols in the sample symbol domain.

Number of common attributes $= \sum_{i=1}^{n} x_i$, where x is the number of the 20 symbols in the sample symbol domain having the configural attribute i. (1)

Number of unique attributes of $c$ $= \sum_{i=1}^{n} y_i$, where y is the number of the 20 symbols in the sample symbol domain not having the configural attribute i. (2)

Number of unique attributes of sample domain $= 54 - z$, where z is the number of common attributes. (There were 54 instances of attributes in total comprising the 20 symbols in the sample domain.) (3)

Taking the standardized regression weights from the multiple regression analysis outlined above,

$D_c = (0.07)$ [number of unique attributes of $c$ + number of unique attributes of sample domain] $- (0.31)$ [number of common attributes]. (4)

For example, consider the first three candidate symbols shown in Figure 3. Candidate Symbol 1 has two configural attributes, a

| CANDIDATE SYMBOL | DISCRIMINABILITY INDEX (Dc) | MEDIAN SEARCH TIME |
|---|---|---|
| 1. MU | 0.73 | 3.04 |
| 2. CEWI | 0.73 | 3.03 |
| 3. P L | 1.23 | 3.94 |
| 4. | 1.63 | 3.83 |
| 5. | 1.63 | 3.68 |
| 6. | 1.63 | 2.61 |
| 7. | 2.13 | 2.93 |
| 8. | 2.13 | 2.39 |
| 9. | 3.03 | 2.59 |
| 10. | 5.28 | 2.69 |
| 11. | 5.33 | 3.08 |
| 12. | 5.68 | 2.67 |
| 13. | 5.73 | 2.47 |
| 14. | 6.63 | 2.12 |
| 15. | 6.68 | 2.21 |
| 16. | 7.58 | 2.11 |
| 17. | 8.03 | 2.34 |
| 18. | 8.03 | 2.29 |

Figure 3. *The 18 candidate symbols used in Experiment 2, their derived discriminability indices, and the median search time to locate the symbols in an array.*

rectangle and alphanumerics. The former attribute is held in common with 11 of the 20 symbols in the sample symbol set shown in Figure 1, whereas the alphanumerics are found in z of the 20 symbols. Thus, from Equation 1, the "number of common attributes" for Candidate Symbol 1 is 13. From Equation 2, the value of "number of unique attributes of $c$" is $(20 - 11 = 9) + (20 - 2 = 18) = 27$. The value of "number of unique attributes of sample domain" is $54 - 13 = 41$, as specified by Equation 3. Therefore, $D_c$ for Candidate 1 using Equation 4 is $(+0.07)[27 + 41] - (0.31)[13] = 0.73$. For comparison, the value of $D_c$ for Candidate Symbol 2 is given by $(+0.07)[29 + 43] - (0.31)[11] = 1.63$, and for Candidate Symbol 3 is $(+0.07)[47 + 41] - (0.31)[13] = 2.13$. Thus, this methodology predicts that Candidate Symbol 3 should be most discriminable from the 20 sample symbols and that Candidate Symbol 1 should be least discriminable. Positive results from tests of predictions such as this one would provide validation for the discriminability-index equation. Work toward this goal is described below.

## EXPERIMENT 2

For purposes of evaluating the discriminability-index formula that was based on configural symbol attributes, 18 candidate symbols were chosen to be studied in a controlled validation experiment. These 18 symbols are presented in Figure 3 along with their respective discriminability indices. The symbols were chosen to provide a wide range of discriminability values. Further, to illustrate the potential diagnosticity of the formula, groups of symbols were embedded in the candidate symbol set, in which each group is composed of three alternative representations of the same concept. For example, in Figure 3, Symbols 2, 6, and 8 all denote combat electronic warfare intelligence and Symbols 5, 7, and 9 all denote air defense. As can be seen from a comparison of the values of $D_c$, certain symbols in each of these two sets are predicted to be more discriminable from the existing sample symbol domain than are others. Thus, the resolution of conflicts between alternative symbols such as these can be offered in terms of the discriminability indices. Specific predictions were evaluated in Experiment 2 so as to provide empirical validation for the formula.

## Method

*Subjects.* The subjects were nine employees of the Perceptronics Corporation who were unfamiliar with Army symbols.

*Procedure.* The experimental procedure was as follows. A 0.6 × 0.9 m magnetic board was used to display the 20 symbols in the sample domain from Experiment 1 in a random array. A battlefield background was drawn on the board with a black grease pencil; otherwise the background was white. Embedded within the array of symbols on each trial were two instances of one of the 18 candidate symbols to be evaluated. This symbol was also presented on a card that was shown to the subject before the trial began. The board was covered until the subject had thoroughly studied the card. The subject's task was to find both instances of the candidate symbol and to pick them from the board using one hand. The time to complete this task, which was recorded with a digital stopwatch, was taken as a measure of the discriminability of the candidate symbol in the context of the sample symbol domain. The experimenter was not aware of the purpose of the study. One trial was conducted, with each candidate symbol yielding 18 trials per subject in all. The spatial arrangement of the 20 symbols from Experiment 1, as well as the positioning of the two instances of the candidate symbol, was randomized across trials. The two instances of the candidate symbol were always separated by 36 cm. This was done to control for proximity effects in finding the two targets across trials. In addition, the order of testing the candidate symbols was randomized across subjects.

## Results and Discussion

The ordering of the 18 candidate symbols on search time was highly regular across the nine subjects, with only 12% of the variation among the search times being accounted for by the interaction between subjects and symbols. The median time to complete the search task for each of the 18 candidate symbols is presented in Figure 3. Attending first to Candidate Symbols 2, 6, and 8, which are alternative representations of the same concept, it can be seen that Symbol 8 has the shortest median search time, whereas Symbol 2 has the longest median search time. This pattern of results is as predicted by the discriminability-index equation. That is, the symbol with the largest discriminability index was found to require the shortest search time. Inspection of Symbols 5, 7, and 9 reveals an analogous pattern, again supporting the predictions of the discriminability-index formula.

Overall, the nine symbols with the highest discriminability indices had an average median search time of 2.44 s, whereas the nine symbols with the lowest indices had an average median search time of 3.12 s. Thus, as predicted, symbols with higher discriminability indices required less time to locate, $t(16) = 3.11, p < 0.01$. In correlational terms, more than 50% of the variance in the median search times could be accounted for with the discriminability indices ($r = 0.71$). A scatterplot of $D_c$ versus search time across subjects is presented in Figure 4. On the basis of these results, we conclude that the discriminability-index formula that was derived from the configural symbol attributes has a reasonable degree of validity.

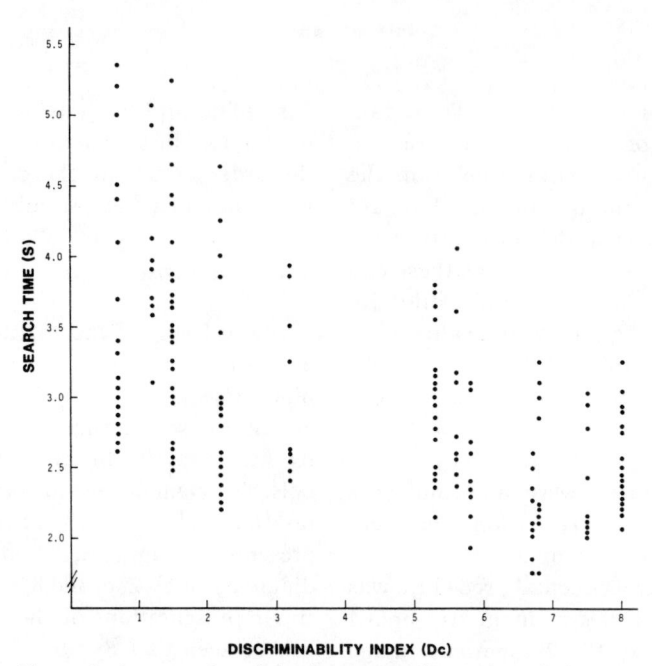

Figure 4. A scatterplot of the discriminability indices ($D_c$) versus search time for the 18 candidate symbols in Experiment 2.

## GENERAL DISCUSSION

The goal of this research was to develop a methodology for choosing among alternative new symbols for inclusion in an existing graphic-symbology data base. Specifically, a formula was derived to predict the discriminability of a new candidate symbol in the context of standard symbols from the Army's conventional display symbology, FM 21-30. This formula, which is easy to apply, was found to account for 50% of the variance in symbol search times in a laboratory task. Thus, the method clearly has promise. Indices obtained from a formula such as the one developed here could be used as part of the basis for choosing among alternative candidate symbols for inclusion in an existing symbol domain. Of course, other factors should also be considered in selecting symbols, such as the degree of association of the symbol with the concept to be portrayed.

Note that the design of a standard display symbology would necessarily be an iterative process. As additional symbols are accepted, the symbol data base for comparison with new symbols is altered. For example, at present, few tactical concepts are represented in FM 21-30 by verbal abbreviations; therefore, such alphanumeric symbols are highly discriminable from the existing symbols. However, the current trend to denote new concepts with alphanumerics will rapidly become an undesirable practice if used too often. Thus, when new concepts *must* be portrayed with alphanumerics, older symbols that include alphanumerics may have to be reevaluated and changed. In this sense, evaluating symbols is a complex iterative process, and certain suggestions for symbol design depend on current trends as well as on past practice. These results suggest that for any iteration, the selection of new symbols can be guided in part by a straightforward analysis of the physical attributes of the existing symbol domain.

If we know which symbol attributes are currently being used and which are being used frequently, then symbol designers might be encouraged to rely on other attributes. That is, the application of results like those reported here need not be restricted to post-design evaluations of symbols; rather, some a priori guidance might be offered. In this regard, both the rectangular external symbol shape and the "X" shape would appear to be symbol attributes to be avoided in FM 21-30 if possible, since they occur most frequently in the sample symbol domain. From the perspective of discriminability alone, all attributes of a new symbol would be made novel to the existing symbol set. To ease learning, however, similar symbol attributes are necessary to portray similar kinds of information. Otherwise, memory for the referents of the different symbols would rapidly become overtaxed. Thus, research is required to identify and catalog symbol attributes that should not be altered because of their organizational properties across symbols. Such work is in progress for the FM 21-30 symbol set (c.f., Landee, Geiselman, and Clark, 1981) and will serve to isolate those symbol attributes that should not be changed to promote intersymbol perceptual discriminability. Within these constraints, the selection of new symbols can be supported with the discriminability-index criterion developed here.

## ACKNOWLEDGMENTS

This work was funded by a contract from the U.S. Army Research Institute for the Behavioral and Social Sciences (ARI, Alexandria, Virginia) awarded to Perceptronics, Inc. Technical support was provided by Dr. Franklin Moses and Ms. Beverly Knapp, both from ARI. The opinions expressed in this paper are those of the authors and do not necessarily reflect the views of ARI, the United States Army, or the Department of Defense.

## REFERENCES

Attneave, F., and Arnoult, M.D. The quantitative study of shape and pattern recognition. In L. Uhr (Ed.) *Pattern recognition*, New York: Wiley, 1966.

Easterby, R. S. The perception of symbols for machine displays. *Ergonomics*, 1970, *13*, 149-158.

Landee, B. M., Geiselman, R. E., and Clark, C. Military symbology: A user community survey. Woodland Hills, CA: Perceptronics Technical Report, April, 1981.

Tversky, A. Features of similarity. *Psychological Review*, 1977, *84*, 327-352.

U.S. Army, *Field Manual 21-30: Military Symbols*. Washington, DC: Author, May, 1970.

Williams, E., and Teichner, W. H. Discriminability of symbols for tactical information displays. Washington DC: Air Force Office of Scientific Research Technical Report 79-1, January, 1979.

# 12

# System Design for Speech Recognition and Generation

CAROL A. SIMPSON,[1] *Psycho-Linguistic Research Associates, Menlo Park, California,*
MICHAEL E. McCAULEY, *Monterey Technologies, Inc., Carmel, California,*
ELLEN F. ROLAND, *Rolands and Associates Corporation, Monterey, California,*
JOHN C. RUTH, *McDonnell-Douglas Electronics Co., St. Charles, Missouri, and*
BEVERLY H. WILLIGES, *Virginia Polytechnic Institute and State University, Blacksburg, Virginia*

*This article reviews human factors research on the design of systems that use speech recognition for human control of the system or that use speech generation for the display of information. Speech technology terms are defined and the current status of the field is reviewed. Included are the performance of current speech recognition and generation algorithms, descriptions of several applications of the technology to particular tasks, and a discussion of research on design principles for speech interfaces. Finally, directions for further research are suggested. The need for better simulation techniques and performance measures is stressed, as is the importance of considering the entire system in which speech technology will function.*

## INTRODUCTION

Language is one of the outstanding capabilities of humans. Human-machine systems have long included written language (e.g., alphanumeric displays and keyboards), but spoken language has been used only for interpersonal communications. Automatic speech recognition and speech generation by machine now offer the promise of person-system transactions via spoken language. Speech input/output (I/O) systems accept spoken input (speech controls), or they "display" information to the user by means of the spoken word (speech displays).

Automatic speech technology is of interest within the human factors community because of its potential as a tool to help the human operator to perform certain tasks. Its potential lies in reducing or reallocating operator workload by providing an alternative I/O channel to the normally overloaded visual-manual channel. But it is only a tool, not a panacea, for the overloaded operator.

The challenge to the human factors field is to determine when, where, and how automated speech technology should be used in person-system transactions. This challenge is formidable because the technology is evolving, and guidelines for its application will depend on many variables. These variables include the characteristics of the users, the physical environment, the communications environment, the operator's workload,

[1] Requests for reprints should be sent to Carol A. Simpson, Psycho-Linguistic Research Associates, 2055 Sterling Ave., Menlo Park, CA 94025.

the constraints imposed by the task, and the stress on the operator.

In general, the strategy for the human factors contribution to the field of speech-interactive systems is three-pronged: (1) to provide methodologies for identifying appropriate applications of speech technology, (2) to select appropriate speech recognition or generation algorithms and system characteristics, and (3) to integrate speech subsystems within the context of the user's task. The current state of the art provides some but not all of the procedures with which to implement this strategy. By their absence, the missing pieces suggest directions for future research.

## TERMS AND DEFINITIONS

A human-machine control and display system is composed of a human, a machine, one or more controls, one or more displays, and an environment (Chapanis, 1976). A *voice-interactive system* is one that includes speech recognition as one form of user control or information input, and speech generation as one form of information display. There will also be systems that use one but not both of these technologies.

A superficial examination of the terminology in speech recognition and in speech generation obscures the commonality of concepts in these two technologies, which are, in many respects, mirror images of each other.

*Speech Recognition Terms*

From a human factors perspective, a *speech-recognition system* is composed of a human speaker, a recognition algorithm, and a device that responds appropriately to the recognized speech. The algorithm recognizes different human speech utterances and translates them into symbol strings. Those utterances could be words, phrases, or, at a lower level, syllables or *phonemes*—the vowel and consonant sounds of the language. The device assigns meaning to the symbol strings in the context of the human's task.

The term *voice recognition* is sometimes used interchangeably with the term *speech recognition*, leading to confusion with the related technology of speaker identification or voice identification. Speaker identification is the automatic identification of a given human speaker. To avoid such confusion, this paper will use the term *speech recognition* exclusively.

*Speaker dependence.* Speech recognition systems vary with respect to several parameters. Speaker dependence refers to the extent to which the system must have data about the voice characteristics of the particular human speaker(s) using it. *Speaker-dependent* recognition systems can recognize the speech of a particular human speaker only if examples of that person's speech have been provided. The vast majority of speech-recognition systems are speaker dependent. *Speaker-independent* systems theoretically can recognize speech spoken by any human in a particular language. Speaker-independent voice recognition is available for small vocabulary sets of from 10 to 20 utterances. In practice, recognition accuracy depends on the similarity of the speech characteristics of the group of users that use the system. So-called speaker-independent systems could be said to be *group dependent*. The less variability among speakers in the user group, the better will be the average recognition accuracy for the group using the system. Speech spoken with a foreign accent, for example, is less reliably recognized than is speech spoken with the accent for which the system has been developed. Also, in practice, it is difficult for a speaker-independent system to recognize both male and female speech (Rollins, 1984).

*Speech variability.* Linguists recognize at least five levels of variability in spoken language, including language families, individual languages, dialects, idiolects, and variations in the speech of individual speakers over time. The categorization of dialects themselves is multidimensional and can be made geographically, by social class, by age, and even by neighborhood (for an introduction to dialectology, see Allen and Underwood, 1971). An *idiolect* is the speech of a single individual. An ideolect varies over time as a function of physiological, psychological, and sociological factors. Similar idiolects can be grouped according to various dimensions, for example, sex, accent, or dialect.

The current practice that distinguishes between speaker-dependent and speaker-independent systems grossly simplifies the range of speaker variability. Even speaker-dependent systems will recognize people who have not enrolled the system, but the recognition accuracy will be poor. The distinction between speaker-dependent and speaker-independent systems is based largely on the engineering strategy for establishing templates. It belies the range of variability in speech and the factors that account for varying amounts of the variability, such as regional accent, sex, stress/workload, and fear. Human speech variability and large vocabulary size are two major challenges for speech-recognition systems. Advances in these areas will depend on fundamental research in linguistics at all levels of language structure (Fujimura, 1984).

*Speaking mode.* Another parameter of recognition systems is the speaking mode, the manner in which utterances are spoken to the system (National Research Council [NRC], 1984). *Isolated word systems* are most prevalent. With isolated word systems, the user must pause briefly (approximately 100 ms) between vocabulary items when speaking to the system. *Connected word systems* are able to recognize words within utterances spoken without artificial pauses between words. However, the individual words are spoken with the same intonation pattern that would be used if they were read from a list. The term *continuous speech recognition* has often been used to refer to what is here called *connected word recognition*. In this article, *continuous speech recognition* is reserved for recognition of utterances spoken with natural speech rhythm and intonation (prosodics). The final term, *continuous speech understanding* adds another dimension to the recognition task. It has been used to refer to systems that attempt to accomplish tasks using continuous speech input (see NRC, 1984).

*Vocabulary size.* A third parameter is vocabulary size. Speech-recognition systems with *fixed vocabulary* must be provided with samples of each word or phrase they are to recognize. They perform acoustic pattern matching at the word and phrase level and typically handle vocabularies of from 100 to 200 utterances (Kersteen and Damos, 1983). Algorithms are under development for *unlimited vocabulary* systems that analyze the speech into phonetic segments, determine the words spoken, and perhaps generate correctly spelled text.

*Enrollment.* A fourth parameter is the type of *enrollment*. Enrollment is the process of providing templates to the recognition system for the different vocabulary items. Speaker-dependent systems must be enrolled separately for each speaker who will use them if good recognition accuracy is to be obtained. Most systems provide a procedure for *user enrollment*. Some systems are more flexible than others in the permissible procedures. Speaker-independent systems, in contrast, may be designed for *vendor enrollment*. This means that the vendor develops the templates that the vendor believes will result in the best speaker-independent recognition accuracy. Some researchers have turned speaker-dependent systems into group-dependent or quasi-speaker-independent systems by means of creative enrollment procedures (e.g., Poock, Schwalm, Martin, and Roland, 1982).

*Speech-Generation Terms*

A speech-generation system is the mirror image of a recognition system. It is composed of a device that generates messages in the form of symbol strings, a speech-generation algorithm that converts the symbol strings to an acoustic imitation of speech, and a human listener. A speech-generation system operates in the context of the user's task environment.

*Method of generation.* Speech generation systems, like recognition systems, vary with respect to several parameters. One is the method of speech generation. The two primary methods are synthesized and digitized speech. *Synthesized speech* refers to speech generated entirely by rule, without the aid of an original human recording. The term *digitized speech* applies to human speech that was originally recorded digitally, and then (usually) transformed into a more compressed data format. The most common compression techniques include, but are not limited to, Fourier Transform, Linear Predictive Coding (LPC), and Waveform Parameter Encoding. Another pair of terms used to describe these methods are *synthesis by rule* for speech synthesis and *synthesis by analysis* for digitized speech generation that uses a data compression technique (Flanagan, 1972).

*Vocabulary size.* Another parameter is vocabulary size. Speech generation systems can have a *fixed vocabulary* or an *unlimited vocabulary*. Fixed vocabulary systems contain a set of words or phrases that can be combined to produce messages. Unlimited vocabulary systems can produce an unlimited number of messages from normally spelled text, from phonemes, or from phonetic segments (Simpson, 1981a; 1981c). Digitized speech systems are limited to fixed vocabularies. Synthesized speech systems can have either a fixed or an unlimited vocabulary. Fixed vocabulary systems are *user programmable* only if the user can change the vocabulary items. They are *vendor programmable* if the user must rely on the manufacturer or some other third party for new vocabulary.

*Voice type.* Digitized speech systems can have an unlimited variety of different voices, since they depend on human speakers for their vocabulary. However, once a particular speaker has been selected for an application, the digitized speech system, in order to sound consistent, is dependent on that same human speaker for new vocabulary. Synthesized speech systems do not depend on a human speaker for new vocabulary, but the number of different voice types than can be obtained from a given system is limited and varies currently from one to about six. Most synthesized voices can be varied under program control with respect to fundamental frequency (perceived as voice pitch) and speaking rate. Most commercially available synthesizers produce male-sounding speech although a few also produce female-sounding speech. With software control of the pronunciation of individual phonemes, some variation in dialect or accent can be obtained. For reviews of the commercially available speech-generation devices see Butler, Manaker and Obert-Thorn (1981), Sherwood (1979), Simpson (1981a), and Smith (1984).

*Data rate, intelligibility, and naturalness.* Three parameters often used to evaluate speech-generation systems are *data rate*, *intelligibility*, and *naturalness*. Data-rate terms are often confusing in the speech product literature because they can refer either to the amount of storage needed to store speech data or to the rate at which speech data are transmitted to the speech device or to the rate at which the resulting speech is actually spoken (Simpson, 1983b). The terms naturalness and intelligibility often are confused in today's product literature and, unfortunately, the scientific literature as well. The term *intelligibility* has a very precise meaning—the percentage of speech units correctly recognized by a human listener out of a set of such units. The units may be words, sentences, individual speech sounds (called phonemes), or even the perceptual acoustic features of those phonemes. (See Kryter [1972] for a review of intelligibility testing.) *Naturalness* refers to a listener's judgment on a scale of the degree to which the speech sounds as though it were spoken by a human. Intelligibility and naturalness can be measured independently, although there are no standardized tests of naturalness (Simpson, 1983b). Further, naturalness and intelligibility are not necessarily correlated (cf. Thomas, Rosson, and Chodorow, 1984). For example, a radio announcer may sound natural in a background of static noise, but the speech may have low intelligibility. Conversely, synthesized speech warning messages that are well-known to a pilot may sound mechanical, yet pilots have rated such messages as seeming more intelligible than are human voice messages transmitted via aircraft radio (Simpson, 1983b; Simpson and Williams, 1980).

*Measures of Algorithm Performance*

Recognition accuracy is the most commonly used measure of performance for speech recognition algorithms. Its counterpart is speech intelligibility, which is the most commonly used performance measure for speech generation algorithms. Both measures are simply the percentage of speech utterances correctly recognized by the "listener" out of a set of such utterances presented under a particular set of listening conditions. When measuring recognition accuracy, the "listener" is the recognition algorithm. Conversely, human listeners are used to measure the intelligibility of speech generated by algorithm.

The classes of errors that occur when speech is presented to either humans or machines are the same, but human and machine performance may differ substantially. Errors fall into one of four mutually exclusive categories: (1) substitution errors (one utterance from the vocabulary is mistaken for another), (2) insertion errors (an utterance is reported that was not spoken), (3) deletion errors (an utterance that was spoken was not reported), and (4) rejection errors (an utterance that is a legal item in the vocabulary is detected but not recognized). Rejection errors are frequently reported in the speech recognition literature. They are not reported as such in the speech intelligibility literature but occur when the subject responds with "don't know."

Both machines and humans also can make correct rejections. For machines (i.e., recognition algorithms), a correct rejection is made when the algorithm refuses to process an utterance that is not in the legal vocabulary, for example, if the user coughed or said something to another human in the work environment. Similarly, human listeners will correctly reject utterances spoken in an unfamiliar foreign language, and, under conditons of poor signal-to-noise ratio, they will also correctly reject nonsense words in their own language and often will then substitute a word that makes sense (Garnes and Bond, 1977, as reported in Bond and Garnes, 1980). This human capability (to substitute a word that makes sense) requires knowledge of syntax, semantics, and pragmatics that is well beyond that found in commercially available speech recognition systems (Fujimura, 1984; NRC, 1984).

Although intelligibility and recognition accuracy are conceptually identical, the performance of speech generation algorithms speaking to human listeners is quantitatively and qualitatively different from the performance of speech recognition algorithms "listening" to human speakers. Accordingly, the remainder of this article treats separately research on speech recognition, on speech generation, and on the integration of recognition and generation into voice-interactive systems.

## SPEECH RECOGNITION RESEARCH

In the introduction, a three-pronged strategy for human factors effort in automatic speech technology was stated. Two of the three levels, namely, (1) identification of speech recognition applications, and (2) selection of appropriate recognition system characteristics, will be the subject of this section on speech recognition research. The third, integration of speech subsystems within the user's task, will be discussed in the section on system integration.

*Applications*

Selection of test-beds for speech technology has not been systematic. Nevertheless, the application research has proven useful in helping to identify characteristics of appropriate applications, potential human-machine interaction problems, required system capabilities, and the need for an integrated systems approach to incorporating speech-recognition systems. A number of application examples (e.g., Breaux, 1977; Grady, 1982; McCauley and Semple, 1980; McCauley, Root, and Muckler, 1982; Moore, Moore, and Ruth, 1984; Poock and Roland, 1984), reviewed in NRC (1984), provide a cross section of attempted applications of speech-recognition technology.

*Observations from case studies.* A review of these and other case studies leads to some observations about speech recognition technology and its integration into operational systems, condensed here from the NRC (1984) report. (1) Recognition accuracy was one of the main limitations. (2) The variability in human speech under stressful conditions contributed to unacceptable performance. (3) The success of voice-interactive systems in most applications arose from their integration with other procedures or automation features. (4) Projects designed from inception to incorporate a voice-interactive system had a greater probability of success than when the capability was added to an existing system. (5) Highly connected systems that depend on accurate speech recognition input tended to amplify the effects of recognition errors. (6) A staged process of voice-interactive system development, including regular checks and tests by users, was more likely to lead to successful systems. (7) Speaker enrollment (in a speaker-dependent system) was sometimes more effective when conducted in the context of the operational task. (8) Other voice-communication functions in the task environment sometimes interfered with the speech recognition task. (9) For externally paced tasks, the timing of the task sequence was disrupted by either long recognition time or recognition errors. (10) The lack of an appropriate recognition feedback mechanism tended to confuse operators regarding the status of the system.

*Speech Recognition Task Selection*

One compelling reason to incorporate speech recognition into complex systems is the potential for reducing the visual-manual task load. However, the decision to use speech for a particular task requires a matching of speech mode features with task characteristics (Simpson, 1984) and analysis of the advantages and constraints of the manual mode versus the speech mode in the context of the tasks to be performed (North and Lea, 1982).

The research on task selection has been conducted on two major fronts. Some researchers have aimed to develop and apply methodologies for selecting appropriate tasks for speech (North and Lea, 1982) and user-preference questionnaires for application of voice recognition and speech generation (Brown, Bertone, and Obermeyer, 1968; Cotton, McCauley, North, and Strieb, 1983; Kersteen and Damos, 1983; Williams and Simpson, 1976). Others have investigated human speech data-entry performance when simultaneous verbal and manual tasks are required (e.g., Wickens, Sandry, and Vidulich 1983).

One study determined that speech is useful primarily for complex tasks requiring cognitive and/or visual effort, whereas simple tasks involving the copying of numeric data were accomplished more quickly and accurately with keyboard entry as compared with voice entry (Welch, 1977). A series of dual-task tracking and data-entry studies (Coler, Plummer, Huff, and Hitchcock, 1977; Simpson, Coler, and Huff, 1982) conducted in the presence of helicopter noise and helicopter motion, respectively, found that, across all noise and motion conditions, tracking performance was less degraded with data entry by speech recognition than it was with data entry by keyboard. Recognition accuracy and keyboard accuracy for the no-noise and no-motion conditions were 99%. Recognition accuracy, however, declined slightly in the presence of noise and motion whereas keyboard accuracy did not. Another study found that in the presence of a simultaneous verbal task, voice data entry resulted in less decrement in tracking performance than did keyed data entry (Harris, North, and Owens, 1977). However, it has also been found that recognition error rates can increase by as much as 39% with concurrent tracking, suggesting that task stress has a sufficiently large effect on human speech production to degrade recognition accuracy (Armstrong, 1980).

Research comparing speed and accuracy of voice versus manual keyboard input has produced conflicting results, depending on the unit of input (alphanumerics or functions) and other task-specific variables. For example, one study on the use of voice input to a computerized war game concluded that the manual method of entry was faster than voice input (McSorley, 1981). Another study, conducted in the same laboratory, to assess speech recognition for operation of a distributed network system, showed speech input to be superior to manual entry with regard to both speed and accuracy (Poock, 1981a). These different results were primarily attributed to task requirements, since the majority of other factors (user group composition, training, equipment, and environment) were constant. The results of these several studies suggest that the benefit to be derived from voice input and output is highly dependent on the specific task and environment.

In summary, the selection of potential tasks for speech recognition should be based on specific task requirements. Speech is not a useful substitute for manual data entry when such tasks already are being performed successfully (Welch, 1977). Speech input is likely to improve system throughput only in complex tasks that involve high cognitive, visual, and manual loading. Such limits on improvements to system throughput using the speech mode are likely to exist irrespective of any future improvements in the technology simply because of the characteristics of speech itself. These characteristics and their implications will be discussed in detail in the section on system integration. Clearly, more research is needed to better understand the complex interaction of the speech mode, voice-recognition technology, the user, and the task being accomplished.

Methods and guidelines are needed for identifying tasks that are amenable for speech recognition applications. Interview and questionnaire techniques are helpful but they are limited in predictive power because the potential user community is familiar with their job but naive with respect to the capabilities and limitations of speech technology.

Finally, no analytic procedure for selecting speech tasks is likely to be accurate enough to enable detailed specification of the speech system requirements. Further work is needed on simulation techniques to establish the speech system requirements early in the system design process. This will be discussed in the next section on the second level of the research strategy, the selection of recognition system characteristics.

*Selecting Speech Recognition System Characteristics*

Given an appropriate task for the speech mode and given a set of performance requirements for the application system that will incorporate that speech task, the characteristics of the speech recognition system must be carefully selected. The algorithm, the human operator, and the interface that links them are all components of the speech recognition system for which the proper characteristics are to be chosen. Therefore, research on algorithm performance and on human-system performance is essential to recognition system selection. Research to date has documented a variety of factors that affect recognition system performance.

*Speech recognition algorithm performance.* Many factors influence recognition accuracy. They can be viewed in terms of the characteristics of the physical speech signal itself and the context in which it is spoken. Today's recognition algorithms, however, are for the most part unable to take advantage of the pragmatic and linguistic context of an utterance. And, their performance is far more fragile than humans' listening performance with respect to degradations or changes in the speech signal or the physical context in which it is spoken. Currently, speaker-dependent isolated-word systems can perform in the laboratory with vocabularies of up to 100 words with an error rate of less than 1%. However, recognizer performance demonstrated favorably in the laboratory often degrades dramatically under the effects of noise, user stress, and operational demands on the user (NRC, 1984).

*User characteristics.* User characteristics can affect speech recognition system performance. Successful applications of speech recognition to date usually involve a small number of carefully selected talkers who have been trained to speak distinctly and to use the equipment correctly. Doddington and Schalk (1981) reported that three-fourths of the talkers they tested had better-than-average recognition scores, indicating that a few people had a majority of the problems.

*Enrollment.* Enrollment is another critical element in speaker-dependent speech recognition systems. Enrollment techniques that avoid any systematic bias in the speech samples seem to be most successful. For example, recognition accuracy is better when the several tokens of each vocabulary item are sampled randomly instead of collecting all tokens of a vocabulary item in sequence (Poock, 1981b). Recognition performance is also enhanced when enrollment occurs in an acoustic or motion environment similar to that of operational conditions (Simpson et al., 1982). In a subsequent study with a different recognition system, it was found that enrollment could be done in a quiet environment for application in cockpit noise levels up to 100 dB SPL with no adverse effects on recognition accuracy (Coler, 1982). In general, performance of different commercial systems varies considerably as a function of enrollment environment (NRC, 1984). For enrollment prompts to the user, the visual mode is usually used. The use of synthesized speech to prompt enrollment has been questioned because some speakers tend to mimic the prompt (McCauley, 1984).

*Adaptive recognition algorithms.* Adaptive recognition algorithms for speaker-dependent systems are one method for dealing with speech variability over time for a given speaker. The algorithm alters its reference template to reflect slow changes in the user's pronunciation over time. To do this, it needs feedback on the accuracy of each recognition attempt. One study (Coler and Plummer, 1974) reported an improvement from 95% to

99.9% recognition accuracy using an adaptive algorithm.

*System feedback.* Feedback by the system to the user may enhance performance, either by altering the user's speech or by allowing for user error correction. Poock, Martin, and Roland (1983) found no conclusive evidence that different levels and types of feedback contributed to changes in speaking patterns or to improved recognition accuracy. However, it was shown that feedback in general affects recognition performance. Recognition performance with subjects not accustomed to feedback improved when some type of feedback was presented, and, conversely, was degraded if the feedback to which a user was accustomed was reduced. In the absence of feedback, a user may incorrectly assume that a sequence of voice commands was executed properly by the system. For example, one study (Schurick, Williges, and Maynard, in press) demonstrated that accuracy in a database entry task using speech could be increased from 70% to 97% correct with feedback and user error correction. Although there is general agreement about the need for feedback, an important issue for human factors integration is how to best provide feedback to avoid interfering with the operator's primary task and to maximize throughput.

*Error correction.* Speech recognition system performance can be improved with two types of error correction. The system can be designed to detect illegal input sequences automatically and to correct them to the most likely legal sequence. It can then optionally present the correction to the user for verification. For example, with syntactically constrained dialogues it has been suggested that the recognizer could select both the first- and second-choice vocabulary items by using standard parsing techniques (Spine, Maynard, and Williges, 1983). Another suggestion is the use of subject-specific confusion matrices as well as the logical "anding" of utterances when users are asked by the system to repeat (Bierman, Rodman, Rubin, and Heidlage, 1984). Although such techniques can improve recognition accuracy, they do not ultimately guarantee a semantically correct message or command. Thus, the human ought to remain in the loop, at least for critical entries.

In addition to automatic error correction, provision should be made for error correction by the user. Three documented types of user errors include failure to remember the vocabulary set, failure to follow the speech cadence restrictions, and conversing with coworkers with an active microphone. Vocabulary errors involve speaking other words outside the vocabulary, including synonyms. Cadence errors include using connected speech with discrete word recognizers. Other types of user errors are to be expected. Lack of a rapid error-correction capability can be frustrating to the user who is engaged in a dynamic, time-critical task, and it can drastically increase the time to achieve a desired system goal via speech recognition.

*Environmental factors.* The task environment comprises a number of factors that must be studied for their effect on human performance and therefore on speech task design. Physical, physiological, emotional, and workload factors can be expected to partially determine the success or failure of a particular speech system design. Only after the effects of these factors are known can speech systems be designed in ways that will enhance rather than hinder human performance and thus systems performance.

The major environmental factor that has been studied is the effect of background noise on recognition accuracy, but little is known of its effect on the performance of humans who are using speech recognition devices. There is qualitative information available on the effects of environmental stress on human speaking performance, but little quantitative data. Relationships between psychophysiological state and voice parameters have been investigated, including changes in laryngeal tension, rise in the fundamental frequency, pitch perturbations, and breath noises (see NRC, 1984, for references). One study manipulated task-induced stress to determine the effects of speaker stress on speech (Hecker, Stevens, von Bismark, and Williams, 1968). This study documented the variety of differences between speech spoken with and without stressful conditions as well as differences in the effects of task-induced stress on the speech of individual speakers. Because stress-related speech changes can take many forms and are neither consistent among people nor tasks, speech recognition performance may vary dramatically as a function of the work environment. This may be why most successful applications of speech recognition do not involve severe time constraints or life-threatening situations.

## Human-System Performance Measurement

Although general methods for performance measurement are available for different levels of human/system performance, the measurement of speech recognition performance in a complex control and display task is more difficult and less understood. In addition to speed and accuracy of operator performance of complex tasks, it is necessary to measure variables such as operator workload and operator ability to deal with novel situations. Also, conflicts between other controls and displays and speech controls and displays have to be assessed.

## Simulating Recognition Systems

By simulating speech recognition hardware, various levels of speech-recognition capability can be controlled and evaluated experimentally. Reseach using simulations of speech controls and displays originated with studies of how people communicate to solve problems (Chapanis, 1975). Problem solution occurred most rapidly whenever the voice link was available. Other modes were typing and handwriting. Because this study did not restrict the speech channel in vocabulary, syntax, or permissible speaking cadence, its relevance to current speech recognition capabilities is limited, but it illustrates the power of voice communication for problem solving, emphasizes the importance of further development of speech recognition technology, and demonstrates simulation of speech recognition as a research methodology.

Since those first studies, several attempts have been made to study system performance and acceptability when the speech channel is restricted in various ways to simulate the use of speech recognition hardware. One study simulated a listening typewriter, where speech was constrained either in terms of vocabulary size or speech pause requirements (Gould, Conti, and Hovanyecz, 1983). Shortcomings of the simulation included slow response time, failure to simulate misrecognition errors as well as nonrecognitions, and inconsistent restriction of discrete data entry when the spelling mode was used to enter words not in the vocabulary. However, the simulation contributes to the development of techniques to simulate speech recognition for human factors research.

Another study demonstrates the difficulty of designing a good simulation of speech recognition. The study attempted to evaluate user acceptance of various levels of recognition accuracy (Poock and Roland, 1982). Because subjects read words in a prescribed order, it was difficult to control appropriate feedback when the subject spoke the wrong word or made a detectable noise. Also, because the subjects had no real task to accomplish, they often failed to read the visual feedback provided and were unaware of errors. As a result, all levels of speech recognition accuracy tested in the simulation were judged acceptable by the subjects, probably indicating simply that they liked the concept of voice input. Avoidance of these and related problems in future simulation designs will be no trivial task.

A study by Zoltan-Ford (1984) demonstrated a simulation technique that was quite believable for subjects and provides encouraging data on successful methods for constraining users' syntax and vocabulary when they speak to a recognition system. Subjects conversing with a computer were not constrained to use any particular syntax or vocabulary. However, the computer, simulated by the experimenter, "responded" with a constrained vacabulary and syntax. The subjects imitated the "computer" and gradually adopted its vocabulary and syntax over the course of the experiment.

*Future Speech Recognition Research*

*Simulation.* Simulation techniques are needed to provide controlled variation along such dimensions as speed of recognition and feedback, recognition accuracy level, and types of recognition errors. In addition, system performance measures must be developed that integrate recognizer performance, human performance, task workload, system utility, and user acceptance.

Important issues to be addressed include the following: speed and accuracy requirements for various applications; criticality of errors, by type; appropriate forms of error correction; the need for speaker independence; the need for connected or continuous speech; the effects of large vocabulary size; and human ability to constrain speech in terms of vocabulary, syntax, and speaking patterns (NRC, 1984). Data from these simulations can be used to determine candidate tasks for speech and the speech recognition performance required for successful use of a speech database. The simulations can provide samples of speech produced under various task conditions, such as noise, mental workload, stress, and various levels of recognition error rate. Finally, the simulation would provide a research environment for developing general guidelines on how speech data entry should be integrated into different task environments.

*Enrollment methods and user training.* Better enrollment methods are needed for speaker-dependent systems. These methods should permit enrollment of the speech recognition system in a benign environment when it is to be used in a more hostile environment. Automatic updating of speech samples while the system is in use may be a partial solution. Solution of this problem will reduce enrollment costs not only in terms of equipment operation, but also with regard to operator time, stress, and fatigue.

Better methods are needed for predicting the speech recognition performance on the basis of user characteristics. For example, the user's dialect may influence recognition performance. Research is needed on techniques for predicting low-performance users and on potential remediating methods. Training users to modify their speech patterns will be difficult because speech is a highly overlearned behavior that is difficult to modify. The extent to which training can reliably alter speaking habits, particularly under stressful conditions, has yet to be determined. This is an important research issue especially for the types of applications envisioned by the military sector.

*Performance measurement.* Improved performance measurement is essential for providing data for decisions about system design and effectiveness. More detailed analysis of recognition algorithm errors will permit a better understanding of the effects of different user characteristics, environmental factors, and task-related factors on recognition accuracy. Errors should be displayed in a confusion matrix format, at the task, utterance, and phoneme levels. High-fidelity quality audio recordings of subjects' utterances spoken to speech recognizers under known, controlled experimental conditions ought to be routinely made and analyzed to discover speech variability factors that affect recognition performance.

Speech recognition performance should be measured within a realistic task scenario, both within the laboratory and in the actual operational setting, including worst-case conditions. Laboratory benchmark tests using standard vocabularies, experienced users, and controlled environments, are useful for comparing recognizers but they are not sufficient for predicting actual performance in operational systems. Adequate methods for the measurement of both human and recognizer performance under realistic conditions remain to be developed. The importance of speed versus accuracy will vary with the application. Speed of command entry will not always be the primary measure of effectiveness when the user is engaged in simultaneous manual tasks. For example, performance on a primary manual task may be facilitated with the use of voice on a secondary task even though that secondary task is then accomplished at a slower but still acceptable rate. Generic measures need to be developed that can be applied to task- or mission-specific events.

Operator workload is an important measure because it can be used to compare system design alternatives. Currently, there is no single reliable method for assessing human workload in a variety of tasks (Wierwille and Connor, 1983). Although some research is being conducted in this area, an emphasis on this topic would be valuable, not only for speech recognition applications, but for many other issues in human-system interface design.

## SPEECH GENERATION RESEARCH

Properly designed voice displays can potentially unload a user's visual system when performing visually demanding tasks. Examples of such tasks are reading technical maintenance or operations manuals while operating or repairing a system, looking through a microscope or other visual system to position one's work, reading flight charts while flying in busy airspace, checking multiple visual readouts while operating a nuclear power station, simultaneously controlling a robotic arm and multiple cameras on board a space station, monitoring multiple vital-sign displays during surgery, and editing text on a visual display. In such situations, not only is the user engaged in a visual task, but efficiency of task performance also depends on the user being able to maintain eye point of regard. Spoken messages, delivered by speech displays, carrying certain information might be more effective and result in more efficient overall task performance than if the same information were displayed visually.

The strategy for effective use of speech generation, like that for speech recognition, is threefold. Methodologies are needed for (1) identification of applications for speech generation, (2) selection of appropriate algorithms and system characteristics, and (3) integration of speech generation into the design of voice-interactive systems.

### Applications

The most common approach for identifying applications for speech generation has been to select a particular human-machine system as a candidate for speech messages and to simulate a version of the system that uses speech messages. Usually, an existing problem such as high visual workload or poor performance is the basis for investigating the speech mode in place of the visual mode. Typically, an experiment is performed using the current system as a control condition, and various measures of task performance are used to determine the relative merits of visual and speech output for the task in question. The results of such studies support decisions regarding the utility of speech displays for that particular application, but they are difficult to generalize to other applications. However, they may suggest areas for more generic research and provide valuable input into human factors issues regarding speech display design.

*General guidelines for use of speech displays.* Despite the limited generalizability of results from such application-specific research, there are some general guidelines for selecting functions for speech. These are based to a small degree on experimental data, but mostly on a combination of deductive and inductive reasoning. For example, Deathridge (1972) lists general guidelines for deciding first between audio and visual displays and then for deciding between speech and nonspeech audio displays. Situations in which auditory (speech or nonspeech) rather than visual displays should be used include: (1) when warning signals are to be given, because the auditory sense is omnidirectional, (2) when there are too many visual displays, (3) when information must be presented independently of head movement or body position, (4) when darkness limits or precludes vision, and (5) when there are conditions of anoxia, because of the greater resistance of auditory sensitivity to anoxia as compared with visual sensitivity. Situations in which speech rather than nonspeech messages should be used are: (1) when flexibility is required, (2) when the message source must be identified, (3) when listeners have no special training in coded signals, (4) when rapid, two-way information exchanges are required, (5) when the message deals with a future time, requiring preparation, and (6) in situations of stress, which might cause the operator to forget the meaning of coded signals. The state of the art in selecting voice functions has not really progressed beyond this philosophical stage.

Simpson (1983a) and Williges and Williges (1982) independently added the same two items to the inventory: (1) spoken information should he highly reliable, and (2) spoken information should be intended for use in the immediate future, due to its poor retainability in short-term memory.

*Selection of Functions for Speech Displays*

It is important to select the best functions for speech displays. These functions can be classified according to the speech acts (Searle, 1969) they represent. Simpson (in press) lists five basic types of information (i.e., speech acts) for which speech displays may be useful. These basic information types transcend specific applications. They are warnings, advisories, responses to user queries, feedback from control inputs, and commands. A sixth class, not listed, comprises spoken prompts from the system to the user to elicit user action, such as data entry. It is unlikely that any particular type of speech act will be amenable to speech output in all situations. Rather, the combination of task and user characteristics associated with a particular application will dictate the applicability of speech displays.

*Warnings.* Of the six types of speech acts, warnings have received most of the attention in speech display research. Results from a series of studies (summarized in Simpson and Navarro, 1984) suggest that voice warnings should be worded as short phrases containing a minimum of four or five syllables to minimize listener attention needed for what they call "perceptual copying" and to ensure high message intelligibility for unexpected messages in the presence of competing noise and speech.

The voice used for cockpit displays needs to be distinctive (Brown et al., 1968; Simpson and Williams, 1980; U.S. Dept. of Defense, 1981) in order to stand out against other human speech. A female voice for environments in which male voices prevail has frequently been suggested for warnings because of its unique voice quality (e.g., Brown et al., 1968), but there are few such environments today. There is also an accumulation of reports from pilots who have served in speech-display flight simulation studies that the voice ought not to sound too human (Simpson, 1981b; Voorhees, Bucher, Huff, Simpson, and Williams, 1983) lest it be confused with human speech. The underlying concept here is that a machine should have a machine voice as a cue to its identity when it speaks.

A main variable in the Voorhees et al. (1983) study was voice type (Simpson, Marchionda-Frost, and Navarro, 1984). Male digitized, female digitized, and a digitized version of synthesizer-generated speech were compared. Pilots reported extreme dissatisfaction with the slow speaking rate of all three digitized voices, caused by the artificial pauses that were introduced by the word-concatenation method used to generate the messages. Direct synthesized speech with more natural prosodics was judged by the same pilots as preferable to both the digitized synthesized and the digitized human female speech used in the flight simulation.

A series of studies has addressed system response time (defined below under human-system performance measurement) for synthesized voice warnings with and without preceding alerting tones or words. First, Simpson and Williams (1980) found that an alerting tone preceding a synthesized voice warning *increased* system response time, whereas lengthening message wording with an extra word to add semantic context did not increase system response time. Hakkinen and Williges (1984) replicated these results but also found that when synthesized voice was used for multiple functions with the alerting tone as a variable only for warning messages, then an alerting tone used exclusively before warnings improved the detection of urgent messages without increasing system response time to these urgent messages. Studies of voice warning prefixes (Bucher, Karl, Voorhees, and Werner, 1984; Bucher et al., reported in Simpson and Navarro, 1984) found no difference in system response time as a function of prefix type, despite differences in actual length of the different prefixes (tone, neutral word, one of three semantic cue words). These studies support the possibility that synthesized speech is somehow distinctive, as compared with human speech, and can perform the alerting function concurrently with the information transfer function. The physical correlates of this distinctiveness remain to be determined experimentally.

*Prompts.* Prompts by the system to the user have been studied by Mountford and her colleagues (Mountford, North, Metz, and Graffunder, 1982). They studied different levels of verbosity for voice messages used as feedback and prompts to users of a simulated voice data-entry system for flight planning and navigation. They found that short dialogues with little prompting and terse feedback provided the best data-entry performance. Future research may well find that the trade-off between verbosity and time spent to complete voice transactions depends on the criticality of an error. The more catastrophic the effects of an error, the more willing users may be to invest the time required for more verbose prompts and feedback. More work is needed in this area.

*Feedback.* Feedback to discrete user control inputs is frequently mentioned as a function for speech displays. Relevant research was discussed in the section of this paper on speech recognition. In passing, it should be noted that feedback can be provided by prompts (cf. the Mountford et al., 1982, study just discussed). That is, if the system prompts the user for a reasonable next data-entry or control input, the user will assume that the system correctly received the previous input. The real-world conditions under which the user can safely make such assumptions, however, need to be understood. A variety of types of feedback should be employed, depending on the time criticality of the control input and the severity of the consequences of a speech recognition error.

*Responses to user queries.* User queries were studied in a computer-graphic simulation of nap-of-the-earth helicopter flight (Voorhees, Marchionda, and Atchison, 1982). Subjects could ask the helicopter to state airspeed, torque, and altitude as they attempted to fly their simulated craft through a maze on a visual display. Maze flying performance was better when subjects used voice queries and received synthesized voice responses than when they had to obtain this information from either a head-up display or conventional dial gauges.

*Advisories.* The advisability of using speech to provide advisories may depend on the other functions for which speech is being employed in a particular application. When advisories were given in conjunction with voice warnings, it was seen, as discussed previously (Hakkinen and Williges, 1984), that warning detection suffered, unless an alerting cue was also used. A study of pilot preferences for warning system design (Williams and Simpson, 1976) found that pilots wanted speech reserved for only the most critical (i.e., warning) information. They preferred to receive advisories visually. If speech is not being used for warnings, then its use for advisories may be appropriate. Further research is needed.

*Commands.* There is some research and discussion in the literature on the advisability of giving commands by automatic speech generation. Simpson and Williams (1975) argue that great caution should be exercised in the use of commands, at least in the aircraft cockpit, because pilots are reluctant to follow a command without knowing the reason for it. In partial support of this argument, a study by DuBord (1982), reported by Palmer and Ellis (1983), found that giving pilots a visual display of traffic situation information reduced their response time to a visual collision avoidance command, as compared with giving them the command without benefit of the traffic situation display. A similar effect is likely for spoken commands. On the other hand, speech commands issued as instructions, in situations that are not time critical or in conjunction with advisories, could well be useful in a variety of applications.

*Simulation of human communications.* The six speech acts just discussed would be performed by machines speaking qua machines to human operators. Another important speech display application is in the simulation of human speech communications; for instance, to eliminate the need for human speakers playing a role in a training situation. For example, speech generation has been proposed and evaluated for training systems for precision-approach radar controllers and for air-intercept controllers (Breaux, 1977; Grady, 1982).

*Comparative display modes.* Comparative speech and visual display research has addressed user preferences, response time, accuracy, and task accomplishment for speech versus visual displays and for speech combined with visual displays, for various speech acts.

Early voice warning research using taped messages found that pilot response time to voice warnings is faster than to visual warning displays (Lilleboe, 1963) and that a visual display augmented with a voice warning results in faster responses to emergencies than does a tone-augmented display (Kemmerling, Geiselhart, Thornburn, and Cronburg, 1969).

Another difference between the visual and speech mode may be users' tolerance for and ability to perform when presented with false information. A study of airline pilots' preferences for design of cockpit warning systems found that pilots expressed less tolerance for false speech messages than for false visual messages (Williams and Simpson, 1976). Moreover, flight performance was poorer in the presence of false voice warnings (Simpson, 1981b) than when voice warnings gave accurate information.

A series of experiments was conducted in flight simulators to evaluate different cockpit display modes, including a large-letter LED display, a synthesized voice display, and a printed paper display (Hilborn, 1975). The airline pilot subjects who flew the simulator preferred visual displays for all but warning information. For warnings, they preferred speech messages. A large-letter LED display was preferred as a recall instrument for currently assigned heading, altitude, and airspeed information. For less time-critical information, which also must be remembered or referred to over a period of time after receipt, an in-cockpit printout was preferred.

In some situations, users may object to the speech mode for certain types of information. For example, a recent study (Stern, 1984) compared speech and visual displays for prompting and giving error messages to users of an automated teller machine. Although there were no performance differences between text and speech displays, subjects did not like spoken error messages because other customers could hear them.

For sensory-handicapped users, the selection of visual or speech displays will depend on the handicap. For systems to be used by the blind, the challenge will be to design a speech interface that will facilitate performance of those functions that are normally better accomplished using visual displays.

*Selecting Speech Generation System Characteristics*

Research on appropriate speech generation systems for particular applications has been done at two levels. The performance of speech generation algorithms has been assessed as a function of multiple factors that influence intelligibility. Also, human-system performance in simulations has been assessed to determine what benefits may derive from using speech displays.

*Speech generation algorithm performance.* Intelligibility is influenced by the physical characteristics of the speech signal and by the context in which the speech is spoken. In addition to intelligibility, comprehension and human information retention and retrieval in the speech mode must be measured.

*Operational intelligibility.* A recent review of research on the intelligibility of computer-generated speech (Simpson and Navarro, 1984) defines three types of context that interact with the speech signal to produce what the authors call the *operational intelligibility* of speech. The operational intelligibility of a particular algorithm is the intelligibility of its speech in a particular set of physical, pragmatic, and linguistic contexts, and it can differ considerably from basic phoneme intelligibility. Figure 1 depicts the four major factors (i.e., the physical signal and the three types of context) that contribute to operational intelligibility.

The physical speech signal can vary with

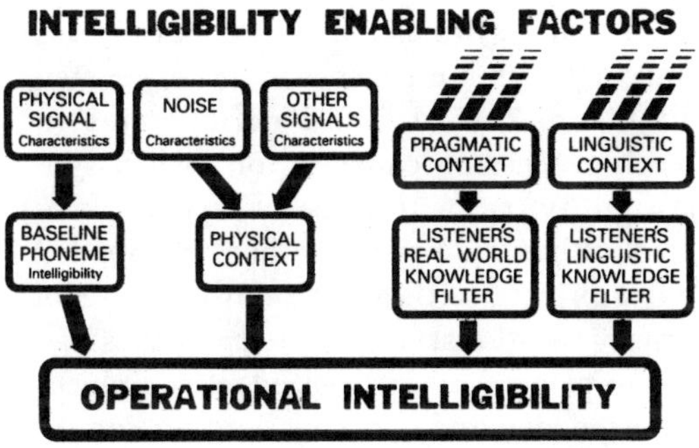

**INTELLIGIBILITY ENABLING FACTORS**

Figure 1. *Factors that contribute to operational intelligibility* (after Simpson and Navarro, 1984).

respect to sex and voice characteristics of the speaker, speaking rate, fundamental frequency, amplitude, accuracy of pronunciation and prosodics, accent, and dialect, among other parameters. The physical context includes aspects of the physical environment such as noise, other audio signals, vibrations, and acceleration forces. The pragmatic context is essentially the real-world situation in which the message is spoken. It includes current events, the ongoing task, time and place, past events, and logically possible future events. The effect of the pragmatic context will be filtered by the listener's knowledge of that pragmatic context. The linguistic context of a speech signal influences intelligibility by providing cues to the listener that limit the possible interpretations of the incoming speech signal. This limit on possible interpretations is a complex type of closed response set. It has long been known that as size of response set decreases, intelligibility of human speech heard in the presence of noise increases, all other factors held constant (Miller, Heise, and Lichten, 1951). Linguistic context limits the size of the response set in more complex ways than does simply limiting message set size. This is due to interactions among the constraints provided by the different levels of linguistic encoding. Simpson and Williams (1975) list these levels and provide references to the literature on the effects of various types of linguistic context on human speech intelligibility. (For an introduction to theories and models of human speech perception see Cole, 1980.) As with pragmatic context, the effects of linguistic context are filtered by the listener's linguistic knowledge of the language being spoken.

Often the effect of factors that enable intelligibility is stronger for synthesized than for human speech (Nye and Gaitenby, 1974; Simpson, 1975). Simpson and Navarro (1984) report that with sufficient assistance from intelligibility-enabling factors, synthesized speech from commercially available devices has been found to be 100% intelligible; without such assistance it has been measured as low as 19%. Factors included as physical characteristics of the speech signal are fundamental frequency, speech rate, prosodics, intonation, learnability of the speech accent, voice type, and phonetic accuracy of the generated speech. In the section of the paper on physical context, the authors review research on effects of background noise and competing speech. Pragmatic context factors include listener familiarity with the speech accent, with the phraseology and vocabulary, and with the real-world situation in which the messages will be spoken. Linguistic context factors include semantic and syntactic context and number of syllables.

The relative importance of the three types of context varies. Under ideal listening conditions, characterized by high signal-to-noise ratio, no competing speech or other audio signals, and listeners familiar with the accent of the machine speech, sentence intelligibility of synthesized speech is from 99 to 100%. Reducing the signal-to-noise ratio and leaving the other factors constant has shown little or no detriment in operational intelligibility, at least for aircraft cockpit messages (Simpson, 1984). High intelligibility (99 to 100%) has been obtained for short, familiar phrases, heard in simulated cockpit noise, using both LPC-encoded digitized speech and synthesis-by-rule speech.

Intelligibility of digitized speech varies as a function of speaker sex. LPC-encoded and Adaptive Predictive Coding (APC) encoded female speech is more susceptible to bit errors, which might be expected during transmission, than is male speech encoded using the same algorithms. The difference is consistent across a wide range of bit error rates (Smith, 1983). Similar comparisons need to be made between female synthesized and male synthesized speech.

When linguistic context or pragmatic context, rather than signal-to-noise ratio, is reduced, substantial degradation of intelligibility occurs (Simpson and Navarro, 1984).

The excellent intelligibility reported by Simpson and Navarro (1984) was achieved at the expense of phonetic hand editing by experts in speech acoustics. The intelligibility of speech generated by text-to-speech algorithms can be poorer and depends on the particular algorithm. For example, the intelligibility of Harvard Psycho-Acoustic Laboratory (PAL) sentences (Egan, 1948) was 93.2% when spoken by one system (Pisoni and Hunnicutt, 1980) and was 87% for PAL sentences spoken by another system (Nusbaum and Schwab, 1983).

The main deficiencies of text-to-speech algorithms are phonetic errors of pronunciation for words that are exceptions to English spelling-to-sound correspondences and limitations of rules for generating correct word stress and sentence intonation. Until these deficiencies are corrected, the need for hand editing of individual speech messages (noted previously) will remain.

*Comprehension.* Although synthesized speech can be 100% intelligible to listeners familiar with its accent, with the phraseology, and with the pragmatically possible messages, further research is needed on comprehension of synthesized speech messages as compared with human speech. Luce, Feustel, and Pisoni (1983) found deficiencies in speech-processing capacity for speech synthesized by one text-to-speech system compared with human speech, when they loaded their subjects with additional short-term memory recall tasks. They interpret these results to mean that synthesized speech places increased demands on encoding and/or rehearsal processes in short-term memory and argue that synthesized speech ought not to be used for cockpit displays. However, their subjects were unfamiliar with the accent of the synthesizer prior to the experiment. The applicability of their findings to pilots' comprehension of familiar messages encoded with sentence-level linguistic context and spoken in a familiar pragmatic context remains to be determined. There is experimental evidence that pilots can store information presented by synthesized speech and later retrieve that information while flying a flight simulator under high workload (Simpson and Marchionda-Frost, 1984). Little is known about how efficiently information in synthesized speech messages can be recalled and under what circumstances listeners will become overloaded in the speech channel. General statements about performance with synthesized speech systems must be made cautiously, with attention to the particular conditions under which the results were obtained.

*Voice characteristics.* Desirable voice characteristics are application dependent. When an inanimate system is speaking qua machine to the user, a machine voice quality is preferred by some user populations (e.g., pilots), as has been discussed. On the other hand, when a system simulates human communications, as in an air traffic control (ATC) training system, a natural-sounding voice, using digitized human speech, is preferred (Cotton and McCauley, 1983). As with machine-sounding speech, it is important to incorporate natural prosodics into the generation process.

Voices can also be varied with respect to pitch and apparent sex of voice. Voice pitch has been suggested for indicating the urgency of a message, with higher pitch signaling greater urgency (Simpson and Marchionda-Frost, 1984). Recent research (Brokx and Nooteboom, 1982) also suggests that differences in voice pitch can help listeners track one or the other of two concurrent messages. The extent to which users can deal with multiple messages needs to be studied and may be a function of the degree of difference among voice types heard on the job.

*Human-System Performance Measurement*

*Operational relevance.* The human factors of speech generation system performance extend far beyond effects on speech intelligibility and recognition accuracy. Message comprehension, human storage and retrieval of information presented in the voice mode, and interactions between speech comprehension and human performance of other concurrent tasks are equally important. Such measures should be "operationally relevant" to the task for which a voice display is used (Simpson, 1981b). An operationally relevant measure of system performance is one that provides users and designers with information about how the system will perform in terms that are meaningful to the operator. For example, one measure of the effectiveness of a navigation computer with voice controls and displays might be a comparison of the amount of time it took a pilot, flying in turbulence in a busy ATC environment, to change a waypoint by means of voice and by means of manual keys and a visual display.

A flight-simulation study to evaluate the concept of a synthesized voice approach callout (SYNCALL) system for airline operations (Simpson, 1981b) measured flight performance in terms of percentage of time out of airline operational tolerance for flight parameters. For the less difficult types of approaches to landing, there were no differences in flight performance attributable to the SYNCALL system. But for the most visually, manually, and cognitively demanding approaches, performance with the synthesized voice system was better than when the normal procedure of pilot-not-flying callouts was used. (Pilot-not-flying callouts are callouts of altitude, airspeed, and other flight parameters that are made by the pilot who is not flying the aircraft as an aid to the pilot who is flying.) For the one approach for which SYNCALL consistently (by experimental design) made false callouts, flight performance was significantly degraded compared with performance on the same approach flown with pilot-not-flying callouts that were correct.

Measures are also needed that will predict the costs and benefits of using speech technology in terms of time saved, more efficient utilization of personnel and equipment, and safer operations. Such measures may follow a generic format but will be application specific in content.

*System response time.* Another operationally relevant measure is system response time. The fact that a speech message takes time to be delivered gives particular importance to what Simpson and Williams (1980) have called *system response time.* The authors defined system response time for voice warnings as the time interval starting with the onset of a warning signal and continuing until the listener has decided upon and initiated his or her first action. System response time thus includes detection, perceptual copying, comprehension, storage, retrieval, and decision making. System response time, rather than simple reaction time or human response latency, is a critical variable for voice warning display systems.

*Future Speech Generation Research*

Research directed toward speech displays in general will support effective design for voice-interactive controls and displays. Specific issues relevant to the design of integrated voice I/O systems are selection of voice type (human- or machine-sounding; male or female), message wording and syntax as a function of speech act, assignment of priorities to functionally different speech display messages, and methods for integrating voice and visual messages when they present the same information. Research on speech-display aspects of dialogue design must also deal with the issue of how to handle concurrent speech messages. Two cases must be handled: (1) user speaking to speech recognition device while speech display is enunciating a message, and (2) triggering more than one speech display message at a time. Speech displays also require improvements to text-to-speech generation algorithms to eliminate the need for hand editing of speech data.

The relative importance of various types of phonetic and prosodic accuracy for synthesized speech intelligibility, learnability, and comprehension is another area that requires further investigation. The degradation of operational intelligibility due to inaccurate vowels, consonants, phoneme transitions, word stress, and prosodics has not been systematically measured. Because of missing perceptual cues in synthesized speech and, to some extent, in human digitized speech in the lower bit rates, the fidelity of audio transmission systems may be more critical than it is for human speech. Just how much redundancy and what type is optimal (syntactic, semantic, phonetic) has not been determined experimentally for all types of speech acts. Also, for listener populations with possible high-frequency hearing loss, computer speech perception may present special problems just because it does not contain all of the perceptual cues of human speech. Specifications for intelligibility of speech to be used for such groups or speech to be used in high-noise environments must take this into account.

## SYSTEM INTEGRATION

System integration, the third level of the research strategy, must consider the research requirements for speech recognition and generation as synergistic technologies. The human visual and manual modalities are commonly associated with perceptual and motor (input/output) characteristics. Similarly, the speech modality has identifiable human speech perception and production characteristics that will become the basis (either unwittingly or by design) for the interface characteristics of speech I/O systems.

The critical issues in human factors integration are task design specifically for the speech modality and human-system dialogue design.

*Task Design*

Applications using the speech modality must be designed around the characteristics of speech. Certain unique features of the speech mode preclude a one-to-one mapping of individual manual controls to speech controls, and of visual display elements to speech display messages (Cotton and McCauley, 1983; Simpson, 1984; Williges and Williges, 1982).

Speech is a discrete, single-channel, omnidirectional, well-known, semantically sophisticated encoding system for the transmission of information. It commands the user's attention and should not be allowed to deliver false information. Used for control of systems, speech can, if properly implemented, reduce the need for the user to learn computer-programming-like languages and can provide an alternative to manual input systems. Speech messages require time to be spoken and may be misunderstood by human or machine "listeners" in the presence of other, competing voice messages, aural signals, or noise. The time and single-channel constraints imposed by the speech mode must be considered in any implementation of speech displays and controls. Further, certain features of speech constrain the way in which it can be used in human-machine systems. Speech may not always provide the most rapid means of interacting with the system. The time required for an operator to execute a speech command is strongly influenced by such variables as vocabulary selection, syntax design, and especially dialogue design.

The receiver of a speech message, whether human or machine, has great difficulty in processing more than one message at a time, with the result that speech is a single-channel code in two senses: neither humans nor current machines can talk and listen accurately at the same time, and both have great difficulty in processing more than one speech message at a time. One implication of this constraint is that speech commands cannot be allowed to interfere with, or to suffer interference from, other speech messages within the system.

Speech messages have a transitory existence unless they are recorded for later playback. The limits of human memory may make it difficult for operators to remember their location in the command structure of a recognition system without the aid of feedback messages and prompts. The task conditions under which this holds true require further investigation, building on previous findings (Mountford et al., 1982).

In general, current speech recognition technology requires a vocabulary that consists of acoustically distinct words. Vocabularies and syntax must also be constrained to be compatible with current recognition technology. These limitations of the technology may be reduced by degrees in the future but cannot be expected to disappear without major advances in fundamental understanding of human speech variability and incorporation of this knowledge into recognition algorithms.

Irrespective of future advances in recognition technology, human performance limitations will dictate vocabulary and syntax constraints. To minimize human cognitive load and the time required to issue speech commands, the number of words in each command should be small. More information is needed on human memory for constrained verbal material and on the effects of such constraints on system performance. Information about the effects of harsh environments and stress on verbal versus motor memory and performance would be particularly relevant. Research in this area would lead to guidelines for establishing vocabularies that are flexible and easy to remember, and also reduce acoustic confusion and minimize awkward speech stylization. Similar guidelines are needed for developing formal grammatical rules that facilitate recognition without placing undue constraints on the user.

*Human-System Dialogue Design*

Careful design of all of the interchanges between the human and the system, not just the speech interchanges, will have major effects on the overall system performance. There are at least two subsets of dialogue design—the dialogue between the user and the speech system and the dialogue between the user and all of the subsystems under the user's control.

The human machine interchanges (i.e., dialogue) must be designed with regard to the total set of control and display options for all subsystems. Mission and task scenarios will have to be analyzed for speech and other audio loads, as well as for the likelihood of concurrent interfering speech messages. The properties of potential functions to be controlled by speech must be assessed, along with the priorities of all speech messages within the system. Voice commands and displays will have to be applied in ways that complement rather than conflict with other controls and displays. Future research and development efforts should address these issues.

To improve system throughput with speech, it is essential to design a speech system dialogue that facilitates rapid information transfer between human and machine. The dialogue design also should minimize the potential for error and the subsequent time required for error correction by the user. Not only the speech commands, but also such dialogue elements as prompts, system feedback, and query responses must be carefully designed and a timeline of the total dialogue evaluated. The desired type and amount of linguistic redundancy for a particular application should be determined experimentally. Syntax design should be viewed as an integral part of speech system design rather than as simply a technique for improving the performance of a marginal recognition or generation system.

Possibly the error rates obtained with current systems can be reduced if system designers provide aids to the user such as tonal prompts for cadence, menus of acceptable entries, consistent feedback, and convenient error-correction commands. The best format for these dialogue elements should be determined by further research.

New techniques are needed to capitalize on syntactic and semantic constraints in the dialogue. These techniques would improve automatic error detection and correction, thereby increasing recognition accuracy and reducing the user's burden of detecting and correcting errors.

At a higher level of dialogue design, speech controls and displays need to be carefully integrated into the total control and display system in order to preclude overloading the speech channel (Simpson, 1984). Certain types of information may be better processed if presented via speech; others may require symbolic information representation. Some basic research has addressed the issue of task/modality compatibility (Wickens et al., 1983) and provides evidence that speech is a better communication mode for some types of tasks, compared with manual input and visual output. When subjects performed two tasks simultaneously—one spatial and the other verbal—spatial task performance was better when the verbal task was accomplished using speech recognition and generation compared with the condition in which both tasks had to compete for the manual and visual channels. This basic research, however, has not involved voice-interactive dialogues. More work is needed on these compatibility issues, using realistic tasks, to support decisions about selecting appropriate tasks for speech-interactive systems with the objective of reducing operator workload. Successful speech system performance for a particular task will not guarantee successful performance of the total application system. Basic limitations of human memory and information processing must be accounted for in the design of any human-machine interface, and especially for those using speech.

Many of the problems of today's complex control and display systems, from the operator's viewpoint, may be solvable by better design at the overall system level. Speech controls and displays may play a role in those solutions, but this can be determined only after considerable analysis or simulation research to compare speech with alternative modes of control and display.

## OVERALL DIRECTIONS FOR FUTURE RESEARCH

Human factors research on the design of integrated voice systems is limited, and reports are spread among conference proceedings, government technical reports, and journal articles (see for example, Cotton and McCauley, 1983; McCauley, 1984; Pallett, 1982; and Simpson, 1984). Although several new design guidelines have been suggested in these reviews, the standard references used by system design engineers, such as U.S. Department of Defense (1981), Van Cott and Kinkade (1972), and Woodson (1981), do not incorporate the new knowledge summarized by these reviews.

If the benefits of speech technology are to be realized, a major effort in human factors research will be needed at many levels of integrated system design: task selection, determination of task-specific recognition and generation system performance requirements, human factors integration to incorporate the speech modality, speech control and display design, task environment effects, and system performance assessment.

A substantial effort in human factors research is needed to develop procedures for selecting appropriate tasks for the voice mode and for integrating voice interaction into the total system design. There is no single area that can be chosen for particular emphasis. However, all of the recommended directions for research should emphasize the total context; that is, the integrated system in which the speech I/O is to be used.

## CONCLUSIONS

Although the human factors literature includes research that supports certain principles of speech system design, this knowledge has not yet been formulated as design guidelines. Human factors methodology *is* sufficiently developed to permit comparison of task-specific speech systems experimentally; however, it does not yet have the tools required for the generation of generic speech system design guidelines. For the near term, simulation of speech system capabilities in conjunction with the development of improved system performance measures should be a productive methodology for accomplishing this work.

Speech generation algorithms may seem to be more advanced than speech recognition algorithms. Reasonably intelligible text-to-speech from standard English spelling is available commercially. The recognition counterpart, speech to text (i.e., machine conversion of human speech to correctly spelled and punctuated text), will not be available commercially in the foreseeable future and is limited to highly constrained laboratory systems. This discrepancy can be interpreted in another way, as merely illustrating the human's great superiority over human-made and machine-processed algorithms when it comes to dealing with variability in the speech signal. Humans quickly learn the strange accent of computer-generated speech, thereby compensating for the deficiences of the algorithm that generates it. On the other hand, when humans speak to current machines, they must eliminate, as much as possible, the normal variability in their speech in order to provide the recognition algorithm with as little variability as possible in the input signal. As knowledge and understanding of the systematic variability in speech increase, recognition algorithms can be expected to perform well over a wider range of speaking contexts, and generation algorithms can be expected to provide speech that contains additional cues for the human listener. Such technology advances will enlarge the overlap between tasks appropriate for the speech mode and speech systems with characteristics that match the task requirements. However, the basic design issues discussed here will apply regardless of the state of speech technology.

For the near term, the current recognition algorithms appear adequate for use in benign environments, characterized by low to moderate noise (up to 85 dB SPL) and motion (up to 5 G), for applications that require small vocabularies and that do not place the user under severe stress. The exact limits of acceptable recognition algorithm performance when the user is under stress are not known. Therefore, great caution must be exercised with current technology for stress-inducing applications. Advances in techniques for dealing with background noise are reducing the impact of this source of variability in the utterances to be recognized.

Speech generation algorithms, on the other hand, have demonstrated acceptable performance under conditions of severe noise and high workload. This technology is ready to be applied appropriately, with careful attention to the human factors integration issues discussed here.

Together, these two technologies offer near-term potential for selected applications. The critical issues for near-term application of voice technology are primarily in the human factors domain. For the longer term, substantial efforts in both algorithm development and human factors will be required in order to extend the range of speech variability that can be accommodated by speech recognition and generation technology and hence the possible applications of speech technology.

## ACKNOWLEDGMENTS

The sections of this article on speech recognition were based largely upon discussions among the authors and on material generated while they served on the Committee for Computerized Speech Recognition Technologies, Commission on Engineering and Technical Systems, of the National Research Council (NRC). The committee was sponsored by members of the Voice SubTechnical Advisory Group (SubTAG) of the Department of Defense. The committee's report, entitled "Automatic Speech Recognition in Severe Environments," was published by the National Research Council in October 1984. James L. Flanagan, AT&T Bell Laboratories, chaired the Committee. From the National Research Council, Dennis F. Miller served as Study Director, and Howard Clark was the Staff Officer. The authors gratefully acknowledge the support of the Voice SubTAG member agencies that funded the NRC Committee and subsequently encouraged the preparation of this article. The knowledge gained from our fellow committee members is gratefully acknowledged. However, the authors take full responsibility for any errors and for the opinions expressed in this article.

## REFERENCES

Allen, H. B., and Underwood, G. N. (Eds.). (1971). *Readings in American dialectology.* New York: Appleton-Century-Crofts.

Armstrong, J. W. (1980). *The effects of concurrent motor tasking on performance of a voice recognition system.* Unpublished masters thesis, Naval Postgraduate School, Monterey, CA.

Bierman, A., Rodman, R., Rubin, D., and Heidlage, F. (1984). *Natural language with discrete speech as a mode for human to machine communication.* Durham, NC: Duke University, Computer Science Department.

Bond, Z. S., and Garnes, S. (1980). Misperceptions of fluent speech. In R. A. Cole (Ed.), *Perception and production of fluent speech* (pp. 115-113). Hillsdale NJ: Erlbaum.

Breaux, R. (1977). Laboratory demonstration of computer speech recognition in training. In R. Breaux, M. Curran, and E. M. Huff (Eds.), *Voice technology of interactive real-time command/control systems applications.* Moffett Field, CA: NASA-Ames Research Center.

Brokx, J. P. L., and Nooteboom, S. G. (1982). Intonation and the perception of simultaneous voices. *Journal of Phonetics, 10,* 23-26.

Brown, J. E., Bertone, C. M., and Obermeyer, R. W. (1968, February). *Army aircraft warning system study* (U.S. Army Technical Memorandum 6-68). Aberdeen Proving Ground, MD: U.S. Army Engineering Laboratories.

Butler, F., Manaker, E., and Obert-Thorn, W. (1981, June). *Investigation of a voice synthesis system for the F-14 aircraft: Final report* (Report No. ACT 81-001). Bethpage, NY: Grumman Aerospace Corp.

Bucher, N. M., Karl, R., Voorhees, J., and Werner, E. (1984, May). Alerting prefixes for speech warning messages. In *Proceedings of the National Aerospace & Electronics Conference (NAECON)* (pp. 924-931). New York: IEEE.

Chapanis, A. (1975). Interactive human communication. *Scientific American, 232*(3), 36-42.

Chapanis, A. (1976). Engineering psychology. In M. D. Dunnette (Ed.), *Handbook of industrial and organizational psychology.* Chicago: Rand McNally.

Cole, R. A. (Ed.). (1980). *Perception and production of fluent speech.* Hillsdale NJ: Erlbaum.

Coler, C. (1982, September/October). Helicopter speech-command systems: Recent noise tests are encouraging. *Speech Technology 1*(3), 76-81.

Coler, C. R., and Plummer, R. P. (1974, May). Development of a computer speech recognition system for flight systems applications. In *Preprints of the 45th Annual Scientific Meeting* (pp. 116-117). Washington, DC: Aerospace Medical Association.

Coler, C., Plummer, R., Huff, E., and Hitchcock, M. (1977, December). Automatic speech recognition research at NASA-Ames Research Center. In *Proceedings of the Voice-Interactive Real-Time Command/Control Systems Application Conference* (pp. 143-163). Moffett Field, CA: NASA-Ames Research Center.

Cotton, J. C., and McCauley, M. E. (1983, March). *Voice technology design guides for Navy training systems: Final report for the period 23 April, 1980–2 January, 1982* (Report No. NAVTRAEQUIPCEN 80-C-0057-1). Orlando, FL: Naval Training Equipment Center.

Cotton, J. C., McCauley, M. E., North, R. A., and Strieb, M. (1983). *Development of speech input/output interfaces for tactical aircraft* (AFWAL-TR-83-3073). Wright-Patterson AFB, OH: Flight Dynamics Laboratory.

Deathridge, B. H. (1972). Auditory and other sensory forms of information presentation. In H. P. Van Cott and R. G. Kinkade (Eds.), *Human engineering guide to equipment design*. Washington, D.C.: U.S. Government Printing Office.

Doddington, G., and Schalk, T. (1981). Speech recognition: Turning theory to practice. *IEEE Spectrum, 18*, 26-32.

DuBord, M. J. (1982, June). *An investigation of response time to collision avoidance commands with a cockpit display of traffic information*. Unpublished masters thesis, San Jose State University, San Jose, CA.

Egan, J. P. (1948). Articulation testing methods. *Laryngoscope, 58*, 955-991.

Flanagan, J. L. (1972). *Speech analysis, synthesis, and perception* (2nd ed). New York: Springer Verlag.

Fujimura, O. (1984, June). The role of linguistics for future speech technology. In *LSA Bulletin 104* (pp. 4-7). Baltimore, MD: Linguistic Society of America.

Garnes, S., and Bond, Z. S. (1977). *The influence of semantics on speech perception*. Paper presented at the 93rd Meeting of the Acoustical Society of America, University Park, PA.

Gould, J. D., Conti, J., and Hovanyecz, J. (1983, April). Composing letters with a simulated listening typewriter. *Communications of the ACM*, 295-308.

Grady, M. W. (1982). *Air intercept controller prototype training system* (NAVTRAEQUIPCEN 78-C-0182-14). Orlando, FL: Naval Training Equipment Center.

Harris, S. D., North, R. A., and Owens, J. M. (1977, November). *A system for the assessment of human performance in concurrent verbal and manual control tasks*. Paper presented at the 7th Annual Meeting of the National Conference on the Use of On-Line Computers in Psychology, Washington, DC.

Hakkinen, M. T., and Williges, B. H. (1984). Synthesized warning messages: Effects of an alerting cue in single- and multiple-function voice synthesis systems. *Human Factors, 26*, 185-195.

Hecker, M. H., Stevens, K. N., von Bismark, G., and Williams, C. E. (1968). Manifestations of task-induced stress in the acoustical speech signal. *Journal of the Acoustical Society of America, 44*, 993-1001.

Hilborn, E. H. (1975). *Human factors experiments for data link: Final report* (FAA-RD-75-170). Cambridge, MA: Department of Transportation Systems Center.

Kemmerling, P., Geiselhart, R., Thornburn, D. E., and Cronburg, J. G. (1969). *A comparison of voice and tone warning systems as a function of task loading* (Technical Report ASD-TR-69-104). Wright-Patterson AFB, OH: U.S. Air Force, ASD.

Kersteen, Z., and Damos, D. (1983, December). *Human factors issues associated with the use of speech technology in the cockpit* (Final Tech. Report, U.S. Army Grant No. NAG2-217). (Available from J. Voorhees, U.S. Army Aeromechanics Laboratory, NASA-Ames Research Center, Moffett Field, CA 94035.)

Kryter, K. (1972). Speech communication. In H. P. Van Cott and R. G. Kinkade (Eds.), *Human engineering guide to equipment design* (pp. 161-226). Washington, DC: U.S. Government Printing Office.

Lilleboe, M. L. (1963, June). *Final Report: evaluation of Astropower, Inc. auditory information display installed in the VA-3B airplane* (Technical Report ST 31-22R-63; AD-831823). Patuxent River, MD: U.S. Naval Air Station, Naval Air Test Center.

Luce, P. A., Feustel, T. C., and Pisoni, D. B. (1983). Capacity demands in short-term memory for synthetic and natural speech. *Human Factors, 25*, 17-32.

McCauley, M. E. (1984). Human factors in voice technology. In F. A. Muckler (Ed.), *Human Factors Review: 1984*. Santa Monica, CA: Human Factors Society.

McCauley, M. E., Root, R. W., and Muckler, F. A. (1982). *Training evaluation of an automated air intercept controller training system* (NAVTRAEQUIPCEN 81-C-0055-1). Orlando, FL: Naval Training Equipment Center.

McCauley, M. E., and Semple, C. A. (1980). *Precision approach radar training system (PARTS)* (NAVTRAEQUIPCEN 79-C-0042-1). Orlando, FL: Naval Training Equipment Center.

McSorley, W. J. (1981, March). *Using voice recognition equipment to run the Warfare Environmental Simulator (WES)*. Unpublished masters thesis, Naval Postgraduate School, Monterey, CA.

Miller, G. A., Heise, G. A., and Lichten, W. (1951). The intelligibility of speech as a function of the context of the test materials. *Journal of Experimental Psychology, 41*, 329-335.

Moore, C. A., Moore, D. R., and Ruth, J. C. (1984, December). Applications of voice interactive systems—Military flight test and the future. In *Proceedings of the Sixth Digital Avionics Systems Conference* (pp. 301-308). New York: IEEE.

Mountford, S. J., North, R. A., Metz, S. V., and Graffunder, K., (1982, April). *Methodology for identifying voice functions for airborne voice-interactive control systems* (Contract No. N62269-81-R-0344). Minneapolis, MN: Honeywell Systems Research Center.

National Research Council, Committee on Computerized Speech Recognition Technologies. (1984). *Automatic speech recognition in severe environments*. Washington, DC: National Research Council, Commission on Engineering and Technical Systems.

North, R. A., and Lea, W. (1982). *Application of advanced speech technology in manned penetration bombers* (AFWAL-TR-82-3004). Wright-Patterson AFB, OH: Flight Dynamics Laboratory.

Nusbaum, H. C., and Schwab, E. C. (1983, May). *The effects of training on intelligibility of synthetic speech: II the learning curve for synthetic speech*. Paper presented at the 105th meeting of the Acoustical Society of America, Cincinnati, OH.

Nye, P. W., and Gaitenby, J. (1974). The intelligibility of synthetic monosyllabic words in short, syntactically normal sentences. In *Status report on speech research* (SR-37/38) (pp. 169-190). New Haven CT: Haskins Laboratories.

Pallett, D. (Ed.). (1982, March). *Proceedings of the workshop on standardization for speech I/O technology*. Gaithersburg, MD: National Bureau of Standards.

Palmer, E., and Ellis, S. R. (1983, October). Potential interactions of collision avoidance advisories and cockpit displays of traffic information (SAE Technical Paper Series 831544). In *Proceedings of the Second Aerospace Behavioral Engineering Technology Conference, Aerospace Congress & Exposition* (pp. 433-443). Warrendale, PA: SAE.

Pisoni, D. B., and Hunnicutt, S. (1980, April). Perceptual evaluation of MITalk: The MIT unrestricted text-to-speech system. In *IEEE International Conference Record on Acoustics, Speech, and Signal Processing* (pp. 572-575). New York: IEEE.

Poock, G. K. (1981a). *A longitudinal study of computer voice*

recognition performance and vocabulary size (NPS-55-81-013). Monterey, CA: Naval Postgraduate School.
Poock, G. K. (1981b, October). To train randomly or all at once—That is the question. In *Proceedings of the Voice Data Entry Systems Applications Conference*. Sunnyvale, CA: Lockheed Missiles & Space Co.
Poock, G. K., Martin, B. J., and Roland, E. F. (1983, February). *The effect of feedback to users of voice recognition equipment* (NPS Technical Report NPS-55-83-003). Monterey, CA: Naval Postgraduate School.
Poock, G. K., and Roland, E. F. (1982, November). *Voice recognition accuracy: What is acceptable?* (NPS Technical Report, NPS55-82-030). Monterey, CA: Naval Postgraduate School.
Poock, G. K., and Roland, E. F. (1984). *A feasibility study for integrated voice recognition input into the Integrated Information Display system (IID)* (NPS Technical Report NPS-55-84-008). Monterey, CA: Naval Postgraduate School.
Poock, G. K., Schwalm, N. D., Martin, B. J., and Roland, E. F. (1982, December). *Trying for speaker independence in the use of speaker dependent voice recognition equipment* (NPS Technical Report NPS-55-82-032). Monterey, CA: Naval Postgraduate School.
Rollins, A. M., (1984). "Composite" templates for speech recognition for small groups. In *Proceedings of the Human Factors Society 28th Annual Meeting* (Vol. 2) (pp. 758-762). Santa Monica, CA: Human Factors Society.
Schurick, J. M., Williges, B. H., and Maynard, J. F. (in press). User feedback requirements with automatic speech recognition. *Ergonomics*.
Searle, J. (1969). *Speech acts*. London: Cambridge University press.
Sherwood, B. A. (1979, August). The computer speaks. *IEEE Spectrum*, pp. 18-25.
Simpson, C. A. (1975). Occupational experience with a specific phraseology: Group differences in intelligibility for synthesized and human speech. *Journal of the Acoustical Society of America, 58* (Supplement 1), 57.
Simpson, C. A. (1981a, April). Access to speech synthesis and its applications. In J. C. Warren (Ed.), *The best of the Computer Faires. Volume VI: Conference proceedings of the Sixth West Coast Computer Faire* (pp. 74-79). Woodside, CA: West Coast Computer Faire.
Simpson, C. A. (1981b). Evaluation of synthesized voice approach callouts (SYNCALL). In J. Moraal and K. F. Kraiss (Eds.), *Manned systems design: Methods, equipment, and applications* (pp. 375-393). New York: Plenum.
Simpson, C. A. (1981c, April). Programming "phoneme" voice synthesizers phonetically. In J. C. Warren (Ed.), *The Best of the Computer Faires, Volume VI: Conference proceedings of the Sixth West Coast Computer Faire* (pp. 84-90). Woodside, CA: West Coast Computer Faire.
Simpson, C. A. (1983a, December). *Advanced technology—New fixes or new problems? Verbal communications in the aviation system.* Paper presented at Beyond Pilot Error: A Symposium of Scientific Focus, sponsored by the Air Line Pilots Association, Washington, DC.
Simpson, C. A. (1983b, March). Evaluating computer speech devices for your application. In J. C. Warren (Ed.), *Proceedings of the Seventh West Coast Computer Faire* (pp. 395-401). Woodside, CA: West Coast Computer Faire.
Simpson, C. A. (1984). Integrated voice controls and speech displays for rotorcraft mission management (SAE Technical Paper Series 831523). *SAE 1983 Transactions, 92*(4), 271-280. Warrendale, PA: SAE.
Simpson, C. A. (in press). *Voice displays for single pilot IFR* (NASA Contract Report CR-172422). Hampton, VA: NASA-Langley Research Center.
Simpson, C. A., Coler, C. R., and Huff, E. M. (1982, March). Human factors of voice I/O for aircraft cockpit controls and displays. In D. Pallett (Ed.), *Proceedings of the Workshop on Standardization for Speech I/O Technology* (pp. 159-166). Gaithersburg, MD: National Bureau of Standards.
Simpson, C. A., and Marchionda-Frost, K. (1984). Synthesized speech rate and pitch effects on intelligibility of warning messages for pilots. *Human Factors, 26*, 509-517.
Simpson, C. A., Marchionda-Frost, K., and Navarro, T. N. (1984, October). Comparison of voice types for helicopter voice warning systems (SAE Technical Paper Series 841611). In *Proceedings of the Third Aerospace Behavioral Engineering Technical Conference, 1984 SAE Aerospace Congress and Exposition*. Warrendale, PA: SAE.
Simpson, C. A., and Navarro, T. N. (1984, May). Intelligibility of computer generated speech as a function of multiple factors. In *Proceedings of the National Aerospace and Electronics Conference* (84CH1984-7 NAECON) (pp. 932-940). New York: IEEE.
Simpson, C. A., and Williams, D. H. (1975, May). Human factors research problems in electronic voice warning system design. In *Proceedings of the 11th Annual Conference on Manual Control* (NASA TMX-62,464) (pp. 94-106). Moffett Field, CA: NASA-Ames Research Center.
Simpson, C. A., and Williams, D. H. (1980). Response time effects of alerting tone and semantic context for synthesized voice cockpit warnings. *Human Factors, 22*, 319-320.
Smith, C. (1983, September). Relating the performance of speech processors to the bit error rate. *Speech Technology, 2*(1), pp. 41-53.
Smith, G. (1984). Five voice synthesizers. *Byte: The Small Systems Journal, 9*(10), 337-347.
Spine, T. M., Maynard, J. F., and Williges, B. H. (1983, September). Error correction strategies for voice recognition. In *Proceedings of the Voice Data Entry Systems Application Conference*, Chicago, IL: American Voice I/O Society.
Stern, K. R. (1984). An evaluation of written, graphics, and voice messages in proceduralized instructions. In *Proceedings of the Human Factors Society 28th Annual Meeting* (Vol. 1) (pp. 314-318). Santa Monica, CA: Human Factors Society.
Thomas, J. C., Rosson, M. B., and Chodorow, M. (1984, October). Human factors and synthetic speech. In *Proceedings of the Human Factors Society 28th Annual Meeting* (Vol. 2) (pp. 763-767). Santa Monica, CA: Human Factors Society.
U.S. Department of Defense. (1981, May). *Human engineering design criteria for military systems, equipment, and facilities* (MIL-STD-1472C). Washington, DC: Author.
Van Cott, H. P., and Kinkade, R. G. (Eds.). (1972). *Human engineering guide to equipment design* (rev. ed). Washington, DC: U.S. Government Printing Office.
Voorhees, J. W., Bucher, N. M., Huff, E. M., Simpson, C. A., and Williams, D. H. (1983). Voice interactive electronic warning system (VIEWS). In *Proceedings of the IEEE/*

*AIAA 5th Digital Avionics Systems Conference* (83CH1839-0) (pp. 3.5.1-3.5.8). New York: IEEE.

Voorhees, J. W., Marchionda, K., and Atchison, V. (1982, March). Auditory display of helicopter cockpit information. In *Proceedings of the Workshop on Standardization for Speech I/O Technology*. Gaithersburg MD: National Bureau of Standards.

Welch, J. R. (1977, September). *Automated data entry analysis* (RADC TR-77-306). Griffiss AFB, New York: Rome Air Development Center.

Wickens, C. D., Sandry, D. L., and Vidulich, M. (1983). Compatibility and resource competition between modalities of input, central processing, and output. *Human Factors, 25*, 227-248.

Wierwille, W. W., and Connor, S. A. (1983). Evaluation of 20 pilot workload measures using a psychomotor task in a moving-base aircraft simulator, *Human Factors, 25*, 1-16.

Williams, D. H., and Simpson, C. A. (1976). A systematic approach to advanced cockpit warning systems for air transport operations: Line pilot preferences. In *Proceedings of the Aircraft Safety and Operating Problems Conference* (NASA SP-416) (pp. 617-644). Norfolk, VA: NASA-Langley Research Center.

Williges, B. H., and Williges, R. C. (1982). Structuring human/computer dialogue using speech technology. In *Proceedings of the Workshop on Standardization for Speech I/O Technology.* (pp. 143-151). Gaithersburg, MD: National Bureau of Standards.

Woodson, W. E. (1981). *Human factors design handbook.* New York: McGraw-Hill.

Zoltan-Ford, E. (1984). Reducing variability in natural language interactions with computers. In *Proceedings of the Human Factors Society 28th Annual Meeting* (Vol. 2.) (pp. 768-772). Santa Monica, CA: Human Factors Society.

# Part IV
# STIMULUS-RESPONSE COMPATIBILITY AND MOTOR CONTROL

A significant aspect of our relationship with the environment is how we act on our perceptions and actively manipulate and control ourselves and objects in the environment. How effectively we execute these manipulations is partly dependent on the relational organization between the stimulus and our action in response to that stimulus. This is known as stimulus-response (S-R) compatibility. The most efficient information processing occurs when the configuration of stimuli needed to perform a task are spatially or conceptually identical to the configuration of alternatives required for response execution. One possible reason for this efficiency is the minimal transformation of information (either spatial or conceptual) that is required when the structure or mapping between stimulus and response is identical or highly similar. This high isomorphism allows the person to efficiently use a mental representation as a basis for action. Optimal S-R compatibility is of obvious importance to system design because it enables high efficiency and relatively low error rate for complex human response to emergencies and high-stress environments.

Two classic articles make up this section on stimulus-response compatibility and motor control. One deals with display-control mapping. (Other relevant selections include Chapters 9 and 10 in Part III, "Information Representation and Displays"). The second selection addresses the control of discrete movements, which is a common way of controlling and interacting with a complex system. Over the years the results of both studies have proven quite useful to the human factors community.

The selection by Paul M. Fitts and Charles M. Seeger (Chapter 13) is one of the early empirical investigations of stimulus-response compatibility. The heart of the issue studied was the degree to which "correspondence of sets of points in the stimulus and the response symbol spaces affects information transfer." A specific type of S-R compatibility—spatial mapping between stimuli and their response alternatives—was investigated using complex spatial arrays of a stimulus and associated response alternatives. The speed and accuracy of responding were superior when a high degree of compatibility existed between the spatial mapping of stimuli and responses, supporting the authors' hypothesis that the requirement to transform information slows the processing involved in perceptual-motor activity. Fitts and Seeger also found that extended practice leads to greater improvement on incompatible mappings but that incompatible mappings do not attain the performance levels of compatible mappings. The importance of this work is obvious in its implications for the design of display-control relationships, in which responses and their associated controls must be mapped in the most natural and efficient manner to the stimuli that control them. It is important to note that compatibility principles have been extended to include conceptual as well as spatial compatibility.

Chapter 14 is a classic article by Paul Fitts and J. R. Peterson which applies Fitts' Law to the execution of discrete movements. Fitts' Law relates movement time to the difficulty of a movement (e.g., distance to a target and target width) and is useful in estimating movement time in situations requiring accuracy. Besides demonstrating the generality of Fitts' Law, the authors were interested in determining the relation between movement time and time to initiate a movement (i.e., reaction time). Results of their experiments showed that reaction time and movement time are independent, which supports the notion that perceptual processes and motor response processes are essentially independent and make use of different information elements. Reaction time was interpreted as reflecting perceptual and cognitive processes in initiating a response. Movement time was interpreted as reflecting the processes required to control the timing and patterning of a movement during its execution.

# 13

## S–R COMPATIBILITY: SPATIAL CHARACTERISTICS OF STIMULUS AND RESPONSE CODES [1]

### PAUL M. FITTS

### AND CHARLES M. SEEGER

The present paper reports the results of two experiments designed to demonstrate the utility of the concept of stimulus-response compatibility [2] in the development of a theory of perceptual-motor behavior.

A task involves compatible S–R relations to the extent that the ensemble of stimulus and response combinations comprising the task results in a high rate of information transfer. Admittedly, degree of compatibility can be defined in terms of operations other than those used to secure a measure of information, for example, it could be specified in terms of measures of speed or accuracy. However, the present writers prefer the preceding definition because of the theoretical interpretation that they wish to give to compatibility effects. This interpretation makes use of the idea of a hypothetical process of information transformation or recoding in the course of a perceptual-motor activity, and assumes that the degree of compatibility is at a maximum when recoding processes are at a minimum. The concept of compatibility can be extended to cover relations between concurrent stimulus activities, such as take place during simultaneous listening and looking, as well as to relations between concurrent motor responses. However, the present paper will be limited to a consideration of stimulus-response compatibility effects in which the relevant information in the stimulus source is that generated by changes in its spatial characteristics, and the relevant aspect of a response is its direction of movement.

One of the earliest studies of the behavioral effects of changes in the spatial correspondence of S–R relations is the well-known experiment of Stratton (12) on vision without inversion of the retinal image. Recently the majority of studies of such effects have dealt with the spatial relations between machine controls and remote visual displays that are connected to them by mechanical or electrical means (1, 3, 5, 9, 13). These relations are important for human engineering. They have also become a matter of considerable interest for learning theory, in part because of Gagné, Foster, and Baker's (2) proposal that a reversal of S–R relations is the only condition leading to negative transfer effects in perceptual-motor learning. However, studies in both of these areas have consistently dealt with only one aspect of the compatibility problem. Investigations in the human-engineering area usually have compared different ways of displaying information when the S responds with a single type

[1] This research was supported in part by the United States Air Force under Contract No. AF 33(038)-10528 with the Ohio State University Research Foundation, monitored by the Human Resources Research Center, and was reported at the 1952 meeting of the Midwestern Psychological Association. Permission is granted for reproduction, publication, use and disposal in whole or in part by or for the United States Government.

[2] The authors wish to credit Dr. A. M. Small for suggesting the use of the term *compatibility* in an unpublished paper presented before the Ergonomics Research Society in 1951.

From *Journal of Experimental Psychology*, 46. This article is in the public domain.

of control, or else have examined the effectiveness of several kinds of controls or control motions when used with a single display. Investigations of transfer effects have typically considered only reversals of the stimulus-response relations within one S-R ensemble, such as changes in the direction of motion of the control on a particular psychomotor test (8), without specifying the location of the original task along a dimension of S-R compatibility. Only two studies (7, 11) have systematically investigated the effects of varying both stimulus sets and response sets. Such an approach is indicated by the concept of compatibility.

Information theory provides a convenient formulation of compatibility in terms of information coding. Shannon (10) and others have pointed out, in the case of physical communication channels, that information can be transmitted at a rate approaching channel capacity only if messages are optimally encoded for the particular channel being used. In such systems optimum encoding requires that messages be expressed in a suitable form and that their probability constraints be matched to the physical constraints of the channel. By analogy, it seems reasonable to hypothesize that man's performance of a perceptual-motor task should be most efficient when the task necessitates a minimum amount of information transformation (encoding and/or decoding), in other words, when the information generated by successive stimulus events is appropriate to the set of responses that must be made in the task, or conversely, when the set of responses is appropriately matched to the stimulus source.[3]

A few of the writers who have discussed the application of information theory to psychology have considered coding problems, such as the possibility of recoding as an aid in remembering. However, interest has been limited to stimulus coding (6).

Since the coding problem is central to the topic of compatibility, it will be worth while to consider briefly the available ways of choosing the sets of stimuli and the sets of responses employed in a visual-motor task. We shall consider only the case of a finite series of discrete code symbols. A stimulus code must utilize one or more stimulus dimensions such as the intensity, the wave length, the duration, or the extent of visible light. A unidimensional code is one in which the required number of unique code symbols is provided by the selection of points along a single stimulus dimension. A multidimensional code is one in which points are selected along two or more stimulus dimensions and each code symbol is defined by specifying a unique combination of several stimulus characteristics. In either case, several code symbols can be combined to form a larger multisymbol series.

A response code can be devised by similar procedures. A unidimensional response code utilizes a single effector member and a specified number of points along one of the physical dimensions of a particular response continuum, such as the direction, the force, or the duration of a movement. A multidimensional response code utilizes the complex response of a single effector member, such as the motion of the arm in positioning of a three-dimensional control, or the responses of several different effectors acting concurrently, such as the simultaneous responses of hands and feet in moving a set of conventional aircraft controls. Both the set of stimuli and the set of responses required in a particular task can thus be specified as

[3] If an incompatible S-R relation exists, then a considerable amount of recoding of information (such as the looking for meaningful associations, etc.) may be highly desirable.

points lying in the multidimensional space comprising the set of all possible discriminable stimuli and motor responses.

Garner and Hake (4) have pointed out that in order to attain maximum average information transmission per symbol, stimulus points should be selected with reference to their position along a scale of equal discriminability. A similar principle undoubtedly holds for the selection of a set of responses. Discriminability, defined without reference to response rate, establishes an upper limit to the maximum average information that can be generated by the selection of particular stimulus or response points from a set of points lying along a specified dimension. The problem of S–R compatibility remains, however, even when sets of stimuli and responses are optimally chosen with respect to discriminability. It concerns the question of how the correspondence of the sets of points in the stimulus and the response symbol spaces affects information transfer.

## Experiment I

The first experiment was planned to test the hypothesis that, in tasks requiring directional motor responses to spatial stimulus patterns, effective performance depends to a large extent upon the unique characteristics of S–R ensembles rather than on specific aspects of particular stimulus or response sets. Three sets of stimuli ($S_a$, $S_b$, $S_c$), each comprising eight easily discriminable light patterns, and three sets of eight responses ($R_a$, $R_b$, $R_c$) were studied in the nine combinations formed by combining each stimulus set with each response set. Within each of these nine S–R ensembles, the pairings of stimuli and responses were those that the $E$s judged would be expected by most $S$s, i.e., would agree with population stereotypes. These sets of stimuli and responses were chosen as abstractions of commonly used spatial patterns of stimuli and responses, i.e., as familiar ways of representing points on a two-dimensional surface.

A further consideration in selecting the sets of stimuli and responses was that three of the nine S–R ensembles ($S_a$–$R_a$, $S_b$–$R_b$, and $S_c$–$R_c$) should represent "corresponding" permutations and combinations. Correspondence, in this case, was judged by the $E$s on the basis of the direct physical similarity of the two patterns. The experiment therefore provides an incidental test of how accurately S–R compatibility can be predicted from a consideration of the correspondence, with respect to the number of coding dimensions employed, between the two sets of points employed in stimulus and response coding.

### Method

*Apparatus.*—The response required of $S$s was to move a stylus quickly in the direction indicated by a stimulus light or lights. The three stimulus and the three response panels used in the study are shown in Fig. 1 and a drawing of the $S$'s position, with the $S_a$–$R_c$ combination in place, is shown in Fig. 2.

Stimulus Set $A$ and Response Set $A$ each consisted of eight permutations of direction from a central reference point. The stimulus panel contained eight lights forming the outline of a circle. The response panel contained eight pathways radiating from a central point like the spokes of a wheel. Each light and each pathway were separated from their neighbors by an angle of 45°. These stimulus and response patterns are characteristic of those provided by a pictorial azimuth or bearing display and an aircraft-type control stick.

Stimulus Panel $B$ consisted of four lights separated by 90°. It provided four single-light positions, plus the four two-light combinations formed by adjacent pairs of lights. Response Panel $B$ consisted of four pathways originating at a central point and separated by 90° intervals. Each path, as seen in Fig. 1, branched in a T and per-

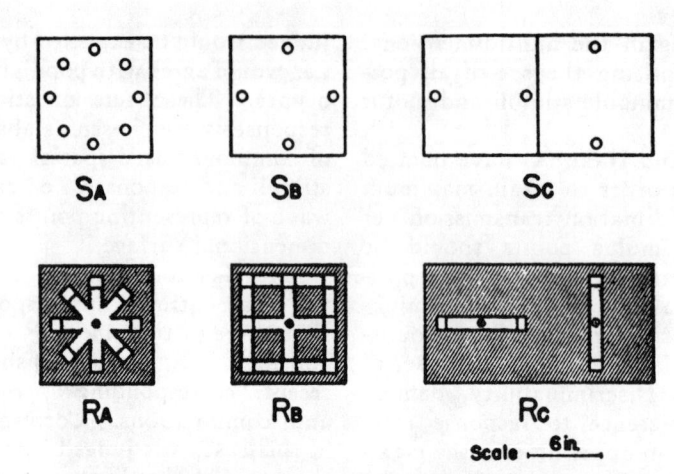

FIG. 1. The three stimulus panels ($S_a$, $S_b$, and $S_c$) and the three response panels ($R_a$, $R_b$, and $R_c$) used in Exp. I. The Ss held a metal stylus on the circular button in the center of the response panel.

mitted Ss to move from the center point to one of eight terminal positions. The four corner points of the response panel could be reached by two alternative pathways; for example, the upper-right corner could be reached either by a right-up sequence or an up-right sequence. The Ss were told that these were equivalent responses. Response Panel B, therefore, involved the choice of a single directional movement, or of a sequence of two successive movements, and permitted Ss to terminate their responses in one of eight end states.

Stimulus Panel C contained a pair of horizontally separated lights and a pair of vertically separated lights. The set of eight stimulus conditions that it provided included the four possibilities that a single light would come on, plus the four two-light combinations that could be produced by the simultaneous presentation of one of each of the two pairs. Response Panel C permitted a left or right response of the left hand, an up or down response of the right hand, plus the four possible combined movements of the two hands. Stimulus Panel C corresponds in general to two separate single-scale instruments and Response Panel C provides a set of responses similar to those present whenever two separate hand controls are used.

At the center of each response panel was a ⅜-in. diameter metal disc, surrounded by a thin nonconductive ring. Reaction time was measured as the time taken by S to move the stylus off this metal button.

The stimulus panels were mounted at a 60° angle to the horizontal. Response panels were 30° to the horizontal. The Ss worked from a seated position. The stimulus panels were 15° downward and 28 in. from their eyes, and the response panels were at a convenient location in front of them. The Ss watched the stimulus panels and seldom looked at their hands or the response panels.

The E's station contained separate selector switches for the eight stimulus combinations and a single noiseless activation switch, which turned on the selected light(s) and simultaneously started a 1/100-sec. timer. The apparatus was designed so that different stimulus and response panels could be substituted at S's station without any change at E's station. The E sat where he could observe S's movements and could record errors as well as reaction time.

FIG. 2. The S's station showing the correct two-handed response on Panel C to the lower right-hand light of Stimulus Set A

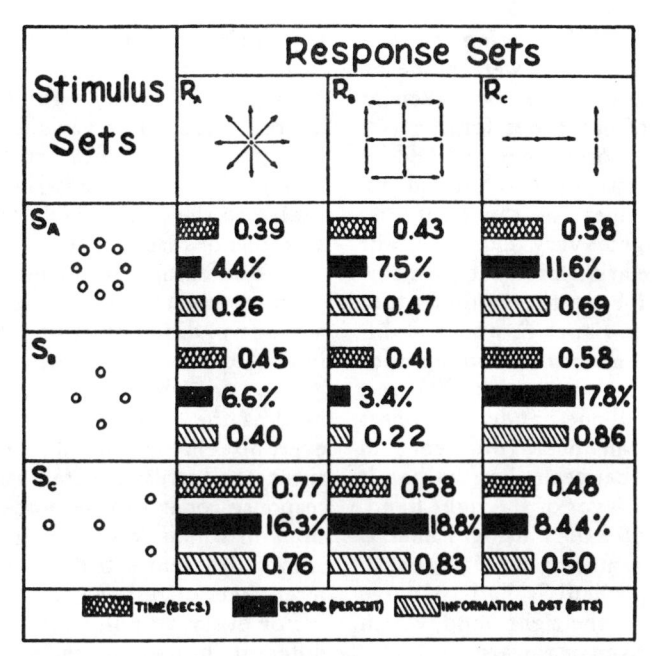

| Stimulus Sets | Response Sets $R_a$ ✳ | $R_b$ ⊞ | $R_c$ —⊥ |
|---|---|---|---|
| $S_A$ (ring of 8) | 0.39 / 4.4% / 0.26 | 0.43 / 7.5% / 0.47 | 0.58 / 11.6% / 0.69 |
| $S_b$ (3 dots) | 0.45 / 6.6% / 0.40 | 0.41 / 3.4% / 0.22 | 0.58 / 17.8% / 0.86 |
| $S_c$ (3 dots) | 0.77 / 16.3% / 0.76 | 0.58 / 18.8% / 0.83 | 0.48 / 8.44% / 0.50 |

TIME (SECS.)   ERRORS (PERCENT)   INFORMATION LOST (BITS)

FIG. 3. Mean scores for the eight $S$s in each of the experimental groups. The datum for information lost is the theoretical information in the stimulus (3 bits) minus the computed value for information transmitted, uncorrected for sample size.

*Subjects.*—The $S$s consisted of 72 airmen at Lockbourne Air Force Base, selected on the basis of two-choice reaction-time measures.[4] Their ages ranged from 18 to 29 years. All were right handed. They were excused from drill during the time spent as $S$s and appeared to be well motivated.

The 72 $S$s were selected from a larger group of 153 men so as to form eight equal-sized strata which had homogeneous within-group average two-choice reaction-time scores. Each of the nine experimental groups was formed by drawing one $S$ at random from each stratum. Each group of eight $S$s was then tested under one of the nine S–R combinations.

*Procedure.*—The instructions for each of the groups were similar. Those for the $S_a$–$R_a$ group were as follows:

"Here is a stimulus panel of eight lights and a response panel in which you can move this stylus to one of eight places. Hold the stylus in your right hand. When I say 'center' place it on this center disc. I shall then say 'ready' and a few seconds later one of the lights will come on. If this light (point) should come on, move the stylus straight up. If this light should come on, move the stylus quickly to this position (indicate upper-right corner). If you start in the wrong direction, correct your movement as soon as possible. Do not try to guess which light will come on as they will be presented in a random order. Work for both speed and accuracy since both reaction time and errors will be recorded."

Each $S$ was given 20 practice trials on his particular S–R combination, followed by 40 test trials. The order of stimuli was randomized, with the restriction of equal frequency for all stimuli at the end of each series, and a further restriction against runs longer than two.

## Results

The experiment provides three measures of the effectiveness of each of the S–R ensembles: (*a*) reaction time, (*b*) percentage of responses that were errors, and (*c*) average information lost per stimulus. The means for all three criterion measures are indicated in Fig. 3.

[4] All $S$s were tested by the second author.

*Reaction time.*—In scoring the two-handed responses that were made on Panel C, reaction time was taken as the average of the times for the two hands. This procedure is justified by the finding that in two-handed responses the times for the right and left hands agree very closely. The average correlation of the two measures was .96 for the three groups that used Response Panel C, and the difference in the mean reaction time for the two hands was only .004 sec. However, for all one-handed responses on Panel C, the mean difference in reaction time between the two hands was .11 sec. in favor of the right hand, and 23 out of 24 Ss using Panel C were faster when using the right hand. In summary, when Ss had to move one hand alone, the right hand, which moved away from or toward the body, was significantly faster (by about .108 sec.) than the left hand, which moved to the right or the left, but when both hands had to be moved together, they had similar reaction times. The time for two-handed responses was approximately the same as the mean for one-hand responses by the left hand.

The means shown in Fig. 3 are for all stimuli in a set combined. The times for movements that were made in the wrong direction (errors) are combined with the data for correct responses, since the mean reaction times for erroneous and for correct responses did not differ significantly.

The mean reaction-time data for the different Ss were tested for homogeneity of variance by Bartlett's test and no significant departure from homogeneity was found, even though variance tended to increase somewhat as the mean reaction time increased (the range of SD's was from .036 sec. for the $S_a$–$R_a$ ensemble to .097 sec. for the $S_c$–$R_a$ combination). A double-classification analysis of variance for matched groups was then carried out (see Table 1). The most important finding is the highly significant interaction effect. The variance that can be attributed to interaction is very much larger than the variance attributable to the primary effects of either stimulus or response sets alone.

The differences in the means for the primary effects are interpreted as significantly different from chance, as indicated by the F ratios shown in Table 1 for which the residual term is used as the estimate of error. However, no reliable generalizations about these arbitrarily selected stimulus or response codes can be made to situations in which comparisons are made among different sets of stimuli or different sets of responses.

For every stimulus set there was a different best-response set, and for every response set there was a different best-stimulus set. For example, Response Set A led to the shortest mean reaction time in combination with Stimulus Set A, but to the longest reaction time in combination with Stimulus Set C. The difference of almost .4 sec. is 21 times as large as the estimate of the standard error of the difference. The three "best" combinations are those that were predicted by Es on the basis of the correspondence of the spatial codes. A

TABLE 1

ANALYSIS OF VARIANCE FOR THE REACTION-TIME DATA

| Source | df | Mean Square | F |
| --- | --- | --- | --- |
| Matched Ss | 7 | 42896 | |
| Stimulus sets | 2 | 86772 | 68.43* |
| Response sets | 2 | 36352 | 28.67* |
| S–R interaction | 4 | 170492 | 134.46* |
| Residual | 56 | 1268 | |
| Total | 71 | | |

* Significant beyond the 1% level of confidence when tested against the residual as an estimate of error.

direct test of the significance of the difference between performance with corresponding and noncorresponding S–R ensembles is provided by a single-classification analysis of variance, which is equivalent to a conventional $t$ test between the means for matched $S$s under the two conditions. Such an analysis was carried out and the difference was found to be highly significant ($p < .001$). The writers feel justified in predicting that if other sets of stimuli and sets of responses should be selected with due consideration to the correspondence of the stimulus and response codes, then it is highly probable that interaction effects would again account for a large portion of the variance and spatially corresponding codes would again give superior performance.

The reaction times for the $S_a$–$R_a$ and the $S_b$–$R_b$ combinations did not differ significantly, but both were superior to that for the $S_c$–$R_c$ combination. It might be hypothesized that a bidimensional stimulus and response coding scheme (two pairs of lights and a two-handed response) is inefficient. It seems appropriate, however, to suggest an alternative hypothesis, that the inferiority may have been due to failure on the part of $E$s to observe some principle of response-response compatibility in selecting the eight alternative movements constituting Response Set $C$. It should be mentioned that forward and back responses made with the right hand only averaged .41 sec. for the $S_c$–$R_c$ combination, which is comparable to the mean reaction times for the $S_a$–$R_a$ and $S_b$–$R_b$ combinations, where the right hand was also used.

*Errors.*—Approximately 10% of all responses were in error, an error being defined as an initial movement in the wrong direction. These error data agree in general with the time data in respect to the rankings assigned to the different S–R ensembles. The three "best" combinations within each row and column of Fig. 3 are the same for the two criteria. The difference between the best and the worst combinations appears to be relatively larger than was the case with the time scores. It is interesting to note that Response Set B, which in combination with its corresponding stimulus set ($S_b$) led to the fewest errors, resulted in the most errors when used in combination with another stimulus set ($S_c$).

The data for responses to separate stimuli revealed two important relations. The first is that those S–R ensembles having lowest mean error scores also tend to have the most uniform time scores from one stimulus to another. The second is that wherever there is marked variability within the responses to a set of stimuli, time and error scores tend to vary together, i.e., are positively correlated. For the four S–R ensembles with the greatest number of errors the rank correlations between time and error scores for the eight stimuli vary from .65 to .93.

*Information lost.*—The average information transmitted per stimulus was computed by Method 1 of Garner and Hake (4). The data for information lost, shown in Fig. 3, are the differences between the theoretical information in each stimulus event (3 bits) and the average information transmitted per stimulation.

The results of the information analysis agree closely with the total error frequencies and, in fact, add little to the grosser error analysis. The ranks of the nine groups are identical on the two criteria except for a reversal of the two last (worst) groups. This agreement is not surprising since the same type of error distribution, a piling up of errors in certain cells of the matrix of transition probabilities, was found for all nine S-R combinations.

It is not possible to compute a meaningful estimate of average rate of information transfer in this experiment because of the relatively long time delay between successive responses. However, short response times were associated with small loss of information both within the eight conditions of each S-R ensemble and between the means for the nine different S-R ensembles. Thus the results of the information or error analysis, considered in relation to the reaction-time analysis, provide empirical support for defining compatibility in terms of the average *rate* of information transmission.

## Experiment II

An important question concerning the results of the preceding experiment is whether the differences between various S-R combinations are transitory or permanent. An extended learning study was carried out in an effort to answer this question.

### Method

The most desirable way to have conducted this study would have been to practice all of the 72 Ss used in Exp. I over an extended period. However, this was not practical. Instead, a single new group was studied for 32 training sessions covering approximately 2½ months. The Ss practiced making a single set of eight responses (Response Set $A$) to each of the three different sets of eight stimuli employed in the previous study. As an alternative Ss could have been asked to make three sets of responses to a single set of stimuli, but this was not done because less initial habit interference is to be expected if the same responses are learned to three sets of stimuli, than if three sets of responses are learned to a single set of stimuli. Response Set $A$ was chosen because there is no ambiguity in the scoring of these responses.

Six male students at Ohio State University were started on the training series but one dropped out after 20 sessions and his data are not reported (although they are comparable to the data that are reported). In order to maintain motivation Ss were scheduled in pairs (except for the last 12 sessions of the odd $S$). One $S$ was given a series of 16 trials on one of the three sets of S-R combinations in an unbroken sequence, while the other $S$ observed. The Ss then exchanged places. This procedure was continued until each $S$ had been tested on each of the three stimulus sets. The sequence of work and rest and the order of trials on the three conditions were balanced. Each stimulus appeared twice in a random order within each run of 16 trials. Each $S$ made a total of 48 responses per session.

Initial instructions and other procedures were the same as in the preceding experiment. At periodic intervals Ss were cautioned to try not to make errors. In addition to reaction time and errors, $E$ recorded movement time, the time to traverse the selected pathway of Panel A. After each response Ss were told their reaction time and if they had made an error, this was pointed out.

On Sessions 27 to 30 inclusive, a secondary task, mental arithmetic, was carried on by Ss concurrently with the perceptual-motor task. The $E$ read aloud a series of numbers at a predetermined rate, and $S$ gave the successive differences between the last two numbers read by $E$. This secondary task was introduced to test the hypothesis that the least compatible S-R combination would show the most deterioration under conditions of additional load or stress. Standard conditions were resumed on Session 31. The experiment was terminated at the end of Session 32.

### Results

The mean reaction-time and movement-time data for the five Ss are shown graphically in Fig. 4. Throughout all of the standard sessions performance was consistently best when Ss responded to Stimulus Set $A$. Stimulus Set $B$ gave almost equally good results. Stimulus Set $C$ was much the worst of the three. At no time during the 32 days did any of the Ss consistently respond as quickly to Stimulus Set $C$ as they did to the other two sets of eight stimuli. The mean times for the three stimulus sets on Days 17 through 26 inclusive were as follows: $S_a$, .272 sec.; $S_b$, .286 sec.; $S_c$, .355 sec.

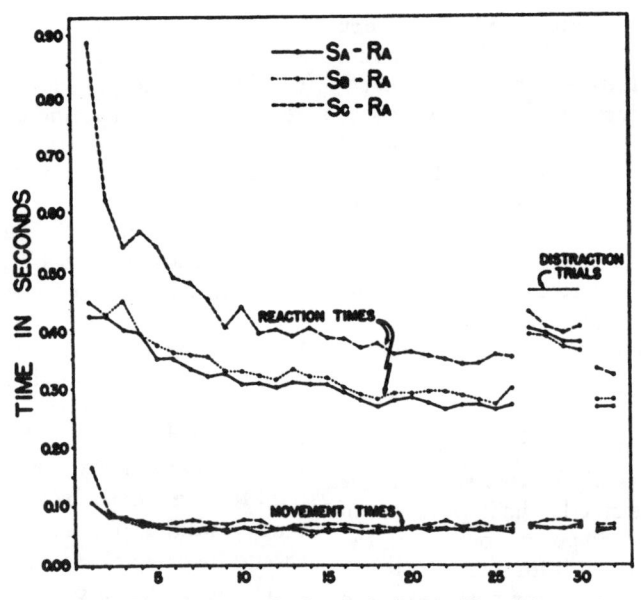

FIG. 4. Learning curve for five Ss during the 32 training sessions of Exp. II. All Ss had 16 practice trials on each of the three S–R combinations each session.

Movement time in responding to Stimulus Set $C$ was slightly but consistently slower than to Sets $A$ and $B$. Averaged over Trials 17 through 26 these times were as follows: $S_a$, .059 sec.; $S_b$, .061 sec.; $S_c$, .067 sec.

The error data, averaged over all five Ss for successive blocks of time, are given in Table 2. It can be seen that the Ss never succeeded in eliminating all errors. In fact, errors occurred more frequently as training progressed, indicating perhaps that S emphasized speed at the expense of accuracy. Errors were made most frequently to Stimulus Set $C$ throughout the training period. Thus both time and error data indicate consistently poorer performance on the $S_c$–$R_a$ condition.

On Days 27–30, when the load on Ss was increased by the addition of a secondary task, reaction times were substantially slower for all three S–R combinations. All five Ss continued to give the slowest reaction to Stimulus $C$; however, the relative differences between groups were much smaller than they had been previously. The frequency of arithmetic errors was approximately the same for all three groups, but there was a large differ-

TABLE 2

PERCENTAGES OF MOTOR RESPONSES THAT WERE IN ERROR DURING DIFFERENT BLOCKS OF TRAINING SESSIONS*

| Sessions | S–R Combination | | |
|---|---|---|---|
| | $S_a$–$R_a$ | $S_b$–$R_a$ | $S_c$–$R_a$ |
| 1–6 | 2.5 | 3.7 | 11.9 |
| 7–16 | 5.6 | 8.7 | 12.5 |
| 17–26 | 6.9 | 10.0 | 11.9 |
| 27–30** | 4.4 | 6.9 | 15.6 |
| 31–32 | 8.1 | 9.4 | 12.5 |

* Sessions consisted of 16 responses per S–R combination for each of the five Ss.
** On Sessions 27, 28, 29, and 30 the Ss responded to stimulus lights and solved mental arithmetic problems concurrently. The number of arithmetic problems attempted during each session was 50 per $S$ and the percentage of arithmetic errors for the three sets of stimulus lights was 4.1, 2.9, and 4.2, respectively.

ence between groups in the frequency of movement errors. The introduction of an additional task late in learning in this case apparently served to reduce the degree of readiness for the motor task, minimizing reaction-time differences, but increasing differences with respect to errors in the motor task. However, the data are not conclusive on these points and the test of the hypothesis regarding the effects of increased load is considered inconclusive.

## Discussion

The results of the two experiments demonstrate clearly the importance of stimulus and response coding for the maximum rate of information transfer in a perceptual-motor task. It also is clear that some S-R compatibility effects are relatively unaffected by extended practice.

An interpretation of the basis for the relative permanence of these effects, which seems appropriate to the concept of compatibility, is one stated in terms of the capacity to learn to deal with sets of probabilities (probability learning). The response that a person makes to a particular stimulus event can be considered to be a function of two sets of probabilities; (a) the probabilities (uncertainties) appropriate to the situational constraints established by $E$'s instructions, by the reinforcements experienced in the experimental situation, and by other aspects of the immediate situation; and (b) the more general and more stable expectancies or habits based on $S$'s experiences in many other situations. It is suggested that extended training will nearly always lead to changes in the former but often will have relatively little effect on the latter.

This view holds that $S$'s behavior, notwithstanding long experience in a particular situation, is never entirely relevant to the specific constraints of that particular situation. Instead, $S$ responds as if additional possibilities were present.

This interpretation supports the view that stimulus and response sets are optimally matched when the resulting ensemble agrees closely with the basic habits or expectancies of individuals, i.e., with individual and with population stereotypes. It must be remembered, however, that the expectancies referred to are those which hold for the particular situation under study, and that population stereotypes should be determined with due regard to the total situation. For example, in the present experiment the $E$s determined, by preliminary trial, that $S$s "preferred" to move toward rather than away from a stimulus light. However, it is known that in many stimulus tasks where the $S$ controls the stimulus, the opposite motion relation is the expected one. When $S$s have to learn to deal with the probabilities inherent in a particular situation, the correspondence of these specific expectancies to the more general expectancies of the individual with respect to that kind of situation is an important aspect of the learning task.

Further support for considering S-R compatibility to be a function of stimulus and response matching comes from the positive correlation between the two criteria, time and errors, used in evaluating performance. This positive correlation would be expected if additional information transformations, or re-encoding steps, were added to a communication system, since each transformation would be likely to add an additional time delay and to increase the total probability of errors. In the human it is hypothesized that the fastest responses may be the most accurate because they involve S-R ensembles in which the transfer of information from stimulus to response is most direct, i.e., involves the minimum number of recoding steps. The concept of intervening information transformations does not attempt to explain how such recoding occurs within the nervous system, but it is in agreement with the subjective reports of Ss who maintained that it was difficult, in the case of the less compatible S-R ensembles used in the present study, to be prepared to respond to all of the eight stimulus possibilities.

## Summary

Experiment I was planned to test the hypothesis that information transfer in a perceptual-motor task is in large measure a function of the matching of sets of stimuli and sets of responses. Nine S-R ensembles, involving variations of the spatial patterns of stimuli and responses, were studied in an eight-choice situation, using groups of matched Ss.

The results, analyzed in terms of reaction time, errors, and information lost, support the hypothesis. They indicate that it is not permissible to conclude that any particular set of stimuli, or set of responses, will provide a high rate of information transfer; it is the ensemble of S-R combinations that must be considered.

Experiment II was planned to test the permanence of three selected S-R compatibility effects. Five Ss were trained for 32 days to make a particular set of responses to each of three sets of stimuli. Differences in reaction time, movement time, and frequency of errors in responding to the three sets of stimuli persisted over the 32 days.

The results are interpreted in terms of probability learning and the necessity for (hypothetical) information transformation or re-encoding steps. It appears that it is very difficult for Ss to learn to deal effectively with the information (uncertainties) characteristic of a specific situation, if these uncertainties are different from the more general set of probabilities which have been learned in similar life situations.

## References

1. FITTS, P. M., & SIMON, C. W. Some relations between stimulus patterns and performance in a continuous dual-pursuit task. *J. exp. Psychol.*, 1952, **43**, 428–436.
2. GAGNÉ, R. M., BAKER, K. E., & FOSTER, H. On the relation between similarity and transfer of training in the learning of discriminative motor tasks. *Psychol. Rev.*, 1950, **57**, 67–79.
3. GARDNER, J. F. Direction of pointer motion in relation to movement of flight controls. Wright Air Development Center, Dayton, Ohio. AF Technical Report No. 6016, 1950.
4. GARNER, W. R., & HAKE, H. W. The amount of information in absolute judgments. *Psychol. Rev.*, 1951, **58**, 446–459.
5. JENKINS, W. L., & OLSON, M. W. The use of levers in making settings on a linear scale. *J. appl. Psychol.*, 1952, **36**, 269–271.
6. KLEMMER, E. T., & FRICK, F. C. Assimilation of information from dot and matrix patterns. *J. exp. Psychol.*, 1953, **45**, 15–19.
7. KNOWLES, W. B., GARVEY, W. D., & NEWLIN, E. P. The effect of "speed" and "load" on display-control relationships. *J. exp. Psychol.*, 1953, **46**, 2, 65–76.
8. LEWIS, D., SMITH, P. N., & McALLISTER, D. E. Retroactive facilitation and interference in performance of the modified two-hand coordinator. *J. exp. Psychol.*, 1952, **44**, 44–50.
9. MITCHELL, M. J. H., & VINCE, M. A. The direction of movement of machine controls. *Quart. J. exp. Psychol.*, 1951, **3**, 24–25.

10. SHANNON, C. E. A mathematical theory of communication. *Bell Syst. Tech. J.*, 1948, **27**, 379–423; 623–656.
11. SIMON, C. W. Instrument-control configurations affecting performance in a compensatory pursuit task. Wright Air Development Center, Dayton, Ohio. AF Technical Report No. 6015, 1952.
12. STRATTON, G. M. Vision without inversion of the retinal image. *Psychol. Rev.*, 1896, **3**, 611–612; 1897, **4**, 342–351, 466–471.
13. WARRICK, M. J. Effects of motion relationships on speed of positioning visual indicators by rotary control knobs. Wright Air Development Center, Dayton, Ohio. AF Technical Report No. 5812, 1949.

(Received for early publication May 22, 1953)

## 14

## INFORMATION CAPACITY OF DISCRETE MOTOR RESPONSES [1]

PAUL M. FITTS AND JAMES R. PETERSON [2]

*University of Michigan*

The effects of response amplitude and terminal accuracy on 2-choice reaction time (RT) and on movement time (MT) were studied. Both the required amplitude (A) of a movement, and the width (W) of the target that S was required to hit, had a large and systematic effect on MT, whereas they had a relatively small effect on RT. Defining an index of movement difficulty as ID = log₂ 2A/W, the correlation between ID and MT was found to be above .99 over the ID range from 2.6 to 7.6 bits per response. Thus the times for discrete movements follow the same type of law as was found earlier to hold for serial responses. The relative independence of RT and MT is interpreted as pointing to the serial and independent nature of perceptual and motor processes.

The relation of response variability and response magnitude has long been one of the major topics of interest in psychophysics. Recently the effects of these two variables plus that of response duration have received renewed emphasis in connection with studies of the information capacity of the human motor system.

For physical communication systems having limited bandwidth ($W$) and signal power ($S$), and perturbed by white Gaussian noise of average power ($N$), Shannon (1948, Theorem 17) showed that channel capacity ($C$) is equal to

$$C = W \log_2 \frac{S + N}{N} \quad \text{bits per second} \quad [1]$$

Arguing by analogy, Fitts (1954) reasoned that the average amplitude ($A$) of a human movement is equivalent to average signal plus noise amplitude, and that half the range of movement variability is equivalent to peak noise amplitude ($n$), and proposed that an index of task difficulty (ID) be defined as

$$\text{ID} = \log_2 \frac{A}{n} \quad [2]$$

In an experiment in which the per-

[1] This research was supported in part by the Air Force Office of Scientific Research, Contracts No. AF 49 (638)-449 and -1235.

[2] Now at Minneapolis-Honeywell Company, Minneapolis.

From *Journal of Experimental Psychology*, 67. Copyright 1964 by the American Psychological Association.

missible plus-and-minus range of terminal movement error is specified as a target band of width ($W$), and $S$ is induced to keep the proportion of his responses exceeding this limit small, it can be assumed further that $n = W/2$ and therefore ID can be evaluated as

$$\text{ID} = \log_2 \frac{2A}{W} \qquad [3]$$

On these grounds it was conjectured that average movement time (MT) should remain constant for different values of $A$ and $W$, within limits, as long as the ID ratio remains constant, i.e.,

$$\frac{\text{ID}}{\text{MT}} = C \qquad [4]$$

where $C$ may be interpreted as analogous to man's capacity for executing a particular class of motor responses in bits per second.[3] Extending the analogy to the case where ID takes on different values, then if motor processes follow the same type of law as do perceptual-motor processes, it would be expected that, within limits,

$$\text{MT} = a + b\,\text{ID} \qquad [5]$$

Fitts (1954) obtained results in agreement with these predictions, using three different self-paced, cyclical tasks. Performance was maximum for a midrange of values of $A$, $W$, and ID and fell off gradually outside these values (optimum performance being obtained in the vicinity of $A = 8$ in. and ID $= 4$–$8$ bits, depending on the particular task). Subsequent investigators (Annett, Golby, & Kay, 1958; Crossman, 1960; Welford, 1958) have, with minor exceptions, reported findings that provide general confirmation of the theory. The times required for different components of a movement sequence appear to follow somewhat different rules, however, and a more complex relation between $A$ and $W$ has been found in certain tasks (Andriessen, 1960; Vredenbregt, 1959). Welford (1960, 1961) has also proposed the adoption of a modified ID ratio. However, all of these results have been obtained in repetitive self-paced tasks, where the only uncertainty confronting $S$ in regard to the requirements of the next response in a series has been the uncertainty resulting from his own amplitude variability in executing the previous response. It therefore was decided to conduct further studies of the generality of the theory when applied to discrete movements. Separate measures of reaction time (RT) and movement time (MT) were taken, and variations introduced in the degree of uncertainty as to what response would be required by the next stimulus.

The experiments were planned to provide answers to the following specific questions: (a) Does a single index of performance apply equally well to both discrete and serial tasks? (b) Are RT and MT affected in the same way by variations in task conditions?

## METHOD

*Apparatus and task.*—The $S$s held a lightweight metal stylus on a small metal starting plate (see Fig. 1), fixated a point midway between two signal lights, and when one of the lights came on attempted to hit the appropriate one of two alternative targets as quickly as possible. Target widths were varied (all were 4 in. long); targets could be located at any desired distance to right or left of the starting point.

An electrical current, sufficient in amount to activate an electronic relay, but below the threshold for detection, passed through $S$'s body whenever the stylus was in contact

---

[3] The analogy with Shannon's Theorem 17 is not exact, since the ID ratio involves an amplitude rather than a power ratio, and since the range of variability is used in estimating noise amplitude.

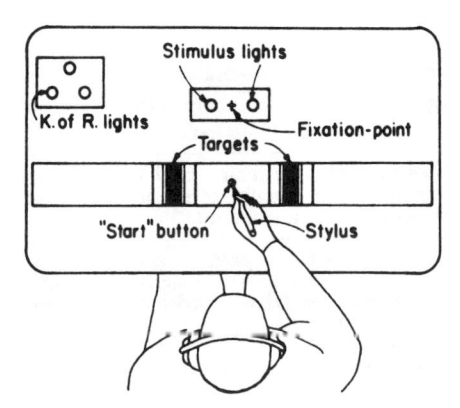

FIG. 1. Plan view of the apparatus.

TABLE 1

TARGET CHARACTERISTICS EMPLOYED IN THE SERIES OF EXPERIMENTS

| Target | Movement Amplitude (A, In.) | Target Width (W, In.) | Index of Difficulty (ID, Bits) |
|---|---|---|---|
| A | 3 | 1.0 | 2.58 |
| B | 3 | 0.5 | 3.58 |
| C | 3 | 0.25 | 4.58 |
| D | 3 | 0.125 | 5.58 |
| E | 6 | 1.0 | 3.58 |
| F | 6 | 0.5 | 4.58 |
| G | 6 | 0.25 | 5.58 |
| H | 6 | 0.125 | 6.58 |
| I | 12 | 1.0 | 4.58 |
| J | 12 | 0.5 | 5.58 |
| K | 12 | 0.25 | 6.58 |
| L | 12 | 0.125 | 7.58 |

either with the starting button, the target plate, or overshoot and undershoot plates on either side of the target. Three time clocks were used to measure RT, MT, and total time to the nearest .01 sec. Lights for knowledge of results provided immediate information regarding hits, overshoot errors, and undershoot errors.

*Subjects.*—Six paid male Ss, 18–25 yr. of age, were used.

*Conditions of A and W.*—Twelve combinations of movement amplitude (A) and target width (W) were provided by using 3-, 6-, and 12-in. values for A, the distances between the starting button and the midline of the target, in combinations with .125-, .25-, .5-, and 1-in. values for W (see Table 1).

*Procedure.*—A series of five studies was carried out (see Table 2). The conditions, including target or stimulus probabilities, were explained fully to Ss. The Ss were instructed to make quick movements aimed at hitting one of two alternative targets as soon as one of the two stimulus lights appeared. Five trials were given per minute, and about 1 min. was required to change targets within blocks of trials. The order of target conditions within experiments was randomized and different for each S. The same six Ss served in all five experiments following a training session.

The basic condition was that used in the Practice Session and in Exp. II (see Table 2). Two identical targets were located to the right and left of the starting button, and the right and left stimulus lights were turned on with equal frequency in random order. This task is thus a standard two-choice B reaction. In Exp. I one of each pair of targets, sometimes the right and sometimes the left one, was designated in advance but S was told that the stimulus indicating he should initiate a movement to that target would follow the ready signal only 50% of the time, and that no stimulus would occur on the other half of the trials. This is similar to an A reaction with 50% "catch" trials; the stimulus is known but there is 1 bit of uncertainty as to whether or not it will occur. In the absence of a better designation this will be referred to as an A reaction. The B reaction was used in Exp. III but unequal probabilities were introduced. In the two remaining experiments, pairs of equally probable but asymmetrical targets were used.

The Ss wore headsets and listened to white masking noise of about 70 db. loudness. A momentary interruption of this noise served as the ready signal, with a stimulus light (when it occurred) appearing exactly 2 sec. later.

The time between the onset of the stimulus light and the breaking of contact between the stylus and the starting button (RT) was recorded, as well as the time between the initiation of the movement and initial contact of the stylus with a target or error plate (MT). The Ss were told their average (RT + MT) time and number of errors after each block of trials. They were not aware of the analysis of response times into RT and MT.

## RESULTS

Results for the Practice Session and for all experiments except Exp. III were highly consistent and will there-

## TABLE 2
### EXPERIMENTAL CONDITIONS FOR THE DIFFERENT EXPERIMENTS

|  | Target Pairs | Summary of Procedures |
| --- | --- | --- |
| Practice Session | 12 pairs of identical targets, on opposite sides of the starting button. | 24 successive trials per target pair. Each target designated randomly and equally often on successive trials. Order of pairs randomized. |
| Exp. I | 12 pairs of identical targets, on opposite sides of the starting button. | 40 successive trials per target pair. One target designated preceding each trial, but the signal to respond given on only half the trials. Order of pairs randomized. |
| Exp. II | 12 pairs of identical targets, on opposite sides of the starting button. | Same procedure followed as used for the Practice Session. |
| Exp. III | 6 pairs of identical targets (C, D, H, I, J, K), on opposite sides of the starting button. | Same procedure followed as for the Practice Session and Exp. II except that one target of each pair designated on the average 50%, 75%, or 92% of the time over blocks of 24 trials. |
| Exp. IV | 3 pairs of heterogeneous targets (C and I, D and J, H and K), each pair of equal difficulty but differing in $A$ and $W$; both targets on the same side of the starting button. | 24 successive trials per target pair. Tests made with both targets to the right and also with both to the left of the starting button. |
| Exp. V | 3 pairs of heterogeneous targets (C and I, D and J, H and K), each pair of equal difficulty but differing in $A$ and $W$; targets on opposite sides of the starting button. | 24 successive trials per target pair. Tests made with each target of a pair alternately to the right and to the left of the starting button on successive blocks of trials. |

fore be discussed together. The standard $B$ reaction (Practice and Exp. II) will serve as the prototype.

*Reaction times.*—In all instances where pairs of identical targets were used RT data were very similar for the right and left targets. Accordingly, the data were combined for all identical pairs of targets.

The correlation between mean RT and ID value for the 12 movement conditions of Exp. II was found to be .79, which is statistically significant. RT increased slightly as movement amplitude ($A$) was increased, and as target width ($W$) was decreased, although only the former effects were significant ($p < .05$). However, the slope of the linear function relating the two variables was only 5.4 msec. per 1-bit change in ID (see Fig. 2). Results for Exp. I, IV, and V were also consistent in indicating that changes in ID values have a consistent but very small effect on RT.

Reaction times were slightly but significantly faster ($p < .01$) for Exp. I ($A$ reaction with 50% stimulus uncertainty) than for Exp. II (two-alternative $B$ reaction). The mean difference, over all 12 target conditions, was only 15 msec. Practice effects alone should have produced a difference in the opposite direction, however, so that the true RT difference between time and event uncertainty may be larger than 15 msec.

The only variable which had an appreciable effect on RT was the relative probability of the two alternative targets (degree of redundancy of a response sequence). These effects (from Exp. III) will be discussed later.

*Movement times.*—Changes in required movement characteristics had large as well as highly reliable effects on MT, in sharp contrast to their small effects on RT. The MT data from the Practice Session, and from Exp. I and II (see Fig. 2), permit a direct comparison with the earlier data from self-paced cyclical tasks (Fitts, 1954). It appears that the index of task difficulty (ID) provides equally as good a prediction of movement times for discrete responses as has been shown previously to hold for serial responses. As long as the level of stimulus uncertainty is held constant, the source of uncertainty (A reaction vs. B reaction) does not change the nature of the function. However, the slope of the function is less steep for discrete than for serial responses. Although individual differences were large, the effects of changes in target distances and widths were highly consistent within Ss.

The movement times were of similar magnitude in Exp. I and II. Five of the six Ss made faster movements under the A reaction condition while one S showed a very small (2 msec.) difference favoring the B reaction. Although the mean difference is statistically significant ($p < .05$), the effect is quite small relative to other experimental effects. Within each experiment about 99% of the variance in mean MT was accounted for by the ID ratio, the correlations between ID and MT for these two experiments being .995 and .994, respectively.

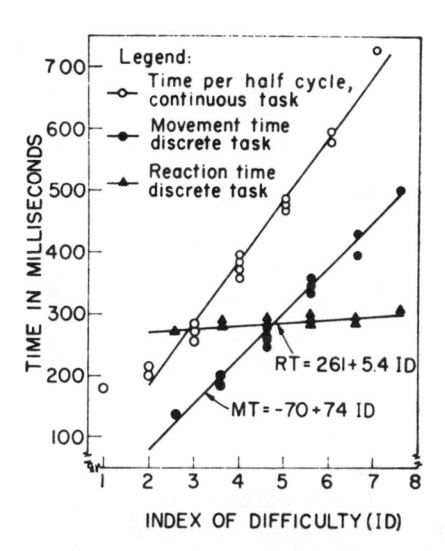

FIG. 2. Relation of reaction time and movement time to the index of task difficulty. (The solid data points show the relation of RT and MT data obtained in Exp. II, to ID— ID = $\log_2 2A/W$. The open circles show mean times per movement in performing a serial tapping task in which target amplitudes and widths were varied in the same manner as in the present experiments; see Fitts, 1954.)

Furthermore, the regression equations for predicting MT on the basis of a knowledge of required movement amplitude and accuracy are very similar for the two experiments as well as for the Practice Session. These three equations are:

MT = 74 ID −42 msec.
(Practice Session) [6]

MT = 70 ID −63 msec.
(Exp. I) [7]

MT = 74 ID −70 msec.
(Exp. II) [8]

Examination of the constants of Equation 6 vs. 8, for comparable data taken at different stages of practice, suggests that practice resulted in a displacement of the function downward without a change in slope. Thus easy and difficult movements became

TABLE 3

MEAN REACTION AND MOVEMENT TIMES FOR COMPARABLE
TARGET PAIRS IN EXP. II, IV, AND V

| Target Pair | ID | Exp. II RT | Exp. II MT | Exp. IV RT | Exp. IV MT | Exp. V RT | Exp. V MT |
|---|---|---|---|---|---|---|---|
| C and I | 4.58 | 28 | 27 | 29 | 25 | 30 | 25 |
| D and J | 5.58 | 29 | 35 | 30 | 31 | 30 | 32 |
| H and K | 6.58 | 29 | 41 | 28 | 38 | 30 | 40 |

Note.—Data are for all $S$s and for right and left targets combined; times are shown to the nearest .01 sec.

slightly faster by similar absolute amounts.

The results of the analyses of movement durations for experiments in which pairs of dissimilar targets were used (Exp. IV and V) are summarized in Table 3. It can be seen that variations in target pairings had a very small effect on RTs. The actual times were very comparable to those found in Exp. II in which identical targets were placed at equal distances on opposite sides of the starting point. However, again it was found that MT increased progressively and by large amounts as a linear function of ID. Movement durations were similar in absolute magnitude to those found for homogeneous pairs of targets in Exp. II, the times for different movements varying over a range of about 150 msec.

MTs in Exp. IV and V were 33 and 23 msec. faster, respectively, than for comparable target conditions in Exp. II. Most or all of this increase could easily have been due to a continuing practice effect, however. Movements to the target on the side of the preferred hand were 20 and 11 msec. faster, respectively, than to the alternative side, whereas movements to the nearer and farther targets of a pair on the same side, equated for ID, differed by only 4 and 6 msec., respectively.

*Errors.*—Error data for the Practice Session and for Exp. I and II are summarized in Table 4. The $S$s failed to hit the target on approximately 10% of their responses, overshoot and undershoot errors being very nearly equal. Error frequencies were found to be essentially independent of movement amplitudes, but were more frequent for the two smaller than for the two larger targets. $A$ responses, where $S$ knew in advance which target he should try to hit, were no more accurate than $B$ responses. (In fact, errors were slightly more frequent for the former.) The percentage of errors in Exp. IV and V were comparable, being 9.5% and 8.2%, respectively, and overshoot and undershoot errors were again almost exactly equal.

*Redundant sequences.*—The results from Exp. III, in which response series of three levels of redundancy were employed, differed from those obtained in other experiments in the series (see Table 5). As redundancy was increased as a consequence of one target of an identical pair being designated more frequently than the other, on the average, both RTs and MTs became slightly faster, for those responses that were made to the more probable target. Accuracy also became somewhat greater for the more probable target.

The differences between the RTs

### TABLE 4

PERCENTAGE OF UNDERSHOOT (U) AND OVERSHOOT (O) ERRORS FOR THE PRACTICE SESSION AND FOR EXP. I AND II

| Target | Practice U | Practice O | Exp. I U | Exp. I O | Exp. II U | Exp. II O |
|---|---|---|---|---|---|---|
| A | 4.2 | 0.7 | 1.7 | 4.2 | 5.6 | 5.6 |
| B | 3.5 | 2.1 | 2.5 | 5.8 | 2.8 | 5.6 |
| C | 6.2 | 4.9 | 10.0 | 6.7 | 5.6 | 3.5 |
| D | 4.2 | 4.9 | 7.5 | 7.5 | 10.4 | 6.9 |
| E | 4.9 | 3.5 | 2.5 | 4.2 | 2.8 | 2.1 |
| F | 2.8 | 3.5 | 7.5 | 8.3 | 3.5 | 4.2 |
| G | 7.6 | 5.6 | 4.2 | 8.3 | 2.8 | 4.2 |
| H | 8.3 | 6.9 | 7.5 | 10.8 | 9.0 | 10.4 |
| I | 1.4 | 1.4 | 2.5 | 4.2 | 5.6 | 2.1 |
| J | 4.2 | 5.6 | 8.3 | 5.8 | 2.8 | 4.2 |
| K | 6.2 | 4.9 | 8.3 | 10.8 | 2.8 | 9.7 |
| L | 6.2 | 5.6 | 8.3 | 9.2 | 6.9 | 7.6 |
| M | 5.0 | 4.1 | 5.9 | 7.2 | 5.0 | 5.5 |

Note.—The Practice Session and Exp. II involved 1,728 trials each; Exp. I involved 1,440 actual and 1,440 "false" trials. In Exp. I, three additional errors occurred as Ss lifted the stylus when a stimulus was not given.

to the alternative targets in each pair increased approximately linearly with redundancy, as has recently been reported by Fitts, Peterson, and Wolpe (1963) for two other tasks, and so did movement times. Although relatively small in magnitude, these effects were consistent for all Ss and for all target pairs. Since time and errors are usually negatively correlated, the MT differences should have been even greater had Ss achieved equal accuracy for the less frequent movements. Gains in speed and accuracy for the more frequent target of each pair, weighted for frequency, just about compensated for losses in speed and accuracy for the less frequent target.

## DISCUSSION

*Independence of reaction time and movement time.*—The present results indicate that RT and MT can be influenced quite independently by (*a*) the degree of uncertainty regarding the stimulus to a

### TABLE 5

SUMMARY OF REACTION TIME, MOVEMENT TIME, AND ERROR DATA FOR MOVEMENTS IN TWO DIRECTIONS IN EXP. III

| Percent Redundancy | Reaction Time (Msec.) N | P | Diff. | Wtd. Aver. | Movement Time (Msec.) N | P | Diff. | Wtd. Aver. | Percentage of Movements Missing Target N | P | Diff. | Overall % Misses |
|---|---|---|---|---|---|---|---|---|---|---|---|---|
| 0.0 | 293 | 279 | 14 | 286 | 342 | 339 | 3 | 340 | 10.0 | 8.3 | 1.7 | 9.1 |
| 18.9 | 315 | 282 | 33 | 290 | 354 | 341 | 13 | 344 | 12.0 | 9.7 | 2.3 | 10.3 |
| 58.7 | 326 | 268 | 58 | 271 | 366 | 343 | 23 | 344 | 22.2 | 8.2 | 14.0 | 9.4 |

Note.—P indicates a movement to the target on the side of the preferred hand and N a movement to the non-preferred side; the target on the preferred side was made the most frequent target under conditions of 18.9% and 58.7% redundancy.

movement, and (b) the degree of uncertainty permitted in executing the movement. This finding supports the view that perceptual processes and motor response processes are relatively independent (see Broadbent, 1958; Welford, 1960), and that human information processing proceeds by a series of essentially independent steps.

Welford's (1958) conclusion that RT and not MT shows the major effect of aging offers strong parallel evidence for the separate nature of perceptual and motor information handling processes, as do results from related experiments of Leonard (1952), Singleton (1954), and Szafran (1951).

Apparently RT reflects the time required for perceptual or cognitive processes, and is determined in part by the preparations which $S$ makes prior to a stimulus, such as those resulting from his knowledge of stimulus probabilities. Movement time, in contrast, appears to reflect the duration of motor system processes that are necessary for the control of the timing and patterning of a movement, and which begin after the decision is made to execute a movement. Advanced preparation for two-alternative movement processes does not appear to lengthen the time required to execute one of the movements, as compared to the situation where $S$ is prepared in advance for only one response which has a 50% probability of being designated.

Several suggestions can be offered regarding processes which might utilize increased time to gain greater accuracy in the control of an output. As an illustration, if neural timing should involve feedback loops or reverberating circuits, then the relative effects of random biological noise in such loops should decrease as the timing interval increases.

*Effects of redundancy and of time vs. event uncertainty.*—The effects of differences in relative stimulus frequencies on RT, although small in absolute magnitude, are similar to those recently reported by Fitts, Peterson, and Wolpe (1963), and offer further support for a stimulus sampling theory of choice behavior. The close similarity of RT and error data for the $A$ and $B$ reactions, where 50% probability obtained in both instances, suggests that the effects of time uncertainty and of event uncertainty are closely equivalent.

*The index of task difficulty.*—Crossman (1960) and Welford (1960) have suggested that instead of actual target width, a corrected estimate of $W$, adjusted for errors, should be used in computing ID values. Applying such an empirical correction (so that $W = \pm 2SD$), the equation fitted to the data for Exp. I becomes

$$RT = 74 \, ID - 57 \text{ msec.} \quad [9]$$

This indicates a slightly less efficient rate of processing information than does Equation 7. However, the correction has no appreciable effect on the correlation between ID and RT (changing it from .995 to .993). The main point for emphasis is an $S$'s remarkable ability for maintaining error rate relatively constant across a wide variety of task conditions, while varying the speed of his movements.

Welford has also suggested that an improved index of task difficulty might be

$$ID' = \log 2 \frac{A + .5W}{W} \quad [10]$$

This suggestion is based in part on the observation that this definition reduces the numerical value of the first constant, $a$, in Equation 5, giving theoretical predictions of MT near zero for an ID' of zero. Accordingly, Equation 5 was re-evaluated for the data of Exp. I, using ID' in place of ID. This expression was found to be

$$MT = 72 \, ID' + 6 \text{ msec.} \quad [11]$$

Near zero MT is now predicted for values of ID = 0 (in place of near zero MT for ID = 1), and the correlation between these modified predictions and actual MTs was found to be .997. These results therefore support Welford's arguments.

It is obvious, however, that neither RT nor MT can ever approach zero in any real task. It also appears reasonable to expect that empirical determinations of human motor performance may indicate that capacity varies over the range of possible response amplitudes and tolerances. Since neither index has been derived formally from a theory, choice between them should rest on heuristic considerations. Some implications of the original index (Equation 3) are indicated below.

*Human channel capacities.*—Accepting Equation 3 as the definition of ID, and Equation 8 as providing a generalized empirical estimate of discrete movement times, the estimates of human performance capacity, as specified in Equation 4, would vary from about 22 bits per second for a value of ID = 2.5 (the least difficult movement studied), to just over 14 bits per second for ID = 7.5 (the most difficult movement studied). Thus it might appear that the motor system is relatively more efficient in producing low-information than high-information responses. Such estimates cannot be extended directly to self-paced cyclical motor tasks, however, since some additional uncertainty is introduced by the requirement that Ss process feedback data in repetitive tasks.

Earlier results (Fitts, 1954) indicate that actual performance rates in self-paced repetitive tasks vary from about 9.5 to 11.5 bits per second for ID values comparable to those studied here, and that maximum performance is attained for intermediate values of $A$, $W$, and ID. It is interesting to note that a linear combination of the equations for RT and MT would predict better performance for more difficult tasks as long as the effect of RT was weighted sufficiently to give a positive value for the intercept constant, $a$. Approximately a 4 to 1 weight for MT relative to RT would give a predicted zero intercept, or equivalent information rates at all difficulty levels.

The view that performance in self-paced cyclical tasks is a combined function of RT plus MT is, of course, an old one and, as mentioned earlier, agrees with the approach taken by Welford (1958) in analyzing age changes in perceptual-motor performance. It is significant that the average total time per response in the self-paced serial task (see Fig. 2) exceeded the present movement times by only about .1–.2 sec., and not by an amount as great as the present reaction times. This suggests that the processing of feedback data can to some extent overlap the processes involved in the control of subsequent movements, or else, as Woodworth (1899) and others have suggested, that a sequence of two or more movements may be programed in advance and executed independently of feedback. Such a finding is also consistent with Licklider's (1960) observation that $S$'s lag in a continuous tracking task is often less than reaction time data might suggest, and with the data from studies bearing on psychological refractory period delays (Welford, 1952) where the increase in RT to the second of two stimuli presented in rapid succession usually is less than a simple reaction time.

In summary, it appears that the processing of feedback data in serial or continuous tasks introduces some small delay relative to simple open-loop movements, but less delay than would be expected if every response involved a separate reaction time.

## REFERENCES

ANDRIESSEN, J. J. Montageproeven bij diverse montagesnelheden (II). Report No. 13, 1960, Institute for Perception Research, Eindhoven, Netherlands.

ANNETT, J., GOLBY, C. W., & KAY, H. The measurement of elements in an assembly task: The information output of the human motor system. *Quart. J. exp. Psychol.*, 1958, 10, 1–11.

BROADBENT, D. E. *Perception and communication.* New York: Pergamon Press, 1958.

CROSSMAN, E. R. F. W. The information capacity of the human motor system in pursuit tracking. *Quart. J. exp. Psychol.*, 1960, 12, 1–16.

FITTS, P. M. The information capacity of the human motor system in controlling the amplitude of movement. *J. exp. Psychol.*, 1954, **47**, 381–391.

FITTS, P. M., PETERSON, J. R., & WOLPE, G. Cognitive aspects of information processing: II. Adjustments to stimulus redundancy. *J. exp. Psychol.*, 1963, **65**, 423–432.

LEONARD, J. A. Some experiments on the temporal relation between information and action. Unpublished doctoral dissertation, Cambridge University, 1952.

LICKLIDER, J. C. R. Quasi-linear operator models in the study of manual tracking. Part 3. In R. D. Luce (Ed.), *Developments in mathematical psychology*. Glencoe, Ill.: Free Press, 1960.

SHANNON, C. A mathematical theory of communication. *Bell Sys. tech. J.*, 1948, **27**, 379–423, 623–656.

SINGLETON, W. T. The change of movement timing with age. *Brit. J. Psychol.*, 1954, **45**, 166–172.

SZAFRAN, J. Changes with age and with exclusion of vision in performance at an aiming task. *Quart. J. exp. Psychol.*, 1951, **3**, 111–118.

VREDENBREGT, J. Metingen van tijden voor het monteren van pennen in gaten. Report No. 2, 1959, Institute for Perception Research, Eindhoven, Netherlands.

WELFORD, A. T. The psychological refractory period and the timing of high speed performance: A review and a theory. *Brit. J. Psychol.*, 1952, **43**, 2–19.

WELFORD, A. T. *Ageing and human skill*. Oxford: Oxford Univer. Press, 1958.

WELFORD, A. T. The measurement of sensory-motor performance: Survey and reappraisal of twelve years' progress. *Ergonomics*, 1960, **3**, 189–230.

WELFORD, A. T. Age changes in the times taken by choice, discrimination and the control of movement. *Gerontologia*, 1961, **5**, 129–145.

WOODWORTH, R. S. The accuracy of voluntary movement. *Psychol. Rev. monogr. Suppl.*, 1899, **3**(2, Whole No. 13).

(Received March 15, 1963)

# Part V
# TIME-SHARING AND MENTAL WORKLOAD

Mental workload refers to the expenditure of mental capacity required to perform a task or combination of tasks. The measurement of mental workload has become increasingly important as systems have become more complex and sophisticated. Technological development has been widely recognized as a double-edged sword in human-systems operation. On one hand, it has greatly enhanced system capability; on the other hand, it has created a significant imposition on the human information-processing system. Modern systems are capable of displaying large amounts of information that are updated at frequent intervals. In addition, they have shifted the kinds of activities required of the human operator from perceptual-motor to cognitive activities such as monitoring, decision making, and diagnosis. Unfortunately for people monitoring and operating these systems, they must integrate and comprehend volumes of information displayed in different formats and different sensory modalities. The information-processing requirements levied by such demands often exceed human abilities.

Concern about exceeding the limitations of the human information-processing system has resulted in intense efforts in both basic and applied research to characterize, measure, and determine the limits of mental workload. Indeed, the concept of workload and determination of workload has come to play a major role in designing for complex human-machine systems. It is often used for important design decisions such as allocation of function, automation, and decision aiding. There are a number of ways to assess mental workload. The three major classes of assessment techniques are behavioral, physiological, and subjective. Chapters 15 and 16 represent early efforts in the area of mental workload. Other selections include an overview of workload assessment techniques and a discussion of scaling the simultaneous performance levels of multiple tasks.

The assessment of mental workload has always been, and continues to be, a difficult undertaking. The selection by William B. Knowles (Chapter 15) suggests that one satisfactory metric of workload may be the measurement of performance of a second task performed concurrently with a primary task. Knowles discusses the rationale for using secondary tasks, including greater realism in mimicking the complexity of the task environment and estimating the spare capacity in the human information-processing system. He also describes characteristics that are desirable in selecting secondary tasks, which include nonintrusiveness and simplicity. Finally, he suggests a number of types of tasks that may be useful as secondary tasks, including mental arithmetic, choice reaction-time tasks, and monitoring tasks. Since the publication of this article in 1963, these tasks have been commonly employed in secondary task assessment techniques. Moreover, the secondary task technique has become a cornerstone in workload research. It has demonstrated its value many times over in the applications and system design environments as well as in theory-based investigations of human information processing.

Because it is crucial for system designers to know human processing capabilities and limitations, as well as when and under what conditions the limitations are likely to be exceeded, research in mental workload often focuses on information-processing bottlenecks, such as attention and memory. In Chapter 16, Douwe B. Yntema reviews his empirical investigations of limitations in working memory. The impetus for the experiments was a task resembling air-traffic control in which large amounts of information must be maintained and updated in working memory. The question asked in this research was how much continuously changing information a human operator could maintain. Yntema found that performance was best when only a few objects, each with many attributes, had to be maintained in working memory. Performance was poor when many objects, each with few attributes, had to be remembered. Memory performance was also superior when each object had its own exclusive set of possible states, which reduced confusability among object states. He provides a number of general design recommendations based on these findings. Empirically based knowledge such as that provided by Yntema is important in human-centered design, in which a machine is built around the capabilities and limitations of the human as a processor of information.

Workload is most often conceptualized in terms of limitations of the human system to process and respond to all of the information necessary to perform a task or combination of tasks. There are a variety of interpretations of the concept of workload and a number of ways of measuring and assessing workload. In Chapter 17, F. Thomas Eggemeier cogently discusses techniques used in assessing workload. He considers data and theory relevant to the major classes of workload assessment (behavioral, physiological, and subjective). His review of metrics is organized around two important properties that significantly affect the usefulness of workload assessment techniques: *sensitivity*, the ability of a technique to detect changes in workload imposed by a task or combination of tasks, and *intrusiveness*, the inadvertent degradation of the task interest (i.e., primary task) caused by the workload assessment procedure. The differential sensitivity of various assessment techniques to task demands placed on different capacity systems (e.g., perceptual/central processing "resources" and response "resources")—known as *diagnosticity*—is also presented. Eggemeier discusses variables that affect the sensitivity and intrusiveness of assessment procedures and notes that several complementary assessment procedures must be used to adequately measure workload.

One of the more difficult aspects of time-sharing and workload is how to characterize and portray the trade-offs inherent in the simultaneous performance of multiple tasks. One way of portraying time-shared tasks and their associated trade-offs is the *performance operating characteristic* (POC). A POC function plots performance of one task on the ordinate and performance of a second task on the abscissa. Theoretically, POCs can be useful in interpreting the expenditure of some hypothetical processing capacity to achieve some specified level of performance.

The selections by Barry H. Kantowitz and Marysue Weldon (Chapter 18) and by Christopher D. Wickens and Yei-Yu Yeh (Chapter 19) provide a spirited discussion of the appropriate scaling of POCs. The interplay between the two selections exposes differences in approaches and provides insight into how such differences and their related controversies lead to the progression of scientific inquiry and, in this case, application of knowledge to system design.

Kantowitz and Weldon review theoretical issues behind POC functions, including the different types of performance resource functions and the various performance properties obtained from the POC function (e.g., point of equal allocation, relative efficiency of the tasks). These authors point out problems with use of single-point POCs and with scaling POC axes (e.g., time-based units on one axis and accuracy-based units on the other). They focus in particular on scaling transformations used by Wickens and his colleagues. Kantowitz and Weldon found that the results of simulations using various performance resource functions did not support the conclusions inferred by Wickens's use of normalized scaling procedures. They express the need for caution in the use of normalized scaling transformations in obtaining and interpreting POCs, as well as in using single-point POCs.

In Chapter 19, Wickens and Yeh respond to the criticisms leveled by Kantowitz and Weldon. They acknowledge theoretical shortcomings of earlier work in scaling POCs and using single-point POCs. However, they maintain that from the perspective of system design, the criticisms of Kantowitz and Weldon are misdirected. Wickens and Yeh argue that although the criticisms are theoretically relevant, they do not address the important practical question of predicting task interference from knowledge of task structure. They imply that what is theoretically appropriate may not always be useful when applied. The authors also provide information about a number of standardization techniques they feel are appropriate for comparing task interference between dissimilar tasks. Wickens and Yeh conclude by reiterating that the factors important for system design are predicting sources of interference in multitask environments and methodologies essential for measuring that interference when different task combinations are used.

# 15

# Operator Loading Tasks

**W. B. KNOWLES,** Hughes Aircraft Company, Culver City, California

*The purpose of this paper is: (1) To review the rationale of measuring operator workload in terms of auxiliary, or secondary task performance scores; (2) To summarize the important characteristics of suitable loading tasks; (3) To describe several loading tasks which have been used or which are potentially useful; and (4) To suggest the development of a set of standardized tasks which would be useful in obtaining more nearly comparable measures over a wide range of primary tasks.*

## INTRODUCTION

In the design of equipment and the development of operating and training procedures it is important to be able to answer questions such as:

How easy is this equipment to operate?
How much attention is required?
How much learning is involved?
How well will the operator be able to perform additional tasks?

All these questions deal with some aspect of what has come to be called operator workload. Essentially, how busy is the operator?

In some instances operator workload can be assessed with sufficient precision by means of task-analysis and related methodologies (Ekstrom, 1962). Siegel and his associates (Siegel and Wolf, 1961) have also developed digital-computer techniques for predicting the effect of different levels of task-induced stress on operator performance that are applicable in situations where sufficient information is available on the detailed structure of the task. But in many cases operator workloads must be assessed empirically and at a stage of equipment development where only part-task simulation techniques are possible.

In these latter situations it has been found that one of the best ways of measuring operator-load is to have the operator perform an auxiliary or secondary task at the same time he is performing the primary task under evaluation. If he is able to perform well on the secondary task, this is taken to indicate that the primary task is relatively easy; if he is unable to perform the secondary task and at the same time maintain his primary-task performance, this is taken to indicate that the primary task is more demanding. Just how easy or how demanding is expressed in terms of loading scores derived from the secondary-task performance scores.

In addition to giving an overall indication of operator loads, secondary-task scores can also be used for other purposes. When properly designed, secondary tasks can be used to indicate how the operator's load varies during the course of a single performance of the primary task. Secondary-task measures can often be used to evaluate the course of learning during primary-task acquisition, since very often primary-task scores will show little appreciable change in performance level while auxiliary-task scores may show progressive improvement indicating better and better mastery of the primary task. Secondary tasks introduced into part-task simulator trainers could also be used to measure the fidelity of the workload aspects of the simulation.

This basic idea of using secondary-task measures to reflect primary-task performance has been used in one or another of the above applications by a number of investigators, but unfortunately the use of different tasks and different measures make it difficult to compare their results directly. These results do indicate, however, that it should be possible to develop a small set of tasks which would be suitable for measuring operator-load with a wide range of primary tasks. Standardization of such a set of tasks would serve to define the concept of operator-load in more operational terms and would provide measures which would be more directly comparable from study to study.

In the following discussion the rationale underlying the use of secondary tasks will be examined in some detail with the view toward describing the characteristics desired in tasks suitable for measuring operator-load, and specifying the research required to develop this powerful and much-needed tool.

## RATIONALE

Secondary or loading tasks are used in part-task simulation studies for two related but basically different reasons, and it is important to differentiate between these uses and the reasons behind them in order to focus clearly on the problem of interest here—the mesaurement of operator-load.

In the first place, the results of part-task simulations are often deficient in that the performance appears unduly good because the operator is permitted to focus all his attention on the part-task and is not required to divide it among several tasks as he would in the total job situation. The first use of secondary tasks is to compensate for this deficiency and to simulate aspects of the total job that may be missing. Ordinarily there is little interest in the secondary-task performance *per se*. The secondary task is used simply to bring pressure on the primary task with the idea that as the operator becomes more heavily stressed his performance on difficult tasks will deteriorate more than will his performance on easy tasks.

Garvey and Taylor (1959) demonstrated this use of secondary tasks by carefully designing two tracking systems which could be operated equally well, as measured by tracking-error scores, but which required different degrees of effort, as indicated by operator-opinion reports. Under the stress of any of a number of loading tasks, e.g., mental arithmetic, tracking, simulated warning-light monitoring, etc., performance decrements for the difficult system were greater than for the easier system.

In this first application of secondary tasks, then, the emphasis is upon stressing the primary task; differences in operator-workload are indicated by differences in primary-task performance measures taken under the stress induced by the auxiliary task. The major methodological difficulty with this use of secondary tasks is that it is impossible to specify or control the degree of stress induced by the secondary task. A second difficulty is that severe stress may disrupt the primary task to the point that the operator's mode of behaviour changes completely.

In the second application of loading tasks, and the one of primary concern here, the auxiliary task is used not so much with the intention of stressing the primary task as with the intention of finding out how much additional work the operator can undertake while still performing the primary task to meet system criteria. Secondary tasks are used because primary part-task performance measures, in and of themselves, seldom reflect operator-load. They usually tell how well some functional system criterion is met, e.g., tracking error, miss-distance, decision accuracy, etc., but they seldom tell the price paid in operator-effort in meeting this criterion.

For example, Ekstrom (1962) measured operator-work-loads during an evaluation of two alternative control modes for the X-15 by having the operators perform an additional self-paced pushbutton task. The pushbutton scores were then converted into an operator-loading index to demonstrate differences in primary-task difficulty. The results of the evaluation showed that, in terms of completing the mission successfully, the pilot could use both modes equally well, but that the more automatic system demanded less of the pilot's attention, particularly during a number of highly critical transition periods.

Knowles and Rose (1962) used a similar self-paced pushbutton task to demonstrate differences in operator-load during simulated lunar landings. The loading scores were sensitive to differences in problem difficulty; they reflected increased ease in handling the control task as a function of practice; they revealed differences in work-load between members of a two-man crew; and they showed that the particular control law under consideration was unsatisfactory because of the extreme buildup of operator-load during the last few seconds of the landing. None of these results was available from system performance criteria, i.e., time, fuel, miss-distances.

Birmingham, Chernikoff and Siegler (1962) have used a self-adaptive tracking system to measure what they call "residual operator bandwidth." Bauerschmidt and Besco (1962) used a forced-pace pushbutton task to evaluate differences in attitude control system configurations but found that the task was insensitive when the rate of presentation was too low. Garvey, who used a mental arithmetic task to stress performance in a display-control compatibility study (Garvey and Knowles, 1954), has suggested that a similar task could be instrumented for use in measuring operator-load.

In all these examples of the second application of secondary tasks, the actual measurement of operation load, the goal has been to use a task which is subtle in its effect on the primary task; one which is demanding enough so that the operator cannot ignore it, yet not so demanding as to stress the primary task to the point of disruption. In fact, the degree of non-performance on the loading task is taken as the measure of operator-loading during what is essentially normal performance of the primary task.

The basic notions of operator-loading and its measurement by loading-task scores can be summarized by comparing the operator to a multiplex communication system, as shown in Fig. 1.

A multiplex system uses a single channel to transmit messages from several sources to several destinations. So long as the channel is connected to a given source and a given destination, messages from other sources to the same or other destinations cannot be transmitted. The basic channel has a fixed capacity, but within this capacity overall rate of information flow can be maximized by proper coding and switching routines.

In measuring operator-load the primary task, $S_1$–$D_1$, represents one set of information to be processed and the loading task, $S_2$–$D_2$, represents another set. It is assumed that the system is so structured that priority is given to primary-task information and only as much loading-task information is processed as is possible within the residual channel capacity.

Two or three interesting and important points can be illustrated by reference to this relatively simple model.

First: The switching points at the input and output represent opportunities for interference between the two tasks that must be minimized in designing the loading task and matching it with the primary task. The input switching shown in this model represents essentially the same concept as the gate in Broadbent's (1957) model illustrating division of attention. Priority is assured to primary task inputs by instruction, by sense modality selection, by apparatus configuration, and by controlling signal intensities and timing, etc. Response interference on the output end is usually easily prevented by using different effectors for the two tasks. Furthermore, most tasks of interest in part-task simulations are limited on the perceptual side, not on the response end.

Second: Mastery of most perceptual-motor skills can be thought of in terms of the adoption on the part of the operator of more efficient methods of coding information. As relevant properties of the input signals are selected and combined in terms of the responses and response sequences to be made, i.e. as the coding becomes

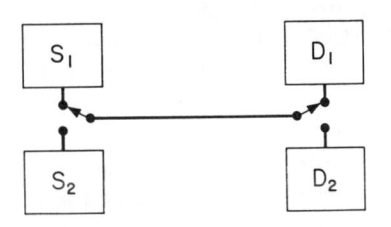

Fig. 1. Simple multiplex model. $S_1$–$D_1$ represents the flow of primary-task information $S_2$–$D_2$ represents the flow of loading-task information.

more efficient, the rate of transmitting information increases. This means that if the rate at which messages are produced is high, more messages per unit time can be transmitted with a given channel capacity; or, if the rate of message production is low, relative to the capacity of the channel, the channel will be open a greater proportion of the time.

This, then, is one way of explaining how loading-task scores can reveal primary task learning in the absence of improvement in system criterion measures. If it is assumed that system performance depends upon the transmission of a certain amount of information at a rate well within the channel capacity, the requirement may be met with very inefficient coding methods. System performance, being dependent simply upon the *effective* transmission of the information, may not show any significant change as the transmission becomes more *efficient*. But loading-task scores should change since the more efficient transmission of primary-task messages leaves the channel free to transmit more loading-task information.

Third: Since the loading-task information must be "sandwiched in," so to speak, whenever there is room for it in the channel, this implies that the loading task message units should be short and efficiently coded. The use of discrete stimulus-response units is probably desirable in meeting the first requirement. Efficient coding is obtained by careful attention to factors such as stimulus-responses compatibility and population stereotypes, and, as discussed above, through learning.

In other words, the loading task, if it is to be sensitive to—and reflect accurately—changes in primary-task information-transmission, should be easy, over-learned, and probably composed of discrete message units.

## CHARACTERISTICS

In the preceding discussions, allusions have been made to a number of properties that are desirable in secondary tasks used as measures of primary task work-loads. The following list summarizes the more important of these characteristics:

### Non-interference

Ideally, the loading task should not physically interfere with, nor otherwise disrupt, primary-task performance. Practically, this is difficult to achieve; some degree of interaction between two tasks is always to be expected. Empirically, it can be determined if the loading-task is too stressful by observing the effect it has on primary-task performance criteria.

### Simplicity

Ideally, the task should require very little learning and should show little inter-subject variability. Again, although difficult to achieve, both of these properties can be evaluated empirically. Furthermore, learning effects can be minimized by practice on the loading-task alone, and subject differences can be controlled by determining the base-line performance for each subject and then computing the loading index for each individual relative to his own base-line.

### Self-pacing

In general, it is preferable that loading-task information be presented at a rate determined by the operator himself. This can be achieved by using a self-paced series of discrete units or by automatic feedback systems which are self-adapting as a function of operator performance. Self-pacing also tends to adjust the attention-demanding properties of the loading task automatically so that, when necessary, the task can be neglected but not ignored.

### Scoring

The index of operator-load that is calculated from the scores of a given loading task should be comparable from situation to situation. The score obtained on the auxiliary task ordinarily will reflect the average rate at which loading-task information is handled over an entire run. In many applications it is also desirable to be able to evaluate the instantaneous rate of flow of information continuously throughout the run. In either case, it appears that automatic recording of loading-task performance is almost a necessity.

## Compatibility

The loading task should be selected so that, if possible, it is different in form from the primary task and, again if possible, so that it will simulate the kinds of tasks that might be required of the operator in addition to the primary task. For example, if the primary task is a tracking task it probably would be unwise to use another tracking task as an auxiliary task because of possible intertask interference. A pushbutton or mental-arithmetic task would probably be less interfering and could be considered to simulate other monitoring or problem-solving functions.

## USEFUL TASKS

Several tasks which appear capable of meeting the above criteria, and which warrant further investigation, are the following:

## Pushbutton Responding

This is the task used so successfully by Ekstrom (1962) and probably represents the standard against which all other loading-tasks might well be compared.

A matrix of sixteen touch-lights was located outside the operator's central field of view as he performed the primary task.

The expression given for the primary task work load is:

$$W = 100 - (W_1 + W_t) \quad (1)$$

where

$W$ = primary task load

$W_1$ = loading task work load

$W_t$ = eye transition time work load.

$W_1$ was computed from

$$W_1 = \frac{N}{N \max} \times 100 \quad (2)$$

$N$ = number of lights handled/sec

$N$ max = calibrated maximum number of lights/sec.

$W_t$ was computed from

$$W_t = \frac{\text{Transitions}}{\text{total time}} \times 100 \times 0 \cdot 14 \quad (3)$$

where $0.14$ = average transition time

The index was interpreted as the "per cent" of the pilot's effort or attention that was devoted to the control-task.

Several variations in the basic pushbutton task can also be considered. Separating the display and the control offers the opportunity of manipulating the difficulty of the task by varying display-control compatibility relationships. Verbal responses to the lights is also another possibility which, in some situations, may overcome response interference problems.

## Mental Arithmetic

In the arithmetic task used by Garvey and Knowles (1954), the subjects were given two digits to add or subtract. When the subject reported his answer he was given another digit to either add or subtract from the previous sum or difference, and so on through the trial. The task is attractive because, unlike the pushbutton task, it is primarily a verbal task. The use of auditory inputs and spoken responses also avoids the possibility of direct response interference with primarily motor tasks. In this form the presentation of stimuli and the recording of responses are somewhat difficult to control. However, the task can be modified and instrumented so that the digits are presented on light panels and the responses keyed out.

## Self-adaptive Tracking

Birmingham et al. (1962) have experimented with tracking systems wherein the level of difficulty is controlled by the operator's level of performance. Difficulty may be varied in a number of ways: by varying the complexity of the input signal, by adjusting the effective order of the control system through variations in "quickening" terms, or by adjusting the upper and lower bounds in a nulling task. Regardless of the exact method of varying difficulty, the essential feature of the task is contained in the self-adjusting feature. A predetermined level of performance is established and, whenever the operator exceeds this level, the task is automatically made more difficult; whenever he falls below the prescribed level, the task is automatically made easier. Ultimately the operator stabilizes out at a particular level of task-difficulty. On the assumption that the stabilization level is a function of the channel-capacity consumed by the primary task, Birmingham then calculated an index which he calls a measure of the "residual operator bandwidth." The index is based upon the frequency-amplitude characteristics of the input, the error characteristics of the output, and certain assumptions concerning the characteristics of the human operator regarded as a servo system.

It would seem desirable to have a tracking task to use in conjuction with some kinds of primary tasks, but the best way of instrumenting and scoring it remains to be worked out.

## Monitoring

Holland (1958), in a vigilance study, used a meter-monitoring task that might be adapted as a loading task. In this task a meter pointer was driven by a slowly varying signal and the subject was asked to report when the reading exceeded a set of prescribed limits. Monitoring responses were recorded by having the subject press a button to illuminate the meter-face. This kind of "peek and report" task might be very useful. Another possibility might be simply to use several meters which the operator is asked to read as often as he can in a manner similar to scanning an instrument panel. The number of "peeks" or the number of readings could be converted into an index of work-load.

There are undoubtedly several other tasks which also have the proper characteristics for loading tasks. However, these four cover a wide range and one or another should be useful in nearly all simulation situations. With refinement and standardization they would provide a much-needed tool for measuring operator-load.

## A SUGGESTED APPROACH

The work required to develop a set of standard loading tasks divide into three phases: selection, evaluation, and standardization.

## Selection

A more complete listing of potential loading tasks than has been given here should be assembled with the goal being to find a number of simple tasks, which meet the criteria previously outlined, and which cover a range of types, i.e., verbal, motor, auditory, monitoring, tracking, etc. From the list, a few tasks, three or four, should then be selected for further refinement.

## Evaluation

Alternative ways of instrumenting these tasks should be investigated thoroughly. It is of extremely great practical importance that the equipment and scoring problems be worked out well and kept simple. The selected tasks should be used in conjunction with primary tasks of different types and levels of apparent difficulty to evaluate their sensitivity as measuring instruments. Learning and subject variances should be evaluated. The end result of this phase would be the detailed specifications for instrumenting, administering, calibrating, and scoring a small but comprehensive set of loading tasks.

## Standardization

The usefulness of the set of tasks would be enhanced if, ultimately, scores on all the tasks could be reduced to a common index of operator work-load, i.e., if the index computed for each task were comparable to the index computed from every other task. There are, of course, severe methodological difficulties to be overcome in achieving this.

First, in a factor analysis sense, the different tasks tap different abilities. This is the basic reason for using different tasks; this is also the basis for subject and learning variances.

Second, although it is assumed that the loading tasks do not interfere with the primary task, it is recognized from the start that, practically, this assumption can only be approximated and, furthermore, that most probably the amount of interference between a loading task and a primary task is a function of the factorial structure of the two tasks. Again, one of the reasons for using different loading tasks is to avoid as much interaction as possible. Presumably, if the structure of the primary and auxiliary tasks were known, an optimum match could be made. But, since the structure of the tasks will probably never be known, it will always be a matter of judgment as to which loading task to use with which primary task.

In the face of these considerations, it is well to look more closely at what may be expected of any measure of operator work-load derived from auxiliary task performance. Fundamentally, such measures yield an ordinal scale; 100 per cent auxiliary task performance does not mean zero operator loading, nor does zero auxiliary task performance mean 100 per cent operator loading. Furthermore, equal increments in loading scores most certainly do not reflect equal increments in work-load. It is therefore most prudent to regard whatever numerical values that are derived with some modesty and to call them what they are—simply indices of operator-load.

The complete standardization of several loading tasks would be an endeavor comparable in magnitude to the cross-cultural standardization of alternative forms of the Stanford–Binet Intelligence Tests, and is certainly not warranted at this time. The immediate problems are (1) to find a few tasks that can be instrumented to give reliable measures, and (2) to demonstrate that these tasks do indeed descriminate between different primary tasks of different degrees of difficulty.

With these tools in hand it should be possible (1) to obtain more meaningful measures of operator-load in the practical context of simulation studies and (2) proceed with such theoretical issues as analysis of the factors which affect operator-load and (3) to investigate the more general problem of task interference.

## REFERENCES

Bauerschmidt, D. K., & Besco, R. O. *Human Engineering criteria for manned space flight: minimal manual systems.* AMRL-TDR62-87, Wright Patterson Air Force Base, Dayton, Ohio, October 1962.

Birmingham, H. P., Chernikoff, R., & Ziegler, P. N. *The design and use of "equalization" teaching machines.* Paper presented at IRE, International Congress on Human Factors Engineering in Electronics, Long Beach, California, May 3–4, 1962.

Broadbent, D. E. A mechanical model for human attention and immediate memory. *Psychol. Rev.*, 1957, **64,** 205–215.

Ekstrom, Phyllis J. *Analysis of pilot work loads in flight control systems with different degrees of automation.* Paper presented at the IRE International Congress on Human Factors Engineering in Electronics, Long Beach, California, May 3–4, 1962.

Garvey, W. D., & Taylor, F. V. Interaction among operator variables, system dynamics and task-induced stress. *J. Appl. Psychol.*, 1959, **43,** 79–85.

Garvey, W. D., & Knowles, W. B. Response time pattern associated with various display-control relationships. *J. Exp. Psychol.*, 1954, **47,** 315–322.

Holland, J. G. Human vigilance. *Science*, 1958, **28,** 61–63.

Knowles, W. B., & Rose, D. J. *Manned lunar landing simulation.* Paper presented at IEE, 1963 National Winter Convention on Military Electronics, Los Angeles, California, January 30–February 1, 1963.

Siegel, A. I., & Wolf, J. J. A technique for evaluating man-machine system designs. *Human Factors*, 1961, **3,** 18–27.

# 16

## Keeping Track of Several Things at Once[1]

**DOUWE B. YNTEMA**, Lincoln Laboratory,[2] Massachusetts Institute of Technology, Lexington, Massachusetts.

*A series of experiments on short-term memory is summarized. The results imply that when possible the following rules should be observed in presenting information to an operator who must keep track of a changing situation: (a) Each variable of which he must keep track should have its own exclusive set of possible states. (b) There should be few variables with many possible states, not many variables with few states. (c) A variable should not change state any more often than necessary. Three other conclusions may be useful to system designers as background information: capacity for random information is low; regularity within the sequence of states assumed by an individual variable is not particularly helpful; and orderly relations among the present states of different variables can be very helpful, at least in the extreme cases that were considered.*

### INTRODUCTION

The design of a command post or a control center often raises questions about how well a person can follow a changing situation, keeping track of it in his head. It may seem strange that the designers should even think of asking an operator to store information in his head—especially if the system is to include a computer that will keep the necessary records and display the information on high-speed electronic devices. Nevertheless, questions about the operator's memory are almost inevitable.

In the first place, he usually does not have a continuous display of all the information that he wants. It is seldom practical to present all at once everything that he may want to know. Some of the information must be relegated to secondary displays where it is available only on demand. There may be a set of buttons that he can press to request special displays, or a telephone on which he can call other operators to ask for information that he needs. Some facts may even be listed on sheets of paper. Getting information from any of these secondary sources takes time and effort; so there is something to be gained by coding the information in such a way that it can be remembered easily.

There is also the question of how far the operator's memory can be trusted. The designers are always under pressure to reduce the amount of information that is continually visible on the primary display. The display can then be cheaper, smaller, and less confusing. Thus there is always a temptation to move part of the information to secondary displays, telling oneself that these are facts that the operator should be able to remember easily. In deciding when to yield to this temptation it would be helpful to have some idea about the human capacity for storage of changing information.

Since these questions can provoke lively discussion, and since the classical psychology of memory is not particularly helpful in providing answers, it seemed a good idea to do some experiments. In this paper I shall summarize the progress that we have made so far and point out the implications for system design.

### GENERAL NATURE OF THE EXPERIMENTS

The sort of situation that we were attempting to abstract and bring into the laboratory is that in which an operator must keep track of several things at once. For example, the information needed by an air-traffic controller might include facts like those displayed in Table 1. He is dealing here with four *objects*, the four hypothetical aircraft whose flight numbers are listed down the left side of the table. These objects have

---

[1] Invited address, Symposium on Information Processing in Man: Research Frontiers, sponsored jointly by the Los Angeles Chapter of the Human Factors Society and the University of Southern California. Held at USC, June 23, 1962.
[2] Operated with support from the U.S. Army, Navy and Air Force.

## TABLE 1

Example of a Situation in Which There are Twelve Variables

(There are 4 *objects*, the 4 fictitious aircraft, each of which has 3 *attributes*. Each attribute of each object is a *variable*.)

|          | *Altitude* | *Next fix* | *Time* |
|----------|------------|------------|--------|
| TWA 123  | 31,000     | Boston     | 14     |
| UA 456   | 35,000     | Albany     | 12     |
| PAA 789  | 31,000     | Boston     | 19     |
| AF 12345 | 41,000     | Hartford   | 23     |

three *attributes*: the altitude at which the airplane is flying, the next radio fix at which it is to report its position, and the time (expressed in minutes after the hour) at which it is expected to arrive there. Thus TWA Flight 123 is at 31,000 ft, its next reporting point is Boston, and the estimated time at which it will arrive there is 14 min after the hour. None of this information is static—altitude, next fix, and estimate can all change—so the three attributes of four objects make twelve *variables* whose current states the controller must know.

This is only an illustration of course. No one is likely to ask a controller to depend on his memory to keep track of this sort of information. But if he did have to keep track of these twelve variables in his head, what would his problem be like?

Figure 1 shows how this sort of task is abstracted to bring it into the laboratory. Instead of four airplanes there are now two nonsense

SHAPE:
O CIRCLE   □ SQUARE   △ TRIANGLE   ♡ HEART

DIRECTION:
↑ UP   ↓ DOWN   → RIGHT   ← LEFT

FOOD:
M MELON   T TOAST   J JELLO   P PEAS

MARK:
✓ CHECK   + PLUS   ∧ HAT   \ STROKE

ANIMAL:
⊲ FISH   ～ BIRD   ～ SNAKE   ⊻ COW

NUMBER:
1 ONE   2 TWO   3 THREE   4 FOUR

WEATHER:
S STORMY   C CLOUDY   F FAIR   U UNSETTLED

COLOR:
R RED   Y YELLOW   G GREEN   B BLUE

Fig. 2. Examples of eight so-called "attributes." In this case each has four possible states.

objects, X and Y, each of which has three abstract attributes—shape, number, and animal. Just as there were a number of possible altitudes (29,000 ft, 31,000 ft, etc.) shape has a number of possible states (circle, square, triangle, heart). The possible shapes, numbers, and animals might be those given in Fig. 2, which also shows five other attributes used in the first experiment discussed below. The states are shown both in the form in which they are spoken and in the form in which the subject writes them down.

Let me digress a moment to point out that these abstract attributes all have their own, mutually exclusive sets of possible states. This is a convention that we have adopted because the attributes of everyday objects are usually specified by different, mutually exclusive sets of words. The size of an apple cannot be red, nor can its shape. Red is exclusively a state of the attribute color. Similarly, in Table 1 Boston cannot be the altitude of an airplane and 31,000 cannot very well be a time. There are of course

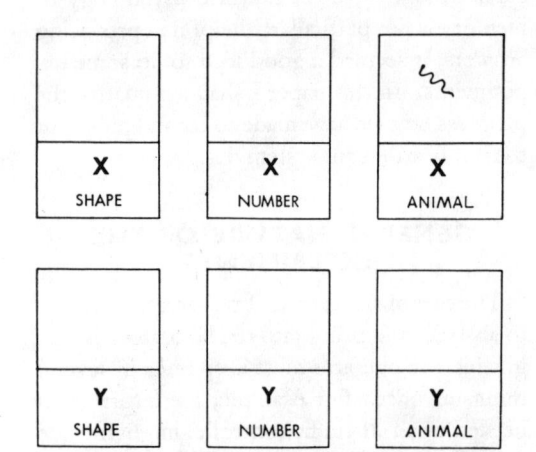

Fig. 1. Illustration of the apparatus. In this example there are six boxes (i.e., six variables) of which the subject must keep track. He has just received the message "X snake" and has written the symbol in the appropriate box.

exceptions, cases where the same word or symbol is in practice used for states of different attributes, but we have nonetheless adopted the convention that the attributes of our nonsense objects shall always have their own exclusive sets of possible states.

Returning to Fig. 1, imagine that the subject sits before an inclined board on which there are six boxes labeled as shown in the figure and holding stacks of blank filing cards. He is read aloud a series of *messages*, each of which names a variable and a state (e.g., "X snake"). He writes the appropriate symbol on the top card in the appropriate box and puts the card on the bottom of the stack where it will be out of sight. From time to time the series of messages is interrupted by *questions* (e.g., "Animal of X?"), each asking for the most recent entry in one of the boxes. Questions occur at random times and ask about randomly chosen boxes; so each box is a variable whose current state he must always try to remember. His responses are not corrected; as soon as he responds the experimenter goes on to the next message or question. The subject is familiar with the possible states of the various boxes, and he is required to guess when he does not know the answer to a question.

He is allowed to go at his own rate, but he is encouraged to work rapidly and is told, "Don't take the time to worry about the other boxes while writing a message or answering a question. Just worry about each box as you come to it." This mild suggestion against rehearsal is included because it seems to stabilize behavior: scores seem to settle down after about 20 min of practice, and the performance of one subject is not very different from that of another. An experimental run consists of about 64 messages and 64 questions (plus a few extra messages at the beginning so that every box will have a state before the questions start). A run takes about 8 to 10 min, and three runs are usually done in a sitting. Subjects are college students or Air Force operators of an experimental air defense center.

In principle the experiment could of course be done without requiring the subject to write the messages. He could just sit with his eyes closed, listen to the messages, and try to answer the questions. Requiring him to put the symbols in the appropriate boxes insures that he will take note of each message. Furthermore, the task seems to be less dreary. In fact it seems to be fun—an important advantage in maintaining good motivation through a series of 10 or 12 runs.

One further comment may help the reader to visualize the task. It should be remembered that questions are asked at random. To be exact, the probability that the next item will be a question is always one-half, and if the item is a question the variable (i.e., the box) about which it will inquire is chosen at random. Thus it sometimes happens that a question follows immediately after a message about the same box. The subject is almost sure to answer such a question correctly. At other times he must reach far back into his memory to find the answer, and in that case he is likely to make a mistake (Yntema and Mueser, 1960). Note too that the subject is not at liberty to dismiss from memory the state of a variable about which a question has been asked. The same question may be asked again before there is another message about the box.

## CAPACITY FOR RANDOM INFORMATION

The first experiment was on keeping track of a completely random situation. The variable (i.e., the box) to which the next message would refer was chosen at random, and the state specified in the message was then picked at random from the four states that the variable might assume. Thus the choice of a message did not depend on the current states of the other boxes nor on the history of the situation[3].

Two cases were considered. In the first the variables were different attributes of one abstract object—e.g., Shape of X, Direction of X, Mark

---

[3] The variables were not represented by boxes in this experiment; there was a different arrangement for hiding what the subject had written (Yntema and Mueser, 1960). For simplicity I shall nevertheless continue to refer to the variables as boxes.

of X, etc. It was as if the boxes were all taken from one row of a large rectangular array like that shown in Fig. 1. The second case was that which would be obtained by taking an equal number of boxes from a column of such an array. The variables were the same attribute of different objects—e.g., Shape of X, Shape of Y, etc.

The results are shown in Fig. 3. In both cases the fraction of the questions answered correctly

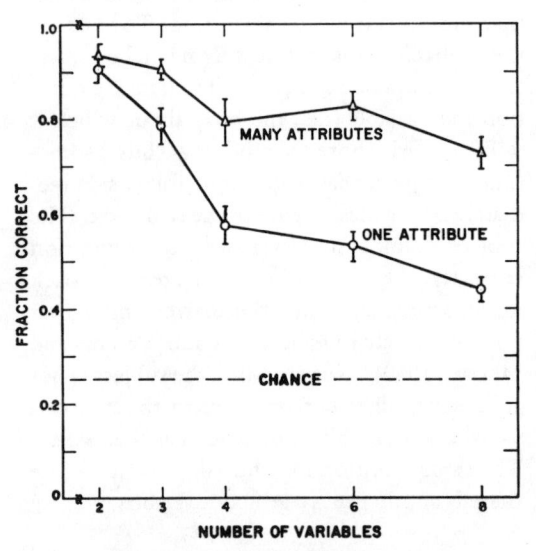

Fig. 3. Results of an experiment on completely random variables (Yntema and Mueser, 1960). Mean fraction of the questions answered correctly is shown as a function of number of variables of which the subject was to keep track. Vertical bars extend plus-and-minus one standard error of the mean. In the upper curve each variable has its own set of four possible states; in the lower, all variables have the same set of four possible states.

decreases with an increase in the number of boxes, just as might be expected. But note that the subject makes a considerable number of mistakes when he has only three variables to keep track of. Even with two variables there are some errors.

We had not expected that people would have quite so much trouble in remembering two or three things at once. Perhaps we were thinking of the archetypical experiments on short-term memory, the experiments on digit-span. If a college student is read a list of four or five digits with the instruction to repeat them immediately he may be expected to perform the task essentially without error. We had supposed that while people might not be able to keep track of as many as five things at once, still there would be some small number of variables whose states could be retained essentially without error. Figure 3 shows that this number must be very small indeed—perhaps no greater than one.

The low level of performance is not peculiar to our method. Lloyd, Reid, and Feallock (1960) have investigated a task that is somewhat like the one considered here but differs from it in several ways. The subject does not write anything down; he simply listens to the messages and attempts to answer the questions. The task is paced; the subject does not work at his own rate. And a question relieves him of further responsibility for the information about which it inquires. A variable about which a question has been asked is, so to say, inactive. No more questions about it may be asked until another message about it has been delivered. Thus the number of things that the subject must try to remember changes from moment to moment, and the fraction of the questions answered correctly is reported as a function of the average number of variables active at one time.

In spite of these considerable differences in conception of the task and in technique, our results are not unlike those of Lloyd et al. They too find a few errors when the average number of things to be remembered is two, and there is a substantial number of errors when the average is three.[4]

The lesson for the system designer is obvious. He must not be optimistic about an operator's ability to keep track of even two things at once —not, at least, when the things change at random.

---

[4] Unfortunately I could not fit into this paper a discussion of the further work of Lloyd, Reid, and their associates. Readers who are interested in memory for changing information should consult the papers by Lloyd (1961), Lloyd and Johnston (in press), and Reid, Lloyd, Brackett, and Hawkins (1961).

## VARIABLES WITH DIFFERENT POSSIBLE STATES

Thus far I have been ignoring the most striking feature of Fig. 3, the difference between the many-attribute curve and the one-attribute curve. In the many-attribute case the boxes represent different attributes of one object—e.g., Shape of X, Direction of X, Mark of X, etc. By our convention each box has therefore its own exclusive set of states. In the other case the variables are the same attribute of different objects—e.g., Shape of X, Shape of Y, etc.—so all boxes have the same possible states. It may be seen that the subject makes about twice as many errors in the one case as in the other. This result was not expected, and it raises some interesting theoretical problems that I cannot digress to discuss here (Yntema and Mueser, 1960).

### Implication of Finding on One "Attribute" vs. Many

Whatever the explanation of this result may be, its practical implication is clear: each variable should if possible have its own exclusive set of states.

An example may be helpful. Suppose that the operator must keep himself informed about a battery of three guns that has four attributes: alert status, amount of ammunition on hand, quality of reception on the radio circuit linking the battery to the control center, and number of guns in working order. Number of guns would naturally be reported as a digit. It might seem convenient to number the alert statuses 0, 1, 2, and 3; number the ammunition levels 0, 1, 2, and 3; and use the same digits, 0, 1, 2, and 3, for the quality of radio reception. All variables would then have the same possible states. It would be better to follow the convention adopted in our experiments and let each attribute have its own set of states. The digits might be reserved for number of guns and the letters A to D used for alert status, W to Z for ammunition, and arbitrary symbols for radio reception. Keeping track of the condition of the battery should then be much easier.

Sometimes it is possible to go even farther and give different states to variables that would normally be regarded as the same attribute of various objects. Suppose that one were planning a control center in which the operators would be concerned about the quality of the data coming in from three radars, one located to the west, one to the north, and one to the east. The designer would probably find it natural to think of the radars as three objects that all had the same attribute, data-quality, and he might let the states of this attribute be H for high quality, M for medium, and L for low. A typical situation would then be, "West H, North H, and East L." A better approach would be to conceive of the whole radar system as one large object with three attributes, quality of the western radar, quality of the northern, and quality of the eastern. The letters A, B, and C could be used for high, medium, and low quality of the data coming from the west; P, Q, and R for high, medium, and low quality from the north; and X, Y, and Z, from the east. A typical situation would then be, "West A, North P, and East Z." The three variables would have different sets of states and keeping track of them should be much easier.

## NUMBER OF ALTERNATIVE STATES AND PROBABILITY OF CHANGE

In the preceding experiment the boxes each had four possible states. Would the task be any different if each had two states, or if it had eight?

As soon as we began to investigate this question we discovered something that should have been obvious beforehand. If the state named in a message is always chosen at random and if each variable has two possible states, then half of the messages do not alter the information that the subject must try to remember. The situation seems to change in a slow and leisurely fashion. But if each variable has eight states, then seven-eighths of the messages are changes, everything seems to be continually in flux, and the task appears much more difficult.

We therefore decided that there was no point in studying the effect of number of states unless we fixed the probability that a message would be a change. Except for that restriction the messages were still chosen at random: the box to which the next message would refer was picked at random, and if the box changed, it changed to a randomly chosen state.

Figure 4 shows the results of three experiments. In Experiment I there were six variables, which were represented by boxes labeled 1 to 6. In any one run they all had the same set of possible states, namely, 2, 3, 5, 8, or 21 consonants. The vertical axis is again the fraction of the questions answered correctly, but this fraction has now been corrected for chance success. (The correction is the familiar one which assumes that the subject really knows the answer or else guesses at random. To the extent that this assumption is true the correction removes the effect of lucky guesses, which are more likely when there are few alternatives, leaving only the fraction of the questions to which the subject really knows the answer.) The two curves are for two different sets of conditions. On the upper, the probability that any given message would change the state of the variable to which it referred was one-quarter; on the lower, every message was a change. The subject knew in advance what the set of possible states would be, and he knew in a general way whether he should expect most of the messages to be changes.

In Experiment II the six variables were six different attributes of one abstract object. Thus each box had its own states, a set of as many as eight symbols like those appearing on one row in Fig. 2. Experiment III was a repetition of what seemed the more important conditions of the first two, but now there were only three boxes.

The results of all three experiments were alike. Errors were more frequent when all of the messages were changes, and the number of possible states had no significant effect, provided the probability of change was fixed and the results were corrected for guessing.

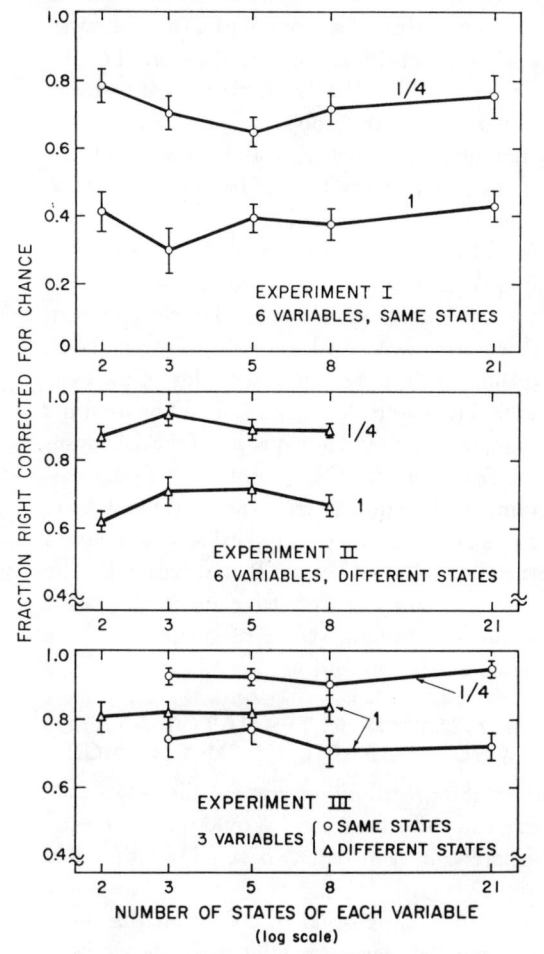

Fig. 4. Results of three experiments showing that number of possible states has no large effect (Yntema and Mueser, 1962). Mean fraction of the questions answered correctly has been corrected for guessing. Vertical bars extend plus-and-minus one standard error of the mean. The parameter is the probability that a message will be a change.

## Implication of the Finding on Number of Alternatives

The conclusion that number of states is not very important has an implication for the coding of reports and displays. When the designer has a choice he should not require the operator to deal with many variables that have few possible states. The information should be compressed into a few variables, each with many states.

Suppose for example that there were two communication channels, and suppose that a channel could be either free or in use and could be set to transmit either data or voice. It might seem natural to display an F or a B to show whether a channel was free or busy and a D or a V to show whether it was set for data or for voice. The information that the operator would then have to remember is illustrated by the example in Table 2 labeled "Expanded code." There would be four variables to keep track of.

**TABLE 2**

Two Ways of Coding the Same Information

|  | *Expanded code* | *Compressed code* |
|---|---|---|
| *Channel 1* | BD | T |
| *Channel 2* | BV | W |

To reduce the number of variables, each of the combinations of free or busy with data or voice might be replaced by a name. Anna might be used instead of FV, Edward instead of FD, Wilma instead of BV, and Thomas instead of BD. When the names are represented by their initial letters the material to be remembered takes the form illustrated under "Compressed code." There are two variables instead of four. The new variables have twice as many possible states, but it was seen that an increase in the number of states has little or no effect. Thus the task should be considerably easier.

How far this sort of compression should be carried in practice will depend on some other considerations. Reducing the number of variables can be useful, quite apart from memory, because the display tends to become simpler and less confusing. On the other hand, too much compression can create a severe training problem. An operator should find it fairly easy to learn the meanings of the four names in the example just discussed, especially since girls' names indicate voice transmission, but suppose that the compression were carried a step further so that all of the information about both channels were coded into a single variable. The memory task would then be very easy, but the variable would have sixteen possible states. Teaching the operator the meanings of so many states might be more trouble than it was worth.

## Implication of the Finding on Frequency of Change

The effect of frequency of change also has an implication for design. The variables with which an operator must deal should not change their states any more often than necessary.

Usually there is not much that the designer can do about the rate of change of the situation that is to be displayed, but there are cases in which he can do something about the way in which the situation is presented. Suppose that several objects were being "counted down" at once and that their progress was to be reported to a central headquarters every few minutes. One way of giving the status of an object would be to report the current count—e.g. "minus twelve minutes and holding" or "minus seven minutes and counting." Another way of giving almost the same information would be to report the current estimate of "time zero," the time at which the countdown was expected to be complete. The choice of the proper method would in part depend on the use that was to be made of the information; but other things being equal it would be better to give the current estimate of time zero. This estimate is a variable whose state does not change as long as the countdown proceeds normally. The count is a variable whose state usually changes with the passage of time; so keeping track of several counts would be much more difficult.

Another way of reducing the frequency of change is to combine states to which the operator reacts in the same way. A computer-generated display for air-traffic control would be likely to show with the current estimate of each airplane's position an indication of the apparent reliability of that estimate. The states of reliability might perhaps be excellent, good, mediocre, and poor. If it developed that the controllers handled airplanes with excellent positions in the same way that they handled airplanes whose positions were only good, then the two states could be combined into a single state, high. All changes from good to excellent and from excellent to good would thus be suppressed, and so the frequency of change would be reduced as far as the controllers were concerned[5].

## REGULARITY WITHIN VARIABLES

The preceding experiments have been concerned with variables that change at random if they change at all. In the real world there are many variables that behave in a much more predictable fashion. The four entries under "Next fix" in Table 1 are good examples: an airplane on a flight plan is expected to pass over a predetermined set of fixes in a predetermined order. The next experiment was done to see whether this sort of regularity makes the task any easier[6].

There were six boxes, identified by the digits 1 to 6. All had same set of seven possible states, the seven days of the week for example. Table 3 shows a typical sequence of messages. A column

### TABLE 3

A Sequence of Messages from the Experiment on Cyclical Variables

(Each column shows the history of a variable, time running down the page.)

| 1 | 2 | 3 | 4 | 5 | 6 |
|---|---|---|---|---|---|
| Mon | Fri | Fri | Tue | Thur | Sat |
|  | Sat |  |  |  |  |
|  |  |  | Wed |  |  |
|  |  |  | Thur |  |  |
|  |  |  |  |  | Sun |
|  | Sun |  |  |  |  |
| Tue |  |  |  |  |  |

gives the history of one of the variables, time going down the page. Let us suppose that at some point in the course of a run the variables were in the states given at the top of the table. The next message happened to be about Variable 2; so the message was "Two Saturday"—i.e., the state changed to the next day of the week. The following message was about Variable 4 and changed it to Wednesday. Variable 4 was then chosen again and changed to Thursday, and so on. In other words, the variables cycled through the seven days: each message was generated by picking a variable at random and advancing it to the next day of the week. As usual, questions about randomly chosen variables were interspersed at random among the messages.

For comparison there was a control condition in which messages and questions appeared in the same places, but the state named in every message was chosen at random with the restriction that, as in the cyclical condition, every message must be a change. The subject was told whether to expect random or cyclical changes, and if the variables were to cycle he knew in advance what the cycle was to be.

In the random condition the fraction of the questions answered correctly was 0.38 after allowance for guessing among the seven alternatives. In the cyclical condition it was 0.42, an increase of only $0.05 \pm 0.03$. (The figure following the symbol "$\pm$" is the standard error of the mean which precedes it.) Making each variable go through a perfectly predictable sequence of states improves performance by a surprisingly small amount, if indeed there is any improvement at all.

The experiment was also done with six variables that were different attributes of a nonsense object—i.e., six boxes that had their own exclusive states. One box cycled through the days of the week, just as before. Another cycled through the musical scale, fa, so, la, ti, etc. Still another cycled through the first seven digits. And so forth. Each variable had its own cycle of seven states. In the random control condition the corrected fraction right was 0.69 and in the cyclical condition it was 0.76, an increase of $0.06 \pm 0.03$. Again the difference is small.

We are left with a rather surprising conclusion: even when each variable will go through a perfectly predictable sequence of states the

---

[5] The fact that superfluous states increase the frequency of change was pointed out by Dr. William P. Harris.

[6] Done in collaboration with Gayle E. Mueser. Full descriptions of procedure and results have not yet been published.

## CORRELATION BETWEEN VARIABLES

The foregoing experiment was concerned with situations in which the successive states of a particular variable were related but the present states of different variables were not. In the next experiment we introduced regularity into the task in the opposite way. The successive states of any one variable were unrelated, but there was a relation between the present states of different variables.[7]

Table 4 shows how the list of messages was constructed. Each column again portrays the

### TABLE 4

**A Sequence of Messages with Correlation between Variables**

(Each column shows the history of a variable, time running down the page.)

| 1 | 2 | 3 | 4 | 5 | 6 |
|---|---|---|---|---|---|
| cow | cow | cow | cow | cow | cow |
|  | fish |  |  |  |  |
|  |  |  | fish |  |  |
|  |  |  |  | fish |  |
|  |  | fish |  |  |  |
| fish |  |  |  |  |  |
|  |  |  |  |  | fish |
|  |  |  |  | snail |  |
|  |  |  | snail |  |  |

Note.—Instead of writing "cow" or "fish" the subject used crude drawings like those shown in Fig. 2.

history of one of the variables. The boxes were labeled 1 to 6, and they all had the same possible states, eight animals that the subject recorded in the form of crude drawings like those shown in Fig. 2. At some point during the course of a run all six boxes might be in the state cow as shown

---

[7] The work discussed in this section was done in collaboration with Hasseltine R. Green and Gayle E. Mueser. Full descriptions of procedure and results have not yet been published.

at the top of the table. A variable was picked at random and its state was changed to some randomly chosen animal other than cow. In this example the message was "Two fish." Another variable (any except Variable 2) was chosen at random and its state was also changed to fish. Still another was then changed to fish, and so on, until all six were in the state fish. Some state other than fish was then chosen at random, and the next six messages changed the boxes in a random order to the new state (snail, in this example). And in general the boxes were all in the same state after every sixth message. Thus there was a fairly strong tendency for different variables to be in the same state at the same time. Questions about randomly selected variables were again interspersed at random among the messages.

In the control condition, messages and questions about the same variables occurred in the same places as in the orderly condition, but the state named in every message was random with the restriction that, as in the orderly condition, every message was a change. The subject knew which condition to expect, orderly or random.

After correction for guessing among the eight alternatives the fraction right was 0.46 in the control condition and 0.93 in the orderly, an increase of $0.47 \pm 0.03$. This kind of regularity has a large effect.

As usual we did a similar experiment with variables that had their own states. There were five boxes labeled Size, Quality, Motion, Color, and Animal. At some point during a run their states might be those shown at the top of Table 5. Reading from left to right the symbols stand for large, placid, ambling, brown, and cow—a set of five words that the subject had been taught to regard as belonging together. The next five messages changed the variables in a random order until, again reading from left to right, the states were tiny, industrious, crawling, red, and ant—another set of words that the subject had been taught to regard as belonging together. After five more messages the states were middle-sized, graceful, floating, white, and swan. And in general every fifth message brought

## TABLE 5

**A Sequence of Messages with Another Kind of Correlation between Variables**

(Each column shows the history of a variable, time running down the page.)

| Size | Quality | Motion | Color | Animal |
|------|---------|--------|-------|--------|
| L | P | A | B | cow* |
| | | | R | |
| | I | | | |
| | | | | ant* |
| | | C | | |
| T | | | | |
| M | | | | |
| | | | W | |

* The subject used crude drawings like those shown in Fig. 2.

the five variables into states that belonged together.

The corrected fraction right was 0.76 in the random control condition and 0.95 in the orderly condition, an increase of $0.20 \pm 0.04$. The improvement is not so large as in the previous experiment, but of course the room for improvement is smaller. Since the boxes now have their own sets of states the fraction right is fairly high even in the random control condition. It is still fair to say that the introduction of orderly relations between the present states of different variables has a large effect.

In sum, the system designer apparently may allow himself to be optimistic about an operator's ability to keep track of a situation that hangs together in the sense that the current states of the variables tend to be related to each other.

## FURTHER QUESTIONS

I began by saying that this paper was a progress report, and before stating the conclusions that have been reached I want to emphasize how much remains to be done.

I have discussed what may be regarded as four ways of reducing the randomness of the situation by decreasing the amount of information contained in a message when the box to which the message refers has been specified. The four ways were: (a) reducing the frequency of change, (b) introducing correlation between the present states of different variables, (c) reducing the number of possible states, and (d) introducing correlation between the successive states of the same variable. The first two have a large effect on performance; the others have little or no effect. The picture that emerges is neither clear nor satisfying. Certainly it is not clear enough to indicate what would happen if other kinds of regularity were introduced. I feel that a study of the types of regularity that do and do not make the task easier should be a matter of considerable practical and theoretical interest[8].

There is another, even more compelling reason for thinking that much remains to be learned. There seem to be situations outside the laboratory in which people perform better than in our experiments. We have been plagued by the thought of a bridge player who keeps track, hand after hand, of the cards that have fallen and the players who held them. He seems to store a large amount of information, and he seems to do it better than any of our subjects. Does the game possess some special regularity that makes his task easy, or does he somehow organize the information so that he can remember it? Or is there some other factor that has not been considered in these experiments?

## CONCLUSIONS

Building a system is a process of making compromises; so rules about good design must be prefaced by some such reservation as "when possible" or "other things being equal." With that understanding, the following recommendations may be made about the way in which information should be coded for presentation to an operator who must deal with a changing situation: (a) Each variable of which he must

---

[8] For a study of a very different kind of regularity see Lloyd and Johnston (in press). They let the series of states named in the messages or in the answers to the questions form an approximation to English.

keep track should have its own exclusive set of possible states. (b) There should be few variables with many possible states, not many variables with few states. (c) The frequency with which a variable changes state should be kept to a minimum.

There are three other conclusions, which though they provide no specific recommendations may nevertheless be useful to the designer as background information: (a) Capacity for random information is low. People make mistakes when keeping track of two or three things at once. (b) Performance is not much improved when each variable goes through a regular, predictable sequence of states. (c) Performance is greatly improved by correlation between the present states of different variables, at least when the correlation is as extreme as in the examples considered here.

## REFERENCES

Lloyd, K. E. Supplementary report: Short-term retention as a function of average storage load. *J. exp. Psychol.*, 1961, **62,** 632.

Lloyd, K. E., & Johnston, W. A. Short-term retention as a function of contextual constraint. *J. exp. Psychol.*, in press.

Lloyd, K. E., Reid, L. S., & Feallock, J. B. Short-term retention as a function of the average number of items presented. *J. exp. Psychol.*, 1960, **60,** 201–207.

Reid, L. S., Lloyd, K. E., Brackett, H. R., & Hawkins, W. F. Short-term retention as a function of average storage load and average load reduction. *J. exp. Psychol.*, 1961, **62,** 518–522.

Yntema, D. B., & Mueser, Gayle E. Remembering the present states of a number of variables. *J. exp. Psychol.*, 1960, **60,** 18–22.

Yntema, D. B., & Mueser, Gayle E. Keeping track of variables that have few or many states. *J. exp. Psychol.*, 1962, **63,** 391–395.

# 17

## PROPERTIES OF WORKLOAD ASSESSMENT TECHNIQUES

*F. Thomas Eggemeier*

University of Dayton
and
Armstrong Aerospace Medical Research Laboratory
Dayton, Ohio
U.S.A.

Workload measurement techniques vary with respect to certain properties that determine the utility of a technique for individual applications. Two particularly critical properties are the sensitivity and intrusiveness of a technique. Present theory and supporting evidence suggest that these properties can be influenced by a number of factors, including the level and type of information processing demands that are imposed on an operator. Such factors emphasize the need for more extensive comparative information regarding the sensitivity and intrusiveness of the major classes of techniques. This chapter discusses theoretical bases of these properties, and reviews some current data that address the sensitivity and intrusiveness of several techniques. The development of a standard evaluation methodology which is designed to provide the required comparative data and refine present workload metric application guidelines is also discussed.

## INTRODUCTION

Applications of sophisticated control and display technologies to modern systems can impose heavy demands on operator information processing capabilities. Such technologies often require the rapid sampling and integration of large volumes of information, and the resulting demands can approach or exceed the limited information processing capacities of the operator. Consequently, the need to assess the load imposed on operator processing capacities is particularly critical in high technology systems. Mental workload refers to the degree of processing capacity that is expended during task performance, and a large number of workload measurement techniques have been developed for application during system design and evaluation (O'Donnell & Eggemeier, 1986; Wierwille & Williges, 1978, 1980).

Workload assessment procedures can be categorized according to the type of response used to derive the index of capacity expenditure. The resulting major classes of measurement techniques include subjective, physiological, and performance-based measures. Although various individual assessment techniques have been developed within each category, all subjective procedures use some report (e.g., rating scale) of experienced effort or capacity expenditure to characterize workload levels, while physiological techniques derive a capacity expenditure estimate from the operator's physiological response (e.g., variations in heart rate) to task demand. Performance-based procedures, which include primary and secondary task measures, are based on operator performance levels. Primary task procedures use the adequacy of performance on the task or system function of interest to characterize capacity expenditure, while secondary task measures are typically derived from the levels of performance on a concurrent or secondary task. Techniques from each major category of procedure have been employed in a range of applications with varying degrees of success (O'Donnell & Eggemeier, 1986).

The capability to assess effort or capacity expenditure with a variety of approaches raises fundamental questions regarding the utility of both classes of measurement procedures and individual techniques. Measurement techniques vary with respect to a number of properties that can be used to evaluate their usefulness for individual applications (Eggemeier, 1984; Eggemeier, Shingledecker, & Crabtree, 1985;

From P. A. Hancock and N. Meshkati (eds.), *Human Mental Workload*. Copyright 1988 by Elsevier Science Publishers B.V.

Shingledecker, 1983; Wickens, 1984a; Wierwille & Williges, 1978). In addition to validity and reliability, two of the most important properties are the sensitivity and intrusiveness of a technique. Sensitivity refers to the capability of a technique to reflect differences in the levels of processing capacity expenditure that are associated with performance of a task or combination of tasks. Intrusiveness, on the other hand, refers to the tendency of a measurement technique to cause unintended degradations in ongoing primary task performance. Because of their importance in determining the utility of a workload measurement procedure, sensitivity and intrusiveness have been the subject of considerable recent research. This work has identified a number of variables which appear to affect the sensitivity and intrusiveness of several metrics, and has provided the basis for some initial general guidelines regarding the application of measurement techniques.

This chapter describes theoretical bases for both sensitivity and intrusiveness, and discusses a number of factors which appear to influence these properties in an assessment technique. Data which address the sensitivity and intrusiveness of several assessment procedures are reviewed, and general application guidelines outlined. The development of a standard metric evaluation methodology for refinement of the comparative data base related to both properties is discussed, as are directions for future research.

## SENSITIVITY

Workload assessment techniques differ in their sensitivity to variations in primary task loading (O'Donnell & Eggemeier, 1986), and such differences significantly affect the utility of a technique for various applications. Current evidence suggests that sensitivity is a complex property that can be influenced by a number of variables. One such variable is the degree of capacity expenditure associated with task performance. A second variable with the potential to affect the sensitivity of some measures is the locus of the demands placed on individual capacities/resources within the human processing system.

### Sensitivity as a Function of Level of Capacity Expenditure

At a general theoretical level, sensitivity can be described in terms of a hypothetical function which relates level of effort/capacity expenditure to the adequacy of primary task performance. Figure 1 depicts a function that consists of two regions which are defined by the relationship of capacity expenditure to a theoretical threshold for unimpaired performance. The first or non-overload region spans those levels of expenditure which do not exceed operator capacity, and is therefore characterized by adequate levels of primary task performance in which both errors and reaction time are relatively low. In this region, the operator has sufficient spare processing capacity to deal with increased levels of demand, and can maintain performance by expending more effort or capacity. Consequently, no direct relationship exists between capacity expenditure and primary task errors or reaction time. Therefore, the increase in capacity expenditure from "A" to "B" noted in Figure 1 will not be reflected by changes in performance levels. In the second or overload region, expenditure levels surpass the capacity of the operator to compensate for increases in demand, and the threshold for unimpaired performance is exceeded. A direct relationship between performance and capacity expenditure is hypothesized in this region, and takes the form of increased reaction time and/or errors with increased demand. Consequently, the increase in capacity expenditure from "C" to "D" will be reflected in performance, even though it is equivalent in magnitude to the previously undetected increase.

One important implication of the hypothesized relationship is that while primary task performance measures will be sensitive to differences in capacity expenditure under overload conditions, they can be relatively insensitive to such differences in the non-overload region. Workload measurement in this latter region is, therefore, dependent upon alternative techniques which can reflect capacity expenditure differences at levels below the threshold for performance breakdown.

Subjective, physiological, and secondary task measures represent alternative assessment procedures which can provide the required capability. Expectations regarding the sensitivity of subjective and physiological techniques are based on the assumption that increased capacity expenditure in either of the noted regions will be accompanied by physiological changes and feelings of exertion or effort that will be

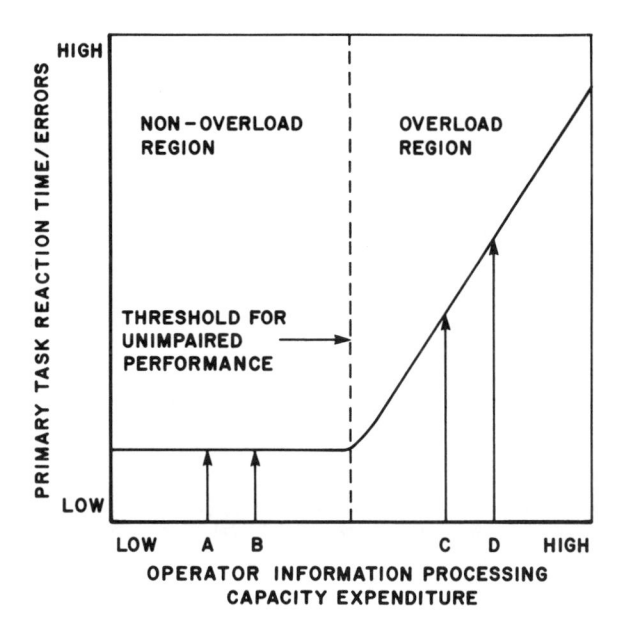

**Figure 1.** Hypothesized relationship between operator capacity expenditure and primary task performance.

reflected in appropriate indices (Johannsen, Moray, Pew, Rasmussen, Sanders, & Wickens, 1979). Secondary task methodology (Knowles, 1963) is based on the expectation that the addition of concurrent secondary task processing demands will be sufficient to shift total capacity usage into the region where performance and expenditure are directly related.

Differences in sensitivity between primary task and alternative measures which are consistent with the noted expectations have been demonstrated in a number of instances (e.g., Bahrick, Noble, & Fitts, 1954; Bell, 1978; Dornic, 1980; Eggemeier, Crabtree, & LaPointe, 1983; Eggemeier, Crabtree, Reid, Zingg, & Shingledecker, 1982; Eggemeier & Stadler, 1984; Schifflet, Linton, & Spicuzza, 1982). Eggemeier et al. (1983), for example, compared the capability of primary task errors and workload ratings obtained from the Subjective Workload Assessment Technique (SWAT) (Reid, Shingledecker, & Eggemeier, 1981; Reid, 1985) to reflect differences in task demand manipulations in a short-term memory update task. Subjects monitored a display and mentally updated the status of several information categories that changed periodically. Categories of information were three letters of the alphabet that were presented in twenty-item sequences, and subjects retained a count of the number of times that each letter occurred. Task demand was manipulated by varying the time interval between the presentation of items, and intervals of 1.0, 2.0, and 3.0 seconds were used. Figure 2 illustrates the effect of the time interval manipulation on both mean SWAT ratings and errors in the memory task. As is clear from Figure 2, SWAT ratings varied substantially with the time interval manipulation, and discriminated the three levels of task difficulty. On the other hand, errors failed to vary systematically with the time manipulation, and demonstrated no significant differences as a function of the demand levels. A similar pattern of results was obtained by Eggemeier and Stadler (1984), who evaluated the sensitivity of SWAT ratings and both primary task reaction time and error measures to demand manipulations in a spatial short-term memory task. In this task, histogram patterns which had been memorized were compared with a test pattern to determine if a match existed. Demand was manipulated by varying both the complexity of the histogram patterns and the length of the memory retention interval. Both SWAT ratings and

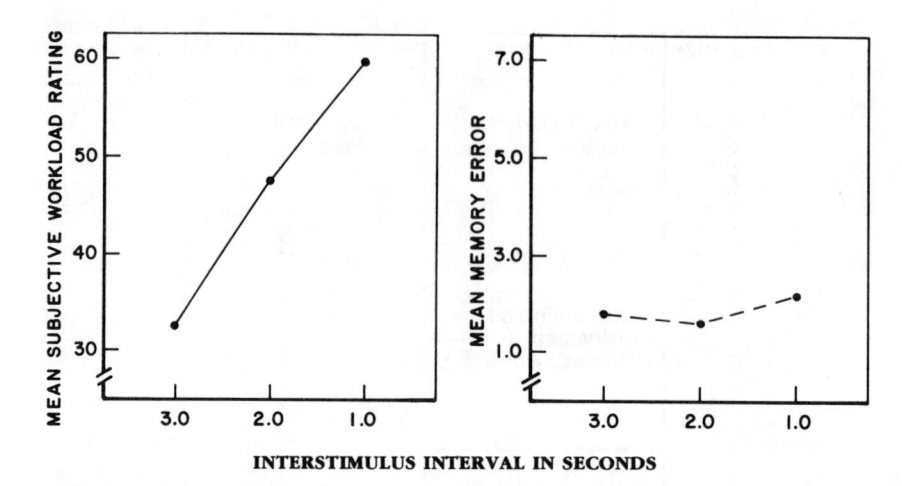

**Figure 2.** Mean subjective workload ratings and mean memory task errors as a function of interstimulus interval. (Redrawn from Eggemeier, Crabtree, & LaPointe, 1983. Reprinted with permission. Copyright 1983, Human Factors Society, Inc.)

reaction time to the test pattern discriminated the differences in histogram complexity. However, SWAT ratings also varied significantly as a function of retention interval, while reaction time failed to do so. Errors in the memory task were not significantly affected by either the retention interval or complexity manipulations.

These and similar patterns of disagreement or dissociation between primary task and alternative measures can be interpreted within the previously described framework by assuming that demand levels in the noted instances fell within that region of expenditure which affords sufficient spare processing capacity to maintain primary task performance. However, maintenance of performance was achieved at the cost of greater effort/capacity expenditure, and this was reflected in the subjective workload ratings. The proposed framework also suggests that primary task measures should demonstrate increased sensitivity at those higher levels of capacity expenditure which fall within the region characterized by a monotonic relationship between expenditure and performance. This type of pattern has been reported by Eggemeier et al. (1982), who manipulated both the number of information categories to be retained and the time interval between information status updates in the short-term memory task described above. Primary task error measures were again less sensitive than subjective workload ratings at lower levels of task demand. However, at the highest level of time demand, error measures equaled the sensitivity of the subjective measure, and actually demonstrated greater sensitivity at the highest level of memory load.

Comparable differences in the sensitivity of primary task and secondary task measures of capacity expenditure have also been noted in a number of instances (e.g., Bahrick et al., 1954; Bell, 1978; Dornic, 1980; Schifflet, et al., 1982). Schifflet et al. (1982), for instance, reported that a secondary task version of the Sternberg (1966) memory search paradigm discriminated differences in the workload associated with two aircraft display options, even though primary flight task performance was equivalent with both displays. These results are consistent with the previously discussed rationale for secondary task methodology, which is to provide a more sensitive index of primary task workload by shifting total task loading into the region where performance and capacity expenditure are related.

The noted framework and data therefore suggest that alternative techniques can provide greater sensitivity than primary task measures in some instances. Ideally, the framework and supporting data should be extended to examine the relative sensitivity of subjective, physiological, and secondary task measures in the region of their maximum sensitivity. However, such data are quite limited (O'Donnell & Eggemeier, 1986), and factors which influence the relative sensitivity of alternative measures have not yet been fully documented by workload metric research. One such factor that has been identified by recent work is related to the locus of demands placed on different capacities within the human processing system, and work related to this factor is discussed in the next section.

### Sensitivity as a Function of the Locus of Processing Demands

A theoretical basis for differences in the sensitivity of some workload assessment techniques can be derived from the multiple resources approach to capacity limitations within the human system (Navon & Gopher, 1979; Wickens, 1979, 1980, 1984b). Essentially, this theory holds that the human processing system can be described as consisting of a number of separate capacities, each with a limited capability to process information. According to this theory, it is possible to exhaust the capacity associated with one processing function (e.g., central processing), while maintaining sufficient independent processing capacity to perform other functions (e.g., motor output). Current multiple resources theory (Wickens, 1984b) suggests that separate capacities may be defined on the basis of three principal dimensions: (1) stages of processing (perceptual/central processing vs. motor output); (2) codes of processing and output (spatial/manual vs. verbal/vocal); and (3) modalities of input (visual vs. auditory). An adequate characterization of workload in this approach is dependent upon the capability to specify the pattern of capacity expenditure associated with each of the proposed processing functions.

Present evidence indicates that some techniques may be capable of discriminating the levels of loading imposed on separate capacities. Such techniques are considered diagnostic (Wickens, 1984a; Wickens & Derrick, 1981) in that they are sensitive to some types (e.g., motor output) of capacity expenditure, but exhibit little or no sensitivity to demands placed on other (e.g., central processing) capacities. Other techniques appear to be less diagnostic, and exhibit relatively uniform levels of sensitivity across different types of capacity expenditure. In general, secondary task methodology and some physiological measures (e.g., the P300 component of the evoked cortical response) can be classified as diagnostic; while primary task measures, subjective procedures, and other physiological techniques (e.g., pupil dilation) appear to be less diagnostic and more globally sensitive to capacity expenditure throughout the human processing system (Eggemeier, 1984).

Secondary task measures provide a clear example of an assessment technique which can exhibit a very selective pattern of sensitivity to different forms of capacity expenditure. As noted above, the basic assumption of secondary task methodology is that additional processing requirements imposed by the concurrent task will shift total loading into the region of the capacity expenditure-performance function which demonstrates a monotonic relationship between the variables. If the concurrent task draws from the same capacity as the primary task, the assumption of an increase in total processing demand can be met for that capacity. Decrements in concurrent task performance relative to single task performance baselines should result in this instance. However, if a mismatch exists between the capacities required by the two tasks, the addition of concurrent processing demands will not shift capacity-specific expenditure into the more sensitive region. In this case, no significant differences between single and dual task performance levels may be evident.

Differences in single to dual task decrements that are consistent with the processing functions outlined by multiple resources theory (Wickens, 1984b) have been reported by several investigators (e.g., Stadler & Eggemeier, 1985; Wickens & Kessel, 1980; Wickens, Mountford, & Schreiner, 1981). Stadler and Eggemeier (1985), for instance, investigated levels of dual task performance as a function of overlap in codes of processing as specified in the current theory. Subjects performed a version of the Sternberg (1966) memory search paradigm which required that a letter probe be compared with items in a memory set. This task was considered predominantly verbal in its coding demands, since it required that letters of the alphabet be processed and retained. The memory search task was performed either singly, or during the retention interval of a concurrent memory task that was either predominantly verbal or spatial in its processing demands. The concurrent verbal memory task required that a list of words be retained and matched with a subsequently presented comparison list. The procedure for the concurrent spatial task was identical, except that word lists were replaced by histogram patterns. Figure 3 shows the percentage of correct responses under single and dual task conditions in the memory search task as a function of concurrent memory task type.

As is evident, the addition of a concurrent demand to retain words led to decrements in memory search performance relative to single task baselines, while the addition of spatial retention demands was not associated with significant performance impairments. These results can be interpreted within the multiple resources and secondary task frameworks outlined above by assuming that verbal and spatially coded tasks draw upon different processing capacities. Under this assumption, the addition of the word task retention demands to memory search requirements was sufficient to overload verbal processing capacity, while the addition of functionally separate spatial demands failed to result in capacity-specific overload. Consequently, performance decrements resulted in the first case but not in the latter. Wickens and Kessel (1980) have demonstrated similar differences in single to dual task decrements that are consistent with the perceptual/central processing and motor output stages of processing proposed by multiple resources theory.

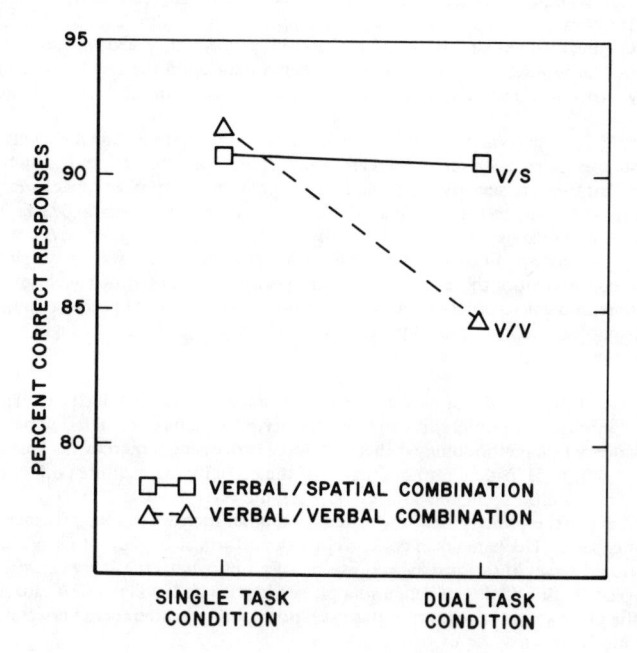

*Figure 3.* Percent correct responses in a verbal memory search task as a function of single vs. dual task performance conditions and the type of concurrent task. (Redrawn from Stadler & Eggemeier, 1985.)

These types of dual task results suggest that the assumptions of the secondary task paradigm will be most readily met in those instances involving substantial overlap in processing demands between the primary and secondary tasks. Consequently, the sensitivity of a secondary task can vary as a function of the locus of processing demands in the primary task, and such variations can be diagnostic of primary task loading patterns. Use of a secondary task which emphasizes a particular form of capacity expenditure can therefore permit some specification of the locus of primary task demands.

The results of work reported by Shingledecker, Acton, and Crabtree (1983) very clearly illustrate the diagnostic sensitivity that can be associated with secondary task applications. Shingledecker et al. used a secondary task version of the Michon (1966) interval production task (IPT) in a series of experiments that involved three primary tasks that differed in their information processing demand patterns. The IPT requires the production of a series of regular finger movements by subjects, and can therefore be assumed to impose demands on motor output functions. The primary tasks used in the three experiments included a probability display monitoring task that had been adapted from Chiles, Alluisi, and Adams (1968), a version of the Sternberg (1966) memory search paradigm, and an unstable tracking task that was similar to the critical tracking task of Jex, McDonnell, and Phatek (1966).

The display monitoring task required that subjects detect the occurrence of visually presented signals. Demand levels were manipulated by varying both the number of displays that were to be monitored (1 vs. 3 vs. 4) and the discriminability of the signals. Each display included a pointer which moved randomly with respect to a center marker under non-signal conditions. A signal occurred when the pointer movement became biased, such that a disproportionate percentage (i.e., 95%, 85%, or 75%) of moves occurred on one side of the center marker. A 95% bias was more discriminable than an 85% bias, which could be more easily discriminated than a 75% bias. Three levels of perceptual loading were achieved with the following combinations of dials and bias levels: (1) one dial at a 95% bias, (2) three dials at an 85% bias, and (3) four dials at a 75% bias. The procedure in the Sternberg memory search task was similar to that which was described previously, and required that subjects determine if a probe letter was a member of a specified memory set. Different loading levels were achieved by manipulating the size (1 vs. 4 items) of the memory search set. The tracking task required that subjects control the movement of a visual target with a joystick controller. Demand was manipulated by varying the instability (lambda levels of 2.4, 3.6, and 6.0) of the target element. Manipulations of demand in the display monitoring and memory tasks were therefore designed to principally involve perceptual/central processing functions, while demand variations in the unstable tracking task were predominantly related to motor output loading.

The results of the three experiments are illustrated in Figure 4, which shows levels of IPT performance as a function of demand level in each of the primary tasks. The IPT workload score was based on the variability of interval durations, and was derived for individual subjects in each demand condition by subtracting a baseline single task score from the dual task score and dividing by the baseline. Therefore, higher scores are associated with larger decrements in performance relative to single task baselines. As is clear, secondary IPT performance varied systematically with manipulations of tracking task demand. However, IPT performance was not significantly affected by demand variations in either the display monitoring or memory search tasks. These results can be interpreted as indicating that the IPT is sensitive to manipulations of motor output demand, but is relatively insensitive to such variations in perceptual/central processing demand.

Similar patterns of differential sensitivity that can be related to the stages of processing dimension have been reported for the P300 component of the evoked cortical response (Isreal, Chesney, Wickens, & Donchin, 1980; Isreal, Wickens, Chesney, & Donchin, 1980). These patterns of specific sensitivity suggest that although selected secondary task and physiological metrics can reflect levels of expenditure within particular capacities of the human system, they can be relatively insensitive to other forms of capacity expenditure. Such diagnostic measures therefore provide a workload index for selected processing functions, and cannot be assumed to reflect general levels of loading throughout the processing system. There are data, however, which indicate that primary task measures and some subjective and physiological procedures may be generally sensitive to capacity expenditure anywhere within the human system. These techniques may, therefore, provide more global measures of load.

Current data which support the global sensitivity of subjective measures are primarily derived from programs that were designed to systematically evaluate the sensitivity of a particular subjective metric (e.g., Hart & Staveland, in press; Reid, 1985; Wierwille & Casali, 1983a). The SWAT development program (Reid, 1985), for example, has included sensitivity evaluations in laboratory, simulator, and field-based environments. A number of the laboratory studies employed tasks designed to place heaviest processing demands on several of the capacities identified by multiple resources theory (Wickens, 1984b), and SWAT has demonstrated its sensitivity across the range of processing functions represented in these experi-

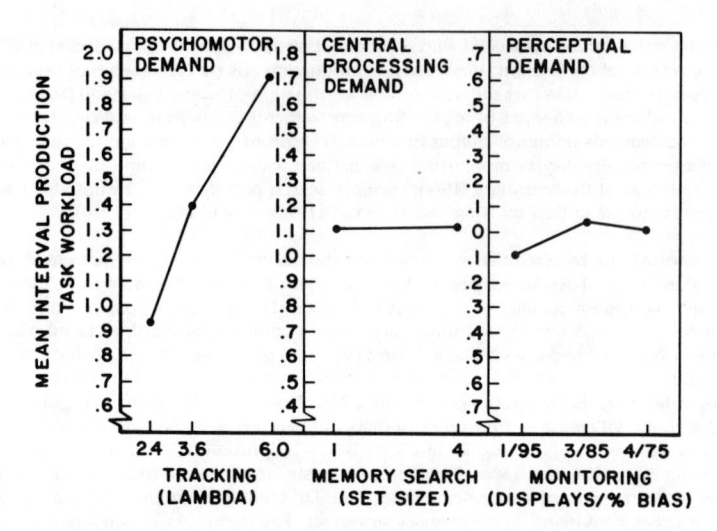

**Figure 4.** Performance in a secondary interval production task as a function of demand levels in three primary tasks emphasizing different processing functions. (Redrawn from Shingledecker, Acton, & Crabtree, 1983. Reprinted with permission. Copyright 1983, Society of Automotive Engineers, Inc.)

ments. A subset of the tasks and associated processing functions to which SWAT has demonstrated its sensitivity include: visual display monitoring (Eggemeier & Amell, 1987; Notestine, 1984) which was designed to heavily load perceptual input capacity; verbal (Eggemeier et al., 1982; Eggemeier et al., 1983) and spatial short-term memory (Eggemeier & Stadler, 1984) which primarily loaded two major central processing coding dimensions; and unstable tracking (Eggemeier & Amell, 1987; Reid et al., 1981) which exerted heavy demands on motor output capacity. Further references to work which supports the sensitivity of SWAT to various forms of capacity expenditure can be found in Reid (1985). Similar patterns of general sensitivity have been reported by Wierwille and Casali (1983a) using a modified version of the Cooper-Harper (1969) aircraft handling characteristics scale, and by Hart and Staveland (in press) with multidimensional workload rating technique developed by the NASA-Ames Research Center. The modified Cooper-Harper (MCH) scale requires direct estimates of workload and effort expenditure by subjects, and proved sensitive to a number of different demand manipulations in a series of flight simulator experiments (Wierwille & Casali, 1983a). Likewise, workload ratings derived from application of the NASA multidimensional procedure demonstrated sensitivity in a variety of laboratory and simulator studies that were conducted as part of the program to develop the technique (Hart & Staveland, in press).

The pattern of sensitivity which has emerged from systematic work with rating scale procedures such as SWAT, the MCH scale, and the NASA multidimensional technique suggests that subjective measures are capable of reflecting variations in effort expenditure across a variety of processing functions, and indicates that these rating scale approaches should be considered global rather than diagnostic in their sensitivity.

Although they exhibit high degrees of sensitivity only at levels of capacity expenditure that exceed the threshold for unimpaired performance, primary task measures appear to represent global indices of workload under such conditions. Theoretically, an overload of any capacity (e.g., central processing, motor output) should lead to performance degradations, since successful performance is dependent on the variety of capacities required by the task. Primary task measures have demonstrated the anticipated sensitivity to a variety of manipulations that would be expected to heavily load perceptual, central processing, and motor output functions within the human system (O'Donnell & Eggemeier, 1986). As a consequence, it appears that such measures should be considered global in their sensitivity. Likewise, those physiological measures with the potential to index levels of activation throughout the processing system could be expected to exhibit global rather than diagnostic sensitivity. Beatty (1982), for example, has reviewed the literature which supports the capability of a pupil dilation measure to reflect levels of loading across a range of processing functions.

Multiple resources theory and the noted data therefore provide a framework which supports a distinction between global and diagnostic metrics. It is probable that results derived from global and diagnostic measures will exhibit some dissociation in those situations that involve a mismatch between primary task demand and the sensitivity area of a diagnostic metric. Therefore, the distinction suggests some caution in interpretation of capacity expenditure estimates derived from application of the two types of measurement procedures.

## INTRUSIVENESS

Intrusiveness (Eggemeier, 1984; Shingledecker, 1983; Wickens, 1984a; Wierwille & Williges, 1978), the tendency to cause unintended degradations in ongoing primary task performance, can pose potentially serious problems in application of a workload measurement technique. Such problems are primarily related to the interpretation of results obtained with an assessment procedure, and with application of techniques to operational environments.

Significant intrusiveness can produce difficulties in interpreting capacity expenditure estimates derived from an assessment procedure. A technique whose use leads to primary task performance decrements would not be expected to accurately reflect the expenditure levels that would be associated with unimpaired performance.

The tendency to intrude on primary task performance can also lead to problems in application of a measurement procedure. Levels of intrusiveness which could be accepted in the laboratory might not be tolerable in operational environments where any compromises in system safety would be unacceptable.

Although systematic evidence regarding the intrusion associated with individual assessment techniques is not extensive, it appears likely that intrusion does not represent a static property of a technique, but may vary as a function of factors such as the type and level of primary task loading. One of the few systematic efforts to compare intrusiveness among techniques (Casali & Wierwille, 1983, 1984; Wierwille & Casali, 1983b; Wierwille & Connor, 1983; Wierwille, Rahimi, & Casali, 1985), for example, demonstrated different patterns of intrusion with a secondary time estimation task in a series of investigations that involved different types (e.g., central processing, motor output) and levels of primary task loading.

The potential for variations in intrusiveness as a function of primary task type is consistent with the multiple resources approach to capacity limitations discussed previously. If some forms of intrusion represent the re-allocation of primary task capacity/resources to information processing requirements that are associated with a measurement technique, then levels of primary task decrement should vary as a function of the degree of overlap in the capacities demanded by the primary task and the assessment procedure. The differences in secondary time estimation intrusiveness reported by Wierwille and Casali (1983b) can be viewed as at least partially related to such overlap if it is assumed that the time estimation task drew heavily on central processing capacities. Time estimation interfered significantly with a flight simulator navigation task which was designed to load central processing capacities, but not with other flight simulator tasks that emphasized perceptual, motor output, or auditory monitoring functions. Within this framework, intrusiveness is similar to sensitivity, in that both properties can vary to some extent with the overlap in the capacities required by the primary task and the measurement procedure. It is important to note, of course, that such capacity-specific interference does not represent the only potential cause of primary task degradation that can be associated with use of an assessment procedure. To the extent that use of a measurement technique is occasioned by distraction or other general interference with the primary task, intrusion that is not attributable to specific capacities will be observed. However, when these general factors are equivalent, the framework predicts relatively more interference in instances of capacity overlap than in those situations where minimal overlap exists.

Intrusion can also be related to the amount of capacity expenditure associated with the combination of the primary task and the assessment procedure. Re-allocation of resources to the measurement technique should be more obvious under high as opposed to low levels of loading. For example, if a subjective rating scale requires the use of central processing capacity to judge and retain the amount of effort experienced during performance of a primary task, this additional capacity expenditure should be more obvious if primary task levels are already near the threshold for degraded performance outlined in Figure 1.

The foregoing discussion is based on the assumption that the degree of intrusion can be significantly affected by the amount and pattern of operator capacity expenditure associated with use of a measurement technique. In this view, secondary task methodology should be the most intrusive of the major categories of techniques, since the capacity expenditure associated with its use should be substantial and would overlap temporally with the demands of the primary task. In fact, secondary task methodology has the potential to suffer not only from such capacity interference, but also from so-called peripheral interference (Wickens, 1984b) which stems from physical input or output constraints (e.g., the inability to generate simultaneous responses to two tasks with the same hand) within the human system. Subjective techniques, whose demands are typically imposed after the completion of primary task performance, and physiological techniques, which would usually minimize processing demands, should demonstrate lower levels of intrusion. Data derived from individual applications of each class of technique are generally consistent with these expectations.

**Intrusion With Secondary Task Techniques**

First, it is evident that there has been a high incidence of intrusion in laboratory applications of secondary task methodology (O'Donnell & Eggemeier, 1986; Ogden, Levine, & Eisner, 1979; Rolfe, 1971; Wierwille & Williges, 1978). The most common application of the methodology is the subsidiary task paradigm (Knowles, 1963), which requires that subjects maintain concurrent primary task performance at single task baseline levels. The intrusion problem in this paradigm has led to application of several techniques (Casali & Wierwille, 1983, 1984; Hart, 1978; Kelly & Wargo, 1967; Shingledecker, 1980a; 1983) which are designed to protect primary task performance.

One such approach (Casali & Wierwille, 1983, 1984; Hart, 1978; Shingledecker, 1980a) has involved investigating the utility of secondary tasks that minimize either perceptual input or response output requirements. This approach attempts to limit or control the degree of peripheral interference by minimizing the input and/or output requirements of a secondary task. The IPT (Michon, 1966; Shingledecker, 1980a; Shingledecker et al., 1983), which was discussed previously, represents an approach which limits the perceptual input requirements of the secondary task. Because it requires a continuous series of regular motor responses which are independent of external cues, this task minimizes the potential for peripheral interference problems associated with stimulus input. As noted above, Shingledecker et al. (1983) have demonstrated the utility of this task in indexing the motor output load imposed by a primary task.

A second approach to protecting primary task performance which was designed to limit intrusion by controlling allocation of processing resources to the secondary task is the embedded task procedure (Shingledecker, 1980a; Shingledecker, Crabtree, Simons, Courtright, & O'Donnell, 1980). This approach uses a task from normal system operational procedures as the secondary task, and is applicable to simulation and operational environments as well as to the laboratory. The technique is designed to minimize intrusion by identifying secondary tasks from system operation functions with a lower priority than primary tasks, thereby controlling the capacity/resource allocation policy of the subject. Use of normal system tasks affords the additional advantages of minimizing secondary task instrumentation requirements, and increasing the likelihood of operator acceptance of the measurement procedure.

Shingledecker et al. (1980) investigated the feasibility of using radio communications as an embedded secondary task. Specifications of input messages and response requirements from sample aircraft communications tasks were obtained through interviews with pilots. The tasks were scaled to derive estimates of the loading associated with each so that quantified levels of subsidiary task demand could be produced.

In order to assess the sensitivity of the scaled tasks, Shingledecker and Crabtree (1982) conducted an experiment in a laboratory analog of a flight simulator. The secondary communications tasks were performed both singly and in combination with a primary tracking task that was intended to represent flight control activities of varying degrees of difficulty. Aircraft communications panels were installed in a fixed-based cockpit with a controller for the primary tracking task. Performance of several communications tasks varied with the presence or absence of the tracking task, and as a function of tracking task difficulty. Results of the study therefore supported the use of some embedded radio communications tasks to assess workload. Additional research is required with operational pilots to further evaluate the sensitivity of these tasks, and to investigate the degree of intrusion that would be associated with them in a high fidelity flight simulator.

### Intrusion With Subjective and Physiological Techniques

As predicted by the framework outlined above, the reported incidence of intrusion with subjective and physiological techniques has been minimal (O'Donnell & Eggemeier, 1986). Current evidence regarding subjective techniques (Casali & Wierwille, 1983, 1984; Eggemeier & Amell, 1987; Wierwille & Conner, 1983; Wierwille et al., 1985) indicates that when applied after the completion of primary task performance, none of the rating scales employed in the experiments conducted to date resulted in significant levels of intrusion.

Eggemeier and Amell (1987), for example, performed two experiments in which the SWAT procedure was used to gather subjective estimates of the workload imposed by several conditions in an unstable tracking task and in a display monitoring task. The first experiment required that subjects perform an unstable tracking task similar to that used by Jex et al. (1966). Several difficulty levels were achieved by varying the instability (lambda levels of 1, 2, and 3) of the target element. SWAT ratings were completed by subjects on one-half of the trials, but were not required on the remaining trials. Root mean square (RMS) tracking error and the number of times that subjects lost control of the target element served as the measures of tracking performance. The results are illustrated in Figure 5, which shows

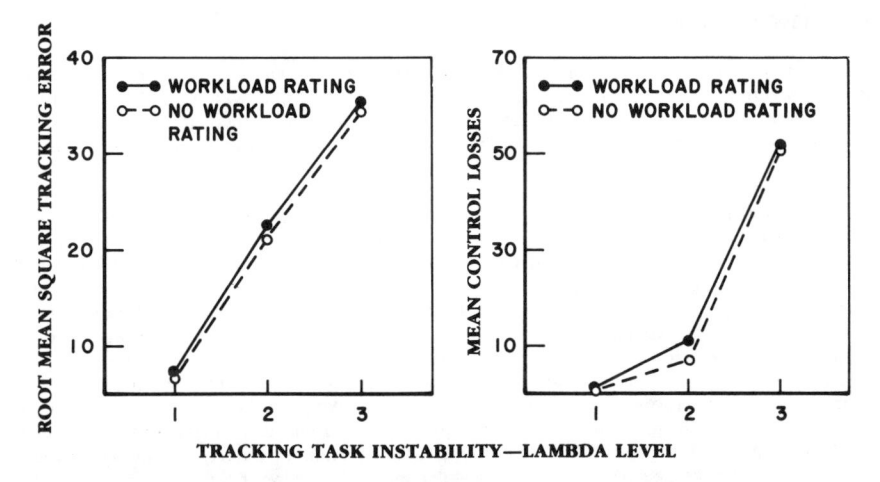

*Figure 5.* Root mean square tracking error and control losses as a function of task demand and workload rating condition. (Redrawn from Eggemeier & Amell, 1987.)

RMS tracking error and the mean number of control losses as a function of task demand under the two rating conditions. As is clear from Figure 5, the requirement to provide SWAT ratings had no significant effect on either RMS error or the mean number of times that subjects lost control of the target element. Subjective workload estimates obtained from the SWAT procedure on those trials which required ratings increased systematically which increases in task demand.

The second experiment followed an identical procedure, except that a display monitoring task replaced the tracking task. The display monitoring task was similar to the previously described variant of the Chiles et al. (1968) procedure. Demand was manipulated by varying the number of displays (1, 2, or 3) to be monitored for the occurrence of signals. The requirement to provide SWAT ratings failed to affect any of the performance indices that were recorded, including mean time to detect signals, the number of missed signals, and the number of false alarms. The SWAT ratings did, however, discriminate the three levels of loading in the monitoring task.

The pattern of results from these experiments is therefore consistent with the expectation that a subjective opinion measure completed subsequent to primary task performance should not be associated with substantial levels of intrusion. It should be noted, however, that the results apply only to the perceptual and motor functions emphasized in the display monitoring and tracking tasks, respectively. It is possible, for instance, that intrusion would occur in a task emphasizing memory functions, since subjective techniques require that judgments regarding experienced levels of effort or capacity expenditure be retained until they are reported at the completion of task performance. Work is currently underway to evaluate this possibility. Finally, although the Eggemeier and Amell (1987) results were obtained with the SWAT procedure, the same pattern of non-intrusiveness has been reported with the MCH workload rating scale in the previously noted flight simulator experiments (Casali & Wierwille, 1983, 1984; Wierwille et al., 1985).

Current information regarding physiological techniques essentially parallels that which is available for subjective assessment procedures. Physiological procedures typically do not require expenditure of operator processing capacity, and for the most part, appear to involve minimal risk of intrusion. Any potential for intrusion from application of physiological techniques would appear to come from possible operator distraction or discomfort that might be associated with recording equipment, but present evidence suggests that this has not represented a significant problem in applications to date (e.g., Wierwille & Casali, 1983b).

## IMPLICATIONS OF PROPERTIES

The theoretical positions and data outlined above indicate that sensitivity and intrusiveness represent complex properties that can be affected by several factors. Techniques differ with respect to both properties, and these differences suggest that no individual metric is capable of meeting the range of sensitivity and intrusion requirements that can be associated with various workload measurement applications.

The noted sensitivity and intrusion patterns, when coupled with instrumentation requirements, can be used to guide the selection of a metric for specific applications (Eggemeier, 1984). Primary task measures should be employed, for instance, when the objective is to determine the adequacy of performance that can be expected with a particular design option. Such measures do, however, require the capability to acquire and record time and error information, and have the potential disadvantage of not discriminating capacity expenditure differences that are below the threshold for unimpaired performance. Consequently, a problem requiring a more sensitive workload evaluation in an operational environment that necessitates minimal intrusion and precludes performance measurement might be more appropriately addressed by subjective techniques. These techniques could meet the objectives and constraints of the noted problem, since they appear to provide global sensitivity, incur little likelihood of intrusion, and also minimize instrumentation requirements. Current data suggest, however, that alternatives to subjective measures would be required for an evaluation conducted to specify the locus of an overload which had been identified with a global metric. This type of application would call for use of more diagnostic secondary task or physiological techniques. The potential capability of such measures to identify the particular processing function or functions (e.g., perceptual, motor) which are most heavily loaded can be useful in specifying the type of design modification that might alleviate the overload. Perceptual overloads, for instance, might suggest reductions in the information content of displays, while high motor output levels would indicate the possible need for modified controls. In many instances, such diagnostic work could be conducted in a simulator or laboratory environment, facilitating the use of physiological recording equipment, and minimizing the practical consequences of any secondary task intrusion.

Considering the variety of objectives and constraints that can be associated with application of workload metrics, it is clear that a comprehensive workload assessment methodology will require the complementary use of several measurement procedures. In fact, the objectives of a particular problem will frequently lead to application of more than one type of technique. It would be typical, for instance, to use primary task measures and one or more additional metrics in an evaluation of alternative designs or operating procedures. Since specification of the operator performance levels that are associated with a design or procedural option is central to most evaluations, primary task measures would be applied to gather such information. Depending upon the objectives and practical constraints of an evaluation, selected subjective, secondary task, or physiological techniques would be employed to provide additional capacity expenditure information. The capacity/effort expenditure data derived from these techniques represent very important supplements to primary task information, since equivalent levels of primary task performance do not provide a strong basis to infer that the workload imposed by design alternatives or tasks is equivalent. The global versus diagnostic capability afforded by the potentially more sensitive alternative measures also suggests complementary application of techniques which differ on this dimension. Globally sensitive techniques might be initially applied, for example, to determine if high levels of loading exist anywhere within a particular design or procedural option. This global evaluation could be followed by use of more diagnostic techniques to pinpoint the locus of any high levels of loading identified in the overall screening. In addition to differences in the objectives to be satisfied by a measurement technique, methodological considerations can also lead to concurrent application of multiple techniques. Proper interpretation of secondary task results, for example, requires measurement of primary task performance under both single task and dual task conditions so that the degree of any intrusion can be assessed (O'Donnell & Eggemeier, 1986).

Although current data provide the basis to evaluate the utility of measurement techniques at the general levels that have been noted, further refinement of selection and application guidelines requires more extensive comparative information on the sensitivity and intrusion properties of individual techniques. As indicated above and in several reviews of the workload measurement literature (O'Donnell & Eggemeier, 1986; Wierwille & Casali, 1983b; Wierwille & Williges, 1978), the data base comparing individual techniques within major categories along these dimensions is quite limited. Available data suggest that differences exist between techniques within some categories, but not in others. Current information comparing alternative subjective techniques (Vidulich & Tsang, 1985; Wierwille & Casali, 1983b), for example, indicates that a high degree of correspondence has been obtained under the conditions that have been evaluated. However, more extensive work is required before firm conclusions can be drawn regarding the degree of comparability among rating scale techniques. In contrast to the results with subjective techniques, current secondary task data demonstrate some differences in sensitivity between techniques (e.g., Wetherell, 1981; Wierwille & Casali, 1983b). Similar patterns of differential sensitivity have been obtained with some physiological metrics (Wierwille & Casali, 1983b; Wilson & Heinrich, 1987). These differences emphasize the need for programmatic research to investigate the sensitivity of individual measures from each of these categories, and suggest that batteries which include a number of both secondary task and physiological techniques might be required to meet the sensitivity requirements of various applications (Eggemeier, 1981; Knowles, 1963; O'Donnell, 1983; Shingledecker, 1983).

Programmatic sensitivity and intrusion research at both the individual technique and category levels requires a standard workload evaluation methodology (Acton, Crabtree, & Shingledecker, 1983; Eggemeier & Reid, 1986; Shingledecker et al., 1983) which will permit comparison of these properties across techniques. The next section describes several elements that are necessary in such a methodology, and also reviews the development of a standardized battery of primary loading tasks which represents the central feature in the recommended methodology.

## WORKLOAD METRIC EVALUATION METHODOLOGY

In order to refine current guidelines for selection and application of workload assessment techniques, systematic research must be conducted to specify the relative sensitivity and intrusiveness that are associated with individual techniques. Without such data, neither a standard set of assessment techniques nor the required guidelines can be developed.

The key elements in a methodology designed to permit comparisons of properties among techniques include standardized testing procedures and a standard set of primary loading tasks which can provide a uniform basis for metric evaluation. The inability to draw detailed comparative data from the existing literature stems largely from the fact that when individual metrics have been applied to evaluate workload in more than one setting, there have typically been variations in the testing procedures, primary tasks, or levels of loading across studies. Therefore, apparent differences in the sensitivity and intrusiveness between techniques cannot be properly interpreted.

Since it is likely that both sensitivity and intrusion will vary as a function of the locus and level of primary task demand, development of an adequate comparative data base requires that these properties be evaluated across a range of information processing functions and loading levels. A standard set of primary loading tasks with known demand levels on each of several processing functions therefore represents an essential component of a workload metric evaluation methodology. Given such a battery, loading levels could be manipulated in individual tasks that emphasize particular processing functions, and the capability of workload metrics to reflect these manipulations assessed. The pattern of sensitivity to the processing functions represented in the battery would provide evidence of the global versus diagnostic nature of a metric, and would specify areas of maximum sensitivity for diagnostic measures. The potential for intrusion as a function of type and level of processing demand could also be evaluated in such an approach.

The Criterion Task Set (CTS) (Shingledecker, 1984; Shingledecker et al., 1983; Shingledecker, Crabtree, & Acton, 1982) is a battery of primary tasks that was developed to provide the required capabilities for comparative evaluation of workload assessment techniques. The original or baseline version of the battery has been instrumented on a microcomputer system (Acton & Crabtree, 1985), and a number of initial applications have been completed. The following sections describe the battery and its development in more detail, and discuss its application to metric evaluation and other performance assessment areas.

### The Criterion Task Set

The baseline version of the CTS (Shingledecker, 1984) included nine primary loading tasks intended to represent a range of human information processing functions involved in performance of complex tasks. The current battery (e.g., Amell, Eggemeier, & Acton, 1987) includes some modifications to the original versions of the same nine tasks. Choice of tasks for the CTS was guided by a model/framework of the human information processing system (Shingledecker, 1984) that had been derived from theoretical positions regarding human processing functions and limits. In developing the model, emphasis was placed on multiple resources approaches (Navon & Gopher, 1979; Wickens, 1980; 1984b) to processing functions.

Figure 6 is adapted from Shingledecker (1984), and depicts the CTS processing framework. As illustrated, three major dimensions of information processing have been incorporated into the model. These include stages of processing, modalities and codes of processing, and functions of central processing. A number of individual processing functions are identified within each dimension. The stages dimension includes perceptual input, central processing, and motor output functions. Within the modality/codes dimension, visual input is distinguished from auditory input, manual output from verbal output, and verbal/symbolic processing from spatial processing. Finally, the central processing dimension differentiates working memory as the locus of central activity from three processing functions: (1) information manipulation or transformation (e.g., pattern analysis, mathematical computation); (2) reasoning activities, which center on extraction of relational rules from information (e.g., logical analysis, problem solving); and (3) planning and scheduling activities involving multi-attribute decision analyses (e.g.,

## CRITERION TASK SET PROCESSING FUNCTION/RESOURCE FRAMEWORK

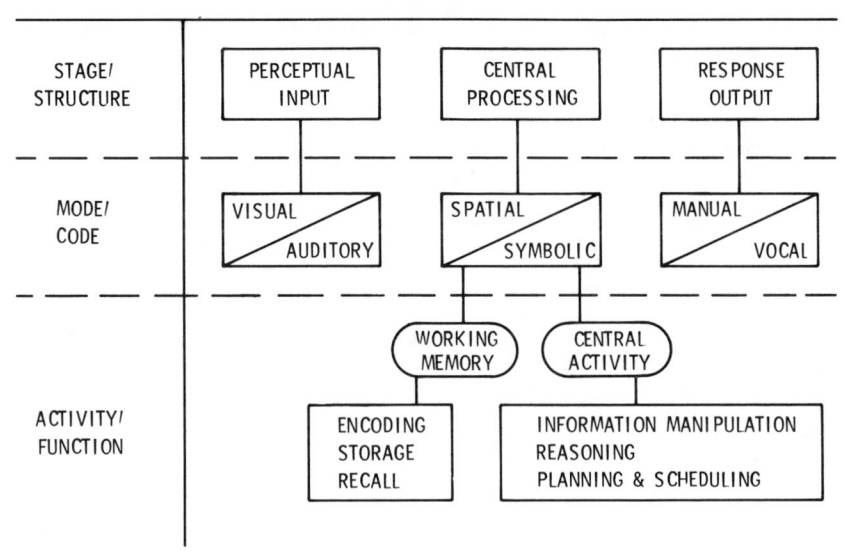

**Figure 6.** *A descriptive model/framework of human information processing functions and resources.* (Adapted from Shingledecker, 1984).

system supervision).

Each task in the battery was chosen to place its heaviest demands on one of the processing functions of the model. Table 1 is adapted from Shingledecker (1984), and lists the tasks and associated processing functions that are included in the current battery.

**Table 1**

**CTS TASKS AND ASSOCIATED PROCESSING FUNCTIONS**

| Task | Processing Function |
|---|---|
| Visual Display Monitoring | Visual Perceptual Input |
| Continuous Recognition | Working Memory Encoding/Storage |
| Memory Search | Working Memory Storage/Retrieval |
| Linguistic Processing | Symbolic Information Manipulation |
| Mathematical Processing | Symbolic Information Manipulation |
| Spatial Processing | Spatial Information Manipulation |
| Grammatical Reasoning | Reasoning |
| Unstable Tracking | Manual Response Speed/Accuracy |
| Interval Production | Manual Response Timing |

*(Adapted from Shingledecker, 1984.)*

Parametric evaluations have been conducted (Amell et al., 1987; Eggemeier & Amell, 1986; Shingledecker, 1984) with each of the tasks in the battery to determine the amount of training required to attain stable performance levels and to establish standard task loading levels. Stable performance levels were considered a prerequisite to use of the tasks to evaluate the sensitivity and intrusiveness of workload measures. Likewise, standard levels of loading were essential to comparisons between metrics, since there is reason to expect that both sensitivity and intrusiveness can vary as a function of primary task demand levels. In these evaluation experiments, loading parameters (e.g., size of the memory search set; number of displays to be monitored) appropriate for each of the tasks were manipulated. Analyses were conducted on both speed and accuracy measures to select three loading levels that were associated with reliably different levels of performance on each task that was evaluated.

Eggemeier and Amell (1986), for example, evaluated a CTS version of the probability display monitoring task (Chiles et al., 1968) that was discussed previously. An initial parametric study was conducted to examine the effects of variations in the number of displays and discriminability of signals on both reaction time and errors. The results of this study indicated that reliably different levels of performance could be obtained by manipulating the number of displays to be monitored (1, 2, or 3) within the condition of highest signal discriminability (95% bias). A subsequent validation study was conducted to verify the effectiveness of this manipulation, and to specify the amount of training that would be required to reach stable levels of performance on this variant of the task. Figure 7 is drawn from the validation experiment (Eggemeier & Amell, 1986), and illustrates mean reaction time and the mean percentage

NUMBER OF DISPLAYS TO BE MONITORED

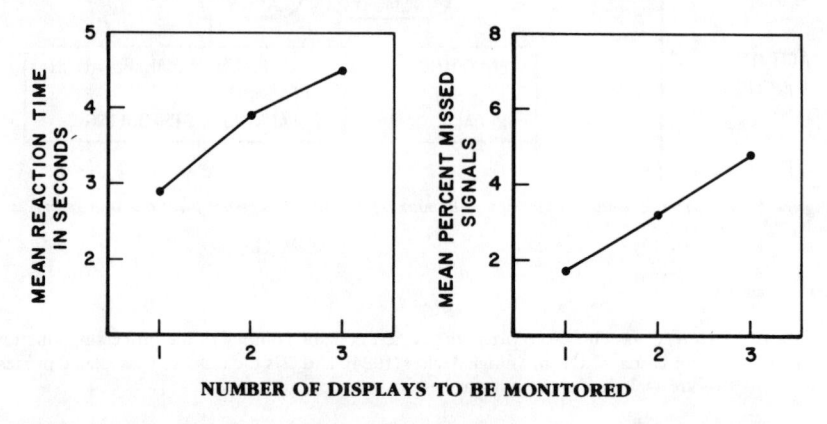

*Figure 7. Mean reaction time and mean percentage of missed signals as a function of the number of displays to be monitored.* (Redrawn from Eggemeier & Amell, 1986.)

of missed signals as a function of the number of displays to be monitored. As is clear from Figure 7, the mean reaction time to signals varied systematically with increases in the number of displays, as did the percentage of missed signals. The differences in reaction time between all three conditions were reliable, and the differences in missed signals between the lowest and highest display conditions were significant. On the basis of these results, standard loading levels of one, two, and three displays were established for the current version of the CTS display monitoring task.

Similar results (Acton et al., 1983; Amell et al., 1987; Shingledecker, 1984; Shingledecker et al., 1982) have permitted specification of three loading levels for seven of the remaining eight CTS tasks. As currently configured, the IPT does not incorporate a difficulty manipulation.

## Applications of the CTS Battery

Elements from the CTS have been employed to investigate properties of several workload measurement techniques (e.g., Eggemeier & Amell, 1987; Potter & Acton, 1985; Shingledecker et al., 1983; Wilson & Heinrich, 1987). The previously cited work on IPT sensitivity (Shingledecker et al., 1983), for example, used variants of elements from the baseline version of the battery as primary loading tasks.

Likewise, the sensitivity and intrusion analyses of the SWAT technique (Eggemeier & Amell, 1987) that were referenced above used the current versions of the CTS unstable tracking and display monitoring tasks to provide primary task loading of motor output and perceptual input functions, respectively.

Potter and Acton (1985) recently investigated the sensitivity of SWAT to demand manipulations in the CTS continuous recognition task, and the technique proved capable of reflecting demand manipulations in this task. Wilson and Heinrich (1987) used the CTS display monitoring and mathematical processing tasks to investigate the sensitivity of the SWAT technique and physiological workload measures derived from heart rate and evoked cortical response indices. SWAT proved sensitive to demand manipulations in each task, while differential patterns of sensitivity were obtained with the heart rate and cortical response measures. This type of result is consistent with the previously outlined framework which suggests that subjective techniques represent global measures of loading, while other techniques may exhibit more restricted patterns of diagnostic sensitivity. Use of the CTS in these types of evaluations provides a basis to generate systematic sensitivity and intrusion patterns for individual techniques, and can also provide the capability to build a data base comparing classes of assessment techniques on relevant properties.

Although application to workload metric evaluation research constitutes a principal use of the CTS, the battery can also be applied to assess the effects of a variety of stressors (e.g., extreme environmental conditions, drugs, fatigue) on operator performance. Evaluations of stress effects typically require a range of loading levels to properly assess potential impacts on performance, since such effects are sometimes detected only at high levels of task demand. While it is not possible to ensure that the range of task demand will be sufficient to detect interactive effects between demand levels and stressors, the multiple loading levels incorporated into CTS tasks increase the likelihood of such sensitivity.

Likewise, the variety of processing functions represented in the battery increase its potential sensitivity in such applications. It is quite possible, for instance, that a particular stressor might significantly affect one information processing function (e.g., motor output, working memory), while leaving other functions unimpaired. The choice of several tasks from the CTS to represent a range of processing functions for initial evaluation of a stressor can increase the likelihood of detecting any effects which are present, thereby increasing the sensitivity of the evaluation. Finally, the capability to detect the potential effects of any given variable on performance can also be facilitated by the stable levels of primary task performance produced by use of the training procedures that have been specified for each of the CTS tasks.

Schlegel, Gilliland, and Schlegel (1986) have reported an initial application of the CTS to evaluate the effects of sleep loss and noise stressors on performance. The noise levels employed in the experiment had no reliable effect on performance of tasks from within the battery. However, sleep loss did significantly impair response times in the central processing tasks, and also degraded both interval production capability and certain levels of tracking performance. The Schlegel et al. (1986) experiment demonstrates the use of the CTS to compare the effects of different types and levels of stressors on performance across a range of processing functions, and illustrates the pattern of stress sensitivity that can result from application of the battery as a primary task assessment device.

**SUMMARY AND CONCLUSIONS**

Sensitivity and intrusiveness are important properties that significantly affect the utility of workload assessment techniques, and current theory and data indicate that a number of variables can affect these properties in an assessment procedure. Present sensitivity and intrusiveness data support a number of general application guidelines for metrics, but a more advanced selection and application methodology will require further evaluation and refinement of these guidelines. Current theoretical frameworks which propose factors that can influence properties of assessment techniques must be tested more extensively, and more definitive comparative information regarding the sensitivity and intrusiveness of individual procedures must also be developed. Present information makes it likely that an advanced metric selection and application methodology will require the complementary use of physiological, subjective, and performance-based techniques.

In addition to programmatic work to develop more extensive comparative data on existing techniques, future research should evaluate procedures that demonstrate the potential to overcome possible deficiencies in the sensitivity or intrusiveness of present techniques. For example, the central role of primary task measurement in workload and performance assessment was discussed previously. An important disadvantage of such measures is their potential inability to reflect capacity expenditure differences below the threshold for unimpaired performance. Therefore, an important area for future research would be to examine approaches which could increase primary task sensitivity prior to actual performance breakdowns.

One such approach which has been discussed by several investigators (Eggemeier, 1980; Shingledecker, 1980b; Williges & Wierwille, 1979) involves examining changes in operator performance strategies which occur with increases in task demand. Traditional primary task measures index the adequacy of performance, but do not examine the approaches or strategies used to achieve those levels of performance. The principal rationale for invariance of primary task performance with increases in demand is that the operator compensates for such increases and is therefore able to maintain performance. If operator compensation involves modifications of the way in which the primary task is performed, these changes could be used as possible indicants of increased demand. Several types of compensatory strategies which permit maintenance of performance have, in fact, been identified (Meister, 1976; Shingledecker, 1980b; Sperandio, 1978; Welford, 1978). Development of primary task metrics which reflect such strategies could potentially increase the sensitivity of these measures, and would represent a significant augmentation of current workload assessment procedures.

A second important area for future research is the investigation of methodological issues associated with applications of the secondary task technique. Because it is designed to measure the spare processing capacity afforded by the primary task, the secondary task technique represents the most direct index of workload as defined within the capacity expenditure framework outlined above. Consequently, secondary task measures represent an important and potentially useful tool for workload assessment applications. The comparative research suggested above will provide a more extensive basis to evaluate differences in intrusiveness among different secondary tasks, but it is likely that intrusion will continue to represent a problem for some applications of the procedure. Since intrusiveness represents a potentially greater problem in operational environments than in simulation or laboratory settings, it is important that this property be evaluated across a range of applications. With relatively few exceptions (e.g., Brown, 1968; Brown, Simmonds, & Tickner, 1967; Schifflet et al., 1982; Wetherell, 1981), secondary task experiments have been conducted in the laboratory, and current intrusion data apply principally to that setting. Additional work of the type reported by Brown (1968), Brown et al., (1967), Schifflet et al., (1982), and Wetherell (1981) should be conducted to assess the intrusion potential of traditional secondary tasks in operational applications, thereby complementing the comparative laboratory research outlined above.

If intrusion does represent a problem in operational and simulation environments, the embedded task method which was discussed earlier represents one promising means of dealing with this difficulty in some situations. However, more extensive testing is required in order to evaluate the general applicability and other essential properties of the technique. Silverstein, Gomer, Crabtree, and Acton (1984) have applied embedded task scaling procedures (Shingledecker et al., 1980) to commercial aviation communications activities, but additional investigations of the applicability of these procedures to other tasks are required. These investigations should be supplemented with research to document levels of intrusiveness and sensitivity that are experienced with the embedded task technique.

Investigation of techniques (e.g., the embedded task procedure; analyses of operator strategies) that demonstrate the potential to address sensitivity and intrusiveness problems of existing metrics can build on information gained from a refined comparative data base, and should contribute to the development of a more advanced and comprehensive workload assessment methodology.

**ACKNOWLEDGEMENTS**
William H. Acton, Herbert A. Colle, Mark S. Crabtree, and Donald J. Polzella made very helpful comments on an earlier version of this manuscript.

## REFERENCES

[1] Acton, W.H., & Crabtree, M.S., *User's guide for the criterion task set,* Harry G. Armstrong Aerospace Medical Research Laboratory Technical Report, (AAMRL-TR-85-034), (Wright-Patterson Air Force Base, Ohio, 1985).

[2] Acton, W.H., Crabtree, M.S., & Shingledecker, C.A., Development of a standardized workload evaluation methodology, *Proceedings of the IEEE National Aerospace and Electronics Conference* (1983) 1086-1089.

[3] Amell, J.R., Eggemeier, F.T., & Acton, W.H., The criterion task set: an updated battery, Paper prepared for presentation at the Thirty-First Annual Meeting of the Human Factors Society (1987).

[4] Bahrick, H.P., Noble, M., & Fitts, P.M., Extra-task performance as a measure of learning in a primary task, *Journal of Experimental Psychology* (1954) *48,* 298-302.

[5] Beatty, J., Task evoked pupillary responses, processing load, and the nature of processing resources, *Psychological Bulletin* (1982) *91,* 276-292.

[6] Bell, P.A. Effects of noise and heat stress on subsidiary task performance, *Human Factors* (1978) *20,* 749-752.

[7] Brown, I.D., Some alternative methods of predicting performance among professional drivers in training, *Ergonomics* (1968) *11,* 13-21.

[8] Brown, I.D., Simmonds, D.C.V., and Tickner, A.H., Measurement of control skills, vigilance, and performance on a subsidiary task during twelve hours of car driving, *Ergonomics* (1967) *10,* 665-673.

[9] Casali, J.G., & Wierwille, W.W., A comparison of rating scale, secondary task, physiological, and primary task workload estimation techniques in a simulated flight task emphasizing communications load, *Human Factors,* (1983) *25,* 623-642.

[10] Casali, J.G., & Wierwille, W.W., On the measurement of pilot perceptual workload: a comparison of assessment techniques addressing sensitivity and intrusion issues, *Ergonomics* (1984) *27,* 1033-1050.

[11] Chiles, W.D., Alluisi, E.A., & Adams, O.S., Work schedules and performance during confinement, *Human Factors* (1968) *10,* 143-196.

[12] Cooper, G.E., & Harper, R.P., Jr., *The use of pilot rating scales in the evaluation of aircraft handling qualities,* (Report No. NASA TN-D-5153), (Moffett Field, California: Ames Research Center, National Aeronautics and Space Administration, 1969).

[13] Dornic, S., Language dominance, spare capacity, and perceived effort in bilinguals, *Ergonomics* (1980) *23,* 366-377.

[14] Eggemeier, F.T., Some current issues in workload assessment, *Proceedings of the Human Factors Society Twenty-Fourth Annual Meeting* (1980) 669-673.

[15] Eggemeier, F.T., Development of a secondary task workload assessment battery, *Proceedings of the IEEE International Conference on Cybernetics and Society* (1981) 410-414.

[16] Eggemeier, F.T., Workload metrics for system evaluation, *Proceedings of the Defense Research Group Panel VIII Workshop "Applications of System Ergonomics to Weapon System Development,"* Shrivenham, England (1984) C/5-C/20.

[17] Eggemeier, F.T., & Amell, J.R., *Visual probability monitoring: effects of display load and signal discriminability,* Paper presented at the Thirtieth Annual Meeting of the Human Factors Society, Dayton, Ohio, (1986).

[18] Eggemeier, F.T., & Amell, J.R., On the sensitivity and intrusiveness of subjective workload assessment techniques, Manuscript in preparation, Armstrong Aerospace Medical Research Laboratory, Wright-Patterson Air Force Base, Ohio (1987).

[19] Eggemeier, F.T., Crabtree, M.S., & LaPointe, P.A., The effect of delayed report on subjective ratings of mental workload, *Proceedings of the Human Factors Society Twenty-Seventh Annual Meeting* (1983) 139-143.

[20] Eggemeier, F.T., Crabtree, M.S., Zingg, J.J., Reid, G.B., & Shingledecker, C.A., Subjective workload assessment in a memory update task, *Proceedings of the Human Factors Society Twenty-Sixth Annual Meeting* (1982) 643-647.

[21] Eggemeier, F.T., & Reid, G.B., Standardization of workload metrics for system design, in D.J. Oborne (ed.), *Contemporary Ergonomics* (London, Taylor & Francis, 1986).

[22] Eggemeier, F.T., Shingledecker, C.A., & Crabtree, M.S., Workload measurement in system design and evaluation, *Proceedings of the Human Factors Society Twenty-Ninth Annual Meeting* (1985) 215-219.

[23] Eggemeier, F.T., & Stadler, M.A., Subjective workload assessment in a spatial memory task, *Proceedings of the Human Factors Society Twenty-Eighth Annual Meeting* (1984) 680-684.

[24] Hart, S.G., Subjective time estimation as an index of workload, *Proceedings of the Airline Pilots Association Symposium on Man-System Interface: Advances in Workload Study,* (Washington, D.C., 1978) 115-131.

[25] Hart, S.G., & Staveland, L.E., Development of a multidimensional workload rating scale: results of empirical and theoretical research, in P.A. Hancock and N. Meshkati (eds.), *Human Mental Workload* (Amsterdam, North Holland Publishers, in press).

[26] Isreal, J.B., Chesney, G.L., Wickens, C.D., & Donchin, E., P 300 and tracking difficulty: Evidence for multiple resources in dual-task performance, *Psychophysiology* (1980) *17,* 259-273.

[27] Isreal, J.B., Wickens, C.D., Chesney, G.L., & Donchin, E., The event-related brain potential as an index of display-monitoring workload, *Human Factors* (1980) *22,* 211-244.

[28] Jex, H.R., McDonnell, J.D., & Phatek, A.V., A critical tracking task for man-machine research related to operator's effective delay time, *Proceedings of the Second Annual NASA—University Conference on Manual Control,* (Report No. NASA-SP-128), (Massachusetts Institute of Technology, 1966).

[29] Johannsen, G., Moray, N., Pew, R., Rasmussen, J., Sanders, A., & Wickens, C., Final report of the experimental psychology group, in N. Moray (ed.), *Mental Workload: Its Theory and Measurement* (New York, Plenum Press, 1979).

[30] Kelly, C.R., & Wargo, M.J., Cross-adaptive operator loading tasks, *Human Factors* (1967) *9,* 395-404.

[31] Knowles, W.B., Operator loading tasks, *Human Factors* (1963) *5,* 151-161.

[32] Meister, D., *Behavioral Foundations of System Development* (New York, Wiley, 1976).

[33] Michon, J.A., Tapping regularity as a measure of perceptual motor load, *Ergonomics* (1966) *9,* 401-412.

[34] Navon, D., & Gopher, D., On the economy of the human processing system, *Psychological Review* (1979) *86,* 214-255.

[35] Notestine, J., Subjective workload assessment in a probability monitoring task and the effect of delayed ratings, *Proceedings of the Human Factors Society Twenty-Eighth Annual Meeting* (1984) 685-689.

[36] O'Donnell, R.D., The U.S. Air Force neurophysiological workload test battery: concept and validation, *Proceedings of the AGARD (AMP) Symposium on Sustained Intensive Air Operations: Physiological and Performance Aspects,* (AGARD-CP-338), (November, 1983).

[37] O'Donnell, R.D., & Eggemeier, F.T., Workload assessment methodology, in K. Boff, L. Kaufman, & J. Thomas (eds.), *Handbook of Perception and Human Performance, Vol. II: Cognitive Processes and Performance,* (New York, John Wiley & Sons, Inc., 1986).

[38] Ogden, G.D., Levine, J.M., & Eisner, E.J., Measurement of workload by secondary tasks, *Human Factors* (1979) *21*, 529-548.

[39] Potter, S.S., & Acton, W.H., Relative contributions of SWAT dimensions to overall subjective workload ratings, *Proceedings of the Third Symposium on Aviation Psychology*, (Columbus, Ohio, Ohio State University, 1985) 231-238.

[40] Reid, G.B., The systematic development of a subjective measure of workload, in I.D. Brown, R. Goldsmith, K. Coombes, & M.A. Sinclair (eds.), *Ergonomics Internationl 85*, (London, Taylor & Francis, 1985).

[41] Reid, G.B., Shingledecker, C.A., & Eggemeier, F.T., Application of conjoint measurement to workload scale development, *Proceedings of the Human Factors Society Twenty-Fifth Annual Meeting* (1981) 522-526.

[42] Rolfe, J.M., The secondary task as a measure of mental load, in W.T. Singleton, J.G. Fox, and D. Whitfield (eds.), *Measurement of Man at Work*, (London, Taylor & Francis, 1971).

[43] Schifflet, S.G., Linton, P.M., & Spicuzza, R.J., Evaluation of a pilot workload assessment device to test alternative display formats and control handling qualities, *Proceedings of the AIAA Workshop on Flight Testing to Identify Pilot Workload and Pilot Dynamics* (1982) 222-233.

[44] Schlegel, R.E., Gilliland, K., & Schlegel, B., Development of the criterion task set performance data base, *Proceedings of the Thirtieth Annual Meeting of the Human Factors Society* (1986) 58-62.

[45] Shingledecker, C.A., Enhancing operator acceptance and noninterference in secondary task measures of workload, *Proceedings of the Twenty-Fourth Annual Meeting of the Human Factors Society* (1980a) 674-677.

[46] Shingledecker, C.A., *Operator strategy: a neglected variable in workload assessment*, Paper presented at the Eighty-Eighth Annual Meeting of the American Psychological Association (1980b).

[47] Shingledecker, C.A., Behavioral and subjective workload metrics for operational environments, *Proceedings of the AGARD (AMP) Symposium on Sustained Intensive Air Operations: Physiological and Performance Aspects*, (AGARD-CP-338), (November, 1983), 6/1-6/10.

[48] Shingledecker, C.A., *A task battery for applied human performance assessment research*, Air Force Aerospace Medical Research Laboratory Technical Report, (Report No. AFAMRL-TR-84-071), (Wright-Patterson Air Force Base, Ohio, November, 1984).

[49] Shingledecker, C.A., Acton, W.H., & Crabtree, M.S., *Development and application of a criterion task set for workload metric evaluation*, (Paper No. 831419), (Warrendale, Pennsylvania, Society of Automotive Engineers, SAE Technical Paper Series, October, 1983).

[50] Shingledecker, C.A., & Crabtree, M.S., *Subsidiary radio communications tasks for workload assessment in R&D simulations: II. Task sensitivity evaluation*, Air Force Aerospace Medical Research Laboratory Technical Report, (Report No. AFAMRL-TR-82-57), (Wright-Patterson Air Force Base, Ohio, 1982).

[51] Shingledecker, C.A., Crabtree, M.S., & Acton, W.H., Standardized tests for the evaluation and classification of workload metrics, *Proceedings of the Human Factors Society Twenty-Sixth Annual Meeting* (1982) 648-651.

[52] Shingledecker, C.A., Crabtree, M.S., Simons, J.C., Courtright, J.F., & O'Donnell, R.D., *Subsidiary radio communications tasks for workload assessment in R&D simulations: I. Task development and workload scaling*, Air Force Aerospace Medical Research Laboratory Technical Report, (Report No. AFAMRL-TR-80-126), (Wright-Patterson Air Force Base, Ohio, 1980).

[53] Silverstein, L.D., Gomer, F.E., Crabtree, M.S., & Acton, W.H. *A comparison of analytic and subjective techniques for estimating communications related workload during commercial transport flight operations*, Report prepared under Contract No. NAS2-11562, (Dayton, Ohio, General Physics Corporation, 1984).

[54] Sperandio, J.C. The regulation of working methods as a function of workload among air traffic controllers, *Ergonomics* (1978) *21*, 195-202.

[55] Stadler, M.A., & Eggemeier, F.T., Codes of processing and timesharing performance, unpublished manuscript, Wright State University, Dayton, Ohio (1985).

[56] Sternberg, S., High-speed scanning in human memory, *Science* (1966) *153*, 652-654.

[57] Vidulich, M.A. & Tsang, P.S., Assessing subjective workload assessment: a comparison of SWAT and the NASA-bipolar methods. *Proceedings of the Human Factors Society Twenty-Ninth Annual Meeting* (1985) 71-75.

[58] Welford, A.T., Mental work-load as a function of demand, capacity, strategy, and skill, *Ergonomics* (1978) *21*, 151-167.

[59] Wetherell, A. The efficacy of some auditory-vocal subsidiary tasks as measures of the mental load of male and female drivers, *Ergonomics* (1981) *24*, 197-214.

[60] Wickens, C.D., Measures of workload, stress, and secondary tasks, in N. Moray (ed.), *Mental Workload: Its Theory and Measurement*, (New York, Plenum Press, 1979).

[61] Wickens, C.D., The structure of attentional resources., in R. Nickerson (ed.), *Attention and Performance VIII*, (Hillsdale, New Jersey, Erlbaum Press, 1980).

[62] Wickens, C.D., *Engineering Psychology and Human Performance*, (Columbus, Ohio, Charles E. Merrill Publishing Company, 1984a).

[63] Wickens, C.D., Processing resources in attention, in R. Parasuraman and R. Davies (eds.), *Varieties of Attention*, (New York, Academic Press, 1984b).

[64] Wickens, C.D., & Derrick, W., Workload measurement and multiple resources, *Proceedings of the IEEE Conference on Cybernetics and Society* (1981) 600-603.

[65] Wickens, C.D., & Kessel, C., The processing resource demands of failure detection in dynamic systems, *Journal of Experimental Psychology: Human Perception and Performance* (1980) *6*, 564-577.

[66] Wickens, C.D., Mountford, S.J., & Schreiner, W., Multiple resources, task-hemispheric integrity, and individual differences in timesharing, *Human Factors* (1981) *23*, 211-229.

[67] Wierwille, W.W., & Casali, J.G., A validated scale for global mental workload measurement applications, *Proceedings of the Human Factors Society Twenty-Seventh Annual Meeting* (1983a) 129-133.

[68] Wierwille, W.W., & Casali, J.G., *The sensitivity and intrusion of mental workload estimation techniques in piloting tasks*, (Report No. 8309), (Blacksburg, Virginia, Virginia Polytechnic Institute and State University, Vehicle Simulation Laboratory, Department of Industrial Engineering and Operations Research, September, 1983b).

[69] Wierwille, W.W., & Connor, S.A., Evaluation of 20 workload measures using a psychomotor task in a moving-base aircraft simulator, *Human Factors* (1983) *25*, 1-16.

[70] Wierwille, W.W., Rahimi, M., & Casali, J.G., Evaluation of 16 measures of mental workload using a simulated flight task emphasizing mediational activity, *Human Factors* (1985) *27*, 489-502.

[71] Wierwille, W.W., & Williges, R., *Survey and analysis of operator workload assessment techniques*, (Report No. 2-78-101), (Blacksburg, Virginia, Systemetrics Corporation, September, 1978).

[72] Wierwille, W.W., & Williges, B.H., *An annotated bibliography of operator mental workload assessment*, (Report No. SY-27R-80), (Patuxent River, Maryland, Naval Air Test Center, March, 1980).

[73] Williges, R.C. & Wierwille, W.W. Behavioral measures of aircrew mental workload, *Human Factors* (1979) *21*, 549-574.

[74] Wilson, G., & Heinrich, T., Steady-state evoked responses used to measure task difficulty in three performance tasks, Technical report in preparation, (Wright-Patterson Air Force Base, Ohio, Armstrong Aerospace Medical Research Laboratory, 1987).

# On Scaling Performance Operating Characteristics: Caveat Emptor

BARRY H. KANTOWITZ[1] and MARYSUE WELDON, *Purdue University, West Lafayette, Indiana*

*Problems associated with scaling and normalizing empirical performance operating characteristics (POCs) are examined. Normalization methods proposed by Wickens (1980) and by Mountford and North (1980) are critically evaluated. Computer simulations are used to generate raw-score and normalized POCs. The interpretation of transformed empirical POCs (Wickens, Mountford, and Schreiner, 1981) is shown to contain inconsistencies. The normalization techniques reviewed fail to resolve POC scaling problems. Caution must be exercised when interpreting transformed POCs.*

The *performance operating characteristic*, or POC, proposed by Norman and Bobrow (1975) has become a popular technique for presenting and analyzing data from dual-task experiments. A POC function plots performance on Task 1 on the ordinate against performance on Task 2 on the abscissa and portrays the trade-off as hypothetical resources are transferred from one task to the other task. As a description of data the POC is theoretically neutral and has no greater implications than any other method of plotting results. However, most authors use POC functions to make inferences about underlying resources that control the locus of dual-task interaction within the POC space (Kantowitz and Knight, 1976). A complete description of the various theories that have been so invoked along with some of the logical difficulties associated with these models of attention and capacity can be found in Kantowitz (1985); here, discussion is limited to a more modest goal of examining problems of scaling POC axes.

Since most POC functions involve two different tasks, different units are plotted on the POC axes when raw-score (i.e., untransformed) data are presented. For example, the abscissa might be scaled in milliseconds for a choice-reaction task, whereas the ordinate might be scored as percentage correct in a memory task. It is obvious that these units are not directly equivalent—reaction time has a lower bound but no upper bound, whereas percentage correct has both a lower and an upper bound—so that there is no direct method for mapping units of reaction time into units of percentage correct. Therefore, researchers, most notably Wickens (1980) and his associates, have proposed scaling transformations to overcome this difficulty, thus increasing the utility of POC functions. The present paper evaluates these proposed scaling operations. In order to ac-

[1] Requests for reprints should be sent to Barry H. Kantowitz, Purdue University, Department of Psychological Sciences, West Lafayette, IN 47907.

complish this evaluation we first review some of the theoretical issues relevant to the generation of POC functions. We then examine the scaling transformations proposed by Wickens (1980) and by Mountford and North (1980) by using computer simulations to generate both raw-score and transformed POC functions.

## THE THEORETICAL GENESIS OF A POC FUNCTION

The actual shape of any POC function is determined by the trade-off between resources or capacity demanded by the two tasks plotted on the function. It is crucial to realize that a direct relationship between capacity and task performance cannot be observed. Capacity is a theoretical construct (Kantowitz, 1985), and any relationship between capacity and performance must be inferred rather than observed. The hypothetical relationship between capacity and behavior has been termed the performance-resource function (Norman and Bobrow, 1975). Several assumptions are required in order to generate such hypothetical functions:

(1) Performance is a monotonically increasing function of the amount of capacity allocated to a process. This axiom was called the *potency principle* by Kantowitz and Knight (1978). This axiom seems to be so obvious that it was taken for granted as a pretheoretical assumption in many older models of attention. Nevertheless, this does not guarantee that the axiom always holds.
(2) The total amount of available capacity is finite and limited. This assumption, when combined with the potency principle, implies that once a process consumes all available capacity, performance will no longer improve.

The preceding two assumptions are necessary before any performance-resource function can be generated. However, in order to generate POC functions from performance-resource functions even more assumptions are required:

(3) The sum of the capacities consumed by each of the two tasks equals total capacity. This was termed the *principle of complimentarity* by Norman and Bobrow (1975). It implies that there is no overhead cost for performing more than one task simultaneously if single-task measures are used as the POC endpoints.
(4) There is only one pool of capacity that is available to serve both tasks. This assumption has been questioned by recent models that postulate multiple sources of capacity (Navon and Gopher, 1979). Therefore, in some circumstances it may be necessary to relax this assumption by postulating that there is at least one common pool of capacity required by both tasks. If there is no common pool of capacity required, then performance of one task will be independent of performance on the other task.

### Three Families of Performance-Resource Functions

Because the shape of a performance-resource function cannot be observed, we have selected three hypothetical shapes to illustrate our arguments (Figure 1). Units of capacity and performance are arbitrary. Linear performance-resource functions (Figure 1a) offer the simplest relationship between performance and capacity. We have used three linear functions: $P = 2R$, $P = R$, and $P = 0.75R$, where P represents performance and R represents capacity. Negatively accelerated performance-resource functions (Figure 1b) are of the form $P = R^{.75}$, and $P = R^{.5}$. Performance still improves as more resources are allocated, but the rate of improvement decreases. Finally, we also use positively accelerated performance-resource functions (Figure 1c) of the form $P = R^{1.3}$ and $P = R^{1.2}$. Although it is unlikely that the rate of improvement increases as more capacity is allocated, these functions will prove useful later in the paper despite their lack of intuitive validity, much as the notion of supercapacity (Townsend, 1974) aids mathematical analysis of reaction time data.

### Slope and Task Efficiency

In general, the slope of a performance-re-

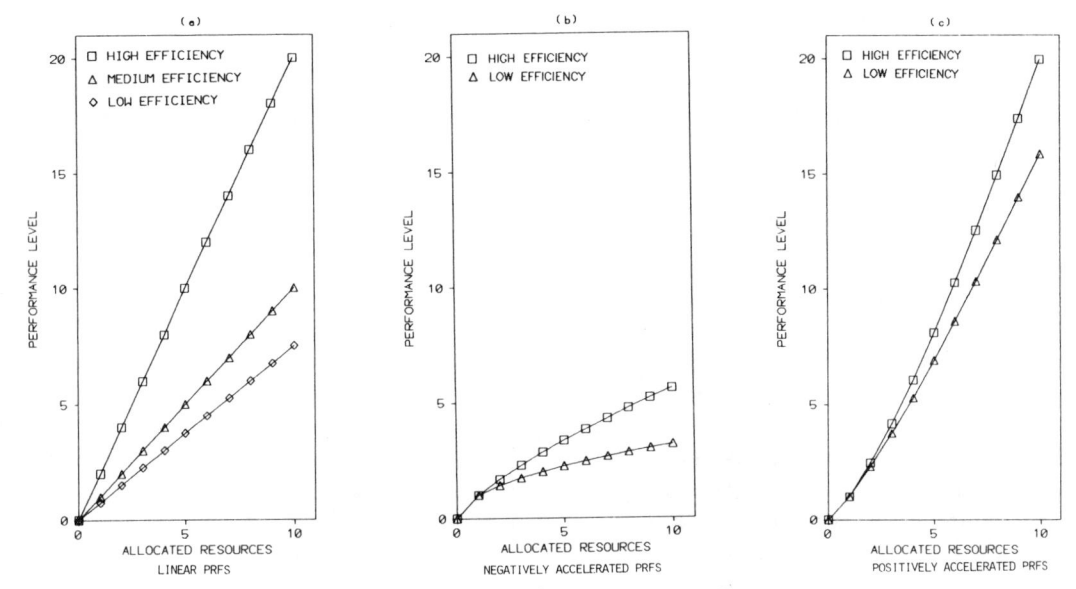

Figure 1. *Hypothetical performance resource functions.*

source function represents the efficiency of resource utilization. Greater efficiency implies greater improvement in task performance (per unit resource) as more units of resources are allocated to the task. Following Navon and Gopher (1979), we distinguish between average efficiency and marginal efficiency. Your average tax rate is simply your total income tax divided by your total income. Your marginal tax rate is the tax paid on an additional dollar of earned income and can be found in a tax table. The marginal tax rate in the United States is higher than the average tax rate. Similarly, average efficiency is the mean change in performance per unit of resources taken over the entire resource domain. Marginal efficiency is the local efficiency; that is, the rate of change in performance for a small increment (or decrement) about the current level of resource allocation.

When the performance-resource function is linear, marginal efficiency is constant over the entire resource domain so that marginal and average efficiencies are equal. Thus, the slope of the performance-resource function can be viewed as an index of both marginal and average efficiency. A greater slope implies a more efficient utilization of resources. Therefore, of the family of linear performance-resource functions plotted in Figure 1a, the most efficient process ($P = 2R$) is shown by the steepest function and the least efficient process ($P = 0.75R$) by the lowest function.

For nonlinear performance-resource functions, one must carefully distinguish between average and marginal efficiency. The average efficiency can be computed as the expected value of marginal efficiency, or the average rate of change of the function, which equals $1/R[f(R) - f(0)]$. The marginal efficiency is the derivative of the function at the point of interest. For the negatively accelerated functions of Figure 1b, marginal efficiency decreases with increasing resource allocation whereas marginal efficiency increases for the positively accelerated functions of Figure 1c.

Whereas the exponent is an index of the relative efficiency of nonlinear functions, it cannot be interpreted directly as an average efficiency as was the case for the linear functions.

## PERFORMANCE OPERATING CHARACTERISTICS

The hypothetical performance-resource functions of Figure 1 were used to generate raw-score POCs illustrated in Figure 2. This was accomplished by selecting appropriate pairs of performance-resource functions and using the assumptions listed in the preceding section to specify the relations between capacity and performance for dual-task situations. Central capacity model interpretations of these POCs are discussed below.

### Interpretation of Raw-Score POCs

*Intercept.* The endpoints of the POC represent performance levels when all resources are allocated to the task represented on that axis. Therefore, the endpoints are equivalent to single-task performance for the respective tasks. This interpretation assumes that there are no concurrence costs or benefits in dual-task conditions.

*Shape.* A *linear* POC is generated by two linear performance resource functions. The linear function in Figure 2a is generated from two linear performance functions with the same parameters, $P = R$.

When a POC is *concave* to the origin, at least one of the underlying performance resource functions is negatively accelerated, such that $P = R^b$, where $0 < b < 1$. The concave function in Figure 2a is generated from two negatively accelerated performance-resource functions with the same parameters, $P = R^{.75}$. As b approaches zero for either performance-resource function, the POC becomes more concave.

When a POC is *convex* to the origin, at least one of the underlying performance-resource

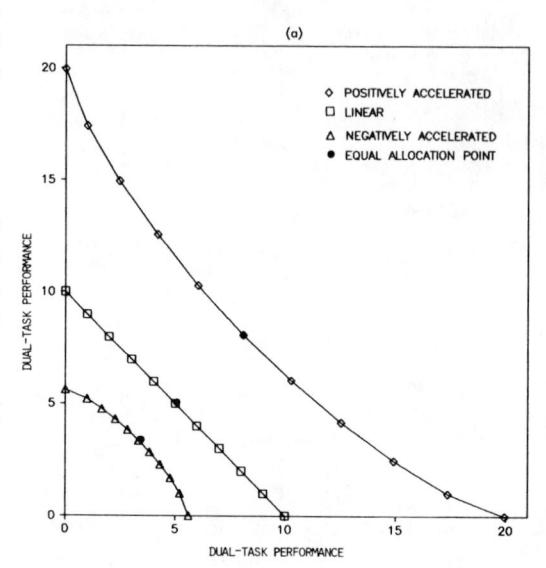

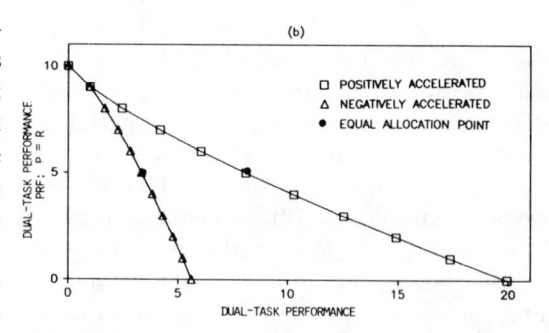

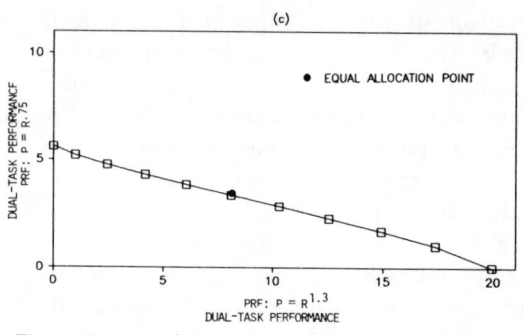

Figure 2. *Hypothetical raw-score performance operating characteristics. Component PRFs are noted on the axes.*

functions is positively accelerated, such that $P = R^b$, where $b > 1$. The convex function in Figure 2a is generated from two positively accelerated functions with the same parameters, $P = R^{1.2}$. As b approaches infinity for either performance-resource function, the POC will become more convex. Empirical convex POCs are extremely rare.

Notice that if the component performance-resource functions are identical, the POC is symmetric. Other combinations of performance-resource functions result in various distortions, as illustrated in Figures 2b and 2c. The degree of distortion will change relative to the parameters of the component performance-resource functions, but the general forms of the POCs generated by any two basic performance-resource functions will remain the same. Figures 3a through 3c illustrate this relationship.

*Point of Equal Allocation*

The point of equal allocation (PEA) on a POC reflects dual-task performance when each task receives 50% of the resources. When the underlying performance-resource functions are identical functions, the point of equal allocation falls on a 45-deg vector from the origin. This is true for both linear and nonlinear POCs, as illustrated in Figure 2a. However, if the underlying performance-resource functions are not identical, the POCs will be asymmetric and the point of equal allocation will not lie on the 45-deg vector, as illustrated in Figures 2b and 2c. In light of the restrictions implicit in symmetric POCs, the point of equal allocation will probably rarely fall on the 45-deg vector of an empirically derived POC. This point is important for the upcoming discussion of the transformation proposed by Wickens, Mountford, and Schreiner (1981), where it is stated incorrectly that normalization equates the point of equal allocation for all POCs.

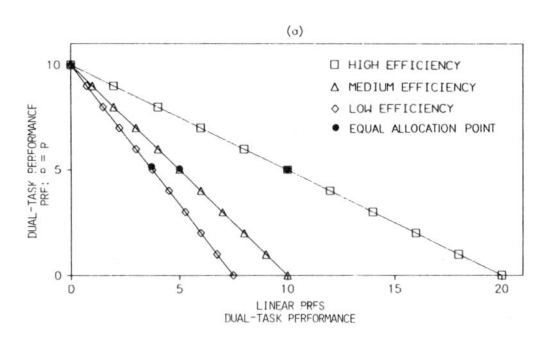

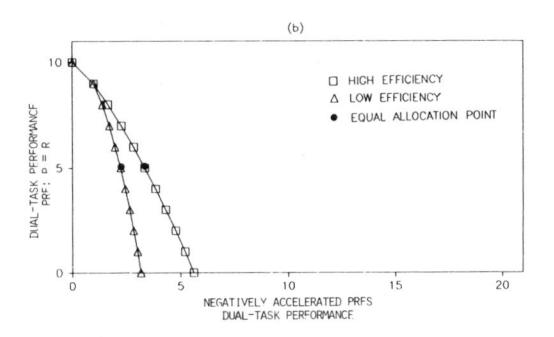

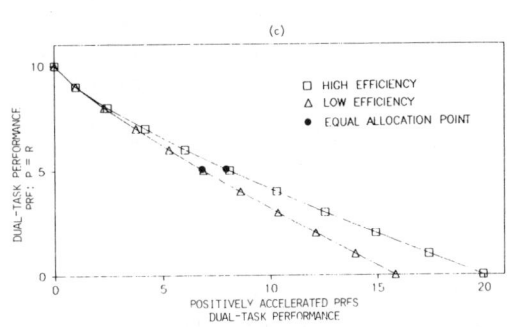

Figure 3. *Families of hypothetical raw-score performance operating characteristics. The component PRFs are noted on the graphs.*

*POC Families and Task Efficiency*

The effect of task efficiency in dual-task conditions can be described by a family of POCs. As task efficiency decreases, the intercept of the POC on the axis representing that task will decrease. These relationships are illustrated in Figures 3a through 3c, where the hypothetical performance-resource functions from the previous section are plotted on the x-axis, and the linear function P = R is plotted on the y-axis. These will be called the hypothetical raw-score POCs. The task represented on the x-axis varies in efficiency. Notice that the POCs that lie on the outside of the family represent the more efficient versions of Task X.

*Objective Substitution Rate and Relative Efficiency*

The slope of the POC provides information about the degree to which performance on one task improves as resources are withdrawn from the other task. Navon and Gopher (1979) refer to this performance shift as the "objective substitution rate" (OSR). The OSR can be defined as the negative of the slope of the POC at a given point. Mathematically, this is the ratio of the partial derivatives of the performance-resource functions with respect to the amount of resources invested in each task. Hence, when resources are withdrawn from Task Y, the performance improvement on Task X is defined as:

$$\text{OSR} = \frac{-\Delta Py}{\Delta Px} = \frac{\delta Py/\delta Ry}{\delta Px/\delta Rx} \quad (1)$$

where:

Py = performance on Task Y
Px = performance on Task X
Ry = resources allocated to Task Y
Rx = resources allocated to Task X
Ry + Rx = 10 (all resources are utilized)

(Navon and Gopher, 1979). For consistency, the OSR will always be expressed as the improvement in Task X as a function of the release of resources from Task Y.

The OSR describes the relative efficiency of the two tasks, or the ratio of marginal increase in performance on one task as a function of the marginal decrease in performance on the other task. When defined as above, the OSR is inversely related to the demand of Task X relative to Task Y; the more Task X demands with respect to Task Y, the larger the negative slope of the POC. Thus, smaller absolute values of the OSRs are associated with more efficient tasks on the x-axis. Table 1 presents the OSRs for the POCs in Figure 3a.

Notice that for nonlinear POCs (e.g., Figures 3b and 3c), the OSR will be a function of the instantaneous change in resource allocation and cannot be expressed as only one number. However, the less Task X demands with respect to Task Y, the smaller the absolute value of the OSR, and the more efficient is Task X. (Note that for the nonlinear functions in Figure 3, this relationship holds only when more than one unit of resources is allocated to Task X.)

## TRANSFORMATION OF POCS

Wickens (1980) attempted to overcome POC scaling problems by transforming dual-

TABLE 1

Objective Substitution Rates (OSR) for Linear Functions in Figure 3a

| Task × Efficiency | f(Rx)* | P | $-\Delta Py/\Delta Px$ = OSR |
|---|---|---|---|
| Low | Px = (0.75)Rx | 0.75 | −1/0.75 = −1.33 |
| Medium | Px = (1)Rx | 1.00 | −1/1.00 = −1.00 |
| High | Px = (2)Rx | 2.00 | −1/2.00 = −0.50 |

*Note.* Px = Performance level on Task X. Rx = Resources allocated to Task X. Computation of OSR is based on withdrawal of 1 unit of resources from Task Y.
* Performance resource function for Task X. The performance resource function for Task Y is Py = (1)Ry for all computations.

task data into decrement scores. This transformation is similar to the z-score transformation. He defined a decrement score as:

$$\text{decrement} = \frac{\overline{X}_s - \overline{X}_d}{s} \quad (2)$$

where:

$\overline{X}_s$ = average single-task performance
$\overline{X}_d$ = average dual-task performance
$s$ = within-trial standard deviation

Although initially this may appear to be a reasonable strategy for equalizing dual-task performance scales, closer inspection of the POCs reveals that the transformation is inappropriate.

The shortcomings of this transformation are discussed in this section. This critique is developed in the following manner. First, the hypothetical "raw-score" POCs from the preceding section are transformed. Next, the interpretations of these transformed hypothetical POCs are compared to those of the original raw-score hypothetical POCs. Then, the original (Wickens, 1980) interpretation of the transformed POC space is presented. Finally, the Wickens et al. (1981) experiment is summarized, the transformed empirical POCs are presented, and the interpretation is critiqued.

*Transforming Families of Hypothetical POCs*

The hypothetical raw-score POCs from Figure 3 were normalized using the transformation in Equation 2. Dual-task decrement scores were computed for each level of each task. Standard deviations for each task were set equal to the square root of 10% of the single-task level of performance on that task. These decrement scores were then used to plot the "normalized" POCs in Figure 4. Note that in this figure, the POCs are plotted in quadrant III in accordance with standard engineering graphics; later graphs are plotted in the format originally used by Wickens et

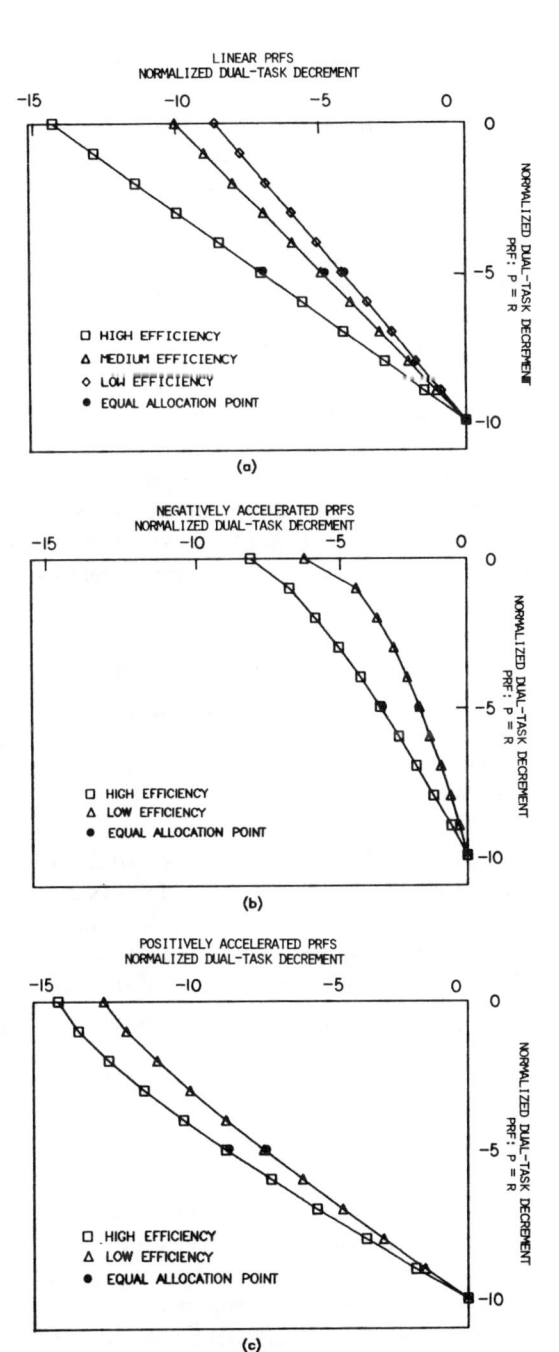

Figure 4. *Families of hypothetical POCs transformed with Wickens's (1980) procedure and plotted in quadrant III. The component PRFs are noted on the graphs.*

al. (1981). The effects of the transformation on the POCs are discussed below.

*Objective Substitution Rate.* The numerical values of the objective substitution rates of the normalized POCs are not the same as those of the raw-score POCs. One can see that the transformation expands the scale of the POCs. The proportion by which each axis expands differs among the shapes *and* among the exemplars of each shape, ranging from a 0% increase for the high-efficiency linear task (P = 2R) to a 122% increase for the low-efficiency negatively accelerated task (P = $R^{.5}$). Of course, these particular proportions are obtained because the divisor in the transformation was set to 10% of the hypothetical single-task performance level. Whatever the divisor, however, the transformation leads to proportionately different estimates of the relative efficiency of tasks in any task pair.

*Interpretation of the Transformed POC Space*

Figure 5 illustrates the original interpretation (Wickens, 1980; Wickens et al., 1981) of the transformed POC space, in which the claim was made that the transformed decrement scores equate the scaling factors and intercepts along both axes. A decrement equal to zero represents single-task performance and defines the endpoint of the axis. Scores close to the origin represent large decrements in performance.

To plot the POC for any pair of tasks, the decrement scores were computed, a single point representing the normalized dual-task performance level was plotted, then the remainder of the POC was extrapolated to the single-task performance level endpoints. Shifts of the POC along the positive diagonal toward the upper-right corner represent improved time-sharing efficiency. Maximum possible dual-task performance will occur when there is no interference between tasks; this is represented by the point "P." According to a multiple-resources model

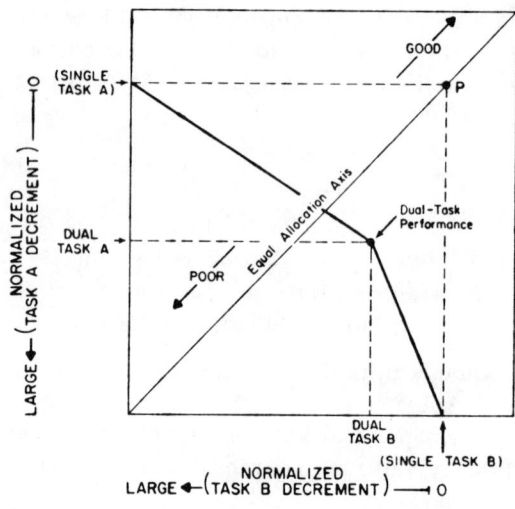

Figure 5. *Wickens's hypothetical representation of the normalized POC space. From Wickens et al. (1981).*

(Wickens, 1980), this point represents perfect parallel processing of two tasks using independent pools of resources. In Norman and Bobrow's framework, this point would be interpreted as indicating that both tasks are operating in data-limited portions of their performance-resource functions.

Shifts of the POC along the positive diagonal toward the origin represent decreased time-sharing efficiency. This shift is interpreted as an indication that the two tasks are competing for a common pool of resources and cannot be performed in parallel (Wickens et al., 1981).

Shifts along the negative diagonal are interpreted as representing changes in resource allocation policy. A shift toward one axis indicates that more resources are allocated toward that task. The further claim is made that the normalization of the data transforms all POCs such that an "equal allocation axis" can be defined. Purportedly, the 45-deg vector from the origin represents equal allocation of resources between the two tasks for all tasks, regardless of the shapes of their re-

TABLE 2

Contrasts of Processing Requirements between Task Groupings

| | | |
|---|---|---|
| 1. Input Modality: | visual<br>⌐———————⌐<br>T  C  L | auditory<br>⌐—⌐<br>A |
| 2. Central Processing: | spatial<br>⌐——⌐<br>T  L | verbal<br>⌐——⌐<br>C  A |
| 3. Response: | response execution<br>analog<br>⌐⌐<br>T | response selection<br>discrete<br>⌐————⌐<br>C  L  A |
| 4. Pacing: | forced<br>⌐——⌐<br>T  A | self<br>⌐——⌐<br>C  L |

Note. From Wickens et al. (1981). T = Tracking; C = Classification; L = Line Judgment; A = Auditory Task.

spective performance-resource functions. We will return to a discussion of these interpretations of the normalized POC after briefly presenting the experiment.

## AN EMPIRICAL EXAMPLE

Wickens et al. (1981) attempted to present evidence supporting a multiple-capacity model of attention. They proposed three separate processing capacities: (1) modality of input and output, (2) stages of processing (encoding and central processing versus response), and (3) code of central processing (spatial versus verbal). In order to demonstrate these separate pools of resources, four tasks were selected that were defined as varying in the degree to which they competed for the resources. Wickens et al. then measured single-task performance and dual-task performance for pairwise combinations of the tasks. The authors predicted that tasks competing for the same resources should show larger dual-task decrements than those using different resources.

The four tasks were: (1) manual tracking (T); (2) auditory short-term memory task (A), in which subjects judged whether auditorily presented letters were in alphabetical order;

TABLE 3

Performance Measures on Wickens et al.'s (1981) Tasks

| Task | Single | With Tracking | With Classification | With Line Judgment | With Auditory |
|---|---|---|---|---|---|
| Tracking (RMS error) | 0.306 | | 0.654 | 0.428 | 0.488 | 0.403 |
| Classification (Number correct) | 152.2 | 131.8 | | 80.6 | 72.4 | 93.2 |
| Line Judgment (Number correct) | 100.7 | 86.6 | 56.5 | | 49.2 | 69.3 |
| Auditory (Correct latency) (in ms) | 1020 | 1014 | 1352 | 1297 | — |

Note. From Wickens et al. (1981).

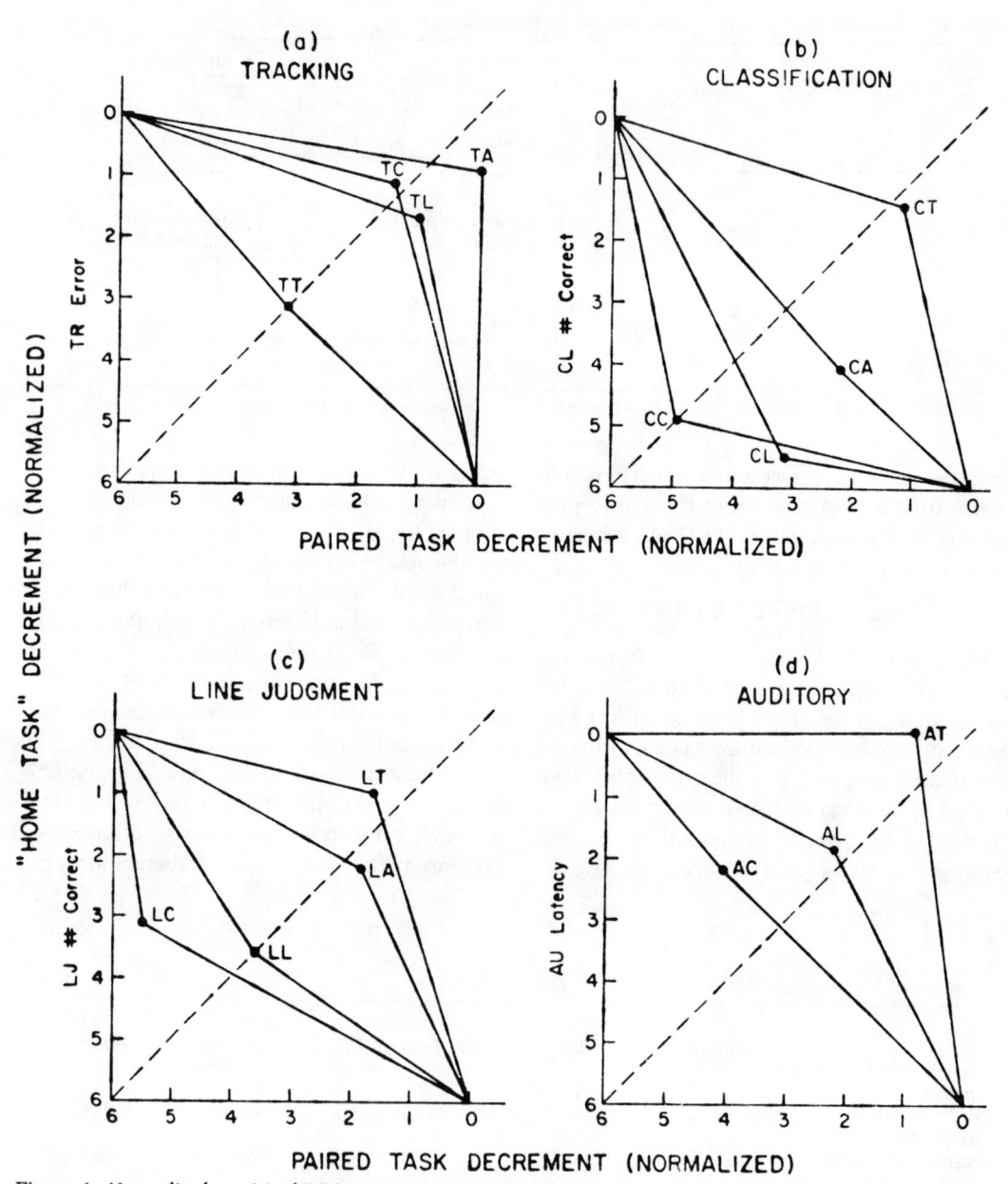

Figure 6. *Normalized empirical POCs representing dual-task performance on the four tasks in Wickens et al.'s experiment. From Wickens et al. (1981).*

(3) digit classification (C), in which subjects made judgments about the values of visually presented digits; and (4) visual line judgment (L). The proposed resource demands of these tasks are illustrated in Table 2.

Subjects performed all tasks in single-task and dual-task conditions. All pairwise combinations of tasks were performed, except for the pairing of the auditory task with itself. Subjects participated in three one-hour sessions on consecutive days, and all tasks were performed with both the left and right hands each day. The performance measures, averaged across Days 2 and 3, are displayed in Table 3. Wickens et al. (1981) transformed these data into decrement scores.

The normalized decrement POCs from the Wickens et al. experiment are plotted in Figure 6. The ordinate of each graph represents performance on the designated "home task." The abscissa represents the task designated by the letter code at the point on the POC. Because each task is paired with all other tasks in each graph, the graphs are redundant except for the POCs that pair each task with itself.

*Critique of the Interpretation of the Normalized POC Space Single-Point POCs*

It is dangerous to extrapolate a POC from one point because the POC should reflect trade-offs in performance as a function of changes in the allocation of resources between the two tasks. It may be misleading to estimate the shape of the POC from only one condition of resource allocation (e.g., 50/50). First, one cannot identify the asymptotic regions of the POC and thus cannot assess resource independence in the performance-resource functions. This point is illustrated in Figure 7a, using POCs from Figure 6. Dotted lines represent alternative shapes that the POCs may assume; these would not be detected with single-point curves. Secondly, many models of resource allocation allow for POCs whose endpoints undershoot or overshoot the single-task level of performance (see Navon and Gopher, 1979, for interpretations). Under these models, single-point POCs would be uninterpretable because they would not allow one to detect the trends that indicate this behavior in the POC. This point is illustrated in Figure 7b using POCs from Figure 6. The dotted lines represent alternative POCs in which dual-task performance undershoots or overshoots single-task performance levels.

Note that the problems with single-point POCs are not due to the transformation technique. These criticisms hold for all single-point POCs, regardless of the scaling procedures employed.

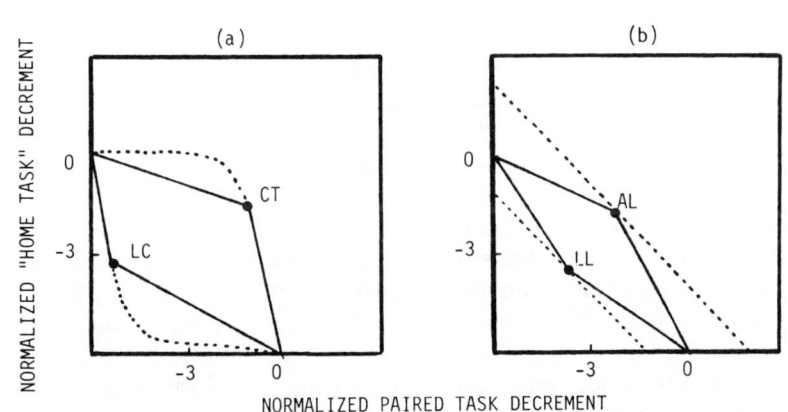

Figure 7. *Alternative extrapolations of single-point POCs.*

*Inferring the Shapes of Component Performance-Resource Functions*

Recall that the general shapes of the component performance-resource functions determine the general shape of a POC; the shape of the POC is not independent of the shape of the theoretical performance-resource functions. Therefore, the shape of a POC constrains the possible shapes the component performance-resource functions may assume. Through a series of deductions, it should be possible to determine the general shapes of the performance-resource functions underlying the Wickens et al. POCs, or at least to determine whether the POCs produce consistent inferences about the shapes of the performance-resource functions.

Because these empirical POCs are transformed, these inferences must be based on the shapes of *transformed* POCs. Therefore, it is important to demonstrate that the inferential value of the POC shape is not lost in the transformation.

Figure 8 illustrates one example of the effect of the transformation on the shape of the POCs. These hypothetical functions are taken from Figures 1a, 1b, 3b, and 4b (now plotted in the format used by Wickens et al., 1981). Panels 8a and 8b illustrate the hypothetical component performance resource functions underlying the raw-score POCs in panel 8c. After normalization, the POCs assume the shapes illustrated in panel 8d. Although the transformation alters many features of the raw-score POC, the general *form* of the POC is maintained. By comparing Figures 1, 3, and 4 (if plotted in the format of Wickens et al., 1981), one can see that for all three combinations of performance-resource functions, the forms of the raw-score POCs are maintained through the transformation. Therefore, the shapes of the raw-score POCs and the transformed POCs produce identical constraints on the shapes that the component performance-resource functions may assume.

These constraints are summarized in Table 4. The following inferences about the shapes of the performance-resource functions underlying Wickens et al.'s POCs are based on these constraints. The inferences are summarized in Table 5.

Let us start with Figure 6a, which plots all tasks against the tracking task, T. Since POC(TT) is linear, performance-resource function T must be linear. If so, performance-resource function L and performance-resource function C must be negatively accelerated, as their POCs with T are concave. The shape of function A is difficult to determine. In this graph, performance on A appears to be independent of the resources allocated to T; A may be in the data-limited portion of its performance-resource function or, according to Wickens' interpretation, A is using a separate pool of resources from that used by T.

Next, look at Figure 6b, which plots dual-task performance of all tasks with the digit classification task, C. Again, POC(CA) is linear, so that both functions C and A must be linear. However, note that POC(CC) is convex, indicating that performance-resource function C must be positively accelerated. Of course, function C cannot be both linear and positively accelerated. Next, notice that POC(CT) is concave, suggesting that at least one underlying performance-resource function is negatively accelerated. If one assumes that function T is linear, as indicated by 6a, then function C must be negatively accelerated. Obviously, performance-resource function C cannot be linear, positively accelerated, and negatively accelerated. Finally, since POC(CL) is convex, function L must be either linear or positively accelerated, which contradicts the negatively accelerated shape of function L suggested by Figure 6a.

The contradictions summarized in Table 5 represent only one possible set of deductions. One would obtain different contradictions if one derived the initial assumptions from a different POC. However, the general conclu-

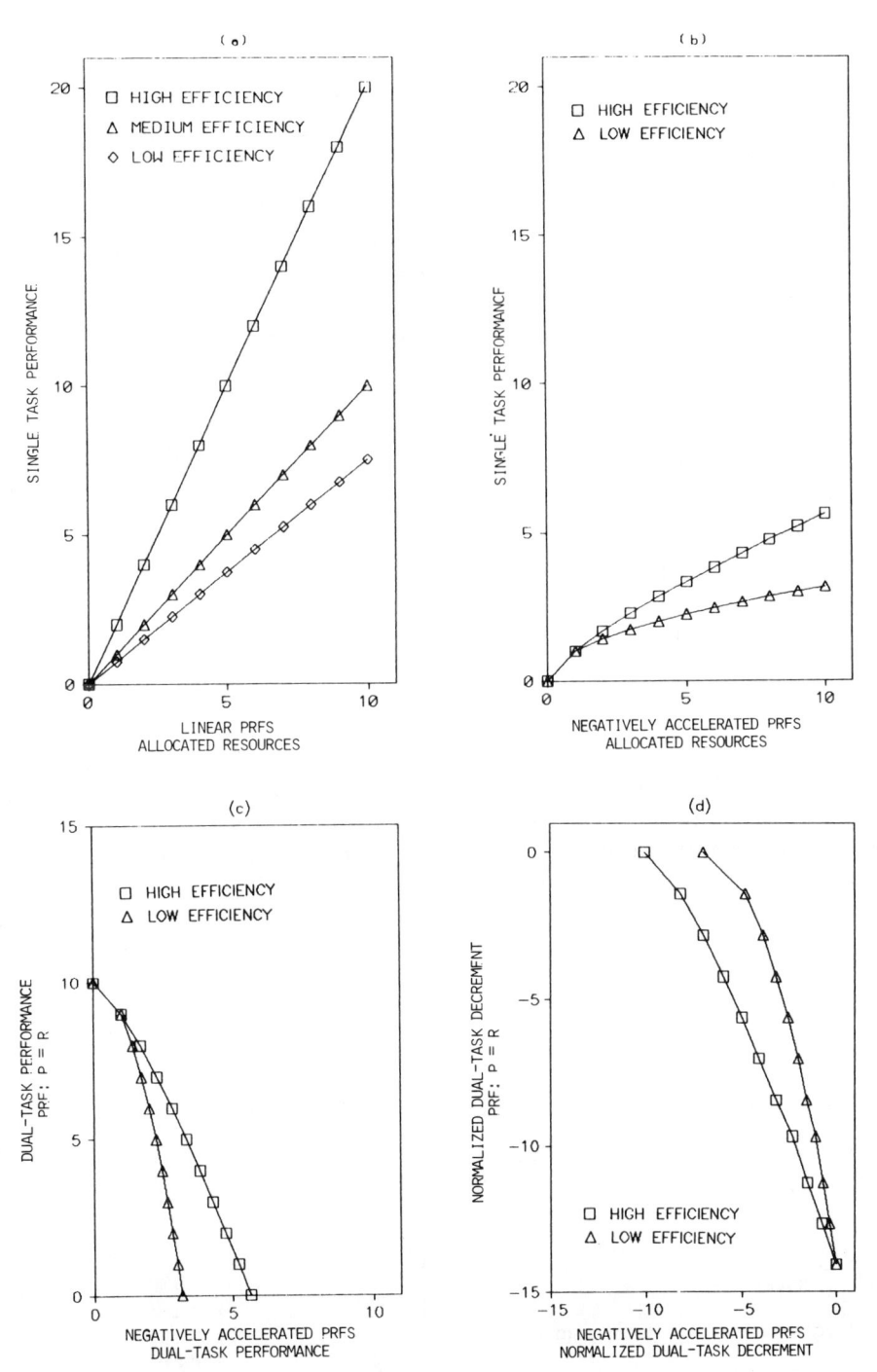

Figure 8. *Consistency between the general forms of raw-score and normalized POCs that have identical component PRFs.*

TABLE 4

Constraints on the Shape of Component Performance Resource Functions (PRF) Based on the Shape of the Transformed and Raw-Score Performance Operating Characteristic (POC)

| POC Shape | PRF Shape |
|---|---|
| Linear | Both PRFs must be linear. |
| Concave to the origin | At least one of the PRFs must be negatively accelerated. If the other is positively accelerated, there may be a point of inflection in the POC.* |
| Convex to the origin | At least one of the PRFs must be positively accelerated. Convex empirical POCs should be rare. If the other PRF is negatively accelerated, there may be a point of inflection in the POC.* |

Note. It is important to note that these relationships hold for both the raw-score and the transformed (if plotted in the format used by Wickens et al., 1981) hypothetical POCs presented in this paper.
* It is impossible to identify a point of inflection in single-point POCs.

sion would be the same: this transformation technique does not provide a consistent set of inferences regarding the performance-resource functions underlying the POCs.

*Equal Allocation Axis*

Recall that the point of equal allocation (PEA) of resources on raw-score POCs lies on the 45-deg vector from the origin *only* if the component performance resource functions are equal. Wickens et al. (1981) claim that when the POC is normalized, the point of equal allocation of resources lies on the 45-degree vector from the origin for *all* POCs. This claim is incorrect.

The points of equal allocation on the normalized POCs are denoted in Figure 4. Note that the location of the 45-deg vector is different for each normalized POC. As with the raw-score POCs, the point of equal allocation on a normalized POC falls on the 45-deg vector from the origin *only* if the component performance-resource functions are equal. In general, it is unlikely that two performance-resource functions will be equal, except perhaps when a task is performed with itself. It is especially interesting to notice this rela-

TABLE 5

Inferred Shapes of the Performance Resource Functions Underlying Wickens et al.'s Transformed POCs in Figure 6

| Home Task | Performance Resource Function ||||
|---|---|---|---|---|
|  | T | C | L | A |
| Tracking (T) | Lin | NA | NA | ? |
| Digit classification (C) | Lin | Lin* and PA* | Lin* or PA* | Lin |
| Line judgment (L) | Lin | PA* | NA and PA* | Lin |
| Auditory STM (A) | ?* | Lin* | NA | Lin |

Note. Lin = linear; NA = negatively accelerated; PA = positively accelerate; ? = indeterminate. * indicates that the inferred shape of the PRF contradicts the original inference.

tionship in the empirical POCs in Figure 6. In all instances in which a task is performed with itself, the dual-task decrement score on the normalized POC does in fact fall on the 45-deg vector. However, the claim that an "equal allocation axis" is produced when dual-task data are normalized is not justified. In fact, the point of equal allocation cannot be determined unless the underlying performance-resource functions are known.

*Summary*

The transformation method discussed above can be criticized on two major grounds. First, the dual-task data transformation is misinterpreted. In particular, the transformed empirical POCs produced contradictory inferences about the shapes of their component performance-resource functions. In addition, it is incorrectly claimed that the transformation produces an axis representing the equal allocation of resources between any two normalized tasks.

Second, it is not clear that this transformation satisfactorily alleviates the POC scaling problems, even when the transformed POCs are interpreted correctly. Contrary to claims, the transformation does not equate the units of measurement of the two performance scales. A comment by Ghiselli, Campbell, and Zedeck (1981) about the distribution assumptions of $z$-scores is germane:

> Comparability is attained not through rendering the units on the various scales equal, but rather through comparing the individual's scores on different variables with the distributions of scores earned by a population of individuals in his or her general class (p. 40).

This suggests that the procedure is a misapplication of the $z$-score transformation. Although $z$ scores allow one to compare an individual's standing within one distribution with his or her standing within another distribution, $z$ scores do not *equate* the distributions themselves. The distributions of the dual-task performance scales are not equated by the transformation of Equation 2.

## PROPORTION SCORES

Mountford and North (1980) represent dual-task performance as a proportion of the single-task level of performance. This linear transformation may seem more appropriate. The hypothetical POCs from Figure 3 are plotted as proportion scores in Figure 9. This transformation changes several important features of the raw-score POC.

First, recall that in raw-score POCs, task efficiency can be represented by the intercept of the POC with the axis. Less efficient tasks intercept the axis closer to the origin. In the proportional POC, however, this information is lost. Single-task performance will always be represented by 100%, regardless of task efficiency.

Second, when POCs are plotted as proportion scores, all linear POCs acquire the same slope (see Figure 9a). This is a problem because linear POCs can no longer be distinguished from one another. Information about the relative task efficiency of the linear functions is lost.

The nonlinear POCs in Figures 9b and 9c are still distinguishable on the basis of their OSRs. Because the curves retain their original (raw-score) general shapes, the OSRs will increase from left to right for the concave POCs in Figure 9b and will decrease from left to right for the convex POCs in Figure 9c. These trends are consistent with the raw-score representation. However, the relative numerical values of the OSRs within a family will have different patterns because (1) the rate of change of the function is altered, and (2) the curves are in different locations relative to each other.

Finally, Mountford and North (1980) claim that POC points falling on the 45-deg vector from the origin represent equal allocation of resources between the two tasks. This claim is not entirely correct. The points of equal allocation (PEA) are denoted in Figure 9. Whereas the PEAs for the linear POCs in

Figure 9a do fall on the 45-deg vector, the PEAs for the nonlinear, asymmetric functions in Figures 9b and 9c do not. Although the proportion transformation produces an equal allocation axis for linear functions regardless of the slopes of the original linear performance-resource functions, the utility of this feature is questionable because the functions are indistinguishable. When nonlinear performance-resource functions compose the POC, the point of equal allocation will lie on the 45-deg vector *only* if the component performance-resource functions are equivalent.

It is clear that proportion scores do not satisfactorily resolve POC scaling problems. Although the nonlinear functions retain some interpretable information, the linear functions become indistinguishable after the transformation. Therefore, this transformation would not be useful for testing models of resource allocation or for gathering information about interference among various types of tasks.

## CONCLUSION

This paper discusses scaling problems associated with the use and interpretation of empirical POC functions. Major criticisms were directed toward the method of normalized decrement scores proposed by Wickens (1980). The claim that "normalized difference scores make the scaling factors and intercepts along both task axes equivalent" (Wickens et al., 1981, p. 220) in general is false. Our simulations of untreated and normalized POC functions yielded results that were completely inconsistent with the conclusions drawn by Wickens et al. (1981). Of course, there might be some combination of performance-resource functions, not considered by us, that could yield consistent results. It is not feasible to simulate all possible performance-resource functions and their pairwise combination. Nevertheless, it appears

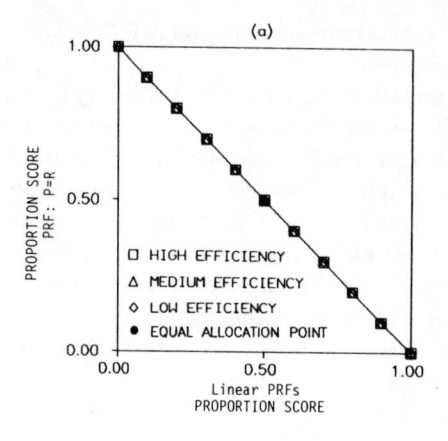

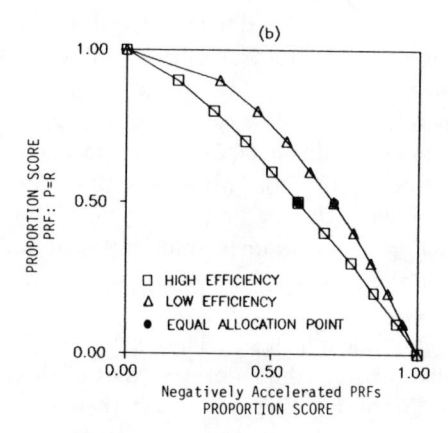

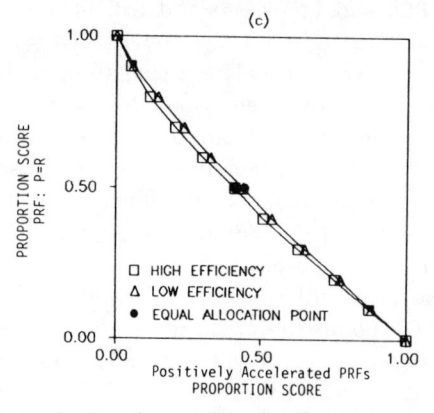

Figure 9. *Families of hypothetical POCs transformed into proportion scores.*

that, in general, scaling POC functions by normalized difference scores, or by proportions, is not a valid solution and that, at the very least, the onus of proof lies with those researchers who use such attempted scaling techniques.

The arguments expressed in this paper do not necessarily imply that researchers should forsake all use of empirical POC functions. Our criticisms apply with greatest force to POC functions that contain two arbitrary tasks that have been combined with little regard for possible correspondence between their underlying performance-resource functions. The hazards of POC interpretation are decreased to the extent that the commonalities between performance-resource functions are known by the experimenter. In particular, studies that utilize the same task on both axes are immune to many of the criticisms raised here. This special type of POC has been termed an *attention operating characteristic* (AOC) by Sperling and Melchner (1978). Although some may think that limiting the scope of POC analysis to only those cases in which the same task is combined with itself unduly narrows the utility of the approach, we point to work summarized by Sperling (1984) as evidence that AOCs are indeed valuable.

Our goal in this paper has been to demonstrate the hazards of dual-task data transformations, especially those performed without an analysis of relevant theoretical considerations. The full effects of such transformations need to be explored in detail before researchers can produce meaningful interpretations of transformed empirical POC functions. One must always ask whether any transformation resolves the scaling problems or merely repackages them.

## ACKNOWLEDGMENT

This research was supported by Cooperative Agreement NCC 2-228 from the National Aeronautics and Space Administration; S. G. Hart was the NASA Technical Officer.

## REFERENCES

Ghiselli, E. E., Campbell, J. P., and Zedeck, S. (1981). *Measurement theory for the behavioral sciences.* San Francisco: W. H. Freeman.

Kahneman, D. (1973). *Attention and effort.* Englewood Cliffs, NJ: Prentice Hall.

Kantowitz, B. H. (1985). Channels and stages in human information processing: A limited analysis of theory and methodology. *Journal of Mathematical Psychology, 29,* 135-174.

Kantowitz, B. H., and Knight, J. L., Jr. (1976). On experimenter-limited processes. *Psychological Review, 83,* 502-507.

Kantowitz, B. H., and Knight, J. L. (1978). When is an easy task difficult and vice versa? *Acta Psychologica, 42,* 163-170.

Mountford, S. J., and North, R. A. (1980). Voice entry for reducing pilot workload. In *Proceedings of the 24th Annual Meeting of the Human Factors Society* (pp. 185-189). Santa Monica, CA: Human Factors Society.

Navon, D., and Gopher, D. (1979). On the economy of the human-processing system. *Psychological Review, 86,* 214-255.

Norman, D. A., and Bobrow, D. J. (1975). On data-limited and resource-limited processes. *Cognitive Psychology, 7,* 44-64.

Sperling, G. (1984). Attention and signal detection. In R. Parasuraman and D. R. Davies (Eds.), *Varieties of attention* (pp. 103-181). New York: Academic Press.

Sperling, G. and Melchner, M. J. (1978). Visual search, visual attention, and the attention operating characteristic. In J. Requin (Ed.), *Attention and performance VII* (pp. 675-686). Hillsdale, N. J.: Lawrence Erlbaum Associates.

Townsend, J. T. (1974). Issues and models concerning the processing of a finite number of inputs. In B. H. Kantowitz (Ed.), *Human information processing: Tutorials in performance and cognition* (pp. 133-185). Hillsdale, NJ: Erlbaum.

Wickens, C. D. (1980). The structure of attentional resources. In R. S. Nickerson (Ed.), *Attention and performance VIII* (pp. 239-257). Hillsdale, NJ: Erlbaum.

Wickens, C. D., Mountford, S. J., and Schreiner, W. (1981). Multiple resources, task-hemispheric integrity, and individual differences in time-sharing. *Human Factors, 23,* 211-229.

# 19

# POCs and Performance Decrements: A Reply to Kantowitz and Weldon

CHRISTOPHER D. WICKENS[1] *and* YEI-YU YEH, *Department of Psychology, University of Illinois at Urbana-Champaign, Champaign, Illinois*

*This paper responds to some of the criticisms presented by Kantowitz and Weldon (1985) that have been directed toward the methodology used in a 1981 article by Wickens, Mountford, and Schreiner. We state here that some of their criticisms are valid: A performance operating characteristic (POC) cannot be derived from a single point in a POC space, and therefore resource competition cannot be separated from concurrence cost as a source of task interference. However, we also note that the primary issue of importance to system designers—how to compare interference between different tasks—is not answered by Kantowitz and Weldon's critique. That issue requires that some technique for standardizing performance decrements across tasks be assumed. Two alternate techniques for standardizing are described in the present paper.*

## OVERVIEW

Elsewhere in this issue of *Human Factors*, Kantowitz and Weldon present an elegant and quantitatively precise critique of the use of performance operating characteristic (POC) methodology in dual-task research. A major focus of their critique is an article that we wrote (Wickens, Mountford, and Schreiner, 1981), the primary purpose of which was to examine dual-task performance as it is affected by (1) individual differences and (2) task structure. The first of these issues addressed the question of whether or not there is a general factor of time-sharing and is not really germane to the current arguments (but see Ackerman, Schneider, and Wickens, 1984, for insightful reanalysis of these data). In the 1981 article we also addressed a second issue: how structural differences between tasks that may be identified a priori by a system designer can predict the degree of interference or time-sharing efficiency between those tasks in a dual-task setting. Such a prediction, if it can be made with reasonable accuracy, is of considerable importance in system design because it will help the designer to specify, early in the design stages, the nature of the task displays, controls, and processing requirements that will produce the most efficient multiple-task performance.

It is unfortunate that most of the criticisms of the 1981 article that are made by Kantowitz and Weldon are directed toward an aspect of our assumptions and analysis that is of relatively minor importance to those system-design questions that we believe are the most concerned with human factors. That

[1] Requests for reprints should be sent to Christopher D. Wickens, Aviation Research Laboratory, Institute of Aviation, University of Illinois, Willard Airport, Savoy, IL. 61874.

is, the authors have addressed most of their criticism toward the use of the POC representation as a means of expressing the degree of interference or time-sharing efficiency between tasks. Therefore, although their criticisms, cautions, and concerns about POC methodology are well founded and are of considerable importance regarding the theoretical adequacy of resource concepts, they shed less light on the broader practical question: How can we predict the degree of interference between tasks from knowledge of the structure of the tasks? One indication of this shift in their focus is suggested by the authors' statement in the final paragraphs; that is, "In particular, studies that utilize the same task on both axes are immune to many of the criticisms raised here" (p. 547). This emphasis on the use of identical tasks explicitly ignores the designer's concerns for how *different* tasks interact.

The remainder of the present article will address two issues: (1) a response to Kantowitz and Weldon's criticism of our use of a POC representation to express task-interference measures, and (2) a consideration of what we believe to be a more important issue not satisfactorily addressed by the authors' critique; that is, the methodology for comparing task-interference measures with different tasks.

## RESPONSE TO THE CRITICISM

### The POC Representation

Kantowitz and Weldon raise the important and fundamental point that there are three components that may contribute to the decrement between two time-shared tasks. The first of these is *resource competition*, the competition between tasks for some supply of mental energy or a limited commodity such as neural processing mechanisms. The second is *resource allocation*, the relative bias of allocating resources between tasks, governed by task priorities and instructions. The third component is a *concurrence cost*, a decrement that appears in the performance of one or both tasks as a result of their being performed concurrently. The size of this decrement is assumed to be unaffected by the trade-off of resources between tasks. Referring to Kantowitz and Weldon's figures, resource competition is revealed by the location and shape of the POC, as the two tasks are time-shared under different conditions of relative task emphasis. Resource allocation is revealed by the positioning of points *along* a given POC, and concurrence cost is reflected by the position of the total POC relative to single-task endpoints on the two axes of the POC space.

Kantowitz and Weldon are absolutely right in asserting that one cannot disentangle the contributions of resource competition and concurrence cost from a single point in the POC space, the nature of our data in our original paper. This point is well illustrated by their Figure 6. In fact, we take responsibility for creating the impression that we were dealing with or presenting POCs by our ambiguous use of terminology. On page 220 of the Wickens et al. (1981) article we explicitly (and correctly) describe the representation as "a single point on a performance operating characteristic (POC) *space* ... [which] represents the decrement in both tasks relative to their respective single-task performance levels" (italics added). A point in the POC's space is not equivalent to a POC, in which performance is plotted as priorities are changed, and we did not intend that equivalence should be assumed. However, in the following paragraph we did convey the impression that we were dealing with POCs by the use of the term *POC representation*. This is unfortunate, and we regret the confusion that our ambiguous use of terminology created.

### Assumptions of a Single Resource

A second point raised by Kantowitz and

Weldon is that standardized decrement-score analysis fails to resolve scaling problems. Unfortunately, the point raised in the article is primarily based on one assumption, that there is only one single, limited resource pool. When they present the genesis of a POC function (p. 532), two of the four assumptions reflect this particular theoretical view: (1) the sum of the capacities consumed by each of the two tasks equals total capacity, and (2) there is only one pool of capacity that is available. Even the authors recognized that the latter assumption has been questioned by other models; however, they relied on this basic assumption in their later discussion of the interpretation of the transformed POC.

*Inferring the Shapes of Component Performance Resource Functions*

In reading the arguments presented by Kantowitz and Weldon, we noticed two interesting points. As they pointed out, "it is important to demonstrate that the inferential value of the POC shape is not lost in the transformation" (p. 542). However, later in the discussion, they assert that "Although the transformation alters many features of the raw-score POC, the general *form* of the POC is maintained ... for all three combinations of performance-resource functions, the forms of the raw-score POCs are maintained through the transformation" (p. 542). If the *form* is maintained, then the concerns regarding the absence of constraints on the performance-resource function (PRF) hold true even for raw-score POCs. Given that the particular transformation we used could not be held responsible for the violation of constraints, we noticed a second interesting point. That is, the absence of constraints on the PRF should only be of concern when a single resource pool is invoked. In part, this lack of consistency in resource trade-offs and PRFs is one impetus for the development of multiple-resource theory (Navon and Gopher, 1979).

*Equal Allocation Axis*

Another major point of Kantowitz and Weldon's criticisms concerns our claim that the 45-deg point in the POC space corresponds to an "equal allocation" axis; that is, the level of joint performance at which resources are equally divided between tasks. We agree with them that this claim assumes that (1) there are equivalent PRFs between both tasks *and* (2) both tasks use the same resources. Neither of these conditions hold in the present data. An alternative approach that we should have taken was to *assume* that, because we had instructed subjects to allocate attention equally between tasks (see Procedure section in Wickens et al., 1981), the points themselves *define* the point of equal allocation. These points will not necessarily lie along the 45-deg line if a multiple-resources conception is adopted. However, we note here that the issue of equal versus nonequal allocation of resources between tasks, as described in half of a paragraph (Wickens et al., 1981, p. 222), represents only a very small component of the main thrust of the original article.

*Questions of Decrement Scaling*

In our view, the real issue to which concern over the 1981 article should be addressed regards whether the assumptions that we made regarding the relative scaling of decrements on different tasks are sound or, if they are not sound, whether different assumptions would change our conclusion. Thus, the real concern should focus on how one scales the decrements in performance resulting from dual-task interference when different tasks with different dependent measures are used: the "apples and oranges" problem. We frame our discussion in the context of Figure 1, which is a representation of the kind of data analyzed in our original study and reanalyzed by Kantowitz and Weldon. In the figure, performance on a home task paired with different

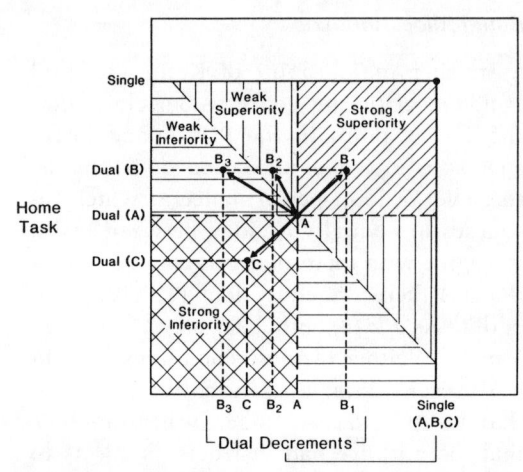

Figure 1. Cross plot of performance of different time-shared task combinations in a POC space. The vertical axis always represents performance on the same home task, time-shared with three different paired tasks (A, B, and C), performance on which is shown on the horizontal axis. Points within the space represent the two-dimensional cross plots of dual-task performance. Points $B_1$, $B_2$, and $B_3$ show the effects of different transformations of the decrement scale for Task B. The four shaded regions represent different relations between performance decrements of the home task with A, and with B or C.

concurrent tasks is shown on the vertical axis of a POC space, and performance on three different paired tasks, A, B, and C is shown on the horizontal axis. (Our arguments here extend logically to four paired tasks.) It should be noted that because all of the single- and dual-task performance measures on the home task are expressed in equivalent units, no transformation that is applied to all of the performance measures of the home task will alter the relative ordering along this axis.

Within the figure, Point A in the middle of the POC space represents the time-sharing of the home task with task A; the surrounding circles represent the time-sharing performance of the home task with Task C and with Task B (the latter showing three different transformations of the Task B decrement: $B_1$, $B_2$, and $B_3$). The relative difference in time-sharing efficiency of the home task with A, B, and C can be assigned to four qualitatively different regions, as indicated by different shadings in the figure. Point B1 is in a region of strong superiority of B over A. Point C is a region of strong inferiority. That is, in both cases the relative decrements of both tasks favor one task combination over the other. Points B2 and B3, however, lie in regions of weak superiority and inferiority of B to A, respectively. Naturally, the lower-right quadrant of Figure 1 can be similarly divided into weak regions of superiority and inferiority. This representation emphasizes that as long as one scale (the home task) is firmly anchored and the relative ordering of points cannot be changed by transformation, then there is no possible way that a differential transformation between the two versions of the paired task decrement scale can shift a relation of strong superiority for one task to that of strong superiority for the other task.

In the 1981 article, all of our discussions and interpretations of differences in time-sharing efficiency were based on relations of strong superiority. Therefore, scale transformations of the paired task could not possibly have reversed any of our conclusions. At best, they could have reduced our effects from strong relations (B1) to weak relations in the same direction (B2), or, with a more dramatic transformation, to weak relations in the opposite direction (B3).

## METHODOLOGY OF COMPARING DECREMENTS

Given the importance of the decrement measure issue in dual-task research involving heterogeneous tasks, it is appropriate to examine in detail the nature of the assumption that we did make to justify our choice of scale equivalence on the paired tasks, and to consider a possible alternative.

Two basic assumptions were made in going

from the physical domain of performance measurement to the psychological domain of task interference or time-sharing efficiency: (1) that the level of performance of a single task with full attention mobilization defines an anchor that is in certain respects psychologically equivalent across a variety of tasks. This assumption is justified by our instructions to the subjects to give full attention to each task in the single-task conditions. Based on this assumption, we aligned all of our single-task performance measures to a single point along the paired task axis. (2) The second and more debatable assumption concerns our standardizing the scales in terms of units of performance variability. Interestingly, Kantowitz and Weldon do not even address the assumption underlying this procedure, which we explicitly stated in our paper: "This procedure requires the assumption that for very stable tasks (little trial-to-trial variability), a given change in performance from single- to dual-task conditions represents a proportionately greater loss in efficiency than for tasks that are highly variable" (Wickens et al. 1981, pp. 219–220). As I have argued elsewhere (Wickens, 1980, 1984) this procedure makes certain assumptions, similar to Fechner's psychological law of subjective intensity, concerning the linear relation between variability and a psychological construct.

An alternative to standardizing by variability is to define equivalence between performance scales in terms of the level of performance reached when a task is time-shared with itself at 50% allocation (i.e., equal priorities between tasks). This performance decrement of a task time-shared with itself ($D_S$), like the variability measure, has some psychological equivalence across all tasks. It defines the performance loss for a given task resulting from the maximum possible resource overlap with another. $D_S$ will be large for difficult, resource-limited tasks and small for easy, data-limited ones. Thus, all time-shared tasks can be compared by asking what proportion of their $D_S$ is lost when shared with a different task.

The decrement scores from the original paper were recalculated using this $D_S$ standardizing procedure, and all but one of the relations of strong superiority in the original figure (replotted in Kantowitz and Weldon's Figure 6) are maintained. This particular relation (LT over LA) is reduced from one of the strong to one of the weak superiority. (In our original experiment, the auditory task was not time-shared with itself. Hence, in renormalizing the data, we assumed that time-sharing of the two auditory tasks would produce a doubling of the RT performance measure—from 1 to 2 s. This assumption may have created the single change in the strength of the relation.) Thus, the relations reported here seem robust to the application of two different plausible transformations. In the absence of strong justification for the choice of one technique over others, this approach (robustness across different plausible transformations) would seem to be the safest means of establishing relative decrements.

To satisfactorily resolve these issues, these different assumptions must be tested through a careful program of simulation. An important goal of these simulations will be to demonstrate whether, and to what degree, different standardization techniques make a difference in the conclusions that are drawn. It is important, however, that any such simulation be carried out within the framework of a multiple-resources assumption. In addition to the simulation work, the identity of these resources should be plausibly grounded in evidence from domains that are independent of the data on task interference (e.g., individual differences, physiology; Wickens, 1984). Such converging evidence from different domains constrains the degrees of freedom of the models and is necessary in order to avoid the circularity of positing resources on the basis of task-interference data that are then used to validate measures of that interference.

In conclusion, we should note that the concerns we have expressed above, regarding Kantowitz and Weldon's criticisms of our analysis, are not meant to suggest that their criticisms are invalid or inappropriate. Theoretical and empirical developments in the five years since our paper was published, reflected in Kantowitz and Weldon's critique, have shed considerable light on the adequacy and limits of the resource concept (see also Navon, 1984). Nor do we wish to convey the impression that questions concerning the theory of resources are unrelated to, and unimportant for, the concerns of the system designer. The authors of both of the articles in question share a common belief in the importance of good theory that must underlie good applications (Kantowitz, in press; Wickens, in press-a). Rather, we suggest that the theory of task interference is a much broader theoretical domain, of which the theory of resources (whether multiple or single) and in particular, the energetics aspects that underlie the use and discussion of POC methodology, are subsets (Wickens, in press-b). At present, these subsets are less germane to the applications for system design than is either the broader theory that predicts the sources of task interference or the methodological issues that enable the amount of interference to be compared across different tasks.

## ACKNOWLEDGMENT

This paper was written under support of Grant # NASA NAG 2-169 from NASA-Ames Research Center. Sandra G. Hart was the technical monitor.

## REFERENCES

Ackerman, P., Schneider, W., and Wickens, C. D. (1984). Deciding the existence of a time-sharing ability: A combined methodological and theoretical approach. *Human Factors, 26*, 71-82.

Kantowitz, B. (in press). Mental workload. In P. Hancock (Ed.), *Human factors in psychology*. Amsterdam: North-Holland.

Kantowitz, B., and Weldon, M. (1985). On scaling performance operating characteristics: Caveat emptor. *Human Factors, 27*, 000-000.

Navon, D. (1984). Multiple resources: A theoretical soupstone. *Psychological Review, 91*, 216-234.

Navon, D., and Gopher, D. (1979). On the economy of the human processing system. *Psychological Review, 86*, 214-255.

Wickens, C. D. (1980). The structure of attentional resources. In R. Nickerson and R. Pew (Eds.), *Attention and performance VIII* (pp. 239-257). Hillsdale, NJ: Erlbaum.

Wickens, C. D. (1984). Processing resources in attention. In R. Parasuraman and R. Davies (Eds.), *Varieties of attention* (pp. 63-101). New York: Academic Press.

Wickens, C. D. (in press-a). Attention. In P. Hancock (Ed.) *Human factors in psychology*. Amsterdam: North-Holland.

Wickens, C. D. (in press-b). Energetics in information processing. In R. Hockey, A. Gaillard, and M. Coles (Eds.), *Adaptation to stress and task demands*. New York: Plenum.

Wickens, C. D., Mountford, S. J., and Schreiner, W. S. (1981). Multiple resources, task-hemispheric integrity, and individual differences in time-sharing efficiency. *Human Factors, 23*, 211-229.

# Part VI
# SKILL ACQUISITION AND SKILLED PERFORMANCE

Training and skill development constitute one of the oldest endeavors in the relationship between humans and tools or machines. In its most basic sense, the function of training is to initiate, organize, and control the learning process necessary for acquiring the skills to successfully operate or interact with some system or machine. In essence, training is the methodical acquisition of skills and knowledge.

Learning and training enjoy an intimate relationship. In his book *Human Performance Engineering: A Guide for System Designers* (Prentice-Hall, 1982), Bailey makes an important distinction between learning theory and training theory. Learning theories are descriptive and specify conditions conducive to acquisition of knowledge, whereas training theories are prescriptive in that they specify effective and efficient ways to obtain knowledge and skills.

The bottom line in training is achieving the most effective training in the most efficient manner. Given that the learning process is intimately related to training and that training is the systematic modulation of the learning process, the question becomes how to organize and control the learning process. A number of factors play a role in this systematic acquisition of skills and knowledge, including part-task training, transfer of training, and realism/fidelity issues. As the sophistication of the human-machine interface grows with advances in technology, the training required to develop complex, high-performance cognitive and perceptual-motor skills becomes more demanding. What should be trained? How should it be trained? Three selections address issues in training, including training in high-performance skills and part-task training.

Paul M. Fitts (Chapter 20) makes the point that technological change is shifting the importance of human skills, which in turn ensures the continued importance of the study of skilled performance and training. The fact that these statements were written almost twenty-five years ago is testimony to Fitts's insight. Even then he noted the emerging importance of perceptual skills and the reduced importance of simple motor skills. (Further technological advances since that time have shifted the emphasis again, and cognitive skills—for example, decision making, diagnosis, and monitoring—have become a primary concern in skill development.) Fitts briefly discussed task characteristics that affect skill acquisition and skilled performance such as task complexity, information coding, and the mapping between stimulus events and response events. He traced hypothetical phases involved in the acquisition of complex skills and discussed the existence of subroutines in complex tasks, the issue of lack of asymptotic functions, and the implications of these factors for training.

As Fitts noted, advances in technology are changing the nature and type of skills used in the human-machine interface. How are designers of training programs keeping up with the changing demands of training? Walter Schneider's thought-provoking article (Chapter 21) identifies erroneous assumptions and misconceptions that often arise when one generalizes the acquisition and training of simple skills to more complex, high-performance skills. Many of the fallacies identified have an empirical basis. Among those discussed by Schneider is the notion that extended practice leads to ever-increasing performance levels, that the whole task should be practiced, and that providing a conceptual understanding leads to immediate proficiency. Schneider contends that designers of training programs should make use of knowledge of prominent features of high-performance skill acquisition, and he provides a number of guidelines for providing training in high-performance skills. Such guidelines provide a useful direction for the changing requirements in training cognitive skills.

Effectiveness and efficiency, the goals of training, may often be at odds. Training is notoriously expensive. One approach that is geared toward efficiency and cost-effectiveness is part-task training. Part-task training involves practice of a subset of tasks or components of the total task, followed by an integration of the component tasks. The article by Dennis C. Wightman and Gavan

Lintern (Chapter 22) is a selective review of part-task training of tracking skills used in manual control. The review focuses on three issues relevant to methodologies and evaluations used in part-task training: *segmentation* (partitioning a task on the basis of temporal or spatial attributes), *fractionation* (partitioning a complex task on the basis of simultaneous subtasks), and *simplification* (adjusting a difficult task to make it easier). Based on their review, the authors point out that not all of these techniques are equally effective. For example, segmentation is shown to be an effective part-task training technique, whereas the interaction of subtasks in the fractionation technique may limit its effectiveness as a part-task training procedure. Wightman and Lintern conclude that many part-task training procedures have some value and may generally allow for more cost-effective training.

# 20

*Factors in Complex Skill Training*[1]

*Paul M. Fitts, University of Michigan*

Skilled performance exhibits the three following characteristics: (*a*) spatial-temporal patterning, (*b*) continuous interaction of response processes with input and feedback processes, and (*c*) learning. This is a broad definition indeed, one which encompasses a large part of all human behavior. It includes so-called "motor" skills, but is consistent with the broader meaning of skill employed by Bartlett (1958) in his book on *Thinking*, by Broadbent (1958) in his book on *Perception and Communication*, and by Woodworth (1958) in his work on the *Dynamics of Behavior*.

The last half-century has seen the emergence, due to modern technology, of many new human tasks which have demanded new kinds of complex skills. Driving automobiles and operating other forms of machinery are common examples. With the further development of technology some of these tasks are now becoming less important than they were a few years ago. However, the total number of human activities requiring complex skills has probably not decreased appreciably, especially when we enumerate such varied activities as those involved in athletic pursuits, walking and running, reading and writing, automobile driving, and industrial tasks.

The point is that specific tasks change rapidly as a result of technological change. For example, at the present time the importance of perceptual skills appears to be increasing while the importance of primarily motor skills may be decreasing. There has also been a trend in effect for some time for an increasing amount of skilled work to be done while

---

[1] Many of the ideas expressed in this chapter are taken from sections of a book on *Skilled Performance* by P. M. Fitts, H. P. Bahrick, M. E. Noble, and G. E. Briggs, which is to be published by Wiley.

From R. Glaser (ed.), *Training Research and Education*. Copyright by R. Glaser.

the individual is seated. As will be emphasized later, skills performed with the body at rest are in one respect simpler than skills that are executed while the body is in motion. The kinds of skills that appear to be increasing in importance are ones in which the individual must keep track of many separate sources of information (stimuli), collate these separate inputs, and sort out effects produced by his own earlier actions from the effects produced by outside agents.

Such considerations lead to the conclusion that the study of skilled performance and skill training will be of continuing importance. Not only is skill important in its own right, but a comprehensive theory of skill and skill learning should provide a basis for understanding many other forms of behavior in which individuals must deal with sequences of events and must organize their own behavior into an effective sequence of actions under time stress.

## Task Taxonomy

The importance of an adequate task taxonomy for skilled tasks is widely recognized in all areas of psychological theorizing today. A taxonomy should identify important correlates of learning rate, performance level, and individual differences. It should be equally applicable to laboratory tasks and to the tasks encountered in industry and in military service. Task taxonomy will therefore receive major emphasis in the present paper. Fleishman has already dealt, in a previous chapter, with several questions of task analysis and classification. The present chapter will extend this analysis, drawing first on results from experimental studies of various task characteristics, and second on results from surveys of the experiences of instructors regarding factors that make the learning of complex skills difficult.

The definition of skill offered at the beginning of this chapter emphasizes the continuous interplay of input, output, and feedback processes. One should therefore seek a taxonomy for *processes* and *activities*, rather than for static elements. In a strict sense it is misleading to assume discrete beginnings and endings of such processes, even though this is often done as a matter of convenience. Keeping this reservation in mind the analysis of skill processes can begin with a consideration of the conditions existing prior to the initiation of some behavior sequence of interest. Here the interest is in the extent to which an individual is prepared or "set" for action, and the relationship of external to self-initiated activity.

*Skill Constancies*

The gross features of a skilled activity can be specified in terms of (a) the degree of gross body involvement and (b) the extent of external pacing of the activity. These two factors specify the nature of the constancies or uniformities that are present in highly skilled patterns of behavior.

In the simplest instance, the body is at rest prior to the beginning of a response sequence, and the individual initiates a behavior pattern which is carried out in relation to a relatively fixed or stable set of environmental objects. Driving a golf ball, picking up a pencil, or threading a needle are simple examples of behavior initiated from such a condition of rest or preparation. The constancies that develop in such behavior patterns are readily apparent and fairly easily measured.

In the next more complex instances, the behavior sequence is initiated either while the body is in motion (with external objects fixed), or while external objects are in motion (with the body fixed or "set"). Examples are the activities of a basketball forward (when shooting while in motion) or of a batter in baseball (when swinging at a thrown ball). Here the uniformities in the individual's behavior patterns are often difficult to observe except in terms of the success or failure of the total sequence (e.g., hitting the ball), since a complex and changing set of relationships is now being dealt with. The sensory-neuromotor activity is also more complex than is true when the body is initially at rest.

Finally, at the most complex level of skill constancy, both the individual and external objects undergo change immediately prior to the time when the particular sequence that is of interest begins. A man who is trying to keep his balance on the deck of a pitching ship and at the same time is training his eyes (or perhaps a gun) on an aircraft that is flying overhead is engaged in such a complex task. A football quarterback who throws a running pass is another example. It obviously would be very difficult to record the complete temporal-spatial patterns of motion involved in such activities, and even more difficult to extract the constancies involved in successive sequences, i.e., to identify anything uniform in the behavior. Only the end result appears to be constant and only by considering means-end relationships is the nature of the constancies revealed.

This admittedly gross classification of tasks requiring skill is mentioned chiefly as a way of putting the rest of this chapter in proper perspective. The remaining discussion deals chiefly with skills that men perform from a seated position and with their bodies in a prepared or set position, at least with respect to their immediate environment such as the vehicle in which they are riding. Emphasis is also upon skills that are performed under time stress, where both speed and accuracy of response are sought.

*Task Characteristics Derived from Feedback Concepts*

The more detailed taxonomic system which follows, and much of the subsequent discussion, is based upon an analytic approach which considers an individual man, engaged in some form of skilled performance,

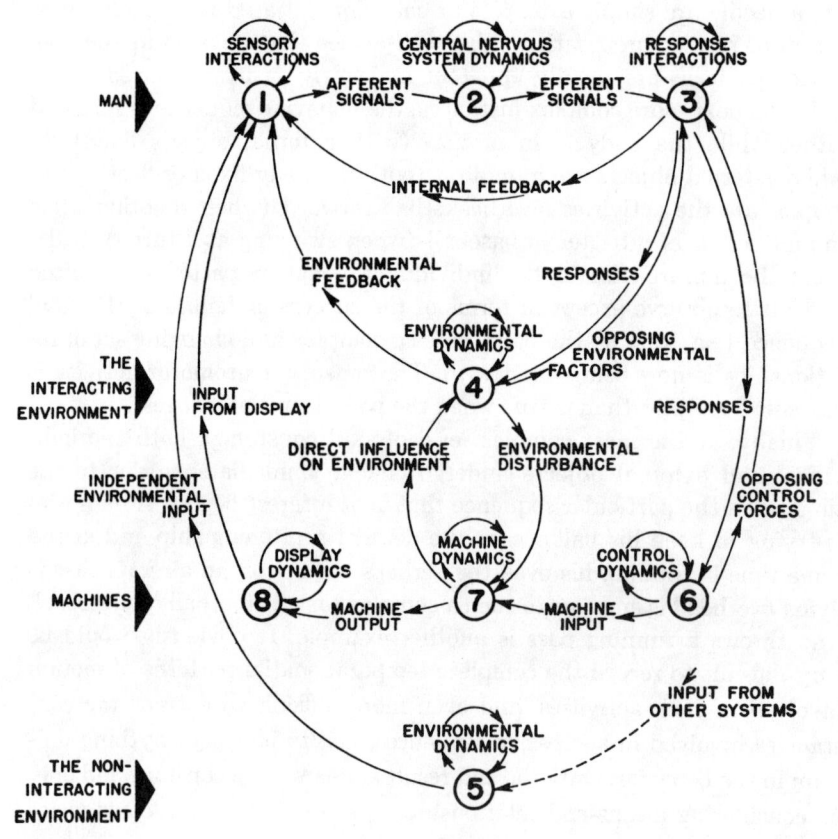

FIGURE 6.1. Illustration of Some of the Dynamic Feed-Back Loops Involved in Skilled Performance. The nodes in the diagram represent the following dynamic processes: (1) receptor, (2) central nervous system, (3) effector, (4) and (5) social environmental, (6) control, (7) machine, and (8) display.

as a closed-loop system. In such a system the feedback loops are equally as important as the inputs. Figure 6.1 is such a schematic representation of the major dynamic interactions or feedback loops involved in skilled performance. Three major loops are shown.

First there is an internal loop (1-2-3-1) whereby a man's responses provide proprioceptive and kinesthetic stimulation that can influence his subsequent responses. Second there is an external loop (1-2-3-4-1) whereby a man's responses influence his social world and other aspects of his environment, and subsequently result in new stimulation or feedback from other people. Third there is the loop (1-2-3-6-7-8-1) whereby man-machine interactions occur. Each node in Figure 6.1, those representing man's receptors, central nervous system, and effectors, and also external systems, has its own peculiar dynamics. The most important of these are found within the central nervous system. Some major characteristics of perceptual-motor tasks can now be enumerated by reference to this diagram.

*Stimulus and Response Sequences.* First, the sequence of stimulus or response events such as those impinging on Node 1 in Figure 6.1 will be considered. Regardless of their specific form, stimulus and/or response sequences can be specified quantitatively by four characteristics —their degree of coherence, continuity, frequency, and complexity.

A sequence is coherent to the degree that there is a specifiable dependence between successive events or values. Thus spoken English, walking movements, and the succession of notes in a classical musical composition are all highly coherent. Degree of coherence can be quantified in several ways, such as by an autocorrelation function or by a coefficient of redundancy. Examples of tasks that require the learning of relatively coherent movement patterns are rotary pursuit, skating, swimming, and handwriting. (At this point a statement of clarification is necessary. A taxonomic system is proposed which can be used to specify, in terms of purely formal properties, similarities and differences in activities that superficially might appear to have little in common, such as playing music and flying an aircraft. Identification of the bases for measures of the coherence of sequences opens up many research possibilities.)

A second characteristic of any type of sequence is its continuity. Task continuity is a function of the duration of sequences of changing events, and the occurrence of pauses between sequences. Stimulus and response sequences can thus be classified as (*a*) continuous and (*b*) discrete. Steering a car is a continuous task; hitting a baseball is a discrete task. From the standpoint of the subject these distinctions probably lie on a continuum. When discrete events follow each other with sufficient rapidity the task may be called a serial one. Typing is a good example of a serial task.

The frequencies of the changes involved in any type of task can also be specified. In the case of continuous sequences, frequency may be specified in terms of the periodic components which the sequence contains (or its power spectrum). In the case of a serial task, frequency may be specified in terms of the spacing of discrete cycles of activity (or the probability densities of events).

Finally, the complexity of a stimulus or a response sequence can be specified in terms of the numbers of different frequencies, time intervals, amplitudes, signals, or other kinds of variations which occur in a cycle of specified duration. Information measures are sometimes applicable. Needless to say, if the properties of a sequence keep changing in an unpredictable fashion, its formal properties cannot be specified precisely.

Referring to the earlier distinction between self-initiated and externally-initiated sequences, it is clear that the specification of a sequence in terms of its coherence, continuity, frequency, and complexity can apply to either type of activity. In one case it is the external, pacing sequence which usually is specified; in the other, it is self-initiated response sequence which is described.

*Stimulus-Response Coding and Code Transformations.* Thus far nothing has been specified about the particular size, color, pitch, or other characteristics of the stimulus, or about the force, amplitude, or other characteristics of the response movements that constitute a sequence or an activity. Tasks can be specified further by the stimulus and response codes employed, and particularly by the transformations required between stimuli and responses, or between responses and knowledge of response effects. Inputs may be via visual, auditory, tactual or other senses; responses may be vocal or manual; and both vocal and manual responses may take many forms. Thus it is often necessary to specify precisely how stimulus events are mapped into response events.

*Nature and Amount of Input and External Feedback Information.* It is often important to specify the kind and quantity of information, both input and feedback, available in a task. Of special interest, for example, are the many forms of knowledge of results.

*Nature of Internal (Proprioceptive) Feedback.* It is convenient to distinguish between internal and external feedback. Internal feedback is much more difficult to measure or to control than is external feedback, and consequently less is known about its effects.

*Dynamics of Physical Systems.* In many of the tasks performed in industry and in military service an important factor is the dynamic characteristics of the physical systems such as submarines, automobiles, or other machines that are operated by a man. The lags and oscillations characteristic of such systems determine part of what a man must learn in controlling them.

*Overall Task Complexity.* Finally it is necessary to specify the complexity of the total task as well as the complexity of particular stimulus-response sequences. This can be done in the same way that the complexity of a single stimulus or response sequence is specified. Overall task complexity thus refers to the number of separate sources of input or feedback information, the number of external systems with separate dynamics, etc., which together constitute the total task. The number of separate actions that must be taken serially as well as concurrently determine complexity. Examples of relatively complex tasks include flying an aircraft, directing several aircraft from a ground-based radar station, and monitoring a panel of many instruments. Few attempts have been made to measure the complexity of different tasks quantitatively, so that one can say how much more complex one is than the other; however, this will obviously be a desirable improvement in task taxonomy.

## Summary of Task Taxonomy

This necessarily short overview of task taxonomy will doubtless be insufficient to provide a clear picture of the task characteristics which determine the rate of learning or the ease or difficulty of performance. However, it is hoped that one conclusion is apparent: it is possible to specify many of the important characteristics of on-going patterns of activity, and to define these characteristics in terms of measures that are operationally independent of the criterion (behavior) measures by means of which the progress of learning and achievement or the "difficulty" of a task is customarily specified. In other words, it is possible to avoid circular definitions of factors in task difficulty and thus to open the door to research on the relation of task characteristics to learning and performance. Task taxonomy has many implications for training and training research, as well as for other research areas such as engineering psychology and individual differences. Before considering some of these implications, however, attention should be turned to an important source of data about the nature of skilled activities and about training problems—the experiences of persons who spend their lives instructing others in skills.

### INSTRUCTORS' OPINIONS REGARDING THE PROBLEMS OF SKILL TRAINING

In the earlier sections of this chapter and in the chapter by Fleishman, two somewhat contrasting approaches to the analysis of skill have been outlined. In the typical individual-difference approach outlined in Chapter 5 many relatively short tests may be given to large numbers of subjects and the interrelations among the dependent variables (scores), and sometimes measures of longer learning changes in a particular task are then studied by factor-analytic techniques. In the typical experimental approach many studies are often conducted, with one or perhaps two or three independent characteristics of a skill task systematically varied in each study, and the effects on performance and learning analyzed. These two approaches differ in important respects and therefore should supplement each other in revealing important dimensions of tasks and dimensions of individual differences.

But there is a third approach to an understanding of the nature of skill and of skill training problems, the use of survey techniques which tap the experiences of the men and women who devote their working lives to the training of young people in various skills. The rationale for studies which take as their data the experiences of instructors is perhaps obvious. Such studies certainly need no special justification. Nevertheless, two points should be made. First, instructors are intensely interested in certain aspects of task taxonomy—they are forced continually to think about factors in skill learning, to try to understand the problems of the learner at various stages of training, and to program their instruction in relation to the nature of the skill task and the nature of the learner. Second, instructors have ample opportunity to study the progress of learners and to try out (albeit perhaps in an unsystematic way) different techniques of instruction. It therefore seems reasonable that much can be learned from the systematic collection and analysis of their experiences.

The results of two studies of instructors' opinions in which the author has been involved in the past should now be considered. The first was an analysis of stenographic reports of the statements made by pilot instructors in the cases of 1000 aviation cadets who were eliminated from Air Force pilot training in 1942 (summarized briefly in Guilford &

Lacey, 1947, p. 9). The second was an unpublished study made by Dr. Alfred Smode and the author in 1957, in which tape-recorded interviews were conducted with 40 coaches and physical education instructors at Ohio State University. The two studies were concerned with quite different skills, and the data collection procedures were also quite different. One concerned the learning of how to fly an aircraft, the other the learning of such sports as swimming, diving, tennis, football, baseball, basketball, fencing, and soccer. The latter activities, it should be mentioned, all involve skills in which the total body is in motion rather than seated (as in the case of the pilot). It is these wide differences in the types of activities which make a comparison of the results of these two studies interesting. In fact, one thing the researchers hoped to do in the 1957 study was to examine skilled activities that were quite different from those required of pilots and the tracking tasks so often studied in the laboratory.

In comparing the results of these two studies it becomes apparent at once that instructors in a wide variety of activities are concerned with very similar problems of skill learning. The apprentice pilot finds himself in a relatively novel environment—but so does the novice swimmer and the diver. New sequences of responses must be planned and executed, new coordinations must be learned, new perceptual habits acquired, new strategies developed. A detailed comparison of the results of these two studies is not here attempted. Instead the major classes of learning problems, with which the results are in close agreement, are pointed out. Respondents in both studies gave greatest emphasis to the following four aspects of skill tasks.

*Cognitive Aspects of Skill Learning.* Most instructors believe that an important aspect of skill learning is the development of an understanding of the nature of the task. This factor is most important early in training. Acting on this belief, they resort to many different procedures in order to help the learner gain such an understanding. The use of demonstrations by experts, movies, lectures, watching oneself in a mirror, and directed attention, are examples. All of the 40 athletic instructors mentioned using such techniques. The important point is that to some extent skills can be intellectualized by learners who previously have acquired adequate verbal concepts. At more advanced levels of skill, cognitive aspects involve strategy, judgment, decision making, and planning.

*Perceptual Aspects of Skill Learning.* Most instructors emphasize the importance of perceptual factors in skill learning. The student must learn what to look for, how to identify important cues, how to make critical discriminations. Much emphasis often is given to training in the use of proprioceptive cues, the discrimination of forces and pressures. Breadth of perception or division of attention also is mentioned frequently.

*Coordination.* Practically all instructors refer to the development of coordination. For the pilot this often means integration of hand and foot movements. For the swimmer it means integration of breathing, stroking and kicking. For the golfer it means integration of body, shoulder, arm, and wrist action. Timing of successive movement patterns, timing of body movements in relation to the movements of external objects, and the development of rhythm are also emphasized.

*Tension—Relaxation.* Although a variety of comments are used in describing the personality and temperamental characteristics of students—ranging from anxiety on the one hand to lack of motivation on the other—by far the most frequent comment of instructors about this aspect of student behavior concerns the degree of tenseness-relaxation which can be observed in their movements. Beginners exhibit overall tension in many muscle groups and appear to be doing an excessive amount of work; as they become more proficient they seem to relax, movements seem to require less effort, and they appear "to have all the time they need for the task at hand." These comments, it should be noted, describe an important change in behavior, but a change that may well be a result of the development of skill, rather than a prerequisite.

On the basis of an examination of the data from these two surveys plus data from the experimental study of skill, it is possible to formulate several broad propositions that have to do with the learning of complex skills. Three such propositions, which concern (*a*) the probable phases in skill learning, (*b*) the importance of learning sub-routines, and (*c*) the extent of improvement possible in skilled performance, will be considered next. The propositions are in the nature of broad generalizations. Emphasis is on complex skills, because the propositions are more readily observed in the learning of complex tasks rather than simple ones.

## Phases in Complex Skill Learning

It is proposed that the learning of a complex skill progresses through three phases which can be identified for convenience under the headings *cognition*, *fixation*, and *automation*. It must be emphasized, however, that these phases clearly overlap and that the progression from one to the other is a continuous rather than a discontinuous process. In fact, improvement in most skills appears to go on continuously without noticeable plateaus or discontinuities.

*Cognitive Phase*

Evidence from many sources indicates that cognitive processes are heavily involved early in the learning of most complex skills. Thus tests of intellectual abilities and tests of specialized knowledge have been found to predict individual rates of learning during early phases of skill acquisition. Students and instructors attempt to analyze tasks and to verbalize about what is being learned. What to expect and what to do is emphasized, procedures are described, and information is provided about errors, which often are frequent.

One of the most significant series of experiments demonstrating the importance of "intellectualization" in the early stages of skill learning was carried out by A. C. Williams and his associates at the University of Illinois Aviation Psychology Laboratory some ten years ago (Williams & Flexman, 1949; Flexman, Matheny, & Brown, 1950). These studies were concerned primarily with comparisons of the use vs. nonuse of a ground trainer in the period of pilot training prior to the first solo flight. The most significant results, however, were obtained from the application of sound principles of learning to the flight situation. As listed by the authors these principles included (*a*) motivation, (*b*) knowledge of results, (*c*) anticipatory set, (*d*) judicious use of both part and whole learning, (*e*) performance of the task while receiving verbal instructions, (*f*) overlearning, (*g*) judicious use of spaced practice, and (*h*) intellectual knowledge of maneuvers. Unfortunately the research program was not continued for a sufficiently long period to determine the independent effects of these different principles, nor of the value of training equipment per se versus the importance of the instructional program per se. The net results were dramatic, however, in one respect. In a separate preliminary study with only six students, time to solo was found to be less than three hours. For the main experiment, with 42 students in two groups, the mean number of hours to solo was slightly less than four hours (3.82 hours). This is strikingly shorter than the accepted time of about eight hours to solo, and can be compared to a mean time of 5.28 hours for 48 students in a previous experiment where less use was made of the special procedures. For purposes of the present discussion it is important to note the extensive use made by these psychologists of procedures designed to promote an understanding of flight problems and procedures, i.e., the use of knowledge of results, the use of procedure for establishing appropriate sets or expectancies, "talking through" maneuvers, and emphasis on "intellectualization."

*Fixation Phase*

It is proposed that the primarily cognitive phase of skill learning is usually followed by a phase in which correct patterns of behavior are fixated by continued practice, and the probability of inappropriate response patterns or errors is reduced nearly to zero. Whereas the cognitive phase may last for hours or days, the fixation phase, if the task is truly complex, may last for weeks or months. This is the stage in which most laboratory experiments are terminated if, in fact, they are ever extended this far. In the case of the aircraft pilot this phase would extend roughly from before initial solo through the time at which a private license is granted and perhaps to the first hundred hours or so of flying. In the case of a typist it would extend from the point at which the student has learned the position of the different keys and how the fingers are used in striking them to the point where he has perhaps graduated from his first typing course, and reduced his errors to less than 1 per cent, and has acquired a fair degree of typing speed.

*Autonomous Phase*

For want of a better word the most advanced level of skill will be called the stage of *automation* of the activity, using a term that was applied by such early psychologists as William James and Münsterberg. This stage is characterized by (*a*) gradually increasing speed of performance in tasks where it is important to improve time or accuracy scores far beyond the point where errors, as ordinarily defined, can be detected, and (*b*) gradually increasing resistance to stress and to interference from other activities that may be performed concurrently.

Recent neurological evidence indicates that there is less and less involvement of cortical associative areas as learning continues in the case of simple conditioned response learning, thus supporting the idea that the stage of autonomous behavior is based on a shift from reliance on visual to reliance on proprioceptive feedback, a shift of control to lower brain centers, and similar changes. However, the present discussion will be confined to the results of a few relevant behavioral studies.

Bahrick and his associates (Bahrick, Noble, & Fitts, 1954; Bahrick & Shelly, 1958) have studied the effects of task variables, such as coherence, and also the effect of extent of practice, on the degree of interference between two activities that are carried on concurrently. In the first study, Ss pressed one of five keys as moving patterns of lights passed behind a crossline. Some Ss were given a random pattern of lights, and others used a cyclical one. When a mental arithmetic task was added early in practice both groups had about equivalent scores on both tasks. Late in practice on the perceptual-motor task, however, mental arithmetic scores were significantly better for the group working with the repetitive or coherent version of the perceptual-motor task.

In a later study a visual and an auditory task were performed together. The visual task consisted of pressing one of four keys in response to one of four stimulus lights. Four light sequences were used, differing in degree of redundancy from 0% to 100%, and 25 practice sessions were given. Again, as predicted, as degree of redundancy increased there was a corresponding decrease in interference between the two tasks, the range in decrement varying from about 40% to as little as 10%.

Additional strong evidence for the presence of a stage in which skills become autonomous comes from the studies of the effects of stress on skilled performance. (See Chapter 7 by Deese.) However, it is worth noting here that a study by R. E. Murphy (1959) and the work of Garvey and Taylor (1959) and others indicates that the magnitude of the effects of variations in task design (e.g., between good and bad designs as indicated by tests under standard conditions) is greatly enhanced by the introduction of stress. It can be assumed that a "good" design of controls, displays, etc., is one that requires the operator to use a highly stereotyped or overlearned response pattern. Thus, the results indicate that highly overlearned, or culturally determined, patterns of behavior are more resistant to stress than are less well learned patterns.

## The Learning of Subroutines

A second general proposition regarding complex skill learning is that such learning can be viewed as the acquisition of skill in a number of semi-independent routines or sequences (subroutines) which may go on successively or concurrently (i.e., in series or in parallel). In view of the original definition of skill, which emphasizes the continuous nature of skilled performance, the idea of viewing a complex skill as an activity involving several semi-independent subroutines seems more appropriate than views which treat of specific S-R elements.

The term subroutine is borrowed from computer programming terminology, and can be defined as a sequence of operations that are called up on the basis of a single cue, once the subroutine itself has been established. Locomotor sequences, that take the individual from one place to another, are examples of important subroutines. Swimming is an excellent example of a task involving several subroutines. Instructors commonly ask their students to practice kicking as one routine, stroking as another, and breathing as still a third. It is also common to practice two of these in combination before trying to per-

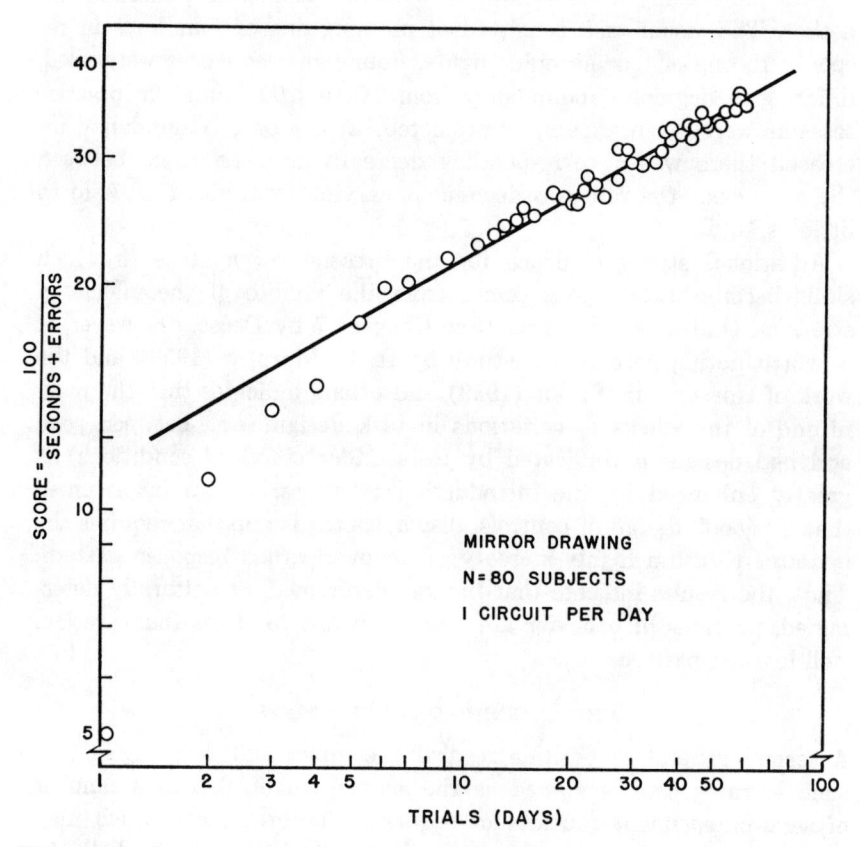

FIGURE 6.2. Improvement in Skill in a Mirror Drawing Task Over 59 Days (after Snoddy, 1926)

form all three at once. So-called "division of attention" tasks also usually involve several subroutines.

## THE ABSENCE OF PLATEAUS AND ASYMPTOTES

The third general observation about the learning of complex skills, borrowing from Keller's (1958) remarks about the "phantom plateau," may be called the "phantom asymptote." The idea is very simple and as far as the present writer has been able to discover was first proposed by Snoddy (1926). Snoddy pointed out that if increments of performance are measured on a logarithmic scale, then proportional (log.) decrements in the time required to perform an activity result from equal (log.) increments in trials. His general learning equation was

$$log\, C = log\, B + n\, log\, x$$

where $C$ is a score based chiefly on the reciprocal of time of performance and $x$ is the number of trials. One set of data published by Snoddy is shown in Figure 6.2.

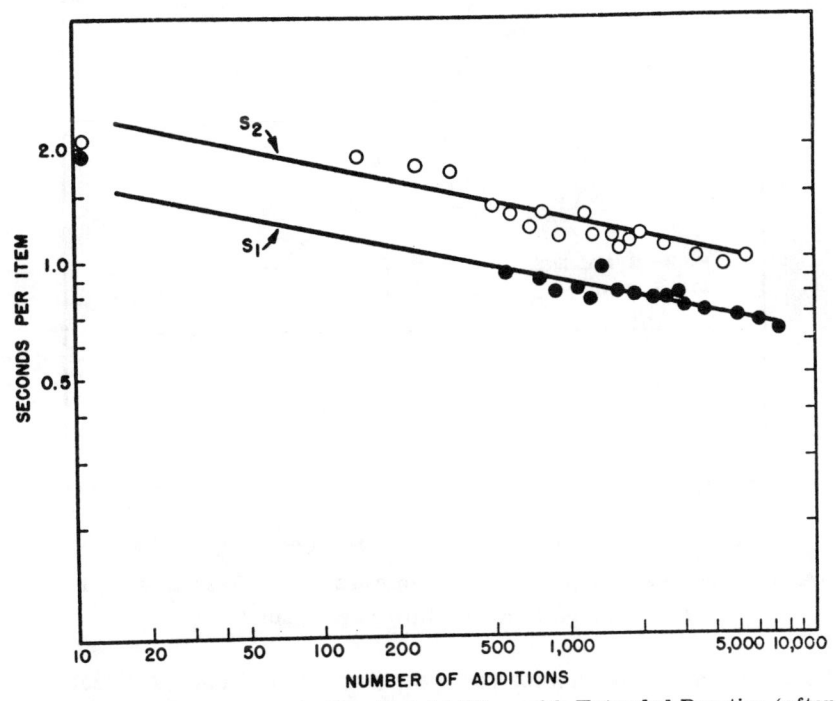

FIGURE 6.3. Improvement in Speed of Addition with Extended Practice (after Blackburn, 1936)

More recently Crossman (1959) has surveyed the evidence for continued slow improvement in performance with continued practice, basing his review primarily on the work of DeJong and Seymour as well as some of his own work. Some typical results are shown in Figures 6.3 and 6.4.

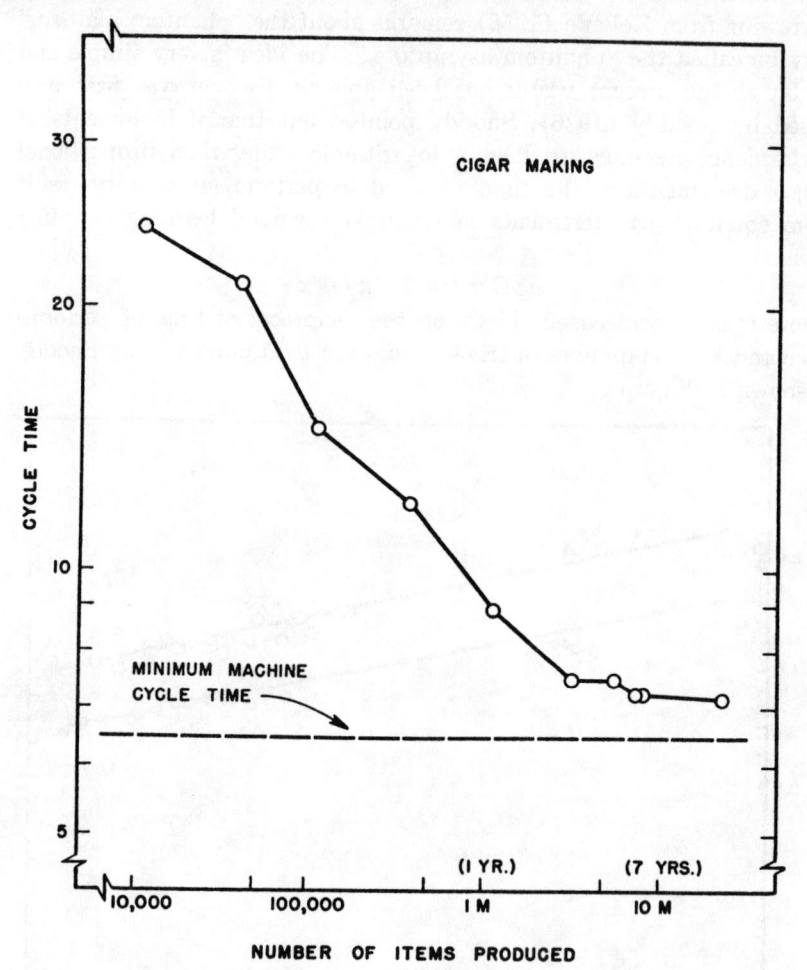

FIGURE 6.4. Increase in Speed of Performance of a Factory Task (cigar making) with Continued Practice (after Crossman, 1959)

The early trials in some of these studies depart from the linear fit of later data points and show more rapid early learning. However, this might be expected on the basis of the high importance of cognitive factors, and the occurrence of errors in early trials. Late trials on some tasks also often show a lack of further improvement which can be attributed to machine limitations.

Figure 6.5 shows some data from a study by Fitts and Seegar (1953) on choice reaction time. These data, for two versions of an eight-alternative task, show continued learning for 26 sessions covering over two months.

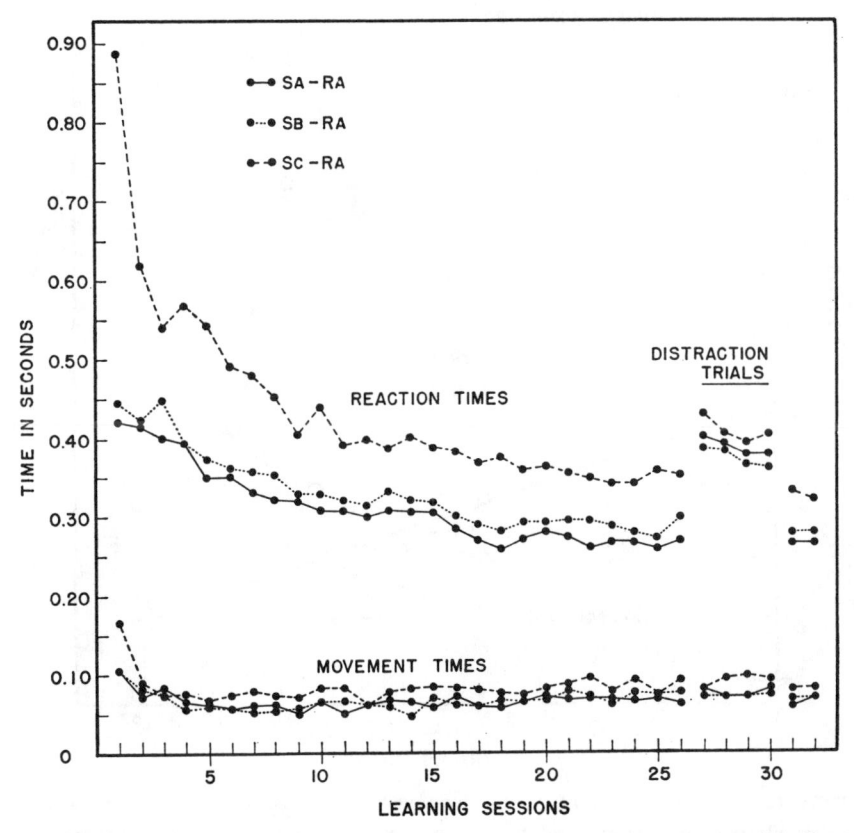

FIGURE 6.5. Increase in Reaction Time in Three Eight-Choice Tasks with Continued One-Hour Practice Sessions (after Fitts & Seegar, 1953)

Another pertinent set of data are those from the perceptual-motor task (the Purdue Pegboard) used by Snyder and Pronko (1952) in their replication of Stratton's classical experiment on the effects of inversion of the retinal image. As far as the author has been able to determine these results are the only data available on the effects of retinal reversal on a task requiring a high degree of skill in a visually controlled task. The results are shown in Figure 6.6. During 28 days of wearing reversing lenses the subject never reached the level of speed which he had achieved during pretests, but on the second trial after

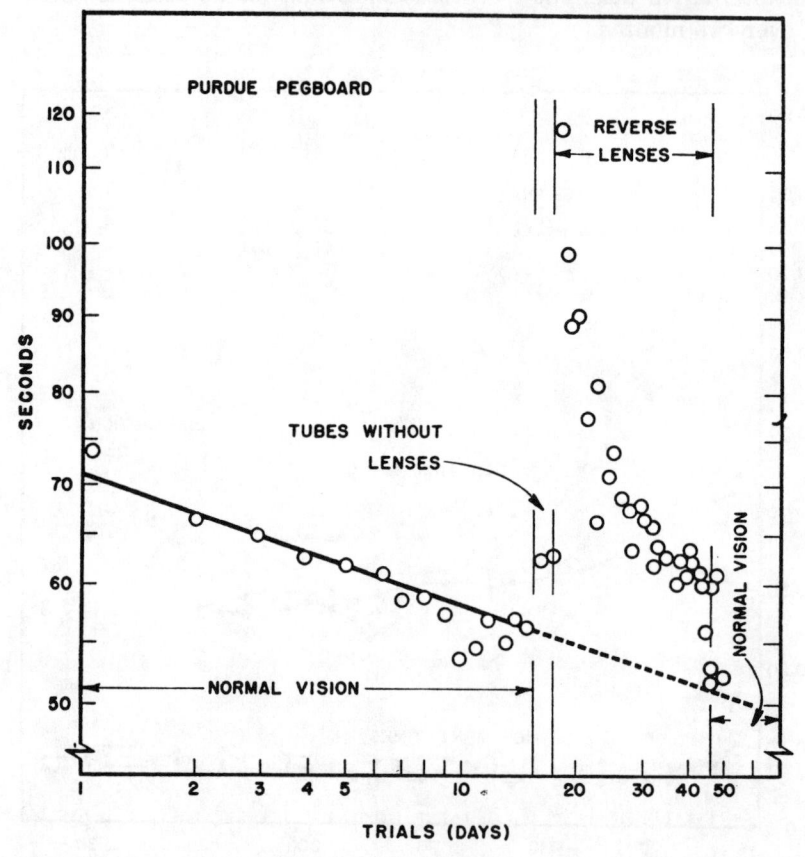

FIGURE 6.6. Performance of a speeded eye-hand coordination task (Purdue Pegboard) before, during, and following the wearing of lenses that reversed the visual field (after Snyder & Pronko, 1952)

removal of the reversing lenses his performance was better than it had ever been, lying almost on the straight-line extrapolation of the data for the original 16 days of pretraining.

In most of these studies of extended training, an increase in skill is evidenced primarily by a decrease in time. Errors are infrequent.

Learning at this stage is seldom investigated by psychologists interested in human learning and yet it is a stage highly important in real life.

One other fact that is obviously true in real life tasks should also be mentioned at this point. It is that the highest achievements in music, in athletic events, and in similar activities often are not attained until five, ten, or often more than ten years of intensive practice. The understanding of such skills poses a great challenge to the learning theorist.

## IMPLICATIONS FOR TRAINING

Several of the points discussed in this chapter have special implications for training in skills. Three of these will now be singled out for consideration.

### Overpractice

The importance of continuing practice far beyond the point in time where some (often arbitrary) criterion is reached cannot be overemphasized. In some types of work, such as most industrial tasks, the individual practices his skill on a daily basis. But in other activities, such as many military tasks, this is not the case. Many military tasks must be practiced under simulated conditions. Realistic conditions of practice (such as firing a real missile, for example) are prohibitively expensive. In such circumstances the amount of practice given to individuals often is the minimum required to reach a criterion. Perhaps only some arbitrary number of hours of practice are given. Individuals who have not had a great deal of practice beyond the stage of initial satisfactory performance probably do not experience the beneficial increase in resistance to stress, fatigue, and interference that comes from extended overlearning.

Overpractice is even more important in tasks which are so designed that individuals are unable to use habit patterns that have been established by life-long experience. When a new task does not conform to a strong population stereotype even very extensive overtraining may not provide the desired level of performance under stressful conditions.

### Training in Subroutines

It is desirable to program training in complex tasks so that extensive practice can be given in separate subroutines. In particular, where invariant subroutines can be identified, considerable gain is to be expected from overlearning these "elements" of the total task. It is also desirable to provide additional training on the total complex task, of course, particularly if there are any interactions between the subroutines. But often it is not feasible to provide facilities for extensive practice on the total task. In such instances the use of "part-task" training is clearly indicated, providing this training can include complete subroutines. According to the general theory developed earlier, overpractice in one or more subroutines should make it much easier for the subject to learn additional new aspects of a complex task. Thus a pilot who has had hundreds of hours of training in a particular aircraft should be able to learn an additional new task (such as a gunnery task) much more readily than a pilot who has only recently mastered the aircraft itself.

*Elimination of Artificial Limits to Performance*

In a great many tasks subjects cease to show improvement, not because they are incapable of further learning, but because some condition of the task restricts the opportunity for improvement. Keller (1958) points out that the plateau in code learning reported by Bryan and Harter was due to the fact that tests were made on a telegraph line over which only slow rates of transmission were used. Performance began to improve as soon as the subject was moved to a main line where transmission rates were higher. Lack of feedback of performance is a frequent factor that limits improvement. Crossman (1959) emphasizes the importance of pressure for increased speed as a requirement for long-term improvement. In some instances the apparent lack of continued improvement is a function of the use of a criterion score which in itself is incapable of measuring further changes in performance.

## REFERENCES

Bahrick, H. P., Noble, M. E., & Fitts, P. M. Extra-task performance as a measure of learning a primary task. *J. exp. Psychol.*, 1954, *48*, 298-302.

Bahrick, H. P. & Shelly, C. Time sharing as an index of automatization. *J. exp. Psychol.*, 1958, *56*, 288-293.

Bartlett, F. C. *Thinking*. London, England: Allen & Unwin, 1958.

Blackburn, J. M. *Acquisition of skill—an analysis of learning curves*. London, England. I.H.R.B. Report, No. 73, 1936.

Broadbent, D. E. *Perception and communication*. New York: Pergamon Press, 1958.

Crossman, E. R. F. W. A theory of acquisition of speed-skill. *Ergonomics*, 1959, *2*, 153-166.

DeJong, J. R. The effects of increasing skill on cycle-time. *Ergonomics*, 1957, *1*, 51-60.

Fitts, P. M., Bahrick, H. P., Noble, M. E., & Briggs, G. E. *Skilled performance*. New York: Wiley, 1961. (In press)

Fitts, P. M. & Seegar, C. M. S-R compatibility: Spatial characteristics of stimulus and response codes. *J. exp. Psychol.*, 1953, *46*, 199-210.

Flexman, R. E., Matheny, W. G., & Brown, E. L. Evaluation of the school link and special methods of instruction. *Univer. of Illinois Bull.*, Vol. 47, No. 80, July 1950.

Garvey, W. D. & Taylor, F. V. The use of "artificial signals" to enhance monitoring performance. In P. M. Fitts (Ed.), *Human engineering concepts and theory*. Ann Arbor: University of Michigan Press, 1959. Pp. 16.1.1 to 16.1.14.

Guilford, J. P. & Lacey, J. I. *Printed classification tests*. Washington, D. C.: U.S. Government Printing Office, 1947.

Keller, F. S. The phantom plateau. *J. exp. Anal. Behavior*, 1958, *1*, 1-13.

Murphy, R. E. Effects of threat of shock, distraction and task design on performance. *J. exp. Psychol.*, 1959, *58*, 134-141.

Snoddy, G. S. Learning and stability. *Applied Psychol.*, 1926, *10*, 1-36.

Snyder, F. W. & Pronko, N. H. *Vision with spatial inversion*. Wichita, Kansas: University of Wichita Press, 1952.

Williams, A. C. & Flexman, R. E. Evaluation of the school link as an aid in primary flight instruction. *Univer. of Illinois Bull.*, Vol. 46, No. 71, June 1949.

Woodworth, R. S. *Dynamics of behavior*. New York: Holt, 1958.

# 21

# Training High-Performance Skills: Fallacies and Guidelines

WALTER SCHNEIDER,[1] *Learning Research and Development Center, University of Pittsburgh, Pittsburgh, Pennsylvania*

> *A high-performance skill is defined as one for which (1) more than 100 hours of training are required, (2) substantial numbers of individuals fail to develop proficiency, and (3) the performance of the expert is qualitatively different from that of the novice. Training programs for developing high-performance skills are often based on assumptions that may be appropriate for simple skills. These assumptions can be fallacious when extended to high-performance skills. Six fallacies of training are described. Empirical characteristics of high-performance skill acquisition are reviewed. These include long acquisition periods, heterogeneity of component learning, development of inappropriate strategies, and training of time-sharing skills. A tentative set of working guidelines for the acquisition of high-performance skills is described.*

## INTRODUCTION

This article examines special considerations and problems associated with high-performance skill acquisition. Much of skill-learning experience and most skill-learning research relate to learning simple skills (e.g., lever positioning). Generalizations based on improvements over short training periods can produce fallacious training assumptions. These assumptions are frequently implicitly assumed in training programs. This paper explicitly identifies some of the more prevalent assumptions. The section on fallacies is written from a devil's advocate position. It is intended to cause the training program designer to question frequently held implicit assumptions. The next section describes empirical results illustrating special considerations for training highly skilled performance.

The recent increased use of microprocessor-based training emphasizes the need to develop explicit guidelines for skill training. Microcomputers can provide feedback, graphic illustrations, and drill on many components of critical tasks. In the past, training amounted to a combination of classroom instruction and laboratory or on-the-job experience in the final work environment. Now microcomputer programs can be easily modified to train individual component skills, graphically represent the problem, provide augmented cues, sequence the training, and so on. If training-program developers blindly make computers perform the same type of simulation activities that were previously done with simulators, there is no reason to expect training efficiency to improve (with the exception of possibly decreasing the

[1] Requests for reprints should be sent to Walter Schneider, LRDC Building, 3939 O'Hara St., Pittsburgh, PA 15260.

number of trainers). For example, an Advanced Controller Exerciser (McCauley, Root, and Muckler, 1982) was developed to replace the traditional multiperson simulation system for training air intercept control. The microprocessor-based system resulted in poorer trainee performance than the original system. Greater awareness of the special considerations of high-performance skill acquisition may enable better use of the flexibility provided by microprocessors.

For the purposes of this paper, high-performance skills will be defined as having three characteristics. First, the trainee must expend considerable time and effort to acquire a high-performance level (i.e., greater than 100 h). Second, the training programs that produce such skill levels will characteristically experience substantial failure rates even among individuals motivated to acquire the skill (i.e., greater than 20%). Third, there will be substantial qualitative differences in performance between a novice and an expert.

Military air traffic and air weapons control provide examples of high-performance skills. To develop proficiency requires from one to two years of training. Washout rates for training programs vary from 25% to 70%, with 50% being typical. Novices and experts show very different performance characteristics. For example, when performing a two-aircraft live intercept, novices have difficulty estimating the turn radii of the aircraft. The novice (13 weeks of training) continues to watch the display for minutes to determine whether the specified turn maneuvers produce the desired effect. In contrast, an expert watching the intercept could specify after only 20 s (two scope sweeps) that the one aircraft is coming in too hot and would pass in front of the aircraft that it was supposed to come in behind. For the novice, decisions are slow and uncertain, and the trainee appears very overtaxed. In contrast, the expert makes decisions quickly and with little effort, and can simultaneously perform other duties.

The training of a fighter pilot provides another example of a high-performance skill. This training typically requires 350 flight hours over two years, and washout rates range in excess of 30% (Griffin and Mosko, 1977).

A more mundane example of a high-performance skill is that shown in professional-level typing. Typical training time necessary to develop a 50 word-per-minute typing speed is in excess of 200 h (Deighton, 1971). Most of the people who try to develop typing skill never obtain that level. A highly skilled typist independently moves his or her fingers to different keys simultaneously, whereas the novice makes individual movements to keys sequentially (Rumelhart and Norman, 1982).

It is difficult to generalize research for the training of highly skilled performance. First, there are few parametric empirical studies. The studies that do exist often confound effects of training procedure, trainers, and subject criterion differences (Eberts, Smith, Dray, and Vestewig, 1982). Also, because performance changes qualitatively over time, training techniques that may be quite useful for initial acquisition may be very ineffective for later skill development. Finally, our theoretical understanding of the nature of performance change with practice is very limited. There are some theoretical perspectives that predict qualitative changes in performance (e.g., Pew, 1966, 1974; Schneider and Fisk, 1983; Shiffrin and Schneider, 1977). However, the theoretical development does not yet specify which training techniques would be best at different stages of skill acquisition.

## TRAINING FALLACIES

Many training programs are based on implicitly assumed fallacies. These are fallacies in the sense that they are misleading and are based on unsound generalizations. The next section provides empirical evidence for the unsoundness of the assumptions. All of these fallacies have some truth. However, when taken to extremes, they often produce inefficient training programs. Examples are provided from the training of military air traffic controllers. Examples could easily be drawn from tasks such as typing, pilot training, or reading. The reader is encouraged to assess whether these generalizations can be seen in training programs familiar to the reader. These generalizations are described from a devil's advocate position to encourage the reader to critically consider some commonly held training assumptions.

*Fallacy 1—Practice Makes Perfect*

"Practice makes perfect" assumes that if individuals continue to perform a task, their performance will improve, reaching near-optimal levels. For learning simple tasks such as memorizing a phone number, practice makes perfect. However, this assumption does not prove to be a valid generalization for high-performance training. For example, in air traffic control training, a large portion of the training time is occupied with the student simply practicing the task. However, many students show only very slow acquisition rates by practicing the task and do not obtain acceptable performance levels by the end of the training program (recall the 50% washout rate).

The statement that practice makes perfect is an overgeneralization. Not only does practice often fail to make perfect, it sometimes produces no improvement in performance at all. For example, if subjects practice a digit-span task for weeks, subjects who do not consistently group the digits show little improvement in their ability to maintain information in memory (see Chase and Ericsson, 1981). Practice on consistent component tasks does improve component skills (see below). Consistent components are those elements of the task where the subject can make the same response to the stimulus whenever it occurs. When given explicit training on using a strategy to consistently encode the incoming stream, subjects' digit span can increase substantially (Chase and Ericsson, 1981).

*Fallacy 2—Training of the Total Skill*

The second fallacy is that it is best to train a skill in a form similar to the final execution of the skill. Total task training is necessary because the final performance is in the target task. However, belief in this fallacy tends to shift most of the training into a target-task format. A belief in this fallacy seduces one to maximize fidelity even when it yields little training benefit (e.g., see Hopkins, 1975). Training an air traffic controller to perceive turn points at which an aircraft should start a turn illustrates the inefficiency of total-task training. A normal aircraft requires four minutes to sweep out a complete turn on the radar screen. It is difficult to learn to perceive turn radii from such observations. First, because of perceptual decay, it is difficult for the controller to integrate more than about 15 s of the display. Hence, the observer must learn to perceive a circular pattern without ever having seen more than about 20 deg of the circle on the display. Second, the trainee receives very little training at this component skill even after long periods of experience. The trainee may experience only eight 90-deg turns in an hour. In contrast, a training module designed to teach this component could expose the trainee to hundreds of accelerated observations of a turn radius in an hour (Vidulich, Yeh, and Schneider, 1983). Third, the trainee receives poor feedback as to the quality of his or her judgment of the turn. The primary feedback indicates how closely the aircraft missed its final destination. There are a number of potential causes that could produce the same final error (e.g., misjudging the wind velocity, misjudging the rollout of the turn, midjudging the initial heading, too sharp a turn, etc.). When trained in the target task, the trainee will have difficulty in determining the source of an error.

Training in the target task can be inefficient. The real situation does not sequence events optimally, results in resource overload, and often produces frustration and panic. Those who support training primarily in the final situation should examine the assumptions that are implied by this "fallacy." If one believes the best way to train is in the target task one believes the following:

(1) The real world optimally presents consistent elements of the task. One is assuming that the world is fortuitously organized such that the typical execution of the skill best illustrates the consistent components of that task for optimal learning.
(2) One assumes that the real world optimally orders the sequence of events for training. Again one is assuming that the world is fortuitously constructed such that the spacing of practice at consistent task elements is optimal for learning.
(3) It is best to train a task when attentional capacities are overloaded. If one wants to learn to drive and converse at the same time, one should begin practicing doing both tasks together.
(4) It is acceptable to be confused about how errors influence performance. Whenever one performs a complex task, it is often difficult to tell which errors caused poor performance or whether those errors were caused due to lapses of attention or an inability to perform the given task.
(5) One assumes that frustration due to errors and poor performance does not reduce student effort.
(6) One assumes that there is little transfer from component task training to total performance.

If this last assumption is true, training the total task is the only way to substantially improve performance. However, in many situations there is substantial transfer of component training. For example, training with cardboard models of the cockpit can produce substantial savings in performing the task in the aircraft (Caro, 1973).

*Fallacy 3—Skill Learning Is Intrinsically Enjoyable*

The third fallacy is that skill training is intrinsically motivating and thus, adding extrinsic motivators is inappropriate. One example is air traffic control training. Air traffic controllers are professionals. Their futures depend on how well they do in the training program. Hence, one would expect little benefit from providing extrinsic motivators. However, being in a darkened room controlling simulated aircraft for 8 h can get boring. As the training day wears on, it can become difficult to concentrate on one's work. The problem with the belief in this fallacy is that it can justify a training program designer's lack of concern about motivating the learner. The problem of motivating the learner is left to the training personnel.

In my laboratory (Human Attention Research Laboratory, University of Illinois), about 3000 subject-training hours are executed per year. Probably the most cost-effective piece of equipment in my laboratory is a noise synthesis chip. This $15 chip can be programmed to emit interesting noises when important events occur. In an air traffic control task, for example, whenever a subject identifies the correct turn point, the aircraft flies the appropriate trajectory with an interesting frequency sweep auditory shot. Before the addition of extrinsic motivators, about 30% of the subjects failed to develop sufficient accuracy in our skill-acquisition experiments. After adding extrinsic motivators (e.g., interesting sound effects, interesting visual display patterns, providing criterion-based feedback), failure rates were reduced to less than 5%.

In many training programs the most important determinant of performance is how long a learner actively practices the task. When designing a training program, one must include motivational events to maintain active participation.

*Fallacy 4—Train for Accurate Performance*

The fourth fallacy is that the primary goal of training a skill is to produce highly accurate performance. In air traffic control, controllers are trained to maintain optimal separation between the aircraft. Training for maximal performance accuracy can be counterproductive. In many skill-training programs the goal should be to obtain acceptable accuracy on a component skill while allowing attention to be allocated to other components of the task. In air traffic control, an operator who can maintain optimal separation of only two aircraft would not be an acceptable controller. What is desired is an operator who can maintain safe separation among 10 aircraft.

Training programs following this fallacy tend to produce operators who can perform individual component skills well but who cannot operate well in high-workload situations. Specialized training may be necessary to develop skills that will operate well under high workload (see below). Also, in order to achieve reliable performance under high workload, substantial overtraining may be necessary. For example, LaBerge (1976) has shown that training subjects to compare symbols when not directly attending to those symbols requires about six times more training than does training them to compare symbols while attending to the task.

*Fallacy 5—Initial Performance Is a Good Predictor of Trainee and Training Program Success*

Belief in this fallacy suggests that if we measure a learner's performance in the first few hours of training, one can predict performance after hundreds of hours of training. In reality, initial performance of complex skills is very unstable and often provides a poor prediction of final performance. For example, the correlation between the first and fifteenth hour of performing a simple grammatical reasoning task was only 0.31 (Kennedy, Jones, and Harbeson, 1980). As the skill becomes more complex, more novel, and requires longer training times, correlations between initial and final performance decrease. Note also that performance may not be a good measure of learning. For example, augmented training may greatly facilitate performance but may slow learning.

This fallacy presents a particular problem in evaluating training programs. Certain techniques may work very poorly in a short training program but be very beneficial in a long training program. For example, in a six-month air traffic control training program, it might be very beneficial to have a six-hour training module on identifying the heading angles of aircraft. However, in a pilot project, the researcher may have to demonstrate the benefit of a particular module with a simulated training program that is only six hours in length. It is likely that whole-task training would be the most effective training in a six-hour time scale even though a combination of part- and whole-task training would be better for a six-month training program.

*Fallacy 6—Once the Learner Has a Conceptual Understanding of the System, Proficiency Will Develop in the Operational Setting*

This fallacy leads to training programs that present technical information in a classroom setting and provide minimal instruction on how to use this information in performing the skill. For example, in air traffic control, the classroom teaching describes the aircraft performance characteristics. However, the student may not be shown explicitly what those performance characteristics look like on the radar scope. Often operators need a great deal of experience with the system even after they have learned to conceptualize it accurately. For example, it is relatively easy to visualize a mental model for a manual transmission. However, many hours have to be spent in a car before gear shifting becomes proficient.

*Fallacy Summary*

Most training programs regard one or more of the preceding fallacies as true principles. If one rejects these fallacies, training design becomes much more difficult, but potentially more successful. First, instead of assuming that practice is sufficient to produce high skill levels (Fallacy 1), one might emphasize practicing consistent components of the task. Second, as opposed to training the learner in the total task (Fallacy 2), one should break down the task and re-represent the task to maximize the learning rate on each component. Then one should sequence the various components to maximize the integration of the task. Third, one cannot assume that the material itself is sufficiently motivating for the learner (Fallacy 3). One may need to design extrinsic motivators into the task. One should find extrinsic methods for motivating the trainee without interfering with the actual teaching process. Fourth, one cannot train for perfect performance (Fallacy 4); one should train to what would be considered an acceptable performance level, but also train so that the learner can perform the task with little or no attention allocated to consistent components of the task. Fifth, one should be very cautious when extrapolating results from short training periods to predicting either successful training procedures or successful trainees (Fallacy 5). Sixth, one should recognize that providing the learner with a theoretical understanding is often only the first stage in developing a high-performance skill (Fallacy 6).

*Empirical Characteristics*

To develop effective training programs, it is useful to know the prominent features of high-performance skill acquisition. The characteristics of developing a high-performance skill are quite different than those of learning declarative information. Teaching declarative information generally includes presenting the information once in a classroom-type setting. In contrast, developing a skill entails presenting comparatively fewer "facts" per unit of time but requires the learner to devote a great deal of effort in developing and practicing component skills. The training program designer must be cautious not to use the academic training model as a model for high-performance skill acquisition. The training program designer should be aware of the nature of skill acquisition functions, the heterogeneity of component tasks, the need to discourage poor strategies, and the need to train time-sharing skills.

*Extended practice function.* The first class of training problems relates to acquisition functions. High-performance skill acquisition is characterized by log-log acquisition functions, improvement over long periods of training, initial instability, and false asymptotes. Practice curves are fit with a variety of functions. Reaction time data are most commonly fit with power functions and exponential functions (see Newell and Rosenbloom, 1981). Performance rating scale data are generally fit by logistic and exponential functions (see Spears, 1982). These various curve-fitting procedures show very high correlations (see Newell and Rosenbloom, 1981). The following discussion uses the power function for illustration, but none of the arguments would change if any of the other curves were utilized, since all show fast initial acquisition rates with gradual approach to an asymptote. The speed of responding is well fit as a power function of the number of trials (see Newell and Rosenbloom, 1981). The power law predicts that the log of the time to complete a response will be a linear function of the log of the number of executions of that particular response (see Figure 1). The power law is stated in the form of:

$$T = BN^{-\alpha} \quad (1)$$

$$\log(T) = \log(B) - \alpha\log(N) \quad (2)$$

T is the time to respond, N is the number of trials, and B and α are constants (with α < 1). The power law predicts that if reaction time to perform a response decreased from 10 s to 5 s over the first 100 trials of training, at 440 trials response time will be 4 s, at 3978 trials response time will be 3 s, and a total of 10 000 trials of training would be necessary to reduce reaction time to 2.5 s. This law predicts that performance will improve rapidly for the initial trials but will continue to improve with a decreasing rate with more and more trials.

Newell and Rosenbloom (1981) refer to the power law as the "ubiquitous law of practice." The power law holds for a wide range of response-time tasks. Predictions from the law fit data including: operating a cigar-rolling machine (Crossman, 1959), adding digits (Crossman, 1959), editing text (Moran, 1980), playing card games (Newell and Rosenbloom, 1981), learning a choice reaction-time task (Seibel, 1963), detecting letter targets (Neisser, Novick, and Lazar, 1963), and performing geometry proofs (Neves and Anderson, 1981). The training-system designer can use the power law to predict performance improvement of component skills as a function of practice (for an excellent example of this type of prediction, see Card, Moran, and Newell, 1983).

A major feature of high-performance skills is that they show improvement over extended periods of time. For example, Crossman's (1959, see Figure 1) subjects showed improvement in operating a cigar-rolling machine over 3 million trials and two years.

The continued improvement after extended practice has two implications. First, high performance requires a great deal of practice even after the trainee understands the nature of the task and can perform the task accurately. Second, it may be beneficial to design training procedures that will allow the trainee many trials of performing critical component tasks.

The third characteristic of acquisition functions is that initial performance (e.g., the first 100 trials) is likely to be an unstable predictor of later performance. For example, Kennedy et al. (1980) found that the correlation between Day 1 and Day 15 of performing a grammatical reasoning task was 0.31. The subjects showed different initial performance levels, acquisition rates, and final asymptotes.

This instability of early acquisition stems from at least four sources. First, the rate of improvement during the first few hundred trials is very rapid, causing a large within-subject variation. Second, subjects with differential experience with related tasks start out at different performance levels. For example, assume one wanted to assess an individual's ability to perform an air traffic control task by running a simulated control session. Assume also that subjects who had played 30 h of a particular video game would start at this task with the equivalent of 2 h of training. In a 1-h test of performance these

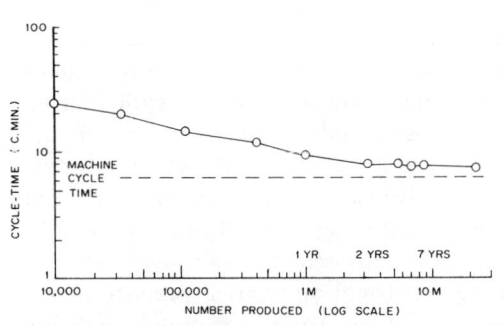

Figure 1. *Time taken to make cigars as a function of practice (Crossman, 1959).*

video-game-wise subjects are likely to perform substantially better than would subjects who had not played video games. However, since the actual training program would require hundreds of hours of training, an individual with a faster learning rate will surpass someone with a 2-h head start in training.

A third source of initial instability is that individuals vary in their rate of acquisition of skills (e.g., see Kennedy et al., 1980). It typically requires hundreds of trials to reliably assess learning rate, and hence it is difficult to get a quick estimate of this parameter. A fourth source of initial instability is that different abilities appear to limit performance at different stages of practice. Early in the training program, general cognitive abilities are critical for following instructions. Later, the basic psychomotor abilities may become the limiting factor (Fleishman and Rich, 1963).

A fourth characteristic of acquisition functions is that the willingness of the learner to continue to practice the task strongly influences final performance level. Most individuals can be motivated to perform even very boring tasks for a few hours. However, many individuals cannot maintain motivated performance when practicing a skill for tens or hundreds of hours. Most of the people who purchase a musical instrument never practice long enough to achieve even basic levels of proficiency with the instrument. In dual-task studies (e.g., Schneider and Fisk, 1984), substantial numbers of college student subjects fail to continue to put their full effort into learning the task after about six hours of training (even when they risk loss of bonus pay). This often does not result in a decrement in performance but rather a plateau or lack of improvement in performance. Bryan and Harter (1899) commented about the difficulties of overcoming plateaus in the development of skill. A training-program designer must help the trainee continue to expend the effort to improve performance over very long practice periods. Note that, with proper motivation, performance plateaus seem less likely (see Keller, 1958).

*Heterogeneity of component improvement rates.* The second class of problems in skill development relates to the heterogeneity of component improvement rates. Performance on most complex tasks is determined by a variety of component skills. For example, in air traffic control, performance is determined by perceptual skills for identifying the locations and trajectories of the aircraft, cognitive skills to predict events and schedule traffic, and output skills relating to handling communications and operating equipment. Improvement rates for these different task components may vary widely. For example, the keying time may decrease by 5% over thousands of trials of training, whereas the time to decide how to schedule traffic may be reduced by 90% in the same number of trials.

Consistent task components show large improvements with practice whereas varied components do not. A consistent component is defined as one in which the subject can make the same response to a particular stimulus situation every time the stimulus situation occurs. For example, in a consistent letter-search task the subject would push a specific button every time the letter *E* appears on the display. In contrast, a varied component is one in which the mapping between the stimulus and response varies across trials. For example, in a varied letter-search task, a subject might search for and respond to *E*s on one trial, but on the next trial, the subject might search for *T*s and not respond to the letter *E*. Figure 2 shows the data in a letter-search experiment manipulating consistent and varied practice at the task. In the consistently mapped condition subjects responded to target stimuli letters

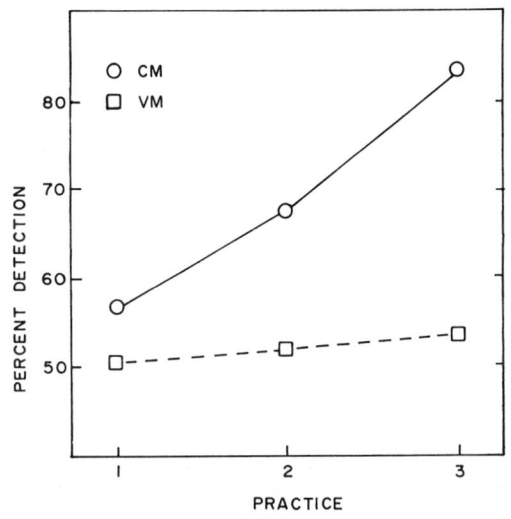

Figure 2. *Detection accuracy as a function of training trials in a letter-search task (from Schneider and Fisk, 1982b). CM refers to a consistently mapped letter search, VM to variably mapped.*

whenever they occurred. Detection accuracy improved substantially over some 840 training trials. In contrast, in the variably mapped condition, in which subjects responded to different stimuli on different trials, there was no improvement over trials (Schneider and Fisk, 1982b).

Similar to letter search, motor responding tasks show improvement primarily on consistent sequences. In a motor output sequential responding task subjects reproduced sequences of eight button-pushes. After the first 10 trials, execution of varied response sequences showed no improvement in speed or accuracy. The execution with consistent sequences improved in accuracy (30%), speed (22%), and response variability (50% relative to the varied sequences) during 50 training trials (see Schneider and Fisk, 1983). Chase and Ericsson (1981) found that subjects who varied in their grouping of digits showed little improvement with practice in a digit-span task. However, when they consistently grouped the digits and associated them with salient classes of events, there was substantial improvement with practice. With a year of practice, one subject was able to increase his digit span to 80 digits.

Consistent task components show substantial improvement in processing speed with practice, whereas varied components do not. In a category-search experiment, Fisk and Schneider (1983) determined the increase in reaction time as a function of the number of category judgments made. The slope relating comparison time to number of comparisons was 200 ms per comparison in the varied search condition and only 2 ms per comparison in the consistent search condition. In this case there was an increase of two orders of magnitude in processing speed for the consistent component relative to the varied component.

Consistent task components can be performed with little or no attention, whereas varied task components are resource sensitive even after extended practice. Figure 3 shows the data from a dual-task experiment (Schneider and Fisk, 1984). The primary task required comparing two digits in memory to two digits on the display that changed every 400 ms. The secondary task required detecting words from a given semantic category. If the category task was consistently mapped, subjects could perform the category task equally well whether they performed the digit task or not. In contrast, if the category task was variably mapped, extended training produced no improvement in the ability of the subjects to time-share the category and digit search tasks. Kennedy and Bittner (1980) provide another example of lack of improvement in time-sharing ability in a task requiring varied responding. They found that when subjects had to count tones on two channels, there was no performance improve-

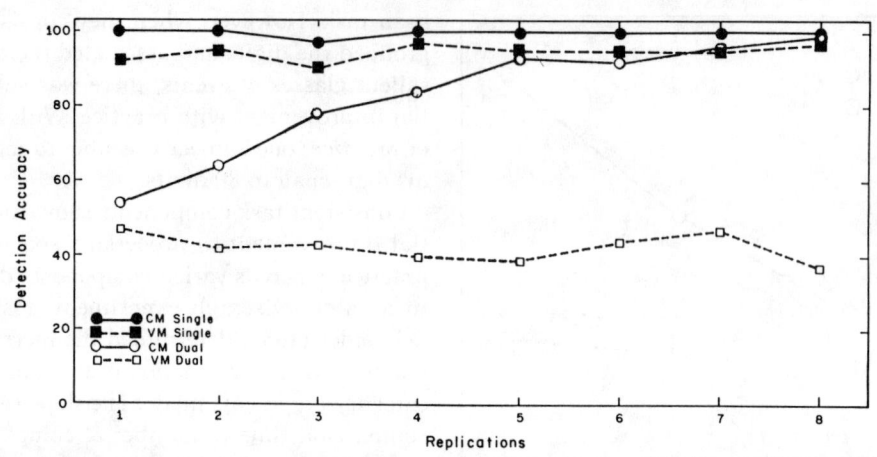

Figure 3. *Single- (filled symbols) and dual- (open symbols) task category-search detection accuracy as a function of sessions of practice (Schneider and Fisk, 1984). Note the elimination of the dual-task deficit in the CM condition (solid lines for consistent category search), and stability of the dual-task deficit for the VM condition (dashed line for varied category search).*

ment over 15 days of practice. Most time-sharing studies have consistent components and show substantial improvement with practice (e.g., Damos and Wickens, 1980; Schneider and Fisk, 1982a).

Heterogeneity of component skills complicates the problem of assessing trainee performance and providing knowledge of results. For example, in air intercept control of a stern attack, the final performance measure is how accurately the fighter is placed behind the enemy aircraft. This single score is determined by perceptual errors in assessing the heading, speed, and turn point of the aircraft; cognitive errors in planning the strategy or deciding the turn point; or motor errors in controlling the equipment and giving commands to the pilot. A single performance score provides the learner with little detail about how to improve performance. In heterogeneous tasks it is important to provide the learner with knowledge of results about the performance of individual component skills (see Newell, 1976). By developing component skill tests, an operator's weaknesses in various phases of a complex task can be illustrated.

Heterogeneity of component skill learning rates may require differential training of components. In the air traffic control training modules, improvement rates range from a 29% improvement during the first 100 trials for identifying the turn point of an aircraft to only a 4% improvement over the first 100 trials at identifying heading angles. After the first 1000 trials at training to identify turn point, inaccuracy in this component no longer limited total performance. In contrast, heading identification would improve for thousands of trials. To optimize final trainee performance, training time should be allocated so as to maximize total performance improvement per unit of training time.

*Eliminating poor strategies.* A third class of problems in high-performance skill training is the need for special training to eliminate poor strategies. In many skills, a variety of strategies may be used to perform a particular task component. However, one strategy usually allows better development of more

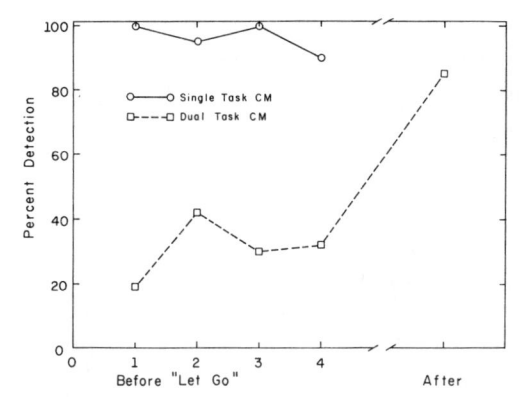

Figure 4. *Subjects' single- and dual-task consistently mapped category-search detection accuracy. After Session 4, subjects were given alternative training to facilitate "letting go" of attentionally processing the words (from Schneider and Fisk, 1983).*

advanced skills. For example, in driving an automobile one can drive by lining up the hood ornament to the road stripe or by estimating the angle of the curve and turning the steering wheel appropriately for that angle. The former strategy is easier to learn but requires many more decisions and results in higher workload.

Trainees may be resistant to discontinuing the use of a strategy that is easy to learn but results in high workload. In laboratory search tasks, some subjects require specialized training in order to enable a low-workload strategy. Most subjects can perform a consistent category search task in combination with a high-workload digit task without deficit (Figure 3, also Schneider and Fisk, 1983). However, occasionally a subject seems unable to perform a category search task under high workload. Figure 4 illustrates data from two such subjects. In dual-task conditions, the subjects' category detection rate was only about 30% of what it was in the single-task conditions. During 4 h of testing there was no evidence that these subjects were improving. This lack of improvement in consistent category search contrasted to the data of most of the subjects (see Figure 3). At the point of Session 4, these subjects would be considered washout subjects. They could not adequately perform this task under high workload. These subjects were then trained to perform an easier semantic search and digit detection task. When the subjects were successful at learning easier categories, they returned to the original category condition in which they were having difficulty. The subjects' dual-task performance increased from the previous 30% to 84% accuracy even though they had had no training on the specific category detection task. The subjects reported that during the interim training they had learned to "let go" and to respond to the words without thinking about them. Once these subjects had learned to "let go," they could perform the category task with high accuracy even while performing a high-workload task (for details, see Schneider and Fisk, 1983).

The acquisition of reading skill provides interesting illustrations of the need to break bad habits. LaBerge and Samuels (1974) report that some readers become overly concerned about word-encoding accuracy. These readers focus too much effort at doing the word-encoding skill and have few attentional resources available for semantic integration of the task. Frederiksen (Frederiksen, Weaver, Warren, Gillotte, Rosebery, Freeman, and Goodman, 1983) reports that some poor readers develop a strategy of looking at the first and last letters of the word and guessing what the word would be. These readers can continue to use this strategy for years without substantial improvement in reading. One method that seems to successfully break this habit is to have the reader identify word units within computer-presented words ("push the button any time the letter pattern *min* appears"). Such training enables the learner to focus on elements of the language that do produce accurate performance and hence show substantial practice effects.

*Developing time-sharing skills.* High-performance tasks often require the development of specialized time-sharing skills. In order to perform two tasks simultaneously, it is critical that the two tasks be practiced together (e.g., Damos and Wickens, 1980). Training with different task priorities may be necessary to help subjects determine the optimal allocation of attention for maximal skill performance (Gopher and North, 1977). It is difficult to train subjects to respond to multiple channels simultaneously (see Duncan, 1980). Schneider and Fisk (unpublished data) have found that practice in conditions requiring a high frequency of simultaneous responding can greatly improve the operator's ability to deal with occasional situations requiring simultaneous responding. It may also be necessary to train subjects so that they can determine how to trade off speed and accuracy. In reading, for example, with full attention allocated to word encoding, word-encoding accuracy may be 98%; however, only a small amount of attentional resources are available for semantic processing. In contrast, if word encoding is done with minimal attention to the word encoding, encoding accuracy may be 90%, but the majority of attentional resources will be available for semantic processing. The latter strategy may result in far better comprehension. Finally, in very high workload situations, the operator must often triage through the list of priorities deciding which tasks must be left undone. Munro, Cody, and Towne (1982) have shown that as workload increases in a simulated air-traffic control task, the operators intentionally ignore information in order to cope with the critical aspects of the situation.

This review illustrates salient features for training in high-performance environments. This review is not intended to be exhaustive (for general reviews on skill acquisition, see Anderson, 1981; Welford, 1976). The emphasis here has been on identifying those features of the training program that enable the novice to become a high-performance practitioner.

## Working Guidelines

The training program designer implicitly or explicitly develops the training program in accordance with certain rules. The six fallacies discussed in this paper indicate the assumptions that the designer should not make. In the last five years at the Human Attention Research Laboratory, subjects have been trained for over 10 000 h in a variety of skill-acquisition experiments. Current laboratory training programs include air traffic control and electronic troubleshooting tasks. The following is a list of rules used in the design effort. The rules developed out of basic research on developing visual search skills (see Schneider, 1982). These rules should be treated as an initial set of working guidelines and are provided to help focus discussion and research in order to develop an explicit set of training rules. The laboratory is engaged in a long-term research project to evaluate the effectiveness of these guidelines in applied training programs. (For a more detailed discussion of these guidelines, see Schneider, 1982.)

These rules are based on the proposition that human performance results from the interaction of two qualitatively different forms of processing (James, 1890; LaBerge, 1976; Norman, 1976; Posner and Snyder, 1975; Schneider and Fisk, 1983; Shiffrin and Schneider, 1977). These two forms are referred to as *automatic* and *controlled* processing. Automatic processing is a fast, parallel, fairly effortless process that is not limited by short-term memory capacity, is not under direct subject control, and performs well-developed, skilled behaviors. Automatic processing typically develops when subjects deal with the stimulus consistently over many trials. Controlled processing is characterized as a slow, generally serial, effortful, capacity-limited, subject-controlled processing mode that must be used to deal with novel or inconsistent information (see Schneider and Shiffrin, 1977; Shiffrin and Schneider, 1977). Controlled processing is expected when the subject's response to the stimulus *varies* from trial to trial. From the automatic/controlled processing perspective, training should develop automatic component skills to perform consistent task components and develop strategies to allocate limited controlled processing resources to inconsistent or poorly developed task components (see Schneider and Fisk, 1983).

*Rule 1*—Present information to promote consistent processing by the operator. In order to develop fast, low-workload processing, the operator must perceive and deal with situations consistently. Developing consistent processing can be done in a variety of ways, including the use of analogies, the provision of specialized representations of the problem, and adaptive training. In teaching electronic circuits it may be beneficial to teach the operator an analogy of a water-flow process for a particular logical element. As the operators visualize the analogy, they consistently make the same response to a given situation, developing automatic component processes. After several hundred trials, the operator can specify the output with little effort and without the use of the analogy. In the air traffic control task for inflight rendezvous (for mid-air refueling) we graphically illustrated all of the possible points at which the two aircraft could rendezvous (see Schneider, Vidulich, and Yeh, 1982). Trainees observe how the total space of rendezvous varies as a function of the intercept angle and displacement of the aircraft. In this way the operators learn to see the consistent relationships among patterns of rendezvous.

*Rule 2*—Design the task to allow many trials of critical skills. Training modules should be designed to provide the learner with many trials of experience in a short period of time. In the air traffic control task, to rapidly train visualization of flight patterns, we compress simulated time by a factor of 100; for example making a judgment of where an aircraft should turn (a maneuver that normally takes about 5 minutes) would take about 0.5 s. By compressing time in this way, we can provide the trainee with more trials at executing this particular component in a single day of training than he or she could get in a year of training with conventional methods. In order to offer extended training experience it may be necessary to compromise on simulation fidelity to increase the number of simulator hours.

*Rule 3*—Do not overload temporary memory and do minimize memory decay. In training the air traffic control task, during initial acquisition the flight path is drawn on the display so that operators need not retain that information in memory. This facilitates the maintenance of a consistent memory representation and speeds the development of automatic component processes to identify turn radii. The number of new tasks to be performed concurrently should be limited to minimize attentional overload.

*Rule 4*—Vary aspects of the task that vary in the operational situation. When developing automatic components, the components must generalize to the entire class of situations to which they are appropriate. For example, when training the operator to identify the turn point for an aircraft, the test intercepts occur at all possible locations on the screen. If all turn identification occurs with the aircraft in the center of the screen, the skill may not generalize well to other positions.

*Rule 5*—Maintain active participation throughout training. Active participation is enhanced if subjects need to respond every few seconds. For example, to train subjects to visualize solution spaces, subjects observe the solution space going through a range of intercept angles and then are presented a test vector. The subject must identify whether that test vector is appropriate for that intercept angle. Without these frequent tests, subjects' observation becomes passive, and there is little improvement with practice.

*Rule 6*—Maintain high motivation throughout the training period. Provide the trainee with extrinsic motivation to maintain high levels of effort. When subjects respond incorrectly, a simulated crash can occur. Adaptive training can sequence subjects to ever more difficult training conditions but still allow them to experience a high degree of success throughout. In order not to significantly increase training time, the motivational feedback should be limited to a small portion of the training period (e.g., less than 5%).

*Rule 7*—Present the information in a context that illustrates more than the to-be-learned task. For example, when subjects identify proper intercept points, feedback shows how the planes would fly to that intercept point, thus illustrating the trajectories of the flight path while the operator tries to perceive the final rendezvous point. Caro (1973) recommends training flight skills within a functional mission context. The trainer must, however, be careful to not overload the subject (Rule 3) and efficiently train component skills (Rule 2).

*Rule 8*—Intermix component training. Intermix the training on various component skills rather than training each component individually before proceeding to the next component. This intermix training distributes the practice and facilitates perception of the interrelationships of the components. The proportion of component and total-task training time should be allocated so as to maximize final total-task performance.

*Rule 9*—Train under mild speed stress. Automatic components are fast processes, probably occurring in less than half a second. Speed stressing subjects improves the development rate. When not speed stressed, subjects tend to use slow, controlled processes that may not be acceptable in the operational environment. For example, in the turn-point identification task, air traffic control operators are expected to make a response in less than 2 s.

*Rule 10*—Train strategies that minimize operator workload. In many tasks there are multiple strategies that involve differential workload. In air traffic control, the operator is allowed only one decision to get the airplanes together in a rendezvous. If operators develop a strategy of many small corrections during training, the workload imposed by that strategy makes it difficult to handle sets of five aircraft.

*Rule 11*—Train time-sharing skills for dealing with high-workload environments. Train operators in situations that require using different speed and accuracy trade-offs, frequent simultaneous responding, and triaging through task priorities. Structure the training so that the expert can perform reliably even during those rare occasions when his or her skills are pushed beyond reasonable limits.

## CONCLUSION

There are special problems associated with training high-performance skills. It is difficult to get an appropriate perspective of the changes that occur during months and years of training. Certain assumptions that work well in short-term training programs may be fallacious when extended to long-term training programs. The training-program designer needs to understand the assumptions underlying each given training procedure. The trainer should be aware of the special problems of acquiring high-performance skills. The research community must work to develop and test an adequate set of guidelines for high-performance skill acquisition. With appropriate perspective, research, and guidelines, the current computer revolutions can flower into a training revolution.

## ACKNOWLEDGMENT

This research was sponsored by Personnel and Training Research Programs, Psychological Sciences Division, Office of Naval Research, under Contract No. N000-14-81-K-0034, Contract Authority Identification No. NR 154-460.

## REFERENCES

Anderson, J. R. (Ed.). (1981). *Cognitive skills and their acquisition.* Hillsdale, NJ: Erlbaum.

Bryan, W. L., and Harter, N. (1899). Studies on the telegraphic language: The acquisition of a hierarchy of habits. *Psychological Review, 6,* 345-375.

Card, S. K., Moran, T. P., and Newell, A. (1983). *The psychology of human-computer interaction.* Hillsdale, NJ: Erlbaum.

Caro, P. W. (1973). Aircraft simulators and pilot training. *Human Factors, 14,* 502-509.

Chase, W. G., and Ericsson, K. G. (1981). Skilled memory. In J. R. Anderson (Ed.), *Cognitive skills and their acquisition* (pp. 141-189). Hillsdale, NJ: Erlbaum.

Crossman, E. R. F. W. (1959). A theory of the acquisition of speed-skill. *Ergonomics, 2,* 153-166.

Damos, D. L., and Wickens, C. D. (1980). The identification and transfer of timesharing skills. *Acta Psychologica, 46,* 15-39.

Deighton, L. (Ed.). (1971). *Encyclopedia of education.* New York: Macmillan.

Duncan, J. (1980). The locus of interference on the perception of simultaneous stimuli. *Psychological Review, 87,* 272-300.

Eberts, R., Smith, D., Dray, S., and Vestewig, R. (1982). *A practical guide to measuring transfer from training devices to weapon systems* (Final Report 82-SRC-13). Minneapolis, MN: Honeywell Systems and Research Center.

Fisk, A. D., and Schneider, W. (1983). Category and word search; Generalizing search principles to complex processing. *Journal of Experimental Psychology: Learning, Memory, and Cognition, 9,* 177-195.

Fleishman, E. A., and Rich, S. (1963). Role of kinesthetic and spatial-visual abilities in perceptual-motor learning. *Journal of Experimental Psychology, 66,* 6-11.

Frederiksen, J. R., Weaver, P. A., Warren, B. M., Gillotte, H. P., Rosebery, A. S., Freeman, B., and Goodman, L. (1983). *A componential approach to training reading skills.* (Final Report 5295). Cambridge, MA: Bolt Beranek and Newman.

Gopher, D., and North, R. A. (1977). Manipulating the conditions of training in time-sharing performance. *Human Factors, 19,* 583-593.

Griffin, G. R., and Mosko, J. D. (1977). *Naval aviation attrition 1950-1976: Implications for the development of future research and evaluation* (Report NAMRL-1237). Pensacola, FL: Naval Aerospace Medical Research Laboratory.

Hopkins, C. O. (1975). How much should you pay for that box? *Human Factors, 17,* 533-541.

James, W. (1890). *Principles of psychology* (Vol. 1). New York: Holt.

Keller, F. S. (1958). The phantom plateau. *Journal of the Experimental Analysis of Behavior, 1,* 1-13.

Kennedy, R. S., Jones, M. B., and Harbeson, M. M. (1980). Assessing productivity and well-being in Navy workplaces. In *Proceedings of the 13th Annual Meeting of the Human Factors Association of Canada,* (pp. 8-13). Ottawa: Human Factors Association of Canada.

Kennedy, R. S., and Bittner, A. C. (1980). Development of performance evaluation tests for environmental research (PETER): Complex counting test. *Aviation, Space, and Environmental Medicine, 51,* 142-144.

LaBerge, D. (1976). Perceptual learning and attention. In W. K. Estes (Ed.) *Handbook of learning and cognitive processes* (Vol. 4) (pp. 237-273). Hillsdale, NJ: Erlbaum.

LaBerge, D., and Samuels, S. J. (1974). Toward a theory of automatic information processing in reading. *Cognitive Psychology, 6,* 293-323.

McCauley, M. E., Root, R. W., and Muckler, F. A. (1982). *Training evaluation of an automated training system for air intercept controllers* (Final Report NAVTRAEQUIPCEN 81-C-0055-1). Westlake Village, CA: Canyon Research Group.

Moran, T. P. (1980). *Compiling cognitive skill* (AIP memo). Palo Alto, CA: Xerox PARC.

Munro, A., Cody, J. A., and Towne, D. M. (1982). *Instruction mode and instruction intrusiveness in dynamic skill training* (Report ONR-99). Los Angeles: Behavioral Technology Laboratories, University of Southern California.

Neisser, U., Novick, R., and Lazar, R. (1963). Searching for ten targets simultaneously. *Perceptual and Motor Skills, 17,* 955-961.

Neves, D. M., and Anderson, J. R. (1981). Knowledge compilation: Mechanisms for the automatization of cognitive skills. In J. R. Anderson (Ed.), *Cognitive skills and their acquisition* (pp. 57-84). Hillsdale, NJ: Erlbaum.

Newell, A., and Rosenbloom, P. S. (1981). Mechanisms of skill acquisition and the law of practice. In J. R. Anderson (Ed.), *Cognitive skills and their acquisition* (pp. 1-55). Hillsdale, NJ: Erlbaum.

Newell, K. M. (1976). Knowledge of results and motor learning. *Exercise and Sport Science Reviews, 4,* 195-228.

Norman, D. A. (1976). *Memory and attention: An introduction to human information processing.* New York: Wiley.

Pew, R. W. (1966). Acquisition of hierarchical control over the temporal organization of a skill. *Journal of Experimental Psychology, 71,* 764-771.

Pew, R. W. (1974). Human perceptual-motor performance. In B. H. Kantowitz (Ed.), *Human information processing: Tutorials in performance and cognition* (pp. 1-39). Hillsdale, NJ: Erlbaum.

Posner, M. I., and Snyder, C. R. (1975). Attention and cognitive control. In R. L. Solso (Ed.), *Information processing and cognition: The Loyola Symposium* (pp. 55-85). Hillsdale, NJ: Erlbaum.

Rumelhart, D. E., and Norman, D. A. (1982). Simulating a skilled typist: A study of skilled cognitive-motor performance. *Cognitive Science, 6,* 1-36.

Schneider, W. (1982). *Automatic/control processing concepts and their implications for the training of skills.* (Tech. Report HARL-ONR-8101). Champaign, IL: University of Illinois, Human Attention Research Laboratory.

Schneider, W., and Fisk, A. D. (1982a). Concurrent automatic and controlled visual search: Can processing occur without resource cost? *Journal of Experimental Psychology: Learning, Memory, and Cognition, 8,* 261-278.

Schneider, W., and Fisk, A. D. (1982b). Degree of consistent training: Improvements in search performance and automatic process development. *Perception and Psychophysics, 31,* 160-168.

Schneider, W., and Fisk, A. D. (1983). Attention theory and mechanisms for skilled performance. In R. A. Magill (Ed.), *Memory and control of action* (pp. 119-143). New York: North-Holland.

Schneider, W., and Fisk, A. D. (1984). Automatic category search and its transfer. *Journal of Experimental Psychology: Learning, Memory, and Cognition, 10,* 1-15.

Schneider, W., and Shiffrin, R. M. (1977). Controlled and automatic human information processing: I. Detection, search, and attention. *Psychological Review, 84,* 1-66.

Schneider, W., Vidulich, M., and Yeh, Y. (1982). Training spatial skills for air-traffic control. In *Proceedings of the Human Factors Society 26th Annual Meeting* (pp. 10-14). Santa Monica, CA: Human Factors Society.

Seibel, R. (1963). Discrimination reaction time for a 1,023 alternative task. *Journal of Experimental Psychology, 66,* 215-226.

Shiffrin, R. M., and Schneider, W. (1977). Controlled and automatic human information processing: II. Perceptual learning, automatic attending, and a general theory. *Psychological Review, 84,* 127-190.

Spears, W. D. (1982). *Processes of skill performance: A foundation for the design of training equipment* (Report NAVTRAEQUIPCEN 78-C-0113-4). Orlando, FL: Naval Training Equipment Center.

Vidulich, M., Yeh, Y., and Schneider, W. (1983). Time compressed components for air intercept control skills. In *Proceedings of the Human Factors Society 27th Annual Meeting* (pp. 161-164). Santa Monica, CA: Human Factors Society.

Welford, A. T. (1976). *Skilled performance.* Glenview, IL: Scott Foresman.

# 22

# Part-Task Training for Tracking and Manual Control

DENNIS C. WIGHTMAN,[1] *Naval Training Equipment Center, Orlando, Florida, and*
GAVAN LINTERN, *Aviation Research Laboratory, University of Illinois at Urbana-Champaign, Savoy, Illinois*

> *Part-task training was defined as practice on some set of components of the whole task as a prelude to performance of the whole task. Part-task procedures are intended to improve learning efficiency and to reduce costs. Our review focused on the instruction of tracking skills for manual control. Transfer of training was emphasized and crucial features of the methodology and of means of assessing transfer were discussed. The part-task procedures of segmentation, fractionation, and simplification were explained, and procedures for reintegrating parts into the whole task were summarized.*

## INTRODUCTION

Part-task training is defined as practice on some set of components of a whole task as a prelude to practice of or performance of the whole task. The rationale for part-task training is that whole-task performance will be improved by practice on task components. Part-task learning is well established as a basic principle underlying education. In mathematics, for example, operations such as addition, subtraction, and multiplication are learned before algebra. These operations, together with special features, are essential components of the whole task of algebra.

The aims of part-task training are to reduce costs and to improve learning efficiency (Adams, 1960; Wheaton, Rose, Fingerman, Korotkin, and Holding, 1976). These economies might be achieved if part-task methods permitted worthwhile learning to occur in devices that were less expensive than the criterion device. Learning would not need to be as efficient or as fast if costs of using the part-task device were sufficiently less than those of using the criterion device. Faster learning is, however, a potential advantage for part-task training and, in the best of both worlds, a less expensive device might promote faster learning.

Basic research has tended to weigh against part-task training. For example, Adams (1960) has noted that results favor whole over part training by two to one. However, reviews of the experimental work have suggested trends that seem important for effective application of part-task procedures. Adams (1960), Holding (1965), and Wheaton et al. (1976) noted that part-task training appears to be more effective with difficult tasks. Schendel, Shields, and Katz (1978) further observed that a difficult task should be partitioned into relatively independent compo-

---

[1] Requests for reprints should be sent to Dennis C. Wightman, Naval Training Equipment Center, Code 711, Orlando, FL 32813.

nents. Part-task training also appears to be more effective for low-aptitude or inexperienced students (Schendel et al., 1978).

The aims of this review are to reexamine these issues and to establish a conceptual structure to guide research. Issues pertaining to tracking in manual control will be emphasized. Key concepts will be explicated, and a rationale for what has been done, and what should be done, will be developed. In particular, we will attempt to point to potentially productive areas for research and to identify effective methods of partitioning the whole task and of reintegrating the parts during learning. Research areas that show little promise will also be noted.

## RESEARCH METHODOLOGY

Tracking is a perceptual motor activity in which an operator is required to match the output of a manually controlled system to a continuously displayed reference signal. Some studies that might seem relevant will not be reviewed, specifically because they do not directly address issues of concern to instruction of tracking and manual control. In particular, the part-task training literature on verbal skills will not be considered. Perceptual and simple psychomotor skills will be considered only in relation to the insight that might be gained for further understanding of tracking skills. We refer occasionally to the techniques of adaptive training and perceptual predifferentiation because they too are concerned with enhancing transfer by first teaching selected components of the whole task (Wheaton et al., 1976).

We concentrate on studies that use a transfer of training (TOT) paradigm to test part-task procedures. As a minimum, the TOT design includes experimental groups that learn the part and then transfer to a criterion or whole task. It also has a control group that learns the whole task during early trials and continues with the whole task in the training session. Nontransfer experiments will be considered only if they suggest principles or techniques that could be tested in a TOT experiment.

This emphasis is justified on the basis of substantial data. Performance differences during training do not imply differential learning in relation to a specific criterion task. For example, comparisons of spaced and massed practice or of various training speeds can show substantial performance differences in training that do not remain after transfer to a criterion schedule (Ammons, Ammons, and Morgan, 1956; Reynolds and Bilodeau, 1952). Even where differences between training conditions are carried over to the transfer test they can be much smaller (Levine, 1953) or even reversed (Dashiell, 1924). As any of these trends are possible in part-task training research, only a TOT design can substantiate the effectiveness of any specific technique.

Further concerns are that the experimental groups have equivalent practice on their designated part task and that the control groups have equivalent practice plus an appropriate testing period on the whole task. This test period for the control group is often referred to as the control group's transfer phase (e.g., Naylor and Briggs, 1963), even though the control group does not transfer to a different task. In this review it will be referred to as the control group's test phase.

In summary, the appropriate TOT design will have two or more groups, including at least one control group that is trained and tested on the whole or criterion task. Each group will be trained for a predetermined period in one and only one condition. Training periods will be equivalent across groups, although the balanced schedule of training periods employed in an incremental transfer design (Bickley, 1980; Povenmire and Roscoe, 1973) is acceptable and can provide important supplementary information. Control subjects remain on a criterion training condition throughout the experiment. They undertake a training and testing schedule that parallels the training and transfer schedules used for the experimental training conditions.

This type of design permits estimates of transfer and of differential transfer. *Transfer* reflects the effects of prior experience of a specific type on performance of the criterion task. The transfer performance of an experimental group is compared with the control group's performance during training. *Differential transfer* estimates the relative effects of equal amounts of experience with experimental and control conditions. The experimental group's transfer performance is compared with the control group's performance in the test phase. Both *transfer* and *differential transfer* provide useful information for basic and applied research.

Formulas for transfer are discussed by Roscoe and Williges (1980). Transfer can be positive or negative, but it cannot be greater than 100%. Differential transfer, which is occasionally reported as transfer (e.g., Briggs and Naylor, 1962), can have a value of more than 100%. Such a value indicates that training with the experimental condition is more efficient for later performance of the criterion task than is training on the criterion task itself. A positive differential transfer value of less than 100% indicates that the experimental training condition is less efficient but does teach some skills that are useful for performing the criterion task. This latter type of finding would lead to cost-effective application only if training on the experimental condition is sufficiently less expensive than training on the criterion task.

## DEFINITIONS AND CONCEPTS

*Segmentation, fractionation* and *simplification* are the three types of part-task manipulations that have been identified in the psychological literature.

*Segmentation* is a procedure that partitions on temporal or spatial dimensions. Many tasks can be considered as a series of subtasks that have identifiable end points. Subtasks can be practiced either in isolation or in small groups and then recombined into the whole task. An example is the backward-chaining procedure of Bailey, Hughes, and Jones (1980), in which the final segment of a bombing task was practiced first and prior segments were successively added during training. Bailey et al. (1980) used spatial segmentation for this task, but temporal segmentation would be possible for some tasks.

*Fractionation* is a part-task manipulation that can be appropriate for a whole task in which two or more subtasks are executed simultaneously. An example is straight-and-level flight, where both pitch and roll must be controlled. A part-task procedure might permit independent practice on pitch and roll before they were combined into the whole task.

*Simplification* is a procedure in which a difficult task is made easier by adjusting one or more characteristics of the task. Reduction in the control-display lag of a tracking system can reduce difficulty (Levine, 1953) and could form the basis of a simplification procedure for part-task training. Lag can also form the basis of an adaptive training manipulation (Norman, 1973; Norman, Lowes and Matheny, 1972) and, in general, many of the task dimensions that have been manipulated in adaptive training (Lintern and Gopher, 1978) could be used for simplification in part-task training.

A central feature of any part-training method is the schedule that is used to reintegrate the parts. Three such schedules have been identified for the fractionation method (Naylor, 1962). Pure-part training refers to a procedure in which parts are practiced in isolation before they are combined into the whole task. In repetitive-part training one part is practiced in isolation, and then another is added. After more practice a third part is added, and this process is continued until the whole task is being practiced. Progressive-part training is similar, except that each new part is practiced in isolation before it is added to any parts that have already been practiced.

These three schedules could also be applied to the segmentation method of part training, and other variations on these reintegration schedules are possible. With simplification the size of the step-increase in difficulty could be varied. Thus, transition from part to whole training might be accomplished in one large step or in a series of smaller steps.

## SEGMENTATION

*Background*

The most obvious advantage of segmentation is that difficult parts of a task can be practiced intensively without spending time on parts that are easier to learn or already are well learned. Aircraft landing instruction offers an example in that the final approach, flare, and touchdown are the segments that are most difficult to learn. In normal flight training a considerable amount of time is consumed during takeoff and pattern flight. A part-task trainer would permit concentrated practice on the final part of the task, thereby increasing the efficiency of training.

*Empirical Results*

Bailey, Hughes, and Jones (1980) compared the backward-chaining technique with whole-task practice of a 30-deg dive-bomb maneuver. These investigators segmented the task based on the commonly used subelements of final approach, rollin, base leg, and downwind leg. Subjects in the backward-chaining group practiced the terminal segment first. Preceding segments were added successively until practice on the whole task was accomplished. A control group practiced the whole task throughout training. Upon transfer to the whole task, the backward-chaining group exhibited significantly fewer errors than did the whole-practice group. Further analysis revealed that in the time taken for 7 of 10 subjects in the backward-chaining group to reach criterion, only 3 of 10 subjects in the whole-practice group reached criterion.

Westra (1982) reported an experiment in which subjects practiced carrier landings in a simulator with a wide-angle visual system. The whole task was a circling approach to landing. A pure-part procedure was used to teach some subjects a straight-in approach before they were tested on the whole task. In this experiment, control time in training was equated for the two groups by extending the distance of the approach beyond what was essential to learn the task.

The part-task procedure resulted in better final-approach lineup performance during the training phase, presumably because it allowed subjects more time to establish themselves on the extended centerline of the landing deck. In testing on the criterion whole task (i.e., circling approach to landing) lineup performance was again superior for the group trained on straight-in approaches. There was no noticeable decrement at the transition from straight-in to circling approaches even though the subjects now had to cope with the new difficulty of establishing lineup after coming out of a turn close to the landing deck. The lineup difference in favor of the part-trained group was substantial and continued through the testing phase.

Wightman (1983) taught straight-in carrier approaches with a repetitive-part technique. The whole task was a straight-in approach to landing from 6000 feet behind the simulated landing deck. Part-task subjects started with approaches from 2000 feet and transitioned to approaches from 4000 feet when they had completed one-third of the training phase. The final third of the training phase involved practice on the whole task. The control subjects were allowed the same number of training trials to practice the whole task and therefore practiced the final 2000 feet of the task for an equal amount of time. However, they did have some advantage over the part-task subjects in that they had 50% more total practice time with glideslope tracking.

Nevertheless, the part-trained subjects had lower RMS error scores for glideslope tracking in the testing phase. There was a significant interaction between training conditions and subject aptitude. The performances of both high- and low-aptitude whole-task subjects suffered in comparison to those of the part-task subjects. High-aptitude subjects overcame this disadvantage before the end of the testing phase, whereas the disadvantage for low-aptitude subjects remained throughout the testing phase. Thus, part-task training appeared to be more critical for the low-aptitude subjects.

Sheppard (1984) also used straight-in simulated carrier approaches as his whole task. His part-task procedure was to freeze the ground position but to otherwise permit full maneuvering around the glideslope so that subjects could learn glideslope control. They were transferred to the whole task after training. This technique was not as effective as that tested by Wightman (1983). Although transfer was positive, Sheppard's part-task subjects had higher RMS glideslope error scores than his whole-task subjects in the testing phase.

*Discussion*

Segmentation appears to be a promising technique. Three of the four experiments reviewed show an advantage for part training. It is possibly significant that the three most favorable results emerged from a backward-chaining technique.

As noted earlier, the most obvious advantage of segmentation is that it permits intensive practice on the most difficult portion of the task and could permit more practice on the difficult portion than would whole-task training, given equal time for the two methods. Note, however, that Wightman (1983) has shown an advantage for backward chaining even though experience with the final and critical segment of the task was equivalent for both part and whole groups, and practice with glideslope tracking was greater overall for the whole group. Thus, practice time is not the only element that enhances the effectiveness of backward chaining. Mere isolation of a critical element for extended practice also does not seem to be particularly useful (Sheppard, 1984).

The nature of the facilitating effect of backward chaining has not been determined, but some hypotheses can be derived from the literature on perceptual-motor learning. The concepts of interference due to activity before knowledge of results (KR), and interference due to activity immediately after KR, are considered in the following paragraphs.

In terminal tasks that converge on a point, such as landing an airplane, gunnery, or bombing, earlier segments may not be learned quickly because they are separated from the potent feedback of the final result. Bilodeau (1956) and Boulter (1964) have shown that activity between action and KR interferes with the progress of learning, possibly because it obscures the association between action and errors. Thus, lengthy perceptual-motor tasks may be naturally acquired in a backward progression in which later task segments, once well learned, become the source of information feedback for earlier segments. Later segments of an extended task may interfere with learning of earlier segments by separating them from

KR. This process could permit the development of inefficient habits in the early segments which, if difficult to correct, would impede whole-task learning.

This view is reminiscent of the response-chaining hypothesis, which might suggest that the effectiveness of backward chaining could result from the fact that responses closest to the reinforcer would be strengthened most (Adams, 1968). Responses earlier in the chain, being further from the reinforcement, would not be learned efficiently, and poor performance of these early responses may interfere with acquisition of later responses in the chain. With the backward-chaining procedure, the final segment is learned first, and can then become a reinforcer for the earlier segment. The more modern view of the feedback in human skill acquisition is that it provides information about errors, rather than reinforcement (Adams, 1971). Nevertheless, the processes underlying learning with backward chaining may be similar in other respects to those postulated by the response-chaining hypothesis. Post-KR processing may also be important (Schendel and Newell, 1976). The post-KR period apparently permits the learner to relate error information to his or her earlier actions. Other activity, such as prompt repetition of earlier task segments, may interfere with this process, whereas immediate performance of the final segment could conceivably facilitate it. Although the evidence for the interfering effects of activity before and after information feedback is sparse, especially for tracking in manual control, these concepts could provide useful hypotheses.

The Treatment × Subject interaction found in Wightman's (1983) data is also noteworthy. Although high-aptitude subjects could quickly overcome the disadvantage of whole training, low-aptitude subjects could not. This appears to be consistent with Holding's (1965) contention that part methods are more useful with difficult tasks. It is possible that part methods may be unnecessary or even counterproductive for very able subjects or with easy tasks.

Whether segmentation is more efficient than whole-task training probably depends to some extent on the nature of the task, as well as its overall difficulty and the aptitude of the students. The previous comments suggest that tasks that have considerable variations in difficulty between segments, or that encourage development of inefficient strategies, are potential candidates for segmentation. Backward chaining has been particularly successful in tests of segmentation, and it remains to be seen whether this sequence offers some unique advantage or whether principles that allow for more flexible sequencing of the parts can be uncovered.

## FRACTIONATION

*Background*

Fractionation has been accomplished in experimental work by partitioning tracking tasks into their control dimensions, their perceptual and motor components, or their continuous and procedural components. Concerns for fractionation are those of the difficulty of each of the components (subtask difficulty) and the need for time-sharing between the components (subtask interaction). In some tasks the time-sharing element may be the only source of difficulty, so that fractionation for training purposes could be counterproductive. In other tasks, many or possibly all of the parts may be too easy to warrant isolated attention.

Naylor and Briggs (1963) have shown the relevance of subtask interaction and subtask difficulty with a prediction task. Their results demonstrated that progressive part training for high subtask difficulty combined with low subtask interaction was superior to whole training. In contrast, progressive part-training with high subtask difficulty and high subtask interaction, low subtask difficulty and low subtask interaction, and low subtask difficulty and high subtask interaction were poorer than for whole learning. Although the relevance of this experiment to tracking in manual control is questionable, the results do show a pattern that might be anticipated in tracking research.

*Empirical Results*

Briggs and Brogden (1954) tested pure-part training with a two-dimensional lever-positioning task. Part groups practiced single dimensions of the task, with some groups practicing only one dimension and others alternating between both. Differential transfer was positive for all part-trained groups, but was less than 100%, possibly because the parts were easy to perform on their own, and the movements required were different from any used in the whole task.

Briggs and Waters (1958) reported two experiments in which subjects practiced pitch and roll tracking in a flight simulator. The second is more relevant to simplification and is discussed later. In the first experiment, subjects practiced pitch and roll tracking in isolation before they practiced them together. Interaction between pitch and roll was manipulated, with errors in roll adding to pitch error in conditions of high subtask interaction. Differential transfer was positive but was never greater than 100%. High subtask interaction was associated with lower differential transfer.

Briggs and Naylor (1962) used a three-dimensional compensatory tracking task to test pure-part and progressive-part procedures (a simplification procedure that was also tested is discussed later). The subtasks were derived by separating the whole task into three single-dimension tracking tasks. Total tracking time was constant for all subjects in this experiment. Differential transfer was less than 100% for both experimental training conditions. Two levels of difficulty were established for the criterion tasks. Differential transfer was higher for the more difficult task. Progressive-part training was better than pure-part training and, for the high-difficulty criterion task, was as good as whole-task training.

Stammers (1980) examined pure-part training with a two-dimensional tracking test. There was a high degree of interaction between the dimensions in that the target's position in relation to one axis could frequently be predicted from its prior position on the other axis. Whole-task difficulty at two levels was obtained by adjusting control-display compatibility. Differential transfer was positive but was less than 100% for both high- and low-difficulty tasks.

In the experiments by Briggs and Brogden (1951), Briggs and Waters (1958), Briggs and Naylor (1962), and Stammers (1980), part- and whole-trained subjects were given an equivalent amount of training. Thus, part-trained subjects had less practice with separate dimensions than did the whole-trained subjects. It could be argued that part-trained subjects should be given the same amount of training on each dimension as control subjects have on the whole task. Stammers (1980) used two training periods in his experiment, so that it is possible to make this comparison from figures contained in his report. Even with this type of comparison, part training was no better than whole training.

Adams (1960) taught experienced pilots a complex bomb-delivery task by partitioning the whole task into continuous tracking elements (controlling the simulated aircraft) and discrete motor responses (setting switches in the cockpit). Control subjects were given 16 training trials on the whole task, and experimental subjects were given 16 training trials on each of the parts. There were no differences between groups in testing on the whole task except that the part-trained groups did not perform the discrete responses well on their first transfer trial. Adams concluded that this kind of part training can be of value when it is less costly than whole training.

Mané (1984) used a pure-part procedure to teach an interactive and relatively complex video game. In this game the goal was to destroy a space fortress with missiles fired from a maneuverable spaceship while evading a variety of missiles from the space fortress. The game had been designed to tax several dimensions of performance, including memory, timing, and psychomotor control. A task decomposition methodology developed by Mané, Coles, Wickens, and Donchin (1983) had been used to identify critical subtasks prior to this experiment (Mané, Coles, Karis, Strayer, and Donchin, 1984). Part-task subjects were given 9 minutes of pretraining on three of those subtasks prior to 100 minutes of practice on the whole task, whereas control subjects were given only the 100 minutes of whole-task practice.

Whole-task subjects required approximately 20 minutes more of whole-task practice to achieve a predetermined performance criterion. In addition, part-trained subjects maintained a higher level of performance throughout their whole-task practice. The advantage appeared to be maintained at a level that represented approximately 20 minutes of extra whole-task practice. Thus there is evidence here of transfer greater than 100%, in which the savings to criterion was more than double the time invested in pretraining.

Adams and Hufford (1961) tested the effectiveness of visual pretraining for teaching landings in an aircraft simulator with a visual display. Their experimental subjects viewed a series of preprogrammed landings and were then tested on their ability to land the simulator. Control subjects were not permitted to view the preprogrammed approaches. There was no statistically significant difference between the landing performances of control and experimental groups. Thus, passive viewing of landings appeared to teach nothing of value for later landing trials.

Although this perceptual manipulation was ineffective, the approach used by Adams and Hufford (1961) is of interest because it constituted a deliberate attempt to teach a crucial perceptual skill that is difficult to learn with normal instructional procedures. The attempt to pretrain perceptual skills has a long history, and the empirical literature has been reviewed by Arnoult (1957) and Gibson (1953, 1969). However, only a small portion of the experiments they reviewed involved a transfer paradigm, and an even smaller portion included a motor task.

Nevertheless these reviews indicate that perceptual skills do improve during training, and that they transfer to a new situation. For example, Gagne and his associates examined pure-part training with a reaction-time apparatus. Subjects were required to activate one of four switches based on a color and position code that was signalled by activating one of four lights. The crucial problem in this task was to learn the correct association between the color-position codes and their respective switches. Gagne and Foster (1949) and Gagne, Baker, and Foster (1950) pretrained experimental subjects on either the position or the color code. This pretraining produced transfer but was not more effective than equal practice on the whole task.

One particularly intriguing result is provided by Vidulich, Yeh, and Schneider (1983). Subjects were taught visual-spatial skills that are a part of a military air traffic controller's task to guide two aircraft into an air-to-air refueling position from several miles apart. The task requires about 5 minutes in real time, but Vidulich et al. (1983) programmed a simulation that completed the problem in approximately 20 s. In 3.5 h of training, control subjects completed approximately 30 real-time trials, whereas experimental subjects completed a few hundred time-compressed trials. In a subsequent real-time transfer test, experimental subjects were able to more accurately judge the point at which an aircraft should start the turn to the desired heading.

*Discussion*

Only one of the experiments that dealt with tracking tasks showed an advantage for part learning over whole learning. Many of the conditions tested did demonstrate positive transfer to the criterion task and could be useful if the part training could be accomplished relatively cheaply.

Subtask interaction appears to be an important variable. Whole tasks having high subtask interaction are poor candidates for part training. Task difficulty also had some impact on the effectiveness of part-task training and, as noted earlier, may generally influence its efficiency. In both experiments in which the difficulty was manipulated, part training was more effective with the more difficult task. Although most of the data reviewed here are discouraging for the application of fractionation methods, the theoretically most efficient combination of low subtask interaction and high task difficulty has not been tested in a manual control context. In general, the approach taken to partitioning the criterion task has been simplistic, and may have contributed to the weakness of the results. Mané's (1984) experiment was the only one to rely on a systematic partitioning procedure, and it seems noteworthy that this effort was rewarded with a strong advantage shown for part-task training.

Other methods of partitioning manual control tasks are also possible. It may be profitable to analyze the nature of the task and establish a part-training schedule that is consistent with that analysis. For example, Briggs (1961) has noted that there is relatively more use made of higher-order error information as tracking skills are acquired. In effect, beginners respond predominantly to displacement error whereas experienced trackers respond to velocity and acceleration errors.

This observation suggests a possible training manipulation. It may be advantageous to follow the natural order with a schedule that teaches responses first to displacement, then to rate, and then to acceleration information. Alternatively, it might be more efficient to concentrate part instruction on the skills that dominate skilled behavior; thus, instruction in responding to acceleration or rate information might speed acquisition of the whole skill.

A further class of manipulations is suggested by the work of Jaeger, Agarwal, and Gottlieb (1980), who have argued that a tracking skill develops through identifiable stages. The directional relationships are learned first, followed by timing, and then by the spatial relationships. Their data and those of Trumbo, Noble, Cross, and Ulrich (1965) and of Noble, Trumbo, Ulrich, and Cross (1966), all from one-dimensional tracking studies, support this view. A three-dimensional tracking study by Lewis, McAllister, and Bechtoldt (1953) showed coordination to be a late-developing factor, whereas an experiment by Pew (1966), specifically designed to study the acquisition of temporal patterning in tracking, showed temporal organization to be a significant feature of skilled performance.

Because so little is known about perceptual-motor skill development, it is not clear whether these data are consistent with a larger overall pattern. Nevertheless, they suggest the possibility that skill development proceeds through a hierarchy of stages and that these stages could be identified. A working hypothesis to emerge from these fragmentary findings is that directional relationships, timing, amplitude, and coordination tend to develop in sequence. Organization, either spatial or temporal, might develop last as the skill becomes automatic.

Identification of stages of learning in this manner may suggest how it is possible to develop special part-task strategies that affect each of these processes. However, even this simple conceptualization does not have a straightforward application. As previously noted in the discussion of progressive development of responses to displacement, rate, and acceleration information, a first supposition is that stages should be taught in their sequence of natural development. However, it is also possible that skill acquisition could be speeded by focusing on the more advanced stages of development before their natural occurrence, possibly forcing the student to progress more rapidly.

A general conclusion that might be drawn from the perceptual predifferentiation literature is that perceptual pretraining could be useful if the perceptual component is critical and if the pretraining can be conducted relatively inexpensively. It also appears that subjects should be actively involved in the search for distinguishing perceptual cues or should make some decision about the visual stimuli during pretraining (Arnoult, 1957). This may explain the ineffectiveness of the passive viewing procedure used by Adams and Hufford (1961).

The research of Vidulich et al. (1983) suggests a further dimension for perceptual pretraining. Time compression as well as active involvement could have contributed to the observed transfer of more than 100%. Time compression has a practical advantage of permitting more practice trials in a set period, and a theoretical advantage of ensuring that all critical events for a single trial occur within the span of working memory. Further development of this type of strategy would seem to be warranted.

## SIMPLIFICATION

*Background*

The notion of an optimum level of difficulty for learning has been emphasized in some part-task research and has formed the basis of the adaptive training strategy (Kelley, 1969). Although a training task that is easier than the criterion task is usually proposed, more difficult training tasks have also been considered (Ammons et al., 1954; Holding, 1965). Although difficult-to-easy transfer is not, in a strict sense, relevant to part-task simplification, any observed advantage for that type of manipulation would seem to provide evidence against a simplification procedure. Thus, those difficult-to-easy transfer results that seem to bear on the issue of simplification will be noted.

Discussions of transfer between easy and difficult tasks can become muddled. Although some experiments show greater transfer from difficult-to-easy than from easy-to-difficult tasks (Day, 1956), this does not necessarily mean that training should be conducted from the outset on the most difficult version of the task (Holding, 1965). It could still be better to use the criterion task for training. An easier or a more difficult training task is warranted only if relative transfer to the criterion task is greater than 100% or if a cost index shows training on the modified task to be more cost-effective. Reviews by Day (1956) and Holding (1962) have failed to clarify this issue.

The most apparent advantage for simplification is with tasks that are too difficult to allow learning to progress or are so difficult that learning is slowed. Some skills learned with an easy version of a task might be applied in learning the more difficult version. House and Zeaman (1960) have, for example, shown that difficult pattern discriminations become easier to learn after practice with easier object discriminations. Similarly, a tracking task could be so difficult that the student would be unable to maintain control for even a short period of time, thereby precluding or limiting the possibility of any meaningful practice on the task.

Gaines (1967) has argued that practice with an easier task could extend students' skills so that performance of the criterion task would no longer be beyond them. It is also possible that practice on an easy task establishes a high performance standard as a goal that can serve to motivate the student after transfer to a more difficult task (Holding, 1965). On the other hand, a more difficult version of the criterion task would force students to extend themselves. That may speed learning of skills that are useful for performance of the criterion task or may establish resistance to forgetting or stress.

Before reviewing the data to assess those arguments, some clarification of the use of the terms *simplification* and *difficulty* seems warranted. We recognize that their use to describe experimental manipulations is not entirely satisfactory. It would be more precise to specify the experimental manipulation. Any resulting change in difficulty would be reflected in performance measures. Holding (1965) has in fact stated that there is no such thing as *difficulty*. Nevertheless, the terms are used so frequently in the literature to be considered that it would be inconvenient to avoid them. However, it should be noted that *difficulty* can be adjusted with a variety of manipulations and it is unlikely that all would have similar effects on learning and transfer.

*Empirical Results*

Briggs and Waters (1958), in the second of a pair of experiments (the first was discussed under the topic of fractionation), manipulated component interaction in a pitch-and-roll tracking task by varying the degree to which control movements on one dimension would affect system response on the other dimension. Subjects were trained on high, medium, and low levels of component interaction and transferred to a criterion task with medium component interaction. Differential transfer was positive from all training conditions, but was less than 100%.

Briggs (1961) examined transfer to a second-order tracking task after practice on zero-order and first-order versions of that task. Again, the differential transfer was positive but was less than 100%. Briggs and Naylor (1962), in a follow-up study, also adjusted system order in their training task and obtained results similar to those of Briggs (1961) for both high- and low-difficulty criterion tasks.

Other data that are relevant to simplification in part-task training have been generated from transfer-of-training and adaptive training experiments. Manipulations of system order, system gain, system lag, and forcing function have been popular. System stability and damping ratio have also been manipulated. Following a comprehensive review of such studies, Lintern and Gopher (1980) concluded that simplification along any of these dimensions does not enhance training efficiency.

Although we generally concur with this analysis, reexamination of those experiments indicates some advantage for transfer from medium- to high-difficulty tasks with manipulations of rotation speed (Ammons et al., 1954) and control-display lag (Levine, 1953). In both of these experiments, subjects were trained on high-, medium-, and low-difficulty tasks and were transferred to one of the same set of high-, medium-, or low-difficulty tasks. Differential transfer from medium to high difficulty was greater than 100%, although transfer from low to medium and from low to high difficulty was not. In only one experiment has a differential advantage for transfer from a difficult to an easier task been claimed, that being in transfer from high- to medium-speed tracking (Williges and Baron, 1973).

Among this generally discouraging evidence, variation of the pursuit versus compensatory nature of a display has emerged as a manipulation that shows some promise. Pursuit displays are easier to track than are compensatory displays (Poulton, 1974). Gordon (1959) has shown that subjects who were trained with a pursuit display performed better on transfer to a compensatory display than did subjects who had equivalent training on the compensatory display. A compensatory tracking system might be simplified for training purposes by transformation into a pursuit system.

Gordon's results were unambiguous and are supported by Jensen (1979), and in a further analysis of Jensen's data by Roscoe, Saad, and Jensen (1979). Nevertheless, they must be balanced against results obtained by Briggs and Rockway (1966) and by Simon and Roscoe (1981) which showed no differential advantage on a compensatory transfer task for groups of subjects trained with degrees of display pursuitedness ranging from zero (fully compensatory) to 100% (fully pursuit).

Although augmented-feedback research does not strictly fall in the domain of part-task training, it would seem remiss to neglect these data entirely. Lintern and Roscoe (1980) have reviewed laboratory and simulator studies of training with augmented feedback and have concluded that it can speed acquisition if students are not permitted to develop dependencies on the supplementary cuing. They suggested an adaptive withdrawal technique to avoid such dependencies. In a study conducted since that review, Lintern, Thomley, Nelson, and Roscoe (1984) have shown a strong effect of adaptive visual cuing on air-to-ground bombing instruction. Differential transfer in favor of augmented-feedback training was greater than 100%.

*Discussion*

The principle of simplification is consistent with common practice in a variety of educational and instructional environments. Nevertheless, it has been difficult to show that simplification procedures are more powerful than whole-task training. These procedures would generally be useful only if they were less expensive than whole-task procedures. However, it is possible that prior training on medium-difficulty tasks would show a differential advantage for later performance on a high-difficulty task, and manipulation of display pursuitedness could also enhance training effectiveness. In addition, augmented feedback may improve the instructional efficiency for some manual control tasks.

The possibility that simplification would be most effective only with a medium-difficulty training task and a high-difficulty criterion task seems to have escaped the attention of part-task researchers. Further tests that are aimed specifically at examining a hypothesis of this type may be productive.

The augmented-feedback and display-pursuitedness manipulations appear to provide students with less ambiguous information about the effects of their control movements on the system being controlled. This might be hypothesized as a general principle that warrants empirical study. Augmented feedback has a large literature, but only recently has it been taken from laboratory tasks to be applied to more practical manual control tasks. As yet, little is known about how to optimize its effectiveness for training.

The confusion about the usefulness of display pursuitedness should also be resolved.

Data from the two experiments that bear most clearly on this issue (Briggs and Rockway, 1966; Gordon, 1959) have markedly different trends. Lintern and Gopher (1978) have observed that Gordon (1959) used a spring-loaded control, whereas Briggs and Rockway (1966) used a quasi-isotonic control. If transfer from pursuit to compensatory tasks depends on proprioceptive cues learned in the pursuit task, the system used by Briggs and Rockway would produce less transfer than the one used by Gordon. This hypothesis needs to be tested as a part of any investigation of display pursuitedness as a training variable.

## ADDITIONAL COMMENTS

Part-task training has recently been popularized in the form of video gaming. Extravagant claims have been made about the transfer of video-game skills to control of complex, high-performance vehicles. The flavor of these discussions suggests a return to the doctrine of formal discipline. This view contended that general abilities such as reasoning, judgment, and memory could be improved through the study of specific subjects such as mathematics and Latin. However, with video gaming, abilities such as timing, psychomotor coordination, and perceptual judgment are discussed. Players of video games are considered to develop those skills in a way that would help them control a high-performance aircraft, to perform accurately with weapons, or to execute all manner of manual control tasks at high levels of skill.

Our review of part-task training has indicated that this is an overly optimistic expectation. There is solid evidence that specific part-task manipulations can speed learning, and we can expect that video-game and microcomputer technology will play a large part in the application of these techniques. In addition, some of the software, or certain dimensions of some video games, may supplement our training procedures. Nevertheless, a comprehensive approach to part-task training must be based on careful analysis of criterion tasks and tailored development of hardware and software for specific tasks.

A fundamental assumption of part-task training is that components of a task can be identified and improved skill on the components will help performance of the whole task. It is evident that proper partitioning of the task is crucial to the success of this technique. Nevertheless, there have been few attempts at systematic task analysis prior to an experiment and, as yet, no attempt to independently show that a useful partitioning of the task had been accomplished.

One promising validation technique is that of backward transfer, in which subjects are taught the whole task and are then tested on the parts that are postulated to be critical to performance of the whole task. Improved performance on the parts, as a result of whole-task training, would seem to validate the partitioning procedure. It seems noteworthy that a recent experiment of this type (Salthouse and Prill, 1983) failed to show any significant improvement in part performance, following training on the whole task. This failure underlines the danger of relying on subjective procedures to partition the task.

Development of part-task methods has been and continues to be restricted by our limited understanding of how tracking skills are learned. The most pertinent issue is that of transfer between instructional and criterion tasks. Although transfer research has a long history, basic processes underlying transfer are poorly understood. There is no comprehensive model to describe transfer relationships between tasks. The simplistic models that do exist (Holding, 1976; Wheaton et al., 1976) offer little guidance for specific manipulations that will ensure high transfer.

In addition to identifying part-task manipulations that do enhance transfer, this review has sought to clarify the principles underlying transfer from part to whole tasks. Although this attempt had only limited success, it is clear that a programmatic approach to part-task training research is possible. Such a research program might uncover many useful principles and establish part-task training as an applied methodology.

## SUMMARY

Part-task trainers offer potential cost savings in flight-training programs, in that relatively inexpensive devices might be used to train critical subskills prior to more comprehensive training in a simulator or in the criterion vehicle. Part-task methods are currently employed in many training programs with apparent success. However, there is no comprehensive statement of principles to guide users towards the best procedures or to help them maximize the effectiveness of procedures already being used. A review of the part-task training literature was undertaken to integrate the existing empirical data. The review was intended to identify the more promising principles and procedures for part-task training and to provide a coherent guide to future research.

Part-task training was defined as practice on some set of components of the whole task as a prelude to performance of the whole task. Part-task procedures are intended to improve learning efficiency and to reduce costs. Our review focused on the instruction of tracking skills for manual control. Transfer of training was emphasized, and crucial features of the methodology and of means of assessing transfer were discussed. The part-task procedures of *segmentation*, *fractionation*, and *simplification* were explained, and procedures for reintegrating parts into the whole task were summarized.

*Segmentation* is a procedure that partitions on the basis of spatial or temporal dimensions. An example is the backward-chaining procedure in which the final segment of a task is practiced first and earlier segments are added progressively throughout training. *Fractionation* partitions a task on the basis of subtasks that are normally executed simultaneously. An example of fractionation is the partitioning of aircraft control during straight-and-level flight into the subtasks of pitch and roll control. *Simplification* is a procedure in which a difficult task is made easier by adjusting one or more characteristics of the task.

The *segmentation* procedure of backward chaining proved to be the most effective of the part-task methods. All available data on backward chaining show it to be superior to whole-task training. It was not possible to ascertain whether this is a general benefit of segmentation or whether backward chaining offers a unique advantage. We recommend further research on backward chaining to identify features that contribute to the power of this technique. In addition, other reintegration sequences for segmentation methods should be tested.

The *fractionation* methods were generally less effective than whole-task training and only once was fractionation shown to be more effective. However, differential transfer was usually positive, so that relatively inexpensive part trainers that employ fractionation methods might be cost-effective. There appears to be some potential for fractionation methods to be more effective, but lack of sufficient information about how perceptual-motor skills develop would seem to be forestalling progress. Consequently, more basic research should be undertaken to identify how perceptual-motor skills develop and how people organize elements of multidimensional tracking tasks. Once a body of knowledge is accumulated about how these skills develop, a more rational determination of how to make fractionation techniques more effective can be made.

*Simplification* techniques resulted in positive transfer, but were generally not superior to whole-task training. Thus, simplification techniques could be useful if the part training was relatively inexpensive. A small number of simplification experiments showed an advantage for part- over whole-task training. Specifically, manipulations of the ratio of pursuit to compensatory components in a display, augmented feedback, and rate and lag variations occasionally led to differential transfer of more than 100%. However, these manipulations did not provide consistent data, and further research is needed to determine the circumstances under which they can be effective.

An additional concern was expressed about the limited knowledge in relation to principles and theory underlying transfer. One conclusion that might be drawn from this review is that the part-task research has often been superficial, and has generally appeared fragmented because it has not been tied to a comprehensive theory. In fact, there is no suitably powerful theory of transfer, and there seems to have been little progress toward developing one during the approximately 30 years of research that has been considered here. A programmatic approach to research and theory development for transfer, particularly in relation to teaching manual skills control, could do much to advance the cause of part-task training.

In conclusion, part-task training has considerable potential to reduce training costs. Almost any part-task method would seem to have some training value, particularly with inexperienced or low-aptitude subjects, and with difficult tasks. However, many procedures are not as effective as their whole-task counterparts, and care is needed to ensure that these procedures are employed in a cost-effective manner. A small number of other part-task procedures were more effective than whole-task procedures, and could probably be less costly. Such training techniques are particularly appealing. We have suggested several lines of research that are needed to develop them.

## ACKNOWLEDGMENTS

This paper was adapted from Technical Report NAVTRAEQUIPCEN 81-C-0105-2 of the Naval Training Equipment Center, Orlando, Florida. The theme developed here was based on a review of literature for the first author's doctoral dissertation. Frank Sistrunk, University of South Florida, was the major advisor for that thesis. His assistance is acknowledged, as is that of Stanley N. Roscoe, New Mexico State University, who reviewed an earlier version of this paper.

## REFERENCES

Adams, J. A. (1960) Part trainers. In G. Finch (Ed.), *Educational and training media: A symposium* (Publication 789). Washington, DC: National Academy of Science, National Research Council.

Adams, J. A. (1968). Response feedback and learning. *Psychological Bulletin, 70,* 486-504.

Adams, J. A. (1971). A closed-loop theory of motor learning. *Journal of Motor Behavior, 3,* 111-149.

Adams, J. A., and Hufford, L. E. (1961). *Effects of programmed perceptual training on the learning of contact landing skills* (NAVTRADEVCEN 247-3). Port Washington, NY: U.S. Naval Training Device Center.

Ammons, R. B., Ammons, C. H., and Morgan, R. L. (1956). Transfer of skill and decremental factors along the speed dimension in rotary pursuit. *Perceptual and Motor Skills, 6,* 43.

Arnoult, M. D. (1957). Stimulus predifferentiation: Some generalizations and hypotheses. *Psychological Bulletin, 54,* 339-350.

Bailey, J. S., Hughes, R. G., and Jones, W. E. (1980). *Application of backward chaining to air-to-surface weapons delivery training* (AFHRL-TR-79-63). Williams AFB, AZ: Operations Training Division, Human Resources Laboratory.

Bickley, W. R. (1980). Optimizing simulator-aircraft training mixes. In *Proceedings of 2nd Interservice/Industry Training Equipment Conference and Exhibition.* Ft. Rucker, AL: Army Research Institute.

Bilodeau, I. M. (1956). Accuracy of a simple positioning response with variation in the number of trials by which knowledge of results is delayed. *American Journal of Psychology, 69,* 434-437.

Boulter, L. R. (1964). Evaluation of mechanisms in delay of knowledge of results. *Canadian Journal of Psychology, 18,* 281-291.

Briggs, G. E. (1961). *On the scheduling of training conditions for the acquisition and transfer of perceptual motor skills* (NAVTRADEVCEN 836-1). Port Washington, NY: Naval Training Device Center.

Briggs, G. E., and Brogden, W. J. (1954). The effect of component practice on performance of a lever-positioning skill. *Journal of Experimental Psychology, 48,* 375-380.

Briggs, G. E., and Naylor, J. C. (1962). The relative efficiency of several training methods as a function of transfer task complexity. *Journal of Experimental Psychology, 64,* 505-512.

Briggs, G. E., and Rockway, M. R. (1966). Learning and performance as a function of the percentage of pursuit component in a tracking display. *Journal of Experimental Psychology, 71,* 165-169.

Briggs, G. E., and Waters, L. K. (1958). Training and transfer as a function of component interaction. *Journal of Experimental Psychology, 56,* 492-500.

Dashiell, J. F. (1924). An experimental isolation of higher level habits. *Journal of Experimental Psychology, 7,* 391-397.

Day, R. H. (1956). Relative task difficulty and transfer of training in skilled performance. *Psychological Bulletin, 53,* 160-168.

Gagne, R. M., Baker, K. E., and Foster, H. (1950). On the relation between similarity and transfer of training in the learning of discriminative motor tasks. *Psychological Review, 57,* 67-79.

Gagne, R. M., and Foster, H. (1949). Transfer of training from practice on components in a motor skill. *Journal of Experimental Psychology, 39,* 47-68.

Gaines, B. R. (1967). Teaching machines for perceptual motor skills. In D. Irwin and J. Leedham (Eds.), *Aspects of educational technology. The proceedings of the Programmed Learning Conference held at Loughborough, 1966.* London: Methuen.

Gibson, E. J. (1953). Improvement in peripheral judgments as a function of controlled practice or learning. *Psychological Bulletin, 50,* 401-431.

Gibson, E. J. (1969). *Principles of perceptual learning and development.* New York: Appleton-Century-Crofts.

Gordon, N. B. (1959). Learning a motor task under varied display conditions. *Journal of Experimental Psychology, 57,* 65-73.

Holding, D. H. (1962). Transfer between difficult and early tasks. *British Journal of Psychology, 53,* 397-402.

Holding, D. H. (1965). *Principles of training.* Oxford: Pergamon Press.

Holding, D. H. (1976). An approximate transfer surface. *Journal of Motor Behavior, 8,* 1-9.

House, B. J., and Zeaman, D. (1960). Transfer of a discrimination from objects to patterns. *Journal of Experimental Psychology, 1960, 59,* 298-302.

Jaeger, R. J., Agarwal, G. C., and Gottlieb, G. L. (1980). Predictor operator in pursuit and compensatory tracking. *Human Factors, 22,* 497-506.

Jensen, R. S. (1979). *Prediction and quickening in perspective flight displays for curved landing approaches.* Unpublished doctoral dissertation, University of Illinois at Urbana-Champaign, Urbana, Illinois.

Kelley, C. R. (1969). What is adaptive training? *Human Factors, 11,* 547-556.

Levine, M. (1953). *Transfer of tracking performance as a function of delay between the control and display* (Tech. Report 53-237). Wright-Patterson AFB, OH. USAF Wright Air Development Center.

Lewis, D., McAllister, D. E., and Bechtoldt, H. D. (1953). Correlational study of performance during successive phases of practice on the standard and reversed tasks on the SAM complex coordinator. *Journal of Psychology, 36,* 111-126.

Lintern, G., and Gopher, D. (1978). Adaptive training of perceptual motor skills: Issues, results, and future directions. *International Journal of Man-Machine Studies, 10,* 521-551.

Lintern, G., and Roscoe, S. N. (1980). Visual cue augmentation in contact flight simulation. In S. N. Roscoe (Ed.), *Aviation Psychology,* Ames, IA: Iowa State University Press.

Lintern, G., Thomley, K., Nelson, B., and Roscoe, S. N. (1984). *Content, variety, and augmentation of simulated visual scenes for teaching air-to-ground attack.* (NAVTRAEQUIPCEN 81-C-0105-3). Orlando, FL: Naval Training Equipment Center.

Mané, A. M. (1984). Acquisition of perceptual-motor skill: Adaptive and part-whole training. In *Proceedings of the Human Factors Society 28th Annual Meeting* (pp. 522-526). Santa Monica, CA: Human Factors Society.

Mané, A. M., Coles, M. G. H., Karis, D., Strayer, D., and Donchin, E. D. (1984, September). The design and use of subtasks in part training and their relationship to the whole task. In *Proceedings of the 20th Annual Conference on Manual Control.* Moffett Field, CA: Ames Research Center.

Mané, A. M., Coles, M. G. H., Wickens, C. D., and Donchin, E. D. (1983). The use of the additive factors methodology in the analysis of skill. In *Proceedings of the Human Factors Society 27th Annual Meeting* (pp. 407-411). Santa Monica, CA: Human Factors Society.

Naylor, J. C. (1962). *Parameters affecting the relative efficiency of part and whole training methods. A review of the literature* (NAVTRADEVCEN 950-1). Columbus, OH: Ohio State University Research Foundation, Laboratory of Aviation Psychology.

Naylor, J. C., and Briggs, G. E. (1963). Effects of task complexity and task organization on the relative efficiency of part and whole training methods. *Journal of Experimental Psychology, 65,* 217-224.

Noble, M., Trumbo, D., Ulrich, L., and Cross, K. (1966). Task predictability and the development of tracking skill under extended practice. *Journal of Experimental Psychology, 72,* 85-94.

Norman, D. A. (1973). *Adaptive training of manual control: Relation of adaptive scheme parameters to task parameters.* (NAVTRAEQUIPCEN 70-C-0215-1). Orlando, FL: Naval Training Equipment Center.

Norman, D. A., Lowes, A. L., and Matheny, W. G. (1972). *Adaptive training of manual control.* (NAVTRADEVCEN 69-C-0156-1). Orlando, FL: Naval Training Device Center.

Pew, R. W. (1966). The acquisition of hierarchical control over the temporal organization of a skill. *Journal of Experimental Psychology, 71,* 764-771.

Poulton, E. C. (1974). *Tracking skill and manual control.* New York: Academic Press.

Povenmire, H. K., and Roscoe, S. N. (1973). Incremental transfer effectiveness of a ground based general aviation trainer. *Human Factors, 15,* 535-542.

Reynolds, B., and Bilodeau, I. M. (1952). Acquisition and retention of three psychomotor tests as a function of distribution of practice during acquisition. *Journal of Experimental Psychology, 44,* 19-26.

Roscoe, S. N., Saad, F., and Jensen, R. S. (1979). *Analysis of intraserial transfer on curved landing approaches with pursuit and compensatory displays* (Tech. Report Illiana 79-1). Champaign, IL: Illiana Aviation Sciences.

Roscoe, S. N., and Williges, B. H. (1980). Measurement of transfer of training. In S. N. Roscoe (Ed.), *Aviation psychology.* Ames, IA: Iowa State University Press.

Salthouse, T. A., and Prill, K. (1983). Analysis of a perceptual skill. *Journal of Experimental Psychology: Human Perception and Performance, 9,* 607-621.

Schendel, J. D., and Newell, K. M. (1976). On processing

the information from knowledge of results. *Journal of Motor Behavior, 8,* 251-255.

Schendel, J. D., Shields, J. L., and Katz, M. S. (1978). *Retention of motor skills: A review.* (Tech. Paper 313). Alexandria, VA: U.S. Army Research Institute for the Behavioral and Social Sciences.

Sheppard, D. J. (1984). *Visual and part-task manipulations for teaching simulated carrier landings* (NAVTRAEQUIPCEN 81-C-0105-9). Orlando, FL: Naval Training Equipment Center.

Simon, C. W., and Roscoe, S. N. (1981). *Application of a multifactor approach to transfer of training research.* (Tech. Report NAVTRAEQUIPCEN 78-C-0060-6). Orlando, FL: Naval Training Equipment Center.

Stammers, R. B. (1980). Part and whole practice for a tracking task: Effects of task variables and amount of practice. *Perceptual and Motor Skills, 50,* 203-210.

Trumbo, D., Noble, M., Cross, K., and Ulrich, R. (1965). Task predictability in the organization, acquisition, and retention of tracking skill. *Journal of Experimental Psychology, 70,* 252-263.

Vidulich, M., Yeh, Y., and Schneider, W. (1983). Time-compressed components for air-intercept control skills. In *Proceedings of the Human Factors Society 27th Annual Meeting* (pp. 161-164). Santa Monica, CA: Human Factors Society.

Westra, D. P. (1982). *Investigation of simulator design features for carrier landing: II. In-simulator transfer of training* (NAVTRAEQUIPCEN 81-C-0105-1). Orlando, FL: Naval Training Equipment Center.

Wheaton, C. R., Rose, A. M., Fingerman, P. W., Korotkin, A. C., and Holding, D. H. (1976). *Evaluation of the effectiveness of training devices: Literature review and preliminary model.* (Research Memorandum 76-6). Alexandria, VA: U.S. Army Research Institute for the Behavioral and Social Sciences.

Wightman, D. C. (1983). *Part-task training strategies in simulated carrier landing final approach training.* (NAVRAEQUIPCEN IH-347). Orlando, FL: Naval Training Equipment Center.

Williges, R. C., and Baron, M. L. (1973). Transfer assessment using a between-subjects central-composite design. *Human Factors, 15,* 311-319.

# Part VII
# HUMAN-COMPUTER INTERACTION

Probably the most pervasive tool in our lives today is the computer. To a great extent it is responsible for the information explosion and the rapid advances in technology we are currently witnessing. It has enabled humans to accomplish remarkable feats, such as walks on the moon and explorations of the solar system. It has allowed medical scientists to construct visual images of brain processes that, in effect, allow us to "see" different kinds of thinking and to observe the functioning of other internal organs. It has facilitated efficient management of extremely large data bases. In effect, it has shrunk the world by enabling satellites to provide instantaneous visual and auditory communication between points all over the globe.

We are now at the point when a computer (or peripheral) sits on nearly every desktop. Along with this luxury has come a number of benefits and problems. The responsibility for developing principles and guidelines for human-computer interface design falls squarely on the shoulders of the human factors community. It should therefore come as no surprise that human-computer interaction is currently one of the fastest-growing areas of research in the field. Human-computer interaction holds great potential for application of existing human factors principles as well as the development of new methodologies and principles.

Issues for human factors engineers include conceptual aspects of the interface, physical organization of the interface, organization and structuring of data base information, efficient retrieval of information, user expertise, and training. The three readings in this section deal with three general areas of the human-computer interface: input devices, text editors, and screen formatting. These selections represent the tip of the iceberg, providing a sample of the important research rather than a survey of important work. Although it is impossible to do justice to this area in a general book of readings, the selections give a taste of the excitement in human-computer interaction research.

An important factor in interacting with computers is the type of interactive devices used. At issue here is which devices allow greater efficiency when people interact with on-screen text, information files, spreadsheets, and so on. The selection by Stuart K. Card, William K. English, and Betty J. Burr (Chapter 23) describes empirical work that evaluates various types of input devices used in pointing to and selecting text on a computer screen. The experiment investigated the utility of four devices: step keys, text keys, the mouse, and a rate-controlled isometric joystick. The results showed that the mouse was superior in speed and accuracy of positioning on a CRT. In addition, relative to the other devices, the mouse afforded the most effective use of the human motor control system. The authors interpret the results in terms of Fitts' Law.

Text editing and word processing are among the most common and frequently used functions of computers. Teresa L. Roberts and Thomas P. Moran (Chapter 24) present a methodology for evaluating text editors. By focusing on common properties and fundamental issues of text editors, the authors found this methodology to be applicable across a wide variety of text editors. The methodology involves four dimensions: time, error, learning, and functionality. The authors aim to "initialize" a data base of information regarding editors and to create a standard against which to evaluate the results of empirical work. The methodology is performance based; the criteria used in creating it include objectivity, thoroughness, and ease of use. Roberts and Moran describe the methodology in detail and present findings of an empirical evaluation of a number of editors using this methodology.

How efficiently and effectively we extract textual information from a display largely depends on how information in that display is formatted. A well-organized and coherently grouped alphanumeric display facilitates rapid comprehension, whereas a more arbitrary format may lead to frustration. How is a display designer to know what principles lead to superior display formats? The final selection, by Thomas S. Tullis (Chapter 25), is an analytic review of alphanumeric formatting on CRTs. Tullis includes both guidelines and the results of empirical studies that used a number of tasks to evaluate various characteristics of display formats. These characteristics included overall density (the amount of total space used), local density (the spacing around each character or word), grouping (items forming perceptually organized groups), and layout complexity (visual predictability afforded by the format or layout of the characters). Tullis presents objective measures that may be helpful in evaluating the usability of a display format.

# 23

# Evaluation of Mouse, Rate-Controlled Isometric Joystick, Step Keys, and Text Keys for Text Selection on a CRT

STUART K. CARD[*], WILLIAM K. ENGLISH, and BETTY J. BURR

Xerox Palo Alto Research Center Palo, Alto, California.

Four devices are evaluated with respect to how rapidly they can be used to select text on a CRT display. The mouse is found to be fastest on all counts and also to have the lowest error rates. It is shown that variations in positioning time with the mouse and joystick are accounted for by Fitts's Law. In the case of the mouse, the measured Fitts's Law slope constant is close to that found in other eye-hand tasks leading to the conclusion that positioning time with this device is almost the minimal achievable. Positioning time for key devices is shown to be proportional to the number of keystrokes which must be typed.

## 1. Introduction

An important element in the design of the man-computer interface is the method of pointing by which the user indicates to the computer his selection of some element on the computer display. This is especially important for computer-based text-editing where the user may repeatedly use a pointing device to select the text he wishes to modify or to invoke a command from a menu displayed on the screen. The choice of pointing device may have a significant impact on the ease with which the selections can be made, and hence, since pointing typically occurs with high frequency, on the success of the entire system.

English, Englebart, and Berman (1967) measured mean pointing times and error rates for the mouse, lightpen, Grafacon tablet, and position and rate joysticks. They found the mouse to be the fastest of the devices, but did not investigate the effect of distance to target. They also gave no indication of the variability of their measures. Goodwin (1975) measured pointing times for the lightpen, lightgun, and Saunders 720 step keys. She found the light pen and lightgun equally fast and much superior to the Saunders 720 step keys. However, she used only one target size and did not investigate distance. In addition, her results also show large learning effects which are confounded with the device comparisons. Both studies were more concerned with the evaluation of devices than with the development of models from which performance could be predicted. In another line of development Fitts and others (Fitts 1954, Fitts and Peterson 1964, Fitts and Radford 1966, Knight and Dagnal 1967, Welford 1968) developed and tested the relation between distance, size of target, and hand movement time. Such a relation might potentially be used to predict pointing times for devices involving continuous hand movements; however this has not been tested directly. In particular it was not known whether Fitts's Law would hold for targets of the shape and character of text strings.

The present report examines text selection performance with four devices: the mouse, a rate-controlled isometric joystick, step keys, and text keys. The study differs from the English et al. and Goodwin studies in that distance, target size, and learning are all simultaneously controlled and a different set of devices is measured. Also, unlike those studies, an attempt is made to give a theoretical account of the results. In particular, performance on the continuous movement devices is tested against the predictions of Fitts's Law.

[*]Reprint requests should be sent to Stuart K. Card, Xerox Palo Alto Research Center, 3333 Coyote Hill Road, Palo Alto, California 94304.

From *Ergonomics*, 21. Copyright 1978 by Taylor & Francis Ltd.

## 2. Method

### 2.1. Subjects

Three men and two women, all undergraduates at Standford University, served as subjects in the experiment. None had ever used any of the devices previously and all had little or no experience with computers. Subjects were paid $3·00 per hour with a $20·00 bonus for completing the experiments. One of the five subjects was very much slower than the others and was eliminated from the experiment.

### 2.2. Pointing Devices

Four pointing devices were tested (see Figure 1). Two were continuous devices: the mouse and a rate-controlled isometric joystick. Two were key operated: the step keys and the text keys. The devices had been optimised informally by testing them on local users, adjusting the device parameters so as to maximise performance.

The mouse, a version of the device described in English *et al.* (1967), was a small device which sat on the table to the right of the keyboard, connected by a thin wire. On the undercarriage were two small wheels, mounted at right angles to each other. As the mouse moved over the table one wheel coded the amount of movement in the X-direction, the other the movement in the Y-direction. As the mouse moved, a cursor moved simultaneously on the CRT, two units of screen movement for each unit of mouse movement.

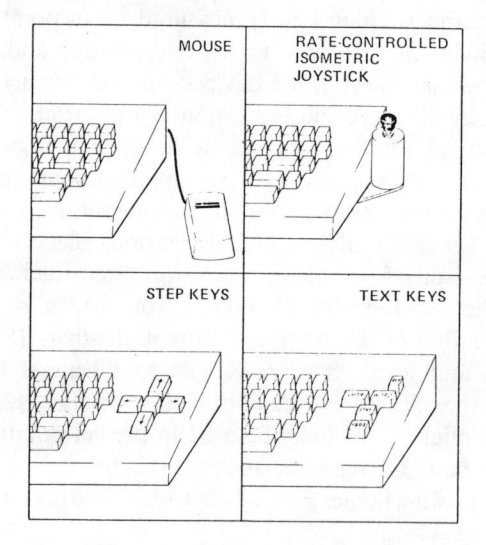

Figure 1. Pointing devices tested.

The joystick used was a small strain gauge on which had been mounted a rubber knob 1·25 cm in diameter. Applying force to the joystick in any direction did not produce noticeable movement in the joystick itself, but caused the cursor to move in the appropriate direction at a rate $= 0·0178$ (force)$^2$ in cm s$^{-1}$, where force is measured in Newtons. For forces less than about 4 Newtons, the cursor did not move at all, and the equation ceased to hold in the neighbourhood of 45 Newtons as the rate approached a ceiling of about 40 cm s$^{-1}$.

The step keys were the ffmiliar five key cluster found on many CRT terminals. Surrounding a central HOME key were keys to move the cursor in each of four directions. Pressing the HOME key caused the cursor to go to the upper left corner of the text. Pressing one of the horizontal keys moved the cursor 1 character (0·246 cm on the average) along the line. Pressing a vertical key moved the cursor one line (0·456 cm) up or down. Holding down one of the keys for more than 0·100 s caused it to go into a repeating mode, producing one step in the vertical direction each 0·133 s or one step in the horizontal direction each 0·067 s (3·43 cm s$^{-1}$ vertical movement, 3·67 cm s$^{-1}$) horizontal movement).

The text keys were similar to keys appearing on several commercial 'word processing' terminals. Depressing the PARAGRAPH key caused the cursor to move to the beginning of the next paragraph. Depressing the LINE key caused the cursor to move downward to the same position in the next line. The WORD key moved the cursor forward one word; the CHARACTER key moved the cursor forward one character. Holding down the REVERSE key while pressing another key caused the cursor to move opposite the direction it would otherwise have moved. The text keys could also be used in a repeating mode. Holding the LINE WORD or CHARACTER keys down for longer than 0·100 s caused that key to repeat at 0·133 s per repeat for the LINE key, 0·100 s per repeat for the WORD key, or 0·067 s per repeat for the CHARACTER key. Since there were 0·456 cm line$^{-1}$, 1·320 word$^{-1}$, and 0·246 cm character$^{-1}$ movement rates were 3·43 cm s$^{-1}$ for the LINE key, 13·20 cm s$^{-1}$ for the WORD key, and 3·67 cm s$^{-1}$ for the CHARACTER key.

## 2.3. *Procedure*

Subjects were seated in front of a computer terminal with a CRT for output, a keyboard for input, and one of the devices for pointing at targets on the screen. On each trial a page of text was displayed on the screen. Within the text a single word or phrase, the target, was highlighted by inverting the black/white values of the text and background in a rectangle surrounding the target. The subject struck the space bar of the keyboard with his right hand, then, with the same hand reached for the pointing device and directed the cursor to the target. The cursor thus positioned, the subject pressed a button 'selecting' the target as he would were he using the device in a text editor. For the mouse, the button was located on the device itself. For the other devices, the subject pressed a special key with his left hand.

## 2.4. *Design*

Text selections and targets were so arranged that there were five different distances from starting position to target, 1, 2, 4, 8, or 16, cm, and four different target sizes, 1, 2, 4, or 10 characters. All targets were words or groups of words. Ten different instances of each distance × target size pair were created, varying the location of the target on the display and the angle of hand movement to give a total of 200, randomly ordered, unique stimuli.

Each subject repeated the experiment with each device. The order in which subjects used the devices was randomised. At the start of each day, the subjects were given approximately twenty warm-up trials to refresh their memory of the procedure. All other trials were recorded as data. At the end of each block of twenty trials they were given feedback on the average positioning time and average number of errors for those trials. This feedback was found to be important in maintaining subjects' motivations. At the end of each 200 trials they were given a rest break of about fifteen minutes. Subjects normally accomplished 600 trials day$^{-1}$ involving about two to three hours of work. They each used a particular device until the positioning time was no longer decreasing significantly with practice (operationally defined as when the first and last thirds of a block of the last 600 trials excluding the first 200 trials of a day did not differ significantly in positioning time at the $p < 0.05$ level using a $t$-test). An approximation to this criterion was reached in from 1200 to 1800 trials (four to six hours) on each device. Of the 20 subject × device pairs, 15 reached this criterion, 3 performed worse in their last trials (largely because some time elapsed between sessions), and only 2 were continuing (slightly) to improve.

## 3. Results
### 3.1. *Improvement of Performance with Practice*

The learning curve which gives positioning time as a function of the amount of practice can be approximated (De Jong 1957) by

$$T_N = T_1 N^{-\alpha} \tag{1}$$

where

$T_1$ = estimated positioning time on the first block of trials,
$T_N$ = estimated positioning time on the $N$th block of trials,
$N$ = trial block number, and
$\alpha$ = an empirically determined constant.

This form is convenient since taking the log of both sides produces an equation linear in $\log N$,

$$\log T_N = \log T_1 - \alpha (\log N). \tag{2}$$

Thus the ease of learning for each device can be described by two numbers $T_1$ and $\alpha$, which numbers may be conveniently determined empirically by regressing $\log T_N$ on $\log N$. Figure 2 shows the results of plotting the data from error-free trials according to Equation 2. Each point on the graph is the average of a block $N$ of twenty contiguous trials from which error trials have been excluded. Only the first 60 trial blocks are shown. Since some subjects reached criterion at this point, not all continued on to further trials. The values predicted by the equation are given as the straight line drawn through the points. The average target size in each block was 4·23 cm (the range of the average targest sizes for different trial blocks was 3·95 to 4·50 cm); the average distance to the target was 6·13 cm (range 5·90 to 6·42 cm).

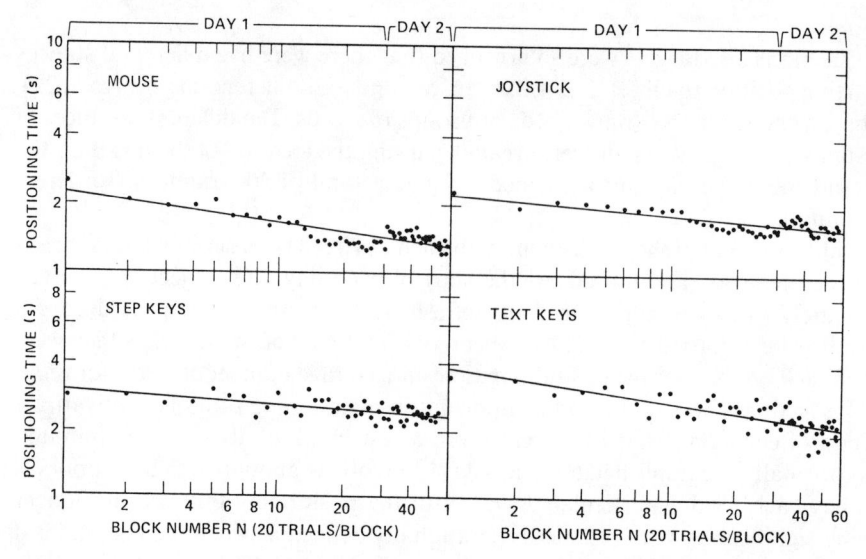

Figure 2. Learning curves for pointing devices.

The parameters $T_1$ and $\alpha$, as determined by the regressions, are given in Table 1, along with the standard error and squared multiple correlation from the regression analysis. Practice causes more improvement in the mouse and text keys than on the other two devices. The step keys, in particular, show very little improvement with practice. Equation 2 explains 39% of the variance in the average positioning time for a block of trials for the step keys, 61% to 66% for the variance for the other devices. The fit, at least for the mouse and the joystick, is actually better than these numbers suggest. Since subjects did 30 blocks of trials on a day typically followed by a pause of a day or two before they could be rescheduled, a break in the learning curve is expected at that point and indeed such a break is quite evident for the mouse and the joystick between the 30th and 31st blocks. Fitting Equation 2 to only the first day increases the percentage of variance explained to 91% for the mouse and 83% for the joystick. In case of the step keys and text keys there is no such obvious day effect.

Table 1. Learning Curve Parameters

| DEVICE | $T_1$ (s) | $\alpha$ | Learning Curve Equation[a] | $s_e$ (s) | $R^2$ |
|---|---|---|---|---|---|
| Mouse | 2·20 | 0·13 | $T_N = 2.20\ N^{-0.13}$ | 0·12 | 0·66 |
| Joystick | 2·19 | 0·08 | $T_N = 2.19\ N^{-0.08}$ | 0·08 | 0·62 |
| Step Keys | 3·03 | 0·07 | $T_N = 3.03\ N^{-0.07}$ | 0·11 | 0·39 |
| Text Keys | 3·86 | 0·15 | $T_N = 3.86\ N^{-0.15}$ | 0·16 | 0·61 |

[a] $N$ is number of trial blocks. There are 20 trials in each block.

### 3.2. Overall Speed

In order to compare the devices after learning has nearly reached asymptote (as would be the case for office workers using them daily), a sample of each subject's performance on each device was examined consisting of the last 600 trials excluding the first 200 trials of a day (in order to diminish warm-up effects). The remaining analyses will be based on this subset of the data, excluding those trials on which errors occurred. Table 2 gives the homing time, positioning time, and total time for each device averaging over all the distances and target sizes. *Homing time* was measured from the time the subject's right hand left the space bar until the cursor had begun to move. *Positioning time* was measured from when the cursor began to move until the selection button had been pressed. From the table, it can be seen that homing time increases slightly with the distance of the device from the keyboard. The longest time required is to reach the mouse, the shortest to reach the step keys. Although the text keys are near the keyboard, they take almost as long to reach as the mouse. Either it is more difficult to position the hands on the text keys or, as seems likely, subjects often spent some time planning the strategy for their move in the time between hitting the space bar to start the clock and the time when they begin pressing the keys. Further evidence for this hypothesis comes from the relatively high standard deviation observed for the homing time of the text keys. While the differences in the homing times among all device pairs except the mouse vs. the text keys are reliable statistically (at $p < 0.05$ or better using a $t$-test), the differences are actually quite small. For example, while the step keys can be reached 0·15 s sooner than the mouse, they take 1·02 s longer to position. Thus the differences in the homing times are insignificant compared to the differences between the positioning times.

Table 2. Overall Times

| Device | Homing Time M | Homing Time SD | Positioning Time M | Positioning Time SD | Total Time M | Total Time SD | Error rate M | Error rate SD |
|---|---|---|---|---|---|---|---|---|
| Mouse | 0·36 | 0·13 | 1·29 | 0·42 | 1·66 | 0·48 | 5% | 22% |
| Joystick | 0·26 | 0·11 | 1·57 | 0·54 | 1·83 | 0·57 | 11% | 31% |
| Step Keys | 0·21 | 0·30 | 2·31 | 1·52 | 2·51 | 1·64 | 13% | 33% |
| Text Keys | 0·32 | 0·61 | 1·95 | 1·30 | 2·26 | 1·70 | 9% | 28% |

Movement time for non-error trials (s)

The mouse is easily the fastest device, the step keys the slowest. As a group, the continuous devices (the mouse and the joystick) are faster than the key-operated devices (the step keys and text keys). Differences between the devices are all reliable at $p \ll 0.001$ using $t$-tests.

3.3 *Effect of Distance and Target Size*

The effect of distance on positioning time is given in Figure 3. At all distances greater than 1cm, the continuous devices are faster. The positioning time for both continuous devices seems to increase approximately with the log of the distance. The time for the step keys increases rapidly as the distance increases, while the time for the text keys increases somewhat less than as the log of the distance, owing to the existence of keys for moving relatively large distances with a single stroke. Again the mouse is the fastest device, and its advantage increases with distance.

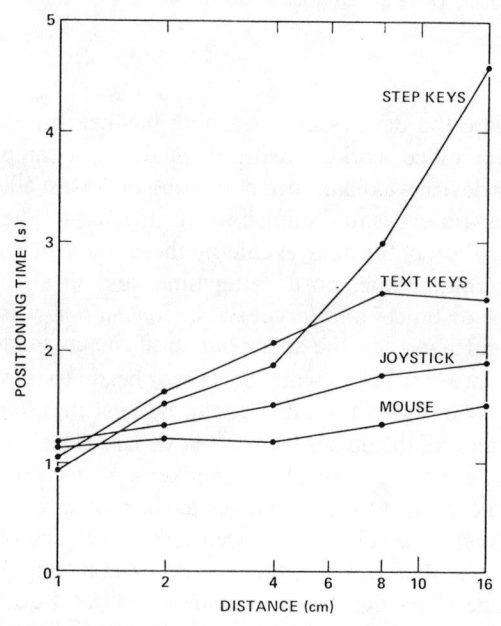

Figure 3. Effect of target distance on positioning time.

Figure 4 shows the effect of target size on positioning time. The positioning time for both the mouse and the joystick decreases with the log of the target size. The time for the text keys is independent of target size and the positioning time for the step keys also decreases roughly with the log of the target size. Again the mouse is the fastest device, and again the continuous devices as a group are faster for all target sizes.

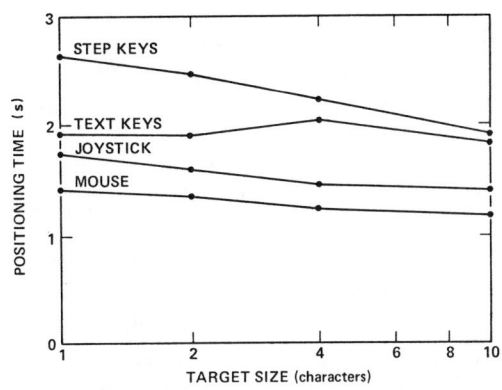

Figure 4. Effect of target size on positioning time.

### 3.4. Effect of Approach Angle

The targets in text editing are rectangles often significantly wider than they are high. Hence they might present a different problem when approached from different angles. In addition, the step keys and text keys work somewhat differently when moving horizontally than when moving vertically. To test if the direction of approach has an effect on positioning time, the target movements were classified according to whether they were vertical (0 to 22·5 degrees), diagonal (22·5 degrees to 67·5 degrees), or horizontal (67·5 degrees to 90 degrees). *Analysis of variance* shows the angle makes a significant difference in every case except for the mouse. The joystick takes slightly longer to position when the target is approached diagonally. The step keys take longer when approached horizontally than when approached vertically, a consequence probably deriving from the fact that a single keystroke would move the cursor almost twice as far vertically as horizontally. By contrast, the text keys take longer to position vertically, reflecting the presence of the WORD key. The differences induced by direction are not of great consequence, however. For the joystick it amounts to 3% of the mean positioning time; for the step keys 9% for the text keys 5%.

### 3.5. Errors

Of the four devices tested, the mouse had the lowest overall error rate, 5%; the step keys had the highest, 13%. The differences are reliable at $p < 0.05$ or better using $t$-tests. There is only a very slight increase in error rate with distance. However, there is a decrease in error rate with target size for every device except the text keys (Figure 5).

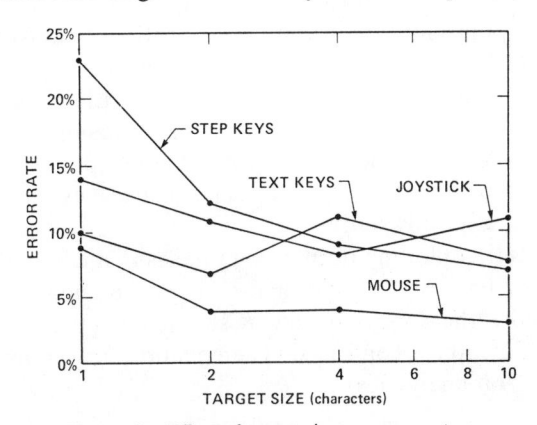

Figure 5. Effect of target size on error rate.

This finding replicates the result of Fitts and Radford (1966). In an investigation of self-initiated, discrete, pointing movements using a stylus, there was a similar marked reduction in errors as the target increased in size, but only a slight increase in error rate as the distance to the target increased.

## 4. Discussion

While these empirical results are of direct use in selecting a pointing device, it would obviously be of greater benefit if a theoretical account of the results could be made. For one thing, the need for some experiments might be obviated; for another, ways of improving pointing performance might be suggested. Fortunately, a first-order account for the devices of this experiment is not hard to give.

### 4.1. Mouse

The time to make a hand movement can be described by a version of Fitt's Law (Welford 1968),

$$T_{pos} = K_0 + K \log_2(D/S + 0.5) \text{ s} \tag{3}$$

where

$T_{pos}$ = Positioning time,

$D$ = Distance to the target,

$S$ = Size of the target,

and

$K_0, K$ = constants.

Here the constant $K_0$ includes within it the time for the hand initially to adjust its grasp on the mouse and the time to make the selection with the selection button. A constant of $K \simeq 0.1 \text{ s bit}^{-1}$ (10 bits s$^{-1}$) appears in a large number of studies on movement. This number is a measure of the information processing capacity of the eye-hand coordinate system. For single, discrete, subject-paced movements, the constant is a little less than $0.1 \text{ s bit}^{-1}$. Fitts and Radford (1966) get a value of $0.078 \text{ s bit}^{-1}$ (12.8 bit s$^{-1}$, recomputed from their Figure 1, Experiment 1, for the experimental condition where accuracy is stressed). Pierce and Karlin (1957) get maximum rates of $0.085 \text{ s bit}^{-1}$ (11.7 bits s$^{-1}$) in a pointing experiment. For continous movement, repetitive, experimenter-paced tasks, such as alternately touching two targets with a stylus or pursuit tracking, the constant is slightly above $0.1 \text{ s bit}^{-1}$. Elkind and Sprague (1961) get maximum rates of $0.135 \text{ s bit}^{-1}$ (7.4 bits s$^{-1}$) for a pursuit tracking task. Fitts's original dotting experiment as replotted by Welford (1968, p. 148) gives a $K$ of $0.120$ bit$^{-1}$ as does Welford's own study using the actual distance between the dots, the same measure of distance used in this study.

Fitts's Law predicts that plotting positioning time as a function of $\log_2(D/S + 0.5)$ should give a straight line. As the solid line in Figure 6 shows, this prediction is confirmed. Furthermore, the slope of the line $K$ should be in the neighborhood of $0.1$ sec/bit. Again the prediction is confirmed. The equation for the line in Figure 6 as determined by regression analysis is

$$T_{pos} = 1.03 + 0.096 \log_2(D/S + 0.5) \text{ s} \tag{4}$$

The equation has a standard error of 0·07 s and explains 83% of the variance of the means for each condition. This is roughly comparable to the percentage of variance explained by Fitts and Radford. The slope of 0·096 bit s$^{-1}$ is in the 0·1 bit s$^{-1}$ range found in other studies. Since the standard error of estimate for $K$ is 0·008 bit s$^{-1}$, the mouse would seem to be close to, but slightly slowerrthan, the optimal rate of around 0·08 bit s$^{-1}$ observed for the stylus and for finger pointing.

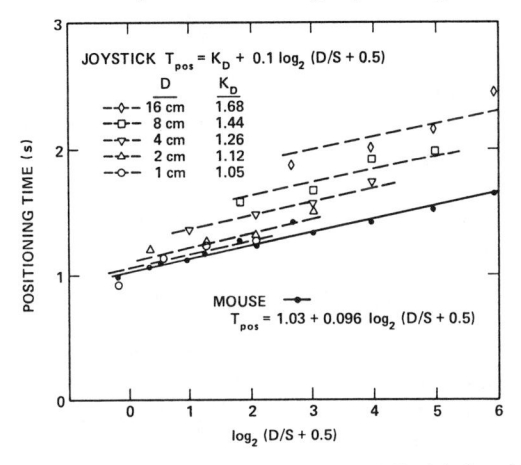

Figure 6. Positioning time for continuous devices as a function of Fitts's index of difficulty $\log_2 (D/S + 0·5)$.

The values for positioning time obtained in this experiment are apparently in good agreement with those obtained by English *et al.* Making the assumption that their CRT characters were about the same width as ours and assuming an intermediate target distance of about 8 cm, Equation 4 (plus the addition of the 0·36 s homing time from Table 2) predicts 1·87 s for 1 character targets (English *et al.* reported 1·93 s) and 1·66 s for 'word' targets of 5 characters (English *et al.* reported 1·68 s).

### 4.2. *Joystick*

Although it is a rate-controlled device instead of a position device, we might wonder if the joystick follows Fitts's Law. Plotting the average time per positioning for each distance × size cell of the experiment according to Equation 3 shows that there is an approximate fit to

$$T_{pos} = 0·99 + 0·220 \log_2 (D/S + 0·5). \tag{5}$$

Equation 5 has a standard error of 0·13 s and explains 89% of the variance of the means. The size of the slope $K$ shows that information is being processed at only half the speed as with the mouse and significantly below the maximum rate. Closer examination gives some insight into the difficulty. The points for the joystick in Figure 6 actually form a series of parallel lines, one for each distance, each with a slope of around 0·1 bit s$^{-1}$. Setting $K$ to 0·1 bit s$^{-1}$, we can therefore write as an alternative model

$$T_{pos} = K_D + 0·1 \log_2 (D/S + 0·5).$$

$K_D$ is the intercept for distance $D$. From the figure, $K_D$ is about 1·05 s for $D = 1$ cm, 1·12 s for 2 cm, 1·26 s for 4 cm, 1·44 s for 8 cm, and 1·68 s for 16 cm. For this model the standard error of the fit is reduced to 0 07 s, the same as for the mouse. (Since the slope was not determined by the regression, a comparable $R^2$ cannot be computed.) Thus the tested joystick can be thought of as a Fitts's Law device with a slope twice that for hand movememts; or it can be thought of as a Fitts's Law device with the expected slope, but having an intercept which increases with distance. The problem with this joystick is probably related to the non-linearity in the control (Poulton 1974, Craik and Vince 1963). It should be noted that for the 1 cm distance (where the effect of non-linearity is slight) the positioning time is virtually the same as for the mouse. Thus the possibility of designing a joystick with performance characteristics comparable to the mouse is by no means excluded.

### 4.3. *Step Keys*

As a first approximation one might expect the time to use the step keys to be governed by the number of keystrokes which must be used to move the cursor to the target. Since the keys can only move the cursor vertically or horizontally, the number of keystrokes is $D_x/0.456 + D_y/0.246$, where $D_x$ and $D_y$ are the horizontal and vertical components of distance to the target; 0·456 cm is the size of a vertical step and 0·246 cm is the size of a horizontal step. Hence positioning time should be

$$T_{pos} = K_0 + C(D_x/0.456 + D_y/0.246). \tag{6}$$

This equation with $K_0 = 1.20$ s and $C = 0.052$ s keystroke$^{-1}$ has a standard error of 0·54 s and explains 84% of the variance of the means.

Since the tapping rate is around 0·15 s keystroke$^{-1}$, $C$ is much too fast to be identified with the pressing of a key. It is also too fast to be identified with the 0·067 s keystroke$^{-1}$ automatic repetition mode. Figure 7 shows positioning time plotted against the predicted number of keystrokes. The long solid line is Equation 6 with the above parameters. The figure shows that positioning time is linear with the number of keystrokes until the predicted number of keystrokes becomes large (that is, the distance to the target is long). In these cases the user often has the opportunity to reduce positioning time by using the HOME key. Fitting Equation 6 to the first part of the graph ($D_x/0.456 + D_y/0.246 < 40$) gives

$$T_{pos} = 0.98 + 0.074(D_x/0.456 + D_y/0.246).$$

The equation, indicated as a short solid line on the figure, has a standard error of 0·18 s and explains 95% of the variance in the means. The reasonable slope of 0·074 s keystroke$^{-1}$ shows that the 0·067 s keystroke$^{-1}$ automatic repetition feature was heavily used.

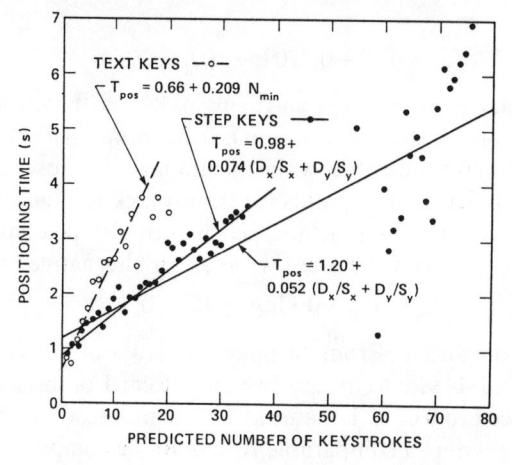

Figure 7. Positioning time for key devices as a function of predicted number of keystrokes.

### 4.4. Text Keys

The text keys present the user on most trials with a choice of methods to reach the target. For example, he might press the PARAGRAPH key repeatedly until the cursor has moved to the paragraph containing the target paragraph. He could then press the LINE key repeatedly until it is on the target line, then use the WORD key to bring it over to the target. Or he might use the PARAGRAPH key to bring it over to the target, then holding, the REVERSE key down, use the LINE key to back up to the line after the target line. And finally, using REVERSE and WORD, back up until he hits the target. In fact, there are 26 different methods for moving the cursor to the target, although only a subset will be possible in a given situation. The fastest method will depend on where the target is located relative to the starting position and the boundaries of surrounding lines and paragraphs.

A reasonable hypothesis would be that positioning time is proportional to the number of keystrokes and that for well practiced subjects the number of keystrokes will be minimum necessary. To test this hypothesis each trial was analysed to determine the minimum number of keystrokes $N_{min}$ necessary to hit the target. The average positioning time as a function of $N_{min}$ is plotted as the open circles in Figure 7. A least squares fit gives

$$T_{pos} = 0.66 + 0.209\, N_{min}.$$

The standard is 0·24 s and the equation explains 89% of the variance of the means. The keystroke rate of 0·209 s keystroke$^{-1}$ is very reasonable, being approximately equal to the typing rate for random words (Devoe 1967). Evidently, the automatic repetition mode was little used. Examination of some statistics on the minimum numbers of keystrokes for each trial shows there was little need for it. For one thing, an average of only six keystrokes was necessary for the text keys to locate a target word. Ten or fewer keystrokes were sufficient for over 90% of the targets. For another, these keystrokes were distributed across several keys, further limiting opportunities to use the repetition mode. The PARAGRAPH key was needed on 48% on the trials, the LINE key on 85%, the word key on 83%, and the REVERSE key on 81%.

### 4.5. Comparison of Devices

Table 3 summarises the models, the standard of the fit, and the percentage of variance between the means explained by the model.

Table 3. Summary of Models for Positioning Time ($T_{pos}$)

| Device | Model (times in s) | $s_e$ | $R^2$ |
|---|---|---|---|
| Mouse | $T_{pos} = 1.03 + 0.096 \log_2 (D/S + 0.5)$ | 0·07 | 0·83 |
| Joystick | $T_{pos} = 0.99 + 0.220 \log_2 (D/S + 0.5)^a$ | 0·13 | 0·89 |
|  | $T_{pos} = K_d + 0.1 \log_2 (D/S + 0.5)^b$ | 0·07 | — |
| Step Keys | $T_{pos} = 1.20 + 0.052 (D_x/S_x + D_y/S_y)^c$ | 0·54 | 0·84 |
|  | $T_{pos} = 0.98 + 0.074 (D_x/S_x + D_y/S_y)^d$ | 0·18 | 0·95 |
| Text Keys | $T_{pos} = 0.66 + 0.209\, N_{min}$ | 0·24 | 0·89 |

[a] Least squares fit to all data points.
[d] Fit for number of keystrokes $(D_x/S_x + D_y/S_y) < 40$,
[c] Least squares fit to all data points.
[b] Fitting a separate line with slope 0·1 bit s$^{-1}$ for each distance.

where HOME key unlikely to be used.

The match of the Fitts's Law slope to the roughly $K \simeq 0.1$ s bit$^{-1}$ constant observed in other hand movement and manual control studies means that positioning time is apparently limited by central information processing capacities of the eye-hand guidance system (cf. Welford 1968, Glencross 1977). Taking $K = 0.08$ s bit$^{-1}$ as the most likely minimum value for a similar movement task, and $K_0 = 1$ s as a typical value observed in this experiment, it would seem unlikely that a continuous movement device could be developed whose positioning time is less than $1 + 0.08 \log_2 (D/S + 0.5)$ s (unless it can somehow reduce the information which must be centrally processed), although something might be done to reduce the value of $K_0$. If this is true, then an optimal device would be expected to be no more than about 5% faster than the mouse in the extreme case of 1 character targets 16 cm distant ($1 + 0.095 \log_2 (16/1 + 0.5) = 1.38$ s vs. $1 + 0.08 \log_2(16/1 + 0.5) = 1.32$ s). Typical differences would be much less. By comparison in this same case, the joystick (in this experiment) is 83% slower than the optimal device, the text keys 107% slower, and the step keys 239% slower. Even if $K_0$ were zero, the mouse would still be only 23% slower than the minimum. While devices might be built which improve on the mouse's homing time, error rate, or ability for fine movement, it is unlikely their positioning times will be significantly faster.

This maximum information processing capacity probably explains the lack of any significant difference in positioning time between the lightpen and the lightgun in Goodwin's experiment. Both are probably Fitts's Law devices, so both can be expected to have the same maximum 0·1 s bit$^{-1}$ rate as the mouse (if they are optimised with respect to control/display ratio and any other relevent variables).

In interpreting these results, highly favourable to the mouse, some qualifications are in order. Of the four devices, the mouse is clearly the most 'compatible' for this task (cf. Poulton 1974, Chapter 16), meaning less mental translation is needed to map intended motion of the cursor into motor movement of the hands than for the other devices. Thus it would be expected to be easier to use, put lower cognitive load on the user, and have lower error rates. There are, however, limits to its compatibility. Inexperienced users are often bewildered about what to do when they run the mouse into the side of the keyboard trying to move the cursor across the screen. They need to be told that their mice can simply be picked up and deposited at a more convenient place on the table without affecting the cursor. Even experienced users are surprised at the results when they hold their mice backwards or sideways.

The greatest difficulty with the mouse for text-editing occurs with small targets. Punctuation marks such as a period are considerably smaller than an average character. The error rate for the mouse, which was already up to 9% for one character targets, would be even higher for these sorts of targets.

## 5. Summary and Conclusion

Of the four devices tested the mouse is clearly the superior device for text selection on a CRT:

1. The positioning time of the mouse is significantly faster than that of the other devices. This is true overall and at every distance and size combination save for single character targets.

2. The error rate of the mouse is significantly lower than that of the other devices.

3. The rate of movement of the mouse is nearly maximal with respect to the information processing capabilities of the eye-hand guidance system.

As a group the continuous movement devices are superior in both speed and error-rate.

For the continuous movement devices, positioning time is given by Fitts's Law. For the key devices it is proportional to the number of keystrokes.

The authors wish to thank J. Elkind, T. Moran, and A. Newell for comments on an earlier draft and E. R. F. W. Crossman for various suggestions.

Quatre dispositifs ont été évalués en fonction de la rapidité de leur utilisation pour une sélection de textes sur l'écran d'un oscilloscope. La balladeuse s'est avérée être la plus rapide et la plus précise. On a montré que les variations dans les temps de positionnement avec la balladeuse et le levier de commande pouvaient être expliquées par la loi de Fitts. Dans le cas de la balladeuse, la pente de la droite de Fitts est proche de celle qui a été trouvée dans d'autres tâches de coordination oeil—main, ce qui semble indiquer que le temps de positionnement avec ce dispositif, est le plus court possible. Les temps de positionnement avec des touches est proportionnel au nombre de frappes nécessaires.

Es wurden vier Einrichtungen untersucht, um festzustellen, wie schnell Textstellen auf einem CRT-Display ausgewählt werden können. Die Einrichtung 'mouse' konnte in allen Fällen als die schnellste bei gleichzeitig geringster Fehlerhäufigkeit ermittelt werden. Die Ergebnisse machen deutlich, daß die Variationen der Positionierungszeiten bei den Einrichtungen 'mouse' und 'joystick' dem Gesetz nach Fitts entsprechen. Bei den Untersuchungen mit 'mouse' entsprach die gemessene Funktionskonstante des Fitt-Gesetzes den Konstanten, die bei anderen Auge-Hand-Tätigkeiten gefunden wurden. Diese Tatsache führt zu dem Schluß, daß bei dieser Einrichtung die minimal möglichen Positionierungszeiten erreicht werden. Die Positionierungszeit für Tasteneinrichtungen ist nach den Ergebnissen proportional zur Anzahl notwendiger Tastungen.

## References

CRAIK, K. J. W., and VINCE, M. A., 1963, Psychological and physiological aspects of control mechanisms. *Ergonomics*, **6**, 419–440.
DEVOE, D. B., 1967, Alternatives to handprinting in the manual entry of data. *The IEEE Transactions on Human Factors in Electronics*, **HFE–8**, 1, 21–31.
DE JONG, J. R., 1957, The effects of increasing skill on cycle time and its consequences for time standards. *Ergonomics*, **1**, 51–60.
ELKIND, J. I. and SPRAGUE, L. T., 1961, Transmission of information in simple manual control systems. *IRE Transaction on Human Factors in Electronics*, **HFE–2**, 1, 58–60.
ENGLISH, W. K., ENGELBART, D. C., and BERMAN, M. L., 1967, Display-selection techniques for text manipulation. *IEEE Transactions on Human factors in Electronics*, **HFE–8**, 1, 21–31.
FITTS, P. M., 1954, The information capacity of the human motor system in controlling amplitude of movement. *Journal of Experimental Psychology*, **47**, 381–391.
FITTS, P. M., and PETERSON, J. R., 1964, Information capacity of discrete motor responses. *Journal of Experimental Psychology*, **67**, 103–112.
FITTS, P. M., and RADFORD, B., 1966, Information capacity of discrete motor responses under different cognitive sets. *Journal of Experimental Psychology*, **71**, 475–482.
GLENCROSS, D. J., 1977, Control of skilled movement. *Psychological Bulletin*, **84**, 14–29.
GOODWIN, N. C., 1975, Cursor positioning on an electronic display using lightpen, lightgun, or keyboard for three basic tasks. *Human Factors*, **17**, 289–295.
KNIGHT, A. A., and DAGNALL, P. R., 1967, Precision in movements. *Ergonomics*, **10**, 321–330.
POULTON, E. C., 1974, *Tracking Skill and Manual Control* (New York: ACADEMIC PRESS).
PIERCE, J. R., and KARLIN, J. E., 1957, Reading rates and the information rate of the human channel. *Bell System Technical Journal*, **36**, 497–516.
WELFORD, A. T., 1968, *Fundamentals of Skill* (London: METHUEN).

Manuscript received 28 August 1977.

# The Evaluation of Text Editors: Methodology and Empirical Results

Teresa L. Roberts  *Xerox Office Systems Division*
Thomas P. Moran  *Xerox Palo Alto Research Center*

**ABSTRACT:** *This paper presents a methodology for evaluating text editors on several dimensions: the time it takes experts to perform basic editing tasks, the time experts spend making and correcting errors, the rate at which novices learn to perform basic editing tasks, and the functionality of editors over more complex tasks. Time, errors, and learning are measured experimentally; functionality is measured analytically; time is also calculated analytically. The methodology has thus far been used to evaluate nine diverse text editors, producing an initial database of performance results. The database is used to tell us not only about the editors but also about the users—the magnitude of individual differences and the factors affecting novice learning.*

## 1. INTRODUCTION

Text editors are the most heavily used programs on interactive computing systems since the advent of time-sharing systems (e.g., [1]). Text editing, or word processing, is also a very pervasive use of personal computers [15]. There are probably hundreds of different text editors in use today: many computation centers have their own local editors, and new computers often come with their own text editors. System programmers cannot seem to resist the temptation to design a better text editor. Heated debates rage over computer networks about text editor design. Yet, remarkably little objective information is known about the relative advantages of different kinds of editing paradigms.

Systematic study of text editors is hampered, at least partially, by the complex of issues surrounding text editor usage. Text editors are flexible tools that are used for a wide variety of purposes, since many kinds of human communication are done by text. Simple informal notes, letters and memoranda, structured text (such as lists and tables), reports and specifications (requiring sophisticated formatting and layout), and program code (structured differently from narrative text) are all applications for which text editors are regularly used. There are many different kinds of editor users—first-time novices, hardened experts, occasional users, and users with specialized applications that lead them to know how to perform some tasks well and other tasks not at all. Finally, there are many different measures of the quality of user-editor interaction, including both objective measures of performance, such as time and errors, and subjective measures of acceptability, such as feelings of enjoyment, clumsiness, and so forth.

The study of text editors up to now has been dominated by functional descriptions of editors, both by proponents of particular systems (e.g., [16]) and by neutral evaluators (e.g., [10, 14, 8]). These reports mainly present subjective opinions as the basis for comparing different systems, either by deciding *a priori* what features are desirable or by informally trying out the systems to get a feel for what works well and what is lacking. Various arguments, which on the surface seem reasonable, are also used to defend the conclusions in these reports, but the validity of these arguments is seldom tested. The purpose of the present study is to obtain objective, replicable results. A survey of related behavioral studies done up to this time is given in [6].

Our purpose in this paper is to present a *standardized evaluation* of text editors. This kind of evaluation may be contrasted with a *specific*

From *Communications of the ACM*, 26. Copyright 1983 by the Association for Computing Machinery.

*evaluation*, which is tailored to a particular purpose or situation, such as the evaluation of a set of editors to determine their utility in a particular working environment. A standardized evaluation does not make assumptions about the particulars of any given situation, nor does it cover all of the various aspects of editor usage. It focuses on the common properties of text editors rather than on the idiosyncracies of particular editors. A standardized evaluation attempts to address the most fundamental issues and is thus applicable to a variety of editors. A familiar example of a standardized evaluation is the EPA rating of automobile gasoline mileage. While the conditions used to obtain the EPA rating do not match the driving conditions of any specific car, the ratings do relate to common driving situations. Thus, the ratings can be used to compare different cars and, to some extent, can be adjusted to tell about specific driving situations.

A benefit of using a standardized evaluation over a period of time is the accumulation of a database of consistent information about editors. This gives a standard for interpreting the results of any new evaluation, a critical factor missing from many specific evaluations (e.g., [7]). One of our goals in proposing a standardized evaluation is to initialize a database of information about the population of existing editors.

The methodology we present here evaluates computer text editors from the viewpoint of the performance of their users— from novices learning the editor for the first time to dedicated experts who have mastered the editor. Objectivity, thoroughness, and ease-of-use were the criteria used in creating this methodology. *Objectivity* implies that the methodology not be biased in favor of any particular editor's conceptual structure. *Thoroughness* implies that multiple aspects of editor usage be considered. The methodology focuses on four dimensions of editor usage that are behaviorally fundamental and practically important.

The *Time* to perform basic editing tasks by experts.
The *Error* cost for experts.
The *Learning* of basic editing tasks by novices.
The *Functionality* over a wide range of editing tasks.

*Ease-of-use* means that the methodology should be usable by editor designers, managers of word processing centers, or other nonpsychologists who need this kind of evaluative information, but who have limited time and equipment resources.

The structure of this paper is as follows: In Sec. 2, we describe the evaluation methodology. In Sec. 3, we apply the methodology to nine different text editors, presenting and discussing the empirical results, and assessing the methodology itself. In Sec. 4, we turn the empirical results around to gain some insight into user performance with computers, particularly in the areas of individual differences and novice learning.

## 2. DESCRIPTION OF THE METHODOLOGY

The methodology is based on the specific kinds of tasks involved in text editing. It consists of experimentally measuring user performance on three dimensions—Time, Error, and Learning—and on an analysis of Functionality. Also, expert performance time can be calculated analytically.

### 2.1 Taxonomy of Editing Tasks

An evaluation scheme for editors needs to have a common ground on which to compare different kinds of editors. Editor design features (e.g., "modeless" insertion of new text vs. having an "insert mode") and design concepts (e.g., table creation using sequential text with formatting characters such as tabs vs. using a two-dimensional structure) cannot serve this role, since the features and concepts differ so much from editor to editor. There is no evidence that one feature is always better than another. In fact, the overall consistency in how well the different design features of the editor fit together may well be more important than any individual feature in determining the quality of the editor.

What is constant across all text editors, in contrast to design features, is the editing tasks they permit their users to accomplish. Thus, the methodology here is based on a taxonomy of 212 editing tasks that can potentially be performed by a text editor. These tasks are specified in terms of their effect on a text document, independent of any specific editor's conceptual model [9]. The organization of the task taxonomy, along with a sample of tasks in each category, is given in Figure 1. The Functionality dimension of an editor is measured with respect to the set of tasks in this taxonomy, by assessing how many of the tasks the editor can perform.

Comparisons between editors on the performance dimensions (Time, Error, and Learning) must be based on tasks that all editors can per-

FIGURE 1. Taxonomy of Editing Tasks on which the Evaluation Methodology is Based.

**Modify Document**
    **Content and structure of text**
        Characters, words, numbers, sentences, paragraphs, lines, sections, document
        References [e.g., keep up-to-date references to section numbers in the document]
        Sources for text or attributes [e.g., make the text layout be the same as in another document]
    **Layout of running text and structure**
        Inside paragraphs [e.g., indent the first line of a paragraph so far from the left margin]
        Headings, random lines [e.g., center]
        Interparagraph layout [e.g., leave so much space between paragraphs]
        General [e.g., lay out document in so many columns]
    **Page layout**
        Every page [e.g., print a page heading that includes the current section number]
        Non-mainline text [e.g., position footnotes at the bottom of the page]
    **Attributes of characters**
        Line break [e.g., automatic hyphenation]
        Shape [e.g., boldface]
    **Tables**
        Column beginning [e.g., columns are equally spaced]
        General alignment [e.g., align the column on the decimal points]
        Modify alignment [e.g., swap the positions of two columns]
        Treatment of table entries [e.g., line up the left and right edges of (justify) each table entry]
    Summary of text [e.g., table of contents]
    Special applications [e.g., mathematical formulas]

**Locate Change (Addressing)**
    Text [e.g., find text which has specified content]
    Structure [e.g., find the next section heading]
    Layout/Attributes [e.g., find a boldface character]
    Misc.

**Program Edits (Control)**
    Command sequences [e.g., invoke a sequence of commands with parameters]
    Control structure [e.g., repeat a sequence of commands a specified number of times]
    Tests [e.g., compare strings for alphabetical order]
    Storage [e.g., store pointers to places in documents]
    User control [e.g., ask user for parameters during execution]
    Preexisting composite commands [e.g., sort a sequence of text strings]

**Find Task or Verify Change (Display)**
    Display text and layout [e.g., show the outline structure of the text]
    Display system state [e.g., show where the selection is relative to the whole document]

**Miscellaneous**
    Hardcopy
        Draft copy [e.g., print with extra space between lines]
        Misc. [e.g., print on envelopes]
    Intermediate Input/Output [e.g., save away the current version of a document]
    Other [e.g., perform arithmetic on numbers in the document]

form. For this purpose, we identify a small set of *core editing tasks* (see Figure 2). The core tasks are the ones that all text editors, by definition, can perform; they are also the most common editing tasks in normal text-editing applications. Most of the core tasks are generated by applying basic text editing operations (e.g., *insert, delete, replace*) to basic text entities (e.g., *characters, words, lines*). Also included in the core set are the tasks of accessing and saving documents and the simplest text-display and text-addressing operations.

A lengthy specification is required to instruct an evaluator to carry out this methodology. In this paper we can give only enough information to make clear the basic structure and procedure of the methodology and the resulting measures. Full instructions and materials for running the evaluation tests and analyses may be found in the report by Roberts [11].

## 2.2 The Time Dimension
The time it takes expert users to accomplish routine text modifications is measured by observ-

FIGURE 2. Core Editing Tasks used in the Methodology for Expert Time Performance and Novice Learning.

Core tasks consist mainly of the cross-product (except for a few obvious semantic anomalies) of the following basic editing operations applied to the following basic text objects:

    Operations:   *insert*    Objects:   *character*
                      *delete*                   *word*
                      *replace*                *line*
                      *move*                  *sentence*
                      *copy*                   *paragraph*
                      *transpose*            *section*
                      *split*
                      *merge*

For example:

    —*insert character(s)*
    —*insert word(s)*
    —*delete character(s)*
    etc.

Core tasks also contain the following miscellaneous tasks:

    —*display a continuous chunk of text*
    —*address a specified place*
    —*address according to content*
    —*make a document available for editing*
    —*put a document away*
    —*start a new document*

Note. The formal definition of the core in the task taxonomy also includes operations on the object *number*; however, no tasks using numbers were included in the experiments. The learning experiments omitted the operation *transpose* since it can be regarded as an optimization of two *moves*.

ing expert users as they perform a set of **benchmark tasks**, which are drawn from the core tasks.

*Benchmark.* There are 53 editing tasks in the benchmark, embedded in four documents: a short interoffice memo, two two-page reports, and a six-page chapter from a philosophy book. The types of tasks in the benchmark are randomly drawn from the core tasks, and the locations and complexities of the benchmark tasks are also randomly distributed. The distribution of tasks in the benchmark is more uniformly distributed than one would observe in normal text-editing work, the benchmark giving more emphasis to the more complex kinds of tasks (most real-world editing tasks are simple text modifications involving a small number of characters). For example, tasks involving "tricky" boundary conditions are over-represented in order to identify special cases, such as insertion at the beginning of a paragraph, which an editor may treat awkwardly. The benchmark also under-represents the typing of lengthy new text, since such typing performance is more a reflection of the skill of the user than of the quality of the editor. We will discuss later how to relate this benchmark to other distributions of tasks.

*Subjects.* Four expert users were tested individually on the benchmark. The evaluator should select the set of subjects to represent the diversity of the exert user community: at least one user should be **nontechnical** (i.e., with no programming background) and at least one should be **technical** (i.e., know how to program). Four is the absolute minimum number of subjects needed to get any reliability of measurement and to get some indication of individual user variation.

*Measurement.* The evaluator measures the performance in the test sessions with a clock and a stopwatch, measuring the overall performance time with the clock and the times spent in error with the stopwatch. The evaluator also notes whether or not each task is performed correctly. When the subject is finished with the tasks, the evaluator asks the subject to make a second pass to complete any incorrectly done tasks. This relatively crude method of measurement is used because it is easy for anyone to run (not everyone has an instrumented editor or a videotape setup, but anyone can acquire a stopwatch) and because stopwatch accuracy is sufficient. [1]

*Error-free and Error Time.* The benchmark typically takes about 30 minutes of steady work to complete. The elapsed time in the experiment is partitioned into error-free time and error time, according to two types of observed behavior. The *error time* is the time the user spends dealing with errors (see below for more detail), and the *error-free time* is the elapsed time minus the error time.

*Scoring.* The individual user's Time score is the average error-free time to perform each task (i.e., the total error-free time divided by the number of tasks). The overall Time score is the average score for the four subjects.

## 2.3 The Error Dimension

The effect of errors in an editor is measured by the *error time*, which is the time cost of errors on the benchmark tasks. The course of a typical error includes committing the error, discovering it, correcting it, and then resuming productive behavior. Error time consists of all the activity up to the resumption of productive activity [4]. Only those errors that take more than about 15 seconds to correct are counted by the evaluator (which is the best that can be done with a stopwatch). Thus, the time for typographical and other simple errors is not included in the error time. We do not know exactly how close this method approximates the true error time, but the true error time is not likely to be dominated by the time in these small errors. In addition to the time for the immediately corrected errors, the time for the second-pass corrections is also counted in the error time.

*Scoring.* The individual Error score for each user is the user's error time expressed as a percentage of his/her error-free Time score. [2] The overall Error score is the average score for the four expert users.

### 2.4 The Learning Dimension
The ease of learning of an editor is tested by actually teaching four novice subjects, individually, to perform the core editing tasks.

*Subjects.* Each subject must be a *novice* to computers (defined as someone with *no* previous experience with computers or word processors). This gives us an easily defined baseline measure of learning, that is, from zero experience. [3]

*Teaching Paradigm.* The learning tests are performed in a one-on-one, oral teaching paradigm, with an instructor individually teaching each novice the editor. Although more expensive than group-teaching or self-teaching paradigms, this paradigm has the crucial advantage that it is adaptable to the individual learner. The other paradigms are more rigid and may tend to magnify the differences between different learners, which obscures the learnability of the editor itself. For example, in a self-teaching paradigm using the editor's documentation, a learner can easily get confused on a point because of a short lapse of attention or because of the particular wording of the documentation and not because the point is inherently difficult. In the one-on-one paradigm, on the other hand, the instructor can respond to the particular difficulties of each learner by explaining things in a different way, by correcting misconceptions, and so forth.

*Teaching Procedure.* The teaching procedure is structured as a series of five instruction-quiz cycles. In each cycle, the instructor first instructs the learner on some new tasks or corrects the learner's difficulties, and during this time the learner is allowed to practice performing tasks on the system; finally, the learner is given a quiz to test what tasks s/he can do independently. The learner paces the session, deciding how much to practice, when to take the quiz, and so on.

The methodology includes a standard syllabus specifying what core tasks are to be taught on each cycle. However, it is up to the instructor to determine which specific editor commands and facilities to teach in order for the subject to be able to accomplish the core tasks. The structure of a particular editor might also make it necessary to slightly alter which tasks are taught in which cycle. The teaching procedure is strongly method-oriented; by "teaching tasks" we mean teaching methods to accomplish the tasks.

The quizzes consist of documents marked with changes to be made (similar to the benchmark performed by the expert users). Only a sample of the core tasks appears on each quiz. Not all tasks on a quiz have necessarily been taught up to that point, which allows learners to figure out, if possible, how to do tasks that have not been explicity taught. During the quizzes, the learners are given access to a one-page summary sheet listing all the editor commands taught. Thus, a learner is not hung up a long time on a quiz because of a simple difficulty, such as not being able to remember the name of a particular command.

*Scoring.* The amount that a subject learns is measured by counting the number of different task types the subject is able to perform on the quizzes. Only half-credit was given if the subject performed a task incompletely or had to look at the summary sheet. The individual Learning score is the amount of time taken for the learning session divided by the total number of tasks learned, that is, the average time it takes to learn how to do a task. The overall Learning score is the average Learning score for the four novice learners.

### 2.5 The Functionality Dimension
The range of functionality available in an editor is measured by analyzing the editor against a checklist of tasks covering the full task taxonomy (Figure 1).

*The Analyst.* The editor is rated on the functionality checklist by a very experienced user of the editor, the *analyst*, who uses whatever documentation material is necessary to ensure accuracy.

*Rating Criteria.* Rating the functionality of an editor on a task involves deciding whether the task can or cannot be done with the editor. This is not a simple binary decision. Almost any task can be performed on almost any editor with enough effort. Consequently, the editor is given full credit for a task only if the task can be done efficiently with the editor. It is given half-credit if the task can be done awkwardly, which can appear in several guises: repetition of commands, excessive typing of text, limitations in parameter values to the task, interference with other functions, substantial planning required of the user, etc. The editor is given no credit for a task if it cannot be done at all (such as trying to specify an italic typeface on a system designed for a line printer) or if doing the task requires as much effort as retyping all the affected text (such as having to manually insert page numbers on every page).

*Scoring.* The overall Functionality score is the percentage of the total number of tasks in the task taxonomy that the editor can do, according to the rating criteria. This score may be broken down into subscores according to the classes of tasks in the taxonomy, to show the strengths and weakness of the editor.

**2.6 Calculation of Expert Performance Time**

The error-free performance time of an expert using an editor can be calculated analytically, using the Keystroke-Level Model [3, 4]. This model predicts expert performance time by counting the number of physical and mental operations required to perform a task and by assigning a standard time for each operation. The model counts operations at the grain-level of keystrokes: typing, pointing at a location on the display with a pointing device, homing the hands onto a device, mentally preparing for a group of physical operations, and waiting for system responses.

The Keystroke-Level Model analysis gives a precise characterization of methods for accomplishing tasks.

When the model is applied to the set of benchmark tasks, it produces a calculated performance time for a "standard expert" that can be compared to the experimentally measured times. However, making this calculation requires the evaluator to predict what methods an expert user would use to perform the benchmark tasks, since the model requires that the methods be specified as input. In the absence of knowledge about the style of expert user interaction, the most useful heuristic is to first identify the common, frequently used commands of the editor and to pick the optimal method for each task within that set of commands. The fact that the experimental subjects sometimes use methods different from those predicted, plus other differences between the assumptions of the Keystroke-Level Model and the test conditions in this methodology (e.g., the inclusion of small errors) leads us to expect small-to-moderate differences between the calculated performance and the experimental results.

**3. EVALUATION OF NINE TEXT EDITORS**

Nine text editors have been evaluated using this methodology, both as a test of the methodology and for the inherent interest in the results. The results of these evaluations provide the beginnings of a database of empirical results giving us behavioral data on user performance, as well as the basis for comparing editors.

**3.1 Description of the Editors**

The nine text editors evaluated are: TECO [20], WYLBUR [24], EMACS [23], NLS [18, 19], BRAVOX [21], BRAVO [22], a WANG word processor [26], STAR [27], and GYPSY [25]. These represent a wide variety of text editors and word processors, some in wide use around the country and some experimental. The first two of these editors were designed for teletypelike terminals, and the rest were designed for display-based terminals or personal computers. The intended users of these editors range from devoted system hackers to publishers and secretaries who have had little or no contact with computers.

Text editors are complex interactive systems. Thus, it is difficult to succinctly describe the design of these nine editors. Figure 3 attempts to characterize the editors according to a set of commonly discussed design features. For example, the Command Invocation column describes the design feature concerned with the ways in which a user designates commands to the system. The nine editors cover a wide range of choices for this feature: (1) type all or part of an English verb, (2) type a one-letter mnemonic for the command name, (3) hold down a control key while typing a one-letter mnemonic, (4) type a one-letter mnemonic on a chordset, (5) press a

**FIGURE 3. Feature Description of Nine Text Editors.**

| Editor [Ref.] | Display | Auto Line Wrap[a] | Strong Line Concept[b] | Text Units | Command Invocation | Insert Mode | Means of Addressing[c] | Addressing Hardware | Computer Processor[d] |
|---|---|---|---|---|---|---|---|---|---|
| TECO [20] | TTY[e] style | No | Yes | Characters, lines | 1-letter mnemonic | Yes | Relative to current position | Keyboard | PDP-10 equivalent, via 3Mb net |
| WYLBUR [24] | TTY[e] style | No | Yes | Characters, lines | English-like, abbreviated | Yes | Absolute line numbers | Keyboard | IBM 370, 1200 baud |
| EMACS [23] | Partial page | Yes | Yes | Characters, words, lines, sentences, paragraphs | 1-letter mnemonic, control keys | No | Relative to current position | Keyboard | PDP-10 equivalent, approximately 1200 baud |
| NLS [18, 19] | Partial page | Yes | No | Characters, words, paragraphs | 1-letter English-like on keyboard or 5-key chordset | Yes | Screen position | Mouse | PDP-10 with local processor |
| BRAVOX [21] | Full page | Yes | No | Characters, words, lines, paragraphs | 1-letter mnemonic, menu, function keys | No | Screen position | Mouse | Xerox Alto personal computer |
| BRAVO [22] | Partial page | Yes | No | Characters, words, lines, paragraphs | 1-letter mnemonic | Yes | Screen position | Mouse | Xerox Alto personal computer |
| WANG [26] | Partial page | Yes | No | Characters | Function keys | Yes | Screen position | Step keys[f] | Stand-alone Wang word processor |
| STAR [27] | Full page | Yes | No | Characters, words, sentences, paragraphs | Function keys, menus | No | Screen position | Mouse | Xerox 8000 processor |
| GYPSY [25] | Partial page | Yes | No | Characters, words, paragraphs | Function keys | No | Screen position | Mouse | Xerox Alto personal computer |

[a] Automatic line wrap means that during type-in a new line is automatically begun when a word overflows the old line, without any intervention from the user.

[b] This refers to editors that require the user to type RETURN at the end of each line of text. Usually, this also means that there is an explicit CARRIAGE-RETURN character at the end of each line in the internal representation of the document.

[c] This refers to the primary means of addressing (all editors have the ability to search).

[d] Time-sharing computers were used under conditions of light load. Terminals and computer displays were all CRTs, except that one WYLBUR user preferred her own hardcopy terminal.

[e] A TTY (teletype) style display is one that does not continuously show the state of the document, but only shows the sequence of commands entered by the user. Snapshots of pieces of the document are displayed when the user explicitly asks for them.

[f] Four keys with arrows on them, which move the cursor up, down, left, and right (see [2]).

special function key, (6) select a command from a menu on the display.

Figure 3 also gives the conditions under which the editors were used for the experiments. For example, TECO was run on a time-sharing machine connected to a terminal over a 3-megabit local network, while the WANG word processor was run on its own stand-alone hardware. Note that the methodology does not provide an evaluation of an editor in the abstract, but only of a particular implementation under a particular set of conditions. It is possible that the particular conditions (e.g., the quality of the terminal or the bandwidth of its connection to the central processor) dominate the abstract characteristics of the editor (e.g., its command language conventions) in determining an expert's performance. Therefore, an attempt was made to run each editor under reasonably optimal conditions, in order to make the overall evaluation results as generally useful as possible. [4]

Figure 4 gives a different characterization of the editors. It shows in detail how a user would go about performing a specific word-replacement task in each of the editors, using the notation of the Keystroke-Level Model (the footnote to the figure lists the different types of Keystroke-Level Model operations). For example, it can be seen that the editors described in Figure 3 as having an insert mode (TECO, WYLBUR, NLS, BRAVO, and WANG) all require the typing of a special character (preceded by a mental operation) after the insertion to terminate the insertion of new text. On the other hand, the "modeless" editors (EMACS, BRAVOX, STAR, and GYPSY) do not require any operations after typing in new text. These methods also show where moving the hands from the keyboard to the pointing device and back (homing) add extra motions to the methods used with editors which have a mouse or step keys (NILS, BRAVOX, BRAVO, WANG, STAR, and GYPSY).

This Keystroke-Level Model analysis can be used to calculate the expected expert performance time for each editor, and to give a detailed quantitative decomposition of the times for each type of operation in each editor. To do this, the Keystroke-Level Model analysis was applied to all the benchmark tasks for each of the nine editors. The calculated task times thus obtained were averaged over the 53 benchmark tasks to give times for an "average editing task" for each editor. Figure 5 presents these first empirical (not experimental) results.

Figure 5(a) gives the calculated average task times for each editor. This leads us to expect a certain pattern of experimental results, for example, for there to be an overall factor of 2.5 between the fastest and the slowest editors. The figure also shows how each average task time is decomposed into the times for each operator type. For instance, the cost of slow system response stands out clearly. If EMACS had been run on a fast terminal, its speed would be faster than NLS's; STAR would be the fastest editor of all if system response times for all editors could be effectively reduced to zero. A weak point of the WANG, on the other hand, is the pointing time required by the step keys; it would be improved at least 2 sec/task (over 10 percent) by using a mouse.

The task time decomposition can also be considered as a percentage of total task time, as shown in Figure 5(b). This shows, for example, that homing time between the keyboard and pointing device is not a major problem (except perhaps with the WANG, which relies heavily on function keys that are separate from the main typing array). An interesting contrast exists between TECO and WYLBUR. Both use the same set of operations: Acquire, Keying, Mental time, and system Response. But TECO, with its emphasis on minimal typing, only spends one-third of its user's time in typing, while WYLBUR spends over half. This is paid for, however, in Mental time, where the ratios are reversed.

### 3.2. Overall Evaluation Results

All nine editors were run through all the evaluation tests. According to the methodology, the overall evaluation of a text editor is a four-tuple of numbers, one numeric score from each dimension. The overall evaluation scores for the nine editors are presented in Figure 6.

Differences were found between the editors on all dimensions. The expert Time results show, for instance, that TECO, WYLBUR, and EMACS, are the slowest editors and that GYPSY and STAR are the fastest. Most of the display-based systems are about twice as fast to use as the non-display systems. The difference between the fastest and slowest system was a factor of 2.5, as the Keystroke-Level Model analysis led us to expect. The Error dimension shows a range of a factor of 5 in the cost of errors between systems. On the Learning dimension, TECO is clearly the slowest to learn, with the next system being a factor of 2 easier to learn, and the rest of the

**FIGURE 4.** Example of the Use of each Text Editor: An Illustrative Method for Accomplishing the Specific Task of Replacing the Word "European" with the Words "Far Eastern".

| Editor | Method (informal) | Method (Keystroke-Level Model encoding)[a] |
|---|---|---|
| TECO | Get task.<br>Place pointer after old word.<br>Delete previous 8 characters.<br>Insert new words.<br>Display line to verify. | A[task]<br>MK[s] 9K[European] MK[ESC]<br>M 3K[-8d]<br>MK[i] 13K[Far Eastern] MK[ESC]<br>M 2K[v ESC] R(0.4) |
| WYLBUR | Get task.<br>Get number of line with old word<br>(system returns line 11).<br>Change old word<br>to new words. | A[task]<br>M 2K[L⏎] 10K[' European] M 3K[' RETURN]<br>R(1.0)<br>M 3K[ch⏎] 10K[' European] M 6K[' ⏎to⏎]<br>14K[' Far Eastern] M 6K[' ⏎in⏎] 2K[11] MK[RETURN] |
| EMACS | Get task and find it on display.<br>Place pointer in old word.<br>Back up to beginning of word.<br>Call Delete Word command.<br>Type new words. | A[task] S[European]<br>M 4K[CTRL S e u] R(2.0)<br>2K[META B]<br>M 2K[META D]<br>13K[Far Eastern] |
| NLS | Get task and find it on display.<br>Call Replace Word command.<br>Point to old word.<br>Type new words. | A[task] S[European]<br>H[chordset and mouse] MK[r] MK[w]<br>P[European] K[OK] H[keyboard]<br>13K[Far Eastern] MK[OK] |
| BRAVOX | Get task and find it on display.<br>Point to old word.<br>Delete old word.<br>Type new words. | A[task] S[European]<br>H[mouse] P[European] K[BUTTON2] H[keyboard]<br>MK[DEL]<br>13K[Far Eastern] |
| BRAVO | Get task and find it on display.<br>Point to old word.<br>Call Replace command.<br>Type new words. | A[task] S[European]<br>H[mouse] P[European] K[BUTTON2] H[keyboard]<br>MK[r]<br>13K[Far Eastern] MK[ESC] R(2.7) |
| WANG | Get task and find it on display.<br>Call Replace command.<br>Select ends of old word.<br>Type new words. | A[task] S[European]<br>H[function keys and step keys] MK[REPLACE]<br>P$_S$[E] K[EXECUTE] P$_S$[n] K[EXECUTE] H[keyboard]<br>13K[Far Eastern] H[function keys] MK[EXECUTE] |
| STAR | Get task and find it on display.<br>Point to old word.<br>Delete old word.<br>Type new words. | A[task] S[European]<br>H[mouse and function keys] P[European] 2K[SELECT SELECT]<br>MK[DELETE]<br>H[keyboard] 14K[Far Eastern⏎] |
| GYPSY | Get task and find it on display.<br>Point to ends of old word.<br>Type new words. | A[task] S[European]<br>H[mouse] P[E] K[BUTTON1] P[n] K[BUTTON1] H[keyboard]<br>13K[Far Eastern] |

[a] Methods are encoded in the Keystroke-Level Model [3] as a sequence of primitive operations that the user must perform. All operations are encoded as one of the following types of operations:

| | |
|---|---|
| A | Acquire a task by looking at the manuscript (1.8 sec). |
| S | Search the display for the location of the task (2.2 sec). |
| K | Type a key or press a button (measured by typing tests; .23 sec used here). |
| P | Point to a location with a mouse (1.1 sec). |
| P$_S$ | Point to a location with step keys (2.3 sec). |
| H | Home the hands on a physical device (.4 sec). |
| M | Mentally prepare for physical actions (1.35 sec). |
| R(n) | Wait n seconds for a system response (measured for each system). |

The notation in square brackets after each operation is an informal comment telling, e.g., what keys are pressed. All operations, except A, S, and P$_S$, are the same as in [3]. The A and S operations used here simply encode [3]'s notion of task acquisition into new operations. P$_S$ represents a type of pointing not covered in [3]. The time attributed to P$_S$ comes from [2].

editors ranging over another factor of 2 in learning speed. We also see large differences in the Functionality dimension, with scores ranging smoothly from under 40 percent of the tasks to almost 80 percent.

We see that no editor is superior on all dimension, indicating that tradeoffs must be made in deciding which editor is most appropriate for a given situation. For example, consider the editor BRAVOX, which was developed at Xerox as an extension to the earlier editor BRAVO. Its purpose was to increase functionality and speed and to try out fashionable design features such as command menus and modeless text insertion. Is BRAVOX really an improvement over BRAVO? From Figure 6 we see that BRAVOX is in-

**FIGURE 5.** Decomposition of the Calculated Editing Times into the Different Types of Keystroke-Level Model Operations.

(a) Average time (in seconds) per core editing task in each type of operation.

| Editor | A | S | K | P | $P_S$ | H | M | R | Total Task |
|---|---|---|---|---|---|---|---|---|---|
| TECO | 4.1 | — | 15.3 | — | — | — | 20.3 | 2.8 | 42.5 |
| WYLBUR | 2.7 | — | 18.3 | — | — | — | 10.1 | 1.4 | 32.5 |
| EMACS | 2.0 | 2.5 | 4.6 | — | — | — | 7.8 | 6.9 | 23.8 |
| NLS | 2.5 | 3.0 | 4.3 | 2.0 | — | 1.0 | 4.9 | 1.3 | 19.0 |
| BRAVOX | 1.9 | 2.3 | 2.7 | 2.0 | — | 0.7 | 2.6 | 3.5 | 15.7 |
| BRAVO | 2.1 | 2.6 | 2.5 | 2.2 | — | 0.4 | 3.0 | 5.6 | 18.4 |
| WANG | 2.3 | 2.8 | 2.0 | — | 4.6 | 2.0 | 3.1 | 2.4 | 19.2 |
| STAR | 2.2 | 2.7 | 2.2 | 2.3 | — | 0.4 | 2.1 | 8.3 | 20.2 |
| GYPSY | 2.1 | 2.6 | 2.2 | 2.6 | — | 0.7 | 2.8 | 3.3 | 16.3 |

(b) Percentage of task time in each type of operation.

| Editor | A | S | K | P | $P_S$ | H | M | R |
|---|---|---|---|---|---|---|---|---|
| TECO | 10% | — | 34% | — | — | — | 48% | 7% |
| WYLBUR | 8% | — | 56% | — | — | — | 31% | 4% |
| EMACS | 8% | 10% | 19% | — | — | — | 33% | 29% |
| NLS | 13% | 16% | 22% | 11% | — | 5% | 26% | 7% |
| BRAVOX | 12% | 15% | 17% | 13% | — | 5% | 17% | 22% |
| BRAVO | 12% | 14% | 14% | 12% | — | 2% | 16% | 30% |
| WANG | 12% | 15% | 11% | — | 24% | 10% | 16% | 13% |
| STAR | 11% | 13% | 11% | 11% | — | 2% | 10% | 41% |
| GYPSY | 13% | 16% | 14% | 16% | — | 5% | 17% | 20% |

deed an improvement over BRAVO in Functionality; it is also faster to learn, possibly justifying the design innovations that were incorporated. The analysis in Figure 5 shows that BRAVOX should be faster than BRAVO, but that improvement does not materialize in the experimental Time score (the reason for this is unknown).

*Reliability.* [5] Thus far we have only been considering the mean evaluation scores for each editor without considering the variability associated with these scores. Figure 6 expresses the variability of each experimentally measured score by the Coefficient of Variation (*CV*), [6] which represents the between-user variability. We see that the variability is very high for the Error scores, but quite moderate for the Time and Learning scores. However, the statistical reliability of the scores depends on the number of subjects as well as on the variability. Since we ran only four subjects, only large differences between scores are statistically reliable. For example, we can say that WYLBUR is reliably faster to learn than TECO, but we cannot say that it is reliably faster to use. [7] We also see that the Learning difference noted above between BRAVOX and BRAVO is reliable, [8] but the Time difference in the other direction is not. None of the differences in the Error dimension are reliable, because the between-subject variation is so high.

The reliability of the scores can be improved by increasing the number of subjects tested. [9] For example, consider the Time difference between WANG and STAR. Although the Time difference between these editors is not reliable with only four subjects per editor, this difference would be reliable if it had been found with ten subjects for each editor.

*Importance.* We want to emphasize the obvious fact that reliability is quite different from importance. Any observed difference between scores, however small, can be made reliable by running enough subjects. The real question is whether the observed difference is *important*, which is a substantive, not a statistical, question. For example, small differences between editors on the Error dimension, even if they were relia-

**FIGURE 6. Overall Evaluation Scores for Nine Text Editors.**

| Editor[a] | Time[b] M ± CV[f] (sec/task) | Error[c] M ± CV (% Time) | Learning[d] M ± CV (min/task) | Functionality[e] (% tasks) |
|---|---|---|---|---|
| TECO   | 49 ± .17 | 15% ± .70  | 19.5 ± .29 | 39% |
| WYLBUR | 42 ± .15 | 18% ± .85  | 8.2 ± .24  | 42% |
| EMACS  | 37 ± .15 | 6% ± 1.16  | 6.6 ± .22  | 49% |
| NLS    | 29 ± .15 | 22% ± .71  | 7.7 ± .26  | 77% |
| BRAVOX | 29 ± .29 | 8% ± 1.03  | 5.4 ± .08  | 70% |
| BRAVO  | 26 ± .32 | 8% ± .75   | 7.3 ± .14  | 59% |
| WANG   | 26 ± .21 | 11% ± 1.11 | 6.2 ± .45  | 50% |
| STAR   | 21 ± .18 | 19% ± .51  | 6.2 ± .42  | 62% |
| GYPSY  | 19 ± .11 | 4% ± 2.00  | 4.3 ± .26  | 37% |
| M(M) M(CV)[g] | 31  .19 | 12%  .98 | 7.9  .26 | 54% |
| CV(M)[g] | .31 | .49 | .53 | .25 |

[a] The evaluations for TECO, WYLBUR, NLS, and WANG are from the first author's thesis [11]; the first author also evaluated STAR. The evaluations of the other editors were done in the second author's laboratory.

[b] The Time score is the average error-free expert performance time per benchmark task on the given editor. A difference between editors with mean values $M_1$ and $M_2$ is statistically reliable (95% confidence) if $|M_1 - M_2| > 0.33 \cdot (M_1 + M_2)/2$.

[c] The Errors score is the average time, as a percentage of the error-free performance time, that experts spend making and correcting errors on the given editor. A difference between editors with mean values $M_1$ and $M_2$ is statistically reliable (95% confidence) if $|M_1 - M_2| > 20\%$. Thus, no differences between editor means are reliable in this data.

[d] The Learning score is the average time for a novice to learn how to do a core editing task on the given editor. A difference between editors with mean values $M_1$ and $M_2$ is statistically reliable (95% confidence) if $|M_1 - M_2| > 0.45 \cdot (M_1 + M_2)/2$.

[e] The Functionality score is the percentage of the tasks in the task taxonomy (Figure 1) that can be accomplished with the given editor.

[f] The *Coefficient of Variation* (CV) = *Standard Deviation / Mean* is a normalized measure of variability. The CVs on the individual scores indicate the amount of between-user variability.

[g] The M(CV)s give the mean *between-user* variability on each evaluation dimension, and the CV(M)s give the mean *between-editor* variability on each dimension.

ble, may not be as important as the fact that the user population is highly variable; even large differences in the Time dimension would not be important in a situation where there were not many dedicated expert users.

In practical situations, small differences are usually not important, for they will be washed out by a host of interacting factors in the larger context. Thus, the fact that small observed differences are unreliable (except in extensive, expensive tests) is of little consequence. The utility of a relatively cheap test, such as the methodology proposed in this paper, is that it reveals potentially important (i.e., large) differences.

Once a potentially important difference is identified, then it is a cost-benefit issue to determine how reliable the difference needs to be. But even if the difference is found to be reliable, it is not as important to be certain that there is some difference as to be certain that the difference is reliably large enough to matter.

One reason that the reliability issue arises is that only overall scores are being considered. Often, an informal visual inspection of the more detailed data comprising the overall scores can tell us more than a formal reliability analysis.

### 3.3 A Closer Look at the Data

The next several figures present breakdowns of the overall evaluation scores in Figure 6. Note that the editors in each of the figures are shown in different orders, corresponding to the order of scores on the different dimensions.

*3.3.1. Time.* Figure 7 is a scatter graph showing each individual expert user's error-free Time score. This graph shows the actual spread of user performance for each editor. The greater

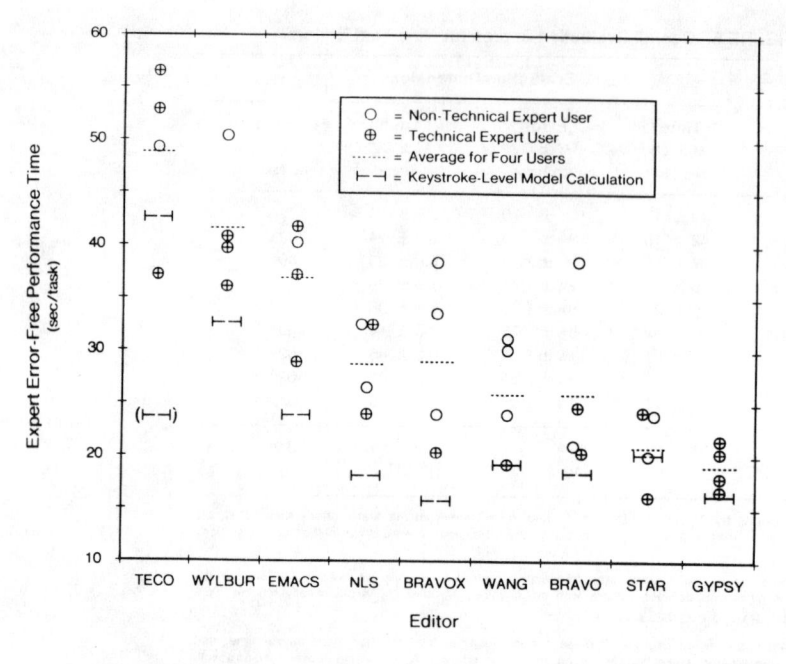

FIGURE 7. Error-Free Time S for Individual Expert Users. T editors are ordered by desce Time score.

the overlap of the performance ranges of two editors, the less likely that the editors are reliably different. The individual points also allow us to identify outliers among the users. An outlier can penalize an editor's score compared to editors that were not unlucky enough to get an unusual user. For instance, the BRAVO outlier suggests that our mean is higher than it would be if the population of subjects had been larger and thus more evenly representative.

Also playing a part in the data is the mix of technical and nontechnical users run on each editor, since the technical users were on the average somewhat faster than the nontechnical users (this will be discussed in Sec. 4.1). We can adjust the overall editor scores to compensate for the different mix of technical and nontechnical users in each editor, but this adjustment does not change any score by more than 2 sec/task and turns out not to change the rank ordering of the editors.

CALCULATED TIME. The task times calculated with the Keystroke-Level Model [Figure 5(a)] are also shown in Figure 7. These calculated times correlate quite well with the empirical Time scores ($R = .90$). The calculated times are on average about 75 percent of the error-free Time scores (the worst case is 54 percent for BRAVOX, and the best case is 96 percent for STAR). The reader will note that there are two calculated times shown for TECO. The original prediction (shown in parentheses) predicted only about 49 percent of the actual error-free time. Because this calculation was so low and because we had time-stamped keystroke records of the users' actual behavior with TECO, we recalculated the task times using the actual methods that the subjects used (rather than trying to predict the methods, as we did for the original calculation). This second calculated time is 87 percent of the actual time. The discrepancy between the method predictions in the two calculations was due to the fact that the users were much more conservative, hence, less optimal, than predicted. The predicted methods used a minimum of searching, displaying, and verifying, while three of the four users were much more careful in their use of this nondisplay-based system. One user was much more daring, and the original calculation was about 70 percent of the actual time for that user—an outcome similar to the calculation results for the other editors.

The reasons for the rather consistent disparity between the Keystroke-Level Model calculations and the actual editing times have to do with the differences between the assumptions of the Keystroke-Level Model and the conditions of our experiments, as noted in Sec. 2.6. There are several differences: (1) The Keystroke-Level Model assumes that the user's method for performing each task is known. However, we cannot always predict the methods, as we saw with TECO. We can usually predict the shorter, easier methods; but the longer, more complex methods are more difficult to predict. Since predicted methods are nearly optimal methods, when a user deviates from a predicted method, it is usually in the direction of using a slower method. (2) Some of the users may have had to engage in problem-solving to perform some of the more complex tasks in some editors (e.g., to transpose phrases with TECO) and their behavior would not be the simple method-execution behavior assumed by the model. (3) The error time for small errors is included in the experimental error-free time, but is not considered in the calculated time. (4) The experimental time includes all the time *between* tasks. Some of this time is not considered in the model, such as page turning time, pauses for rest, etc. But even without such differences, it should be remembered that the Keystroke-Level Model is an approximate model, and we should not expect its calculations to be perfect.

The data for individual users show that, for most editors, one user comes very close to the level of performance represented by the Keystroke-Level Model calculation. Since the calculations were based on predictions of optimal methods, this suggests that only a minority of users are likely to approach optimal performance. [10]

*3.3.2. Error.* Figure 8 is a scatter plot of the individual expert users' Error scores. This data shows a factor of 5 difference between the best and the worst editors; even so, these differences are swamped by the large ranges of error within editors. The relative variabilities are summarized in Figure 6: the between-editor $CV$ is .49, whereas the between-user $CV$ averages .98. Thus, no conclusions can be drawn about the differences between editors in error cost.

It might be noted that the individual users who have large Error scores do not have them because they were unfortunate enough to be struck by rare, disastrous errors; rather, these users merited their Error scores by committing several errors throughout the experiment. Among the seven users whose Error scores were greater than 20 percent, the error time came from an average of 7.4 individual errors: 3.1 during the first pass over the benchmark and 4.3 incomplete tasks that had to be fixed up on the second pass. The errors during both passes took an average of over 70 seconds each.

*3.3.3 Learning.* The overall Learning scores are broken down in two ways: by time and by individual learners. Figure 9 gives learning curves over time for all of the editors, each curve being the average of four learners. Each learning curve is drawn in a stylized fashion as a series of five steps, one step for each cycle in

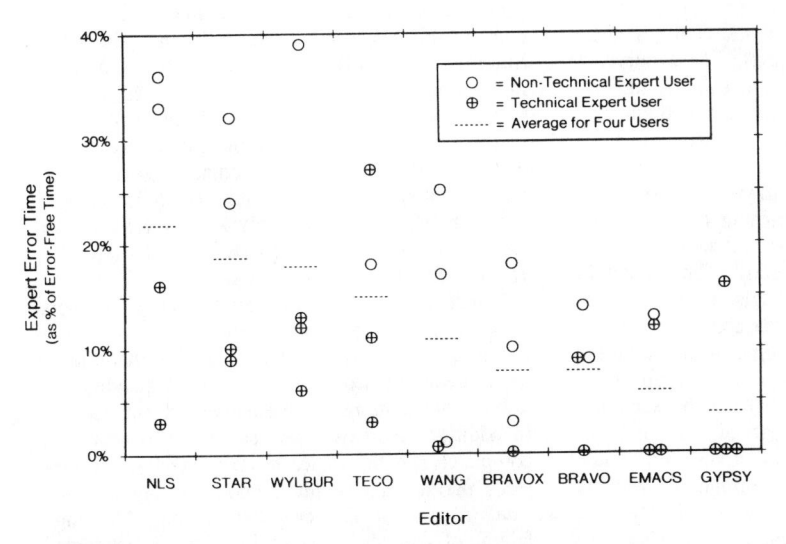

FIGURE 8. Error Time Scores for Individual Expert Users. The editors are ordered by descending Error score.

FIGURE 9. Average Learning Curves over all Learners on each Editor. The two TECO curves were produced by different instructors.

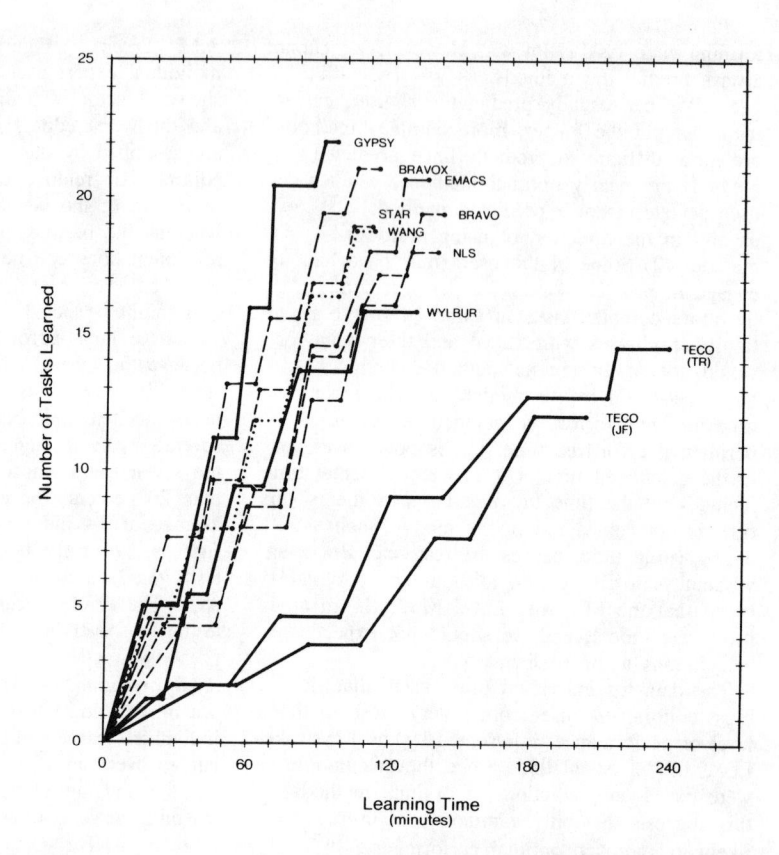

the learning session. The instruction part of a cycle is represented by the sloped part of the step, and the quiz part of the cycle is represented by the flat part of the step (as if no learning occurs during the quiz). These curves can be seen to be fairly straight overall, indicating that it is reasonable to summarize them using their overall slopes, which is just what the Learning scores are.

The reader will note that there are two learning curves for TECO. The learning test was replicated for TECO with a second instructor, who ran the test completely independently. The second instructor, using only the materials in [11], taught a slightly different set of TECO commands than the first instructor and of course taught a different set of *four* subjects. The results of this second evaluation test (marked JF) can be seen to be quite close to the first (marked TR).

Figure 10 is a scatter graph of the individual novices' Learning scores. This graph, as well as Figure 9, shows large differences in the learnability of the different editors. TECO is clearly different from all the others, taking over twice as long to learn as the next editor (WYLBUR). The rest of the editors lie in a tight group with considerable overlap between adjacent editors. But this group still covers another factor of two in learning time, so GYPSY is four times as fast to learn as TECO. The large amounts of overlap in the range of learners within editors indicate that the differences between adjacent editors are mostly not reliable. The difference in Learning scores between TECO and WYLBUR is reliable, as are the differences between GYPSY and each of TECO, WYLBUR, NLS, and BRAVO.

Figure 10 allows us to identify outlier learners, as we did with the Time scores. One such outlier is a STAR learner, which suggests that the mean Learning score for STAR might be slightly lower from a more representative subject sample. In addition, there was one subject who was completely unable to learn TECO at all (that subject's partial data is not included in any of our data or graphs). The fact that the only learning failure of the whole set of learning experiments

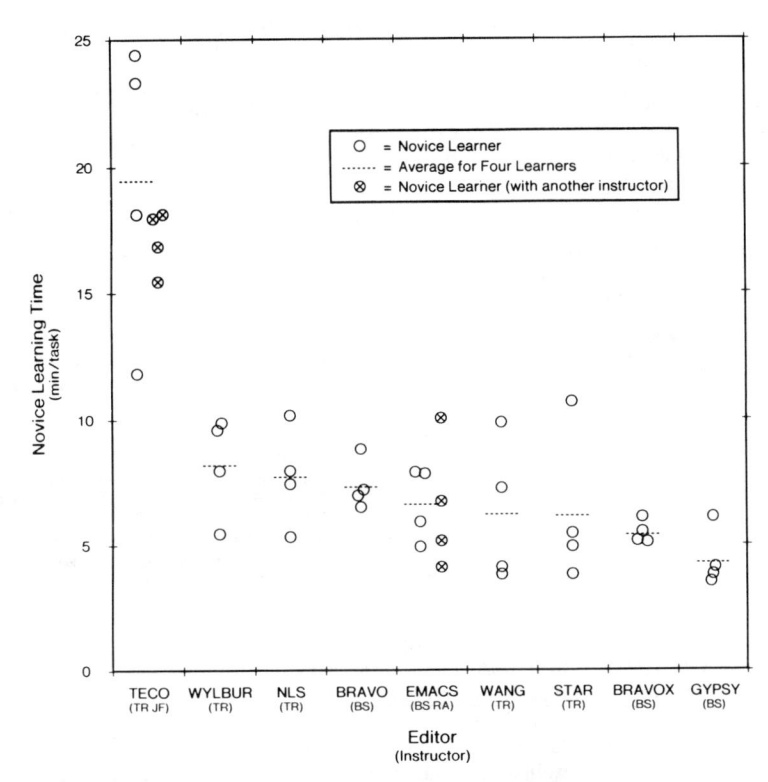

FIGURE 10. Learning Scores for Individual Novice Learners. The editors are ordered by descending Learning score. The instructors are noted below each editor.

occurred with TECO reinforces the notion that TECO is more difficult to learn than the rest.

**INSTRUCTOR EFFECTS.** The instructor plays a strong role in the learning experiments—s/he decides what subset of commands to teach, and s/he tries to maximize the learning rate by keeping the subject from getting bogged down in nonproductive efforts. Thus, the instructor could have a potentially strong effect on the learning results. To show instructor effects, the specific instructors are noted in Figure 10. Since the scores for the different editors overlap so much, it seems that no instructor is consistently faster or slower than the others. This can be seen most clearly in the cases where the learning tests have been replicated. In the TECO case (mentioned above), the second instructor obtained a mean Learning score within 12 percent of the score obtained by the first instructor. In the second case, the EMACS learning tests were replicated in a different laboratory, obtaining a virtually identical overall Learning score [13].

The differences in teaching style of the different instructors can, on the other hand, be seen in the between-subject variations. The two TECO data sets show this difference most clearly—the second instructor has very much less between-subject variation. This can also be seen in the between-subject *CV*s in the editor evaluations run by TR and BS, the two instructors who ran most of the tests. TR's *CV*s range from .24 to .45, while BS's *CV*s range from .08 to .26. The instructors seem to be exerting different amounts of control over the learners. However, this does not seem to affect the mean Learning scores.

*3.3.4. Functionality.* Figure 11 gives a breakdown of the Functionality scores by the different categories in the task taxonomy. These functionality results show that most of the editors can perform about half of the tasks in the task taxonomy. Each system has its areas of strength and weakness. To show this, the scores are broken down into subscores in Figure 11. For instance, EMACS is excellent in programming capability, while NLS and BRAVOX are especially good in formatting and layout tasks. Because the number of tasks in the taxonomy was weighted more toward text layout than programming, the

**FIGURE 11. Functionality Subscores for the Nine Text Editors.**

| Task Category[a]<br>(No. of Tasks)[b] | NLS | BRAVOX | STAR | BRAVO | WANG | EMACS | WYLBUR | TECO | GYPSY | All Editors[d]<br>M±CV |
|---|---|---|---|---|---|---|---|---|---|---|
| TOTAL (212)[b] | 77% | 70% | 62% | 59% | 50% | 49% | 42% | 39% | 37% | 54%±.25 |
| Modification | | | | | | | | | | |
| Content (66) | 94% | 89% | 93% | 90% | 87% | 74% | 63% | 88% | 80% | 84%±.13 |
| Text Layout (19) | 89% | 71% | 66% | 71% | 37% | 37% | 26% | 3% | 26% | 47%±.56 |
| Page Layout (25) | 74% | 62% | 56% | 40% | 34% | 2% | 6% | 4% | 4% | 31%±.85 |
| Characters (21) | 43% | 76% | 57% | 62% | 38% | 14% | 21% | 0% | 17% | 36%±.66 |
| Other (16) | 53% | 59% | 50% | 22% | 34% | 0% | 16% | 3% | 0% | 26%±.84 |
| Addressing (22) | 68% | 36% | 30% | 30% | 16% | 61% | 34% | 25% | 18% | 35%±.48 |
| Control (23) | 56% | 37% | 24% | 20% | 24% | 89% | 61% | 48% | 9% | 41%±.58 |
| Display (8) | 94% | 94% | 63% | 69% | 19% | 81% | 62% | 38% | 50% | 63%±.42 |
| Misc. (12) | 100% | 88% | 100% | 71% | 71% | 46% | 71% | 25% | 42% | 68%±.38 |

[a] The Task Categories are described in the task taxonomy shown in Figure 1.

[b] The number in parentheses after the task category name gives the total number of tasks in that task category. The Functionality scores and sub-scores are given as a percentage of the total number of tasks in each task category. The scores in the TOTAL row are the same as in Figure 6.

[c] The editors are ordered in descending order of their overall Functionality scores.

[d] The numbers in the All Editors column tell how well the task categories are handled by the whole collection of editors and the amount of between-editor variability there is.

document-oriented editors generally scored somewhat better overall than EMACS. But NLS, which tries to cover all needs, is clearly superior in overall functionality.

We can question the reliability of these Functionality scores, as well as the other scores generated by this methodology. An analyst's rating of the functionality of an editor is partly a matter of judgment, as was noted in Sec. 2.5, and partly a matter of detailed knowledge of the editor (e.g., knowing about limitations that may not be apparent from the documentation). To quantify the variation between analysts, three different analysts were asked to independently rate WYLBUR. The overall Functionality scores for the three analysts were 42 percent, 45 percent, and 39 percent. Scores within task categories differed more, but the differences between the analysts tended to be averaged out over the total set of tasks. Thus, as a rule of thumb, we can consider the overall Functionality scores to be accurate to around 10 percent.

### 3.4 Assessment of the Methodology

The above results show that diverse editors can indeed be evaluated and compared. As a whole, the evaluation methodology seems to successfully provide an objective, multidimensional picture of text editors. This methodology is also quite practical. For an experienced evaluator, about one week of time is required to evaluate a new editor. Thus, it should be practical for a system designer or a potential buyer.

Several other issues surrounding the methodology deserve discussion.

*3.4.1. Reliability.* The main drawback in the use of this methodology is that the small number of subjects used for each of the tests makes the results very coarse. In addition, the results point out that the Error dimension needs a more reliable measure to differentiate editors, which will have to take into account the effect of large differences among the users.

Another way to increase reliability, besides increasing the number of subjects, is to decrease the between-user variability by homogenizing the subject sample. For instance, potential subjects could take a pretest, and only people who scored within a certain range could be used. This, however, specializes the results so that they only represent a small segment of the user population, decreasing the generality of the methodology.[11]

Given that the methodology accepts a wide range of subjects, we can check whether the methodology is being applied to a restricted sample. If the between-user variance is ever substantially less than in the data here, the reason may be that the evaluator has picked a restricted sample of subjects. This is a useful caution for designers who are testing their own systems and who especially have to guard against bias. For example, in the data presented here, we note that the Time data for GYPSY does in fact have a lower than normal *CV*, which in this case is largely explained by the fact that only technical subjects were used.

### 3.4.2. Coverage.
Although the methodology covers several basic aspects of editor usage, there are still aspects not covered. When this methodology was being developed [11], a variety of easy-to-obtain measures of other aspects were explored. Some examples are: (1) The error-proneness of an editor was measured by putting external stress on expert users while they performed editing tasks. (2) The possibility of disastrous errors in an editor was measured by a procedure for analyzing the editor's command language. (3) The display capabilities of an editor were measured by users performing proofreading tasks. (4) The learning and use of advanced features was addressed by using a questionnaire to measure experts' knowledge of how to perform complex editing tasks. Unfortunately, all of these attempts turned out to be too crude to be reliable and too unproductive in differentiating systems. The tests presented in this paper are the only ones we know currently that work well enough to be included in a methodology.

### 3.4.3. Representativeness.

TIME. A general criticism of benchmark testing is that the items in the benchmark are not appropriate or appropriately weighted for any particular application. Specifically, the benchmark used in the present methodology has been criticized for not representing the true mix of tasks in real text-editing situations [17]. This is true, as we noted in Sec. 2.2. However, we are skeptical that there is a single benchmark set representing the majority of text-editing situations. This is an empirical issue, and we know of no data currently that settles it. But there remains the issue of how to use the results of the present methodology if one is interested in a particular situation that has a different mix of tasks from the benchmark.

We propose an analytic procedure for adjusting the Time score from the benchmark test to correspond to a new situation, which is characterized as a new set of tasks (weighted by the frequency of the individual tasks). This adjustment procedure is based on the assumption that there is a constant ratio between the experimentally measured Time score and the time calculated with the Keystroke-Level Model. This can be expressed in a formula:

$$T/C = T' - C'$$

where $T$ is the Time score on the benchmark, $C$ is the calculated time on the same benchmark (as in Figure 5), $C'$ is the calculated time for the new mix of tasks, and $T'$ is the Time score we would expect from an experimental test on the new mix of tasks. $T$ and $C$ are given by the present methodology. $T'$ is the desired result. It can be estimated by calculating $C'$, which is done by using the Keystroke-Level Model on the new (weighted) set of tasks. One must be cautious about the assumption behind this adjustment procedure, especially if the new task set contains many complex editing tasks, for the assumptions behind the Keystroke-Level Model (see [3]) might be violated (such as was our experience with the first TECO calculation).

LEARNING. The particular set of tasks chosen for the learning experiments undoubtedly affects the results obtained here, but it is likely to be less influential than which teaching paradigm is used. For example, we would expect the results of a self-teaching paradigm to be mostly determined by the quality of documentation. We do not in general know how teaching paradigms differ, but there is one preliminary result in a recent study by Robertson and Akscyn [13] comparing different teaching paradigms. They applied the present learning methodology to the ZOG frame editor, using an instructor and using two self-teaching paradigms by substituting online and offline documentation for the instructor. They found that the instructor produced about 13 percent faster learning than the self-teaching documentation; and they found that the offline documentation was about 6 percent faster than the online documentation. The reason for the small difference caused by mode of documentation was that all the learners used the documentation in the same way in both cases—by reading through it at the beginning of the session. The lesson here is that real learners do not necessarily follow the paradigms laid out for them by the system documenters.

FUNCTIONALITY. Finally, the issue of representativeness also applies to the checklist of tasks for testing functionality; the tasks in the checklist do not represent the needs of any particular situation. The degree of elaboration of the tasks in the task taxonomy was influenced by the capabilities of the editors existing or being envisioned at the time the taxonomy was being created. Thus, there are eight tasks relating to the layout of paragraphs but only one about the ability to typeset mathematical formulas properly. An editor that performs both functions equally well gets far more credit for one than the other. This problem is best addressed by using the functionality subscores; for a given application more weight can be given to the areas relevant to the application.

### 3.4.4. Applicability.

**EXTRAPOLATION TO A LARGER CONTEXT.** All of the data we have gathered have been from people performing a small number of preset tasks in a laboratory environment. What relationship do these results have to productivity in an office where the tasks may be different (e.g., proofreading and editing one's own work) and the environmental conditions may be different (e.g., a receptionist with constant small interruptions from people walking by)? A 20 percent improvement in the Time score for this methodology would not necessarily translate into a 20 percent improvement in overall office productivity. This is because an improvement in editing speed may not be accompanied by a proportional improvement in the speed of other activities that the user is doing along with editing, such as thinking about the proper wording of the text, typing in large amounts of new text, or proofreading for errors. Another possible factor is that the intense concentration on the editing task allowed by laboratory conditions, but often not allowed by real situations, may differentially affect the performance of different editors. Such problems beset all laboratory work, and the questions raised can only by answered when laboratory studies are supplemented by on-site studies to determine the relationship between the two.

**USE BY EDITOR DESIGNERS.** The full methodology requires an implemented text editor that has been running long enough to have at least a few expert users, which suggests that the methodology is not useful for a designer of a new editor. However, the designer can use parts of the methodology to get an early indication of how well the proposed editor compares with existing editors and where the strengths and weaknesses of the new editor lie. Two of the evaluation measures, Time and Functionality, can be obtained analytically, when the design is still on paper. Learning can be measured experimentally on a prototype (that need only be complete enough to cover the core tasks). The Error measure is the only one that cannot be obtained easily; this should pose no problem, since editors cannot be differentiated on this dimension anyhow.

On the Time dimension, the Keystroke-Level Model can be used to produce a calculated task time, along with a decomposition of the time into the times for the different operations. These times can be compared to the calculated task times for other editors in Figure 5 to see whether the times are in line with similar editors and to reveal possible bottlenecks on some operations. (The calculated task time can also be adjusted, by multiplying by 1.3, to compensate for the model's tendency to underpredict the experimental Time scores. The adjusted time can than be compared to the Time scores in Figure 6). In this analysis, the only parameters which must be estimated are the system response times. If these are not available, this analysis can be turned around to provide the designer with a specification for acceptable limits for the response times (by showing how different response times make the proposed editor compare to other editors). Finally, if a prototype system is available, experimental benchmark tests can be run using the designers and implementors themselves as subjects. These data would be useful to provide a check on the calculated times and the predicted methods that the times are based on.

## 4. BEHAVIORAL RESULTS

The database of results from the experimental studies gives us information not only about the specific editors, but about user behavior in general, such as the gross levels of user performance in text editing. The data show that the core editing tasks require about 20-45 seconds per task for most expert users on most systems, and it shows that a period of about two hours of one-on-one training is enough to teach novice users about 20 core tasks in most editors. These results should be of interest to researchers in office productivity, for example, to measure the cost-effectiveness of word processing. More detailed results are interesting in two principal ways: for the light they shed on (1) the individual differences in performance between users and (2) the factors influencing novice learning.

## 4.1 Individual User Differences

### 4.1.1. Magnitude of Individual User Differences.
The greatest individual differences by far are found in Error time scores (ranging from 0 to 39 percent), which reflects a wide variation among expert users in how careful they are in avoiding errors and in performing tasks completely. There is much less variation among experts in speed of editing—about a factor of 1.5 to 2 between the fastest and slowest users' Time scores within each editor. This range is much smaller than the factor of 3.5 reported in [4]. However, [4] tested a more diverse sample of users, including casual users as well as dedicated expert users.

A somewhat surprising result is that the variation among novice learners is not much greater than among expert users. Learners exhibit about the same range of variation (up to a factor of 2.5 between the fastest and slowest learners within an editor) and $CV$ (.19 for experts and .26 for novice learners). This is partly due, no doubt, to the fact that the learning tests are designed to minimize variation due to idiosyncratic learners (e.g., the command summary sheet and the always present instructor). A self-teaching paradigm is likely to yield much more variation among learners.

### 4.1.2. Time vs. Errors.
It is common wisdom that there is a speed-accuracy tradeoff: that when people work faster, they make more errors. Our data can be used to investigate whether the users who spend more time in error do so because they are working faster, that is, whether users with higher Error time scores have lower error-free Time scores. We cannot directly compare scores of users on different editors, however, unless we normalize over editors. A user's score on an editor can be normalized by dividing it by the overall (mean) score for the editor. That is, a normalized score of 1.0 indicates an average user, and a score of .5 indicates a user twice as good as the average. Figure 12 plots the normalized Time vs. Error scores for all the expert users. What is immediately obvious from this plot is the much larger variation on the Error dimension than on the Time dimension. However, we do not see the tradeoff between Time and Error scores that a speed-accuracy tradeoff would suggest, but rather a modest positive correlation between them ($R = .58$). Some users tend to be better than others on both dimensions.

### 4.1.3. Technical vs. Nontechnical Expert Users.
The individual users plotted in Figure 12 are marked as being technical or nontechnical. The technical users are clearly the better users on both Time and Error (clustering in the lower left quadrant). Also plotted in the figure is the average technical user and the average nontechnical user. These two fictitious average users account for the major features of the plot. The average nontechnical user is 15 percent slower than the average technical user (.94 vs. 1.08) and spends a factor of 3 more time in error (.50 vs. 1.56). [12] The factor 1.15 difference between technical and nontechnical users on the Time dimension is comparable to the factor of 1.3 reported in [4].

The underlying reason for the difference between technical and nontechnical users is not known. It is not due to physical skill factors, such as typing proficiency, for which nontechnical users are superior. [13] It could just be due to a difference in general intelligence or education, rather than anything due to technical experience per se. (The programmers we used as technical subjects have been preselected to be very bright and highly educated, whereas the secretarial and

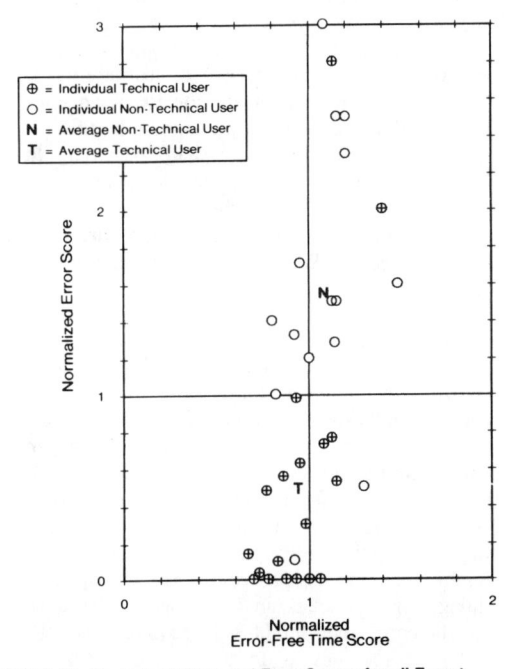

FIGURE 12. Normalized Time and Error Scores for all Expert Users. A user's score is normalized by dividing it by the average score in the editor.

support personnel we used as nontechnical subjects have undergone less of such preselection.) Other possible factors, suggested by a recent study [5], are that technical users might have more spatial ability or be younger than nontechnical users. These two factors have been shown to affect editor learning rates, and they are also likely to apply to expert performance.

### 4.2. Novice Learning

Learning behavior is less well understood than expert performance. The Keystroke-Level Model [3] (along with its theoretical underpinnings [4]) provides a usefully accurate account of the time performance of expert users. However, we have no similar account of why some editors are easier for novices to learn than others. Our learning data provide the opportunity to test some ideas about the main factors affecting learnability.

#### 4.2.1. Factors Affecting Editor Learnability.

How does the structure of an editor affect its learnability? Perhaps the most obvious hypothesis to consider is that the command languages of some editors are more complex. One measure of command language complexity is the number of distinct commands in an editor. According to this hypothesis, the editors with fewer commands should be faster to learn. (This might be called the "weigh-the-manual" theory of learnability, since most reference manuals consist of an enumeration of the different commands.) In this methodology, since only commands necessary to do core editing tasks are taught, we restrict our measure to the number of these "core commands." Figure 13 shows that this measure correlates poorly ($R = .37$) with the Learning scores. [14]

The crucial point missed by this hypothesis is that commands are not useful in isolation, rather they are used in the context of methods or procedures to accomplish editing tasks. Thus, the second hypothesis to consider as a predictor of learnability is that learning is related to the *procedural complexity* of a command language. This is quite different from command language complexity. For example, a "simple" command language with only three commands might require lengthy and intricate procedures to accomplish editing tasks, whereas an editor with a large variety of commands might only require a couple of those commands to do any one task. The procedural complexity hypothesis says that a user must learn not just what each command does, but how each command is used in various ways in different methods. This leads us to consider the number of distinct uses of commands, which is related to the length of the methods (rather than the length of the list of commands).

One way to approximate the procedural complexity of an editor is to compute the average number of steps in the methods for accomplishing a representative set of tasks, such as the benchmark used in the Time and Error dimensions of our methodology. [15] The physical operations in the Keystroke-Level Model encodings of methods (see Figure 4) provide a simple, unambiguous set of steps to count. Figure 13 shows that the average number of physical operations per task correlates substantially better with the Learning scores ($R = .68$) than do the commands, although the correlation is still modest.

FIGURE 13. Correlations of Learning Scores with Various Measures.

| Measure | Correlation (R) | |
|---|---|---|
| | All Nine Editors | All Editors except TECO[a] |
| Number of Core Commands in Editor | .37 | .19 |
| Number of Physical Operations per Task | .68 | .58 |
| Number of Method Chunks (M's + A's) per Task | .93 | .65 |
| Expert Time Score | .79 | .67 |

[a] Since the Learning score for TECO is an extreme value, it has a large influence on the correlations. Hence, it is useful to present a separate set of correlations with the influence of the TECO score removed.

The length (in physical operations) of a method, although it may correlate with procedural complexity, can be a misleading indicator. For example, a method requiring the user to type D E L E T E RETURN is not seven times more complex than a method requiring only D to be typed. Thus, we see that procedural complexity has more to do with the *mental* "chunking" of physical steps into coherent fragments than the physical steps themselves. To operationalize this notion, let us return to the Keystroke-Level Model encoding of methods. This model has two kinds of mental operations, **A**'s and **M**'s. When a large editing task is broken into subtasks, the subtasks are each preceded by an **A** operation, representing the user's having to acquire a mental representation of the subtask. Within a subtask, the sequence of physical operations is punctuated with **M** operations, which represents small mental preparations for the upcoming physical operations (rules for placing **M** operations are given in [3]). The **A** and **M** operations have the effect of breaking the sequence of physical operations into procedural chunks. For example, consider the method encodings of the example task in Figure 4. The method for WYLBUR is:

**A M** 12K **M** 3K R **M** 13K **M** 20K **M** 8K **M** K

Here the physical operations are divided into seven chunks by the **A**'s and **M**'s. The methods for the same task in EMACS and STAR contain only three and two chunks, respectively.

**A** S **M** 4K R 2K **M** 15K
**A** S H P 2K **M** K H 14K

The number of chunks in a method, which can be estimated by simply counting the **A**'s and **M**'s, should be a better indicator of the procedural complexity of the method than the physical operations we counted before. In fact, the mental chunking measure correlates better with the Learning scores ($R = .93$) than do the physical operations, as Figure 13 shows. It is the best correlate we have of Learning time.

This notion of procedural complexity as determined by mentally defined chunks is an instance of the "zeroth-order theory of learning" [4]: that learning time is proportional to the number of chunks of information that must be learned. To make this theory operational, we must be able to specify what the chunks are. In this case, the chunks ar the procedural fragments bounded by mental operations.

Figure 14 shows a plot of the mental-chunking measure of procedural complexity against the Learning scores. This plot shows how raw correlations must be interpreted with caution, for we see that the learning score for TECO, which lies far out from the others, has great leverage on the correlation (which is why we also give the correlations excluding TECO in Figure 13). What we see in Figure 14 is that procedural complexity accounts for the difference between the fastest and slowest editors, but that it tells us little about the observed differences among the set of fastest editors. Procedural complexity is not the only factor affecting learnability; in fact, it seems to be dominated by other factors among fast editors.[16] However, procedural complexity may be the most dominant factor in learning overall, statistically accounting for about half the variance between editors.

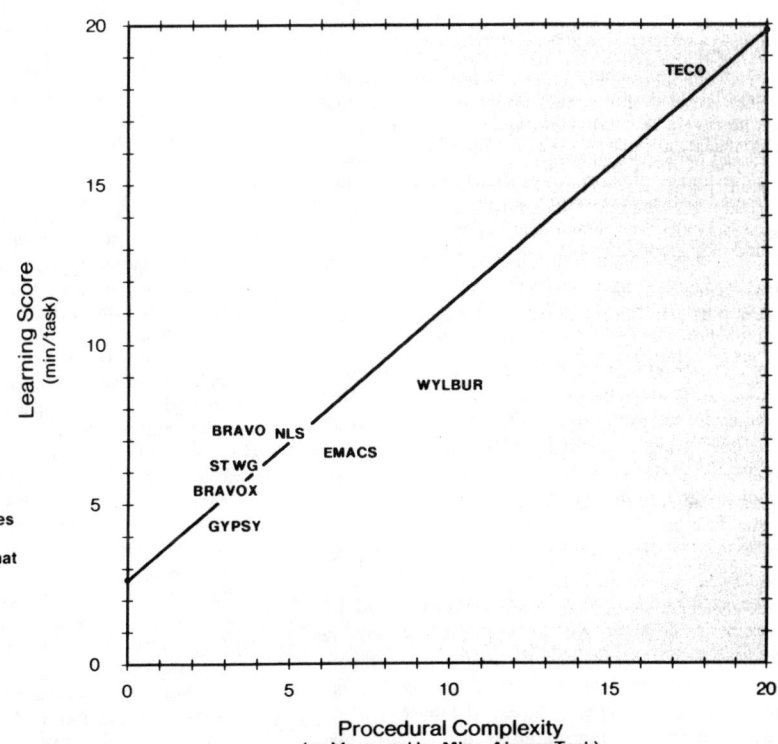

FIGURE 14. Plot of Learning Scores vs. the Mental-Chunks Measure of Procedural Complexity. (Note that STAR is abbreviated as ST and WANG as WG.)

*4.2.2. Learning vs. Time.* The conventional wisdom among designers is that there is a tradeoff between systems that are easy to learn by novices and systems that are efficient to use by experts. However, if we correlate the Learning scores with the Time scores, we see exactly the opposite. The data from our study shows a high positive correlation ($R = .79$, Figure 13) between the Time and Learning scores. [17] The concept of procedural complexity introduced in the last section explains this correlation. It says that the same factor—procedural complexity— underlies both expert performance (longer methods take longer to execute) and novice learning (longer methods imply that there are more chunks to learn). [18]

## 5. CONCLUSION

A standardized four-dimensional methodology for evaluating text editors has been presented and applied to nine different editors. The methodology seems to be an effective tool for the empirical evaluation of text editors along the dimensions of Time, Error, Learning, and Functionality. Of course, the methodology has limitations—having to do with reliability, coverage, representativeness, and applicability—which is the price of keeping the methodology simple to use. It is obvious that the methodology could be improved by both refinement and extension. However, even in its present form, it provides for the generation of a valuable user-editor performance database of objective measures. We would urge others who need to do evaluations of editors to use this methodology. Its main advantage is that the numbers produced can be put in the context of the database of already evaluated editors (without such a context, numbers are difficult to interpret). At the same time, the additional evaluations (either replications of existing evaluations or evaluations of new editors) would be contributing to extending the database, allowing our knowledge of editor performance to systematically accumulate.

We have also shown how the database of results can help us understand user performance, by making clear the magnitude of individual differences of both experts and novices, and by providing a testing ground for understanding the factors affecting learning. Although we presently favor a theory of learning based on the notion of procedural complexity, a larger database will show whether this theory holds up. Finally, we have shown that Keystroke-Level Model calculations of editor performance, which also belong in the database, are useful analyses against which to compare and interpret the experimental results.

*Acknowledgements.* We thank Betsey Summers for organizing and running many of these evaluation studies and for helping us analyze the data. We thank Allen Newell and Stu Card for many helpful discussions and Allen Newell for commenting on drafts of this paper.

This paper is based in part on the first author's thesis research (reported in [11]) which was done under the supervision of the second author, and on continuing research by the second author. A short, preliminary version of this paper was published as [12]. The authors are listed in reverse-alphabetic order.

## NOTES

[1] The reliability of the measurements is determined more by the small number of subjects than by the accuracy of measurement.

[2] Thus, the total time to perform an average benchmark task is $T + Te$, where $T$ is the error-free Time score and $e$ is the Error score.

[3] More and more people today have some exposure to computers, and it may become more important to look at the learning users experienced in other systems. However, this would present difficult methodological problems in assessing their degree of experience and the similarity of their experience to the editor to be learned.

[4] EMACS was the only system for which optimal conditions were not found. The workstation used was actually a personal computer running a rather slow terminal-emulation package. This cut the effective communication rate between the main computer and the workstation to around 1200 baud, which is much slower than is often available with EMACS.

[5] In this paper we use the term "reliability" instead of the more usual term "(statistical) significance," since we are trying to emphasize the difference between *statistical* and *substantive* significance, the latter of which we call "importance."

[6] We use the *CV*, which is the Standard Deviation normalized by the Mean, instead of the Standard Deviation, because *CV*s are more constant across the different scores. That is to say, the absolute size of the variation is approximately proportional to the mean.

[7] Quantitative formulas for computing which differences between scores are reliable (derived from the standard statistical concept of confidence limits) are given in the notes to Figure 6.

[8] This result was obtained using the actual variances of the BRAVOX and BRAVO data, rather than by using the general formulas given in Figure 6.

[9] Reliability, as measured by the confidence interval around a score, is approximately inversely proportional to the square root of the number of subjects used to determine the score.

[10] The one exception to this observation is in STAR, which had one user who performed much better than the Keystroke-Level Model calculation. We believe that that is because the user constantly overlapped his actions with STAR's long system response times: he often did not wait for the machine to catch up with him between tasks, but typed ahead whenever possible.

[11] Another way to increase reliability is to use all the subjects, but to use the pretest scores to normalize the overall results. This would require a model of the relation between pretest scores and performance results.

[12] This data allows us to calculate an adjustment for the effects of using different proportions of technical and nontechnical subjects in different editors. As mentioned in Sec. 3.3.1. such an adjustment does not change the rank ordering of the editors of the Time dimension. A similar adjustment on the Error dimension also makes little difference in the results: the range of Error scores becomes a factor of 4 instead of a factor of 5, and differences between editors are still not statistically reliable.

[13] The nontechnical users were 1.4 times faster than the technical users. Given that an average of about 22 percent of the time is spent in typing [Figure 5(b)], this would give the nontechnical users about a 7 percent advantage over the technical users.

[14] One problem with this measure is deciding what a command is (e.g., is a preselection a command itself or just an argument to a command that follows it?). This issue can be sidestepped somewhat by counting parts of commands, such as commands names, arguments, terminators, etc. However, this "finer" measure does no better than just counting "whole" commands (see [11]).

[15] It may seem paradoxical that we are using the expert benchmark test to measure learnability by novices. But note that we are only using the benchmark test as a convenient sample of tasks to get at the procedural complexity *required by the core functions of the editor*. Since the novices are trying to acquire this same expertise, it represents the target competence they are trying to achieve.

[16] A candidate for one of the other factors is what we might call "conceptual unfamiliarity," which taps how well novice users understand, *a priori*, the conceptual constructs involved in an editor. This notion is currently being explored by the second author and Sally Douglas in *Learning to Text Edit: Semantics in Procedural Skill Acquisition*. Ph.D dissertation. Stanford University, March 83.

[17] This is *the* only substantial correlation between scores on the methodology's dimensions. Correlations between the other dimensions range between .24 and .36. All of these correlations are positive, in the sense that editors tend to improve in the two dimensions together, with the exception that there is a tradeoff between Error and Functionality.

[18] We can use this result to conjecture that the main reason for the superiority of display-based systems, on both the Time and Learning dimension, over nondisplay systems is not the display itself, but rather that the display-based systems permit much less complex procedures.

## REFERENCES

1. Boies, S. J. User behavior in an interactive computer system. *IBM Systems Journal 13* (1974) 1-18.
2. Card, S. K., English, W. K., and Burr, B. J. Evaluation of mouse, rate-controlled isometric joystick, step keys, and text keys for text selection on a CRT. *Ergonomics 21* (1978) 601-613.
3. Card, S. K., Moran, T. P., and Newell, A. The Keystroke-Level Model for user performance time with interactive systems. *Comm. ACM 23, 7* (July 1980) 396-410.
4. Card, S. K., Moran, T. P., and Newell, A. *The Psychology of Human-Computer Interaction*. Lawrence Erlbaum Associates, Hillsdale, NJ, 1983.
5. Egan, D. E., Bowers, C., and Gomez, L. M. Learner characteristics that predict success in using a text-editor tutorial. *Proc. Conference on Human Factors in Computer Systems*. Gaithersburg, MD. (March 1982), 337-340.
6. Embley, D. W., and Nagy, G. Behavioral aspects of text editors. *Computing Surveys 13*, 1 (March 1981) 33-70.
7. Good, M. An ease of use evaluation of an integrated document processing system. *Proc. Conference on Human Factors in Computer Systems*. Gaithersburg, MD, (March 1982), 142-147.
8. Meyrowitz, N., and van Dam, A. Interactive editing systems. *Computing Surveys 14*, 3 (Sept. 1982) 321-415.
9. Moran, T.P. The Command Language Grammar: A representation for the user interface of interactive computer systems. *Int. Journal of Man-Machine Studies 15*. 1 (July 1981) 3-50.
10. Riddle, E. A. *Comparative Study of Various Text Editors and Formatting Systems*. Report AD-A029 050, Air Force Data Services Center, The Pentagon, Washington, D.C., (Aug. 1976).
11. Roberts, T. L. *Evaluation of Computer Text Editors*, Ph.D. dissertation, Department of Computer Science, Stanford University, Stanford, Calif., (1980). Available as Report AAD 80-11699 from University Microfilms, Ann Arbor, Mich.
12. Roberts, T. L., and Moran, T. P. Evaluation of text editors. *Proc. Conference on Human Factors in Computer Systems*, Gaithersburg, MD, (March 1982), 136-141.
13. Robertson, C. K., and Akscyn, R. Experimental evaluation of tools for teaching the ZOG frame editor. Computer Science Department, Carnegie-Mellon University, Pittsburgh, PA, (1982).
14. *The Seybold Report on Office Systems* (through 1981 called *The Seybold Report on Word Process-*

*ing*). Media, PA.
15. *The Seybold Report on Word Processing.* 4. 4. (April 1981). Issue on Personal Computers: Word Processing Packages.
16. Smith, D. C., Irby, C., Kimball, R., Verplank, W., and Harslem, E. Designing the Star user interface. *Byte* 7, 4 (April 1982) 242-282.
17. Whiteside, J., Archer, N., Wixon, D., and Good, M. How do people really use text editors? *Proc. SIGOA Conference on Office Information Systems*, Philadelphia, (1982) 29-40.

**References (for Editor Documentation)**
18. Augmentation Research Center. *NLS-8 Command Summary.* Stanford Research Institute. Menlo Park, Calif., (May 1975).
19. Augmentation Research Center. *NLS-8 Glossary.* Stanford Research Institute. Menlo Park, Calif., (July 1975).
20. Bolt, Beranek, and Newman, Inc. *TENEX Text Editor and Corrector* (Manual DEC10-NGZEB-D). Cambridge, Mass., (1973). (Documents TECO.)
21. Garcia, K. *Xerox Document System Reference Manual.* Xerox Office Products Division. Palo Alto, Calif. (1980). (Documents BRAVOX.)
22. Lampson, B. Bravo manual. *Alto User's Handbook.* Xerox Palo Alto Research Center, Palo Alto, Calif., (1979).
23. Stallman, R. M. *EMACS Manual for ITS Users.* AI Lab Memo 554, MIT, Cambridge, Mass., (1980).
24. Stanford Center for Information Processing, *Wylbur/370 The Stanford Timesharing System Reference Manual, 3rd ed.* Stanford University, Stanford, Calif., (1975).
25. Tesler, L. The Smalltalk environment. *Byte* 6, 8, (Aug. 1981) 90-147. (There is no available GYPSY documentation. This paper describes the Smalltalk editor, which is based on many of the same design ideas as GYPSY.)
26. Wang Laboratories, Inc. *Wang Word Processor Operator's Guide, 3rd release.* Lowell, Mass., (1978).
27. Xerox Corporation. *8010 Star Information System Reference Guide.* Dallas, Texas. (1981). (See also [16].)

**CR Categories and Subject Descriptors:** H.1.2 [**Models and Principles**]: User/Machine Systems— *human factors*; I.7.1 [**Text Processing:**] Text Editing— *languages*; I.7.2 [**Text Processing**]: Document Preparation— *languages*

**General Terms:** Experimentation. Human Factors.

**Additional Key Words and Phrases:** human-computer interface, human-computer interaction, user model, user performance, user psychology, ergonomics, human factors, system design, system evaluation, text editing.

*Received 3/82; revised and accepted 1/83*

Thomas J. Moran's major research interests are in mental models of systems, the learning of systems, and the nature of expertise in using systems, as well as the formalization of the issues and processes of designing systems. Teresa L. Roberts received her Ph.D. in Computer Science from Stanford University in 1979.

Authors' Present Addresses: Teresa Roberts. Xerox Office Systems Division. 3333 Coyote Hill Road. Palo Alto, CA 94304 Arpanet Roberts. PA©PARC-MAXC: Thomas Moran. Xerox Palo Alto Research Center. 3333 Coyote Hill Road. Palo Alto, CA 94304 Arpanet Moran. PA©PARC-MAXC.

# 25

# The Formatting of Alphanumeric Displays: A Review and Analysis

THOMAS S. TULLIS,[1] *Bell Laboratories, Whippany, New Jersey, and Rice University, Houston, Texas*

*This paper surveys the literature on alphanumeric display formatting, focusing primarily on computer-generated displays. Two general areas are included: guidelines addressing display design and empirical studies of displays. Four characteristics of display formats are described: overall density, local density, grouping, and layout complexity. Objective measurement techniques for these characteristics are proposed and are applied to two different display formats. The results suggest that these measures could provide the basis for objectively evaluating a display without collecting performance data.*

## INTRODUCTION

People extract information from alphanumeric displays every day. They scan newspapers, read highway signs, look up telephone numbers, or read the latest best-sellers. In addition, a growing number of people spend most of their days working with computer-generated alphanumeric displays. In each of these situations, the individual is presented with a frame of information, such as a newspaper page or a CRT screen, that must be processed according to the demands of the task. Each of these frames is somehow formatted to aid the viewer in processing the information. The purpose of this review is to determine what characteristics of these formats affect the user's ability to process the information.

[1] Requests for reprints should be sent to Thomas S. Tullis, now at Burroughs Corporation, 25725 Jeronimo Road, Mission Viejo, CA 92691.

*Scope of the Review*

To reduce this topic to a manageable size, some restrictions on its scope were adopted. This review focuses on the following types of displays:

(1) *Computer-generated displays, especially CRT displays.* The reason for focusing on computer-generated displays is their widespread use and the consequent importance of understanding their effect on human performance. Many of the topics addressed, however, will be equally relevant to other types of displays.

(2) *Alphanumeric displays.* Alphanumeric displays were selected primarily because most computer-generated displays in commercial use are alphanumeric. This is not intended to deny the importance of graphic displays, which have been shown to be beneficial to human performance under certain circumstances (Tullis, 1981).

(3) *Monochromatic displays.* As with alphanumeric displays, the main reason for emphasizing monochromatic displays is simply that most of the computer-generated displays currently in use are monochromatic. In addition, the use of color in displays has been discussed extensively elsewhere (Carter, 1982; Carter

371

and Cahill, 1979; Christ, 1975; Christ and Corso, 1983).

(4) *Formatted displays.* The primary difference between formatted displays (Rosenthal, 1979) and narrative displays is that the viewer's task with a formatted display is usually *not* reading the frame from left to right and from top to bottom. Instead, the task generally involves searching and selectively encoding parts of the display (e.g., searching a computer-displayed menu for the desired function).

*Impact of Display Design*

Placing these restrictions on the type of displays to be covered may give the reader the impression that the scope of the review has been reduced to almost trivial proportions. However, the number of such displays in use and the amount of time people spend in working with them is overwhelming. Galitz (1980, pp. 105-106) reported the results of a study which projected that a single computer system for an insurance company would process 4.8 million screens per year. Analogous estimates for a Bell System computer system, the Automated Repair Service Bureau (ARSB), indicate that employees using the system must extract information from 344 million distinct frames (screens, print-outs) per year. The importance of designing these frames effectively becomes clear when one considers that if the ARSB users took only 1 s longer to extract information from each frame, an additional 55 person-years would be required just to extract the information.

Can the design of such a display actually make a difference in how rapidly the user extracts information from it? Consider the displays shown in Figures 1 and 2, which show two different formats for presenting results from computerized tests of a telephone line (Tullis, 1981). Figure 1 shows a "narrative" format originally designed to convey the test results, and Figure 2 shows a "structured" format in which the test results were redesigned using a variety of techniques (eliminating unnecessary information, grouping related data, etc.). Bell system employees were trained on the interpretation of these displays and then were tested using questions that they would have to answer for themselves on the job. After practice, mean time to answer a question about the display was 8.3 s for the narrative format and 5.0 s for the structured format—a statistically significant difference. That savings of 3.3 s per display translates to 79 person-years saved.

## METHOD OF THE REVIEW

Several reviews of the literature on human factors in computer systems were particularly useful in conducting this survey. Ramsey and Atwood (1979) published an extensive review of human factors in computer systems, along with an associated bibliography of that literature compiled by Ramsey, Atwood, and Kirshbaum (1978). Ramsey and Atwood (1979) provide a particularly good overview of the research on "informational properties of displays," which provided a starting point for this review. More recently, Williges and Williges (1981) published a compilation of user considerations in computer-based information systems.

The literature on displays can be divided into two general categories: guidelines and empirical data.

*Guidelines*

Guidelines for alphanumeric display design are commonly presented as either highly specific lists of rules for information display (Bailey, 1982; Engel and Granda, 1975; Galitz, 1980; MIL-STD-1472c, 1981; NASA, 1980; Smith, 1980, 1981, 1982; Smith and Aucella, 1983), or more conceptual discussions of display design in general (Bonsiepe, 1968; Cakir, Hart, and Stewart, 1980; Cropper and Evans, 1968; Danchak, 1976; Grace, 1966; Green, 1976; Jones, 1978; Marcus, 1981, 1982; Mehlmann, 1981; Miller and Thomas, 1977; Pakin and Wray, 1982; Peterson, 1979; Ro-

Formatting of Alphanumeric Displays 373

```
TEST RESULTS    SUMMARY: GROUND

   GROUND, FAULT T-G
   3 TERMINAL DC RESISTANCE
      >  3500.00 K OHMS  T-R
      =    14.21 K OHMS  T-G
      >  3500.00 K OHMS  R-G
   3 TERMINAL DC VOLTAGE
      =     0.00 VOLTS   T-G
      =     0.00 VOLTS   R-G
   VALID AC SIGNATURE
   3 TERMINAL AC RESISTANCE
      =     8.82 K OHMS  T-R
      =    14.17 K OHMS  T-G
      =   628.52 K OHMS  R-G
   LONGITUDINAL BALANCE POOR
      =     39   DB
   COULD NOT COUNT RINGERS DUE TO
     LOW RESISTANCE
   VALID LINE CKT CONFIGURATION
   CAN DRAW AND BREAK DIAL TONE
```

Figure 1. *Example of narrative format from Tullis (1981).*

```
      ******************************
      *                            *
      *   TIP GROUND      14 K     *
      *                            *
      ******************************

DC RESISTANCE       DC VOLTAGE          AC SIGNATURE

3500 K T-R                               9 K T-R
  14 K T-G           0 V T-G            14 K T-G
3500 K R-G           0 V R-G           629 K R-G


  BALANCE                              CENTRAL OFFICE

   39 DB                               VALID LINE CKT
                                       DIAL TONE OK
```

Figure 2. *Example of structured format from Tullis (1981).*

senthal, 1979; Stewart, 1976; Uber, Williams, Hisey, and Siekert, 1968). Problems are often encountered when applying these guidelines. The lists of rules are commonly too specific to a particular type of display or system to be applicable to one's own problem, or else they address the details of a display (e.g., "use a 'MM/DD/YY' format for dates") without adequately addressing the display as a whole. On the other hand, the more conceptual guidelines are often too general to be directly applicable to the design of a given display (e.g., "the format should be simple and straightforward"). What is lacking is a middle level of guidelines that are general enough to be applicable to a variety of displays but specific enough to be directly usable. Part of the goal of this review is to search for guidelines that fall within this middle level.

Another major problem with the present guidelines is that they are often based on the author's own ideas about display design and are only occasionally supported by referenced data.

*Empirical Studies*

Empirical studies related to display design can be categorized in two ways: by the type of display and the type of task. In general, two types of displays have been studied: simple, artificial displays, and more complex, realistic displays.

*Simple, artificial displays.* The simpler displays usually involve arrays of individual letters or numbers (e.g., Atkinson, Holmgren, and Juola, 1969) or individual symbols such as dots and squares (e.g., Mackworth, 1976). The number of items in each display is typically small (from 1 to 5 in Atkinson et al., 1969), although some do involve larger numbers (up to 81 in Treisman, 1982). Most studies using the simpler displays involve a visual search task. Typically, participants are instructed to indicate the presence or absence of a target in each display (e.g., Egeth, Atkinson, Gilmore, and Marcus, 1973) or to indicate what target from a predefined set appeared (e.g., Banks and Prinzmetal, 1976). For more complete reviews of visual search, see Teichner and Krebs (1974) and Teichner and Mocharnuk (1979).

*Complex, realistic displays.* The more complex displays usually involve arrays of words, numeric data, or alphanumeric codes. Often, these studies use displays proposed for a computer system (Dodson and Shields, 1978; Grace, 1966; Tullis, 1981). The number of items in each display is typically large (100 to 250 items in Ringel and Hammer, 1964), and there are often complex relationships among the items (e.g., currency conversion tables and travel timetables in Wright, 1968, 1977).

The complexity of these displays allows for greater task diversity. The studies that used such displays will be categorized into five task types:

(1) *Visual search.* As with the simple displays, a common task is to report a well-defined item on the display. In some cases, the observer simply indicates the location of an item (e.g., Card, 1982). In other cases, the observer is given a label on the display and then reports the data associated with that label (e.g., Callan, Curran and Lane, 1977; Dodson and Shields, 1978; Vartabedian, 1971).
(2) *Question answering.* Another common technique is to ask a variety of questions about the displays (Grace, 1966; Ringel and Hammer, 1964; Tullis, 1981; Wright, 1968, 1977). These range from simple questions that can be answered by retrieving only one item from the display (thus reducing to a simple search task) to complex questions involving the integration of numerous items on the display. For example, Ringel and Hammer (1964), using displays of the status of military units, asked questions like, "Which unit has an armor equipment status of 95 and is combat experienced?" This type of question required participants to find a specific conjunction of characteristics in two separate columns of a table.

(3) *Problem solving/decision making.* Another technique is to pose a problem to the participants in the study and have them solve that problem using the displays (Baker and Goldstein, 1966; Cicchinelli and Lantz, 1978; Dorris, Sadosky, and Connolly, 1977; Landis, Slivka, and Jones, 1967; Silver, Jones, and Landis, 1966). Sometimes the problem can be solved using only one display (e.g., Cicchinelli and Lantz, 1978), and sometimes it requires a sequence of displays (e.g., Baker and Goldstein, 1966). The important distinction between this technique and the previous one (question answering) is that problem solving always involves the same problem on all displays. For example, Silver et al. (1966) described a hypothetical trucking company to their participants, who were then given a complex display describing the current status of the company's truck loads, drivers, and trucks. Given the destination for each of the loads, the participants were instructed to assign loads to drivers and trucks to keep costs at a minimum.

(4) *Reading.* A few studies using a reading task manipulated variables of interest to the design of formatted displays (Kolers, Duchnicky, and Ferguson, 1981; Poulton and Brown, 1968; Tinker, 1955). Typically, participants in such studies are instructed to read the text and then are tested for comprehension. One study (Kolers et al., 1981) monitored eye movements to determine the pattern of fixations.

(5) *Subjective ratings.* In some studies, the participants' primary task is to make qualitative ratings of the displays. Observers have been instructed to rate each display on a scale of overall quality (Christie, 1981, pp. 202-205), to rate the similarity of pairs of displays (Siegel and Fischl, 1971), or to rank order their preferences for a set of displays (Vitz, 1966).

*Selection of Display Characteristics*

The literature was studied to determine what underlying characteristics of displays are addressed by either the guidelines or the empirical studies. The following criteria for defining and selecting these underlying characteristics were adopted:

*The characteristic must be related to the spatial array of characters on the display.* This eliminates a variety of highlighting techniques (e.g., blinking, increased intensity, reverse video) that clearly affect the user's processing of the display. These were eliminated simply because they represent a qualitatively different aspect of display design. Blink coding in particular has been discussed in detail by Smith and Goodwin (1971, 1972). Characteristics related to the legibility of individual characters have also been eliminated. The effects on character legibility of such factors as luminance contrast, dot matrix size, and raster scan resolution have been discussed thoroughly by Shurtleff (1980).

*The characteristic must be objectively defined, or must at least have the potential for it.* The main criterion used for deciding this was to ask, "Could a computer program be written to assess this characteristic?" If the answer was either "yes" or "probably," the characteristic was included. This criterion eliminates a wide variety of guidelines that are dependent on semantic or contextual information (e.g., presenting information in a "logical" sequence according to its semantic content). The elimination of these semantic characteristics is not meant to deny their importance; they clearly are critical to the usability of a display. However, semantic characteristics represent a different realm from the spatial characteristics considered in this paper.

*The characteristic must be applicable to any alphanumeric display.* This eliminates many guidelines that apply only to certain types of displays (e.g., guidelines addressing the format of specific items, such as a date, that not all displays contain).

## CHARACTERISTICS OF DISPLAYS

By applying the preceding criteria to the guidelines and empirical data, four basic characteristics of alphanumeric display formats were identified:

(1) *Overall density*—the number of characters displayed, often expressed as a percentage of the total character spaces available.
(2) *Local density*—the number of filled character spaces near each character, often manipulated by altering line spacing.
(3) *Grouping*—the extent to which items form well-defined perceptual groups.
(4) *Layout complexity*—the extent to which the arrangement of items on the frame follows a predictable visual scheme.

These four characteristics are not necessarily independent of each other. For example, in the set of real-world displays, overall density and local density have a high positive correlation. Likewise, increasing the overall density tends to decrease the extent to which items can be arranged into distinctly separate groups.

This derivation of characteristics from the guidelines and empirical data has not always been a well-defined process. Specifically, there were some situations in which a new characteristic could have been defined, but, for a variety of reasons, was not. One example of a characteristic that could have been included is the letter case (upper or lower) of items on the display. Numerous authors have proposed that normal upper- and lowercase should be used for presentation of text while uppercase alone should be used for labels and visual search tasks (Engel and Granda, 1975; Galitz, 1980, p. 111; Mehlmann, 1981, p. 118; Smith, 1982, p. 97). These guidelines are based on studies by Poulton and Brown (1968) and Tinker (1955) which showed that combined upper- and lowercase text was read about 13% faster than text in all capitals, and a study by Vartabedian (1971) which showed that search time to find a word on a CRT display was about 13% shorter for uppercase words than for lowercase words. The characteristic of "letter case" was not included because it is only indirectly related to the spatial array of characters on the screen. One could argue that letter case has an effect on the spatial array since uppercase letters are, on the average, larger than lowercase letters, but this seems to be stretching the point.

Another example of a characteristic that could have been included is the consistency of related displays. Numerous guidelines have advocated that the formatting of items on related displays should be consistent: "When using the same items on different displays, make an attempt to locate them in the same place on all displays" (Bailey, 1982, p. 333); "The ordering and layout of corresponding data fields should be consistent from one display to the next" (Smith, 1982, p. 104). Although such consistency is clearly important, it is only defined on the basis of a set of displays. Consistency was not included in this analysis because it represents a level of organization beyond a single display.

Each of the four characteristics of displays will now be considered in detail. The discussion of each characteristic will first cover the relevant guidelines, followed by the empirical data, and then a synthesis of the two sets of information. Much of the discussion will center on ways of measuring these characteristics.

## OVERALL DENSITY

### Guidelines

A common theme in many of the display design guidelines is that only "relevant" information should be displayed (Cakir et al., 1980, p. 114; Galitz, 1980, p. 108), or that the display should not appear "cluttered" (Green, 1976; Peterson, 1979). These guidelines are addressing the same basic concept: the total amount of information displayed on a single frame should be kept to a minimum. Some of the authors go on to rationalize this guideline by claiming that high information density causes "the human perceptual channels [to] become overloaded" (Cropper and Evans, 1968, p. 96), "leads to confusion and an increased error rate" (Engel and Granda,

1975, p. 8), causes "greater ... competition among screen components for a person's attention" (Galitz, 1980, p. 108), causes a "psychological strain" (Green, 1976, p. 145), or "increases search time" (Stewart, 1976, p. 142).

Three of the authors take this idea a step further and discuss specific values for overall density. Danchak (1976, p. 33) states, "Experience shows that display loading (the percentage of active screen area) should not exceed 25 percent." He goes on to state that "an analysis of existing CRT displays that were qualitatively judged 'good' revealed a loading on the order of 15 percent" (p. 33).

In a set of guidelines for the design of Space Shuttle displays, NASA (1980, p. 3-26) states that "density generally should not exceed 60% of the available character spaces." They support this guideline by claiming that "empirical tests ... indicate that response time and accuracy begin to degrade rapidly when data presented is above 60% density" (p. 3-26). Apparently this refers to the Dodson and Shields (1978) study of Space Shuttle displays. They manipulated density using values of 30%, 50%, and 70% and found increases in search time with increasing density. However, the support for the assertion that performance begins to degrade rapidly above 60% density is not clear, since Dodson and Shield's (1978) data appear to be fit reasonably well by a simple linear function over the range they studied.

Smith (1980, 1981, 1982) does not provide a specific upper limit for display density, but in a checklist for "data display" he refers to three levels of density for tabular data and data forms (1982, p. 53):

| | |
|---|---|
| high | (>600 char) |
| moderate | |
| low | (<300 char). |

Assuming a standard 24 × 80 character CRT, these values correspond to the following densities:

| | |
|---|---|
| high | (>31.2%) |
| moderate | |
| low | (<15.6%). |

Interestingly, Smith's threshold for high density of 31.2% is not too far from Danchak's density limit of 25%. Likewise, Smith's threshold for low density of 15.6% is essentially the same as Danchak's optimal density of 15%.

*Empirical Data*

Studies have repeatedly shown that human performance deteriorates with increasing display density. The most common finding of visual search studies is that increasing the number of displayed items increases time and errors in locating the target. This has been shown in search studies using simple displays (Atkinson et al., 1969; Burns, 1979; Egeth et al., 1973, Mackworth, 1976; Treisman, 1982) as well as complex displays (Callan et al., 1977; Dodson and Shields, 1978). Similar results have been found in question-answering studies (Coffey, 1961; Ringel and Hammer, 1964) and in problem-solving studies (Baker and Goldstein, 1966; Cicchinelli and Lantz, 1978; Dorris et al., 1977; Landis et al., 1967).

A few studies have suggested that the detrimental effect of increasing display density only holds for higher levels of complexity. For example, Landis et al. (1967) found that quality of performance in a simple logistics game *increased* as the number of facts shown increased, as opposed to the more common finding that performance in a complex reconnaissance game decreased as the number of facts shown increased. This led them to propose that the general function relating quality of performance and display density has an inverted U shape. In other words, at low levels of density, increasing the number of items increases effectiveness, while the reverse is true at higher levels of density. A similar result was found by Vitz (1966) using a very different technique. He asked observers to rank order their preferences for a set of displays. The displays were either "random walks" varying in number of steps or random patterns of straight lines varying in number of lines. He found that for both types of displays, the observers' preferences increased up to a moderate level of complexity and then decreased with higher complexities.

*Synthesis*

The guidelines proposing that display density be kept as low as possible, but still retaining the relevant information, are clearly supported by the data. Assuming that the information necessary for the task is displayed, there can be little doubt that increasing the number of items beyond that level will have a detrimental effect on performance.

However, the recommendations for specific values of display density are not so clearly supported (e.g., Danchak's [1976] recommendation that display density not exceed 25%). The main problem is that it is not always possible to convert the measures of density used in the various studies to a common measure for comparison purposes. The different studies used their own operational definitions of density—such as total number of characters, number of rows or columns in an array, number of lines in a table, or number of "facts." For most of these studies it is not possible to derive a percentage of the sort discussed by Danchak (1976). One study that did manipulate density as a percentage of spaces available (Dodson and Shields, 1978) started at 30%, which is above Danchak's recommended maximum of 25%. They found that performance deteriorated with increasing density; however, the effect of densities under 30% was not studied. One would expect, based on Danchak's recommendation, that increases in density up to about 25% would have little effect on performance, whereas further increases would have a more substantial impact.

Danchak reported that his analysis of "good" CRT displays indicated an average density of 15%. To corroborate that figure, a similar analysis of CRT displays from the ARSB system mentioned earlier was conducted. Although these displays have not necessarily been judged as "good," they are displays from a successful, currently operational system. A randomly selected sample of 20 different CRT displays from this system had a mean density of 14.2%, standard deviation of 7.1%, and range of from 0.9% to 27.9%. The close agreement between this mean of 14.2% and Danchak's 15% is surprising, considering the different populations of displays involved. In addition, the fact that only 2 of the 20 ARSB displays exceeded 25% density (i.e., 25.3% and 27.9%) lends credence to Danchak's recommendation that display density not exceed 25%.

## LOCAL DENSITY

*Guidelines*

Some of the guidelines mention that a display should contain ample blank spaces between the items. This concept is closely related to overall density but is not identical to it. For example, it is possible to have two displays with the same overall density, but in one case the items could be packed into one corner of the display while in the other case the items could be evenly dispersed across the entire display. The latter case would provide more blank spaces between the items. This concept of how "tightly packed" the items are will be called *local density*.

Several guidelines have advocated such use of blank spaces on a display: "Blank spaces can ... be used to provide structure in the display" (Cakir et al., 1980, p. 114); "Space makes it easier to find one's way around by breaking up the text into logical segments" (Jones, 1978, p. 159); "Spacing and blanks in a display ... are important, both to emphasize and maintain the logical sequencing or structure" (Stewart, 1976, p. 142).

In spite of these admonitions that spacing is important in the design of a display, none of the guidelines has offered a general way of quantifying its use. Several of the guidelines have, however, offered the specific recommendation that groups of items be separated by three to five rows or columns of blank spaces (Bailey, 1982, p. 347; Engel and Granda, 1975, p. 8; Galitz, 1980, p. 107).

*Empirical Data*

Several experiments have studied local density by manipulating the spacing between lines of a display. Ringel and Hammer (1964) manipulated the ratio of letter height to space between lines in a table from 1:4 for low density to 1:2 for high density. They found that the time to answer a question about the display decreased slightly, but significantly, with greater density of lines. Thus, higher local density enhanced performance. On the other hand, Kolers et al. (1981), in comparing single-spaced with double-spaced CRT displays of text, found that single spacing required more eye fixations per line, resulted in fewer words read per fixation, and required longer total reading time. Thus, higher local density degraded performance.

The apparent conflict between these two studies can be clarified by a closer examination of the stimuli. Whereas Ringel and Hammer (1964) varied the ratio of letter height to space between lines from 1:2 to 1:4, Kolers et al. (1981) did not provide this measure for their stimuli. However, measurements made from their photographs of the stimuli reveal that single spacing was a ratio of about 1:0.3 (i.e., the bottom of one line almost touched the top of the next), and double spacing was a ratio of about 1:1.7, approximating Ringel and Hammer's 1:2. Thus, the two studies revealed that double spacing (approximately 1:2) yields optimal performance, whereas performance degrades on either side of that point. This sort of function relating performance with local density is reminiscent of the inverted U-shaped function proposed by Landis et al. (1967) for the effect of overall density on performance.

Several visual search studies have manipulated what may be called local density using a variety of other techniques. Brown and Monk (1975) manipulated the number of background dots in the $3 \times 3$ matrix of character spaces centered around a target "double dot." They found that search time increased as the number of local background dots increased from 0 to 8. Egeth et al. (1973) manipulated local density by using either a circular or a linear array of from 1 to 5 characters. In the circular array the minimum separation between characters was 0.024 rad (1.37 deg), while in the linear array it was 0.009 rad (0.53 deg). Thus, local density was higher for the linear array. They found that time to detect the target character increased more rapidly with increasing total number of characters when the linear array was used than when the circular array was used. Thus, higher local density caused a slower rate of searching.

Treisman (1982) manipulated local density by varying the distance between groups of characters. She found that the search time to find a target character was slightly, but significantly, longer with the less dense displays. Thus, contrary to the other search studies (but consistent with Ringel and Hammer, 1964), she found that higher local density enhanced performance.

Here again the conflict between Treisman's (1982) findings and those of the other search studies (Brown and Monk, 1975; Egeth et al., 1973) can be clarified somewhat by a consideration of the stimuli. In the Brown and Monk (1975) study, the target was separated from the background dots by only 0.004 rad (0.21 deg). In the Egeth et al. (1973) study, the target was separated from the other characters by only 0.009 rad (0.53 deg) or 0.024 rad (1.37 deg). On the other hand, Treisman (1982) manipulated the separation of groups of characters from the fixation point over a range of 0.037 rad (2.14 deg) to 0.075 rad (4.28 deg). Thus, Treisman studied much lower local densities than did the others. These findings are consistent with the type of inverted U-shaped function relating performance and local density described earlier: at low levels of local density, raising the density enhances performance (Ringel and Hammer, 1964; Treisman, 1982), while at high levels of local density, raising the density degrades performance (Brown and Monk, 1975; Egeth et al., 1973; Kolers et al., 1981). Perhaps such a function could be explained by lateral masking of characters at high local densities (Bouma, 1970; Collins and Eriksen, 1967) and by increased eye-movement time at low local densities.

*Synthesis*

The relationship between the guidelines related to local density and the empirical data is difficult to assess, primarily because the guidelines are poorly defined, stating only that spacing helps to structure a screen. Certainly, none of the guidelines suggests what the empirical data seem to suggest: that there may be an optimal level of local density, below or above which performance degrades (i.e., the peak of the inverted U).

What is lacking in both the guidelines and the empirical studies is a definition of local density applicable to any alphanumeric display. Conceptually, the term is used to mean how "tightly packed" the display is, but a variety of measures have been used (e.g., line spacing, separation of adjacent characters, separation of groups). Most of these measures are only applicable to particular types of displays. However, the measure used by Brown and Monk (1975) shows promise for being generalizable. They manipulated local density by varying the number of background dots in the 3 × 3 matrix of spaces surrounding the target. In essence, this is a measure of how many background symbols there are near the target. This could be converted to a percentage, since there are eight character spaces in the surrounding 3 × 3 matrix. To generalize this measure to other tasks besides visual search (i.e., tasks in which there is not a specific target character), one could calculate an average percentage of filled spaces in the 3 × 3 matrix surrounding every character on the display.

This measure of local density has an arbitrary component in the selection of a 3 × 3 matrix surrounding each character. That selection of the surrounding matrix defines what is meant by "near" a character. One would like to make that selection based upon some characteristic of the human visual system. A somewhat less arbitrary choice would be to define the area "near" each character as being the area surrounding the character to which the eye is most sensitive. It is well known that visual acuity falls off rapidly as the visual angle from the point of fixation increases (Anstis, 1974; Blackwell and Moldauer, 1958; Taylor, 1961). In fact, averaging the data of Blackwell and Moldauer (1958) and Taylor (1961) shows that relative visual acuity has approximately halved at a distance of 0.044 rad (2.5 deg) from the point of fixation. This is consistent with the data of Bouma (1970), which showed that when a letter was flanked on either side by other letters and presented at 0.044 rad (2.5 deg), it was reported with half the accuracy of a letter at the fixation point. Thus, a circle with a 0.088-rad (5-deg) diameter centered around the character may be a reasonable choice for the area "near" that character. This choice of a 0.088-rad (5-deg) circle is consistent with Danchak (1976) who selected a 0.088-rad (5-deg) circle as the basis for calculating the recommended maximum length for a displayed word.

If one assumes that the average CRT-viewing distance is 475 mm (which is the middle of the 450- to 500-mm "optimum" viewing range stated by Cakir et al., 1980, p. 173), then the 0.088-rad (5-deg) visual angle translates to a circle with 41.8-mm diameter on the face of a CRT. Likewise, if one assumes that the average distances between character centers are 2.8 mm horizontally and 5.6 mm vertically (based on the average dimensions of characters displayed on three different vendors' CRTs), then the 0.088-rad (5-deg) visual angle includes about 88 spaces centered around the point of fixation. This is illustrated in Figure 3.

A possible index for local density, then, could be the average percentage of characters in these 88 spaces surrounding each character on the screen. Such an index, however, would fail to account for the different sensitivities of the eye within the 0.088-rad (5-deg) visual angle. The effect of characters closer to the center of the 0.088-rad (5-deg) circle is clearly greater than the effect of those at the perimeter, due to different sensitivities of the eye and lateral masking. Thus, a more realistic index of local density would weight those characters closer to the center more heavily than those farther out. For ease of calculation, a linear weighting scheme could be chosen, whereby the weight assigned to each character space is inversely proportional to its distance from the fixation point. Such a scheme of weights is illustrated in Figure 3. Arbitrarily, the center (fixation) character has been assigned a value of 10, and those character spaces outside the 0.088-rad (5-deg) circle have been assigned a value of 0.

The proposed index of local density would be the sum of the weights assigned to filled

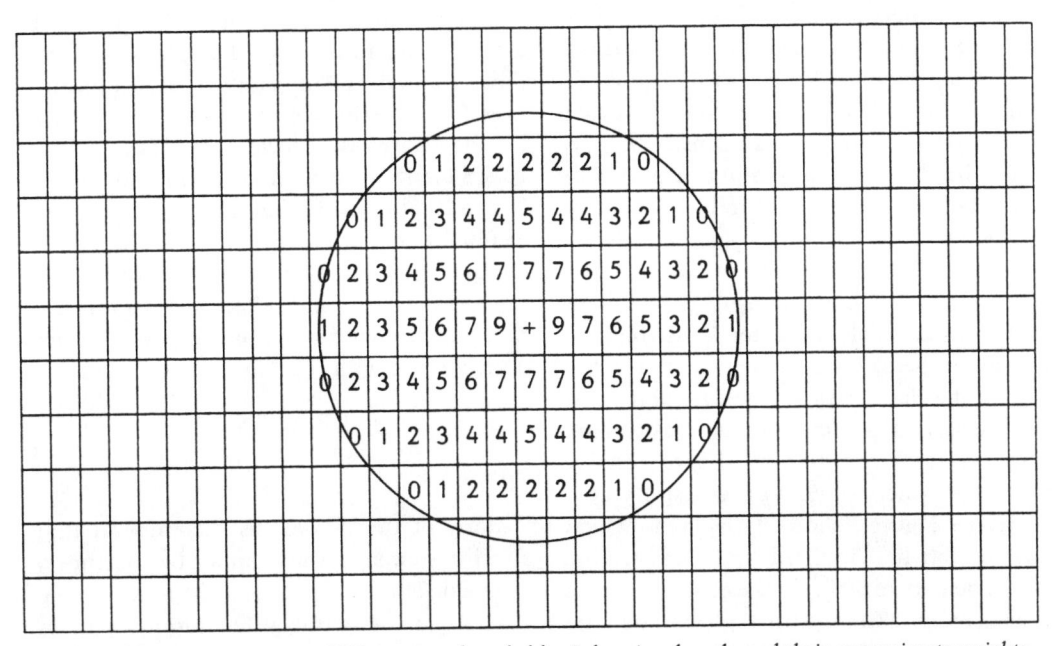

Figure 3. *Character spaces on CRT screen subtended by 5-deg visual angle and their approximate weights.*

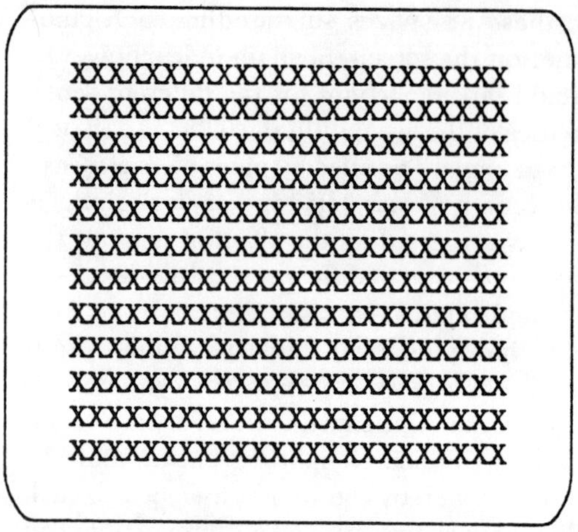

Figure 4. *A completely filled display. Overall density = 100%; local density = 81%.*

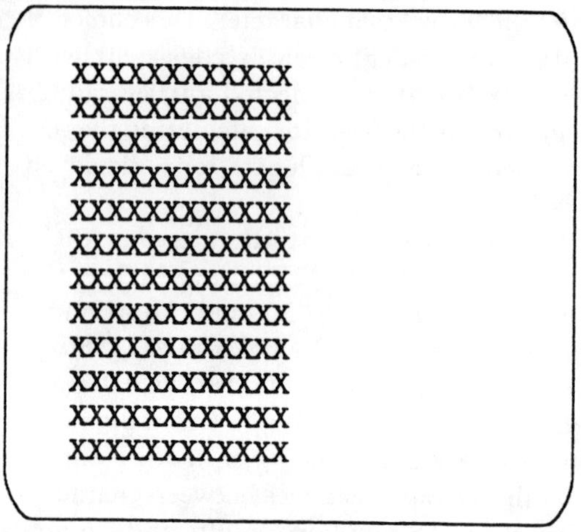

Figure 5. *A display with the left half filled. Overall density = 50%; local density = 72%.*

character spaces around each character, expressed as a percentage of the total possible weight. Conceptually, this index can be viewed as the average percentage of other characters near each character, with those closer being weighted more heavily.

A better understanding of this index and its relationship to overall density can be gained by studying Figures 4 through 6. These are examples of various displays that illustrate how local density and overall density covary. In the simplest case, an empty display, obviously both overall density and local density are 0%. Figure 4 shows the opposite case: a completely filled display. Overall density, obviously, is 100%. Local density is also high (81%) because each character is surrounded by many others. Local density is not 100% because the characters at the edges of the display are viewed as being surrounded by blank spaces outside the display. Local density would approach 100% as the display gets very large. Figure 5 shows a display in which only the left half is filled, thus halving the overall density to 50%. On the other hand, the local density, 72%, is still high because the characters are densely packed. Figure 6

shows a display that also has only half of the character spaces filled, but they are distributed uniformly across the entire display. Obviously, the overall density is still 50%, but the local density has now been reduced to 39%.

It is also instructive to apply this index of local density to real-world displays, such as those studied by Tullis (1981), shown in Figures 1 and 2. The overall densities are 17.9% for the "narrative" format of Figure 1 and 10.8% for the "structured" format of Figure 2. The local densities, on the other hand, are 58.0% for the "narrative" format and 35.6% for the "structured" format. This difference in local density could reflect at least one underlying reason for the participants' better performance with the "structured" format.

## GROUPING

*Guidelines*

Many of the guidelines recommend that similar items on the display be distinctly grouped. This is closely related to local density, since the primary technique used for grouping items is to leave blank spaces be-

Formatting of Alphanumeric Displays 383

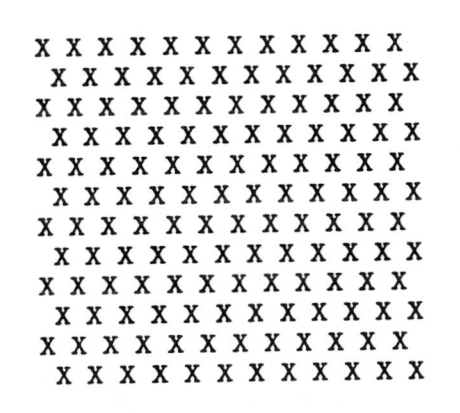

```
X X X X X X X X X X X
 X X X X X X X X X X X
X X X X X X X X X X X
 X X X X X X X X X X X
X X X X X X X X X X X
 X X X X X X X X X X X
X X X X X X X X X X X
 X X X X X X X X X X X
X X X X X X X X X X X
 X X X X X X X X X X X
X X X X X X X X X X X
 X X X X X X X X X X X
```

Figure 6. *A display with half the spaces filled uniformly across the display. Overall density = 50%; local density = 39%.*

tween groups. Most of the guidelines claim that grouping enhances the structure of the display: "Grouping techniques are important in helping to organize information" (Bailey, 1982, p. 330); "Grouping similar items together in a display format improves their readability and can highlight relationships between different groups of data" (Cakir et al., 1980, p. 114); "Screens should provide cohesive groupings of screen elements so that people perceive large screens to have identifiable pieces" (Galitz, 1980, p. 108).

Two of the references take this guideline a step further and propose in general terms how the grouping should be done. Both Cropper and Evans (1968) and Danchak (1976) state that the 0.088-rad (5-deg) visual angle to which the eye is most sensitive (called the "span of attention" by Danchak) defines discrete areas on the screen, and that the display should be structured with this in mind. "The presentation of information in 'chunks' ... which can be taken in at one fixation will help to overcome the limitations in the human input system in searching tasks" (Cropper and Evans, 1968, p. 96). Likewise,

"since the span of attention defines discrete areas of the CRT, it is advisable to have each area contain only one piece of information" (Danchak, 1976, p. 34).

*Empirical Data*

The empirical evidence directly relevant to grouping on visual displays is somewhat sparse. Although grouping effects on short-term memory have been studied extensively (e.g., Kahneman and Henik, 1977; Mayzner and Gabriel, 1963; Severin and Rigby, 1963; Winzenz, 1972), such studies are not really relevant to the tasks involved in the use of complex real-world displays.

Several studies have investigated the effects of different semantic bases for groupings on real-world displays. For example, Dodson and Shields (1978) found that the time to locate an item on a display was shorter when the items were grouped by function (i.e., by instrument involved) than when the groups had no functional basis. Likewise, Card (1982) found that the time to select an item from a menu varied with the semantic basis of the groups: alphabetical grouping was fastest, functional grouping was next, and random grouping was slowest. Card also found that participants tended to recall menu items in "chunks," which corresponded to the menu groups. Although these studies are informative, they do not address the primary topic of this discussion, which is the *spatial* aspect of grouping (e.g., grouping versus lack of grouping) as opposed to the semantic aspect.

A few studies have manipulated the spatial component of grouping. Woodward (1972) found that the time to compare three-digit numbers in pairs was shorter when the numbers were presented side by side (proximally) than when they were presented end to end (distally). Woodward pointed out that both numbers fell within a 0.088-rad (5-deg) visual angle in the proximal arrangement (thus forming a "group"), while only one number fell within that space in the distal arrangement.

Banks and Prinzmetal (1976) found that the time to detect a target letter was shorter when the letter was in a group by itself than when it was part of a group of noise characters. A group was defined as being an arrangement of characters in "good form" according to the definition used by Garner (1970, 1974): a good form generates a small number of different forms when reflected about an axis or rotated 90 deg (i.e., it has symmetry). Banks and Prinzmetal's finding cannot be attributed to target-noise proximity (i.e., local density for the target) because in the "grouped with noise" conditions, the target was just as far from the noise characters as it was when grouped separately.

Banks and Prinzmetal also provided an interesting test of their assumptions about the participants' perception of groups (i.e., that characters in good form are perceived as a group). They simply asked the participants to draw boundaries around items that seemed to group together on the displays. They derived a measure of target-noise grouping by counting the number of boundaries drawn between the target and noise characters and then dividing this by the number of noise characters. The higher this number was, the more isolated the target was. As expected, they found that this grouping index was twice as large for the condition in which they intended the target to be perceived as being separate than the condition in which the target was part of a good form with noise characters.

Treisman (1982) provided one of the most extensive studies of grouping. She manipulated grouping by displaying 36 characters in either 1, 4, 9, 18, or 36 groups. Each group was composed of homogeneous letters (i.e., all green $X$s or red $H$s), except for the group containing the target (i.e., a green $H$). She found that the time to detect a target letter requiring a conjunction of features (i.e., color and letter shape) increased as the number of *groups* increased, even though the total number of characters remained the same. The function relating reaction time to number of groups was negatively accelerated, with increases in number of groups at the low end (i.e., 1 to 9 groups) having the largest effect on reaction time. On the other hand, she found that number of groups had little effect on time to detect a target letter defined by a disjunctive feature (e.g., a blue $H$ among red $H$s and green $X$s). This is consistent with her earlier finding (Treisman and Gelade, 1980) that visual search for targets defined by one or more *disjunctive* features occurs in parallel.

It is not particularly clear what conclusion is to be drawn from these various studies of grouping. Woodward (1972) found that grouping numbers together enhanced the ability to compare them. Banks and Prinzmetal (1976) found that grouping a target separately from the noise enhanced the ability to detect the target. Treisman (1982) found that grouping characters into larger groups enhanced the ability to detect a conjunctively defined target. The problem is that one cannot really make comparisons between these studies because of the differences in the tasks and the differences in the types of grouping. Each of the studies used its own operational definition of grouping: Woodward (1972) viewed a group as being two three-digit numbers displayed proximally to each other; Banks and Prinzmetal (1976) viewed a group as being an arrangement of characters having "good form"; Treisman (1982) viewed a group as being a set of adjacent, homogeneous characters. In addition, only Banks and Prinzmetal (1976) took the step to show empirically that their operationally defined groups corresponded to groups perceived by the participants.

*Synthesis*

The empirical data seem to support the idea that grouping of items is beneficial to performance. A smaller number of groups is better than a larger number of individual items (Treisman, 1982). In another sense, grouping is beneficial if the key item can be grouped by itself (Banks and Prinzmetal, 1976). However, neither the guidelines nor the empirical studies have presented a general definition of grouping. Perhaps the closest to that is the definition used by Banks and Prinzmetal (1976), derived from Garner (1970, 1974): a group is a collection of symbols constituting a "good form." Such a definition, however, seems limited in its generalizability to complex real-world displays composed of words and alphanumeric data with a variety of spatial relationships.

Another type of definition of grouping was proposed by Cropper and Evans (1968) and by Danchak (1976), who proposed that a screen should be designed in discrete "chunks," each of which subtends a visual angle of less than 0.088 rad (5 deg). Precisely how such a definition could be applied, however, is not clear. For example, the definition is circular, in that it invokes the concept of a "discrete chunk" (which is apparently the same thing as a group) in defining what it is that must fall within a 0.088-rad (5-deg) visual angle. Obviously, it is not enough to say that anything that falls within a 0.088-rad (5-deg) visual angle is a group, since *every* character on *any* display would fall within a 0.088-rad (5-deg) visual angle centered on that character. The key is the term "discrete," which implies that the character or set of characters has a boundary that separates it from other characters. Perhaps that boundary is defined by blank spaces (but how many?), by some special characters (e.g., asterisks), by a change from upper- to lowercase, or by some other technique altogether.

This question of what defines a "group" is certainly not a new one in psychology. The Gestalt psychologists were the first to study the problem extensively. They attempted to understand perception in terms of a series of organizational laws or principles, including the laws of proximity, similarity, continuity, and common fate (Koffka, 1935; Wertheimer, 1923).

Some attempts have been made to expand the Gestalt laws and to implement them in computer programs for detecting groups. For example, Zahn (1971) described a technique for implementing the law of proximity. Although he used a complex technique for detecting groups of dots, the following simplification may be sufficient for detecting groups of alphanumeric items. Consider the display shown in Figure 7. First, compute the distance between each character and its nearest neighbor. Using on-center distances between characters of 1 unit horizontally and 2 units vertically, this results in a mean of 1.42. Then form a graph by connecting any pair of characters separated by less than a threshold value depending on that mean. A threshold value of twice that mean seems to work well for alphanumeric CRT displays. Such a graph is shown in Figure 8. A group is then defined as any interconnected set of characters. Thus, Figure 8 represents two groups. Although this technique seems to identify groups that match with intuition, Zahn (1971) does not give any empirical data to demonstrate its validity.

Some insights can be gained into this technique for identifying groups by applying it to real-world CRT displays. Once again, the displays from the Tullis (1981) study shown in

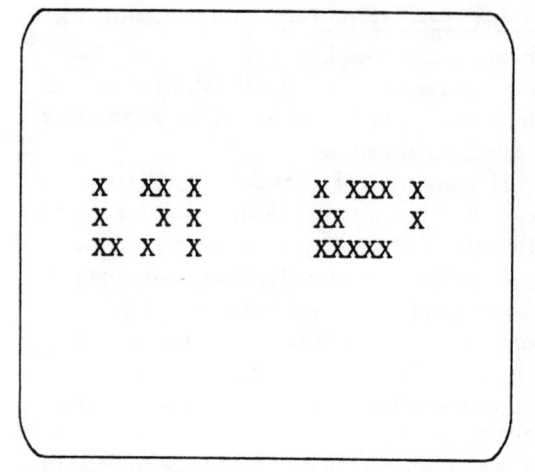

Figure 7. Sample display to illustrate grouping algorithm.

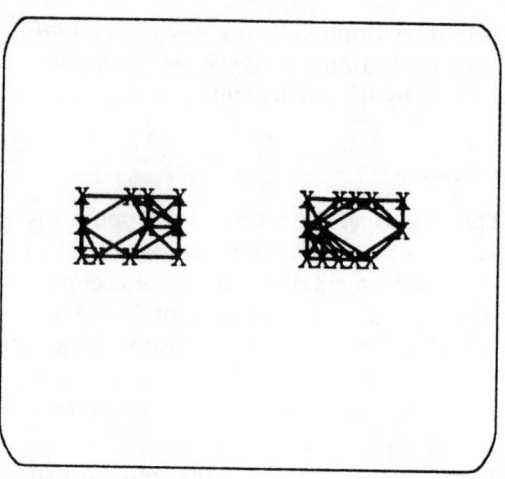

Figure 8. Sample display with lines connecting all pairs of characters separated by less than a threshold distance.

Figures 1 and 2 will be used. The "narrative" format of Figure 1 has a mean distance between neighboring characters of 1.05 (using the same units as in the example of Figures 7 and 8). The "structured" format of Figure 2 has a mean distance between neighboring characters of 1.09. Connecting those pairs of characters separated by less than twice the mean (that is, 2.10 for Figure 1 and 2.18 for Figure 2) results in the configurations shown in Figures 9 and 10.

Figure 9 shows that the "narrative" format contains only three groups of connected characters. On the other hand, Figure 10 shows that the "structured" format contains thirteen groups of connected characters. The design of the "structured" format, then, is more consistent with the various guidelines stating that a large screen should be broken into a number of small, discrete groups. Perhaps this difference in the number of groups could be another factor (like differences in local density, discussed earlier) mediating the participants' better performance with the "structured" format.

The obvious question this raises is, "What is the optimum number of groups?", if such a number exists. Treisman's (1982) studies would seem to suggest that the fewer groups the better. One should be careful, however, in making such a generalization from her studies. For example, her largest groups were composed of only 36 characters, unlike the 319 characters in the largest group of Figure 9. Perhaps if she had manipulated grouping over a wider range she would have found the same sort of inverted U-shaped function discussed for the other characteristics: when using a few large groups, dividing the information into smaller groups might enhance performance; but when using many small groups, dividing the information into even more groups might degrade performance.

Another aspect of the groupings proposed by Cropper and Evans (1968) and by Danchak (1976) is the size of the groups. It is possible to measure the visual angle subtended by each of the groups on the display and then to derive an average by weighting each group's visual angle by the number of characters in the group. Applying this technique to the "narrative" format of Figure 9 results in an

Figure 9. *Narrative format from Tullis (1981) with grouping indicated.*

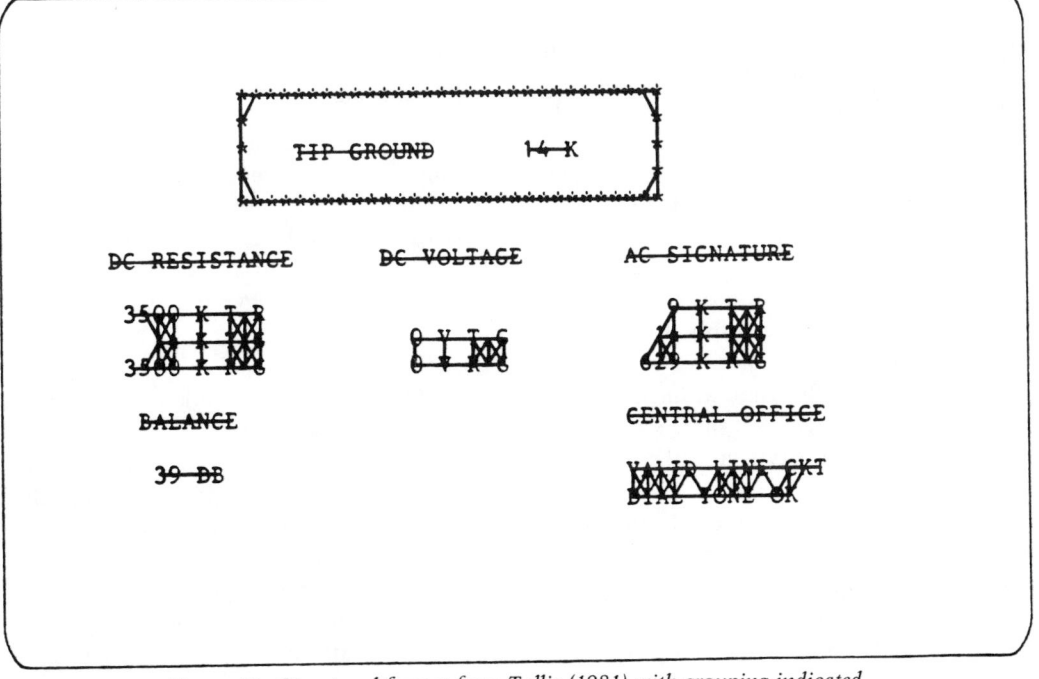

Figure 10. *Structured format from Tullis (1981) with grouping indicated.*

average visual angle of 0.232 rad (13.3 deg). Likewise, the "structured" format of Figure 10 results in 0.091 rad (5.2 deg). Obviously, the "structured" format more closely adheres to the recommendations (Cropper and Evans, 1968; Danchak, 1976) that a group should fit within a 0.088-rad (5-deg) visual angle. Perhaps this difference could be another factor mediating the differences in performance between these two formats. Possibly this measure of visual angle could be a more predictive index of grouping than simply the absolute number of groups.

## LAYOUT COMPLEXITY

### Guidelines

One of the most common themes in the guidelines, and perhaps the most difficult to characterize, is that the overall display format should minimize the complexity of the layout or maximize the visual predictability. That is, based on a knowledge of the location of some items on the screen, one should be able to predict the locations of others. This concept is reflected by the guidelines in a variety of ways: "People seem to be able to scan for a certain item of information more quickly and accurately if a tabular format . . . is provided" (Bailey, 1982, p. 345); "Use vertically aligned lists with left justification for most rapid scanning" (Engel and Granda, 1976, p. 6); "An almost visual motion can be created by either implicit or explicit 'lines' formed by the display elements" (Green, 1976, p. 147); "Tabular formats of alphanumeric data have been shown to be most usable and accurately readable" (NASA, 1980, p. 3-20).

In addition to these general recommendations about using tables, columnar lists, and vertical alignments, a number of the guidelines make the specific recommendation that words and alphanumeric data should be left-justified, whereas numeric data should be right-justified on the decimal point (e.g., Bailey, 1982, p. 346; Engel and Granda, 1976, p. 7; Galitz, 1980, p. 113).

The effect of all these recommendations is to increase the predictability of the locations of items on the display (or, with numbers, the predictability of the decimal point's location). For example, in a tabular format, the location of any entry in the table can be predicted from a knowledge of the column and row positions. By contrast, the location of any item in a textual format cannot be predicted so efficiently.

Marcus (1981, 1982) has incorporated this concept of minimizing layout complexity into a general system for the design of an interface. He proposes a "grid system" that uses a few imaginary vertical and horizontal lines to determine the positioning of elements on the display. In essence, this approach limits the amount of spatial variation between display elements and enhances visual predictability.

### Empirical Data

Despite the number of guidelines addressing this topic, there have been virtually no studies directly addressing it. The only study that comes close is that by Brown and Monk (1975). They used two different patterns of background dots in a visual search task: random or constrained. This was manipulated by the probability, P, of transition from "dot" to "no dot" in adjacent positions of the background matrix. In the random condition, $P = 0.5$ (i.e., the transition from dot to no dot was just as likely as the opposite transition). In the constrained condition, $P = 0.25$ (i.e., the transition from dot to no dot was less likely than the opposite transition—so that once the condition "dot" was established in the pattern, it was likely to continue for a while). This manipulation resulted in a less complex layout for the constrained condition. They found that search time to find a target "double dot" was greater with the random background than with the constrained background. (This effect was independent of local density of background dots surrounding the target.) In essence, then, the constrained background enhanced the search process.

Although this study is interesting, it is only marginally relevant. The manipulation of random versus constrained background does not address exactly the same kind of layout complexity as described in the guidelines. The guidelines focus on reducing layout complexity by aligning data items vertically and horizontally, while Brown and Monk (1975) used a probabilistic approach to reducing layout complexity.

*Synthesis*

Although Brown and Monk's (1975) study lends some support to the guidelines addressing layout complexity, the support is weak at best. Perhaps what is needed to stimulate research in this area is a general technique for measuring layout complexity.

Bonsiepe (1968) proposed a method for quantifying the layout complexity of a typographically designed page that he used for the comparison of "before" and "after" versions of a page from a catalog. The technique involves first drawing rectangles around all the items on the page. Bonsiepe derived measures of two types of order from these rectangles: system order and distribution order. The "system order" is determined by counting the number of *unique* widths and heights for the rectangles on a page. Bonsiepe then used the following formula adapted from information theory (Shannon and Weaver, 1949) to calculate the complexity of the system:

$$C = -N \sum_{n=1}^{m} p_n \log_2 p_n$$

where:

C = complexity of the system, expressed in bits
N = number of events (i.e., widths or heights)
m = number of event classes (i.e., number of unique widths or heights)
$p_n$ = Probability of occurrence of the nth event class (based on the frequency of events within that class)

The second type of order, distribution order, involves the layout of the items on the page. This layout can be specified by measuring the horizontal and vertical distances of each item (or, actually, its rectangle) from some starting point on the page. Arbitrarily, Bonsiepe chose to measure the horizontal distance of the rectangle's left side from the left edge of the page, and the vertical distance of the rectangle's top side from the top edge of the page. The same formula from information theory is then used to calculate the complexity of the distribution of these vertical and horizontal distances.

In attempting to apply Bonsiepe's technique for measuring layout complexity to CRT displays, one encounters some problems. One problem is deciding what to draw the rectangles around. Bonsiepe never defines what he means by an "item." Another problem is deciding exactly how to draw the rectangles around whatever items are decided upon. Bonsiepe specified that "the items were to be inscribed in rectangles corresponding to their real or maximum possible extents" (Bonsiepe, 1968, p. 209). But how does one objectively determine the "real or maximum possible extent" of each item?

These problems with Bonsiepe's technique led to the adoption of a modified technique for application to CRT displays. First, the concept of "system order," or the order that is dependent on the size of each item, was dropped. This was done primarily because of the ill-defined nature of an item's "maximum possible extent." In addition, it appears that the other type of order, distribution order, is more appropriate to CRT displays because of the tasks for which they are commonly used. Since many of the tasks involve searching for and then encoding items on the display, it would appear that the predictability of the beginning of each item (i.e., where one would usually want to start encoding) is more important than the width and height of the item.

The second modification to Bonsiepe's technique involves *what* items on the display to consider in measuring the distribution order. Formatted CRT displays almost always contain two types of items: labels and data. The labels remain basically the same on different representations of the same display, whereas the data change. A single label as well as a single data item may be composed of more than one "word" (group of contiguous characters). These labels and data items are the units upon which the distribution order will be measured, since they appear to be the units a user would search for and encode.

To illustrate this modified measure of the layout complexity of a CRT display, consider the displays shown in Figures 11 and 12, taken from Stewart (1976). Stewart presented Figure 12 as a redesigned (better) version of Figure 11. Although he did not discuss layout complexity per se, his redesign presents a striking example of the use of techniques to minimize layout complexity. The labels and data items on both displays have been inscribed by rectangles. The same basic items are inscribed on both figures, although Stewart occasionally changed the wording. Also, the redesigned version has fewer labels and data items. An analysis of the distribution order results in the following:

Figure 11—original version:

   36 horizontal distances in 22
      unique classes       = 140 bits
   36 vertical distances in 11
      unique classes       = 122 bits
        overall complexity = 262 bits

Figure 12—redesigned version:

   30 horizontal distances in 6
      unique classes       =  67 bits
   30 vertical distances in 10
      unique classes       =  98 bits
        overall complexity = 165 bits

Thus, the distribution order of the redesigned version is about 37% simpler than the original version. Most of the reduction in layout complexity resulted from the adoption of a small number of horizontal positions (i.e., "tab stops") for the beginning of data items, thus reducing the horizontal complexity by more than half.

Regrettably, Stewart (1976) does not present any empirical evidence related to the use of these displays. Thus, the validity of the layout complexity measure cannot be addressed.

Since the measurement techniques described for all of the other characteristics (overall density, local density, grouping) have been applied to the displays from Tullis (1981), this measure of layout complexity will be applied to them as well. Figures 13 and 14 show the "narrative" and "structured" formats from that study, with the labels and data items inscribed by rectangles. The same basic items are inscribed in both cases, although the "narrative" format has more labels. The technique used for inscribing numeric data was based on the maximum values that the data could assume.

The results of applying Bonsiepe's (1968) technique for measuring distribution order are as follows:

Figure 13—narrative format:

   22 horizontal distances in 6
      unique classes       =  41 bits

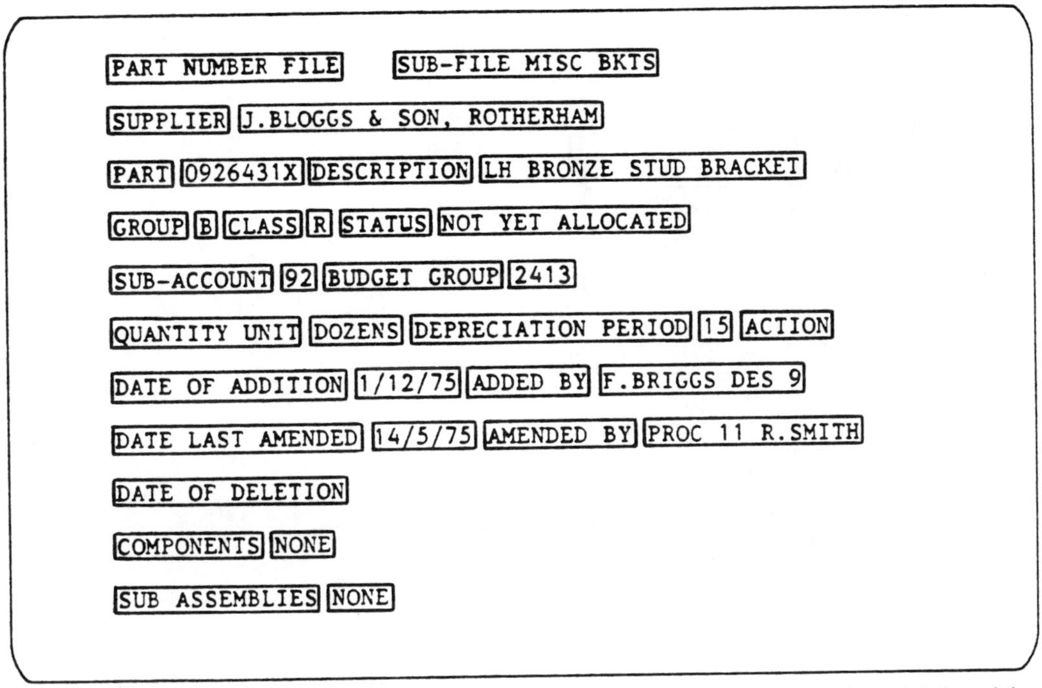

Formatting of Alphanumeric Displays 391

```
PART NUMBER FILE    SUB-FILE MISC BKTS

SUPPLIER  J.BLOGGS & SON, ROTHERHAM

PART  0926431X  DESCRIPTION  LH BRONZE STUD BRACKET

GROUP  B  CLASS  R  STATUS  NOT YET ALLOCATED

SUB-ACCOUNT  92  BUDGET GROUP  2413

QUANTITY UNIT  DOZENS  DEPRECIATION PERIOD  15  ACTION

DATE OF ADDITION  1/12/75  ADDED BY  F.BRIGGS DES 9

DATE LAST AMENDED  14/5/75  AMENDED BY  PROC 11 R.SMITH

DATE OF DELETION

COMPONENTS  NONE

SUB ASSEMBLIES  NONE
```

Figure 11. *Original version of display from Stewart (1976) with rectangles added to indicate labels and data items.* (Reprinted from *Applied Ergonomics, Vol. 7.3*, p. 142, with permission of the publisher, Butterworth Scientific Limited, Guildford, Surrey, U.K.)

```
PART NUMBER FILE:                MISCELLANEOUS BRACKETS

PART:    0926431X        LH BRONZE STUD BRACKET
GROUP:   B               BUDGET GROUP:         2413
CLASS:   R               SUB-ACCOUNT:          92
UNITS:   DOZENS          DEPRECIATION PERIOD:  15
ACTION   ___             PRODUCT STATUS:       NOT YET ALLOCATED
ADDITION DATE:           1 DEC 75     F.BRIGGS DES 9
LAST AMENDED:            14 MAY 75    R.SMITH PROC 11
DELETION DATE:           NONE

MAIN SUPPLIER:           J.BLOGGS & SON, ROTHERHAM
```

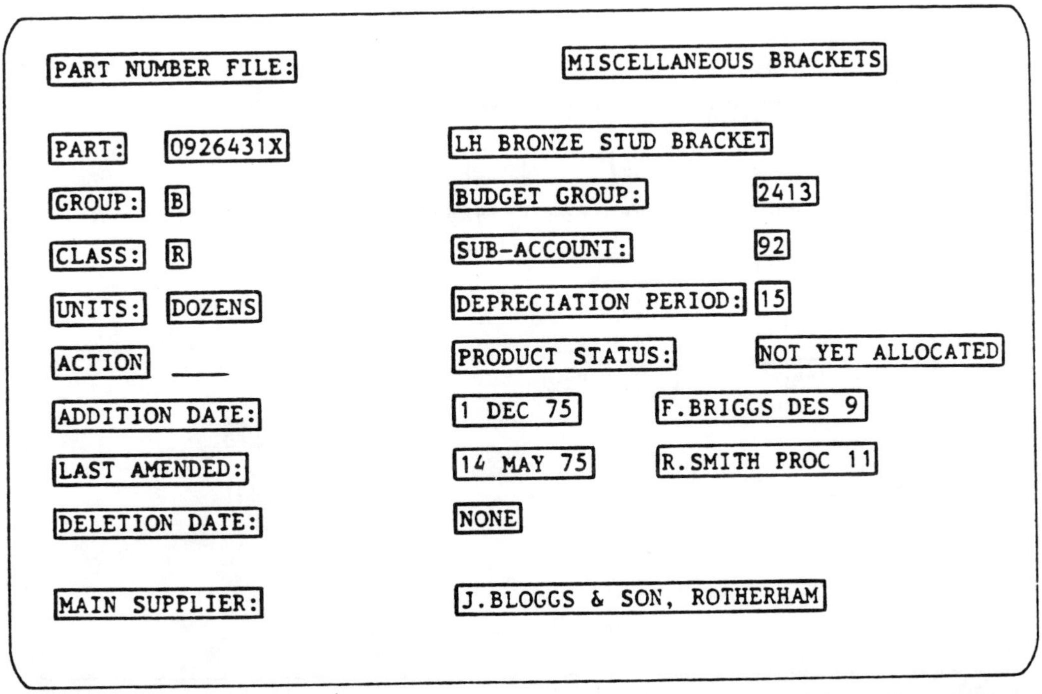

Figure 12. *Redesigned version of display from Stewart (1976) with rectangles added to indicate labels and data items.* (Reprinted from *Applied Ergonomics, Vol. 7.3*, p. 142, with permission of the publisher, Butterworth Scientific Limited, Guildford, Surrey, U.K.)

392  Tullis

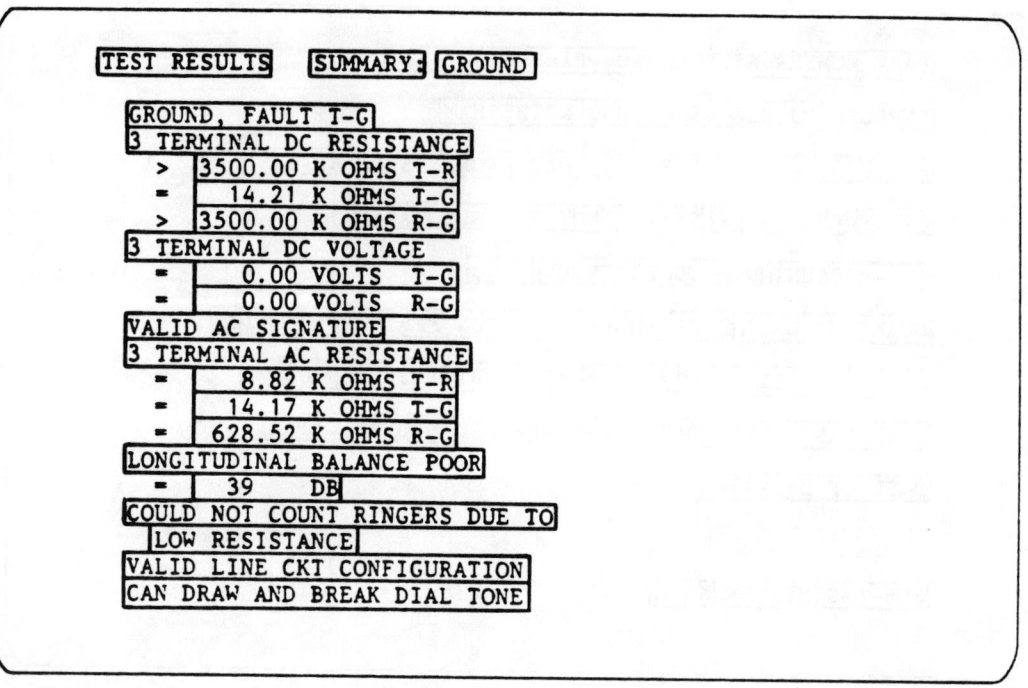

```
TEST RESULTS    SUMMARY:  GROUND
  GROUND, FAULT T-G
  3 TERMINAL DC RESISTANCE
    >   3500.00 K OHMS T-R
    =     14.21 K OHMS T-G
    >   3500.00 K OHMS R-G
  3 TERMINAL DC VOLTAGE
    =      0.00 VOLTS   T-G
    =      0.00 VOLTS   R-G
  VALID AC SIGNATURE
  3 TERMINAL AC RESISTANCE
    =      8.82 K OHMS T-R
    =     14.17 K OHMS T-G
    =    628.52 K OHMS R-G
  LONGITUDINAL BALANCE POOR
    =     39    DB
  COULD NOT COUNT RINGERS DUE TO
    LOW RESISTANCE
  VALID LINE CKT CONFIGURATION
  CAN DRAW AND BREAK DIAL TONE
```

Figure 13. *Narrative format from Tullis (1981) with labels and data items inscribed by rectangles.*

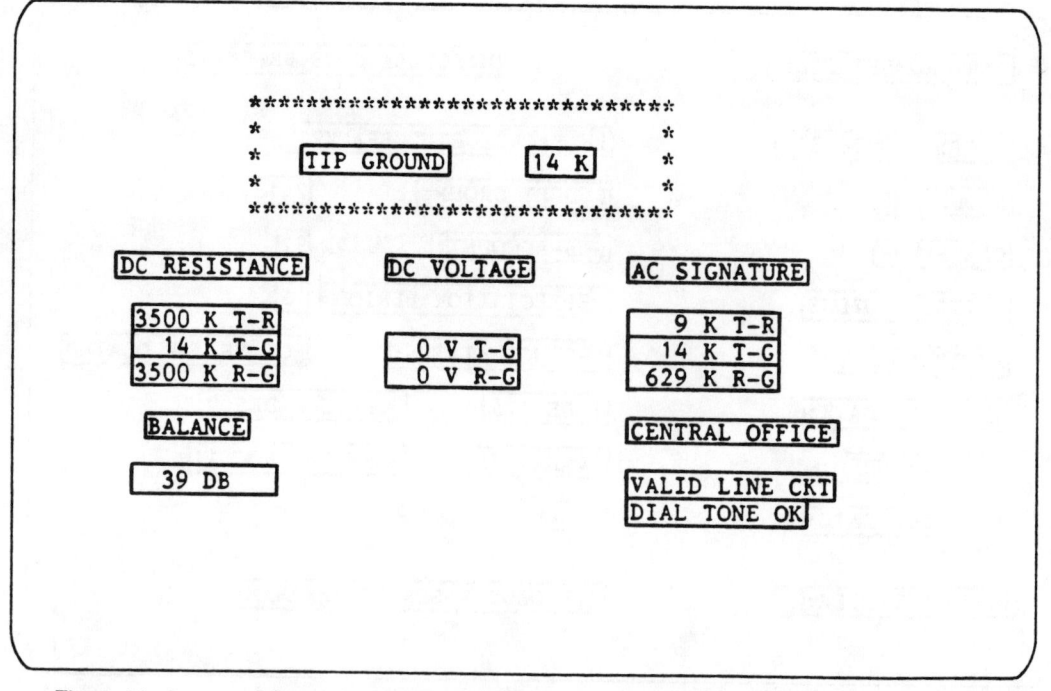

```
**********************************
*                                *
*    TIP GROUND        14 K      *
*                                *
**********************************

DC RESISTANCE     DC VOLTAGE      AC SIGNATURE

3500 K T-R                          9 K T-R
  14 K T-G        0 V T-G          14 K T-G
3500 K R-G        0 V R-G         629 K R-G

  BALANCE                         CENTRAL OFFICE

   39 DB                          VALID LINE CKT
                                  DIAL TONE OK
```

Figure 14. *Structured format from Tullis (1981) with labels and data items inscribed by rectangles.*

TABLE 1

Measures of Each Characteristic Applied to the Narrative and Structured Displays from Tullis (1981)

| Characteristic | Definition of Measure | Narrative Display | Structured Display |
|---|---|---|---|
| Overall density | Number of filled character spaces as a percentage of total spaces available | 17.9% | 10.8% |
| Local density | Average number of filled character spaces in a 0.088 rad (5 deg) visual angle around each character, expressed as a percentage of available spaces in the circle and weighted by distance from the character | 58.0% | 35.6% |
| Grouping | (1) Number of groups of "connected" characters, where a connection is any pair of characters separated by less than twice the mean of the distances between each character and its nearest neighbor | 3 | 13 |
|  | (2) Average visual angle subtended by groups (as defined above), weighted by number of characters in the group | 0.232 rad (13.3 deg) | 0.091 rad (5.2 deg) |
| Layout complexity | The complexity, as defined in information theory, of the distribution of horizontal and vertical distances of each label and data item from a standard point on the display | 134 bits | 96 bits |

22 vertical distances in 20 unique classes = 93 bits
overall complexity = 134 bits

Figure 14—structured format:
18 horizontal distances in 7 unique classes = 43 bits
18 vertical distances in 8 unique classes = 53 bits
overall complexity = 96 bits

Thus, the distribution order of the structured format is about 28% simpler than the narrative format. The reduction in layout complexity resulted from the lower vertical complexity of the structured format's tabular layout compared to the narrative format's list layout. Here again, perhaps this difference could be another factor mediating the participants' better performance with the structured format.

## SUMMARY AND CONCLUSIONS

Four characteristics of alphanumeric display formats have been discussed: overall density, local density, grouping, and layout complexity. For the first three of these, there is some empirical evidence indicating that the characteristic has an effect on human performance. The precise nature of the effect, however, is not clear. For each of these three characteristics, it is suggested that the function relating performance to a particular measure of the characteristic may have an inverted U-shape. Thus, at low levels of the measure, increases may have a beneficial effect on performance, while at high levels of the measure, increases may have a detrimental effect. The problem with determining the validity of this assertion, however, is that no studies have manipulated these characteristics over a wide enough range.

For the last characteristic discussed, layout complexity, there is virtually no empirical evidence directly addressing its effect on human performance. Numerous guidelines suggest, however, that increasing the layout complexity may have a detrimental effect on human performance.

Much of the discussion has focused on deriving objective ways of measuring these four characteristics. As a summary of these measures, Table 1 presents a definition of each and shows the results of applying them to the narrative and structured displays (Figures 1 and 2) from the Tullis (1981) study.

All of the measures showed a difference between the "narrative" and "structured" formats. The differences indicate that these measures, or some combination of them, could provide the basis for objectively evaluating the usability of a display, since Tullis (1981) did find statistically significant performance differences between the two formats. The predictive validity of these measures, however, cannot be assessed from the Tullis (1981) study since the characteristics were confounded with each other. The differences in performance could have arisen from the differences in some of the characteristics, all of the characteristics, or even some other characteristics not currently defined. A study that manipulates these characteristics in a controlled fashion needs to be conducted. Such a study could provide the basis for a "display evaluation tool" that could be used to predict the usability of a display without the cost of collecting performance data.

## REFERENCES

Anstis, S. M. A chart demonstrating variations in acuity with retinal position. *Vision Research*, 1974, *14*, 589-592.

Atkinson, R. C., Holmgren, J. E., and Juola, J. F. Processing time as influenced by the number of elements in a visual display. *Perception & Psychophysics*, 1969, *6*, 321-326.

Bailey, R. W. *Human performance engineering: A guide for system designers.* Englewood Cliffs, NJ: Prentice-Hall, 1982.

Baker, J. D., and Goldstein, I. Batch vs sequential displays: Effects on human problem solving. *Human Factors*, 1966, *8*, 225-235.

Banks, W., and Prinzmetal, W. Configurational effects in visual information processing. *Perception & Psychophysics*, 1976, *19*, 361-367.

Blackwell, H. R., and Moldauer, A. B. Detection thresholds for point sources in the near periphery (Project 2455). Ann Arbor: University of Michigan Engineering Research Institute, 1958. Described in W. F. Grether and C. A. Baker. Visual presentation of information. In H. P. Van Cott and R. G. Kinkade (Eds.), *Human engineering guide to equipment design* (Rev. ed.). Washington, DC: U.S. Government Printing Office, 1972.

Bonsiepe, G. A method of quantifying order in typographic design. *Journal of Typographic Research*, 1968, *2*, 203-220.

Bouma, H. Interaction effects in parafoveal letter recognition. *Nature*, 1970, *226*, 177-178.

Brown, B., and Monk, T. H. The effect of local target surround and whole background constraint on visual search times. *Human Factors*, 1975, *17*, 81-88.

Burns, D. A dual-task analysis of detection accuracy for the case of high target-distractor similarity: Further evidence for independent processing. *Perception & Psychophysics*, 1979, *25*, 185-196.

Cakir, A., Hart, D. J., and Stewart, T. F. M. *Visual display terminals: A manual covering ergonomics, workplace design, health and safety, task organization.* England: Wiley, 1980.

Callan, J. R., Curran, L. E., and Lane, J. L. Visual search times for Navy tactical information displays (Report NPRDC-TR-77-32). San Diego, CA: Navy Personnel Research and Development Center, 1977. (NTIS No. AD A040 543)

Card, S. K. User perceptual mechanisms in the search of computer command menus. In *Proceedings: Human factors in computer systems,* Washington, DC: Association for Computing Machinery, 1982, 190-196.

Carter, R. C. Search time with a color display: Analysis of distribution functions. *Human Factors*, 1982, *24*, 203-212.

Carter, R. C., and Cahill, M.-C. Regression models of search time for color-coded information displays. *Human Factors*, 1979, *21*, 293-302.

Christ, R. E. Review and analysis of color coding research for visual displays. *Human Factors*, 1975, *17*, 542-570.

Christ, R. E., and Corso, G. M. The effects of extended practice on the evaluation of visual display codes. *Human Factors*, 1983, *25*, 71-84.

Christie, B. *Face to file communication.* New York: Wiley, 1981.

Cicchinelli, L. F., and Lantz, A. E. The elimination of irrelevant information in a multidimensional stimulus classification task. *Human Factors*, 1978, *20*, 75-82.

Coffey, J. L. A comparison of vertical and horizontal arrangements of alpha-numeric material—Experiment 1. *Human Factors*, 1961, *3*, 93-98.

Collins, J. F., and Eriksen, C. W. The perception of multiple, simultaneously presented forms as a function of foveal spacing. *Perception & Psychophysics*, 1967, *2*, 369-373.

Cropper, A. G., and Evans, S. J. W. Ergonomics and computer display design. *The Computer Bulletin*, 1968, *12*(3), 94-98.

Danchak, M. M. CRT displays for power plants. *Instrumentation Technology*, 1976, *23*(10), 29-36.

Dodson, D. W., and Shields, N. L., Jr. Development of user guidelines for ECAS display design (Vol. 1) (Report No. NASA-CR-150877). Huntsville, AL: Essex Corp., 1978.

Dorris, A. L., Sadosky, T. L., and Connolly, T. Varying data and information in a decision making task. *Ergonomics*, 1977, *20*, 643-649.

Egeth, H., Atkinson, J., Gilmore, G., and Marcus, N. Factors affecting processing mode in visual search. *Perception & Psychophysics*, 1973, *13*, 394-402.

Engel, S. E., and Granda, R. E. Guidelines for man/display interfaces (Technical Report TR 00.2720). Poughkeepsie, NY: IBM, 1975.

Galitz, W. O. *Human factors in office automation*. Atlanta, GA: Life Office Management Assn., 1980.

Garner, W. R. Good patterns have few alternatives. *American Scientist*, 1970, *58*, 34-42.

Garner, W. R. *Processing of information and structure*. Potomac, MD: Erlbaum, 1974.

Grace, G. L. Application of empirical methods to computer-based system design. *Journal of Applied Psychology*, 1966, *50*, 442-450.

Green, E. E. Message design—Graphic display strategies for instruction. In *Proceedings of the Annual Conference*. New York: Association for Computing Machinery, 1976, 144-148.

Jones, P. F. Four principles of man-computer dialog. *IEEE Transactions on Professional Communication*, 1978, *PC-21*(4), 154-159.

Kahneman, D., and Henik, A. Effects of visual grouping on immediate recall and selective attention. In S. Dornic (Ed.) *Attention and performance VI*. Hillsdale, NJ: Erlbaum, 1977.

Koffka, K. *Principles of Gestalt psychology*. New York: Harcourt, Brace, and World, 1935.

Kolers, P. A., Duchnicky, R. L., and Ferguson, D. C. Eye movement measurement of readability of CRT displays. *Human Factors*, 1981, *23*, 517-527.

Landis, D., Slivka, R. M., and Jones, J. M. Evaluation of large scale visual displays. Griffiss Air Force Base, NY: Rome Air Development Center, 1967. (NTIS No. AD 651 372)

Mackworth, N. H. Stimulus density limits the useful field of view. In R. A. Monty and J. W. Senders (Eds.) *Eye movements and psychological processes*. Hillsdale, NJ: Erlbaum, 1976.

Marcus, A. Designing the face of an interface. In *Proceedings of the 2nd Annual Conference and Exhibition of the National Computer Graphics Association*, Baltimore, MD: National Computer Graphics Assn., 1981, 207-215.

Marcus, A. Typographic design for interfaces of information systems. In *Proceedings: Human factors in computer systems*. Gaithersburg, MD: Association for Computing Machinery, 1982, 26-30.

Mayzner, M. S., and Gabriel, R. F. Information "chunking" and short-term retention. *Journal of Psychology*, 1963, *56*, 161-164.

Mehlmann, M. *When people use computers*. Englewood Cliffs, NJ: Prentice-Hall, 1981.

MIL-STD-1472C. Military standard: Human engineering design criteria for military systems, equipment and facilities. Washington, DC: Department of Defense, 1981.

Miller, L. A., and Thomas, J. C. Behavioral issues in the use of interactive systems. *International Journal of Man-Machine Studies*, 1977, *9*, 509-536.

NASA. Spacelab display design and command usage guidelines (Report MSFC-PROC-711A). Huntsville, AL: George C. Marshall Space Flight Center, 1980.

Pakin, S. E., and Wray, P. Designing screens for people to use easily. *Data Management*, July, 1982, 36-41.

Peterson, D. E. Screen design guidelines. *Small Systems World*, February, 1979, pp. 19-21; 34-37.

Poulton, E. C., and Brown, C. H. Rate of comprehension of an existing teleprinter output and of possible alternatives. *Journal of Applied Psychology*, 1968, *52*, 16-21.

Ramsey, H. R., and Atwood, M. E. Human factors in computer systems: A review of the literature (Technical Report SAI-78-071-DEN). Englewood, CO: Science Applications, Inc., 1979. (NTIS No. AD A075 679)

Ramsey, H. R., Atwood, M. E., and Kirshbaum, P. J. A critically annotated bibliography of the literature of human factors in computer systems (Technical Report SAI-78-070-DEN). Englewood, CO: Science Applications, Inc., 1978. (NTIS No. AD A058 081)

Ringel, S., and Hammer, C. Information assimilation from alphanumeric displays: Amount and density of information presented (Tech. Report TRN141). Washington, DC: U.S. Army Personnel Research Office, 1964. (NTIS No. AD 601 973)

Rosenthal, R. I. The design of technological displays (tutorial paper). In P. A. Kolers, M. E. Wrolstad, and H. Bouma (Eds.) *Processing of visible language* (Vol. 1). New York: Plenum, 1979.

Severin, F. T., and Rigby, M. K. Influence of digit grouping on memory for telephone numbers. *Journal of Applied Psychology*, 1963, *47*, 117-119.

Shannon, C. E., and Weaver, W. *The mathematical theory of communication*. Urbana, IL: The University of Illinois Press, 1949.

Shurtleff, D. A. *How to make displays legible*. La Mirada, CA: Human Interface Design, 1980.

Siegel, A. I., and Fischl, M. A. Dimensions of visual information displays. *Journal of Applied Psychology*, 1971, *55*, 470-476.

Silver, C. A., Jones, J. M., and Landis, D. Decision quality as a measure of visual display effectiveness. *Journal of Applied Psychology*, 1966, *50*, 109-113.

Smith, S. L. Requirements definition and design guidelines for the man-machine interface in $C^3$ system acquisition (Technical Report ESD-TR-80-122). Bedford, MA: USAF Electronic Systems Division, 1980. (NTIS No. AD A087 258)

Smith, S. L. Man-machine interface (MMI) requirements definition and design guidelines: A progress report (Technical Report ESD-TR-81-113). Bedford, MA: USAF Electronic Systems Division, 1981. (NTIS No. AD A096 705)

Smith, S. L. User-system interface design for computer-based information systems (Technical Report ESD-TR-82-132). Bedford, MA: USAF Electronic Systems Division, 1982. (NTIS No. AD A115 853)

Smith, S. L., and Aucella, A. F. Design guidelines for the user interface to computer-based information systems (Technical Report ESD-TR-83-122). Hanscom Air Force Base, MA: USAF Electronic Systems Division, 1983. (NTIS No. AD A127 345)

Smith, S. L., and Goodwin, N. C. Blink coding for information display. *Human Factors*, 1971, *13*, 283-290.

Smith, S. L., and Goodwin, N. C. Another look at blinking displays. *Human Factors*, 1972, *14*, 345-347.

Stewart, T. F. M. Displays and the software interface. *Applied Ergonomics*, 1976, 7.3, 137-146.

Taylor, J. H. Contrast thresholds as a function of retinal position and target size for the light-adapted eye (REF 61-10). Scripps Institution of Oceanography, 1961. Described in W. F. Grether and C. A. Baker, Visual presentation of information. In H. P. Van Cott and R. G. Kinkade (Eds.) *Human engineering guide to equipment design* (Rev. ed.). Washington, DC: U.S. Government Printing Office, 1972.

Teichner, W. H., and Krebs, M. J. Visual search for simple targets. *Psychological Bulletin*, 1974, *81*, 15-28.

Teichner, W. H., and Mocharnuk, J. B. Visual search for complex targets. *Human Factors*, 1979, *21*, 259-275.

Tinker, M. A. Prolonged reading tasks in visual research. *Journal of Applied Psychology*, 1955, *39*, 444-446.

Treisman, A. Perceptual grouping and attention in visual search for features and for objects. *Journal of Experimental Psychology: Human Perception and Performance*, 1982, *8*, 194-214.

Treisman, A., and Gelade, G. A feature integration theory of attention. *Cognitive Psychology*, 1980, *12*, 97-136.

Tullis, T. S. An evaluation of alphanumeric, graphic, and color information displays. *Human Factors*, 1981, *23*, 541-550.

Uber, G. T., Williams, P. E., Hisey, B. L., and Seikert, R. G. The organization and formatting of hierarchical displays for the on-line input of data. *AFIPS Fall Joint Computer Conference Proceedings*, 1968, *33*, Part 1, 219-226.

Vartabedian, A. G. The effects of letter size, case, and generation method on CRT display search time. *Human Factors*, 1971, *13*, 363-368.

Vitz, P. C. Preference for different amounts of visual complexity. *Behavioral Science*, 1966, *11*, 105-114.

Wertheimer, Max. Untersuchungen zur lehre von der Gestalt, II. *Psychologische Forschung*, 1923, *4*, 301-350. Abridged translation by Michael Wertheimer in D. C. Beardslee and Michael Wertheimer (Eds.), *Readings in perception*. Princeton, NJ: Van Nostrand, 1958.

Williges, B. H., and Williges, R. C. User considerations in computer-based information systems (Tech. Report CSIE-81-2). Blacksburg, VA: Department of Industrial Engineering and Operations Research, Virginia Polytechnic Institute and State University, September, 1981. (NTIS No. AD A106 194)

Winzenz, D. Group structure and coding in serial learning. *Journal of Experimental Psychology*, 1972, *92*, 8-19.

Woodward, R. M. Proximity and direction of arrangement in numeric display. *Human Factors*, 1972, *14*, 337-343.

Wright, P. Using tabulated information. *Ergonomics*, 1968, *11*, 331-343.

Wright, P. Decision making as a factor in the ease of using numerical tables. *Ergonomics*, 1977, *20*, 91-96.

Zahn, C. T. Graph-theoretical methods for detecting and describing Gestalt clusters. *IEEE Transactions on Computers*, 1971, *C-20*, 68-86.

# Suggested Reading

## Prologue

Gopher, D., and Kimchi, R. (1989). Engineering psychology. *Annual Review of Psychology, 40,* 431-455.
Hammond, K. R. (1986). Generalization in operational contexts: What does it mean? Can it be done? *IEEE Transactions on Systems, Man and Cybernetics, SMC-16,* 428-433.
Kantowitz, B. W. (1982). Interfacing human information processing and engineering psychology. In W. C. Howell and E. A. Fleishman (Eds.), *Human performance and productivity* (vol. 2, pp. 31-81). Hillsdale, NJ: Erlbaum.
Rouse, W. B. (1985). On better mousetraps and basic research: Getting the applied world to the laboratory door. *IEEE Transactions on Systems, Man and Cybernetics, SMC-15,* 2-8.
Rouse, W. B., and Boff, K. R. (1986). *System design: Behavioral perspectives on designers, tools, and organizations.* New York: North-Holland.
Wickens, C. D., and Kramer, A. F. (1985). Engineering psychology. *Annual Review of Psychology, 36,* 307-348.

## Human-Machine Systems

Adams, J. A. (1982). Issues in human reliability. *Human Factors, 24,* 1-10.
Fleishman, E. A. (1982). Systems for describing human tasks. *American Psychologist, 37,* 821-834.
Hollnagel, E., and Woods, D. D. (1983). Cognitive systems engineering: New wine in new bottles. *International Journal of Man-Machine Studies, 18,* 583-600.
Miller, D. P., and Swain A. D. (1987). Human error and human reliability. In G. Salvendy (Ed.), *Handbook of human factors.* New York: Wiley.
Moray, N. (1986). Monitoring behavior and supervisory control. In K. R. Boff, L. Kauffman, and J. P. Thomas (Eds.), *Handbook of perception and human performance* (vol. II, pp. 40-1-40-51). New York: Wiley.
Parasuraman, R. (1986). Vigilance, monitoring, and search. In K. R. Boff, L. Kauffman, and J. P. Thomas (Eds.), *Handbook of perception and human performance* (vol. II, pp. 43-1-43-49). New York: Wiley.
Pew, R. W., and Baron, S. (1983). Perspectives on human performance modeling. *Automatica, 19,* 663-676.
Price, H. E. (1985). The allocation of function in systems. *Human Factors, 27,* 33-46.
Rasmussen, J. (1986). *Information processing and human-machine interaction: An approach to cognitive engineering.* New York: North-Holland.
Rasmussen, J., and Vicente, K. J. (1989). Coping with human errors through system design: Implications for ecological interface design. *International Journal of Man-Machine Studies, 31,* 517-534.
Sage, A. P. (1981). Behavioral and organizational considerations in the design of information systems and processes for planning and support. *IEEE Transactions on Systems, Man and Cybernetics, SMC-11,* 640-678.
Sheridan, T. B. (1988). The system perspective. In E. L. Wiener and D. C. Nagel (Eds.), *Human factors in aviation* (pp. 27-51). New York: Academic.
Warm, J. S. (Ed.). (1984). *Sustained attention in human performance.* New York: Wiley.
Warm, J. S., and Parasuraman, R. (Eds.). (1987). Vigilance: Basic and applied research. *Human Factors, 29* (special issue).
Wilson, J. R., and Rutherford, A. (1989). Mental models: Theory and application in human factors. *Human Factors, 31,* 617-634.

## Information Representation and Displays

Carswell, C. M., and Wickens, C. D. (1987). Information integration and the object display: An interaction of task demands and display superiority. *Ergonomics, 30,* 511-527.
Coury, B. G., Boulette, M. D., and Smith, R. A. (1989). Effect of uncertainty and diagnosticity on classification of multidimensional data with integral and separable displays of system status. *Human Factors, 31,* 551-569.
Deutsch, D. (1986). Auditory pattern perception. In K. R. Boff, L. Kauffman, and J. P. Thomas (Eds.), *Handbook of perception and human performance* (vol. II, pp. 32-1-32-49). New York: Wiley.
Doll, T. J., and Hanna, T. E. (1989). Enhanced detection with bimodal sonar displays. *Human Factors, 31,* 539-550.
Hakkinen, M. T., and Williges, B. H. (1985). Synthesized warning messages: Effects of an alerting cue in single-and multiple-function voice synthesis systems. *Human Factors, 26,* 185-195.
Hennessy, R. T. (1975). Instrument myopia. *Journal of the Optical Society of America, 65,* 1114-1120.

Jacob, R. J., Egeth, H. E., and Bevan, W. (1976). The face as a data display. *Human Factors, 18*, 189-200.
Marics, M. A., and Williges, B. A. (1988). The intelligibility of synthesized speech in data inquiry systems. *Human Factors, 30*, 719-732.
McGreevy, M. W., and Ellis, S. R. (1986). The effect of perspective geometry on judged direction in spatial information instruments. *Human Factors, 28*, 439-456.
Robinson, C. P., and Eberts, R. E. (1987). Comparison of speech and pictorial displays in a cockpit environment. *Human Factors, 29*, 31-44.
Sanderson, P. M., Flach, J. M., Buttigieg, M. A., and Casey, E. J. (1989). Object displays do not always support integrated task performance. *Human Factors, 31*, 183-198.
Slowiaczek, L. M., and Nusbaum, H. C. (1985). Effects of speech and pitch contour on the perception of synthetic speech. *Human Factors, 27*, 701-712.
Smith, S. L. (1979). Letter size and legibility. *Human Factors, 21*, 661-670.
Smith, S. L. (1981). Exploring compatibility with words and pictures. *Human Factors, 23*, 305-315.
Sorkin, R. D., Kantowitz, B. H., and Kantowitz, S. C. (1988). Likelihood alarm displays. *Human Factors, 30*, 445-459.
Stokes, A. F., and Wickens, C. D. (1988). Aviation displays. In E. L. Wiener and D. C. Nagel (Eds.), *Human factors in aviation* (pp. 387-431). New York: Academic.
Whitehurst, H. O. (1982). Screening designs used to estimate the relative effects of display factors on dial reading. *Human Factors, 24*, 301-310.

## Stimulus-Response Compatibility and Controls

Andres, R. O., and Hartung, K. J. (1987). Prediction of head movement time using Fitts' Law. *Human Factors, 31*, 703-713.
Baron, S., and Kleinman, D. L. (1969). The human as an optimal controller and information processor. *IEEE Transactions on Man-Machine Systems, MMS-10*, 9-17.
Downing, J. V., and Sanders, M. S. (1987). The effects of panel arrangement and locus of attention on performance. *Human Factors, 29*, 551-562.
Drury, C. G. (1975). Application of Fitts' Law to foot pedal design. *Human Factors, 17*, 368-373.
Jagacinski, R. J., Plamondon, B. D., and Miller, R. A. (1987). Describing movement control at two levels of abstraction. In P. A. Hancock (Ed.), *Human factors psychology*. New York: Elsevier.
Jex, H. R., McDonnel, J. P., and Phatak, A. V. (1966). A "critical" tracking task for manual control research. *IEEE Transactions on Human Factors in Electronics, HFE-7*, 138-144.
Kantowitz, B. W., Triggs, T. J., and Barnes, V. (1989). Stimulus-response compatibility and human factors. In R. W. Proctor and T. G. Reeves (Eds.), *Stimulus-response compatibility*. Amsterdam: North-Holland.
Keele, S. W. (1986). Motor control. In K. R. Boff, L. Kauffman, and J. P. Thomas (Eds.), *Handbook of perception and human performance* (vol. II, pp. 30-1-30-60). New York: Wiley.
Pew, R. W. (1974). Human perceptual-motor performance. In B. W. Kantowitz (Ed.), *Human information processing: Tutorials in performance and cognition* (pp. 1-39). Hillsdale, NJ: Erlbaum.
Wickens, C. D. (1986). The effects of control dynamics on performance. In K. R. Boff, L. Kauffman, and J. P. Thomas (Eds.), *Handbook of perception and human performance* (vol. II, pp. 39-1-39-60). New York: Wiley.
Young, L. R. (1969). On adaptive manual control. *IEEE Transactions on Man-Machine Systems, MMS-10*, 292-331.

## Time-Sharing and Mental Workload

Damos, D., and Wickens, C. D. (1980). The acquisition and transfer of time-sharing skills. *Acta Psychologica, 6*, 569-577.
Derrick, W. L. (1988). Dimensions of operator workload. *Human Factors, 30*, 95-110.
Gopher, D., and Donchin, E. (1986). Workload: An examination of the concept. In K. R. Boff, L. Kauffman, and J. P. Thomas (Eds.), *Handbook of perception and human performance* (vol. II, pp. 41-1-41-49). New York: Wiley.
Hancock, P. A., and Meshkati, N. (Eds.). (1988). *Human mental workload*. New York: Elsevier.
Kantowitz, B. (1985). Channels and stages in human information processing: A limited analysis of theory and methodology. *Journal of Mathematical Psychology, 29*, 135-174.

Kramer, A. F. Sirevaag, E. J., and Braune, R. (1987). A psychophysiological assessment of operator workload during simulated flight missions. *Human Factors, 29,* 145–160.
Lysaght, R. J., Hill, S. G., Dick, A. O., Plamondon, B. D., Linton, P. M., Wierwille, W. W., Zaklad, A. L., Bittner, A. C., and Wherry, R. J. (1989). *Operator workload: Comprehensive review and evaluation of operator workload methodologies* (Tech. Report No. 851). U.S. Army Research Institute.
Moray, N. (1982). Subjective mental workload. *Human Factors, 23,* 25–40.
O'Donnell, R. D., and Eggemeier, F. T. (1986). Workload assessment methodology. In K. R. Boff, L. Kauffman, and J. P. Thomas (Eds.), *Handbook of perception and human performance* (vol. II, pp. 42-1–42-49). New York: Wiley.
Thackray, R. I., and Touchstone, R. M. (1989). Effects of high visual taskload on the behaviours involved in complex monitoring. *Ergonomics, 32,* 27–38.
Wickens, C. D. (1984a). Processing resources in attention. In R. Parasuraman and D. R. Davies (Eds.), *Varieties of attention* (pp. 63–102). New York: Academic.
Wickens, C. D. (1984b). *Engineering psychology.* Columbus, OH: Merrill
Wickens, C. D., Sandry, D. L., and Vidulich, M. A. (1983). Compatibility and resource competition between modalities of input, central processing, and output: Testing a model of complex task performance. *Human Factors, 25,* 227–248.
Wierwille, W. W. (1979). Physiological measures of aircrew mental workload. *Human Factors, 21,* 575–593.
Williges, R. C., and Wierwille, W. W. (1979). Behavioral measures of aircrew mental workload. *Human Factors, 21,* 549–574.

# Training

Carlson, R. A., Sullivan, M. A., and Schneider, W. (1989). Component fluency in a problem-solving context. *Human Factors, 31,* 489–502.
Fisk, A. D., and Rogers, W. A. (1988). The role of situational context in the development of high-performance skills. *Human Factors, 30,* 703–712.
Kessel, C. J., and Wickens, C. D. (1982). The transfer of failure detection skills between monitoring and controlling dynamic systems. *Human Factors, 24,* 49–60.
Schneider, W., and Fisk, A. D. (1982). Degree of consistent training: Improvements in search performance and automatic process development. *Perception & Psychophysics, 31,* 160–168.
Schumacher, R. M., and Gentner, D. (1988). Transfer of training as analogical mapping. *IEEE Transactions on Systems, Man and Cybernetics, SMC-18,* 592–599.

# Human-Computer Interaction

Baecker, R. M., and Buxton, W. A. S. (1987). *Readings in human-computer interaction: A multidisciplinary approach.* San Mateo, CA: Morgan Kaufmann.
Card, S. K., Moran, T. P., and Newell, A. (1983). *The psychology of human-computer interaction.* Hillsdale, NJ: Erlbaum.
Curtis, P. (Ed.). (1981). *Human factors in computer systems.* Los Angeles: IEEE Computing Society.
Gould, J. D., Boies, S. J., Levy, S., Richards, S. T., and Schoonard, J. (1987). The 1984 Olympic Message System: A test of behavioral principles of system design. *Communications of the ACM, 30,* 758–769.
Grandjean, E., Hunting, W., and Piedermann, M. (1983). VDT workstation design: Preferred settings and their effects. *Human Factors, 25,* 161–175.
Helander, M. (1988). *Handbook of human-computer interaction.* New York: North-Holland
Kelly, M. J., and Chapanis, A. (1977). Limited natural language dialogue. *International Journal of Man-Machine Studies, 9,* 479–501.
Neal, A. S., and Simons, R. M. (1984). Playback: A method for evaluating the usability of software and its documentation. *IBM Systems Journal, 23,* 82–96.
Norman, D. A., and Draper, S. W. (1986). *User-centered system design: New perspectives in human-computer interaction.* Hillsdale, NJ: Erlbaum.
Shneiderman, B. (1986). *Designing the user interface: Strategies for effective human-computer interaction.* Reading, MA: Addison-Wesley.

# Index

Action slips
  activation-trigger-schema (ATS) system, 73
  associative activation, 79
  and computer system errors, 80-81
  data-driven, 78-79
  defined, 46, 71
  description errors, 77
  detection of, 81-83
  feedback mechanisms, 81-83, 84
  mode error, 76-77
  sources of, 75-81
  schemas, 73-75
  triggering conditions, 73, 74, 80
  verbal, 71, 72
Action scenarios, 32
Aggregation, 66
Airborne displays, 119-130
  coding information for, 120
  digital vs. spatial analog presentation, 123
  hierarchy of flight tasks, 120-121
  integrated vs. separated, 123
  integration, 121-122
  map-type displays, 121-123
  moving vs. fixed, 123-124, 125-126
  principle of frequency separation, 128-129
  principle of the moving part, 123-127
  principle of optimum scaling, 129-130
  pursuit vs. compensatory, 127-128
  and speech integration, 153-179
Air traffic control displays, 131-142
  as example of skill training, 299, 300, 301, 304, 306, 308, 309
  and data tags, 132
  horizontal vs. vertical avoidance maneuvers, 132, 137-140
  perspective format, 132, 137-140
  plan-view format, 132, 135, 137-140
  problem of superimposition, 137, 140-141
  and shape encoding, 132
Allocation of function, 45, 55, 56
Alphanumeric displays
  characteristics of, 375-376
  vs. color and color coding, 89-117
  computer-generated, 371
  examples of, 371
  grouping in, 376-393
  guidelines for, 372-374
  letter case (upper or lower), 376
Analogies, 66
Applied research, 6
  generalizability of, 12-13
Attention
  multiple-capacity model, 257
  *See also* Action slips; Memory; Performance
Augmented feedback, in training, 324
Automatic processing, in training, 308
Automatic speech technology. *See* Speech technology
Automation, 9, 51, 58
  design of systems, 58, 61-70
  *See also* Speech technology

Backward chaining, in training, 315, 316, 317
Backward transfer, in training, 325
Basic research, 6
  generalizability of, 12-13
Blink coding, 375

Capacity. *See* Performance operating characteristic
Capacity expenditure. *See* Workload
Capture slips. *See* Action slips
Coefficient of variation, 356
Cognitive load, 207-213, 215-225
  with pointing devices, 344
Color coding, 89-117
  bibliography of research, 111-113
  in unidimensional and multidimensional visual displays, 89-117
  vs. other target attributes (e.g., shapes, sizes, achromatic/alphanumeric symbols, position, brightness), 89-117
  knowledge gaps in research, 110-111
Comparability
  of humans and machines, 56-57
Computer-aided design (CAD)
  effects of design process on, 27-28, 42
  personalized expert systems, 38
Computers
  and text selection techniques, 333-345
  color coding for displays, 89-117
  designing for usability, 27-28, 30, 33, 38
  evaluation of text editors for, 347-370
  formatting of alphanumeric displays, 371-396
  guidelines for training on, 297-298
Construction task
  consequences of ill-designed tasks, 31-32
  defined, 31
Continuous movement devices, 333-334, 338, 344-345
Control
  defined, 47
  and discrete motor responses, 183-194, 195-204
  systems development, 53
  via voice recognition, 153-179
Controlled processing, in training, 308-309
Coordination, 284
Criterion Task Set (CTS), 240-243
  *See also* Workload

Data-driven slips. *See* Action slips
Degradation of design, 58
Design process
  dimensions of sketching, 36-42
  evaluation of systems, 69
  patterns of problem solving, 27, 34-42
  planning during, 32, 36
  sequential model of, 28-31
  of technical systems, 66
  and usability of computer systems, 27-28, 30, 33, 38
  views of, 27, 31-34

401

Design tasks
  as ill-defined construction tasks, 31–32
  as visual tasks, 32–33
  as a series of information transactions, 33–34
Diagnosticity, 206
Displays
  air traffic control, 131–142
  complex, realistic, 374
  computer-generated, 371
  for instrument flight, 119–130
  formats, 68, 372
  grouping, 382–388
  importance of design, 372
  informational properties of, 372
  layout complexity, 388–393
  local density, 378–382
  monochromatic, 371
  overall density, 376–378
  narrative format, 372–373, 386–387, 390–394
  perspective vs. plan-view in pilot traffic avoidance, 131–142
  related, formatting items in, 376
  simple, artificial, 374
  speech, 153–179
  structured format, 372–373, 386–387, 390–394
  symbols used in, 143–151
  tasks used in evaluation of, 374–375
  *See also* Airborne displays; Alphanumeric displays; Speech technology
Dual-task performance, 249–265, 267–272, 305
  *See also* Primary tasks; Secondary tasks; Time-sharing; Workload

Engineering psychology
  applications of, 5–6
  defined, 3
  educational foci, 6–7
  and experimentation, 7–9
  history of development, 3–5
  organizations, 9
  research methods, 7–9
  and technology, 53–54
Error
  and memory, 215–225
  modeling, 68
  monitoring, 81–82
  naturalistic vs. laboratory-induced, 83–84
  in stimulus-response activity, 182, 189–190
  theory, 72
  *See also* Action slips; Workload
External representation, 61–70
  *See also* Visual representation
External validity of studies, 18–20

Feedback
  in maintaining motivation, 335
  in motor response studies, 203

Feedback concepts
  task characteristics derived from, 278–281
Feedforward control, 63
Fitts' Law, 333, 340–342
Fitts' list, 56, 57
Flight displays. *See* Airborne displays
Fractionation, in training, 274, 315, 318–322, 326
Frame of information
  formatting, 371


Generalizability
  defined, 1, 11
Generalization
  about conceptual variables, 14–15
  and design guidelines, 14
  designing studies for, 20–24
  empirical evidence for, 15–18
  fallacies about, 11, 12–15
  of knowledge to technology, 49
  in learning, 15–17
  limiting factors, 18–20
  in performance analyses, 69
  through replication, 17–18, 23–24
  about training tasks, 298–299
Gestalt psychology
  laws of proximity, similarity, continuity, common fate, 385
Graphacon tablet, 333
Grouping in alphanumeric displays, 376, 393
  effect on performance, 383–388
  functions of, 382–383
  operational definitions of, 384–385
  semantic components of, 383
  spatial components of, 383–384


Heterogeneity
  in design of studies, 22–23
Human-computer interaction, 333–345, 347–370
  and air traffic control displays, 131–142
  in design of flight displays, 119–130
  and human peformance models, 61–70
  and voice recognition, 153–179
Human-machine comparability, 56
Human-machine complementarity, 57, 58
Human-machine systems, 56
  analysis of, 57
  problems in design, 69


Individual differences
  in acquiring skills, 304
  in selecting text editors, 365
Industrial design
  as a construction task, 31
Information
  capacity in motor responses, 195–204
  coding and memory, 7, 120, 220, 224–225

"demassification" of, 52
management during design, 40-42
as signals, signs, and symbols, 64, 65
states, and memory, 215-225
(technology) bomb, 51
theory, 389
transaction, as medium of exchange in design, 33
translation, 30-31
Intention formation, 75
Intentional models, 67
Interaction matrix, in design studies, 29-30
Interference
 between tasks, 268, 270-272
 in training, 317-318
 *See also* Intrusiveness
Intermix training, 310
Internal validity of studies, 18
Interval production task (ITP), 233, 236, 242
 *See also* Workload
Intrusiveness
 impairing primary-task performance, 206, 228, 235-240
 *See also* Interference; Workload
Invention
 defined, 67
 during design, 39

Joystick, 333-334
 effect of approach angle, 339
 information-processing speed with, 341
 practice with, 337
 strain gauge, 334

Keystroke-level model, 206
Knowledge acquisition, 47-54
Knowledge-based behavior, 62, 63-64, 68
 and training, 68

Lateral masking, 381
Layout complexity in displays, 376, 393
 distribution order, 389-393
 effect on performance, 388-389
 guidelines for, 388
 quantifying, 389
 system order, 389-393
Loading tasks, 207-213, 215-225, 231, 233, 242
 *See also* Secondary tasks; Speech technology; Workload
Locus of demands. *See* Workload

Machines
 defined, 57-58
 and evolution of technology, 47-54
 manual backup of, 58
Managing information, in design process, 40-42
 combining pattern, 41-42

grouping pattern, 41
 labeling pattern, 41
 partitioning pattern, 40-41
Measurement
 of human performance, 61
 of motor responses, 195-204
 necessitated by technology, 48
 and POC, 249-265, 267-272
Memory, 215-225
 coding information, 220, 224-225
 frequency of change, 221-222
 lucky guesses, 220
 and number of states, 220-225
 and rehearsal, 217
 schemas, and action slips, 73
 search paradigm, 230, 231, 233
 secondary sources of information, 215
 short-term, 218, 229, 234
 variables, 216-225
Mental arithmetic, as secondary task, 211
Mental models, 52, 53, 63, 65, 68
 and action slips, 71-85
 of knowledge acquisition, 47-54
 related to displays, 119-130, 131-142
Mental workload. *See* Workload
Mode error, 76-77
Model transformations, 65
 strategies for, 65-66
Modified Cooper-Harper scale, 234
Monitoring, as secondary task, 212
Motivation, 59 in training, 300
Motor responses
 effects of redundancy and uncertainty, 202-203
 errors, 200-201
 and feedback data, 203
 as a function of displays, 119-130, 131-142
 and index of task difficulty, 202-203
 information capacity of, 195-204
 movement times, 199-200, 201-202, 203
 reaction times, 198-199, 201-202, 203
 text selection methods, 333-345
 variability and magnitude, 195
Mouse, 333-334
 compared with stylus and finger pointing, 341
 effect of approach angle, 339
 practice with, 337
 time to use, 340
Multiple capacity model, 257
Multiple resources theory, 231-232, 233, 235, 256, 269

Operator workload. *See* Workload

Part-task simulation, 207, 208
Part-task training, 313-329
 adaptive training strategy, 322
 aims of, 313
 and backward chaining, 315, 316, 317-318

and backward transfer, 325
defined, 273, 313, 326
differential transfer, 315
effect of pretraining, 320, 322
fractionation, 315, 318–322, 326
and interference, 317–318
response-chaining hypothesis, 318
segmentation, 315, 316–318, 326
simplification, 315, 322–325, 327
and stages of tracking skill development, 321–322
and subject aptitude, 317, 318
and time-sharing, 318
with tracking tasks, 313–329
and transfer of training, 314–315, 323–324
types of, 315–316, 319
vs. whole-task training, 313–329
Perceptual-motor tasks, 279
Performance
behavioral levels, 62
capacity, 250
concurrence cost, 268
and discrete motor responses, 183–194, 195–204
efficiency, average and marginal, 251
interaction with technology, 47
knowledge-based, 61–70
measurement, 61
and memory, 215–225
practice effects, 336–337
prediction, 333
qualitative models of, 67–68, 69
quantitative models of, 67, 69
skill-based, 62–63
skills, rules, and knowledge, 61–70
and tracking tasks, 313–329
warm-up effects, 337
See also Workload
Performance operating characteristic, 206, 249–265, 267–272
attention operating characteristic, 265
equal allocation axis, 256, 262–263, 269
families, 253–254
linear/nonlinear, 252–253, 254, 260
multiple-capacity model of attention, 257
objective substitution rate, 254, 256
performance resource function, 250
point of equal allocation, 253
potency principle, 250
principle of complimentarity, 250
as proportion scores, 263–264
scaling, 249, 250, 267–272
shape, 252, 260, 269
symmetry/asymmetry of, 253
and task efficiency, 250–252
time-sharing efficiency, 270
transformation of, 254–257, 260
Physical models of human behavior, 50
Pointing devices
for text selection on a computer, 333–335, 340, 343
times, 333
Power law of training, 302–303

Practice
with consistent component tasks, 299, 304–305, 309
effects with text-editing devices, 336–337
and fixation, 286
fallacy, in learning high-performance tasks, 299
identifying information on displays, 107
and learning subroutines, 289–290, 293–294
and overpractice, 292
with tracking tasks, 313–329
See also Skill learning; Skill training
Primary tasks, 207–213, 215–225, 227–248, 249–265
See also Secondary tasks; Workload
Proportion scores, 263–264


Relaxation, 284
Replication
and generalizability, 17–18, 23–24
Research criteria, 19
Resource allocation
and resource competition, 268
See also Performance operating characteristic
Rule-based performance, 62, 63


Sampling
and design of studies, 19
Secondary tasks, 207–213, 227–248, 249–265, 267–272
characteristics of, 210–211
development of standard tasks, 212–213
in measurement of workload, 207–213
types of, 211–212
Segmentation, in training, 274, 315, 316–318, 326
Sensitivity
of workload assessment techniques, 206, 228–235, 240
See also Workload
Similarity, 143–151
and design of studies, 21–22
Simplification, in training, 274, 315, 322–325, 327
Simulation
fidelity of, 17
in training high-performance skills, 297–312
in training tracking skills, 313–329
Single-task performance. See Performance operating characteristic; Primary tasks; Secondary tasks; Workload
Sketching, in the design process, 36–40
coherence, 37, 38–39
inclusion, 37, 38
precision, 37, 39–40
selective refinement, 37
sloppiness hypothesis, 39
Skill
constancy, 277
high-performance, defined, 298
Skill development, 275–295, 302–308
and motivation, 304, 310

power law, 302–303
and practice, 303
and rate of acquisition, 304
reading, 307, 308
time-sharing in, 308, 310
transfer of, 313–329
Skilled performance, 275–294, 297–312
characteristics of, 275
effect of stress on, 287
subroutines, 287–288, 293–294
Skill learning
autonomous phase of, 286–287
cognitive aspects of, 283, 285–286
complex, 284–285
enjoyment of, 300
fixation phase of, 286
of high-performance tasks, 297–312
perceptual aspects, 283–284
phases of, 63
Skill training, 276–294
fallacies of, 298–302
instructors' opinions regarding, 282–284
transfer of, 313–329
Slips. *See* Action slips
Speed-accuracy trade-off
in text selection methods, 365
Speech technology, 153–179
applied to system design, 153–179
comprehension of synthesized speech, 170
integrated into displays, 165–172
generation system, defined, 155–156
input/output (I/O), 153
interactive systems strategy, 154
measures of algorithm performance, 157
operational intelligibility, defined, 168
operational relevance of, 171
recognition system, defined, 154
review of research, 157–172
and system response time, 171
and voice characteristics, 170–171
Step keys, 337
effect of approach angle, 339
positioning time, 338
practice with, 337
Stimulus and response sequences
and task characteristics, 279–280
Stimulus-response coding, 184
unidimensional codes, 184
multidimensional codes, 184
in task taxonomy, 280
Stimulus-response compatibility, 183–194, 210
discriminability, 185
in displays, 119–130, 131–142
and errors, 187–190, 192
information coding, 184–185
and lost information, 189
and reaction time, 187–190, 192
and secondary task loading, 191
transfer of information, 183, 192–193

Stress
and skilled performance, 287
task-induced, 207
in workload, 243
Stroop phenomenon, 79
Subjective Workload Assessment Technique (SWAT), 229–230, 233–234, 237–238, 243
Subsidiary task paradigm, 236
*See also* Secondary tasks
Symbols, 64, 65, 88, 143–151
color coding of, in displays, 89–117
configural properties of, 145, 146
discriminability of, 143
discriminability index formula, 144, 147–149
meaningfulness of, 143
perceptual discriminability as selection basis for displays, 143–151
primitive attributes, 146
Symbolism
and human performance, 63–64
System design, 55–59, 61–70
incorporating speech recognition and generation, 153–179
Systems criteria, 19

Tasks
average efficiency of, 251
characteristics of, and feedback concepts, 278–281
color coding and, 89–117
complexity of, 281
flight, 119–130, 131–142
loading, 207–213, 231, 233, 242
marginal efficiency of, 251
performance, measurement of, 249–265, 267–272
taxonomy, 276–282
*See also* Time-sharing; Workload
Technology
history of, 47–50
and human performance, 47
and task change, 275
Teleological behavior, defined, 61
Text editing
computer-based, 333
with mouse, 344
and screen formats, 371–396
*See also* Text selection techniques
Text editors
evaluated, 347–370
dimensions of usage (time, error, learning, functionality), defined, 348
as interactive systems, 352
Keystroke-level model calculations, 358–359, 363, 366, 368
methodology, 348–352
overall results, 354–357
task taxonomy, 348–349
Text keys, 333–335
effect of approach angle, 339

positioning time, 338
practice with, 337
Text selection techniques
light gun, 333
light pen, 333
joystick, 333–334, 339, 341–342
mouse, 333–334, 339, 341–342
Saunders 720 step keys, 333
Step keys, 337–339
Time-sharing, 7, 207–213, 227–248, 249–265, 267–272
and concurrence cost, 268
efficiency, 270
with high-performance training tasks, 306, 308, 310
and resource allocation, 268
and resource competition, 268
Tools, defined, 57
Tracking
defined, 314
self-adaptive, defined, 211–212
training for, 313–329
Training
backward-chaining procedure, 315
and design of studies, 18
experience in operational setting, 301
fallacies, 298–302
of high-performance skills, 297–312
and initial performance, 301
intermix training, 310
with microprocessor-based systems, 297–298
for maximal accuracy, 300–301
motivation and, 300, 310
novice vs. expert performance, 298
plateaus, 304
power law, 302–303
and practice, 299
rules, guidelines for, 308–310
speed stress training, 310
total task, 299–300
*See also* Part-task training; Transfer of training
Transfer of training, 16–17, 297–312, 313–329
differential transfer, 315
paradigm, 314–315
from video games, 325
*See also* Part-task training

Verbal slips. *See* Action slips
Visual acuity
as a function of local density, 380
Visual representation, in the design process, 27, 32–33
in air traffic control displays, 131–142
in color displays, 89–117
dimensions, 33
in flight displays, 119–130
matrices, 32–33
notations, 33
orthographic projections, 33
procedural representations, 32
solid models, 32
and systems, 61–70
Visual search, 374, 384
Voice I/O systems. *See* Speech technology

Workload
assessment techniques, 227–248
capacity expenditure, 227, 228, 236, 250, 257
Criterion Task Set (CTS), 240–243
effect of secondary tasks, 207–213, 227–248
effects of speech techology, 153–179
effects of stress, 207
effects on training, 306–307
interval production task (ITP), 233, 236, 242
locus of demands, 228, 231–235, 240, 249–265, 267–272
measurement of, 209–210, 227–248
memory search paradigm, 230–231, 233
metric evaluation methdology, 240–243
Modified Cooper-Harper scale, 234
multiple resources theory, 231–232, 233, 235
and primary and secondary tasks, 227–248
Subjective Workload Assessment Technique (SWAT), 229–230, 233–234, 237–238, 243
task loading, 207–213, 231, 233, 242
*See also* Secondary tasks; Workload

# NOTES

# NOTES